DATE DUE

APR 1 5 2010		
JUN 0 3 2010		
NOV 1 0 2010		
SEP 2 0 2011		

Demco, Inc. 38-293

FEB 0 5 2010

The Handbook of Spanish Language Media

With the rise of Spanish language media around the world, *The Handbook of Spanish Language Media* provides an overview of the field and its emerging issues. This Handbook will serve as the definitive source for scholars interested in this emerging field of study; not only to provide background knowledge of the various issues and topics relevant to Spanish language media, but also to establish directions for future research in this rapidly growing area.

This volume draws on the expertise of authors and collaborators across the globe. It is an essential reference work for graduate students, scholars, and media practitioners interested in Spanish language media, and is certain to influence the course of future research in this growing and increasingly prominent area.

Alan B. Albarran is Professor of Radio, Television and Film and Director of the Center for Spanish Language Media at the University of North Texas. He has extensive experience as an editor and author and is widely recognized as an international scholar in the area of media management and economics. He is former editor of both the *Journal of Media Economics* and the *International Journal for Media Management*.

The Handbook of
Spanish Language Media

Edited by Alan B. Albarran

R Routledge
Taylor & Francis Group

NEW YORK AND LONDON

First published 2009
by Routledge
270 Madison Ave, New York, NY 10016

Simultaneously published in the UK
by Routledge
2 Park Square, Milton Park, Abingdon, Oxon OX14 4RN

Routledge is an imprint of the Taylor & Francis Group, an informa business

© 2009 Taylor & Francis

Typeset in Minion by
Keystroke, 28 High Street, Tettenhall, Wolverhampton
Printed by
CPI Antony Rowe, Chippenham, Wiltshire

Library of Congress Cataloging in Publication Data
Handbook of Spanish language media / [edited] by Alan B. Albarran.
    p. cm.
    Includes bibliographical references and index.
  1. Mass media—Latin America. 2. Hispanic American mass media.
3. Mass media—Spain.
P92.L3H36 2009
302.23098—dc22   2008054971

ISBN 10: 0–415–99044–0 (hbk)
ISBN 10: 0–415–99101–3 (pbk)
ISBN 10: 0–203–92647–1 (ebk)

ISBN 13: 978–0–415–99044–8 (hbk)
ISBN 13: 978–0–415–99101–8 (pbk)
ISBN 13: 978–0–203–92647–5 (ebk)

This book is dedicated to the memory of my dear mother,
Jean M. Albarran (1932–2008)

Contents

List of illustrations   xi
Foreword: *Félix F. Gutiérrez*   xv
Preface: *Alan B. Albarran*   xvii

**PART I: SPANISH LANGUAGE MEDIA: A COUNTRY-BY-COUNTRY
EXAMINATION**   1

1. Spanish Language Media in the United States   3
    KENTON T. WILKINSON

2. The Media in Spain: Three Decades of Transformation   17
    ÁNGEL ARRESE, JUAN PABLO ARTERO and MÓNICA HERRERO

3. The Media Industry in Mexico   34
    MARÍA ELENA GUTIÉRREZ RENTERÍA

4. The Media in Central America: Costa Rica, El Salvador, Guatemala,
    Honduras, Nicaragua and Panama   47
    CATHERINE SALZMAN and RYAN SALZMAN

5. The Media in Colombia   63
    GERMÁN ARANGO FORERO, LILIANA GUTIÉRREZ COBA,
    ALFONSO FORERO GUTIÉRREZ, JAIRO VALDERRAMA VALDERRAMA,
    RODOLFO PRADA PENAGOS, LUZ CARMEN BARRERA AVELLANEDA and
    ADRIANA GUZMÁN DE REYES

6. The Mass Media in Venezuela: History, Politics and Freedom   77
    GUILLERMO GIBENS

7. The Mass Media in Bolivia   88
    GONZALO SORUCO and JULIET PINTO

8. The Media in Ecuador   103
   RODRIGO JORDÁN TOBAR and ALLEN PANCHANA MACAY

9. The Media in Peru   125
   ROSA ZETA DE POZO

10. The Chilean Media Landscape   139
    CRISTÓBAL BENAVIDES, MARIA IGNACIA ERRÁZURIZ, DAVID KIMBER,
    ISABEL SANTA MARÍA and ALDO VAN WEEZEL

11. Media and Entertainment in Argentina: Doing Business in a Fragmented
    Society   151
    LUCIANA SILVESTRI and ROBERTO S. VASSOLO

12. The Media in Uruguay   171
    EILEEN HUDSON, FERNANDO SALAS, LUCILA CARBAJAL and FLORENCIA TRAIBEL

13. The Media in Paraguay: A Locked Nation in Times of Change   183
    LIGIA GARCÍA BÉJAR

14. The Media in Cuba, the Dominican Republic and Puerto Rico   189
    JUAN PABLO ARTERO

PART II: TOPICS AND ISSUES IN SPANISH LANGUAGE MEDIA   201

15. Growth and Trends in Spanish Language Television in the United States   203
    AMY JO COFFEY

16. Television News: Spain, Mexico, Colombia and the United States   218
    PHYLLIS SLOCUM

17. Univision and Telemundo: Spanish Language Television Leaders in the
    United States   237
    GUILLERMO GIBENS

18. The Latinos and Media Project   245
    FEDERICO SUBERVI

19. Advertising in Spanish Language Media   249
    CRISTINA ETAYO and ÁNGELA PRECIADO HOYOS

20. Hispanic Advertising, Marketing and New Media   266
    LAUREN BOYLE

21. The Potential of Book Publishing in Iberian American and African Countries:
The Portuguese Perspective   277
PAULO FAUSTINO

22. Assessing the State of Spanish Language Media: A Summary and Future Directions   294
ALAN B. ALBARRAN

Contributors   300
Index   305

List of illustrations

Figures

5.1	Media Consumption in Colombia, 1999–2007	67
9.1	Presence of Peruvian Media on the Internet, 2006	135
11.1	Socioeconomic Pyramids in Developed Markets and Emerging Markets: An Illustration of Vertical Fragmentation	156
11.2	Socioeconomic Segments in Argentina as Considered in Our Study	158
11.3	Emerging Framework: Dimensions Generating Structural Differences among Groups of Consumers	162
11.4	Middle-Market Consumers: Relationship Building with Technology According to Lifecycle Stage	164
11.5	Middle-Market Consumers: Relationship Building with Content and Preferred Platforms According to Lifecycle Stage	165
11.6	Middle-Market Consumers vis-à-vis High-Income and Low-Income Consumers: Relationship Building with Technology According to Lifecycle Stage	167
15.1	US Hispanic Population versus Number of Hispanic Networks, 1986–2004	204
15.2	US Hispanic Population versus Number of Local Hispanic Television Stations, 1995–2004	205
15.3	US Hispanic Population versus Total Hispanic Television Advertising Revenue, 1997–2004	210
15.4	US Hispanic Population versus Total Hispanic Spot TV Advertising Revenue, 1997–2004	211
15.5	US Hispanic Population versus Total Hispanic Network TV Advertising Revenue, 1997–2004	211
15.6	Hispanic versus General Market Total Broadcast Television Advertising Revenue, 1997–2004	212
15.7	Hispanic Spot versus General Market Spot TV Advertising Revenue, 1997–2004	212
15.8	Hispanic versus General Market Broadcast Network TV Advertising Revenue, 1997–2004	213
19.1	Advertising Intensity in Relation to Time and GDP in Each Country	253

Tables

1.1	Top Ten Spanish Language Newspapers by Gross Ad Revenue, 2007	6
1.2	Top Ten Hispanic/Latino-Oriented Magazines by Gross Ad Revenue, 2007	6
2.1	Main Newspapers in Spain, 2008	25
2.2	Main Spanish Consumer Magazines, 2008	26
2.3	Evolution of Audience Shares of Spanish Television Channels, 2000–2007	27
2.4	Total Turnover of the Spanish Television Industry, 2005–2007 (€ millions)	29
2.5	Pay Television in Spain: Subscribers and Revenues, 2005–2007	29
2.6	Radio Stations in Spain, 2008	30
2.7	Total Revenues of the Spanish Radio Industry, 2005–2007 (€ millions)	31
2.8	Audience and Traffic of the Main Spanish Media Websites, 2008	32
3.1	Integration of Socioeconomic Levels in Mexico, 2007	36
3.2	Market Segmentation by Value, 2007	37
3.3	Principal Channels on Open Television in Mexico, 2008	39
3.4	The Twenty Papers with the Highest Published Tariffs, 2004	41
3.5	Principal Dailies with Certified Circulation above 18,000, 2004	42
3.6	Leading Main Communication Firms in Mexico, 2008	44
4.1	Demographics, 2008	50
4.2	Index Scores, Ranks and Evaluations	51
4.3	Freedom of the Press, 1980–2005	55
4.4	User Data, 2005	59
7.1	Principal Newspapers of Bolivia, 2008	98
7.2	Main Television Networks in Bolivia, 2008	99
8.1	Sales of the Top Nine Media Groups in Ecuador, 2007 (millions of US$)	111
8.2	Open (Free) Television Channels in Ecuador, 2008	114
8.5	Radio Groups with the Most Frequencies, 2008	117
8.6	Number of Printed Copies, 2007	119
8.7	Internet Access in Ecuador, 2008	120
8.8	Ranking of the Twenty Most Visited Websites, 2008	121
9.1	Household Media Equipment, 2005–2007 (in % of Households)	126
9.2	Media Consumption (Lima only), 2007	126
9.3	Media Advertising in Peru, 2007	126
9.4	Top Five Dailies According to Circulation, 2007	128
9.5	Top Radio Stations and Audience (Metropolitan Lima Only), 2008	132
9.6	Television Audience Program Habits: I Watch . . . (%), 2008	133
9.7	Growth of Press on the Internet and Cybermedia, 1997–2004	136
10.1	Readership and Circulation of Newspapers, January–June 2007	142
10.2	Market Share of Magazines, 2007	142
10.3	Main Radio Networks in Chile, 2008	143
10.4	Internet Access Statistics in Chile, 2000–2007	145
10.5	Top Fifteen Chilean Websites Ranked by Unique Visitors, January 2008	145
10.6	Advertising Expenditure in Chile, 1995–2006 (US$ millions) (constant 2007 prices)	145
10.7	Advertising Expenditure by Medium, 1995–2007	146
11.1	A Socioeconomic Portrait of Argentina, 2008	152
11.2	Focus Group Participants: Middle-Market Consumers (Profiles and Demographic Data)	159

11.3	Focus Group Interview Guidelines	160
11.4	Participants of Personalized, Semi-Structured Interviews: High-Income and Low-Income Consumers (Profiles and Demographic Data)	161
13.1	Total Number of Users and Percentage of Media Products, 2005	184
14.1	Main Newspapers in Cuba, 2008	191
14.2	Main Magazines in Cuba, 2008	191
14.3	Main Radio Stations in Cuba, 2008	192
14.4	Main Television Channels in Cuba, 2008	192
14.5	Main Newspapers in Dominican Republic, 2008	194
14.6	Main Radio Stations in Dominican Republic, 2008	194
14.7	Main Television Channels in Dominican Republic, 2008	195
14.8	Main News Websites in Dominican Republic, 2008	195
14.9	Main Newspapers in Puerto Rico, 2008	197
14.10	Main Radio Stations in Puerto Rico, 2008	197
14.11	Main Television Channels in Puerto Rico, 2008	198
15.1	Hispanic Networks and Launch Dates, 1961–2008	205
19.1	Percentage of GDP Allotted to Advertising per Country, 1995–2004	250
19.2	Correlation between Advertising Intensity and Time, 2008	251
19.3	Correlation between Growth in Advertising Investment and GDP, 2008	252
19.4	Participation of Each Media in the Total Investment, 2008	254
19.5	Evolution of Advertising Commitment to Newspapers, 1995–2004	255
19.6	Correlation between Newspaper Advertising and Time, 2008	255
19.7	Evolution of Advertising Commitment to Magazines, 1995–2004	256
19.8	Correlation between Magazine Advertising and Time, 2008	256
19.9	Evolution of Television Advertising Commitment, 1995–2004	257
19.10	Correlation between Advertising Commitment to Magazines and Time, 2008	257
19.11	Evolution of Commitment to Radio Advertising, 1995–2004	258
19.12	Correlation between Radio Advertising and Time, 2008	258
19.13	Advertising Agencies with Presence in Spanish-Speaking Countries, 2008	260
19.14	Media Agencies in Spanish-Speaking Countries, 2008	261
21.1	Objectives of the Iberian American Cultural Charter, 2006	282
21.2	Opportunities and Threats within the Iberian American Area	282
21.3	Revenues of Spanish Companies in Portugal, 2007–2008 (€ 000)	284
21.4	Global Media and Entertainment Markets by Region, 2007–2012 ($US millions)	284
21.5	Book Publishing Market Trends, 2003–2012 (US$ millions)	287
21.7	Consumer and Educational Book Publishing Market, 2003–2012* ($US millions)	288
22.1	Highest and Lowest Birth Rates among Spanish Language Nations, 2007	295
22.2	Best Places to Do Business (country followed by 2009 ranking)	297

Foreword

Félix F. Gutiérrez

Annenberg School for Communication, University of Southern California, USA

The publication of *The Handbook of Spanish Language Media* comes at an important time for media scholars and professionals interested in putting into focus the continuing growth, impact and influence of Spanish language media reaching audiences all around the world. Though the subject is Spanish language media, the fact that the book is being published in English is a reflection of the widespread interest in these media. It also means that awareness and understanding of the growing importance of Spanish language media will be raised among key audiences who are primarily conversant in English.

The breadth and depth of the chapters in the book will help readers understand that Spanish language media in Europe, South America, the Caribbean and the United States share more than a common language as they look to the future. Though their history may be rooted in disparate national and political backgrounds, their growth is increasingly linked to developments in marketing, technology and globalization that affect all of them and in which they all can share.

This is not the first time that the technology and globalization have shaped the growth of Spanish language media. Before the 1492 arrival of the Spanish in what is now called the Americas, the indigenous people of the continent had developed elaborate systems of reporting and recording information of importance and interest, though not always disseminating it widely. Though much of the understanding of the uses of these media was destroyed by the Spanish during the conquest and colonization of the Americas, those elements of pre-Hispanic civilization that remain are reminders that the indigenous people had developed their own elaborate communication systems. In fact, some early Spanish language media included bilingual books using the sounds of native languages that were read to indigenous people.

It was globalization and technology that brought the first printing press to America in the 1500s. But it may surprise some readers to learn that Spanish language media and printed news reporting in America predates the English colonies by more than a century. The first printing press in America came from Spain to Mexico City by the mid-1530s, more than 100 years before English colonists brought their first printing press to New England 1638.

The first printed news in America was from Mexico City; an eight-page *hoja volante* (flying page) news booklet reporting a natural disaster that destroyed Guatemala City in 1541. Giving readers a foretaste of the lively journalism that would follow it over the centuries, the front page featured attention-getting large bold type promising a "Report of the Terrifying Earthquake Which Has Reoccurred in the Indies in a City Called Guatemala." Issued irregularly to report news of major announcements or word of world events arriving via ships docking at Veracruz, the *hojas volantes* were the beginning of printed news reporting in America.

This book's completion also coincides with the bicentennial year of the first Spanish language newspaper in the United States, *El Misisipí*, founded in New Orleans, Louisiana in 1808. Founded as a result of the international impact of the Napoleonic wars, *El Misisipí* was a fiercely anti-Napoleon newspaper published by those opposing his occupation of Spain and claim on the Spanish colonies in the Americas. Once again reflecting the global reach of Spanish language media, *El Misisipí*'s outspoken criticism of Napoleon's regime reached and was quoted in newspapers as far away as New York and London.

Sadly, much of the Spanish language media history has been either lost or ignored by those who write in English, though this has not always been the case. Writing in 1810, New England journalist and historian Isaiah Thomas began his book, *The History of Printing in America*, with a ten-page chapter on printing in Spanish America. The chapter was deleted in later editions of the book, denying English language readers an accurate account of the development of print media in America and an understanding of the evolution of Spanish language media on this continent.

Much more recently, some scholars writing in English have included references to the Spanish language roots of American media in their texts, have studied the development of Spanish language media across the globe, including the United States, and have taken a transnational approach to studying these media. In so doing, they and scholars writing in Spanish have bridged boundaries of oceans and national borders that had earlier been barriers to understanding links and connections between Spanish language media around the world. Current scholars in both languages are building borderlands of understanding where earlier generations followed borderlines of division.

This book comes at a critical time in the development of this scholarship and reflects the truly international scope of Spanish language media by taking a building block approach to constructing a wider understanding across several key dimensions. Part I, Spanish Language Media: A Country-by-Country Examination, features chapters that begin in the United States and Spain, then take the reader southward through Mexico and Central America into South America and back north to the Caribbean. Part II, Topics and Issues in Spanish Language Media, uses both national and international perspectives to examine key issues in of television, broadcast news, research, advertising, marketing and book publishing. The insightful chapters in these two parts provide both important information and perceptive analyses regarding these media and the forces shaping their development.

The concluding chapter by the editor, Alan B. Albarran, provides a well-informed and thoughtful assessment of the contents of the book and discusses possible future directions for Spanish language media. Although it provides an alternative, concluding summation to be read and digested after reading the chapters in the book, it could just as well serve as a stage setter for the readings that precede it. Those who have read so far may want to consider reading Albarran's contribution before diving into the chapters between this foreword and the final chapter.

Those of us who have been involved with the study of Spanish language media over the decades owe a great debt of gratitude to Professor Albarran and his author colleagues for their work in producing this comprehensive compilation of scholarship on Spanish language media around the world. It is a most welcome addition to the field and will no doubt serve as an insightful guide for future scholarship and the works that will no doubt follow.

Preface

University of North Texas, USA

On behalf of the approximately forty contributors who participated in the research and writing of this research volume, I am pleased to introduce you to *The Handbook of Spanish Language Media*. The genesis for this project came about in the fall of 2006, during the inaugural year of a new Center for Spanish Language Media at the University of North Texas. One of the goals of the Center is to promote understanding of Spanish language media, not only in the United States but also throughout the globe.

The first speaker we invited to the campus of the University of North Texas (UNT) was Dr. María Elena Gutiérrez, a scholar from Mexico whom I first met in 2002 at the University of Navarra in Pamplona, Spain during her doctoral studies. María Elena came to UNT to present a lecture on the Mexican media conglomerate Grupo Televisa, the topic of her dissertation.

During her visit, we were talking about the challenges of doing research in Mexico due to the lack of publicly available data sources, and very limited literature on the media industries in Mexico. María Elena explained to me the situation in Mexico was similar to many Latin American countries, and more research was needed. I was aware that there was not a great deal of literature on Spanish language media, not only inside but also outside United States. Our conversation struck a chord—that we needed a research volume that could perhaps serve as a beginning, or a baseline, on Spanish language media, but from an industry-driven perspective. I remember saying to her, "We need a handbook about Spanish language media," and she agreed.

Now the idea for a handbook was not original. I served as editor, along with my good colleagues Sylvia Chan-Olmsted and Mike Wirth, for a *Handbook of Media Management and Economics* that was published by Lawrence Erlbaum Associates (LEA) and well received by its audience. I wondered if such a project might be considered for Spanish language media.

Well, by the time these ideas came together, it was now 2007, and I had some conversations with Linda Bathgate at Taylor and Francis about such a project. Linda was part of LEA before it was acquired by Taylor and Francis. I have worked together with Linda in many different roles since the mid-1990s, and she is a consummate professional. She was very encouraging, and suggested I put together a proposal for such a project.

Over the next few weeks I assembled the makings of a proposal, and came to realize that this was not going to be a "small" project. The question was how to proceed. By now the Center for Spanish Language Media had hosted several speakers both within and outside the United States, and I talked up this idea with many people, including colleagues at the University of Navarra, and other scholars in Mexico, Colombia, Chile and Argentina.

The vision was fairly simple—to put together a volume that offered a country-by-country examination of the media industries in the various Spanish-speaking countries, and to have a few chapters look at topics and issues in the United States, as well as those that applied to all Spanish language countries—such as advertising, news and marketing. Another colleague who visited the Center during its initial year was Dr Paulo Faustino from Lisbon, Portugal, who was able to enlighten me on the importance of the Spanish language market to the countries where Portuguese is the primary language, notably Portugal and Brazil, but also several African countries.

I am not an expert on Spanish language media, as most of my close colleagues know. But it is an area I am very interested in and have developed a passion for. Part of that is due to what is happening with Spanish language media in the United States, but it is also part of my own roots. While I am of Hispanic descent, I was not raised in a Spanish-speaking home. Nevertheless, there is a connection, one that I feel deeply whenever I visit Mexico, Spain and Latin America.

Therefore, it was critical to me that my challenge was to find authors who could write with authority, and have a connection with the various countries and topics they were addressing. Luckily, with the help of a strong and established contact base, I was able to put together a wonderful collection of scholars to author the various chapters in the handbook, limiting my primary role as editor of this volume and authoring this brief preface as well as a summary chapter.

Eventually the proposal was formulated, reviewed, revised and ultimately given the green light by Taylor and Francis. Authors were solicited and acquired through various networks and contacts. Not every chapter has an author who has lived in the featured country, but all of the authors share a deep interest in Spanish language media. Thus, we are proud to share with you *The Handbook of Spanish Language Media*.

The book consists of two large parts. Part I is a country-by-country examination of the media industries and the key issues found in each nation. There are twenty-one countries around the globe that have a significant Spanish-speaking population; all are represented in this project. However, some countries are small, not only in population, but also in terms of their indigenous media industries. As such, there is a single chapter devoted to Central America, and a single chapter devoted to the Spanish-dominant Caribbean nations of Cuba, the Dominican Republic and Puerto Rico. The only Spanish-dominant country omitted from the handbook is Equatorial Guinea, which is an African nation with fewer than 600,000 population and no distinct media industries of its own.

Part II looks at various topics and issues in Spanish language media, with most of the areas of investigation concerning the United States. There are eight chapters in Part II, including a summary chapter that wraps up the entire handbook.

It is my personal hope, as well as that of the many authors represented in this project, that this handbook serves two key goals: to provide a baseline of research on Spanish language media from a global perspective, and also to provide an agenda for future study that might be considered by students and scholars attracted to this field.

As editor, I am grateful to Linda Bathgate for her courage and faith to develop this idea into the finished product you now hold. The staff at Taylor and Francis have been a pleasure to work with as well. I appreciate all of the hard work and effort by each of the authors, many of whom were asked to write in English as opposed to their native language, and to do their best to adhere to all of my editing suggestions and style checks. Christine Paswan and the research assistants at the Center for Spanish Language Media have been a source of help and encouragement for all of us involved with this project.

Finally, on a personal note, my thanks go to my chair in the Department of Radio, Television and Film, Professor Melinda Levin, for supporting a faculty development leave that made it possible for me to devote time to finish this project in the fall of 2008. I deeply appreciate the love and support of my wife and best friend Beverly as I was working on this and other projects during my leave.

It is my hope this volume of research will be useful to new students and scholars interested in Spanish language media, and will generate more inquiry and analysis that goes far beyond what we have accomplished in these pages. Spanish language media are global phenomena and deserve continuing study and investigation.

I
Spanish Language Media
A Country-by-Country Examination

1

Spanish Language Media in the United States

Kenton T. Wilkinson
Texas Tech University, USA

Spanish language media have long been important channels for reaching people of Latin American or Iberian origin in the United States. English language and bilingual media, which also communicate with this population group, are beyond the scope of this chapter. Historically, language difference has been a key marker of Hispanic/Latino identity and is likely to remain so well into the future. Spanish language media are typically used by recent immigrants (first and second generation) to the United States, though interest in recovering or re-establishing their roots are leading Hispanics and Latinos of subsequent generations to use Spanish language media. People from other ethnic groups are also attracted to these media to improve their Spanish and learn more about the culture of a growing and increasingly influential segment of the population.

The Hispanic and Latino population of the United States has been difficult to measure precisely due to changing ethnic categories and counting methods at the US Census Bureau, and the elusiveness of some population members, among other factors. Yet even the estimated figures reflect tremendous growth. The 1940 census placed the Hispanic and Latino population at 1.9 million; by 1980 it had reached 14.6 million (6.4 percent of the US population) and by 2000 it was 35.3 million (12.5 percent of the US population). A widely reported announcement by the Census Bureau claimed that Hispanics and Latinos surpassed African Americans as the country's largest minority group in 2003. Certainly not all of these Hispanics and Latinos speak Spanish regularly (or at all) or use Spanish media consistently. The Census Bureau estimates that 12 percent of the US Hispanic/Latino population age 5 and over speak Spanish at home. According to a Simmons Market Research Bureau (2003) National Hispanic Consumer Study, 19 percent speak only Spanish, 9 percent speak only English, 55 percent have limited English proficiency and 17 percent are fully English–Spanish bilingual. Where available, media use statistics are included in the following discussion of specific media.

The steady growth of the Hispanic/Latino population has significant political, economic and social implications for the United States, and Spanish language media play a noteworthy role. National political parties have actively sought the Hispanic/Latino vote since the 1980s, with Spanish language media as part of the strategy. As the number of registered Hispanic/Latino voters has grown, so has the group's potential for constituting a swing vote in local, state and national elections. Thus Hispanic/Latino-oriented media have received increased attention—and advertising revenues—for their ability to reach a sizeable portion of the electorate. Politicians are also increasingly wary of their stands on issues that may impact Hispanic/Latino voting patterns such as the immigration reform debate in spring 2006, which was closely covered by US Spanish language media and prompted a swing against some Republican candidates in the national elections that year.

Although its growth has been steady, the Hispanic/Latino market has garnered fluctuating attention from the press and major corporations since the 1980s, the so-called "Decade of the Hispanic." Demographic factors such as larger family size, higher-than-average household spending on consumer products, and long-term brand loyalty have attracted large corporations to the Hispanic/Latino market and to advertising in Spanish language media. The market growth and recognition of the profit potential it offers are likely to increase throughout the twenty-first century. Nevertheless, the percentage of total advertising spending in Hispanic/Latino-oriented media has always lagged behind the group's population percentage. Numerous scholars and community leaders have decried this imbalance and noted a tendency for mainstream US society to welcome Hispanic/Latino spending into the economy but not the people into US political and social systems. Not surprisingly, there is particular resistance to Spanish-dominant citizens and residents who are expected to assimilate to mainstream US culture and language as prior generations of non-English-speakers have.

Before we examine each of the US Spanish language media in turn, their collective place in broader historical changes should be noted. Investment, content and business models from other countries have been influential in the development of these media. Likewise, investment, content and business practices from the United States influence Spanish language media in other countries, especially within the Western Hemisphere. US Spanish language market growth has coincided with the hemispheric and global expansion of markets and media which in turn have been facilitated by freer trade, economic reform and technological change. Communication technologies, transformed since the 1980s by the advent of digitalization, are at the forefront of change. The latter part of this chapter reviews developments in new technology as they have impacted Spanish language media in the United States.

The Press

As noted in Chapter 3 regarding Mexico, the first print press in the Americas began publishing Spanish copy in Mexico City in 1533. The first publications in Spanish within the United States territory were *El Misisipí* (1808) and *El Mensagero Luisianés* (1809), both from New Orleans (Kanellos, 2000). Significantly, these followed on the heels of the Louisiana Purchase (1803) whereby the United States acquired 828,000 square miles of French territory in the center of the North American continent. Thus the buffer was largely erased between the expansionist United States with its growing territories to the east and Spanish, later Mexican, territory to the west. Kanellos (2000) recounts the founding of Spanish language newspapers in Texas (1813), Florida (1817), the north-east (1824) and New Mexico and California (1834).

Preceding, during and following the War for Texas Independence (1835–1836) and Mexican–American War (1846–1848) regional newspapers were important sources of information for Spanish-speaking audiences in US and Mexican territories whose citizenship status, social standing and titles to property would be influenced or determined by the outcome. Newspapers established in this period continued disseminating important political, economic and social news that helped inform and unify Spanish-speaking communities well after the conflicts. Over time, and at different places, the newspapers began the transition from an immigrant press emphasizing news from the country of origin and its relationship with the United States, to a minority press focusing coverage on community development and advocating for civil rights of their readers as well as greater influence over local, regional and national affairs (Miller, 1987). A number of US-based publications also advocated change in foreign lands. Exiles and expatriates from Latin America took advantage of press freedom and access to publishing resources in the United States to create an exile press which supported movements against governments, political and economic elites, religious institutions, etc. Thus US press freedoms influenced consequential political processes such as Spanish American independence from Spain, the French intervention in Mexico, the Spanish–American War, the Mexican Revolution, the Spanish Civil War and the Cuban Revolution (Kanellos, 2000). When other non-English publications waned in number during the middle decades of the twentieth century, the Spanish language press remained strong as immigration continued and government efforts such as the Bracero program (1942–1964) brought Mexican workers to the United States to meet unmet demand for labor. Similar programs brought labor from Puerto Rico and other areas of the Caribbean to the US mainland beginning in the World War I era.

As the prior discussion suggests, Hispanic/Latino communities in the United States differed from other immigrant populations because some families and population centers were established long before Mexico gained its independence from Spain, the United States imposed its dominion over Mexican Territories through the Treaty of Guadalupe-Hidalgo (1848) or Puerto Ricans were granted US citizenship in 1917. Geographic proximity facilitating fluid movement between the United States and the homeland as well as active family ties differentiate these ethnic minority communities from others. Many readers sought news from their country of origin and information that would help them adjust to life in their host country, as readers with different orientations still sought information in Spanish. This dynamic persists to the present day.

Spanish language publications have served as forums for political communication within the United States as well. They have communicated information about parties, candidates, legislation, law enforcement and similar mainstream political topics as most publications do. However, because they have served a minority population (on the national scale) they have also engaged in advocacy. For example, early in the twentieth century, as Hollywood produced and distributed so-called "greaser" films containing pejorative representations of Mexicans and Mexican-Americans, some newspaper owners along the US-Mexican border helped raise awareness and organize protests that succeeded in changing the representations (Keller, 1994). Print media also played central roles in the farm worker and Chicano power movements of the 1960s and 1970s.

Growth of the US Hispanic/Latino population has helped many Spanish language newspapers maintain or increase circulation and advertising revenues at a time when numerous English language publications are in decline due to an aging audience base, competition from various forms of electronic media and other factors. Bendixen and Associates (2005) report 20 percent of Hispanic/Latino adults prefer newspapers in Spanish over those in English. Between 1970 and 2002 the number of Spanish language daily newspapers grew from around 240 to over 650 and during the same period, according to Latino Print Network, their combined circulation increased from 140,000 to over 1.7 million (cited in Nealy, 2008). *La Opinión* in Los Angeles and *El Diario La Prensa* in New York, two of the leading newspapers in circulation, are properties of ImpreMedia, which in 2008 owned twenty-six print and online outlets including newspapers in seven of the top ten Latino/Hispanic metropolitan markets. Spanish language print media, while growing at a higher rate than English counterparts, is undergoing similar processes of ownership consolidation. Table 1.1 shows the top ten Spanish language newspapers in 2007 based on gross advertising revenues.

Table 1.1 Top Ten Spanish Language Newspapers by Gross Ad Revenue, 2007

Rank	Newspaper	2007 Ad Revenue (Gross) (US dollars)
1	*El Nuevo Herald* (Miami)	90,450,600
2	*La Opinión* (Los Angeles)	45,910,300
3	*El Diario* (Juárez, Mexico)	33,712,800
4	*El Diario La Prensa* (New York)	25,710,300
5	*Hoy* (Chicago)	20,088,600
6	*Hoy* (Los Angeles)	12,929,600
7	*La Raza* (Chicago)	11,649,500
8	*El Norte* (El Paso, TX/Juárez, Mexico)	10,754,100
9	*Hoy* (New York)	10,625,400
10	*Washington Hispanic*	10,393,200

Source: Adapted from *Advertising Age* (2008)

Although newspapers have historically had greater impact on Spanish-speaking communities in the United States than magazines, since the last quarter of the twentieth century magazines have grown in number and circulation. General interest English language magazines like *Hispanic* and specialized titles like *Hispanic Business*, founded in 1987 and 1979 respectively, increased their circulation in the 1980s and 1990s as the Hispanic/Latino market garnered more attention. This trend helped congeal a national Hispanic/Latino market, a process that is still underway and which is challenged by significant diversity within the United States. Among the most popular titles are Spanish versions of well-known English magazines such as *People en Español* and *Selecciones* (*Reader's Digest*); other such as *TV y Novelas* and *Vanidades* have their headquarters in other countries. Many titles reflect the audience segmentation trend in media from the 1990s onward that has led to a splintering based on demographic factors such as age, interests and lifestyle. Examples published in the United States include *Estrenos* (Hollywood and celebrities), *ESPN Deportes* (sports), *Iguana* (children aged 7 to 12) and *Siempre Mujer* (for US women to stay connected with Hispanic/Latina culture) which reported that its advertising revenue increased 39 percent from 2007 to 2008. By way of comparison, *Ladies' Home Journal*'s ad revenue decreased about 10 percent over the same period (Nealy, 2008). Table 1.2 reports the top ten Hispanic/Latino-oriented magazines in 2007 based on gross advertising revenues.

Table 1.2 Top Ten Hispanic/Latino-Oriented Magazines by Gross Ad Revenue, 2007

Rank	Magazine	2007 Ad Revenue (Gross) (US dollars)
1	*People en Español*	49,692,500
2	*Latina* (English)	36,042,100
3	*TV y Novelas* (Mexico)	16,152,800
4	*Selecciones* (Reader's Digest)	15,330,400
5	*Siempre Mujer*	12,890,500
6	*Vanidades* (Mexico)	12,607,800
7	*Ser Padres*	9,699,400
8	*Hispanic Business* (English)	8,055,200
9	*Mira*	7,942,200
10	*Sports Illustrated Latino*	6,670,300

Source: Adapted from *Advertising Age* (2008)

Special interest magazines have also benefited from the growth of the Internet, a topic discussed later in this chapter.

Radio

Once radio emerged as a commercial medium in the 1920s and 1930s, Spanish was heard full-time over the airwaves only in small markets; in larger markets it was relegated to off-peak hours on stations broadcasting in English. As described by Gutiérrez and Schement (1979), brokers purchased airtime from English language stations wishing to increase revenues at times of low listenership. The broker arranged the programming—usually consisting of live music (later recorded music), drama, discussion and community calendar items—and sold advertising in the form of announcements read during the program. Early on it was a small group of businesses that were interested in reaching the Spanish-speaking Hispanic/Latino audience and could be convinced that off-peak radio was a legitimate medium for doing so. Some brokers like Rodolfo Hoyos, heard in Los Angeles from 1932 to 1967, also played musical instruments and/or sang as part of the entertainment (Gutiérrez & Schement, 1979, p. 6). Another way for Spanish to cross the airwaves was for an English language station that was not competitive in a particular market to switch language formats in search of listeners, advertising revenue and, ultimately, profit.

A content analysis of Spanish language radio programs conducted in 1941 by Arnheim and Bayne (cited in Gutiérrez & Schement, 1979, p. 7) estimated that 264 hours of Spanish language content was broadcast weekly in the United States. The stations in New York, Arizona, Texas and California which the researchers analyzed were dominated by music content at 88 percent of airtime followed by news (4 percent), talk (3 percent), drama (3 percent) and other (2 percent). The news broadcast in Spanish placed heavy emphasis (80 percent) on international reports. The most common products advertised were medicines followed by movies, food, clothing and furniture. Arnheim and Bayne also noted the strong appeals to Hispanic/Latino unity and listeners' nations of origin in much of the advertising. In reviewing the 1941 study, Gutiérrez and Schement (1979) note the political sensitivity of non-English radio broadcast during wartime as well as the difficulty it represented for people whose lives are lived in more than one culture and language. (This is not an unfamiliar dynamic in the post-September 11, 2001 environment where immigration status and border security have become volatile issues.)

The first Spanish language radio station to be owned and operated by a Hispanic/Latino is believed to be KCOR in San Antonio, Texas, which began broadcasting in 1946. Spanish content had been available to San Antonio residents since at least 1928 through the broker system described above. The struggle to increase radio station ownership and management by Hispanics/Latinos dates from the origins of commercial radio and continues into the twenty-first century. A related issue among US Hispanics/Latinos in the radio industry concerns achieving better balance between United States and foreign-born talent and management. On-air talent and entrepreneurs, especially from Mexico, Puerto Rico and Cuba, have participated in the US industry since its inception, and prior to the growth of Miami as a Spanish language production center (Sinclair, 2003), a vast majority of the music played on air originated from overseas. At times this has sparked tensions, even walkouts, especially when jobs or promotions have appeared to go to non-US workers, or issues of accent or linguistic purity have been raised.

In the 1950s and 1960s US Spanish language radio began to institutionalize along network, advertising and promotional lines. Groups of radio stations with holdings in multiple markets began to standardize programming so as to reduce costs and increase efficiency. Agencies specializing in Spanish language media began offering spot sales in multiple markets and targeted larger entities having more substantial advertising budgets than the local, community focused businesses that had sustained Spanish language radio in the early decades. The challenge was to convince deep-pocketed corporations that there were solid long-term dividends to be earned from investing in the Hispanic/Latino market, and that Spanish language radio was an effective medium to reach Hispanic/Latino consumers. The challenge of selling the Hispanic/Latino market to advertisers continues in the twenty-first century when advertising spending on Hispanic/Latino-oriented media (whether in English, Spanish or bilingual) remains far from parity with the group's population or consumer-spending figures.

The 1970s and 1980s saw a deepening of the institutionalization trend. Although, as Gutiérrez and Schement (1979) point out, non-Latino/Hispanic investors had been involved in the industry from its inception, bigger players with deeper pockets began expressing and acting on serious interest in the Spanish language market. Some of the credit for this growth must be attributed to firms representing networks and stations, or "radio reps," four of which dominated the market in the 1980s and 1990s: Caballero Spanish Media, Katz Hispanic Radio, Spanish Broadcasting System and Lotus Hispanic Reps. Of course corporate interest was also spurred by the remarkable growth and performance of Spanish language stations which garnered number one ratings in influential markets like Los Angeles, Miami and San Antonio (Adelson, 1993) and were covered closely in the business press. Significant gains were also made by stations in other markets such as New York and Chicago. *Hispanic Business* reported in the late 1980s and early 1990s that stations in these five cities consistently dominated the top ten of Hispanic/Latino radio billings.

The Telecommunications Act of 1996 endeavored to increase competition in broadcasting by easing restrictions on station ownership and permitting greater cross-ownership of different media outlets by a single entity. In the wake of the Act, Spanish language radio underwent a similar process of ownership consolidation as did English language radio. In 2003 Univision Radio purchased Hispanic Broadcasting Corp. for nearly $3 billion acquiring sixty-eight stations (eighteen AM and fifty FM). Clear Channel Communications, the company most closely associated with post-1996 ownership consolidation, sold its shares in the Univision group and began converting stations in select markets to Spanish in order to capture more of the Hispanic/Latino revenue stream. In 2008 Univision Radio owned and/or operated seventy stations whereas Entravision Communication Corp. owned and operated forty-eight, Liberman Broadcasting twenty-one, Clear Channel eighteen and Spanish Broadcasting System had ten in the mainland United States and five in Puerto Rico, according to company websites. It should be noted that Univision stations were in sixteen of the top twenty-five markets and all but one of Spanish Broadcasting's mainland properties were in a top five Hispanic/Latino market. By contrast, all of Clear Channel's were in smaller markets. Of the top five Spanish language stations in 2007 (measured by cumulative audience), numbers one, three and five were located in Los Angeles and two and four in New York: three of the stations were Spanish Broadcasting System properties, and two were Univision (*Advertising Age*, 2008).

Important shifts in Spanish radio formats are also worth noting. New musical genres such as Reggaetón developed in the 2000s while institutional shifts led to new ways of packaging and delivering news and entertainment in Spanish. According to a report by Arbitron Corp. (2008), the largest ratings service for commercial radio in the United States, there were 872 Spanish language radio stations operating in the United States as of 2007; the majority used a Mexican Regional format (302) followed by Spanish Variety (146) and Spanish Contemporary

(126). In 2008 *Advertising Age*'s annual guide to Hispanic marketing and media identified the top seven formats for Spanish language radio—in terms of audience percentage reached—in descending order: Mexican Regional, Spanish Contemporary, Spanish Adult, Spanish Tropical, Spanish News/Talk, Latino Urban and Spanish Variety. Bendixen and Associates (2005) found that on average 55 percent of US Hispanics/Latinos tune in Spanish language radio regularly, and the majority of them prefer Spanish as their primary language format. At time of writing the economic downturn of 2008–2009 had slowed market growth, but Spanish language radio will be poised to continue its remarkable expansion when the economy recovers.

Television

Like radio, Spanish language television began rather sporadically with content aired at non-peak hours on predominantly English language stations located in cities with significant Hispanic/Latino populations. A brokering system for television functioned much like that for radio described above. The host typically performed and was sufficiently well connected in the community to draw a variety of high-profile guests to the show. Due to the higher costs of television production and distribution compared to radio, the barriers to access were more formidable. Nonetheless, Spanish language programming began airing at non-peak hours in the 1950s, especially on stations in the south-west.

The significant capital investment required delayed entrepreneurs' recognition of the potential for full-time TV broadcasting in Spanish in the United States. The initial capital and programming originated from Mexico. Rene Anselmo, an international program sales executive for Telesistema Mexicana (now Televisa), convinced the company's president, Emilio Azcárraga Vidaurreta, to explore the possibilities of US Spanish language television. In the early 1960s Azcárraga Vidaurreta organized a group of investors from both countries so as to comply with Federal Communications Commission regulations limiting foreign ownership and control of broadcast entities to 25 percent (United States Communication Act, Section 310[b]). The investors formed two companies, Spanish International Communications Corp. (SICC), which held licenses for television stations, and Spanish International Network (SIN), which provided programming and advertising sales for the SICC owned and operated stations. SICC began acquiring ultra-high frequency (UHF) stations in cities with high Hispanic/Latino populations beginning in San Antonio (1961) and Los Angeles (1962). SICC and SIN grew in step with the Spanish-speaking population during the 1960s, expanding to other key markets such as New York, Chicago, Miami and San Francisco, but did not become profitable until the 1970s.

With profit came problems. The Azcárraga family and other Mexican investors sought to recover their considerable investments in the US market while some of the US investors preferred to fold profits back into the Spanish International companies. Internal disagreements led to two legal processes: a stockholder derivative lawsuit claiming breach of fiduciary duty by the SICC/SIN executive leadership (Fouce v. SICC, 1976), and an inquiry into illegal control by foreign nationals of US broadcasting entities, in this case the SICC stations (In re SICC, 1986). The cases took a full decade to adjudicate before being settled in 1986. A federal judge found that control of the five full-power and five low-power SICC stations had indeed exceeded the limit allowed by law; as a result SICC was sold to the highest bidder in a sales process overseen by the court (SIN was exempt from the ownership and control limits because networks are regulated differently than broadcast stations). The court's selection of a $301.5 million bid by Hallmark Cards Corp. and its partner First Chicago was controversial in that a higher though less secure bid had been tendered by a group of Hispanic/Latino investors. At the time of the transfer to Hallmark, the SICC stations group, which had recently been renamed Univision, consisted of ten owned-and-operated stations, yet reached hundreds of communities through affiliated stations, satellite translator stations and cable systems. Within months of purchasing SICC, Hallmark paid another $300 million for the Univision *network* in order to guarantee a regular supply of programs from Mexico's prolific producer, Televisa.

The acquisition of SIN was likely inspired by an important simultaneous development: competition arrived in the form of the Telemundo network. The Telemundo Group was majority shareholder in station KVEA in Los Angeles which demonstrated phenomenal audience growth shortly after switching to a Spanish language format in 1985. So much pent-up interest was released that Univision's LA station, KMEX-TV, saw an *increase* in its audience at the same time KVEA's ratings spiked. This success encouraged the Telemundo Group to acquire Spanish language television stations in Miami and San Juan, Puerto Rico in 1986, then two more in New York/New Jersey and San Francisco/San Jose the following year. By 1992, Telemundo owned and operated six full-power and four low-power stations while its programming appeared on twenty-two affiliated US stations, three affiliated Mexican stations along the US border, and on cable systems in fourteen states as well as Washington DC (Esparza, 1998). Telemundo's station acquisition slowed for a time as competition with Univision put more pressure on program content that would attract audiences and advertising revenue.

Competition led to expansion of Spanish language program production within the United States and efforts to sell such programs on the international market. (Most Spanish language productions within the United States prior to the late 1980s were news programs which do not "travel" well to other societies.) Many of the early shows produced in the United States were Spanish language versions of popular English language programs—courtroom shows and talk shows, for example. Industry representatives reasoned that programs which appealed to diverse Hispanic/Latino audiences in the United States would attract diverse viewers in international markets as well. However, several US-based *telenovelas* (soap operas) featuring multicultural Hispanic/Latino casts were unsuccessful internationally. Other programs like the variety show *Sabado Gigante*, which relocated its production from Chile to Miami in 1986, became an international success. So did *El Show de Cristina*, a talk show hosted by Cristina Saralegui that sometimes covered controversial topics such as homosexuality and child abuse which had been taboo to broadcast in most Latin American countries. This closer integration among the United States' Spanish language sector and international markets was intertwined with the movements toward globalization and technological convergence discussed below.

With their production facilities firmly established in South Florida and program export operations underway, Univision and Telemundo focused on expanding their reach and revenues domestically. In 1992 Univision underwent a second ownership change as Hallmark, disappointed with its investment, sought to divest of Spanish language television. It agreed to sell the network and station group for $550 million to a partnership of A. Jerrold Perenchio, a Hollywood producer and investor, a Venezuelan TV network named Venevision, and Televisa, the same entity whose principals had launched the US industry through the Spanish International companies three decades earlier. The Latin American entities held small percentages of the station group in order to comply with the ownership restrictions discussed above. The partnership oversaw steady growth of Univision, which was headed for a time by Henry Cisneros, the first Hispanic/Latino elected mayor of a major US city (San Antonio) and Secretary of Housing and Urban Development (1993–1997). Another ownership change occurred in 2006 when the Perenchio-Venevision-Televisa partnership sold Univision to Broadcast Media Partners for $12.3 billion. The

$11.75 million difference in the selling price of Univision from 1992 to 2006 is clear evidence of the increased profitability of Hispanic broadcasting.

The Telemundo network also saw key ownership changes in the 1990s and 2000s. Telemundo was never on as solid financial footings as its competitor and even underwent Chapter 11 bankruptcy protection during 1993–1994. In 1997 a partnership of Sony Corp. and Liberty Media paid $539 million to acquire controlling interest (about 70 percent) of the network and station group. By increasing their investment in the network, Sony and Liberty Media aimed to improve programming, marketing and distribution, thereby making it a viable competitor with Univision. In 2001 NBC paid $1.98 billion for Telemundo's ten stations and took on another $700 million in debt as part of the agreement (the network also had forty affiliated stations at the time). Thus Telemundo has become part of the NBC-Universal conglomerate and is a key media property involved in cross-promotions with other NBC networks, synergies with Internet-based properties and a variety of advertising sales deals.

As is the case with other non-mainstream media, convincing advertisers of Spanish language television's reach and persuasiveness has been a challenge since the industry's inception. In the early years, audience measurement was comparatively unsophisticated as researchers went door-to-door to interview viewers or had members of selected Spanish-speaking households complete diaries concerning their media use. These methods led to disagreements between network or station representatives and advertisers concerning the veracity of the self-report data, thereby complicating the sensitive process of determining advertising rates. In 1989, the television ratings company Nielsen announced a new Spanish language service which began with 150 meters connected to televisions in Los Angeles households, then expanded to other key markets. In order to secure more accurate counts of Spanish language viewership and thereby facilitate the negotiations over advertising rates, Univision and Telemundo subsidized the service, some-thing English language networks had never done. As technology advanced and the Spanish language market matured, new methods for linking television viewing to specific members of a household, such as the People Meter, were employed. In 2007, Nielsen underscored the growth and stability of the market by disbanding the separate Spanish language service and drawing its Hispanic/Latino viewing statistics from the same national People Meter sample as the general market service. Nielsen reported that the number of Hispanic television households was projected to increase 4.3 percent to 12.6 million in 2008, a rate three times greater than for the general population (Bachman, 2008).

A third competitor, Azteca América, entered the US Spanish language market in 2001 through a partnership with Pappas Broadcasting of Visalia, California. By 2005 the network reached forty-two US media markets; in 2008 the network claimed to reach fifty-seven markets through twelve over-the-air-outlets and forty-five cable and/or satellite systems (Azteca América, 2008; Romano, 2005). Azteca América is a principal international arm of Grupo Televisión Azteca, based in Mexico, a network that emerged from the privatization of the government-owned network Imevisión in 1993. An investment group headed by the Salinas Pliego family purchased the network for $642 million in a 1993 sale that was controversial for its political ramifications and charges of influence peddling leveled by unsuccessful bidders. Televisión Azteca has a formidable competitor in Televisa within Mexico and, as we have seen, in the US Spanish language sector as well.

Although over-the-air networks, especially Univision and Telemundo, laid the groundwork for Spanish language television in the United States, pay television services have grown in scope and influence, especially as the Hispanic/Latino audience has fragmented along demographic lines. Galavisión, a cable-based cousin of the Spanish International and Univision companies, was launched in 1979 as the first national-level Spanish language cable service. It originally offered *telenovelas*, comedies and talk shows, later expanding into news, sports and special programs, sometimes transmitted live from Mexico and other areas of Latin America. In the 1980s and 1990s, a number of large players in US television launched Spanish language services to open new revenue streams from their programming libraries, take advantage of higher capacity, lower-cost satellite services, and establish a presence as media globalized in a new digital age. Most of these services were available on US cable systems as well as in Latin America. This was the genesis of program services such as ESPN Latin America (1989), HBO Olé (1990), TNT Latin America (1991), Canal de Noticias NBC ("NBC News Channel," 1993), Cine Canal ("Movie Channel," a partnership including Paramount, MGM, Universal and Twentieth Century Fox, 1993), Discovery Channel Latin America (1993), Fox Latin America (1993), Gems (female-focused, 1993), MTV Latino (1993), Tele-Uno (Spelling Entertainment, 1993) and USA Network (1994).

As confidence in—and revenues from—Spanish language television grew during the 1990s and 2000s, more demographically streamlined services appeared, and they began to be bundled together and sold as Spanish language packages on cable and satellite systems. New music and lifestyle channels targeted pre-teens and adolescents, talk and lifestyle channels sought women, and sports channels were geared toward men. Another important development in this period was bilingual and English language networks aimed at Hispanic/Latino viewers. SíTV launched in 2004 with the intent of attracting young "English-speaking Latinos who consume English media, but still want shows that speak to their Latino roots" (PR.com, 2008). Mun2, a project of Telemundo began in 2001, also with the intent of attracting English-speaking Hispanic/Latino youth, though some Spanish and so-called "Spanglish" is also spoken. The network's name is a play on the world *mundo* meaning "world;" viewers inhabit and often blend influences from two worlds: a Hispanic/Latino one in Spanish and a mainstream US one in English. *Advertising Age* (2008) reported that all of the top ten cable TV Spanish language programs measured by Nielsen People Meters in Hispanic households April 28–May 25, 2008 appeared on two networks: Galavisión and Fox Sports en Español. The top five most viewed Spanish language cable networks were, in descending order: Galavisión, Mun2, Fox Sports en Español, ESPN Deportes (Sports) and Discovery en Español (*Advertising Age*, 2008).

Boom in the Age of Digital Media

The 1990s and 2000s saw an interesting confluence of Hispanic/Latino influence on mainstream US popular culture, accelerated growth in the Hispanic/Latino consumer market, rapid change in communication technologies through digitization, and a blurring of boundaries among media industries through a process known as convergence. Spanish language media both influenced and were affected by these forces. The so-called "Latin Boom" in US popular culture was fueled in part by successful Spanish language singers such as Marc Anthony, Shakira and Ricky Martin crossing over to the English market. Actors like Edward James Olmos, Jennifer Lopez, Jimmy Smits, Selma Hayek and Antonio Banderas made Hispanics/Latinos more visible in Hollywood. Some English language performers also crossed over (if briefly) to the Spanish market; examples are Linda Ronstadt, Bon Jovi, Wyclef Jean, Beyonce, Dr. Dre and Christina Aguilera. Certainly expansion of the US Spanish language market is a motivating factor for these cross-language forays, and one that is likely to persist. In 2007, ad spending for Hispanic/Latino media grew 4.2 percent compared to just 0.6 percent for US media as a whole (*Advertising Age*, 2008). Prior to the 2008–2009 economic downturn, the Association of Hispanic Advertising Agencies (2008) projected that consumer spending by Hispanics/Latinos would reach $992 billion by 2009.

Spanish language media has been changed by the technological shifts that began transforming media industries around the globe in the late 1980s. The analog-to-digital transition in technologies used for production, distribution and receiving/playback has improved image and sound quality, increased the number of available channels, and augmented storage capacity while at the same time lowering costs and placing more power with the audience to provide feedback and create their own high-fidelity content at ever-decreasing prices.

Globalization is another key development. Recall from the prior sections of this chapter that throughout their history, US Spanish language media have maintained significant connections with industries in other countries, especially Mexico. These connections became the pathways to market expansion as content producers, distributors and advertisers sought to knit together markets in the Spanish-speaking world. The spread of newer communication technologies such as direct-to-home television, Internet and mobile telephony is predicated upon international corporations and/or consortiums building ever-larger customer bases. A shared language and common cultural roots are central factors in initiating and sustaining such international ventures.

Because of the high rate of pay television penetration in US households, direct-to-home television has had less impact on the US Spanish language sector than many Latin American countries. A larger challenge for US companies has been to establish a strong presence on the World Wide Web and to make sound strategic alliances with new media companies that will direct consumers to their television channels, websites and other media properties. In 1999 Univision became the first US Spanish language television network to launch its website, univision.com. It was cited in one study as the most visited US Spanish language website from 2000 to 2006 (Univision.com touts ranking, 2006). However, *Advertising Age* (2008) lists telemundo.yahoo.com as the leading recipient of Internet advertising revenues among US-based Spanish language websites in 2007 (over $180 million). Telemundo's site edged out univision.com, the second highest earner, by $13 million. It should be noted that significant Spanish language Internet use is likely conducted by bilingual and even some English-dominant users: only one-third of Spanish-dominant Hispanics/Latinos were found to use the Internet (Fox & Livingston, 2007).

In 2007 univision.com added a video portal providing users access to clips from Univision TV shows, interviews with Hispanic celebrities, music videos and news clips. For its part, Telemundo partnered with multiple Internet portals including espanol.com and quepasa.com early in the 2000s, before it established a more consistent presence with telemundo.yahoo.com in 2006. Like the Univision site, it features promotional material for Telemundo television shows and links to other media under its NBC corporate umbrella. Azteca América has similar intentions, but did not appear in *Advertising Age*'s (2008) list of the top ten advertising recipients.

The networks have also endeavored to encourage interaction with and among viewers via the Internet. In 2003 Univision aired *Rebeca*, a *telenovela* in which plot lines were determined in part by audience input through univision.com. Thus, viewer's preferences expressed online influenced the outcome of three male characters' competition for the affections of the female protagonist. On Valentine's Day, 2008 Telemundo launched *holamun2.com: El Show*, a 30-minute weekly magazine program that encourages viewers to integrate their television viewing with Internet and mobile phone use. Such programs may be expected to increase in number and frequency as more Spanish-speaking Hispanics/Latinos gain broadband access to the Internet and the networks gain experience in linking their television and Internet interests. Both networks have launched digital media divisions to reach consumers through interactive technologies such as cellular telephones and iPods. Martinez Ruiz-Velasco (2007) reports about 15.7 million Hispanics own a mobile phone. Not all those devices have video capabilities, of course, although a 2007 Forrester Research report indicated that Hispanic mobile-data users are three times more likely to download videos than non-Hispanics (Martinez Ruiz-Velasco, 2007). *Advertising Age* (2008) reported that Hispanics/Latinos use mobile data services more frequently than the general US population in nine out of ten service categories. Univision Móvil launched in 2004 providing mobile games, ring tones, wallpaper, news snippets and mobile greeting applications; it has subsequently expanded to offer more extensive audio and video services requiring higher bandwidth. Telemundo dedicated a new company division to digital technology in 2005. In April, 2007 the network, along with parent company NBC, became a founding member of the Open Mobile Video Coalition, a group organized to promote the development of technical standards for mobile digital broadcast TV in the United States (Bachman, 2007).

Conclusion

Since its origin early in the nineteenth century, Spanish language media in the United States has helped its audiences stay connected with their cultures of origin, informed about their local communities and the nation, and entertained. Constant themes across the different time periods and media covered in this chapter are population expansion, market growth and commercialism. Publicly supported media in Spanish are few and far between, likely because of the general expectation that immigrants to the United States learn English, the largely commercial nature of US media, and the sensitivity in some regions about dedicating public funds to non-English initiatives.

Several topics discussed in the body of this chapter are likely to occupy the attention and activity of US Spanish language media researchers at least through the middle of the twenty-first century. The same technological revolution which has enabled a proliferation of media channels and information services has also facilitated audience research, the creation of detailed demographic databases and data mining for commercial purposes. Thus, increasing segmentation of the Hispanic/Latino media audience is as much a result of more and better data being available to content producers, marketers and advertisers as of any natural maturation of the market and its industries. Narrower segments of the audience are likely to be identified by combinations of demographic data: age, country of origin, geographic region within the United States and lifestyle preferences (see Korzenny & Korzenny, 2005). As a result, analytical research concerning US Spanish language media is likely to focus on that market research, how it is being conducted and how it is being used (preferably not abused) by industry participants.

We may also reasonably expect that new communication technologies will continue to be developed and introduced at a rapid pace. Some of these will promote further convergence, the erosion of barriers between distinct media. One factor in accelerating convergence is conglomeration—fewer corporations are owning and controlling a larger percentage of media outlets. This will encourage studies of how power is concentrating within US Spanish language media and the resulting influences on content. Given the projected growth of the Hispanic/Latino population through the first half of the twenty-first century, influence within media industries and, by extension, over the audience, will be an increasingly important issue. A related concern is likely to be how audiences use Spanish language media, and for what purposes, in the complex context of convergence.

Future research will probably emphasize complicated language dynamics among the audience. This chapter has noted that bilingual media appeared in the 1990s; we may expect that trend to continue and even deepen as immigration continues to add native speakers of Spanish to the population and larger numbers of US citizens and residents become bilingual. Therefore, analyses of media content will probably focus on Spanish, English and bilingual content directed to the Hispanic/Latino audience. This also suggests greater emphasis on how and why media influences relations among different subgroups within the Hispanic/Latino population. There is likely to be more emphasis given qualitative aspects of the audience as researchers endeavor to move beyond the access, exposure and consumption questions that have driven much of the audience research through the 2000s.

We may expect that Spanish-speaking communities will continue to exist in the United States throughout the twenty-first century, and that English-dominant and bilingual Hispanics/Latinos will maintain an interest in recovering, maintaining and/or reinvigorating their cultural roots through Spanish language media. Mainstream US society, in recognition of its history as a nation of immigrants, should support the existence and use of such media—it is quite clear that corporate America will, as long as the profits continue to flow.

References

Adelson, A. (1993, January 25). Spanish radio leads in Los Angeles. *New York Times.* Retrieved September 14, 2008 from http://query.nytimes.com/gst/fullpage.html?res=9F0CE1D6113AF936A15752C0A965958260.

Advertising Age. (2008, July 28). *Hispanic Fact Pack: Annual guide to Hispanic marketing and media.* (2008 edition). Crain Communications. Retrieved September 14, 2008 from http://adage.com/images/random/datacenter/2008/hispfactpack08.pdf.

Arbitron Corp. (2008). *Hispanic Radio Today: How America listens to radio* (2008 edition). Retrieved September 15, 2008 from www.arbitron.com/downloads/hispanicradiotoday08.pdf.

Association of Hispanic Advertising Agencies. (2008). *Hispanic Media and Marketing Factoids.* Retrieved September 21, 2008 from www.ahaa.org/media/Finalfacts04.htm.

Azteca América. (2008). Cobertura de canales [Channel coverage]. Retrieved September 22, 2008 from http://azteca america.terra.com/cobertura-canales.htm.

Bachman, K. (2007, July 24). More stations join Open Mobile Video Coalition. *Mediaweek.* Retrieved October 27, 2007 through Lexis-Nexis database.

Bachman, K. (2008, August 28). Nielsen: TV households to increase 1.5 percent for 2008–09 season. *Mediaweek.* Retrieved September 21, 2008 from www.mediaweek.com/mw/content_display/news/media-agencies-research/e3i1ceb 4468ca0772e7143529f7fa375d45.

Bendixen and Associates. (2005). *The Ethnic Media in America: The giant hidden in plain sight.* Retrieved September 14, 2008 from www.ncmonline.com/polls/full_em_poll.pdf.

Esparza, E. (1998, January–February). The Telemundo takeover: Can a corporate coup save the embattled network? *Hispanic.* Retrieved May 20, 2000 from www.hisp.com/janfeb98/telemundo.html.

Fouce Entertainment Enterprises v. Spanish International Communications Corp. (1976). U.S. District Court, Central District of California, Los Angeles – CV 76-3451 (November 4, 1976).

Fox, S. & Livingston, G. (2007, March 17). *Latinos online.* Pew Hispanic Center and Pew Internet Project Report. Retrieved October 12, 2007 from www.pewinternet.org/pdfs/Latinos_Online_March_14_2007.pdf.

Gutiérrez, F. F. & Schement, J. R. (1979). *Spanish Language Radio in the Southwestern United States.* Austin, TX: Center for Mexican American Studies, University of Texas at Austin.

In re Spanish International Communications Corp. (1986). Federal Communications Commission Release no. 86D-1. (January 8, 1986).

Kanellos, N. (2000). *Hispanic Periodicals in the United States, Origins to 1960: A brief history and comprehensive bibliography.* Houston, TX: Arte Público.

Keller, G. D. (1994). *Hispanics and United States Film: An overview and handbook.* Tempe, AZ: Bilingual Press/Editorial Bilingüe.

Korzenny, F. & Korzenny, B. A. (2005). *Hispanic Marketing: A cultural perspective.* Burlington, MA: Elsevier Butterworth-Heinemann.

Martinez Ruiz-Velasco, L. (2007, April 23). Mobile video booms among Latinos. *Advertising Age,* S-5.

Miller, S. M. (1987). Introduction. In S. M. Miller (Ed.) *The Ethnic Press in the United States: A historical analysis and handbook* (pp. xi–xxii). New York: Greenwood.

Nealy, M. J. (2008, July 24). Spanish language media market in a growth phase. *Diverse Issues in Higher Education.* Retrieved September 14, 2008 from www.diverseeducation.com/artman/publish/article_11437.shtml.

PR.com (2008). *SiTV company overview.* Retrieved September 21, 2008 from www.pr.com/company-profile/overview/3104

. (2005, November 21). Station to station. *Broadcasting & Cable, 135*, p. 10.

Market Research Bureau. (2003). *National Hispanic Consumer Survey.* Retrieved October 1, 2008 from w.smrb.com/aspx/content.aspx?pid=4&sid=46&page=Core_Solutions_National_Hispanic_Consumer_Survey

Sinclair, j. (2003). The Hollywood of Latin America: Miami as regional center in the television trade. *Television and New Media*, 4(3), 211–229.

Univision touts ranking as no. 1 most visited Spanish-language website (2006, September 18). *Wireless News.* Retrieved October 10, 2007, from LexisNexis database.

2
The Media in Spain
Three Decades of Transformation

Ángel Arrese, Juan Pablo Artero and Mónica Herrero
University of Navarra, Spain

Introduction

Since the 1970s, Spain has seen a series of profound changes. In that period, the country has managed to get out of the dark tunnel in which it has laid for half a century, due to the civil war and Franco's military dictatorship, and has become a modern nation, adopting a more significant role both in Europe and the rest of the world. In almost every social, political and economic sphere, there have been fundamental changes thanks to that process of opening up to the world, to the release of energies and to an ever-increasing optimistic view of Spain's potential.

There is a debate as to whether this quarter of a century has undergone a revolution, an evolution, or some other kind of process. The idea of transformation, a change in forms, no matter how deep that change may be, best reflects the fact that, at the same time that it seems that everything has changed, some deeply rooted Spanish cultural, social and political customs remain unchanged. In that transformation process, the mass media have played a key role, and they themselves constitute a proof of the modernization process the country is undergoing, which has helped Spain become a "normal country," like any other developed nation, in almost any field considered.

Given the close ties between the mass media and the events that take place in society—in a kind of continuous and interchangeable cause–effect relationship—a parallel will be established between the main transformations which have occurred in the country and their impact on the mass media. In order to do that, it is necessary to begin by referring briefly to the political transition, economic modernization and socio-cultural "liberation" that has taken place since the mid-1970s.

All Changes and Quite a Lot Remains

The political transition which Spain underwent from 1975, following the death of General Franco, is well known. It brought about a peaceful and orderly transition from a dictatorship to a democracy, to a parliamentary monarchy in particular. At the same time, a second transition took place, less spectacular but significant nevertheless, which has not yet concluded. It consisted in giving way to a decentralized government creating what has been termed State of Autonomies (*Estado de las Autonomías*): seventeen autonomous regions, each with its own degree of autonomy and hopes for self-government.

Both processes brought an end to the Franco regime, which had kept Spain isolated from the ongoing historical changes affecting the Western world. Since then, very distinct governments have ruled the country: centre-right governments (1978–1982), left-wing governments (1982–1996), right-wing governments (1996–2004) and back to left-wing governments (2004 to the present).

All have managed to consolidate the Spanish democracy, though not without problems, many of them in relation to the fact that now and again Spain has relived events and attitudes pertaining to a certain "culture of regime," with some authoritarian reminiscences. Some of them, as it will be explained, have to do with the way the mass media have been treated in some specific situations.

Along with political transition, the second main transformation has been economic modernization. In fact, the process of eradication of the autarchic economic system—a self-sufficient economy—was initiated in the 1960s, although only the downfall of the political regime enabled Spain to achieve an economy both open and integrated in the international economic system. Spain's entry to the European Economic Community in 1986 gave rise to complete economic normalization. It was from that very moment, while a neoliberal wave was sweeping across the Western world, that the free market economy was accepted as the right economic system for the future. The Spanish economy was moving away from its agricultural and industrial past, positioning itself as an economy of services. As a consequence, foreign investment steadily began to pour into Spain, a large number of state monopolies started to crash to the tune of long live the people's capitalism and privatization, while Spanish managers and companies discovered (by the 1990s) their own particular yet risky paradise in the globalization era: the Latin American markets.

Having left the autarchic economy, Spain obviously learned along the way of ever-present diseases such as inflation, unemployment or stockmarket crashes and there was no chance for the state to disguise or correct them. In any case, whether past or present, beyond or near the inexorable market logic, the economic modernization has not prevented one of the country's essential economic values from being a subtle way of defining quality of life, which is more related with enjoying life than with creating and accumulating wealth.

Finally, as in the case of political and economic changes, the downfall of the regime meant an enormous social and cultural liberation. A traditional, conservative, demure society let its hair down, seemingly overnight, and tried to gulp down anything coming from abroad, good or bad: "Sex & drugs & rock & roll," as Ian Dury was singing by then. Fortunately, these centrifugal forces have been calmed down by centripetal ones and traditional pillars of the Spanish society such as family (although it is being eroded more and more), solidarity (even though individualism is on the rampage) and a dominant Catholic tradition (with an increasing decline of followers) still constitute the backbone of this society. Also, after the death of Franco, a particular and historically well-known political and cultural movement, a nationalistic one, began to emerge once again with great force, perhaps excessive. Basques, Catalans and Galicians set forth on a journey of cultural reconstruction which would soon clash with the typical Spanish image which the Franco regime had so earnestly created.

All the above is, of course, just a brief review of a very complex process, which cannot be simplified in a few ideas. But, accepting the simplification, some of these few ideas are essential to understand what has happened with the Spanish mass media since Franco's death (see Barrera, 1995a, 1995b; Gunther, Montero & Wert, 1999).

The media system has moved away from a closed and hijacked system, with censorship at all levels and a rigid governmental control of editors and company managers; a media system in which newspapers, television and radio were used as a big propagandistic machine, not as much to spread any sort of ideology as much as to work for the reduction of the influence of politics in society. From that situation, a system of modern, free, diverse and plural mass media has finally emerged. But the process of transformation has also had a special development. Since the late 1970s, the state has slowly stepped down in its role as media manager and owner, although politics, especially partisan politics, may have played too excessive a role in the state's endeavor to free and favor the reconstruction of the sector. In fact, the abolition of certain monopolies by the government has produced too much servitude in specific moments, giving rise to powerful mass media groups which hold strong ties with the reigning political power. This is especially true of the television industry, which, strictly speaking, is the only traditional media that was in the past a monopoly and is now a very competitive market. At the same time that this process of liberalization occurs, the decentralization of power and the creation of autonomies have giving rise to new problems in some of the main Spanish regions, in which new media groups have been created under the control of regional governments.

From State-Controlled to a Business-Oriented Media

From 1976 to 2000, two fundamental stages in the development of mass media in Spain can be distinguished. These stages changed the operations of the media industries in Spain.

The first stage, from 1976 to 1989, can be identified as the "normative/legal development," that enabled a shift from censorship to freedom of expression, from a state-run system to a system in which private-run media has increasing protagonism, and from a centralized media and communication policy to a decentralized one, in the context of a common European media policy. The year 1989 marked the closing of this period, when the first three licenses were granted for commercial television channels (Villagrasa, 1992).

The second stage, from 1989 to 2000, can be defined as the stage of managerial development of the sector, characterized by the formation of big media and multimedia groups, and in more recent years, by the creation of an information hyper-sector, highly globalized, in the midst of the spectacular development of information technologies and the liberalization of telecommunication markets.

The Road towards Freedom of Information: 1976–1989

In 1976 the only media in which private ownership existed were the press and radio, but licenses had been granted during the Franco's regime only to those individuals and institutions closely related to the regime (particularly Catholic organizations). In that year, La Prensa del Movimiento, Franco's group of newspapers, along with Radio Nacional de España (RNE) (Spanish official radio network), were at the forefront of the news sector. In regards to television, there were only two state-run channels, TVE1 (Spanish Television First Channel) and TVE2 (Spanish Television Second Channel).

Since 1966 there was a tinge of freedom in the Ministry of Information, and political debate had appeared diffidently in some newspaper and magazine pages, but the truth of the matter is that news and other mass media contents were subject to several forms of censorship. By then, international news and certain foreign films, as well as tourism, were the sole channels which helped the public envisage what Spain could be without Franco.

The death of Franco in 1975, and the law of political reform in 1976, opened to the gradual eradication of the limits which constrained the written press and the whole journalistic activity, but it was not until the Constitution in 1978 that those limits definitively disappeared and that the right to freedom of information was fully granted.

The years 1976 to 1978 saw the birth of several newspapers which would turn out to play a vital role in the transition period. The most significant was *El País*, which became the leading Spanish newspaper, founded in 1976. That very same year another emblematic newspaper appeared: *Diario 16*. Even before the Constitution blessed the autonomies system, in some regions newspapers of a nationalist nature cropped up in languages other than Spanish: some examples were the dailies *Deia* and *Egin* (in Basque) and *Avui* (in Catalan). In the meantime, the onset of new newspapers saw the closure of several others, primarily those closely related to the previous regime, all leading to a transformation of the national press.

During that process, the number of newspapers (around ninety) was not altered substantially, and the number of readers remained almost the same, a third of the population, which is a bit lower than today's rate. However, what did change were readers' votes: the new and the old newspapers which identified themselves fully with the new political system displaced all the rest. This transformation process ended in the 1980s when La Prensa del Movimiento (the chain of state-owned newspapers, among them a sports newspaper called *Marca*) was auctioned and also some newspapers belonging to a Catholic publishing house were sold. These transactions spawned several new journalistic groups, for instance Recoletos and Grupo Correo, which occupy a leading position in the contemporary Spanish media market under new corporate names Unedisa and Vocento (for a detailed description of those groups, see Alférez, 1986).

The magazine sector also experienced frenetic activity in the early years of democracy. In fact, magazines had played a key role in helping to create a critical attitude towards the regime in its last decade, and the new airs of freedom enabled new publications to be born, some of them unthinkable in previous years. One of the most outstanding and symbolic cases was the debut of *Interviú* in 1976. This magazine was a strange mixture of news magazine and pornographic material; the combination of a long-sought political freedom and unknown sexual freedom. Its success was extraordinary with a circulation of almost 1 million copies in 1978, although soon after, its popularity fell. The success of this title was the seed of another media group, Grupo Zeta, also one of the leading Spanish media companies at the moment.

The magazine market would be one of the first to warmly welcome foreign firms, some of which had already arrived during the Franco regime. During the 1980s the number rose so sharply that some publishing houses such as Hachette, Bertelsmann and Springer, along with many others, ended up dominating the sector.

The freedom of expression and the renewal of the press led to a rapid transformation of Spanish journalistic practices and media sector actors. However, it did not manage to have a significant impact on some media consumption habits which held their ground.

In 1975, just over one-third of Spaniards read newspapers while almost 90 percent watched television and around 40 percent listened to radio. Moreover, TV and radio were the media most trusted by the public, despite the Franco regime's far tighter control over them in comparison to that of the press.

From 1976 onwards, television and radio became crucial tools for democratic and political education. They constituted in some way a part of the new political system and, just as had happened under the Franco regime, the tradition of putting those media at the service of the ruling party was somehow kept alive. The only difference was that the way in which these tools were used was now supervised and criticized by all other political forces. This was particularly the case of television, perhaps one of the reasons why the private sector was condemned to wait for over a decade before appearing.

It remains paradoxical that the renovating effect of the audiovisual market was brought about by the state, reinforcing its media structure before promoting the commercial one. In fact, when the State of Autonomies appeared on the scene, new regional public television services were set up. All this came about in 1983. As a consequence, the public television service was greatly strengthened during the 1980s (see Maxwell, 1995).

Regarding radio, in contrast with the rest of Europe, where the state monopoly had a long tradition, in Spain there had always been a certain balance between state- and privately-run radio stations. However, with the arrival of democracy this balance was broken, at least during the first years, in favor of state-owned radio stations, precisely when in Europe the winds were changing in the opposite direction. One private group, Antena 3, set up in 1982, stood out among the rest of the leading stations, namely a chain called SER, which was state-controlled, and a chain owned by the Spanish Catholic Church, COPE.

After a decade, defined by the driving forces already mentioned, Spain's entry in the European Economic Community in 1986 was yet another catalyst to normalize the mass media sector. After 1986, Spanish media needed to get on the same standing as their European counterparts in order to compete as a single market. This would bring about further significant changes in the sector, some of which were to grant the private sector a large role in the television market, as was the trend in other countries during the 1980s, pave the way for the creation of large communication groups to compete in the new European market, and open the gates to a larger number of foreign companies and groups in the sector. Perhaps the clearest result of all these market requirements would be the granting of licenses to commercial television channels in 1989, which could be considered the concluding decision in the process of opening up the media system, and at the same time the starting point of the second phase in the transformation of Spanish media during this period.

On the Road towards Managerial Mass Media: 1989–2000

In 1989, two free-to-air television channels (Antena 3 and Telecinco) along with one pay television channel (Canal Plus) were each granted a ten-year license. The granting process was surrounded by many controversies on the political and professional qualifications of the candidates. Finally, the groups that received the licenses represented quite well the diversity of the Spanish media companies which wanted to be in the TV business. However, some signs of favoritism were clear.

The license given for a pay television channel to Prisa group, editor of the daily *El País* and main shareholder of one of the largest radio stations, SER (which was still state-participated at 25 percent), led to the establishment of the first and biggest private multimedia group in Spain. In fact, Prisa group, which was closely related to the socialist government in power at that time, managed to achieve a complete monopoly over paid TV for almost a decade. The other two channels were to be owned by quite a diverse group of shareholders—press and radio companies, banks, building companies, etc., none with more than 25 percent ownership as law determined. Most noteworthy was the active presence of foreign firms in these new TV companies, among them the Italian group Mediaset in Telecinco and Canal Plus France in Canal Plus, both of which introduced the commercial TV formats used in their countries of origin into Spain. By 1995, Spaniards had increased their time viewing television significantly, to 214 minutes a day per person, watching state-run television as much as commercial TV. The dominant role of television in the Spanish market, already obvious during the last years of the dictatorship, was reinforced with its new channels.

Meanwhile, the press sector, which continued having quite a small readership, was being reorganized around regional media groups, which were reinforced after the sale of an important number of newspapers owned by the state and the church. The fact that these regional newspaper chains appeared was only natural, due to the fact that two-thirds of all newspapers sold were regional. Among these new press groups, the most important was Grupo Correo, which slowly managed to acquire some of the most profitable newspapers, capturing around 15 percent of all newspaper sales. In 2008, Grupo Correo owned eleven newspapers, most of them leaders in their regions. Other press groups based their growth on the specialized press and the magazine market, such as Recoletos group, with the sports daily *Marca* and the economic newspaper *Expansión*, and the already mentioned Zeta group, one of the main magazine publishers in Spain.

Finally, since the late 1980s another quality daily newspaper, *El Mundo*, made its way into the market which brought back the journalistic style of the hard-fighting press against the government. In some way, this was a phenomenon quite new in a market where the necessary defense of the democratic system had maintained a low profile of political criticism. Several other media joined *El Mundo*, especially some radio stations, and together orchestrated a campaign to overthrow the socialist government, which had been in power for fourteen years and was riddled with corruption in its last ruling stages.

As in the case of television, in the creation and growth of some of these new press companies, foreign investment began to play an important role. Two good examples are the role played by the Italian group Rizzoli-Corriere della Sera in the development of the daily *El Mundo*, and by the British group Pearson in the extraordinary growth of the group Recoletos. After the disinvestment operation of Pearson, both Spanish subsidiaries merged into Unedisa in 2007.

From a journalistic point of view, radio may possibly have been at the forefront of the media discourse during the first half of the 1990s. The fact that the government stopped running several radio stations and three large private groups appeared—SER, COPE and Onda Cero—had a revitalizing effect on the sector, enabling it to reach new peaks in terms of audience and social influence. The commercial radio sector ended up holding two-thirds of radio audiences, in stark contrast to the previous decade. The influence of radio news and radio-star anchors in public opinion was so important that political battles affected radio's market structure. For example, in 1992 a noteworthy political and managerial event took place when the Grupo Prisa bought its main radio competitor, Antena 3, closing it shortly after. It is said that one of the reasons for this closure—besides the business strategy of Prisa—was that Antena 3 had been a slap in the face of the socialist government. There is no doubt that Antena 3 had been the main protagonist of the sector in the 1980s and early 1990s, and one of the main reasons why Spanish political journalism on the radio became so successful.

The media landscape changed again significantly in the second half of the decade. A change in government in 1996 occurred when a right-wing government replaced Felipe Gonzalez's reigning socialist party, coinciding with sweeping changes in the audiovisual sector. First, it was the regulation and introduction of new TV services such as cable TV, digital satellite TV and terrestrial digital TV. Second, at the same time, it started a bitter fight for TV rights to broadcast some content, especially football (soccer), and it also started the liberalization process of the telecommunications sector. All these were going to be the driving forces which determined the evolution of media markets in the second half of the 1990s. They even would constitute a new political and media battlefield, limited only by the European Union's supervision and regulation.

The arrival of new television operators, and the development of the rest of the media in that context, was conditioned by Telefónica's entry into the communication sector. The privatization of the company which had the monopoly of the telephone market, a process finished by the government led by José María Aznar, gave rise to an ambitious strategy to internationalize the firm and widen its business interests, especially entering the content and media markets.

In 1997 a hard-fought battle was waged between Grupo Prisa, with a pro-socialist tendency, and Telefónica, supported by the Aznar government, with the purpose of controlling the entire digital satellite TV business. As far as the control of public opinion was concerned, Prisa had been in some ways the former socialist government's spearhead, so the new right-wing government hoped Telefónica would be theirs. Eventually, the two groups would compete against each other with their own digital platforms: Canal Satelite Digital belonging to the Prisa group and Via Digital belonging to Telefónica. The third potential contender, Grupo Correo, dropped out in the fight as it opted to increase its scope of activities in the free-to-air television, Tele 5, becoming the main Spanish investor in that channel, along with Mediaset and the German group Kirch.

But the arrival of Telefónica to the media market shocked the sector in many other ways. The liberalization of the telecommunication market enabled other firms to materialize, such as Retevisión, which would start to play a key role in new television services, notably cable and terrestrial digital television.

Apart from Vía Digital, the digital satellite platform, Telefónica gained control of Antena 3 TV in 1997, which at the time was the leading commercial network in Spain. From then on, its endeavors to foster a strong division of media business continued, both in Spain and abroad. Telefónica became the main Spanish shareholder of the Recoletos Group, and as a consequence, one of the key private shareholders of the British Group Pearson Group. The company also bought the second private radio station in Spain, Onda Cero, purchased one of the leading European TV producers, Endemol, and, finally, replicated its strategy for Spain in other Latin American countries, especially Argentina, where Telefónica has become in a key media player.

Almost overnight, by 1998 Telefónica was the leading firm in the media sector, and what is more important, it set the guidelines for the media appetite of other telecommunications firms such as Retevisión, which hoped to play a special role in digital terrestrial TV. Furthermore, Telefónica possessed great financial potential, unequalled by any other mass media group: its total revenues are almost four times those of the rest of the media sector combined. In addition, its international strategy gave Telefónica a strong competitive advantage over other Spanish media companies.

Hence, facing a somewhat alarming situation, the rest of the big media groups had sought to boost their position by forming national and international alliances, play a greater role in Latin America (a natural market for Spanish firms) and foster joint ventures with Telefónica and other telecommunications companies to develop certain business areas. As of 2008, Telefónica is almost completely out of the media sector. The dotcom crash of 2001 as well as other internal factors led the company to abandon its strategy of immersion in the media, while concentrating on mobile phones, Internet access and ADSL (asymmetric digital subscriber line) pay TV both in Europe and Latin America.

In the meantime, the state-run television channels, both national and autonomous, entered the end of the twentieth century suffering from a profound identity crisis. On the one hand, they were too dependent, from a journalistic point of view, on whatever government was in power, while on the other hand they practically worked as commercial channels in all other aspects, a motive attracting continuous criticism both by their commercial competitors who thought that the commercialization of the public television services meant a corruption of its function.

In summary, it can be said that that between 1976 and the final years of the twentieth century, Spanish people witnessed an almost complete transformation of the Spanish mass media markets. The Spanish media industry had become as complex and modern as any other Western media market (Nieto, 1998; Reig, 1998). With the arrival of the twenty-first century, the sector experienced an intense process of development driven by the challenges of the digital revolution.

Media in the New Century

The media in contemporary Spain is characterized by strong competition in all parts of the market. The audiovisual sector is the dominant industry, with around 50 percent of the advertising investment in conventional media (8 billion euros in 2007, around 1.8 percent of GDP). Television and radio are also the media with higher penetration of the audience (television reaches 90 percent of the Spanish population and radio 55 percent). Far behind are the daily press (41 percent), magazines (51 percent) and Internet (27 percent of daily users). Spaniards dedicate, on average, almost 4 hours a day to watching television, 2 hours to listening to radio, and 25 minutes to reading newspapers.

The Press

There are around 140 newspapers in Spain. They are as free from government control as those of any other democratic country. Every day 4.2 million issues are sold and read by around 40 percent of the population (which represents around 100 readers per 1,000 inhabitants). There are just twelve newspapers with a circulation above 100,000, most of them national dailies (the national press represents 40 percent of the total circulation). The best-selling paper, El País, is a national quality daily and sells about 440,000 copies per issue. The next best-selling titles are El Mundo, with 340,000 copies, and Marca, a daily sports newspaper, with 315,000 copies. Marca has the higher readership with around 2.4 million people. As for the business press, four titles compete in a small market of around 150,000 daily copies, and a readership of 300,000. Spain's leading newspapers are predominantly located in the capital, Madrid, though the major regional newspapers in those areas with more political autonomy, particularly Catalonia and the Basque country, have an important role in local and national life (Asociación de Editores de Diarios Españoles (AEDE), 2008).

In contrast with other European markets, the market for paid newspapers in Spain has been stagnant, even expansive, since the late 1990s. In that market, six big media groups, Vocento, Prisa, Unidad Editorial, Zeta, Godó and Prensa Ibérica, control about 75 percent of the total revenue of the press industry, and a similar percentage of total circulation. The process of concentration in the press industry has become clearer since the beginning of the twenty-first century.

However, the most remarkable event since the late 1990s has been the extraordinary success of the free newspapers. Four titles, 20 Minutos, Metro, Qué! and ADN, distribute around 4.2 million copies every day, practically the same number of daily paid newspapers. The phenomenon is more impressive if we consider that the first of those titles (20 Minutos) was introduced in 2001. The arrival of free newspapers has set off a revolution, expanding the number of readers to reach new groups such as younger people, lower class segments and immigrants. This has allowed the launching in 2007 of a new popular and low-cost newspaper, Público. This left-leaning new title achieved a circulation of 70,000 in less than six months.

The fierce competition in the daily market has lead to aggressive marketing and promotional practices by the majority of newspapers. For instance, in the business press sector, where a free daily, Negocio, was also launched successfully in 2007, three of the four paid newspapers have become partly free (at least 20 percent of circulation at full cover price, and the rest highly discounted). Table 2.1 contains basic data on the main newspapers in Spain.

Table 2.1 Main Newspapers in Spain, 2008

	Circulation (OJD)	Audience (EGM)	Owner group
National newspapers			
El País	435,083	2,234,000	Prisa
El Mundo	338,286	1,398,000	U. Editorial
ABC	228,258	662,000	Vocento
La Razón	153,024	407,000	Planeta
Regional newspapers			
La Vanguardia	213,413	712,000	Godó
El Periódico	174,649	793,000	Grupo Zeta
El Correo	118,107	520,000	Vocento
La Voz de Galicia	103,341	580,000	Grupo Voz
Sport newspapers			
Marca	315,279	2,379,000	U. Editorial
As	233,530	1,170,000	Prisa
Sport	101,633	625,000	Grupo Zeta
Mundo Deportivo	99,368	576,000	Godó
Business newspapers			
Expansión	50,128	175,000	U. Editorial
Cinco Días	40,554	72,000	Prisa
Free dailies*			
Qué!	1,062,187	1,955,000	Vocento
ADN	1,063,236	1,417,000	Planeta
Metro	940,289	1,721,000	Metro Ed.
20 Minutos	1,174,620	2,507,000	Schibsted

Sources: Estudio General de Medios (EGM—October 2007) (AIMC, 2008); Oficina de Justificación de la Difusión (OJD), January–December 2007
Note: *Free dailies: publishers' data (April 2008)

As for the magazine market, it is becoming increasingly fragmented. This has had a negative impact on the circulation of individual titles, with weekly magazines losing readers in favor of monthlies.

There are about 350 periodicals with a controlled circulation, and many more with circulation unknown. Most Spanish magazines have a small circulation, with only a few exceeding 500,000 copies. Among these are *Pronto* and *Hola*, representing the so-called *prensa del corazón* (gossip and celebrities magazines), selling about 900,000 and 600,000 copies per issue respectively.

According to data derived from Estudio General de Medios (EGM: General Media Study) the magazine audience in 2007 reached 18.7 million readers, 49.4 percent of the population. This level was significantly lower than the penetration achieved at the beginning of the century (53.6 percent in 2000). From a business perspective, according to Infoadex (the research company which periodically assesses advertising investments in all communication media), magazine investment stood at 722 million euros, or 9 percent of overall media investment.

The most relevant trend in the Spanish magazine market during the first decade of the twenty-first century has been the striking growth of the weekly gossip magazines (Bueno, Cárdenas & Esquivias, 2007). The main titles are the leaders in circulation, as well as readership and advertising revenues. There are six gossip magazines among the top ten titles which were most widely read in 2007, accounting for 11 million people who admit reading these magazines on a weekly basis. All of them have a readership over 1 million, a level achieved by only a few monthlies, two of which are TV guides for the main pay television platforms (see Table 2.2).

Table 2.2 Main Spanish Consumer Magazines, 2008

	Circulation (OJD)	Audience (EGM)	Owner group	Category
Weekly magazines				
Pronto	974,254	3,423,000	Grupo Heres	Gossip and celebrities
Hola	537,270	2,408,000	Hola SA	Gossip and celebrities
Diez Minutos	376,101	1,381,000	Hachette	Gossip and celebrities
Qúe me dices	309,039	1,094,000	Hachette	Gossip and celebrities
Cuore	216,959	715,000	Grupo Zeta	Gossip and celebrities
Semana	205,069	1,357,000	RBA Edipresse	Gossip and celebrities
Lecturas	198,931	1,196,000	RBA Edipresse	Gossip and celebrities
Mía	163,955	583,000	G+J	Women's
Interviú	94,461	905,000	Grupo Zeta	News, gossip and erotic
El Jueves	77,495	723,000	RBA Edipresse	Humour
Monthly magazines				
Digital +	1,933,342	3,076,000	Sogecable	Satellite TV guide
Ono	977,890	1,957,000	Ono	Cable TV guide
Saber Vivir	281,904	1,352,000	RBA Edipresse	Health and epicurean
Glamour	253,000	580,000	Condé Nast	Fashion and women's
Muy Interesante	245,815	2,368,000	G+J	Science and divulgation
El Mueble	217,435	1,371,000	RBA Edipresse	Deco and household
National Geographic	196,478	1,556,000	RBA Edipresse	Science and nature
Cosmopolitan	194,887	822,000	G+J	Fashion and women's
Cosas de casa	183,117	812,000	RBA Edipresse	Deco and household
Telva	180,473	402,000	U. Editorial	Fashion and women

Sources: Estudio General de Medios (EGM—May 2008) (AIMC, 2008); Oficina de Justificación de la Difusión (OJD), January–December 2007

Traditionally, foreign companies have had an important presence in the magazine industry in Spain. The main international publishing houses, Hachette, G+J and Condé Nast, are leaders in key market segments. However, the more popular titles are published by Spanish groups, such as Hola, Edipresse, RBA and Grupo Zeta. Around 70 percent of the total market (more than 1 billion euros in circulation and advertising revenues) is controlled by ten groups, which publish 120 titles.

Television

The Spanish television market has experienced increasing fragmentation. As of 2008, there are six big national television networks, a dozen regional channels, hundreds of small local television channels, two private terrestrial national channels, one merged digital satellite television network and a big cable operator. The battle for the audience, based on the acquisition of the rights to broadcast the main sporting events, has created a very competitive environment, worsened by the "unfair" participation of public television channels in the advertising business. Private channels argue that public broadcasting companies are unfairly using public funds (considered as state aid) to strengthen their commercial activities (Uteca, 2007).

In fact, after 2000, a new stage was inaugurated in the Spanish television market. The two free private channels became publicly traded companies, listed on the stock market. While Telecinco was still dominated by the Italian group Mediaset, Antena 3 fell into the hands of Planeta, which in 2003 became the leading shareholder. At the same time, RTVE became attached to the state-owned industrial holding company Sociedad Estatal de Participaciones Industriales (SEPI). New management models were introduced that were specially focused on a more active sales management.

In 2005, Digital Terrestrial Television (DTT) licences were handed out among the already known channels, Veo Televisión, Net TV and La Sexta, a new channel that would also broadcast in analog format. Canal Plus, the first terrestrial pay television channel, converted to digital and gave its terrestrial frequency to Cuatro, Sogecable's (Prisa) new free-to-air television channel.

Between 2000 and 2004, the three major channels continued to dominate the airwaves with audience shares above 29 points, with TVE being the solid leader. Only Telecinco managed to top TVE by the end of the period. Advertising was more erratic; it grew considerably in 1999 and 2000, diminished in 2001 and did not recover until 2003. Telecinco was the leader in advertising income. It surpassed the two TVE channels combined, which had even increased their marketing pressure. In any respect, the economic control maintained by these major channels was around 80 percent of the market.

This concentration of advertising was partly due to the regulation of the market. The initial model had already led the generalist channels to form an oligopoly and a monopoly was directly formed by the sole pay channel (Artero, 2008). Later, various European directives tried, rather unsuccessfully, to put order in the market and moderate the unfair competition of Spanish public television.

This situation changed when the new socialist government granted the two new licences for two free national channels, Cuatro (2005) and La Sexta (2006). A new battle for football rights started between Sogecable, Cuatro's owner, and Mediapro, main shareholder of La Sexta. As a consequence, the share of audience of the main channels—the old, and the new ones—was quickly modified. The fragmentation of the market, due to the two new channels and to the steady growth of thematic channels in pay television offers, has negatively affected the share of public television. See Table 2.3 for the evolution of the channels' audience shares between 2000 and 2007.

This growing fragmentation happened in the middle of the difficult process of switching from analog to digital broadcast television, a conversion that must be completed by the end of 2010 (Arrese & Herrero, 2005).

Table 2.3 Evolution of Audience Shares of Spanish Television Channels, 2000–2007

	2000	2001	2002	2003	2004	2005	2006	2007
Sofres/ Universe	38,634,000	39,280,000	39,280,000	39,429,000	40,806,000	41,266,000	41,555,000	42,022,000
Minutes per day	210	208	211	213	218	217	217	223
TVE1	24.5	24.8	24.7	23.4	21.4	19.6	18.3	17.2
La2	7.9	7.8	7.7	7.2	6.8	5.8	4.8	4.6
TVE	32.4	32.6	32.4	30.6	28.2	25.3	23.1	21.8
Telecinco	22.3	21.1	20.3	21.4	22.1	22.3	21.2	20.3
Antena 3	21.6	20.5	20.3	19.5	20.8	21.3	19.4	17.4
Cuatro	–	–	–	–	–	0.8	6.4	7.7
La Sexta	–	–	–	–	–	–	1.8	4
Canal Plus	2.4	2.6	2.3	2.4	2.1	1.6	–	–
Privadas	46.2	44.2	43	43.3	45	45.9	48.8	49.4
Forta*	17	17.2	17.9	18.4	17.7	17.6	15.4	14.7
Temáticas	1.8	2.6	2.8	2.8	5.9	7.4	8.9	11.3
Locales	1.5	1.9	2.2	2.7	3	3.5	3.4	2.6
Otras	1.2	1.6	1.6	2.1	0.2	0.2	0.4	0.1
Rest of channels	21.5	23.3	24.5	26	26.8	28.7	28.1	28.7

Source: Anuario de la Televisión en España 2007 (Sofres, 2008); Note: *Forta-Federation of state-owned regional television channels

The development of DTT has finally arrived. Between 2006 and 2008 the number of DTT decoders in Spanish households grew extraordinarily. According to the latest monthly report from Impulsa TDT (the non-profit organization which promotes the implementation of DTT in Spain), a total of 1,412,000 DTT households were added in the first quarter of 2008. As a result, the penetration rate was 31.85 percent, or more than 5 million households. The Spanish DTT network reached 85.4 percent of the population, or over 38 million people, by 2008.

In parallel, the penetration of pay television services—satellite, cable and broadband—had continued growing. The slow development of cable and the failure of the first experience of digital terrestrial television (a pay television channel called Quiero TV) enabled satellite service providers to be the main competitors for the broadcasting rights. It was hardly surprising that Canal Satélite Digital and Vía Digital announced their decision to merge in May 2002 under the commercial name of Digital Plus. The digital satellite market for pay services became a monopoly.

Since coaxial cable had just been implemented in Spain, when the government allowed cable providers to expand their businesses in the middle of the 1990s, they started using optical fiber, making use of all the benefits of digital technology. In fact, since the very beginning cable was a multiservice integrated offer, as providers could serve their subscribers with triple-play services of telephone, multichannel television and Internet access.

Nevertheless, legislation did not allow big groups to operate in the cable market, and the market structure was very much a regional one, although Ono and Auna were positioning themselves as the main cable providers. This made it difficult for the cable providers to negotiate film and sport rights and therefore to build an attractive television scheduling for potential subscribers. Moreover, the construction of infrastructures was very slow, as there had not been cable networks in Spain before.

In this context, uncertainty surrounded the development of cable television services when the merger of the two digital satellite platforms was completed. The green light given by the government to this operation, without satisfying the limitations regarding the control that they have on key contents for pay television, caused a great discontent among cable companies. The consequence was that Ono and Auna, the main cable operators, entered into negotiations to merge, a process that concluded in 2005 with Ono's acquisition of Auna.

Finally, regarding Internet Protocol Television (IPTV) penetration, Telefónica maintains a clear leader in that market. At the beginning of 2008, the telecommunication company estimated its Imagenio service had a domestic market share of 13 percent, with a subscriber base of 575,558. Telefónica's Imagenio IPTV service was one of the world's leading commercial IPTV service offerings, providing all-digital, DVD-quality delivery of television and audio content to subscribers in Spain. Imagenio's interactive video-on-demand service enables subscribers to watch movies, documentaries, concerts, television shows and newscasts at any time of day, and features DVD-like controls (including play, stop, fast forward, rewind, pause and automatic language selection). Telefónica is also positioned to play a very relevant role in the development of webcasting, not yet a hot topic in the Spanish media market (Herrero & Sádaba, 2007).

In general terms, things have been very positive for the television industry as a whole. For example, 2007 closed with a total turnover of 6.3 billion euros including subsidies from national and regional governments. The industry continues to be driven by free-to-air television, with a total turnover of 4.3 billion euros, although pay television has maintained a clear upward trend, with a turnover of 2 billion euros. In 2007, there were 3.9 million subscribers to pay television services, almost half of them to satellite television. Tables 2.4 and 2.5 present the basic economic data of the Spanish television industry (see Comisión del Mercado de las Telecomunicaciones (CMT), 2008).

Table 2.4 Total Turnover of the Spanish Television Industry, 2005–2007 (€ millions)

	2005	2006	2007
Advertising	3,066.82	3,290.57	3,582.48
	53.90%	50.30%	52.80%
Pay television fees	1,225.87	1,323.90	1,393.86
	21.50%	20.30%	20.50%
Pay-per-view and VOD	151.07	184.91	227.7
	2.70%	2.80%	3.40%
Subventions	660.9	1,190.92	1,017.70
	11.60%	18.20%	15.00%
Other	584.55	546.88	564.34
	10.30%	8.40%	8.30%
Total	5,689.21	6,537.18	6,786.07

Source: CMT (2008)

Table 2.5 Pay Television in Spain: Subscribers and Revenues, 2005–2007

		2005		2006		2007	
	Technology	Subscribers	Revenue (€ millions)	Subscribers	Revenue (€ millions)	Subscribers	Revenue (€ millions)
Digital Plus	Satellite	1,960,030	1,495	2,044,000	1,474	2,065,093	1,522
Ono	Cable	871,817	234	949,152	255	964,822	262
Imagenio	IPTV	206,572	18	380,634	79	508,766	123
Telecable	Cable	108,003	20	96,062	23	110,304	24
R Cable	Cable	62,481	18	60,988	19	63,831	19
Procono	Cable	45,780	9	32,490	7	28,252	7
Euskaltel	Cable	30,086	10	38,851	13	40,414	12
Orange	IPTV			9,759	0	53,747	7
Jazztel	IPTV			5,448	0	6,682	1
Rest of Pay TV		104,102	37	127,673	36	138,313	33
Total		3,388,871	1,842	3,745,057	1,906	3,980,224	2,010

Source: CMT (2008)

Radio

Second to television, radio is the most popular medium in Spain. Approximately 55 percent of all Spaniards usually listen to a vast array of radio stations: state-run or private, national or regional, analogical or digital, and spend around 100 minutes per day listening. As a result, especially from an information perspective, radio networks have a significant influence on the Spanish political and social life. This has been very notorious during the government of José Luis Rodríguez Zapatero, between 2004 and 2008, when the ideological polarization of the main networks has influenced the whole journalistic activity and the political climate.

The Spanish radio industry is dominated by three large private groups. Prisa controls the main national network, Cadena SER, and the biggest musical format, Cadena 40. Grupo Popular is the owner of the second network in audience, Cadena COPE, and Grupo Planeta of the third, Onda Cero. Another important player in the market is Radio Nacional de España (RNE), a public radio station with national coverage that also runs several local and regional public radio stations. RNE does not air advertisements, and its costs are covered by the Corporation Radio Television Española (RTVE).

As in the case of print media and television, radio has played an important role in consolidating culture and identity in Spain's regions and autonomous communities. This has been especially clear in the Basque country, Galicia and Catalonia. Euskadi Irratia (Basque Radio) broadcasts throughout the Basque region in Basque. Radio Galega, part of RTVG (Compañía de Radiotelevisión de Galicia), broadcasts exclusively in Galician. In Catalonia, Catalunya Radio, owned by the Corporació Catalána de Radio Televisio (CCRTV), has contributed to the expansion of Catalan language over the airways.

With regard to radio audiences, general interest radio accounts for half of the audience, and the rest belongs to thematic radio, more than 90 percent of which corresponds to music formats. SER, with an audience share of 38.7 percent, leads the general-interest radio market. COPE with 18.2 percent and Onda Cero with 14.3 percent are some distance behind. The public radio, RNE, reaches 8 percent of the audience, and the most important regional station, Catalunya Radio, 3.6 percent. As for thematic radio stations, music formats dominate the market, led by Cadena 40 with a 24.2 percent audience share (see Asociación para la Investigación de Medios de Comunicacíon (AIMC), 2008).

In 2007, the radio broadcasting market, with a turnover of 445 million euros, was the audiovisual market with the greatest growth, an annual rate of 10 percent (Infoadex, 2008). Of the three major operators in the market, Prisa (SER) continued to lead the sector with a turnover of 220 million euros, followed by Grupo Popular (COPE) with 105 million euros and Planeta (Onda Cero) with 99 million euros. The main data on the Spanish radio market are presented in Tables 2.6 and 2.7.

Table 2.6 Radio Stations in Spain, 2008

General interest format	Audience (EGM)	Audience share (%)	Type of station	Owner group
SER	4,636,000	43	Private	Prisa
COPE	1,916,000	18	Private	Grupo Cope
Onda Cero	1,823,000	17	Private	Uniprex/Planeta
RNE 1	1,000,000	9	Public	Corp. RTVE
Catalunya Radio	495,000	5	Public	CCRTV
Punto Radio	450,000	4		Vocento
Sur Radio	319,000	3	Public	RTVA
Rac I	290,000	3	Private	Grupo Godó
Radio Euskadi	205,000	2	Public	Grupo EITB
Radio Galega	138,000	1	Public	CRTVG

(Total daily listeners: 10,672,000)

Thematic formats	Audience (EGM)	Audience share (%)	Type of format	Owner group
C40	3,173,000	29	Music	Prisa
Dial	1,510,000	14	Music	Prisa
Kiss FM	1,143,000	11	Music	Kiss SA
Cadena 100	872,000	8	Music	Grupo Voz
Europa FM	760,000	7	Music	Uniprex/Planeta
M80	556,000	5	Music	Prisa
Radio Olé	413,000	4	Music	Prisa
R5TN	401,000	4	Music	RTVE
Radio Marca	363,000	3	Sports	U. Editorial
Máxima FM	322,000	3	Music	Prisa

(Total daily listeners: 10,848,000)
Sources: Estudio General de Medios (EGM—May 2008) (AIMC, 2008)

Table 2.7 Total Revenues of the Spanish Radio Industry, 2005–2007 (€ millions)

	2005	2006	2007
Cadena SER	186.8	201.5	219.5
	49.77%	49.89%	49.47%
Cadena COPE	88.8	96.9	105.4
	23.63%	23.95%	23.71%
Onda Cero	91.9	95.2	99.5
	24.44%	23.51%	22.37%
Rest of stations	7.8	10.3	19.3
	2.07%	2.54%	4.34%
Total	376.28	404.87	444.66

Source: CMT (2008)

The Internet

The Internet is already a big information and entertainment provider in the Spanish media market. Most of the traditional media brands and other new online media business have developed an intense Internet activity since the late 1990s.

According to the last available data from AIMC the mass media research association which is the most reliable source regarding Internet usage and penetration in Spain), in 2007 the medium reached a monthly average of 41 percent of the population (15,563,000 Spaniards aged 14 years and over). These figures have been growing steadily, from a 20.5 percent in 2000. However, according to the same source, only 26.2 percent of the total population stated they had used the Internet "yesterday" (AIMC, 2008).

The Spanish Internet user profile is an urban man (58 percent), aged 25–44 (51 percent), of a middle economic class (44 percent). The access takes place mainly from home (76 percent), while at work Internet usage declines to 28 percent. Accessing the web (95 percent) and email (86 percent) are the preferred Internet applications, with instant messaging reaching 41 percent of penetration. On average, the Internet user dedicates 35 minutes per day to the medium.

Since home is the main place to access the Internet, the number of broadband connections has risen steadily, reaching 8 million lines in 2007 (18 lines per 100 inhabitants). DSL (digital subscriber line) is the main way to access the Internet from home, despite the fact that prices are much higher than other European countries. Telefónica was the dominant player in the broadband market with 4.5 million lines, followed by cable operator Ono (1.3 million) and Orange (1.1 million) (CMT, 2008).

The growth of Internet penetration is reflected in the advertising investments in that medium. According to Infoadex data for 2007, the Internet received 6 percent of the total advertising investment in conventional media, 500 million euros out of 7.9 billion. One more year, it was the media with a highest annual rate of growth (55 percent).

The audience of online media is dominated by the websites of the main offline media brands, although some new purely online projects, such as Libertad Digital, Periodista Digital or El Confidencial Digital, have reached a significant penetration. One of the main problems of this market is the ongoing debate between media outlets and media research companies and organizations about the best way to measure audiences on the net.

There are several sources of data on audience and web traffic in Spain. The AIMC (Mass Media Research Association) publishes the most recognized study on media consumption in this market. The EGM (General Media Study) is conducted four times a year and provides interesting and updated information about the evolution of media and Internet use in Spain.

Web traffic research is more complex. Media companies rely on the Oficina de Justificación de la Difusión (OJD: Audit Bureau of Circulation) as a source of information for the offline media to get information about web traffic. The online version of OJD has an important weakness: not all media-related websites are audited by OJD. In some cases, such as with the media of Grupo Prisa (including *El País* and Cadena SER), the reason has been a dispute about the method used to measure web traffic. OJD's audit includes web platforms, portals and entertainment sites, which offers a varied picture of the traffic.

Nielsen Net Ratings has developed a system of panels in Spain, based on households. The information emerging from it is very useful but, of course, limited. Advertising agencies and media buying groups also develop *ad-hoc* studies, and ad server technology is used to monitor user behavior.

As a result of this variety of data sources, the radiography of the traffic and audience of online media is not very accurate, although the basic image about the leading media websites is quite clear. Table 2.8, on the main media websites, according to different research providers, shows the map of media audiences in the Internet.

Table 2.8 Audience and Traffic of the Main Spanish Media Websites, 2008

	Traffic (OJD)					
	Unique users	Visits	Pages viewed	Audience (EGM)	Offline media	Owner group
El Mundo	11,576,073	57,373,355	360,907,605	–	Daily	U. Editorial
Marca	7,702,387	80,980,500	422,732,129	2,519,000	Daily	U. Editorial
20 Minutos	5,735,700	19,475,401	135,225,607	–	Free daily	Schibsted
ABC	4,236,086	11,362,240	55,859,430	329,000	Daily	Vocento
Telecinco	3,645,251	9,317,850	83,200,388	1,887,000	TV	Mediaset
Periodista Digital	2,249,207	4,296,781	12,621,347	–	Only online	Periodista D. SL
Antena 3	2,154,971	5,235,333	23,809,873	1,104,000	TV	Planeta
TVE	1,848,721	3,590,311	17,188,252	–	TV	RTVE
Libertad Digital	1,768,955	7,603,296	25,200,082	–	Only online	Libertad D. SA
El Confidencial	1,288,125	5,371,592	22,664,825	–	Only online	Titania Co.
ADN	1,064,372	1,557,177	5,876,738	–	Free daily	Planeta
El País	–	–	–	1,911,000	Daily	Prisa
As	–	–	–	1,098,000	Daily	Prisa
Ser	–	–	–	923,000	Radio	Prisa
Cuatro	–	–	–	904,000	TV	Prisa

Sources: Estudio General de Medios (EGM—May 2008) (AIMC, 2008); OJD, June 2008 (OJD, 2008)
EGM: Unique visitors/last 30 days
OJD: Monthly traffic
Note: OJD does not control Prisa media; EGM does not offer data for El Mundo, RTVE, and free and exclusively online newspapers.

Conclusion

Any transformation is complex and more so when it involves changes which are as profound as the ones discussed in this chapter. Yet beneath those changes projecting Spanish media into the future, there still seem to remain ties with the past, which is possibly an essential condition for the success of all development processes.

Much progress must yet be made to eliminate certain dangerous old tendencies such as the close ties between the media and different types of power. Complete dependence on the state is long gone, yet has somehow brought about a dependence on specific political interests, which has gradually led to a dependence on the economic interest of leading firms.

Fortunately, in respct to these dependences, Spain is not such a different country as it was in the 1970s. For instance, the debate on the consequences of concentration, in the midst of growing convergence and globalization of businesses, is very vibrant in many other places, in fact in any developed media market.

The debates will also continue about the role, structure and operations of state-owned media, especially in the television market, where the commercialization of the public channels distorts the competition in a more and more cluttered sector. Of course, the numerous technological challenges—DTT, webcasting, mobile TV, new online media, etc.—will dominate the evolution of these industries, but always, at least in Spain, with that peculiar tension between political and business interests that has marked the latest developments in the Spanish media markets.

References

Alférez, A. (1986). *El cuarto poder en España*. Barcelona: Plaza y Janés.

Arrese, A. & Herrero, M. (2005). Spain: A market in turmoil. In A. Brown & R. Picard (Eds.), *Digital Terrestrial Television in Europe* (pp. 181–202). Mahwah, NJ: Lawrence Erlbaum Associates.

Artero, J. P. (2008). *El mercado de la televisión en España: Oligopolio*. Barcelona: Deusto.

Asociación de Editores de Diarios Españoles (AEDE). (2008). *Libro Blanco de la prensa diaria 2008*. Madrid: AEDE/CIEC.

Asociación para la Investigación de Medios de Comunicacíon (AIMC) (2008). *Marco general de los medios en España 2008*. Madrid: AIMC.

Barrera, C. (1995a). *Periodismo y franquismo: De la censura a la apertura*. Pamplona: Ediciones Internacionales Universitarias.

Barrera, C. (1995b). *Sin mordaza: Veinte años de prensa en democracia*. Madrid: Temas de hoy.

Bueno, M., Cárdenas, M. L. & Esquivias, L. (2007). The rise of the gossip press in Spain. *Journalism Studies*, 8(4), 621–633.

Comisión del Mercado de las Telecomunicaciones (CMT) (2008). *Informe anual del mercado de las telecomunicaciones en España 2007*. Madrid: CMT.

Gunther, R., Montero, J. R. & Wert, J. I. (1999). *The Media and Politics in Spain: From Dictatorship to Democracy*. Working Paper 176. Barcelona: Institut de Cienciès Polítiques i Socials.

Herrero, M. & Sádaba, C. (2007). Spain: An emerging market still taking its first steps. In L. Ha & R. J. Ganahl III (Eds.), *Webcasting Worldwide: Business Models of an Emerging Global Medium* (pp. 155–170). Mahwah, NJ: Lawrence Erlbaum Associates.

Infoadex. (2008). *Estudio de inversión publicitaria en España 2007*. Madrid: Infoadex.

Maxwell, R. (1995). *The Spectacle of Democracy: Spanish Television, Nationalism and Political Transition*. Minneapolis, MN: University of Minnesota Press.

Nieto, A. (1998). Spain. In A. Albarran and S. Chan-Olmsted (Eds.), *Global Media Economics* (pp. 137–149). Ames, IA: Iowa State University Press.

Oficina de justificación de la difusión (OJD). www.ojd.es.

Reig, R. (1998). *Medios de comunicación y poder en España. Prensa, radio, televisión y mundo editorial*. Barcelona: Paidós.

Sofres. (2008). *Anuario de la audiencia de televisión 2007*. Madrid: Sofres-TNS.

Uteca. (2007). *La televisión en España: Informe 2007*. Madrid: Uteca/Deusto/CIEC.

Villagrasa, J. M. (1992). Spain: The emergence of commercial television. In A. Silj (Ed.), *The New Television in Europe* (pp. 337–426). London: John Libbey.

3

The Media Industry in Mexico

María Elena Gutiérrez Rentería
Universidad Panamericana, Guadalajara, Mexico

Introduction

The year 2000 saw an event the likes of which Mexico had not experienced in almost seventy years. For the first time since 1929, a party different from the Partido Revolucionario Institucional (PRI: Institutional Revolutionary Party) won the presidential elections. Partido Acción Nacional (PAN: National Action Party), represented by Vicente Fox Quesada, was the winner. For the majority of Mexicans, this event promised the end of a presidential system that had characterized the government for seven decades, and also influenced the economy and the actions of the country's media industry.

The concentration of the economic, political, media industry and social structure in Mexico has been one of the consequences of the relationships, at times harmonious, at times conflicted, between the president, the ruling party (PRI), big business and, of course, the media. In the media industry, there was never a clear, effective judicial framework that would set the standards for social communications in the country (Gutiérrez, 2004).

Some of the great topics that have dominated discussion since 2000 are related to the judicial regime, under which the information industry must operate. The principal topics for debate have been informational transparency on the part of the government, access to the media by the principal government institutions, and the healthy economic independence of some media with regards to financing and influence from the government (Villanueva, 2001).

Also under discussion and change has been the topic of telecommunications. The Federal Law for Radio and Television, established in 1960, has also been under permanent discussion in Mexico. The debate has centered on assigning radio and television concessions, as well as causes for revoking the same. This is a permanent source of linkage between the media and the party regime (Corral, 2007; Fuentes-Berrain, 2001). Finally, the use of fiscal time on television and radio, that is, airtime conceded to government authorities, also came under discussion. During the term of President Gustavo Díaz Ordaz (1964–1970), there were confrontations between political groups and media managers. Commercial TV was slowly gaining more influence in society: Díaz Ordaz wanted to have access to the media, and he created new rules related to broadcasting. The fiscal tax that he pretended to establish was transformed in an exchange. Broadcasters ceded a total of 12 percent of programming time to the government authorities; in this way the state managed access to radio and television. In 2003, authorities approved a reduction in fiscal time to 2.5 percent of programming time given to authorities (Gutiérrez, 2004, pp. 72–75).

Some studies have addressed the influence of the audiovisual industry given the maximum level of concentration on informational pluralism, diversity and cultural content in the country (see Amyot, 1995; Clarke & Riddell 1995; Fadul & Solis, 1995). In Mexico there has been little research and few sources of information that study the communications sector from a perspective related to economy or strategic management (e.g., Gutiérrez, 2001, 2004, 2007, 2008; Hernández, 2001; Sánchez-Ruíz, 2000; Sánchez-Ruíz & Hernández, 2001).

This chapter offers a brief description of the principal actors and characteristics that define the media sector in Mexico with the greatest influence on the Hispanic market. The importance of this examination is based on the fact that Mexico is the largest country in Latin America, and the birthplace of the majority of Hispanic residents in the United States.

This chapter is divided into three sections. The first section presents the main macroeconomic variables that influence the media. The second section deals with media content, as well as audience preferences and tastes in terms of information and entertainment. Finally, the third section describes the principal leaders in each sector.

Macroeconomic Environment

Mexico is characterized as a mosaic of realities. This region of Latin America exemplifies the existence of distinct and separate worlds, with the tensions and contradictions characteristic of inequality. There is rural Mexico, poor and predominantly indigenous. In contrast, there is modern Mexico, urban, globalized, with the prosperity of the countries of the first world. The Mexican media are considered among one of the most trustworthy and credible six institutions in the country (Consulta Mitofsky, 2005).

Since the 1930s, Mexico allowed the development of firms that learned to participate in a market structure with high levels of concentration. This gave rise to large monopolies, both private and public. Some examples are Vitro, Cemex, Grupo Carso, Gruma, Maseca and Telmex, among others. Economic neoliberalism and a period of industry deregulation began in the early 1990s. The first half of this decade saw the creation of the Federal Law for Economic Competition (COFETEL) and the Federal Law for Telecommunications; both directly impact the Mexican media sector. At present, there are no legal limits to vertical or horizontal integration in multi-media groups, which has favored the concentration of the audiovisual industry.

Throughout its history, the Mexican economy has been greatly dependent on the United States. Beginning in the 1990s, Mexico began a period of liberalization deregulation and market privatization. This has helped the country grow economically and become a competitive market, not only on the domestic front, but also internationally. The country has also felt the consequences of market globalization.

For several years, the Mexican economy has been seen as low risk for national or foreign investment. More institutional reforms are expected, and these should allow for a more competitive role on the markets, and for a stronger political system.

The telecommunications sector is more open to foreign investment. Job growth is stable, in spite of the negative effects of the current economic situation in the neighboring northern country. However, there are still problems that have been hard to solve, such as drug trafficking, insecurity, and informal commercial activities. As to the media, negative feelings remain due to the high level of concentration found in national television.

Table 3.1 Integration of Socioeconomic Levels in Mexico, 2007

Classification	Mexico City (%)	Monterrey (%)	Guadalajara (%)
A/B	7	12	8
C+	11	16	15
C	15	18	20
D+	41	32	40
D/E	27	22	17
Total	100	100	100

Source: Compiled by the author with information from AMAI

The population of Mexico is young. According to the Consejo Nacional de Población (Conapo: National Council of Population) it is made up of 105,790,725 persons (Consejo Nacional de Población, 2007). Of these, 56,066,743 are men and 53,723,982 are women. About 62 percent of the population is under 29 years of age. The average life expectancy is 75 years.

Mexico is considered the third country in Latin America in terms of median human and social development (Consejo Nacional de Población, 2000). In 2000, 91.8 percent of the total population of children and teenagers (aged 6 to 14) were attending school; only 55.3 percent of young people aged 15 to 17 were, while barely 22.3 percent of 18 to 24 year olds still attended school. In general 95 percent of the younger population is literate.

Cities with the strongest economic, political and social influences are Mexico City, Monterrey and Guadalajara. Table 3.1 shows the socioeconomic level of these three cities in 2007, according to research carried out by the Agencia Mexicana de Investigación Aplicada (Mexican Agency of Applied Research) (2007).

Table 3.1 illustrates how most of the Mexican population, located in the three largest cities, is largely made up of socioeconomic levels D+ and D/E. According to the classification by Asociación Mexicana de Agencias de Investigación de Mercado y Opinión Pública (AMAI: Mexican Association of Market Research Agencies and Public Opinion), the main characteristics of D+ households are that the head of the family is a person who has finished secondary or at least primary school. Their homes are, for the most part, owned, though in some cases they are rented, and in others, they are acquired through a government credit program. On the other hand, levels D/E are represented by those households where the head has an average primary school education. Level E is the lowest segment, and is not often included in market segmentation. The heads of these families lack basic education; they do not own their homes and are very austere people.

Main Sources of Entertainment and Information

Commercial television with nationwide coverage is the most influential means of communication in Mexican society; it is the means chosen by advertisers, and it is the one that has had an influence on the evolution of the behaviors, values and customs of the Mexican public. Television constitutes the largest source of entertainment and information for the people. This is due, in large part, to the political environment that characterized Mexico during the one-party dictatorship, to the current situation of transition to democratic life, to the socioeconomic level of the population, and to the low level of readership. In a world comparison, investment in open access television is Mexico is much higher than the average. It is close to 58 percent, while the world average is around 38 percent, according to the Asociación de Radiodifusores del Valle de Mexico (ARVM: Association of Radio Broadcasters of the Valley of Mexico, 2008, p. 9).

Table 3.2 Market Segmentation by Value, 2007

Segment	% share
Television	58.0
Outdoor	11.0
Radio	8.0
Newspapers	8.0
Magazines	5.0
Pay television	5.0
Cinema	2.0
Internet	1.0
Others	2.0
Total	100

Source: Compiled by the author with information from AMAP

At the same time, new technologies and opening markets have contributed to rethinking the ways that media companies in Mexico entertain and inform. In Mexico, there have also been changes in consumer habits, especially due to the arrival of Internet, and also due to digital convergence that allows pay and cable television to begin looking for packaging triple-play services (digital television, telephone and Internet).

For their part, advertisers have become more selective in deciding where to advertise. Audience fragmentation is a challenge for reaching key groups. There is a segment of the national market whose source of information and entertainment is the Internet. Table 3.2 shows the investment preferences of advertisers.

Commercial television is the means most selected by advertisers, followed by billboards, radio and the national press. In spite of the fact that online advertising acquires only 1 percent of the total advertising pie, it is an industry that is growing exponentially year by year (Asociación Mexicana de Agencias de Publicidad (AMAP: Mexican Association of Advertising Agencies), 2005).

The audiovisual industry has remained almost the same since 2000. However, some media were affected by decreasing government investment in advertising and by the arrival of new technologies. The three main communications groups in the country are Grupo Televisa, TV Azteca and Grupo Radio Centro; together they account for more than 50 percent of all advertising revenues (ARVM, 2008, p. 9).

Penetration by pay television in Mexico is approximately 28 percent (Cámara Nacional de la Industria de las Telecomunicaciones (CANITEC: National Chamber of Cable Telecommunication Industry), 2008). At present, there are roughly 1,100 concessions controlled by some 200 companies throughout the country. Mexican legislation established in 1960 considers radio and television to be a public service. Media managers are allowed to charge freely to advertisers, and to admit or reject advertisers. The law gives concessions to radio and television stations up to thirty years to operate commercially. Article 13 of Radio and Television law warns about the nature and the purpose of the stations, which can be commercial, cultural or experimental. Broadcast stations are required to have concessions. Official, cultural, experimental, school stations or other kinds of public stations are required to have permissions. Throughout the country, companies offer digital services, and are currently prepared to offer the services that make up the triple play.

Mexico's cable telecommunications industry grew from 1.9 million subscribers in 2003 to more than 4.3 million in pay television by 2007 (Cámara Nacional de la Industria de las Telecomunicaciones, 2008, p. 44). According to CANITEC, the industry expects to reach 1.1 million Internet subscribers and 200,000 subscribers to telephone services. As of 2008, the country was awaiting reform of the telecommunications law. Companies who participate in this sector are hoping that Telmex, the main provider of telephone services in Mexico, will not be an obstacle to interconnection. Cable providers have joined together hoping to get more coverage, to take advantage of convergence, and to encourage competition. According to CANITEC, the largest cable provider in Mexico is Megacable Telecomunicaciones, followed by Cablemás and Cablevisión, which belong to Grupo Televisa.

In 2007, the Internet boasted 19.5 percent of national penetration. That is, in that year, there were around 20.4 million users among the total population over 6 years of age (Fundación Telefónica, 2007). Socioeconomic levels ABC+ and C account for approximately 70 percent of the total users among that population; the age profile is between 13 and 35 years of age. Approximate connection time is around 2 hours per day. The majority of young people use that time to listen or download music and to play online games.

Television

The media industry model is characterized as a commercial enterprise, as it is in the United States. Mexican television and radio had the same nuances as to legislation as they did in the northern neighboring country, unlike the majority of European countries, with decades of audiovisual monopolies under the direction of the state. Mexico had a private television monopoly for twenty years (1973–1993) controlled by the Azcarraga family; this company is Televisa. Public television has never had the same acceptance among the audience. In 1993 the government decided to sell Imevisión—the public television network—to Ricardo Salinas Pliego, who is the main owner of TV Azteca. Currently, the main broadcast networks are Televisa and TV Azteca.

The typical Mexican spends about four and a half hours watching television (Jara & Garnica, 2007, p. 61). Prime time in Mexico is between 9 p.m. and 10 p.m. During this period, the average percentage of viewers is between 68 and 70 percent. According to Grupo Televisa, in 2007 the company aired 78 percent of the top hundred programs, and forty-five of the top fifty programs in Mexico. In addition, its average sign-on to sign-off audience share was 70.9 percent of the network's prime-time hours. The content, in particular soap operas, brought Univision some of its best ratings during the year (Grupo Televisa, 2007). However, TV Azteca reported in 2007 an average share of 27.9 percent of the prime-time hours on weekdays (Grupo TV Azteca, 2007).

According to Jara & Garnica (2007, p. 71), Mexican television as a whole broadcasts around 22 million minutes a year. Of this total, roughly 80 percent of the time is devoted to programming, and the rest is devoted to advertising. Nevertheless, the average viewer watches less than 2 percent of the total broadcast time. This explains the enormous competition that exists between open and pay television vying for audience attention.

Broadcast television with its national coverage devotes the greater part of its time to programming in genres such as magazine shows, marketing programs, news programs and foreign movies. With regard to pay television, the majority of the channels devote almost two-thirds of their total broadcast time to movies, musical programs or series.

Melodramas (soap operas) are not the most important part of Mexican production. This genre, as well as soccer matches, has helped generate audiences for advertisers, and has been the most important Mexican export in audiovisual material for several decades. In fact, the most important daily news programs on both Televisa and TV Azteca begin as soon as their major soap operas end. Televisa's Channel 2 ("the channel of the stars") and TV Azteca's Channel 13 devote a large part of their programming to the production and broadcasting of soap operas.

Soap opera viewers are mainly women; men, though, also habitually watch them. According to Jara & Garnica (2007, pp. 87–88), there are two women for every man in the audience. The dominant age group is over 45 years of age. In general terms, older viewers in a lower socio-economic group are Televisa's target audience. In spite of this, TV Azteca has captured audience attention through the production of melodramas targeted to the middle class.

Table 3.3 includes the principal television channels in Mexico. There are numerous affiliates, for the most part, to Televisa and to TV Azteca. In the past few years, state television has tried to

Table 3.3 Principal Channels on Open Television in Mexico, 2008

Channel	Institution	Coverage	Type
Canal 11-XEIPN	Instituto Politécnico Nacional	Mexico City and Federal District	Cultural and educational
Canal 22	Consejo Nacional para la Cultura y las artes	Mexico City and Federal District	Cultural and educational
TV UNAM	Universidad Autónoma de México	Mexico City and Federal District	Cultural and educational
Canal 2, Canal 4, Canal 5 and Canal 9	Televisa	National	Commercial
Canal 7 and Canal 13, Proyecto 40 (Mexico City)	TV Azteca	National	Commercial
Canal 28	Imagen Telecomunicaciones	Mexico City and Federal District	Commercial
Canal 34	Sistema de Radio y Televisión Mexiquense	Mexico City and Federal District	Public

Source: Compiled by the author from various sources

increase audience participation, though it has not been able to create content that is attractive to its target audience.

Radio

Programming and supply of radio content in Mexico is made up of a mix of information—talk radio, news programs, opinion programs—and entertainment, which is primarily musical content depending on the region where the station is located. There are 855 AM stations and 616 FM stations in the country; most of them are affiliated to one of the main radio groups.

The main radio groups operating in the country are Organización Radiorama, with more than 220 stations, distributed all over the country; Grupo ACIR (Association of Independent Radio Concessionaires), associated with the Clear Channel group and with 160 stations throughout the country; MVS Radio; Grupo Radio Fórmula (belonging to the Ramsa chain), with 101 stations and coverage in the southern United States; and Grupo Radio Centro, with 14 stations. Grupo Radio Centro trades on the stock markets in both Mexico and New York.

According to the Asociación de Radiodifusores del Valle de México, in the Federal District and in Mexico City, radio is a key companion medium, because of the amount of time people spend commuting in that part of the country (ARVM, 2008).

The industry has given rise to several journalists who are considered as leaders of public opinion in Mexico. Among the most important are Jacobo Zabludovsky, Joaquín López Dóriga, Ciro Gómez Leyva, Eduardo Ruiz Healy, Denise Maerker, Jorge Zarza, Adela Micha, Alejandro Alfaro, Sergio Sarmiento and Pedro Ferris de Con. In fact, radio has been used by political parties to carry out their campaigns (Ibope AGB, 2008). Some of the radio programs are also broadcast on pay television channels.

Mexican radio is experiencing a high rate of audience segmentation and it has also been undergoing a learning process with respect to the new political era in the country. There are some radio stations without an established political position; there are others that have been criticized for maintaining editorial stances according to economic interests related to political parties or powerful groups.

Audience participation is active: Mexican radio continues to be a local or regional strategy that allows a community to remain in touch. Talk radio is predominant and has the most impact among adult listeners, as well as stations devoted to certain types of music: Grupera, pop in English or Spanish; ballads, English pop-rock, or mainstream Spanish music. The scheduling period with the highest number of listeners is 7 a.m. to 3 p.m.

Radio has been one of the means of communication that has been most affected by new technologies, and by the unfortunate practice known as *payola*, whereby certain radio stations enter into pacts with record companies to broadcast songs and lodge them in the audience's mind, regardless of audience acceptance. Listeners are tiring of this practice and are opting for the new broadcasting options.

Newspapers

Perhaps it is the newspaper industry that has most been affected by the arrival of the Internet and the new information technologies, political changes and the socioeconomic level of the people. Mexico has always been noted for its low readership numbers, and for the direct links that existed between some of the more important papers and the country's political leaders.

One of the main features of the history and development of Mexico's principal newspapers during the PRI era was strong party influence on editorial issues, through loans, concessions or, in some cases, government manipulation. At the same time, the various recurring economic crises caused a considerable decrease in the funding available to the government for self-promotion in the media. Newspapers that depended on federal funds have been disappearing little by little, since their main source of income came from government advertising, or from enterprises directed linked to the government.

Beginning in the 1990s, diverse institutions such as the Comisión Intersecretarial para la Transparencia y el Combate a la Corrupción (Intersecretary Commission for Transparency and Combatting Corruption) and Instituto Federal de Acceso a la Información Pública (IFAI: Federal Institute of Access to Public Information) have been involved in different legal processes that have helped to bring about informational transparency.

The country's main newspapers have redoubled efforts to improve their content, and have changed editorial and commercial strategies. Most newspapers have no official editorial stance to favor a particular political party. There has been a notable change in the principal newspapers, as they try to develop strategies appropriate to the market, while they attend to their readers' needs. New papers have sprung up, and the current supply even includes some foreign papers. Beginning in 2000, free newspapers began to circulate locally. There are those devoted to sensationalism or to sports, with the intention of capturing a non-reading audience. For example, *El Gráfico*, a sporting paper certified by Institute for the Verification of Media the Instituto Verificador de Medios (IVM), has become one of the nation's most popular dailies. According to *El Gráfico*'s director, Eduardo Vorhauer of *El Universal*, 29 percent of the readers did not previously read any newspaper. These papers have opened up a fertile and previously non-existent market for the press, at low cost and with considerable reach (Méndez, 2006, p. 51).

The Mexican press is predominantly regional or local. The most important journalistic enterprises handle different brands distributed by region. Others simply locate their operations in Mexico City, Monterrey and Guadalajara, where the political decisions that impact society are made. Some of the industry leaders have made strategic alliances with each other, while others have made these alliances with international organizations. This has contributed to changing the

Table 3.4 The Twenty Papers with the Highest Published Tariffs, 2004

Rank	Newspaper name	Publishing group	Location
1	*El Financiero*	El Financiero	Metropolitan Mexico City
2	*El Universal*	El Universal Cía. Periodística Nacional	Metropolitan Mexico City
3	*Reforma*	Grupo Reforma	Metropolitan Mexico City
4	*Rumbo de México*	MAC Ediciones y Publicaciones	Metropolitan Mexico City
5	*La Crónica de Hoy*	Grupo Empresarial Periodístico	Metropolitan Mexico City
6	*La Jornada*	Desarrollo de Medios	Metropolitan Mexico City
7	*Milenio Diario*	Milenio Diario	Metropolitan Mexico City
8	*El Diario DF*	MAC Ediciones y Publicaciones	Metropolitan Mexico City
9	*El Economista*	El Economista	Metropolitan Mexico City
10	*Diario Monitor*	Infored	Metropolitan Mexico City
11	*Excélsior*	Excélsior	Metropolitan Mexico City
12	*Unomásuno*	Impulsora de Periodismo Mexicano	Metropolitan Mexico City
13	*Mural*	Grupo Reforma	Guadalajara
14	*Milenio*	Grupo Mulimedios	Monterrey
15	*El Mexicano*	Editorial Kino	Tijuana
16	*Diario de Yucatán*	Cía. Tipográfica Yucateca	Mérida
17	*El Informador*	Unión Editorialista	Guadalajara
18	*El Nuevo Siglo de Guadalajara*	El Nuevo Siglo de Guadalajara	Guadalajara
19	*El Sol de México*	Cía. Periodística del Sol de México	Metropolitan Mexico City
20	*El Diario de Juárez*	Publicaciones Paso del Norte	Cd. Juárez

Source: Compiled by the author with information from Zapata (2004)
Note: 283 dailies, both morning and evening editions, were analyzed.

way information is handled, and to professionalizing these institutions. Table 3.4 presents the top twenty papers as ranked by advertisers.

Mexican society is more actively involved in the political life of the country, promoting editorial quality. The media are now under the scrutiny of their principal clients: readers and advertisers. The press has given signs of positive change, and has made an effort to support the political transition towards democracy. The most important and renowned information enterprises have tried to accomplish their social roles in the way they handle information.

In 2006 Mexico had 462 newspapers registered with the Secretariat of the Interior; the majority are dailies. Some foreign papers are included in these, such as *Señales*, a magazine from Colombia, *El País*, the Spanish newspaper, and *Diario de México* and *Rumbo de Texas*, both from the United States.

Currently, the newspapers with the strongest influence and the best positioning and market participation are financed through advertising revenues, especially from financial groups, the automotive industry and service institutions. These papers have been considered more attractive to advertisers because they also have their own websites, which complements their offerings. Subscribers do not form part of the principal source of income for these newspapers.

There is no official institution to monitor circulation; the data come from each paper, or from registration in the Institution for the Verification of the Media, and from private audits undertaken by outside consultants. Table 3.5 shows the certified dailies with the largest national circulation.

Most newspapers are associated with the Union of Distributors. Grupo Reforma stands out for being one of the first groups to develop its own distribution channels.

Table 3.5 Principal Dailies with Certified Circulation above 18,000, 2004

Daily	City	Verifying institution	Daily circul.
El Gráfico	Metropolitan Mexico City	Instituto Verificador de Medios	225,469
El Universal	Metropolitan Mexico City	Instituto Verificador de Medios	170,356
Ovaciones	Metropolitan Mexico City	Ferral, de la Fuente y Asoc.	152,388
Reforma	Metropolitan Mexico City	PriceWaterhouseCoopers	150,569
El Norte	Monterrey	PriceWaterhouseCoopers	146,039
Diario de Yucatán	Mérida	Instituto Verificador de Medios	78,117
Metro	Metropolitan Mexico City	PriceWaterhouseCoopers	73,970
Excelsior	Metropolitan Mexico City	Instituto Verificador de Medios	55,493
Metro	Monterrey	PriceWaterhouseCoopers	54,108
El Sol Regiomontano	Monterrey	PriceWaterhouseCoopers	52,258
El Diario de Juárez	Cd. Juárez	Instituto Verificador de Medios	47,702
La Crónica de Hoy	Metropolitan Mexico City	Check Media	43,020
El Debate	Culiacán	Instituto Verificador de Medios	38,406
Mural	Guadalajara	PriceWaterhouseCoopers	38,311
El Guardián	Saltillo	Daniel Moreno y Asoc.	37,847
a.m.	León	Instituto Verificador de Medios	34,776
El Economista	Metropolitan Mexico City	Instituto Verificador de Medios	32,689
El Imparcial	Hermosillo	Instituto Verificador de Medios	32,365
Récord	Metropolitan Mexico City	Instituto Verificador de Medios	32,330
El Siglo de Torreón	Torreón	Instituto Verificador de Medios	30,572
Provincia	Morelia	Instituto Verificador de Medios	30,000
El Diario	Toluca	Instituto Verificador de Medios	28,734
Novedades Acapulco	Acapulco	Instituto Verificador de Medios	25,562
Tribuna del Carmen	Ciudad del Carmen	Notario público 20	24,750
Vanguardia	Saltillo	Daniel Moreno y Asoc.	24,062
Noroeste Mazatlán	Mazatlán	PriceWaterhouseCoopers	24,026
El Dictamen	Veracruz	Reyes del Valle y Asoc.	23,356
La Voz de la Frontera	Mexicali	Instituto Verificador de Medios	22,548
Dirario de México	Metropolitan Mexico City	Universidad Autónoma de Morelos	18,473
Noroeste	Culiacán	PriceWaterhouseCoopers	18,381
Imagen	Zacatecas	Instituto Verificador de Medios	18,000

Source: Complied by the author with information from Zapata (2004) and Centro Interamericano de Marketing Aplicado, plus information from the press.
Note: 283 dailies, both morning and evening editions, were analyzed.

Magazines

The national trend is toward title segmentation on the part of the publishers who participate in the sector. Grupo Televisa is considered the most influential publisher in Latin America. The group publishes eighty different titles in nineteen countries, with a circulation of 127 million issues monthly. Their principal distinguishing strategy is branch generation, advertising strategies and subscriptions (Méndez, 2006, p. 51). The seven companies with the largest number of titles are Editorial Televisa, Grupo Expansión, Grupo Editorial Vid, Corporativo Mina, Servicios Editoriales Sayrols, Editora Cinco and Ediciones PLM (Ayala, 2001, p. 53).

The editorial content with the most demand by readers in the Mexican market is sensational stories, comics or love stories. Another popular product is a summary of the content of soap operas, principally those broadcast by Televisa. The five weekly magazines with the greatest circulation in Mexico are *Libro Semanal* and *Libro Vaquero*, both from Nueva Impresora y Editora Mexicana; *Libro Policiaco*, *TV y Novelas* and *TV Notas* (Ayala, 2001, p. 53). The specialized magazines sector is even smaller than the popular market. The five magazines with the greatest monthly circulation are *Selecciones de Reader's Digest, Tú, Cosmopolitan, Muy Interesante* and *Escala.*

A large part of the income from magazines with a nationwide weekly distribution comes from direct purchasing by the reader. However, the same cannot be said for the specialized magazines: these survive thanks to advertising sales.

Industry Leaders

Mexico's media market has evolved positively in part by the actions of the principal industry leaders. Since the 1990s, the heads of the principal companies have used different strategies that have strengthened them against competition. Other important companies are diversifying in order to participate actively in the national media industry. The main communications companies have maintained their important presence in Mexico from the beginning of the industry to today's more dynamic and competitive environment.

The different economic, political and social stages in Mexico's history have also played a role as macroeconomic factors that have influenced company owners' strategies and actions. Depending on the medium, the competitive structure differs. It is similar to the present structure in the United States. The television sector shows excessive market concentration. With regard to pay television, in spite of increasing participation by more companies, the structure remains a very dynamic oligopoly, especially now that companies can participate in offering triple-play services.

Local or regional press follows a model of monopolistic competition. However, an analysis of the owners of the principal papers that are produced and distributed by locality shows that they belong to a small group of enterprises.

Some of the most important communication groups in Mexico entered the business in a single medium. At present, they have modified their strategy to form large multimedia groups organized around their greatest source of revenue. Other entrepreneurs have decided not to enter into related business, preferring to concentrate on their star medium. Nevertheless, they are all present on the Internet. Table 3.6 (p. 44) shows industry leaders in Mexico, grouped according to their level of influence and market penetration, as well as the medium, and the president or director of the company.

Conclusion

The economic, political and social situation that Mexico experienced after the Mexican Revolution (1910) through a one-party dictatorship influenced the media industry in Mexico. Given this fact, the media market in Mexico grew in an environment of high levels of economic and political concentration.

The Mexican economy represents an oligopoly structure, where the main source of demand has been placed in a domestic market, centered in the highest spheres of the society. Mexican authorities never had a clear vision for the mass media, as in the United States and other countries. It was not until the 1990s with the passage of the Federal Law of Telecommunications that the market found the environment to establish a competitive market in Mexico, given the rise of globalization and other international factors.

Economical liberalization and financial globalization created the right conditions for some private companies like Televisa Group, MVS, TV Azteca, Carso Group, Telmex and America Movil (Carlos Slim Helú), to start plans for international strategies through joint investments with foreign companies, and the simple trading and exportation of media content that had been already proven in the domestic market.

Table 3.6 Leading Main Communication Firms in Mexico, 2008

Company	Media	President or CEO
América Móvil	Wireless operator and prepaid card for cellphone	Carlos Slim Helú, CEO
CIE-OCESA	Entertainment (shows)	Alejandro Soberón Kuri, CEO
Cinemark	Motion picture distributor	Roberto Jenkins de Landa, CEO
Cinemex	Motion picture distributor	Alma Rosa García Puig, CEO; Miguel Ángel Dávila, main owner
Cinépolis	Motion picture distributor	Enrique Ramírez Miguel, President
Editorial Notimusa	Sports newspaper, magazines	Carlos M. Flores, President
Editorial Progreso	Books	Joaquín Flores Segura, CEO
El Universal	Press, Internet	Juan Francisco Ely Ortiz, President
Grupo Acir	Radio, Internet	Francisco Ibarra López, President
Grupo Carso	Diversified company; press: new stakeholder of *New York Times*; music store: Mixup.	Carlos Slim Helú, CEO
Grupo Editorial Expansión	Business magazines	John Reuter, CEO; Clemente Serna Alvear, main owner
Grupo Fórmula	Radio, pay television, Internet	Rogerio Azcárraga Madero, President
Grupo Imagen y Excélsior	Radio, press, Internet	Olegario Vázquez Raña, President
Grupo Mundo Ejecutivo	Magazines, radio, television, press	Walter Coratella, CEO
Grupo Radio Centro	Radio, Internet, television, printed media	Francisco Aguirre, President
Grupo Reforma	Press, Internet	Alejandro Junco de la Vega, President
Grupo Santillana	Books	Jorge Delkáder, CEO México
Grupo Televisa	Open and pay television, magazines, radio, video, Internet	Emilio Azcárraga Jean, President
Megacable	Cable television, Internet and telephony (triple play)	Enrique Yamuni Robles, President
MMCinemas	Motion picture distributor	Germán Larrea, President
Multimedios Estrella de Oro	Press, radio, television, Internet, magazines	Francisco A. González, President
MVS Comunicaciones	Radio, television, magazines, books	Joaquín Vargas, President
Nueva Impresora y Editora Mexicana	Magazines: comics "Libro Vaquero"	Fernando Varela Robles, CEO
Organización Editorial Mexicana	Press, Internet	Mario Vázquez Raña, President
TV Azteca	Television, Internet	Ricardo Salinas Pliego, President
Telmex	Telecommunications and Internet	Carlos Slim Helú, CEO

Source: Compiled by the author from various sources

The economic and political system in Mexico has had a lack of democratic tradition similar to most Latin American countries, until 2000 when a different political party won the presidential elections. This helps explain the long absence of professionalism in the mass media, which is an essential function to guarantee political pluralism and reflect the cultural diversity of society.

The main providers of entertainment and information of Mexicans are a few huge multimedia groups. Nevertheless, this environment has changed thanks to the arrival of new technologies that give the audience numerous options for information and entertainment. Nowadays the media industry faces the advantages and competitive risks that offer digital convergence. Mexico has started a battle to win the audience, and media managers have realized the importance of paying attention to fragmented audiences that demand more specialized options in media content. The triple play is one example: it is taking an important role as a competitive factor, driving the expansion of strategic alliances between national and international media companies.

Media companies in Mexico started around the 1960s to conquer Latino audiences in the United States. The companies have worked the strategy of selling content to television networks, the launching of television and radio stations and newspapers, the exporting of Mexican newspapers, and even print editions of Mexican magazines.

Communication companies have entered the digital stage, and it is expected that the switch from analog will alter the offer and demand of information and entertainment. The total switch to digital technologies is expected to occur by 2017.

The work of media professionals is not well valued in Mexico. The main challenge for universities is to educate communicators with ample knowledge of the media industry, reflexive and critic thinking, and entrepreneurship skills.

Mexico is a country with a high level of influence on the media industry in the United States and across Latin America. More research and study are needed, not only to strengthen links between scholars and entrepreneurs, but also to give the Hispanic market higher levels of quality and diverse options in information and entertainment content.

References

Agencia Mexicana de Investigación Aplicada. (2007). Medición del Nivel Socio Económico en México. Retrieved April 15, 2008, from www.amai.org/NSE/NSE_2007_AMAI.pdf.

Amyot, G. (1995). Une conquête en retour: Les télévisions hispaniques aux États-Unis. In G. Schneider (Ed.), *L'Amérique Latine et ses télévisions du local au mondial* (pp. 91–100). Paris: Anthropodos/INA.

Asociación de Radiodifusores del Valle de México (ARVM). (2008). Inversión en medios: Del manjar a dieta [Media investment: From treat to diet]. *Media Book*, special edition. *Merca 2.0.*

Asociación Mexicana de Agencias de Investigación de Mercado y Opinión Pública (AMAI). (2007). NSE Medición Nivel Socioeconómico 2007. Retrieved May 12, 2008, from www.amai.org/nse/nse_2007_amai.pdf.

Asociación Mexicana de Agencias de Publicidad (AMAP). (2005). Hábitos de los usuarios de Internet en México. Retrieved May 12, 2008, from www.amap.com.mx/archivosdownload/Habitos_de_los_usuarios_de_internet_en_Mexico_2005.pdf.

Ayala, A. (2001). Revistas 2000, diario de una circulación [Circulation of diary]. *Adcebra*, México.

Cámara Nacional de la Industria de las Telecomuniciones (CANITEC) (2008). *Balance Latino*. Retrieved July 11, 2008, from www.canitec.org/faq.php

Clarke, N. & Riddell, E. (1995). Un baron interstellaire: El cacique Azcárraga. In G. Schneider (Ed.), *L'Amérique Latine et ses télévisions du local au mondial* (pp. 67–71). Paris: Anthropodos/INA.

Consejo Nacional de la Población. (2000). Índices de Desarrollo Humano y Social [Index of Human and Social Development]. Retrieved April 15, 2008, from www.conapo.gob.mx/00cifras/6.htm.

Consejo Nacional de la Población. (2007). Indicadores demográficos básicos [Basic demographic indicators]. Retrieved April 15, 2008, from www.conapo.gob.mx/00cifras/00indicadores.htm.

Consulta Mitofsky. (2005). Encuesta: Índice de confianza en las instituciones [Poll: Index of trust in the institutions]. Retrieved May 11, 2008, from www.amai.org/dato1.php?ID_textos=223.

Corral, J. (2007, May 22). Censura y mentira [Censorship and lies]. Retrieved May 13, 2008, from www.el-universal.com.mx/editoriales/37649.html.

Fadul, L. & Solis, B. (1995). Televisa, première chaîne hispanique du monde. In G. Schneider (Ed.), *L'Amérique Latine et ses télévisions du local au mondial* (pp. 77–84). Paris: Anthropos/INA.

Fuentes-Berrain, R. (2001). Prensa y poder político en México [Press and political power in Mexico]. Retrieved June 16, 2008, from www.cem.itesm.mx/dacs/publicaciones/logos/anteriores/n23/23_rfuentes.html.

Fundación Telefónica. (2007). *Medios de comunicación: El escenario Iberoaméricano* [Mass media: Iberian American scenario]. Madrid: Ariel.

Grupo Televisa. (2007). Annual report. Retrieved September 15, 2008, from www.esmas.com/documento/0/000/002/030/Business_Eng.pdf.

Grupo TV Azteca. (2007). Annual report. Retrieved September 15, 2008, from https://www.irtvazteca.com/downloads/investors.aspx?lang=es.

Gutiérrez, M. (2001). Comunicación en América Latina [Communication in Latin America]: Mexican summary. *Revista Latinoamericana de Comunicación.* Chasqui, Quito: CIESPAL.

Gutiérrez, M. (2004). Las estrategias de Grupo Televisa: Del monopolio audiovisual a la competencia [The strategies of Televisa Group: From audiovisual monopoly to competition]. Unpublished doctoral dissertation, University of Navarra, Pamplona, Spain.

Gutiérrez, M. (2007). Media concentration in the Hispanic market: A case study of TV Azteca vs. Televisa. *International Journal on Media Management,* 9(2), 70–76.

Gutiérrez, M. (2008). Globalization with Latin flavor. *Journal of Spanish Language Media,* 1. Denton, TX: University of North Texas.

Hernández, J. (2001). La expansion internacional de la industria Mexicana de television [The international expansion of the Mexican television industry]. Unpublished doctoral dissertation. Universidad Complutense, Spain.

Ibope AGB. (2008). *Anuario 2007–2008: Audiencias y medios en México* [Audiences and media in Mexico]. Mexico: Ibope AGB.

Jara, E. & Garnica, A. (2007). *¿Cómo la ves? La televisión mexicana y su público* [How do you watch it? Mexican television and its audience]. Mexico: Ibope AGB.

Méndez, M. (2006). El mejor medio [The best medium]. *Merca2.0,* 45.

Sánchez-Ruíz, E. (2000). Las industrias culturales latinoamericanas en tiempos de la globalización [Latin American cultural industries in times of globalization]. *Revista Mexicana de la Comunicación,* 12 (64), 40–43.

Sánchez-Ruíz. E. & Hernández, F. (2001). *Televisión y mercados: Una perspectiva Mexicana* [Television and markets: A Mexican perspective]. Mexico: Universidad de Guadalajara.

Villanueva, E. (2001, October 1). Primero transparencia y luego más impuestos [First transparency, then more taxes]. Retrieved May 13, 2008, from http://gruporeforma.com/mural/Documentos/DocumentoImpresa.aspx?ValoresForma=496192025,ernesto+villanueva+tiempo+fiscal+y+acceso+a+la+informaci%u00f3n

Zapata, M. (2004, December). Un año de buenas notas [One year of good news]. *Merca2.0,* 32, 32–35.

4

The Media in Central America
Costa Rica, El Salvador, Guatemala, Honduras, Nicaragua and Panama

Catherine Salzman and Ryan Salzman
University of North Texas, USA

Introduction

The circumstances and roles of the media in Central America are both regionally consistent and country specific. The interplay between the media industry, society and government offers a unique perspective of media in developing countries like those in Central America. A mix of oligarchic ownership, oscillating regime types, economic and technological development, and user adoption cause Central America to stand alone as a uniquely comparative region for studying the media industry in Latin America. By investigating the media in Costa Rica, El Salvador, Guatemala, Honduras, Nicaragua and Panama together, distinctions, similarities and trends will all be highlighted.

This chapter endeavors to provide a thematic and country-specific set of observations and analyses of the media in Central America. These observational and analytical goals will be met by first considering the common history of the countries in the region, with specific attention given to the oligarchic ownership structure of the media industries. Next, the general level of media freedom of each country will be examined. Then, the media industry itself will be discussed. This section will focus on the continued oligarchic trend of ownership, advertising structures and the globalization of Central American media. Next, this chapter will take a more individual-level look at media consumption within each nation. Finally, there will be a discussion where observations are brought to light and evaluated to encourage further research.

Common History

Like many historically colonial regions of the world, states in Central America, a region comparable in size and population to the state of California and composed of Costa Rica, El Salvador, Guatemala, Honduras, Nicaragua and Panama, share a common history across many dimensions. The entire region of Central America was colonized by the Spanish beginning in 1522. The initial settlement involved the areas that are now El Salvador, Guatemala, Honduras and Nicaragua, which left large areas of what is now Costa Rica and Panama initially untouched (Booth, Wade & Walker, 2006). As in much of the Americas, many of the indigenous people were killed outright, which led to the Iberianization of the Central American isthmus. Culture and politics developed along stratified lines that are still evident nowadays. Variable levels of attention were given by the Spaniards depending on location and available resources. Specific geographic areas were the initial divisions upon which variable development was established between the states in the region. Regardless of the developmental variation of each distinct area, independence was sought and won by all by 1823 (Booth et al., 2006). The one exception to this common history of independence is Panama, which gained independence from Colombia in 1903 with the assistance of the United States for the explicit purpose of securing the trans-isthmus waterway now known as the Panama Canal (Central Intelligence Agency (CIA), 2008).

As in many developing nations, elites, the individuals who control either political or economic power (or both) within each state, shaped the economies and political systems of each state. Agriculture-based economies began to promote the hacienda system in which large landholders organized and controlled resources (Booth et al., 2006). This system introduced and maintained stratified land distribution that has continued to the present day. Poverty became widespread with little opportunity for upward mobility for citizens in each of the six countries. Similar political systems also developed in each of the countries in the nineteenth and twentieth centuries (again with the exception of Panama, which was still part of Colombia). A conservative–liberal political division developed with elites aligning themselves with one side or the other. The difference in initial policy orientation does not need elaboration since these early genuine party differences have degenerated over time into "ideologically indistinguishable clan-based political factions" (Booth et al., 2006, p. 46). What is important to recognize is that until the revolutionary period of the late twentieth century, the economies and political systems of each of the states of Central America were similar in their overtly elite-led orientation. The lasting effects of this orientation would lead to political revolution and structural adjustment for the contemporary states of Costa Rica, El Salvador, Guatemala, Honduras, Nicaragua and Panama.

The Revolutionary Period

From the beginning of the Costa Rican revolution in 1949 through the termination of the Guatemalan civil war in 1996, Central America continually experienced violent, armed conflict in some form. The height of this period of conflict was the 1980s. During this decade, Guatemala, Nicaragua and El Salvador were all involved in civil conflict with Honduras, experiencing high levels of violence. Many of the revolutions that occurred in the region were in response to the high levels of inequality that had developed over the 400-plus year history of Central America. This inequality was exacerbated by the collapse of many of the countries' economies that will be discussed further in a later section.

During these decades of violence, the media played various roles. While the media in Costa Rica were able to operate in a politico-cultural system that was relatively stable, the media in countries like El Salvador were receiving threats from both sides of the conflict and were subsequently pushed into non-influential roles. In Nicaragua, the role of the media was more mixed. The opposition paper, *La Prensa*, was allowed to continue operating but was, at times, subject to extreme censorship (Rockwell & Janus, 2003). Regardless of direct government initiatives, high levels of violence depressed much of the media industry, especially during the height of civil conflict in the region.

The Role of the United States in Central American Revolutions

For the most part, the United States stood in opposition to the popular revolutions of Central America. During the Sandinista revolution in Nicaragua and the civil war in El Salvador, the United States stood against the Sandinista National Liberation Front (FSLN) and the Farabundo Martí National Liberation Front (FMLN) (see Smith, 2000; Walker, 2003). By providing funding and military resources to the counterinsurgents, often Central American governments, the United States initiated a prolonged stalemate which led to the loss of thousands of lives. For example, in El Salvador alone 80 percent of the 70,000 deaths were attributed to the military, police or other US-supported counterinsurgency groups (Booth et al., 2006). This culture of violence that became region-wide impeded the progress of the media industry as non-governmental violent threats, so often a tool of revolutions, continued against media into the modern day.

The one exception of US involvement being pro-state is the fight for independence in Panama. There, the United States mobilized economic and military resources, including a payoff to Colombia, for the eventual success achieved in the fight for independence by the Panamanians (Smith, 2000). Although this case differs in many aspects from the fighting that would break out almost seventy-five years later in Central America, it is necessary to point out that Panama is a historically unique state in Central America. After gaining its independence, Panama remained a virtual protectorate of the United States due to US interest in the Panama Canal (Smith, 2000). This prompts the exclusion of Panama from most of this historical analysis but should not be seen as necessary for exclusion in the sections dealing with the contemporary media industry.

Economics

The economies of Central America are historically agrarian with a specific focus on products such as coffee and tropical fruit (CIA, 2008). This agrarian developmental path was initiated by the colonizing Spanish and carries through to the present day. In an effort to break what many leaders in the region thought of as a pattern of dependent development (Vanden & Prevost, 2006), the governments in the region implemented an economic policy of import substitution industrialization (ISI). Under ISI, countries would produce products that had normally been imported. The three purported goals related to this policy were "to assert economic independence, to create jobs for a burgeoning work force, and to promote economic growth" (Smith, 2005, p. 214). Ultimately, this economic policy led to severe over-inflation of the state apparatus and created an economically vacuous reality sustained only by international loans. After the petroleum shocks of the 1970s, many states were unable to pay their international debts and were forced to seek further relief from international organizations and lender countries. This inspired the current system of neoliberal structural adjustments to be put into place.

Neoliberalism became broadly understood as a set of structural adjustment mandates, induced by the failure of ISI policies, designed to reintroduce pure market forces into the national economies of Central America. It is patterned after the liberal economic system that was in place in the late nineteenth century. As elaborated on by Booth et al. (2006), neoliberal adjustments include

> (1) downsizing government by laying off public employees, (2) balancing public budgets by cutting programs and subsidies to food, transport, and public services, (3) privatization of state-owned enterprises, (4) deregulation of private enterprise, (5) currency devaluations to discourage imports and encourage investment, and (6) sharp reduction of tariff barriers to foreign trade.
>
> (Booth et al., 2006, p. 25)

Proponents of these measures believed that they would provide the necessary economic structure to promote foreign investment and genuine economic growth. The effects of the adoption of neoliberal policies were state-wide. Since governments were left with few options of what to implement and how to implement them, changes were drastic and often of high immediate political cost. Social services and infrastructure upgrades languished which further exacerbated the social unrest already present in Central America. As of today, the effectiveness of these policies remains questionable (Huber & Solt, 2004).

Contemporary Demographic Rankings

The relative development of each of the six Central American countries is the subject of this section. It is important to understand where these states and the region lie relative to other states in the region as well as all other states worldwide (especially developing states). The best way to demonstrate the relative development of Costa Rica, El Salvador, Guatemala, Honduras, Nicaragua and Panama is to employ a number of indexes and data sources, including Freedom House (2006), Transparency International (2007) Corruption Perceptions Index, Human Development Index (United Nations, 2007), Polity IV (Center for Systemic Peace, 2006) and the *CIA world factbook* (CIA, 2008). Table 4.1 shows the demographic characteristics of each Central American state.

To move beyond absolute numbers, in order to determine the true level of development of each state in Central America, the 2005 Human Development Index (HDI) is examined. This index combines many demographic statistics in order to score and rank most countries. According to HDI, Costa Rica (at no. 48) and Panama (62) are fairly well developed with their scores falling in the upper one-third of all 177 countries. El Salvador (103), Nicaragua (110), Honduras (115) and Guatemala (118) are each below the top 50 percent of all countries as rated by HDI. Most importantly, all six countries have experienced positive growth since 1975 in their HDI scores. Out of the 180 countries rated by the Corruption Perceptions Index, the Central American states show a good deal of variation within the middle 50 percent of all countries. Costa Rica (46) has the best score, followed by El Salvador (67), Panama (94), Guatemala (111), Nicaragua (123) and Honduras (131). Corruption is important to consider when looking at the media industry because it often involves facets of the industry such as licensing, regulation lobbying and ownership.

To assess the ability of individuals to act freely within society, Freedom House (2006) offers scores and ratings that classify countries as "free," "partially free" and "not free." All countries in Central America were "free" (Costa Rica, El Salvador, Panama) or "partially free" (Guatemala, Honduras, Nicaragua). In order to further rate the ability of individuals to affect influence on their governments, the Polity IV democracy scores in Table 4.2 show these states' relative level of

Table 4.1 Demographics, 2008

	Population	Size rank (in Central America)	GDP (per capita)	Literacy (%)	Life expectancy (years)
Costa Rica	4,195,914	5	$13,500	96	77.4
El Salvador	7,066,403	3	$5,200	80.2	72.06
Guatemala	13,002,206	1	$5,400	69.1	69.99
Honduras	7,639,327	2	$3,300	80	69.37
Nicaragua	5,785,846	4	$3,200	67.5	71.21
Panama	3,292,693	6	$9,000	91.9	75.17

Source: CIA (2008)

Table 4.2 Index Scores, Ranks and Evaluations

	HDI 2005 (rank)	CPI 2007 (rank)	Freedom House 2006	Polity IV 2006
Costa Rica	48	46	Free	10
El Salvador	103	67	Free	7
Guatemala	118	111	Partially free	8
Honduras	115	131	Partially free	7
Nicaragua	110	123	Partially free	8
Panama	62	94	Free	9

Sources: Center for Systemic Peace (2006); Freedom House (2006); Transparency International (2007); United Nations (2007)

democracy. A score of 10 denotes a pure democracy with a score of −10 representing a pure autocracy. Generally, a score equal to or greater than 7 is accepted as a democracy by most researchers.

A Brief History of Media in Central America

Information is disseminated through the media in all societies. This is no different in Central America. A successful media industry provides the necessary information to individuals regarding issues of government and world affairs (Rockwell & Janus, 2003). In addition, a successful media industry aids in the education of individuals and provides entertainment, which may improve the quality of life for its consumers. Additionally, the media provide jobs.

Media industries exist in all Central American nations in varying capacities. Newspapers were initially the only real form of national and regional information, with some dating back to the early 1800s. Many of these papers have had a turbulent past operating during wars and oppressive governmental regimes. Some are openly political, while others portray an unbiased orientation (Rockwell & Janus, 2003). For example, Nicaragua's Radio Ya was started by the liberal Sandinista party. This radio station continues to be openly biased and a mouthpiece for the party. In contrast, Costa Rica, with its longtime separation of government and media, maintains a number of successful media enterprises that display little political bias (Rockwell & Janus, 2003).

Newspaper production and consumption is difficult due to low literacy rates throughout significant parts of the region. For example, only 69.1 percent of Guatemala's population is literate (CIA, 2008). Also, there are complications dealing with the physical distribution of papers because of the rugged terrain and primitive transportation routes. Radio has become the preferred media throughout the region. Radios are relatively cheap, and do not need electricity if battery powered. Delivery is obtainable regardless of terrain, and there is a social aspect that enables large numbers of individuals to be exposed at once. Also, an individual does not need to be literate to use radio. Upwards of 90 percent of the population of Central America is exposed to radio on a daily basis. However, compared to more developed countries (e.g. the United States), the dissemination of radio receivers in the region is still relatively low (Rockwell & Janus, 2003).

It is important to note that the radio spectrum was unregulated in several of these countries throughout the twentieth century, which has led to problems. These problems include interference, oversaturation and an amount of competition that cannot be supported by these small nations. Due to civil wars and ineffective rulers, radio stations were begun with little regulation. This is the case for Guatemala, Nicaragua and El Salvador (Rockwell & Janus, 2003).

Television also remains relatively low in its level of consumption compared to developed nations. Much of this is due to low incomes in the region. Many households in this region do not have electricity, or the ability to purchase a television set. For this reason, television offerings have historically been sparse, and reserved for those few individuals and families in higher classes and urban areas. However, this is changing with low-cost television receivers and the increase of wages across all sectors of Central American society. Computers and Internet access also remain low in the region. As of 2004, computers per 1,000 inhabitants ranged from a high of 219 in Costa Rica to a low of 16 in Honduras (United Nations, 2007). Public Internet cafés can be found throughout the region and are growing in number, but most citizens do not have the ways, means or the need to embrace computers (Rockwell & Janus, 2003).

Although these countries share a similar colonial history, they do differ in their degrees of development in politics, economics and media (Booth et al., 2006). Costa Rica has maintained a relatively successful newspaper and radio industry since the 1950s, in contrast to Guatemala, which still struggles to develop and maintain successful media enterprises (Rockwell & Janus, 2003).

Media Oligarchies

When an industry, including the media, is begun, capital and knowledge must be obtained. These resources are mostly available to those already benefiting from the society. Therefore, as media developed in Central America, enterprises were often begun to promote political goals and aspirations from those who could afford it. Even as power changed hands over time, the survival of these media was dependent on the government and the nation's elite for assistance and advertising support. Since most of this region's population is poor, the citizens themselves do not have the economic capabilities to financially support a media industry, and as a result, a media oligarchy exists in most of these nations where there is little distinction between the political, economic and media elites. While it is the job of many media producers, even in Central America, to produce valuable and necessary information to be used by consumers, it is not easy to separate the owners from the information.

Media oligarchies are present throughout many of Central America's nations. The Chamorro and Sacassa families in Nicaragua have been involved in both media and politics since the nation's beginning nearly 200 years ago (in 1821). A Chamorro was the first president of Nicaragua, and the family also owns one of the most popular and oldest newspapers in the nation, *La Prensa* (Rockwell & Janus, 2003). These media oligarchies are also sometimes tied to the wealthy landowning elites who endorsed much of the violence in the later part of the twentieth century throughout the region. Twelve families in El Salvador, whose money was initially made through the production of agricultural products such as coffee and bananas, then invested in media not only as a potentially profitable enterprise, but also as a platform from which they could promote their interests and agendas.

In Honduras, five families control the majority of the media industry. Known as the "Turkos" because of their Arabic heritage, this group of families obtained their wealth through entre-preneurship and investments in industries including the media (Rockwell & Janus, 2003). In addition to media ownership, these families are heavily involved in politics, which has historically resulted in a relatively biased media.

Panama's media oligarchy is referred to as the "twenty families." Also biased, but in a manner different from the Honduran system, these families are ideologically split and have engaged in political and economic disagreement for a prolonged period of time. Because of this divide among elites, media in Panama look as though they provide multiple viewpoints and active discussion, but in actuality, there is not much more than an elite battle being carried out on the newsstands.

Both the Honduran and Panamanian media are historically oligarchic but we see that the two systems are manifestly different beyond their centralized ownership.

Twelve families and two business groups control all television, most radio, and all but one newspaper in Guatemala. One unique characteristic of Guatemala's media oligarchy is the presence of foreign investment. A Mexican, Ángel González González, owns much of the media. As of 2003, González controlled twenty-one radio stations, four of the five national television stations (the fifth being the government's) and most of the cinemas in the region. González has a relationship with the Mexican television giant, Televisa, which is where most Guatemalan programming originates. This transition to foreign-led media investment is occurring in other nations as well, indicating a new trend in oligarchic media ownership.

Costa Rica, in contrast, has seen a variety of successful, non-partisan media enterprises throughout its contemporary history. Media, in this case, appear to be reflective of the democratic environment of the nation in which it exists. Most media have been historically owned by three different groups. The Pecado Cozza and Jimenez families are longtime elites. González of Mexico, the same individual who owns media in Guatemala, is the third large media owner in Costa Rica. These groups are not directly tied to the government and do not have a history of repression; therefore, it is in the media's interest to appeal to the population and not political parties. Additionally, ad spending in Costa Rica is much higher than the rest of the region. Because profit is obtained through advertising, it is vital for these media owners to appeal to their audience, instead of governments or elites, to survive. Although media are oligarchic in ownership structure, Costa Rica's media industry is market driven.

Press Freedom

Each of the Central American states discussed to this point has active constitutions in place that guarantee basic rights in clear and concise terms. This is true specifically for the media as well as more broadly for anyone wishing to exercise their right to expression. Although the realization of these freedoms is significantly more tentative, the letter of the law stands to reinforce the rights of expression and the press. The regular changing of political regimes in these countries, while positive for democracy, often ushers in changes in media regulations which can have either positive or negative effects depending on the policy orientation of the specific regime. However, instead of focusing on the carousel of media regulations per country and per regime, we will report on the general state of the freedom of the press. In short, the information below represents a summation and generalization of state–press and society–press relations specifically as it relates to the ability of information within Central American societies to be spread.

In order to make an assessment regarding the level of press freedom in each of the Central American states, we employ the World Press Freedom Index 2007 (Reporters Without Borders, 2007) and the Freedom of the Press Index 2006 (Freedom House, 2006). Out of the 169 countries that were rated in the World Press Freedom Index 2007, Costa Rica (at no. 21), Nicaragua (47), Panama (54) and El Salvador (64) fell in the top half, with Honduras (87) near the half-way point, and Guatemala (104) landing well in the bottom half of the rankings.

Costa Rica has the highest press-freedom rank in the region. In fact, it is high for the entire world, ranking above the United States. Nicaragua's press freedom is second to Costa Rica within the region. It is still considered in the satisfactory level of press freedom. Reporters Without Borders (2007) found no incidents of violence against media professionals in 2007. This favorable ranking reveals that the press in Nicaragua continues to encourage the growth of a quality consumer base.

Panama also has a "satisfactory environment" regarding press freedom. While this nation has many benefits, in March 2007, President Torrijos endorsed two articles in the amended criminal code that inhibit press freedom. These prohibitions include the publication of documents not intended for publication and the revealing of secrets. Laws such as these, which are punishable by both fines and imprisonment, diminish freedom and security of media professionals in Panama by putting reporters at risk when publishing material not in the reigning government's interest (Reporters Without Borders, 2007).

El Salvadorans have a somewhat free press. While this nation has endured a history of violence, Reporters Without Borders (2007) reports that El Salvador has a satisfactory rating in regards to press freedom. This satisfactory situation may be attributable in part to the death of a radio personality in 2007. It was later suspected that gang members, whom the journalist regularly covered, were to blame for the murder. Additionally, a freelance reporter was arrested for violating anti-terrorism laws in 2007. These two occurrences demonstrate the pressure placed on media professionals by both state and society.

Honduras has a lower press-freedom rank due to a perceived corrupt government and suspicions of government involvement and censorship. Media professionals claim that the president tries to control the media. Two reporters were severely threatened, and one was killed. A poor relationship between the government and media industry, an unsafe environment for reporters, and incidents of censorship by the government all prevent the Honduran media industry from achieving greater stability (Reporters Without Borders, 2007).

Guatemala has the worst reported level of press freedom in the region. In 2007 alone, two media professionals were killed, and another was threatened with guns after reporting a traffic accident. There were also threats phoned into a television station, two armed attacks on a radio station and one kidnapping of a reporter. Incidents of violence against media professionals in Guatemala grossly exceeded all other nations in the region. Guatemala is the only nation in the region to be classified in the "Noticeable Problems" category of the press-freedom rankings (Reporters Without Borders, 2007).

The Freedom of the Press Index 2006 gives a more temporal perspective but offers more ambiguous classifications than the ranking of the World Press Freedom Index 2007. As of 2005, only Costa Rica's press was rated as "free." Guatemala, Nicaragua, El Salvador, Panama and Honduras were all rated as "partly free" (Freedom House, 2006). Costa Rica, Guatemala and El Salvador have maintained a stable rating since the index was begun in 1980. Honduras has seen degeneration from a rating of "free" (1980–87, 1992–93) to today's stable rating of "partly free." Both Nicaragua and Panama have seen their ratings fluctuate regularly on almost a year-to-year basis. More accurately, the fluctuations seem to be in line with regime transitions. For example, the only time that Panama is rated as "not free" is in 1989 and 1990 when it was undergoing a forced transition from the rule of Manuel Noriega to open democracy (see Table 4.3).

Some of the specific attributes of press regulations that have led to the variable ratings of different Central American states include the criminalization of libel, slander and defamation in the press, censorship and registration or licensing of journalists. While the implementation of criminal penalties for libel, slander and defamation have significantly decreased in recent years, their continued presence in the legislative code of Central American states renders them a continued threat in their readiness for use. The registration or licensing of journalists is still enforced but the abuse of this regulation by the state appears on the decline region-wide. Overt censorship by the state also appears on the decline but similar proclamations about self-censorship should be less readily asserted. Consistent levels of societal violence constantly force journalists to carefully choose the information that they report.

Table 4.3 Freedom of the Press, 1980–2005

	1980	1985	1990	1995	2000	2005
Costa Rica	Free	Free	Free	Free	Free	Free
El Salvador	Partly free	Partly free	Partly free	Partly free	Partly free	Partly free
Guatemala	Partly free	Partly free	Partly free	Partly free	Partly free	Partly free
Honduras	Free	Free	Partly free	N/A	N/A	Partly free
Nicaragua	Free	Partly free	Not free	Partly free	Partly free	Partly free
Panama	Partly free	Partly free	Not free	Free	Free	Partly free

Source: Freedom House (2006)

To further the assessment of the relationship between the press and governments, economic and social policies are examined to determine if the leadership in these nations is proactively attempting to better the economic and social situation in these nations. The World Bank (2008) provides some information regarding government activities in relation to economic development. While much of the information is not directly related to the media, this industry is affected by the actions of the government that may enable or inhibit competitive advantage and profitability within the media.

According to the World Bank (2008), the Arias administration in Costa Rica views overarching reforms and investment in education, infrastructure, telecommunications and energy as primary for growth and poverty reduction. While the effects of these promises have yet to be realized, Costa Rica's proactive government has produced several initiatives that, if carried out correctly, will provide significant competitive advantage for the media.

Following the civil war in the 1980s, El Salvador's government has made many economic reforms to encourage investment, privatize industries such as electricity and telecommunications, and improve its level of competitiveness (World Bank, 2008). Remittances were disseminated throughout the population through 2006 and 2007. This money has resulted in a boost in consumption. However, crime and violence have hindered the continued implementation and success of these governmental and economic incentives. In late 2006, El Salvador's government signed a $461 million compact intended to both stimulate growth and reduce poverty by increasing education, enterprise development and transportation infrastructure.

Guatemala continues to suffer from the unequal distribution of income and resources. The government is combating this and a past of corruption by encouraging transparency and legitimacy. The government is also encouraging privately led growth and investment in human capital. Although Guatemala's GDP is higher than other nations in the region, social indicators remain low. While wealth continues to be concentrated with a few, the spread and growth of a media industry cannot be achieved (World Bank, 2008).

Honduras benefits from the most diversified economy in the region. Both agriculture and manufacturing are valuable industries in Honduras. However, poverty remains high, and there is a large disparity in incomes (World Bank, 2008). Honduras was devastated in 1998 by Hurricane Mitch. Following this great loss of life and assets, Honduras implemented a program to help prevent such destruction from recurring. While Honduras remains poor, the most recent hurricane claimed far fewer lives, indicating improvement in disaster awareness and response, much of which is initiated and disseminated through the media.

Since 2001, Nicaragua has seen moderate continuous growth in its economy, as well as a low level of inflation. According to the World Bank (2008), President Ortega's main objectives are stabilizing the economy and reducing poverty. Additionally, creating a positive investment environment in the private sector and the development of small and medium businesses are issues that Ortega intends to address in his term. Sustaining quality social programs to improve the overall well-being of citizens is a priority as well. While no specific issues regarding the media are addressed, all of these programs, if implemented appropriately, can contribute to a healthy media industry in Nicaragua.

Panama has one of the fastest-growing and best-managed economies in Latin America (World Bank, 2008). It is estimated that the expansion of the canal and the new trade relationships established since 2007 will lead to even further economic development in the future. While this economic expansion is promising, the presence of large discrepancies in wealth and education among Panama's citizens continues to demonstrate that unresolved issues remain. In addition to the general well-being of the Panamanian economy, growth is needed to develop a media industry that not only is economically successful, but also serves all citizens of the nation.

The Media Industry

The media serve as information sources to citizens and necessary institutions for the success of democracy. However, money must still be made if the media are to operate independently of the government and ruling elites. "Fundamentally, mass media are economic institutions that produce and distribute communication content and services to members of a society" (Albarran & Chan-Olmsted, 1998, p. 3). Advertising, ownership and globalization are three areas that may have an effect on a media industry's ability to produce content and services for its consumers. Also, these issues can affect programming and profitability. This chapter has previously examined the political environment of Central America and the relationship that the media have with government and media professionals. This section examines the media industries, or the producers and distributors of media content for economic gain, within Central America.

Advertising

Media organizations in Central America, like much of the world, need money to operate. In addition to the necessary equipment, personnel must be adequately compensated for quality content. To do this, monetary funds must be available. Media industries possess a unique quality known as the dual product market (Picard, 1989). Media actually produce the same products but for two different groups—one for consumers and one for advertisers. Central American media industries operate in this dual product market; however, since little money is spent by consumers on media, the role of the advertiser is of primary importance.

The advertising industry can have both positive and negative effects on the media in Central America. Without advertising revenues, media are left either to receive subsidies from the government or to survive solely by support from the citizenry. Financial ties of the advertisers, often business-owning elites, to the government leads to corruption and censorship. While many nations rely somewhat on a mix of government subsidies and advertising to support the media (Albarran & Chan-Olmsted, 1998), government corruption and instability in Central America have made media companies who accept this funding subject to government control over content. This leaves private companies to support the media through advertising. While this method works in many nations that are economically advanced, certain problems arise in small and economically struggling nations like most of the states in Central America. For example, often there is little distinction between government and private-sector interests. In these small oligarchic economies, companies and individuals who purchase advertising may have a similar agenda and intentions as the governmental regime. Also, reporters may feel threatened to speak out against private interests who buy advertising. In fear of losing the revenues from an advertiser, various levels of self-censorship regarding the company in question or the ideological beliefs of that advertiser may influence reporting (Rockwell & Janus, 2003).

In addition to powerful private-sector advertisers supporting the media, the government is often one of the largest purchasers of advertising in these nations (Rockwell & Janus, 2003). Similar to the self-censorship effects that private companies can have on media organizations and reporters, the government may threaten to pull advertising dollars from a media organization that does not please the regime in power. Advertising boycotts have also been used by the government in an attempt to quiet opposition media outlets. Since there is often little distinction between the private sector and the government, private advertisers who want to stay in favor with the government follow suit and also boycott these outlets. This technique has been successfully employed in El Salvador and Guatemala, but was ineffective in the late 1990s when Nicaraguan President Alemán pulled all advertising from opposing media outlets run by the Sandinistas (Rockwell & Janus, 2003). While the opposition media in Nicaragua displayed some losses, they managed to stay afloat due to large circulations, a good listener base, and the support of private companies willing to disagree with the government boycott and continue purchasing advertising space.

Finally, political parties and candidates may be purchasers of advertising as well. Paid editorials are an advertising technique used by political parties. Often, it can be difficult to distinguish between real news and these paid editorials. This is a way for political parties to insert themselves into an otherwise non-partisan media outlet. This was a popular campaign strategy for Flores in El Salvador in 1999. By purchasing editorial time and space known as *campos pagados* on radio stations and newspapers, citizens were exposed to political advertisements disguised as news. This idea of paid news stories is not strictly limited to political campaigning either. There are examples of media organizations in need of funds charging private companies and organizations for news coverage, and in some cases having these outside parties actually author the content themselves (Rockwell & Janus, 2003).

Globalization

The world is becoming increasingly connected as technology advances and economies become more international. This is seen in media industries through an increase in foreign ownership and new technologies that enable rapid content distribution across nations to occur (Albarran & Chan-Olmsted, 1998). Foreign investment is a central aspect of developing the growing economies of Central America. With the adoption of the Central American Free Trade Agreement (CAFTA), trade and international business relationships have been promoted. The media worldwide are becoming an increasingly global industry as well. Media were once tied strictly to the society and nation that it served; however, today media are viewed as an economic enterprise that can span borders and cultures.

Additionally, Central America's citizens, with their increasing economic development, progressively liberal markets, and increased buying power, have become a popular target for foreign investment. The strongest example of this trend toward foreign media ownership is centered on the media investments of one individual. Ángel González González, a prominent Mexican media executive who has a relationship with Mexican television giant Televisa, owns much of the media in Guatemala. As of 2003, Mr. González had a virtual television monopoly in Guatemala, mostly importing programming from Mexico. González holds interests in radio, and owns many of the cinemas in Guatemala as well. In addition to owning media enterprises in Guatemala, González owns media properties in other Central American nations including Honduras, Nicaragua and Costa Rica (Rockwell & Janus, 2003).

Costa Rica is the most desirable market for foreign investors in Central America. Because of its stable government and relatively stable consumer base, as compared to the rest of the region, there is profit potential in Costa Rica that far exceeds that of other nations in Central America. Not only does González own some media properties in Costa Rica, but another large media owner in Costa Rica is a Canadian company, who owns one of the largest newspapers in the region (Rockwell & Janus, 2003). Costa Ricans, with their longstanding stable media industry, are torn between the advancement and globalization of society and the undesirability of foreigners owning their media. For the time being, globalization appears unstoppable.

Content

Central American television stations import much of their entertainment programming from Mexico, other parts of Latin America and the United States. For example, Benitez (2003) reported that 82 percent of television programming in El Salvador was from foreign producers. Often this programming is legitimately acquired through syndication; however, there are cases of foreign programming being acquired illegally. Satellite signals are known to be intercepted and programming is then shown without the provider's knowledge.

Content is also easier to access as technology expands throughout the region. Cable allows for more variation in content than the few national broadcasts, and the Internet and computer technology provide an even greater potential for variable content in the region. The Internet may not be manipulated as easily as traditional media outlets because content is not necessarily produced by the providers. Also, the amount of content is endless and the price to produce it is low. Therefore, more content is easily available potentially rendering the gatekeepers of traditional Central American media obsolete. There is a concern for the ambiguity of content on the Internet. Sometimes it is difficult to recognize the origin or motives behind the producers. While motivational factors may not be of great concern in a nation such as the United States, who has had a trusted media system for decades, in Central America, the media industry as a whole must always be questioned.

Media and Society

Media creates information for consumers. A media industry will not be very successful or profitable if no one uses it. It is necessary to investigate the people of Central America to understand how and to what extent they use media. As mentioned earlier, radio is the most popular media format in the region. Following radio consumption, in terms of quantity, is television use. Newspapers, which have existed in the region for a long time, do not obtain high circulation numbers relative to the consumption levels of radio and television. Internet and computer use is on the rise, but has not reached widespread diffusion. While Table 4.4 provides data on the number of televisions and radios per thousand inhabitants, it is important to recognize that one of these devices can often be used by multiple people. There are also public places where different media can be used. For example, public buses often air radio programming; also, a household may share one device among multiple family members. Newspapers can be read and passed along to other individuals.

Technology ownership and use has increased since the late 1990s. The *World statistics pocketbook* (United Nations, 2005) provides information regarding device ownership. This

Table 4.4 User Data, 2005

	Television receivers (per 1,000)	Radio receivers (per 1,000)	Computers (per 1,000)	Newspapers (per 1,000)	Internet users (%)
Costa Rica	144	816	197.2	94	29.37
El Salvador	679	481	25.2	28	9.17
Guatemala	61	79	14.4	33	10.37
Honduras	96	411	13.6	55	4.51
Nicaragua	68	270	27.9	30	2.73
Panama	183	300	38.3	62	6.80
Average	205	393	52.8	50	10.49

Source: United Nations (2005)

information is also available from 1995 and in that time, all media ownership has increased, and the number of Internet users has grown as seen in Table 4.4. Although only a small percentage of the population are considered Internet users according to the *CIA world factbook* (CIA, 2008), there is great growth potential as the economies of these nations continue to develop and expand.

Costa Rica

Similar to Costa Rica's democratic and economic success relative to the rest of the region, this country also contains more media devices and users than the rest of the region (see Table 4.4). Costa Rica's media consumers are more able to obtain and use media which can result in more profitable media industries. While television and radio ownership numbers may be deceiving because of the variable size of the household and the potential for use without ownership, computer ownership and users are telling of the progress of this nation. Compared to the other five countries in this region, Costa Rica has a more developed computer user base. Additionally, newspaper circulation is higher in Costa Rica. This can be explained by the high rate of literacy, the longtime credibility of Costa Rican newspapers, and a population more economically able to purchase newspapers than other poorer nations in the region.

El Salvador

The United Nations (2005) reported that El Salvador has more television receivers per capita than any other nation in the region. Radio device ownership is also high with almost one radio for every two citizens. This rate of dissemination indicates that radio is easily accessible. Newspaper readership, Internet users and computer ownership are all low but growth can be anticipated in computer ownership and Internet users as infrastructure improves and the cost of computers continues to decrease. El Salvador's highly concentrated and urban population (Booth et al., 2006) also provides potential benefits for the growth of media in the region. Geographic concentration can lead to the ability to share devices such as computers with Internet access.

Guatemala

Television ownership is lower here than in the rest of the region. Television may still be seen by many Guatemalans on a regular basis; however, the options for doing so may be limited to public places and gatherings. Radio ownership is also low in the region. Relatively low incomes and the lack of fluent Spanish speakers in some regions may be responsible for these numbers. It is important to note that by absolute population numbers, Guatemala is the largest nation in the region (see Table 4.1). Therefore, even though the dissemination of radio and television receivers may be low, the total number of people exposed to television and radio is higher than the less populated nations in the region. Newspaper circulation is very low due to a combination of low literacy rates, rugged terrain and primitive roadways. The percentage of Internet users is second only to Costa Rica in the region at around 10 percent of the population. Even though Costa Rica has about three times the percentage of users, Guatemala has about three times the total number of citizens. Therefore, the absolute number of Internet users in Guatemala and Costa Rica are about equal, making the current Internet market size comparable. One huge benefit for Guatemala over Costa Rica, in this respect, is the size of the potential market due to its large population.

Honduras

Other than Honduras' relatively large dissemination of radio receivers, the rest of the media are lacking in terms of consumption (see Table 4.4). Television dissemination is low, but not as low as some other nations. With about one television for every ten people, it can be assumed that television is available, but perhaps not in as many locations as in other nations like El Salvador. Computer ownership is the lowest in Central America with about 1 percent of the population owning a computer. This low dissemination of computers is also evident in the small number of Internet users. Newspaper circulation is higher than in some other nations in the region, but with only about one newspaper for every twenty citizens, there does not seem to be an active newspaper readership. Honduras does have the second largest population in the region (although a distant second to Guatemala) meaning that there is a potentially larger base of consumers in this nation. However, due to its relatively large land mass and slow economic growth, it may be difficult to increase the media audience.

Nicaragua

Nicaragua has the second poorest economy in Latin America and the Caribbean, second only to Haiti (United Nations, 2007). This means that Nicaraguans struggle economically more than any other nation in Central America. Most of the data regarding their media users reflect a dim economic environment. For example, Nicaragua's television receiver dissemination is less than 10 percent. This number is slightly higher than Guatemala, but Nicaragua's population is less than half the size of Guatemala making the television audience smaller in absolute numbers. There is about one radio for every three citizens in Nicaragua. This number is high enough to assume that most people have regular access to a radio. Newspaper circulation is low. This may be explained by a low literacy rate, and low disposable income to spend on items such as newspapers. There are fewer Internet users in Nicaragua than any other Central American nation. This number is contradictory when examining the dissemination of computers, which although only around 3 percent, is higher than Guatemala and Honduras, both of which have higher rates of Internet users. Perhaps computers are not shared outside the home, there are not as many public options for Internet use, or Nicaraguan citizens who do not own a computer are not as willing or able to pay for Internet use.

Panama

Panama displays some promising characteristics when looking at its media consumers. Television dissemination is similar to Costa Rica, with about one television for every twenty citizens. While this is not enough for every household to have its own television, they are not nearly as sparse when compared to other Central American nations. Radio dissemination is around 30 percent. Newspaper circulation is the second highest after Costa Rica. However, Panama does have the smallest population of any nation in the region making the absolute number of papers circulated quite small. Panama also has the second highest number of computers, but falls short in the percentage of Internet users.

Conclusion

Although the media industries of the Central American states are unique and variable in their production, consumption and regulation, there are some consistent trends and realities, not only as each state relates to the other but also as the region relates to the surrounding regions and the world as a whole. Generally, Central American states should be viewed as peripheral to the larger nations of Latin and North America. Positive trends in human development and media usership at the individual level contrast with stable production and regulation at the institutional level of these states. The lack of purchasing power by consumers has left the media industry in Central America subject to elite design both nationally and internationally. Costa Rica stands as the single exception to this regional rule. While subject to international movement, Costa Rican media also looks to its citizenry for developmental direction. While this is the hoped-for projection for the rest of the region, certainty is elusive. As we will further discuss below, the trends of ownership, consumption and regulation hold the key for defining the place of Central American media.

Ownership of media industries in Central America is limited. This oligarchic ownership structure, familial in nature, has continued as such with the introduction of international ownership. International media owners, such as Ángel González González of Mexico, have made a pronounced move to acquire media industries throughout Central America. Given the lack of domestic programming in most of these states, this international reorientation has exacted little change in the product received by consumers.

As the conditions of the citizens of Central America continue to improve, consumption of goods and services trends steadily upward. This is no different for the consumption of media. The existence of a relatively free press and the existent trend toward an even freer press should encourage consumption and industry growth. While the possibility of region destabilization always stands, the current political and economic movement of these states is toward greater stability, like that already achieved by Costa Rica. Even the country that ranks at or near the bottom in almost every category, Guatemala, finds itself in a grossly better situation today than in the immediate past. Growth, both general and industry specific, is present in all of Central America.

To further add to the discussion of media in Central America, it may be useful to highlight two new trends in media. The first is the continued prominence of radio in Central America. More than any other medium, radio stands far above television, newspapers and Internet in terms of consumption. The ability to circumvent traditional Central American realities, such as rough terrain, low literacy rates, electricity interruption and general accessibility, allows radio to remain as the most used medium. However, research has shown that this is not a stagnant reality. Agosta (2007) discusses the role of community radio in encouraging development and political participation in El Salvador. This community-based movement has shown the continued vitality of radio in the region. Therefore, we should not be so obsessed with the globalization of media markets through television and Internet growth to ignore the continued embrace of traditional media in the region.

Like media ownership, the role of globalization is paramount in this peripheral region. Besides increases in consumption and the expansion of medium choice throughout the states of Central America, globalization has proven broader than ever. The implementation of economic structural adjustment programs has encouraged foreign investment. Now, both ownership and programming is international. However, other effects of globalization can be seen. Kumar (2006) claims international assistance for the promotion of an independent media has been ongoing for over two decades. The purpose of this assistance is "to promote democratization by facilitating the free flow of information, transparency, accountability in the government, and economic growth" (Kumar, 2006, p. 652). Training of journalists and general improvements in the media industry by international organizations has had far-reaching, developmental effects. Globalization, therefore, must be understood to be broader than simple economic take-over.

No matter what facet of Central American media one intends to focus on, the generality of positive growth and peripheral international placement must be understood. The states of Costa Rica, El Salvador, Guatemala, Honduras, Nicaragua and Panama continue to be assimilated into Latin America as a whole as their ownership and programming demonstrates. None of these countries, individually, will lead the Latin American region in media advancement. However, the positive consumption trend will move the countries toward the Costa Rican model of consumer-led media.

References

Agosta, D. E. (2007). Constructing civil society, supporting local development: A case study of community radio in postwar El Salvador. *Democratic Communiqué, 21*(1), 4–26.

Albarran, A. B. & Chan-Olmsted, S. M. (1998). *Global media economics: Commercialization, concentration, and integration of world media markets.* Ames, IA: Iowa State University Press.

Benitez, J. L. (2003, May). *Television in El Salvador: Foreign investment, loss of local control?* Paper presented at MIT3 International Conference, Television in Transition, Cambridge, MA.

Booth, J. A., Wade, C. J. & Walker, T. W. (2006). *Understanding Central America.* Boulder, CO: Westview Press.

Center for Systemic Peace (2006). *Polity IV project: Political regime characteristics and transitions, 1800–2006.* Retrieved June 1, 2008, from www.systemicpeace.org/polity/polity4.htm.

Central Intelligence Agency (CIA) (2008). *The CIA world factbook.* Retrieved May 8, 2008, from https://www.cia.gov/library/publications/the-world-factbook/.

European Union (2007). *European Union election observation mission: Guatemala.* Retrieved June 1, 2008, from http://ec.europa.eu/external_relations/human_rights/eu_election_ass_observ/guatemala/index.htm.

Freedom House (2006). *Freedom of the press.* Retrieved June 1, 2008, from www.freedomhouse.org/template.cfm?page=16.

Freedominfo.org (2004). *Global survey.* Retrieved June 16, 2008, from www.freedominfo.org/documents/global_survey2006.pdf.

Huber, E. & Solt, F. (2004). Successes and failures of neoliberalism. *Latin American Research Review, 39*(3), 150–164.

Kumar, K. (2006). International assistance to promote independent media in transition and post-conflict societies. *Democratization, 13*(4), 652–667.

Picard, R. G. (1989). *Media economics: Concepts and issues.* Newbury Park, CA: Sage.

Reporters Without Borders (2007). *World Press Freedom Index.* Retrieved June 16, 2008, from www.rsf.org/article.php3?id_article=19388.

Rockwell, R. & Janus, N. (2003). *Media power in Central America.* Urbana, IL: University of Illinois Press.

Smith, P. H. (2000). *Talons of the eagle: Dynamics of US–Latin American relations* (2nd ed.). New York: Oxford University Press.

Smith, P. H. (2005). *Democracy in Latin America: Political change in comparative perspective.* New York: Oxford University Press.

Transparency International (2007) Corruption Perceptions Index. Retrieved March 3, 2009, from www.transparency.org/policy_research/surveys_indices/cpi.

United Nations (2005). *World statistics pocketbook: Containing data available as of 30 Nov. 2004.* New York: UN Department of Economic and Social Affairs.

United Nations (2007). *Human development reports.* Retrieved December 12, 2007, from http://hdr.undp.org/en/statistics/.

Vanden, H. E. & Prevost, G. (2006). *Politics of Latin America: The power game* (2nd ed.). New York: Oxford University Press.

Walker, T. W. (2003). *Nicaragua: Living in the shadow of the eagle* (4th ed.). Boulder, CO: Westview Press.

World Bank (2008). *Country briefs.* Retrieved June 16, 2008, from http://web.worldbank.org/WBSITE/EXTERNAL/COUNTRIES/0,,pagePK:180619~theSitePK:136917,00.html.

5

The Media in Colombia

**Germán Arango Forero, Liliana Gutiérrez Coba,
Alfonso Forero Gutiérrez, Jairo Valderrama Valderrama,
Rodolfo Prada Penagos, Luz Carmen Barrera Avellaneda
and Adriana Guzmán de Reyes**
Universidad de La Sabana, Colombia

Introduction

Colombia lies on the north-west corner of South America. It has coasts on both the Pacific and Atlantic oceans. Panama (on the north-west), Venezuela (on the north-east), Brazil (on the south-east) and Peru and Ecuador (on the south) share borders with Colombia. Colombia extends over 1,141,178 square kilometers. In 2005 the population was 42.8 million people and it is projected to increase to 45.5 million by 2010, with life expectancy reaching 70.6 years for men and 77.5 for women (Departamento Administrativo Nacional de Estadística (DANE), 2005).

Colombia is the third most populated country in Latin America, after Brazil and Mexico. In 2005, 76.6 percent of the population lived in or around urban areas; that is expected to increase to 78.5 percent by 2010 percent. The Colombian economy ranks fifth in Latin America. In 2000 the unemployment rate was the highest in the region at 17.2 percent, dropping to 11.6 percent in 2007, second only to the Dominican Republic, whose unemployment rose to 15.6 percent. In 2006, 20.9 percent of the population worked in agricultural activities, 19.8 percent in the industry sector and 59.4 percent in the service sector (Economic Commission for Latin America and the Caribbean (ECLAC), 2007).

The main exports are petroleum, coal and some metals such as ferrous nickel. At the same time, the main commercial trade partners include the United States, Venezuela, the European Union, Ecuador and Peru.

A Country of Violence

Despite having the longest-standing and most stable democracy in the continent, Colombia's social and political history has been laden with difficult periods of violence, especially since the 1960s, when the so-called left-wing guerrillas were formed. These appeared in the aftermath of armed militias created by the traditional political parties, *liberales* and *conservadores* (liberals and conservatives), which began clashing in the nineteenth century and agreed to cease hostilities with the Benidorm (1956) and Sitges (1957) agreements, which in their turn led to the Frente Nacional, a period of sixteen years in which *liberales* and *conservadores* agreed to alternate the presidency, and hence political power, from 1958 to 1974 (Sánchez, 2007).

Although these agreements reduced the traditional bipartisan confrontation, it also inspired the foundation of the left-wing illegal armed groups, such as the Fuerzas Armadas Revolucionarias de Colombia (FARC: Colombian Revolutionary Armed Forces), a farmer's movement inspired by Marxism-Leninism, and the Ejército de Liberación Nacional (ELN: National Freedom Army), formed by the urban student movements inspired by the Cuban revolution.

In the 1980s another spur of violence took place. Organizations dedicated to the production and distribution of illegal substances became hierarchically established, following their birth during the late 1970s with exports of marihuana to the United States. The drug cartels created their own armed bands, which began fighting the guerrilla for the control of harvesting fields of illegal substances, routes and drug markets. These armed bands later became known later as paramilitary organizations (Franco, 1999).

After failed peace negotiations with FARC, encouraged by President Andrés Pastrana Arango during his term in office (1998–2002), Álvaro Uribe Vélez won the presidential election in 2002. In 2006 President Uribe was re-elected for a second term of four years. During his tenure he has implemented the policy of democratic security, backed by US political, economic and military support. This policy has achieved considerable progress in weakening the drug cartels and guerrilla organizations. It has also demobilized and reincorporated to civil society a considerable number of paramilitary ex-combatants and tried some of their masterminds, fourteen of whom were extradited to the United States in 2008 on charges of organizing the smuggling of illegal substances to America.

Life in a country like Colombia has to carry on amidst these problems of violence, but regardless, the country struggles as a whole to develop a proper environment for business and entrepreneurship. The efforts of the government and the civil society have focused on recovering national confidence and projecting a positive image on the international sphere. This in its turn has made the country competitive as an emerging market, as it has also become an important market for international investment.

Colombian Media: In the Hands of a Few

The arrival in Colombia of foreign enterprises as the main stockholder of the most relevant national media reflects the broader trend of national media conglomerates to develop mergers and alliances to widen their coverage and influence. The first relevant international acquisition took place in 1999, when the Spanish-based Grupo Prisa bought 19 percent of the stock of Cadena Radial Colombiana (Caracol), then owned by a Colombian mogul, Julio Mario Santodomingo. In 2002, Prisa increased to 60 percent its participation in a Colombian investment group to create Grupo Latino de Radio, an international subsidiary of the Unión Radio system, which owns 1,240 stations in seventeen countries. Prisa's share in Union Radio stock is 86.7 percent, and it holds 13.3 percent of Valores Bavaria, owned by Santodomingo.

One of the most important moves took place in 2007, when Spain's Grupo Editorial Planeta acquired 55 percent percent of the stock of Casa Editorial El Tiempo (CEET), owner of *El Tiempo* for $338 million. *El Tiempo* has the largest circulation of any newspaper in the country, and is the owner of the most visited Colombian Internet website, www.eltiempo.com.co, according to Alexa (2008). The purchase included 40 percent of the television channel City TV, owned by Casa Editorial El Tiempo, limited by Colombian legislation, which limits ownership by foreign companies. Casa Editorial also owns *Portafolio*, a newspaper dealing with economics; the regional newspapers *Tolima 7 días, Boyacá 7 días, Llano 7 días* and *Café 7 días*; the publishers Multirrevistas and Círculo de Lectores, and the websites Metrocuadrado.com and el Empleo.com.

A Mexican Conglomerate Looks South

In the field of telecommunications, Mexican conglomerate Telmex purchased a group of cable television companies to become the largest Colombian cable television provider. Starting in 2005, Telmex took over several cable television providers: TV Cable, Superview, Cablepacífico, Satelcaribe and Cablecentro. In February, 2008, Telmex held 44 percent coverage of the cable TV market in Colombia (La gran encuesta de la televisión en Colombia, 2008: The great survey about Colombian television). By owning less than 50 percent of the market, the Comisión Nacional de Televisión (CNTV: National Television Commission) does not consider Telmex to be engaged in a monopolistic practice (Rueda, 2008).

The CNTV allowed cable television providers Cablecentro, Supercable, Satelcaribe, Cablevista, EPM Televisión, Cablepacífico and Cable Unión de Occidente opportunities to widen their coverage to the whole country in 2007. However, the Consejo de Estado (National Council), which has no mandatory power, rejected the decision on the grounds that it created a monopolistic move.

As the judicial battle ensues, Telmex remains the main cable television provider in Colombia. Its main competition is the Spanish-based multinational Telefónica-Telecom, which has started to offer satellite television along with telephone and broadband Internet access, matching Telmex "triple play" packages.

The Moguls

On Sunday, May 11, 2008, *El Espectador*, a newspaper owned by Comunican SA, returned to daily production, eight years after it had become a weekly newspaper. The 1986 assassination of its director, Guillermo Cano, led to a severe financial crisis following repeated threats by the drug mafia. Those eight years as a weekly newspaper allowed the newspaper to remain in existence and continue as one of the oldest newspapers in Colombia.

In 1998 the Santodomingo group, one of the biggest industrial corporations in Colombia and owner of *Cromos* magazine, took over *El Espectador*, as the Cano Isaza family, who held ownership, declared that they were unable to retain the newspaper. Going back to a daily print run meant an investment of around US$12 million for Santodomingo, through Comunican SA. Santodomingo also owns Canal Caracol, a TV channel and broadcaster that formed a strategic alliance with the American Spanish language channel Telemundo, to broadcast novellas and news shows in various Latin American countries and the United States.

RCN radio network and RCN television channel, both owned by Organización Carlos Ardila Lulle, have formed international alliances with other radio and television stations in the continent with Televisa and Univision, respectively. Just like its main competitor, Caracol, RCN looks to widen its audience and to co-produce novellas to broadcast to the Spanish-speaking audience in the Americas.

Some other radio networks like Todelar, Super, Olímpica, Colmundo and Líder, which had an important place in Colombia's radio history, have died out or almost disappeared after selling some of their frequencies, due to the pressure of the financially stronger media groups such as Caracol and RCN. New radio broadcasters have emerged, including La WV Radio. The name of the station comes from the initials of its owner, journalist and sports commentator William Vinasco, who handles the programming of both radio stations, Candela and Vibra. However, the advertising sales on the network have been controlled by Caracol since 2006. This means that although the stations remain property of Vinasco, they are broadcast by Caracol, who rents the airtime to them.

In the field of newspapers in the Colombian regions, Santander-based Grupo Galvis, the original owner since 1921 of Bucaramanga's *Vanguardia Liberal* newspaper, has become a conglomerate which also owns other local newspapers, such as *El Liberal*, from Popayán, *El Universal*, from

Cartagena, and *La Tarde*, from Pereira. With those acquisitions Grupo Galvis has increased its coverage in four strategic areas of the country: the eastern plains, the Caribbean coast, the south and the coffee region.

The Digital Divide

As in many nations, the digital revolution in Colombia has brought media, telecommunications companies and the information and computer industries closer together (Herman & McChesney, 1999). As Ocampo (2004) explains, when one analyzes the phenomena of media concentration,

> in a competitive market economy, in which the value of money stands out, it is hard to build communication alternatives which contribute to dignify the human being and raise the socio-cultural level of those majorities which make up the media audience. The alternative falls on the hands of the small independent media which have reduced audiences anxious to go back to everything local, to access information closer to their everyday [lives. This leads to] less massive media and, thus, is less attractive for the big conglomerates.
>
> (Ocampo, 2004, p. 110)

The concentration of the major media in a handful on industrial groups has led to reflection in different parts of society, especially in academia, about the homogenization of information and content agendas, their lower quality and the consumption practices headed by this phenomenon. In reference to media globalization, Eduardo Galeano (1995), in his presentation *Apuntes sobre los medios de incomunicación* held at the World Association for Christian Communication (WACC) Congress in Mexico City, stated:

> the dictatorship of the single word and the single image, even more devastating that a single party, is imposing a life whose model citizen is a feeble consumer and a passive spectator, built on the production belt according to the US American model of commercial television.
>
> (Galeano, 1995)

Media Consumption

Against this picture of concentration of media in a few hands, it is interesting to analyze the consumer trends in Colombia, and the aspects of the information system in the country. The picture described below is supported by different media consumption studies, especially in the data provided by the Estudio General de Medios (EGM: General Media Study), that is undertaken bi-annually by the Asociación Colombiana de Investigación de Medios (ACIM: Colombian Association of Media Research). This is considered the most elaborate and methodologically accurate research about audiences in Colombia. The study was conducted with a sample of over ten thousand people from seventeen main Colombian cities, belonging to the socioeconomic strata 2 to 6,[1] and examines media consumer trends, which shows stable numbers for television audiences, with radio showing a declining number of listeners. The Internet is the only medium which shows a permanent and accelerated increase in the number of users (see Figure 5.1). The factors which determine this diagnosis of the Colombian media are addressed in the following section.

Television

Colombian television, similar to other Latin American countries, started out as a governmental initiative with the aim of providing educational, artistic and cultural programming to distant

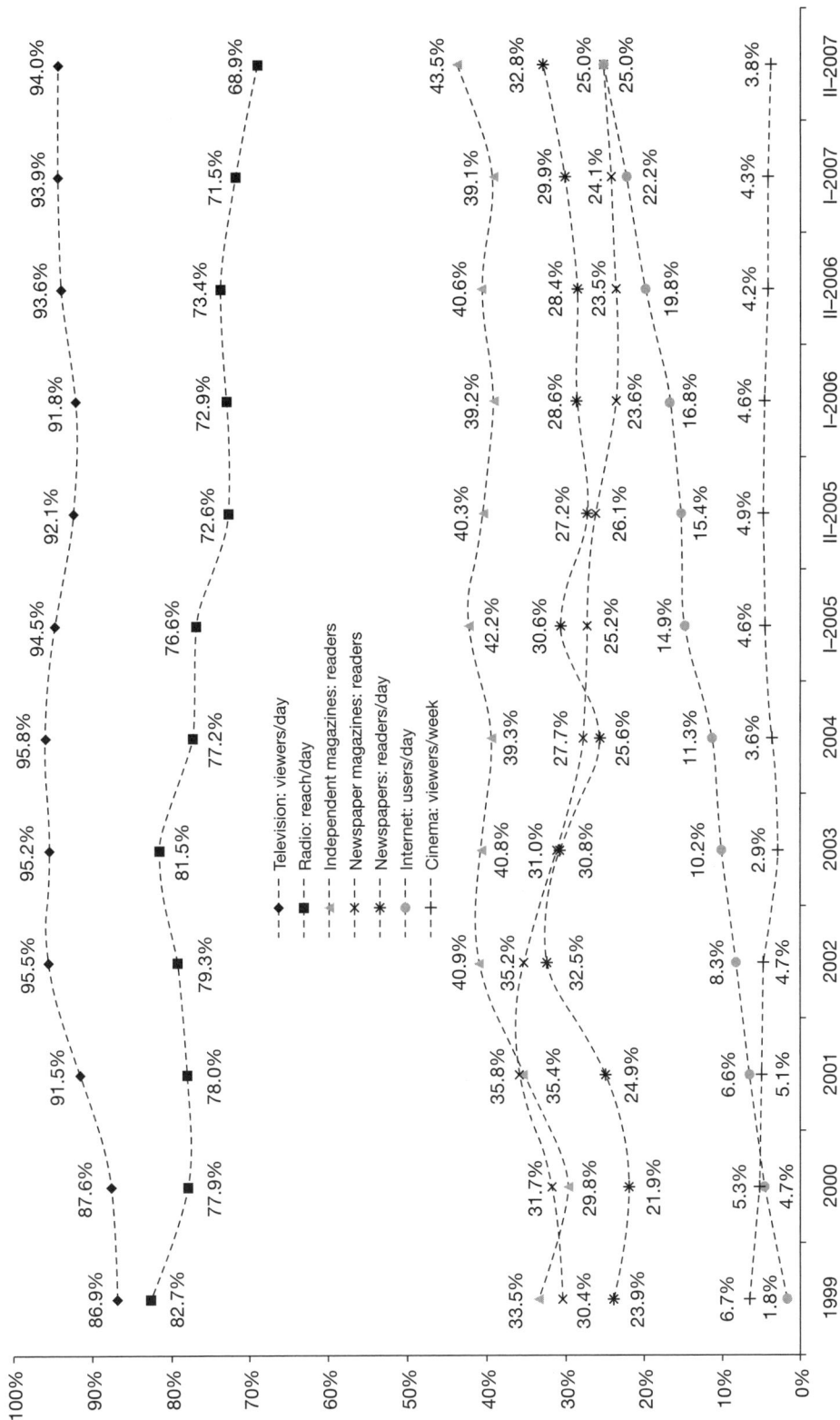

Figure 5.1 Media Consumption in Colombia, 1999–2007

Source: ACIM (2007)

regions where state presence was lacking. Hence, Colombian television has been predominantly public, and the first local, regional and national frequencies were managed solely by the state.[2]

The nationally produced content for the first broadcast had to do mainly with agricultural education programs about field labor and technical education programs for worker training. However, only one year after it had been started, state national television began to give away part of its programming to commercially oriented spaces, not only due to pressure from advertising agencies, but also to satisfy viewers' demands. The growing number of viewers voiced that they were tired of watching only institutional shows and foreign movies. The latter were constantly criticized because of their excess of violence. Although television was a public medium, the main private television channels were established at that time. By 1958, Caracol and RCN had formed the Televisora Nacional Ltda and managed to get 50 percent of the television programs to include commercial time.

What the government kept for over forty-five years was the total control of the radio frequencies and the television networks, enabling different channels for state-defined programming and frequencies in which program slots were leased to privately owned companies, which undertook the job of producing and programming. This was achieved through lease contracts for a defined length of time and a determined set of programming options. Thus, Colombian television maintained a monopoly scheme on state ownership of the medium, while it was an oligopoly in its commercial broadcasting (producers and programmers), until 1995, when the CNTV was established in the reform of the 1991 constitution.

Beyond the institution of the CNTV, law 182 on January 20, 1995, defined the rules of procedure for the medium, issued policies for its development, made access democratic, enacted ordnances for service contracts, modified the structures of the dependencies involved and set guidelines in issues regarding telecommunications. The law widened the traditional spectrum of Colombian television and produced the following classification, according to their coverage level:

1. According to the country of origin and destiny of the signal:
   (a) *International television.* This refers to the television signals which are originated outside the national boundaries and which can be received in Colombia, or those which have Colombia as their origin, but can be received in other countries.
   (b) *Colombian television.* This is originated and received within the national boundaries.
2. According to its level of regional coverage:
   (a) *Public service national television.* This refers to the television signals operated by the state, and are entitled to cover the whole national territory.
   (b) *Private service national television.* This is authorized as a private and open-to-the-public alternative to cover in a permanent way the audience needs and, provide efficient and competitive service in the whole national territory.
   (c) *Regional television.* This is the television service which covers a determined geographical area, made up by the Capital District or any other area which is smaller than the national territory while not yet local. These are public access frequencies.
   (d) *Local television.* This is the television service on a continuous geographical area, as long as this does not go over the municipal or district borders, its metropolitan area or township associations. The frequencies can be either public or private.
   (e) *Community not-for-profit television.* These are the not-for-profit frequencies operated by a community and with coverage of an area of influence.

This classification of systems and frequencies has allowed for growth in the Colombian television market since 1995. By June, 2008, the television operators recognized by CNTV were three public service channels (one of which receives its programming from independent and commercial producers), two national private channels, eight public regional channels, one private local channel, forty-seven local not-for-profit channels, 915 community frequencies, sixty-two cable television providers, and two satellite television providers (CNTV, 2008) reaching about 94 percent of the national population (ACIM, 2007).

Furthermore, the licenses for the national private channels RCN and Caracol were due for renewal in 2008. An open public contest has been held for one more national private channel starting in 2009. International conglomerates—Grupo Prisa and Grupo Planeta from Spain, Ángel González González and Televisa from Mexico, the Cisneros organization from Venezuela and RTI Telemundo (General Electric) from the United States—are competing to obtain the license for the third private television channel. In August 2008, CNTV chose the European digital standard television DVB-T that will replace the current analog system.

Colombian television has been considerably increased by the high penetration of subscription model (paid television), setting Colombia in first place in Latin America with over 74.6 percent of market penetration, followed by Argentina with 65.3 percent, Peru with 48.7 percent, Venezuela with 40.8 percent and Chile with 32.5 percent (Concilio Latino Americano de Publicidad en Multicanales (LAMAC), 2007).

The Gran Encuesta de la Televisión en Colombia (Great Colombian Television Survey), carried out by the independent firm Napoleón Franco (2008), set the level of subscription television penetration at 72 percent, while at the same time research undertaken by the Observatorio de Medios (2008) at the Universidad de La Sabana sets at 84.3 percent the level of penetration at university students' households, in the eight largest cities. Cali is the Colombian city with the highest penetration of subscription television, with 92.7 percent, followed by Manizales at 90.8 percent, Pereira at 90.2 percent, Armenia at 86.8 percent and Bucaramanga at 86.0 percent. Bogotá, the country's capital city, holds eighth place at 77.1 percent (ACIM, 2007).

The New Colombian Television Layout

After more than forty years with a concentrated television system, Colombia now displays a multichannel layout. This has increased channels and simplified access to television products and also spread the rating measurements that had been highly favorable for the national private television channels RCN and Caracol. Ibope, the company in charge of daily rating measurement of Colombian television, was criticized by Caracol and RCN, which announced in June, 2008, that they were no longer going to participate in the Brazilian multinational's measurements any more. To determine viewer ratings in Colombia, Ibope uses the people meter system, installed in 1,850 television sets, in 1,001 TV households, in twenty-three cities that encompass six different regions of the country: Centro, Pacífico, Café, Antioquia, Caribe and Oriente.

Regardless of the high impact that private national channels achieve with their soap operas, their prime-time strength in the international service has widened, promoting the consumption of themed channels. This demographic and psychographic increase is evident, especially among younger audiences, who are drawn in by the aesthetics, presentation, variety and production patterns of the programs on subscription television.

The trend towards an increase of international television consumption helps explain the audience fragmentation phenomenon. The information gathered reflect the principles poised by Webster (2005): programming is more diverse, programming is more specific in its contents in relation to the nature of the channel and its topic, and the entry of television in the household is nowadays more differential, depending on access possibilities and content offer of each programming system.

Radio

In 1929, during the government of Miguel Abadía Méndez, radio was the major mass medium in Colombia. Their environment was different from that of newspapers. The latter concentrated on a much more profound information display than what had been broadcast by radio the day before. The details of the reports, the newest, versions of the news, the different foci and the various opinions provided by the printed media enriched the information provided by radio (Ministerio de Comunicaciones, 2004).

Main Commercial Radio Stations

Radio in Colombia has experienced a decrease in the size of its audience. In 1999, 82.7 percent of the population listened to the radio; by 2007, this percentage fell to 68.9 percent (ACIM, 2007). Nevertheless, radio remains the second most consumed media after television, and it has begun to broadcast its contents through Internet platforms

The most recognized Colombian radio companies are Radio Cadena Nacional (RCN), founded in 1949, which owns 106 radio stations. It constitutes about 20 percent of all national radio. RCN owns 26 stations in the AM spectrum, mainly news stations, and has a presence in Latin America and the United States through RCN International. Caracol, established in 1956, currently manages 236 radio stations, of which 182 are in Colombia; 113 are owned and operated, while 64 are affiliates. The third radio company is Todelar, based on the name of its originating founder, Bernardo Tobón de la Roche. Todelar began broadcasting in 1953 with La Voz de Cali, to reach the western part of the country. In 1956 the circuit Todelar was properly constituted and in 1963 acquired its first FM license.

The procedures to gain access to radio are set by the national government, which also controls access to the electromagnetic spectrum. In general, the legal aspects are focused on the following considerations: license lease for radio stations, frequency allocation for public service, commercial and community broadcasters; and the details of programming and contents.

Commercial radio, mostly in the hands of the private sector, has 656 stations: 257 FM and 399 in AM. For these kinds of stations there is a public contest. When the license has been obtained, the freedom to determine content, slot and advertisement allocation, schedules, programming and even coverage is total. The government receives its main tax intake from this kind of broadcaster; hence, flexibility remains in place.

Public and Community Radio Stations

There are public service stations, which are under the management of governmental bodies. There are 106 such stations on FM, 61 on AM. They total 167 stations, with a share of 12.9 percent. This kind of radio involves special regulations because the broadcasters and producers are schools, public universities, city councils, the national police and the military. Any civil servant may have access to this scheme, under some basic conditions: daily broadcasting shall not exceed 12 hours and the strength of the signal must be lower than 50 watts.

Since 1997 there are also community stations in Colombia; there are 469 as of 2008. They broadcast entirely on the FM spectrum. A total of 199 new stations have had their frequencies assigned, meaning they have met the requirements to begin operation. The government has announced that it wishes to create 1,000 community radio stations.

These stations appeared because of the empowerment of communities to champion for a collaborative tool for their members and with the aim of providing an alternate educational method, based on the provisions made in the 1991 National Constitution. However, the demands by the government make its maintenance difficult, and its development, even more so. For example, the community broadcasters are entitled to have only official advertisements, the lease contests are made whenever the government wishes to do so and for as long as the goverment mandates; a signal tower cannot be more than 10 meters in height and must be placed further than 100 meters away from the broadcasting location. They also demand all the equipment to have been purchased and the community needs to guarantee funds for their maintenance.

Current Market Trends in Radio

In Colombia there are thirty-two *departamentos* (which are similar to states, provinces or prefectures in other countries). In Bogotá, the capital, there are about 6.77 million people. With that in mind, the Estudio General de Medios 2007-II reveals that the penetration of radio in Colombia is high (68.9 percent), but there is a clear tendency towards a decrease in radio consumption in recent years. This is seen as a warning signal for the sector.

Regardless, it is possible to say that radio is one of the media which shows a higher consumption rate in all social and economic level in the whole country, because there is a wide variety of programming, from current affairs to different musical genres, and going from religious stations to more specific, single-topic radio. That is to say, there are stations for all kinds of tastes and interests, which ensure high radio consumption by the different layers of society.

Radio news broadcasts have been pushed aside by entertainment radio, in particular by music. A study of media consumption by young people, undertaken in 2006 by the Observatorio de Medios (Media Observer) at Universidad de La Sabana, shows that 75 percent of those interviewed listen to music on the radio, whereas only 5 percent listen to the news and other informational broadcasts.

Newspapers

Up until the end of the nineteenth century, newspaper activity was closely related to political activity. They either used to belong or remain in the hands of families whose importance in the society of the time was relevant to public life. There is evidence of how, since 1886, a total of twenty-one presidents were former directors, owners or editors of periodical publications (Herrán, 1991, p. 57). But the arrival of private capital, coming from large enterprises, drove a good deal of printed media away from the doctrine and political currents that had defined them.

Newspapers in the Twentieth Century

Newspapers in Colombia went towards the so-called liberal press at the end of industrialization and at the dawn of the information society. The most renowned case is *El Tiempo*, owned by Planeta Group and Casa Editorial El Tiempo, one of the largest media conglomerates in the country, which owns the tabloid *Hoy*, the free newspaper *ADN* and the magazine *Cambio*, on national circulation.

Every capital city in Colombia has at least one newspaper in national circulation. Among the most renowned are *El Tiempo*, *El Colombiano* (Medellín), *El Heraldo* (Barranquilla), *Vanguardia Liberal* (Bucaramanga) and *El País* (Cali).

Although the conglomerates have acquired stock from the newspaper enterprises, most major newspapers are still associated with the last names of a few families that have sat behind their editorial focus. Those are, for example, *El País* with the Lloreda family, *El Tiempo* with the Santos family and *El Nuevo Siglo* with the Gómez family.

Printed Media versus the Digital World

The research results regarding reading habits and printed media consumption in Colombia pinpoint to the new reality arising from the so-called media convergence. The results obtained by the Estudio General de Medios, undertaken in 2007, ranks access and consumption of newspapers fourth after television, radio and independent magazines. Newspapers show a slight increase in readers, opposed to the steep decline of newspaper magazines (which are circulated along with the newspapers). Of the 32.8 percent of Colombians who read newspapers, the majority prefer *El Tiempo* (1,098,000 readers), followed by *El Espectador* (687,900), *El Espacio* (345,000), *Hoy* (327,000) and *El Colombiano* (323,000). *El Tiempo* belongs to the CEE (Casa Editorial El Tiempo) merger with the Spanish-based group Planeta. CEE also owns *Hoy* and *Portafolio*, and the regionals *Tolima 7 Días*, *Boyacá 7 Días*, *Llano 7 Días* and *Café 7 Días*.

El Espectador belongs to the national group Santodomingo, which is the major Colombian industrial emporium holding investments in various fields, including banks, hotels, petrochemical industry, automotive industry, gastronomy and the food sector. *El Espacio* constitutes the main tabloid and shows, in comparison with its competition, a constant increase of readers. *El Colombiano* belongs to a group called Periódicos Asociados (Associated Newspapers) made up of the regional newspapers *El País*, from Cali, and *Vanguardia Liberal*, from Bucaramanga. *Hoy* belongs to *El Tiempo*, circulates in Bogotá and competes for the tabloid share of *El Espacio*.

The so-called small print, mainly regional newspapers, deals mostly with citizenship journalism and it tends to concentrate on strategic places of the national geography, including the eastern plains, the Caribbean coast, the south and the coffee-growing regions. The future perspective for regional newspapers shows them joining forces to create a popular newspaper of national distribution, originally aimed to circulate in Bogotá, and whose objective is to compete with the tabloids *El Espacio* and *Hoy*.

Colombian newspapers are in decline in terms of use and consumption as consumers choose different media. *El Tiempo* lost over 100,000 readers since 2006. Ten major regional newspapers have ceased to exist since 2003 and, for the first time in history, the main national newspaper was auctioned and acquired by a foreign investment group (Planeta). It cannot go unnoticed that in Colombia, a country with more than 42 million people and with a renowned tradition of literature, has only two national newspapers.

Independent Magazines

Regarding independent magazines, it must be mentioned that their considerably high consumption, surpassing newspapers, turns out to be somewhat paradoxical. Readership takes place on all socioeconomic levels, when one would expect the lower income end of the socioeconomic spectrum to consider such magazines as unnecessary luxury.

According to Estudio General de Medios, the magazine *TV y Novelas*, printed by a Mexican consortium and devoted to entertainment news, holds first place in number of readers (1,159,700), whereas *Semana* (owned by Semana Publishing Group) ranks second among Colombians' preferences (927,900). The latter has recognition and prestige in national journalism perceptions and deals with weekly issues concerning public opinion matters. In third place is the magazine *Soho*, part of the Semana Publishing group, with a mixture of literary genres (chronicles and interviews) with erotic and trivial topics and a readership of 817,200. The youth magazine *Tú* is in fourth place (511,100), while *Cromos* magazine (475,800) dealing with current affairs and the entertainment magazine *Caras* (457,100 readers) rank fifth and sixth, respectively.

The large circulation by entertainment and erotic-literary magazines displays a sustained increase that seems to play against opinion and information magazines. The latter face a clear disadvantage by facing competition from the new media. Although they try to break deals with each other through convergence, their decline is evident.

Finally, it is important to note that the birth of the information superhighway has altered the media. As pointed out by García-Avilés (2006):

> there is no doubt that digitalization and the strengthening of interactive nets have altered the traditional structure of the media. The daily habits and, especially, information consumption and entertainment habits of the citizens are changing rapidly. Increasingly, users want to access the news through these diverse media, everywhere and at any moment.
>
> (p. 37)

All of this supposes a change in consumer habits and thus a modification in the way media will face these new challenges. One challenge in Colombian printed media involves the synergy produced inside multimedia groups, which enable the integration of production processes and the circulation of contents between print, audiovisual and digital media, coordinating publishing strategies and engaging in cross-promotion, as *El Tiempo* has done.

The Internet

Similar to global trends, Internet use in Colombia continues to increase. In 2000 less than 5 percent of the population used the Internet; by 2008 the percentage has grown to 25 percent, as more than 9 million Colombians go online daily.

Internet penetration will continue to rise, judging by the improving accessibility conditions for citizens, such as more concern by educationalists with the use of new technologies in the classroom, the increasing bilingualism in high schools and universities, a decrease in desktop and laptop prices and the competition between the companies that offer Internet access. The last factor has led to a stabilization of connection costs and the optimization of service, which was formerly done through commuted systems (telephone lines) whereas now there is clear evidence of a migrating trend towards a dedicated service, which is faster and more affordable. According to the Comisión de Regulación de las Telecomunicaciones (Commission for Telecommunication Regulation), by December 2007, Colombia had 174,383 subscribers to commute (dial-up) Internet access. By March 2008, the number dropped 13.5 percent to 150,894. Meanwhile, broadband subscribers (xDSL, Cable, wimax and wireless, among others) increased by 17.5 percent in the same period of time, going from 1,207,090 people in December, 2007, to 1,418,232 by March, 2008.

According to the Comisión de Regulación de las Telecomunicaciones, the number of Internet subscribers increased 13.6 percent during the first three months of 2008, reaching 1.56 million people and attaining, according to the population estimates offered by DANE (2008), a subscription penetration of 3.53 percent. While Colombia remains at the back of the race in comparison with countries such as the United States, these data suggest the digital gap is being bridged. This is especially evident when looking at the weekly intake of Internet in various Latin

American countries. According to Estudio General de Medios, Colombia reaches 35 percent of weekly Internet users, surpassed only by Chile, with 40 percent, and followed by Argentina, with 33 percent.

However, significant inequalities are revealed in the educational and socioeconomic level of users. The Estudio General de Medios points out that only 20 percent of the lowest-income population state they have access to Internet, while 66 percent of the highest income population has access. Most of the consumers range between 18 and 34 years of age.

Bringing the Internet to Everyone

Like many countries, Colombia wants to ensure that people at the less favored socioeconomic end of the spectrum have access to the Internet, knowing that part of the country's development depends on achieving equal access to the information and knowledge provided by the web. In 2005 DANE, along with the Ministries of Culture and Education, the Instituto Distrital de Cultura y Turismo (Municipal Institute for Culture and Tourism), the Cámara Colombiana del Libro (Colombian Book Chamber) and Fundalectura, with the support of the Centro Regional para el Fomento del Libro en América del Latina y el Caribe (CERLALC: Regional Center for the Encouragement of Books in Latin America and the Caribbean), decided to include a module about reading habits and book consumption in the Encuesta Continua de Hogares (Continuous Home Survey).

The survey revealed that young people use the Internet to search for information to help with high school and college homework, to chat, to check email and to play games and music. As age increases, Internet reading interests change; people between 25 and 55 years of age use the web to search for work-related information and to remain updated. On the other hand, although the increase in Internet users can be seen as positive, it is clear that this takes users away from traditional media. Research undertaken by the Stanford Institute for the Quantitative Study of Society mentioned in 2000 what is now evident in the whole world and specifically in Colombia (Nie & Erbring, 2000, p. 3).

Conclusion

Data on media consumption in Colombia show a similar behavior to that of the whole Western world—the need to adapt traditional media to information and communication technologies, the struggle between the information and entertainment agendas, audience segmentation and the consolidation of media conglomerates.

Changes in the Media

Newspapers have a disadvantage in the race of fast-paced information. Reading habits have declined and only a privileged few, in terms of financial power or socio-cultural status, prefer daily newspapers over other media. This explains why newspaper circulation has declined or, at best, remained at the same levels. Newspapers cannot compete with the lightning-fast response of audiovisual media and the Internet. Facing these facts, some newspapers have turned to making their content more analytical, explaining causes and consequences of the facts addressed, and hoping to overcome the plain informative record by giving broader details to their readers.

This is also the case for specialized magazines, which have risen in consumption due to their specific topic area, or to the depth of their research concerning everyday issues. As reader segmentation becomes evident, magazines which cover specific areas of public interest have started to appear (e.g. celebrities, sport, culture, economics).

Television remains the main medium in terms of audience penetration and influence. Apart from national audiovisual products, subscription-based television has a rising penetration, placing Colombia at the top of paid television consumption in Latin America. Themed channels, based on demographic interests, have been shown to be especially attractive to children and teenagers (Observatorio de Medios, 2008).

On the other hand, the Internet has become strong competition against both written and audiovisual media, as many consumers prefer to look for the news online, at any time of day. Consumers have stopped buying newspapers and magazines, and dedicate longer periods of time surfing and browsing through the Internet instead of watching television or listening to radio. Even on the entertainment arena, where radio and television were heading the race, Internet has stepped up, offering an alternative with online radio stations and downloadable music, while forums and chats seem more interesting for young people than the old magic box.

Finally, Colombia does not escape the trend of media conglomerates, which prove to be dangerous because the concentration of the media in a few hands may lead to a reduction in the visions of reality. There are one or few dominant ideologies and, therefore, it is difficult to find contrasting views. If what the general population expects is for media to provide guidance, it would at least require opposite or balanced views, which enable them to make free choices, because otherwise there would only be manipulation.

Further Scholarship

Although debates criticizing the rise of monopolies abound, the situation shows no change. On the contrary, major media negotiations transcend borders and the main dish is strategic alliances, mergers and acquisitions of enterprises with large digits on the price tag.

Within this media context, along with the world trends, Colombia faces other risks. There is pressure to crack down freedom of the press, pushed by external factors such as the guerrilla and the paramilitaries, and inside factors, such as the economic or political interests of the media owners, confronting freedom of speech. Media challenges in Colombia remain linked to other factors like educational and economic levels of the potential consumers. This requires that the government and the media conglomerates lead democratic access endeavors, including alphabetization programs and reading promotion, as well as training in the use of new technologies and a reduction in the cable television and Internet connection fees.

Topics for Future Research

Media research needs to find out more about how audiences, especially younger members, consume audiovisual products and how does this have an affect on the traditional Colombian media market. It is worthwhile to figure out the ownership models and their impact on the industry, due to the penetration of foreign investment on major national media which has promoted new entrepreneurial dynamics regarding editorial policies, value chains, exhibition windows and distribution. Finally, the decision to embrace the European standard of digital television pinpoints the need to study its possibilities, impact, business models and audience interaction, as outlined by the model.

Notes

1 For those new to the Colombian stratification system, a brief explanation is warranted. In Colombia, urban areas are divided into six categories (*estratos*) according to the quality and quantity of the surrounding infrastructure (including recreational facilities and hospitals). The level of stratification defines the costs paid for public utilities. Strata 1 and 2 (the lowest) are given support, reducing the cost of their bills. Strata 3 and 4 pay the average value of their consumption, whereas strata 5 and 6 are charged a "subsidy fee" to cover the cost reduction of the lower strata. Thus, this stratification system is also used as a general reference to consider average income of those leaving in the respective neighborhoods, and their inherent acquisition power.

2 The date chosen for the first Colombian television broadcast was June 13, 1954, to commemorate the first year in office of General Gustavo Rojas Pinilla, who took power through a military coup over President Laureano Gómez.

References

Alexa. (2008). *Top web sites Colombia*. Retrieved May 25, 2008, from www.alexa.com/site/ds/top_sites?cc=CO&ts_mode=country&lang=none.

Asociación Colombiana de Investigación de Medios (ACIM). (2007, December). *Estudio General de Medios (EGM), Ola 2007-II*. Bogotá: ACIM.

Comisión Nacional de Televisión (CNTV). (2008, June). *Directorio de operadores*. Bogotá: CNTV.

Concilio Latino Americano de Publicidad en Multicanales (LAMAC). (2007). *Colombia supera a Argentina en penetración de TV paga*. Marketing Evolution, 7. Retrieved June 18, 2008, from www.lamac.org/assets/documents/Colombia/2007/Newsletters/col_sep_2007.pdf.

Departamento Administrativo Nacional de Estadística (DANE). (2005). *Censo Nacional 2005 Nivel Nacional. Dirección de difusión, mercadeo y cultura estadística*. Bogotá: DANE.

Departamento Administrativo Nacional de Estadística (DANE). (2007a). *Proyecciones nacionales y departamentales de población 2006–2020. Dirección de Censos y Demografía*. Bogotá: DANE.

Departamento Administrativo Nacional de Estadística (DANE). (2007b). *Principales Indicadores del mercado laboral mayo de 2008. Dirección de difusión, mercadeo y cultura estadística*. Bogotá: DANE.

Departamento Administrativo Nacional de Estadística (DANE). (2008). *Encuesta de Consumo Cultural 2007. Dirección de difusión, mercadeo y cultura estadística*. Bogotá: DANE.

Economic Commission for Latin America and the Caribbean (ECLAC). (2007). *Statistical yearbook for Latin American and the Caribbean*. Santiago de Chile, Chile: ECLAC.

Franco, S. (1999). *El Quinto: No matar*. Bogotá: Tercer Mundo Editores.

Fundalectura, Ministerio de Cultura, Ministerio de Educación, DANE & CERLALC. (2006). *Hábitos de lectura, asistencia a bibliotecas y consumo de libros en Colombia*. Bogotá: Cámara Colombiana del Libro.

Galeano, E. (1995, October). *Apuntes sobre los medios de incomunicación*. [Notes about miscommunication media]. Presentation held at WACC 1995 Congress. Mexico City.

García-Avilés, J. A. (2006). *Desmitificando la convergencia periodística. Chasqui (Revista Latinoamericana de Comunicación)*, 94, 34–39.

Herman, E. S. & McChesney, R. W. (1999). *Los medios globales, los nuevos misioneros del capitalismo corporativo*. Madrid: Ediciones Cátedra.

Herrán, M. (1991). *La Industria de los Medios Masivos de Comunicación en Colombia*. Bogotá: Fescol.

Ministerio de Comunicaciones. (2004). *Políticas para radiodifusión en Colombia: Cuadernos de política sectorial*. Bogotá: Ministerio de Comunicaciones.

Napoleón Franco. (2008, March). *La Gran Encuesta de la Televisión en Colombia*. Bogotá: Ipsos-Napoleón Franco. Retrieved July 16, 2008, from www.cntv.org.co/cntv%5Fbop/noticias/2008/abril/gran_encuesta.pdf.

Nie, N. H. & Erbring, L. (2000). *Internet and society: A preliminary report [online]*. Stanford Institute for the Quantitative Study of Society (SIQSS). Stanford University, and Intersurvey Inc. Retrieved March 13, 2008, from www.stanford.edu/group/siqss/Press_Release/Preliminary_Report.pdf.

Observatorio de Medios. (2008). *Tendencias y hábitos de consumo en televisión y expectativas del público objetivo frente al proyecto de creación del Canal Nacional Universitario*. Facultad de Comunicación, Universidad de La Sabana. Retrieved June 18, 2008, from www.cntv.org.co/cntv%5Fbop/noticias/2008/junio/investigacion.pdf.

Ocampo, M. C. (2004). *Conglomerados multimedia: La nueva tendencia empresarial de los medios de comunicación*. Palabra Clave (Revista Facultad de Comunicación, Universidad de La Sabana), 11, 93–111.

Rueda, I. E. (2008, May). *El "monopolio" Telmex. En Directo (Periódico Facultad de Comunicación, Universidad de La Sabana)*, I38, p. 8.

Sánchez, F. (2007). *Las cuentas de la violencia*. Bogotá: Grupo Editorial Norma Universidad Sergio Arboleda (2008) Observatorio Económico, Financiero y Empresarial. Retrieved July 20, 2008, from www.usergioarboleda.edu.co/observatorio_economico/index.htm.

Webster, J. G. (2005). Beneath the veneer of fragmentation: Television audience polarization in a multichannel world. *Journal of Communication, 55*(2), 366–382.

6

The Mass Media in Venezuela
History, Politics and Freedom

Guillermo Gibens
William Penn University, Iowa, USA

Introduction

Venezuela, located in the northernmost section of South America, has been called the "gateway to South America" for it faces the Caribbean Sea, offering visitors the first view of the mainland of the continent. According to data obtained from the online edition of the *Encyclopedia Britannica* (2006), Venezuela can be described as follows:

- Name: República Bolivariana de Venezuela (Bolivarian Republic of Venezuela).
- Government: multi-party system with executive, judicial and legislative branches under a federal republic. The legislature is unicameral and called the National Assembly.
- The head of the government is the president. The capital is Caracas. The official language is Spanish, but a number of indigenous Indian languages are also considered official since May 2002. There is no official religion.
- The country is divided into twenty-three states, covering a total area of about 353,841 square miles. It is larger than France and Germany together.
- It borders the Caribbean Sea in the north, Guyana in the east, Brazil in the south and Colombia in the west.
- Venezuela's population was calculated at 26,749,000 people in 2005. People living in urban areas made up about 87.7 percent and rural population totaled 12.3 percent in 2003. In 2001, sex distribution was male, 49.46 percent, and female, 50.54 percent.
- Approximately 33 percent of the population is under 15 years old; 27.5 percent is between 15 and 29 years old; about 21 percent is 30 to 44 years old; almost 12 percent is 45 to 59 years old; about 5 percent is between 60 and 74 years old; and 1.9 percent is 75 and older, according to 2001 Venezuelan vital statistics.
- Figures from 2000 indicate that ethnic composition is about 64 percent for mestizo, 20 percent for white, 10 percent for black, 1.3 percent for Amerindian and 1.7 percent for other races.

Economy

The Venezuelan economy is mainly based in the extraordinary revenues brought about by the oil industry (the largest in the country with the most exports), representing 67.3 percent of the ordinary income (*Encyclopedia Britannica Online*, 2006). The rest comes from agricultural production that includes products such as corn, rice, bananas, plantains and potatoes in addition to livestock and fish. Venezuela also has a mining industry with a sizable production of iron, bauxite, gold and diamonds.

The fact that agriculture and livestock take second place after oil production is noticeable in the low percentage of land use for those segments of the national economy. Data from the *Encyclopedia Britannica Online* (2006) indicate that in 2000, 2.9 percent of the land was used in temporary crops, 0.9 percent was for permanent crops and 20.7 percent for pasture.

Venezuela's gross domestic product was estimated at $12,200 per capita in 2007, as indicated in the Central Intelligence Agency (CIA 2008) *World factbook*, and imports in 2007 were calculated at $45.46 billion, with 2006 figures indicating imports from the United States being the largest (27 percent), followed by Colombia (9.8 percent), Brazil (9.6 percent), China (7.2 percent), Mexico (5.7 percent) and Panama (4.6 percent). Its exports, also according to figures from the *CIA world factbook*, were estimated at $69.17 billion in 2007. The United States is the largest importer (44.1 percent)of Venezuelan products, especially oil, followed by the Netherlands Antilles (14.5 percent) and China (3.1 percent), according to 2006 figures.

The president of Venezuela, Hugo Chávez, praised his own administration for raising Venezuelan literacy to 93 percent, a figure confirmed by Venezuelan 2001 census data and indicated in the *CIA world factbook* (CIA 2008).

Brief Political History

As early as 1810, the people of Venezuela started to reflect on the idea of independence from Spain's colonial power. The war for independence would continue until June 24, 1821, when Venezuelan forces defeated the Spaniards in the Battle of Carabobo. Two years earlier, in 1819, the countries of what is now known as Colombia, Panama, Ecuador and Venezuela had come together to form the new Gran Colombia whose capital was Bogotá.

From 1819 until its disintegration in 1830, Gran Colombia was overtaken by political turmoil, a product of civilian and military unrest. There were political leaders who wanted a centralist government, while others wanted a federalist association. In the end, the countries parted ways.

It was in 1830, after the death of the Venezuelan leader and liberator Simón Bolívar, that Venezuela began its life as an independent republic, but the confrontation between conservative and liberal ideas, centralism and federalism would continue to plague Venezuela's political landscape for many years. Conservatives ruled from 1830 until 1846, with General José Antonio Páez leading this period as president of Venezuela from 1831 to 1835 (Arráiz Lucca, 2008). The liberals came to power between 1847 and 1858, with General José Tadeo Monagas as Venezuela's president between 1847 and 1851 (Arráiz Lucca, 2008).

Significant events that left a definitive mark in Venezuela's political history were to happen in the following years: the Federal War, the presidency of Antonio Guzmán Blanco, the hegemony of Táchira state generals (a succession of Venezuelan presidents who were generals and all born in Táchira state) and the beginning of a genuine democratic system. It is important to notice that Venezuela's political life in the nineteenth century was many times written by the presence of *caudillos* (regional leaders and veterans of the Independence War and the Federal War) who believed they were endowed to rule Venezuela.

The Federal War began in 1859 and lasted until 1863. It started with several revolts against the administration of President Julián Castro. Second only to the war for independence, over 200,000 people were killed, and the country was left devastated and impoverished (Arráiz Lucca, 2008).

The presidencies of General Antonio Guzmán Blanco (1870–1877, 1879–1884, 1886–1888) were notable because of the many reforms within the civic life of the country (free public education, civil marriage, divorce law). The president also initiated a number of modernization projects, including railroads, public roads, public lighting and telephone service (Arráiz Lucca, 2008).

Historian Rafael Arráiz Lucca (2008) states that the ruling of Táchira state generals began with General Cipriano Castro entering with his troops in Caracas, on October 22, 1899, and would end with the presidency of General Isaías Medina Angarita, who was overthrown by a civic-military coup on October 18, 1945. One dictator who stood out during this period was General Juan Vicente Gómez, who ruled Venezuela from 1908 to 1935 after ousting his *compadre* (a Spanish word that signifies the friendly relationship brought about by one man baptizing the son or daughter of another), General Cipriano Castro. Gómez's dictatorship is the longest in Venezuelan history at twenty-seven years. He died in office on December 17, 1935.

A few years later, in 1945, an alliance between Acción Democrática (AD: Democratic Action), a political party, and the military ousted General Medina Angarita and began what Arráiz Lucca (2008, p. 139) calls "democracy by way of military weapons." This experiment in democracy would not last long, and in 1948, elected President Rómulo Gallegos was removed from power by a military junta that included General Marcos Pérez Jiménez.

General Pérez Jiménez was overthrown by a coup d'état on January 23, 1958. This date marked for many Venezuelans the true beginning of a democratic system in the country. The upcoming years proved to be beneficial for the rising democracy but at times tumultuous as well.

In 1958, Rómulo Betancourt, a civilian and leader of Democratic Action, was elected by popular vote as president for the 1959–1964 term. That same year, the political parties agreed to always respect the results of any election and form government alliances with the opposition as to consolidate the democratic system and minimize the possibility of another dictatorship. This agreement was officially signed by leaders of the main political parties on October 31, 1958, in what is known as the Punto Fijo Pact. In addition to AD, Unión Republicana Democrática (URD: Democratic Republican Union) and COPEI (Social Christian Party) signed the agreement. The Partido Comunista Venezolano (PCV: Venezuelan Communist Party) was not invited because of its ties with the Soviet Union, which was not considered desirable in a democratic government, and because Betancourt had explicitly expressed his desire not to enter into any association with the communists (Arráiz Lucca, 2008).

The years of the Betancourt administration were marked by a growing respect for democratic institutions, despite several attempts by a few military officers to overthrow the legitimate government. It is during this presidency that the Organization of Petroleum Exporting Countries (OPEC) was created by the Minister of Mines and Hydrocarbons, Juan Pablo Pérez Alfonzo. Betancourt also saw the birth of a guerrilla movement in Venezuela that was supported by Cuba's Fidel Castro (Arráiz Lucca, 2008).

As democracy continued to settle in Venezuela, more political parties were founded, some as a result of internal party divisions, but the democratic road was sustained by new elections in 1963, with Raúl Leoni elected president for the 1964–1969 term. For the first time in Venezuela, a democratically elected president transferred the presidential office to another one also democratically elected by popular vote. Betancourt and Leoni were both AD leaders, and in 1969 Leoni gave the presidency to his rival and winner of the 1968 elections, Rafael Caldera of the opposition party COPEI, who was elected for the 1969–1974 term. Caldera's biggest accomplishment may have been the pacification policy of the communist guerrilla movement that had started during the Betancourt administration in the early 1960s. According to Arráiz Lucca (2008):

> Caldera's goal was to incorporate the guerrilla into the peaceful and democratic life, that they surrendered their weapons. In turn, the government promised to pardon them, changing their crimes from civil offenses to political ones.
>
> (Arráiz Lucca, 2008, p. 174)

With the consolidation of democratic institutions, many small political parties disappeared, leaving the political arena in the hands of two major parties: AD and COPEI. From 1973 to 1999, the two parties would rule Venezuela by winning elections. Carlos Andrés Pérez (AD) was elected president in 1973 for the 1974–1979 term followed by Luis Herrera Campíns (COPEI) for the 1979–1984 period, then Jaime Lusinchi (AD) took office for the 1984–1993 term. Carlos Andrés Pérez (AD) would again win a general election and served as president from 1989 until 1993, when he was accused of corruption and embezzlement. Pérez was impeached, and Ramón J. Velásquez assumed the presidency for the rest of Pérez's term until 1994, when Caldera of COPEI was elected for a second term from 1994 to 1999 (Arráiz Lucca, 2008).

Throughout these democratic administrations, however, corruption and embezzlement were what many Venezuelan citizens would call the "cancer of the nation." Although Pérez was the only president impeached for misdeeds, for Venezuelans the democratic governments did not do enough to stop the "bleeding" of the national treasury. The last chapter of these years was written by Pérez during his second administration, before being impeached. Pérez tried to change the economic model of the nation to a very liberal approach that brought higher prices for consumer goods, and disgruntled Venezuelans took to the streets of Caracas on February 27, 1989, in what is well known among Venezuelans as "El Caracazo." Riots went on for several days in many cities besides Caracas. The National Guard and the Army were called to restore order, and hundreds of people were killed.

It is against this political backdrop that a not yet well-known Lieutenant-Colonel Hugo Chávez tried to oust President Pérez on February 3, 1992, but the coup failed, and he was arrested along with his followers. President Caldera pardoned Chávez during his second term. In 1998, Chávez was elected president with 56.26 percent of the popular vote after a very successful presidential campaign, was reelected in 2000 under a new constitution and reelected again in 2006 for the period 2007–2013 (Arráiz Lucca, 2008).

Although President Chávez has been elected by popular vote, many believe his ruling has the color of a dictatorship because he has been in office since 1999. His government can be characterized by a turn toward what he calls "Socialism of the twenty-first century," the loss of power and popularity of the traditional parties (AD and COPEI), a weak opposition and a conflicting approach to the news media.

Venezuelan Media

The sometimes confrontational nature of the relationship between Venezuelan presidents and the news media is intrinsically linked to the diversity of social responsibilities that each president thought was necessary to respond to his citizens' demands and to protect his administration from the attacks of the opposition. At the same time, the news media have looked at themselves as the watchful eye of the government's actions and have defended fervently their right to freedom of the press.

This section reviews the development of the media in Venezuela (print, radio and television), and then presents some of the key issues, with special consideration to the Chávez–media relationship.

Marcelino Bisbal is a well-known communication researcher in Venezuela and director of the School of Graduate Studies in Social Communication at the Catholic University Andrés Bello in Caracas. Bisbal's recollection of the history and current landscape of the Venezuelan media, along with unpublished material and his book *Televisión, pan nuestro de cada día* (Television, our daily bread) published in Spanish in 2005, were used to provide a profile of the media in Venezuela. I personally interviewed him and several other Venezuelan journalists in early March and mid-July 2008 to get a closer and critical view of the current state of affairs in the Venezuelan media.

The Press

Venezuela's experience with the print media can be dated back to the colonial years, when the country was part of the Spanish empire. *La Gazeta de Caracas* (The Caracas Gazette) began to be published in 1808. A common practice for this newspaper was to take the side of those winning the Independence War at a given time. When the colonial authorities seemed to be the winners, it would support them; when the revolutionaries were the ones winning, then it would switch to their side (Bisbal, personal communication, 2008) Another important newspaper was *El Correo del Orinoco* (The Orinoco Post), which began in June 1818 as the voice of the new republic.

During the nineteenth century, the Venezuelan press became the vehicle for different political factions to express their opinions, and the newspapers were not always as objective as they could have been. For instance, during José Antonio Páez's second term, *El Venezolano* (The Venezuelan), a weekly newspaper founded in August 1840, was critical of the Páez administration and became the voice of the Liberal Party (Arráiz Lucca, 2008). At the dawn of the twentieth century, President Castro had his own newspaper, *El Constitucional* (The Constitutional). Founded in November 1899, the newspaper would bring to the readers the issues, opinions and ideas held by Castro. The "oppositional" press suffered "suspensions, closedowns and its reporters prison, every time General Castro and his closed associates felt annoyed by the other press" (Díaz Rangel, 2007, p. 15).

The twentieth century continued to see a growing print media in Venezuela, some newspapers were considered independent while others were associated with the president in office at the time. The Gómez government that began in 1908 allowed certain freedom for the press and tolerated somewhat criticism of his administration. Many newspapers that had disappeared during Castro's regime began to appear again, and there were new ones, including national and regional newspapers such as *El Liberal* (The Liberal), *La Prensa* (The Press) and *Unión Obrera* (Worker Union), all in Caracas in 1909; *La Mañana* (The Morning) in Maracaibo and *El Republicano* (The Republican) in Barquisimeto, all in 1912 (Díaz Rangel, 2007).

But relative freedom of the press during the Gómez administration did not mean that future governments were going to be tolerant of an independent press. The Gómez government itself sent to prison several reporters when it disagreed with what they wrote. It was easy to see throughout the first half of the twentieth century that an independent press was not going to enjoy full freedom. Nevertheless, the newspaper industry continued to grow. Some newspapers would disappear after a few years in the market; others solidified their presence and continue to exist today.

One example is *El Universal* (The Universal) founded in 1909. Owned by the Mata family, the newspaper is considered somewhat conservative and pro free market (Vanden Heuvel & Dennis,

1995). According to the latest figures from the Asociación Nacional de Anunciantes (ANDA: National Association of Advertisers, 2008), a Venezuelan private business organization, *El Universal* had an average circulation of 80,370 copies nationwide in 2006.

El Nacional (The National) is another national newspaper with a long history in Venezuela. It was founded in 1943 and is owned by the Otero family (Díaz Rangel, 2007). It had an average circulation in 2006 of 89,847 copies, according to ANDA figures. *Ultimas Noticias* (Last News) founded in 1941 and owned by the Capriles Network, a news media group, is another national paper with a circulation on average of 189,576 copies in 2006 (ANDA records).

Despite their significance and influence, however, these papers had experienced the censoring arm of the government in office. For instance, *El Nacional* was closed down in April 1950 by General Pérez Jiménez for referring to the three members of the Military Junta as "the three little pigs" (Botía, 2007, p. 14) and *El Universal* was also suspended for three days in May 1950 for being critical of the government in a story on the front page (García Ponce, as cited in Botía, 2007).

But one of the most peculiar confrontations with a newspaper happened in 1961 under the democratic government of Betancourt; the situation did not involve the government but businesses that advertised in *El Nacional*. The editorial board of the newspaper wanted to keep an independent line in reference to the powerful economic groups in the country. These groups, under the umbrella of the National Association of Advertisers, requested a boycott of the newspaper. Members of the organization were asked not to advertise any products in the newspaper. *El Nacional* tried to confront the boycott with dignity, using its own revenues to publish the daily newspaper. The number of pages was reduced. Nevertheless, after two years and serious economic loses, the newspaper gave up. The advertisers returned their ads in 1964 (Díaz Rangel, 2007).

Since then, there has not been any other situation like this within the Venezuelan media, and the newspaper industry in particular has had a healthy growth, nationally and regionally. Bisbal (n.d.) indicates two news groups that would bring sensationalism to popular information: Cadena Capriles (Capriles Network), founded in 1959, and Bloque de Armas (de Armas Bloc), founded in 1970. Both networks own a number of newspapers and magazines. Bisbal added that in 1975 there were 59 newspapers in Venezuela. By 1986, that number grew to 70 newspapers. In 2008 the industry had a total of 111 newspapers.

In the second half of the twentieth century, freedom of the press would gain ground thanks to a more democratic society, but as illustrated by the boycott of *El Nacional* in 1961 and a few more instances of either self-censoring or government censorship, complete independence and autonomy seems to be nonexistent in the news media. Take for example the case of *El Mundo* (The World), a daily newspaper which was confiscated on October 1, 1971, by the democratic government of Caldera because of a report of a possible invasion of Venezuela by Colombia (Catalá & Díaz Rangel, 2003). Further, on February 4, 1992, during the Pérez administration, all civil rights were suspended after Chávez's military coup attempt. Freedom of expression was also suspended, and *El Nacional* and the magazines *Elite* and *Zeta* were confiscated. A radio station, YVKE Mundial (YVKE World), was also closed, according to Catalá and Díaz Rangel (2003).

Radio

Radio started in Venezuela about the same time as it began in the United States. It was during the dictatorship of Gómez, on May 23, 1926, that the first Venezuelan radio station, Broadcasting Central de Caracas, also known as AYRE, initiated its transmission (Bisbal, n.d.). Bisbal said the work of this first station was irregular, and it would cease to broadcast in 1928 as the revenues obtained from the use of radio receivers by listeners were not enough to support the station financially (Vidal, 2004). Programming was poor, and it included reading news from a newspaper, popular music from 78 rpm records, some live music in the evening, comedy and classic music (Cortina, 1995).

In 1930 the radio industry in Venezuela began to develop with the creation of Broadcasting Caracas, now known as Radio Caracas Radio (YV1BC). This station was the first to use a commercial approach to its operation (Bisbal, n.d.). Edgar Anzola, in association with businessman William Phelps, initiated the station with a variety of programs, including an earlier version of present-day soap operas (Bisbal, n.d.; Cortina, 1995). Cortina said the managing of this station under Anzola's direction was an example of what a radio station should be like even today. Cortina (1995, p. 34) added, "Broadcasting Caracas spread culture and knowledge with a well-coordinated and adequate programming." Bisbal also noted that the first public radio station, funded by the Venezuelan government began operating in 1936 under the name Radio Nacional de Venezuela (Venezuela's National Radio).

The number of commercial stations would continue to grow, and in 1935 the country had 13 AM radio stations. By 1955, that number grew to 50 radio stations. In the 1960s, 128 stations were operating and, by 1975, 137. In 1989, 173 radio stations were broadcasting. The latest figures from the National Telecommunications Commission (CONATEL) indicate a total of 209 AM stations in 2005. FM radio stations began to operate in the late 1980s, and by 2005 there were 521 of them, for a total of 730 radio stations. Bisbal (n.d.) also reported the existence in Venezuela of radio networks that operate with a central station located in Caracas and a number of affiliates and owned stations in the rest of the country. The main radio networks are Unión Radio Noticias (Union Radio News) composed of 42 stations nationwide, and AM Center that counts 54 radio stations across the country (Bisbal, n.d.).

Television

Television began around the same time it started in the United States. In 1952, the first television station, Televisora Nacional de Venezuela (National Television of Venezuela), owned by the Venezuelan government, went on the air, but a drop in the signal would delay the official start until January 1953 (Bisbal, 2005). The first commercial television station also began in 1953. Televisa (Channel 4) marked the starting point of Venezuelan television stations entering in partnership with US television networks. Televisa's association was with NBC. But in the early 1960s, Televisa's financial problems forced the owners to sell it to Diego Cisneros, a Cuban-Venezuelan entrepreneur and founder of a powerful media group. Televisa's partnership with NBC ended, and it switched to ABC. It would also change its name to Venevisión in 1961 (Bisbal, 2005).

The Phelps Group (owners of Radio Caracas Radio) founded Radio Caracas Televisión (Channel 2) in 1953 and entered into a partnership with NBC (Bisbal, 2005). Venevisión and Radio Caracas Televisión were targeting national audiences, but in the 1950s, there was also an attempt to regionalize television. From 1956 to 1960, Televisa of Zulia state began broadcasting as a subsidiary of Televisa Channel 4 in Caracas. Ondas del Lago Televisión (Radio Waves of the Lake) broadcast from 1957 until 1960, and Radio Valencia Televisión began in 1958 and ended in 1962 (Bisbal, 2005).

The number of homes with television sets increased from 200,000 in the 1950s to 439,000 in 1965. This growth stimulated the expansion of commercial television, allowing the foundation of three new television stations: Cadena Venezolana de Televisión (VTV: Venezuelan Television Network), in 1964, which was going to be associated with CBS; Cisneros Group's Teletrece (Telethirteen), former Radio Valencia Televisión, began in 1963 and finished in 1969; and Canal Once de Televisión (Channel Eleven Television), which started in 1966 and disappeared in 1967. VTV ownership was transferred to the Venezuelan government in 1974, becoming the second public television station (Bisbal, 2005).

Satellite transmissions began in 1971 and color television arrived in 1979, adopting the US NTSC system. Another attempt to regionalize television occurred in 1976 with TeleBoconó in the state of Trujillo. This effort to decentralize television from Caracas, the capital city, would continue from the late 1980s to the late 1990s with the creation of many TV stations around the country, including Televisora Andina de Mérida (Andean Television of Mérida) in 1982 in Mérida state, Amavisión in 1984 in Amazonas state and TV Guayana in 1993 to cover southern Venezuela (Bisbal, 2005).

Throughout these years, television audiences continued to grow. In 1970, there were 820,000 homes with television; by 1991, that figure increased to 3.49 million; and by 2005, homes with television sets were estimated at 4.94 million (Bisbal, n.d.).

It is important to mention the powerful presence of two groups in Venezuela that have dominated the telecommunication market for many years: the Phelps/Granier and the Cisneros groups (Vanden Heuvel & Dennis, 1995).

In addition to Radio Caracas Radio and Radio Caracas Televisión, the Phelps/Granier Group includes interests in the recording and music industry, legal representation of music shows and international marketing of television programs. Also, the group owns Gems Television in Florida (United States), which broadcasts entertainment programs for Hispanic audiences via satellite, and two television production centers (Bisbal, 2005).

The Cisneros Group has associations and partnerships with seventy companies worldwide, including organizations like AOL Time Warner, GM Hughes Electronics, Coca Cola and Hicks, AOL Latin America, Direct TV Latin America, Univision and Venevisión. The latter, through its distributors Venevisión International and Venevisión Continental, brings programming to more than 900 million viewers in sixty-one countries (Bisbal, 2005).

Cable television service began in the late 1980s, and in 2006 there were about 1.17 million subscribers. The service is offered by six companies: Omnivision, Cablevision, Supercable, Cabletel, Direct TV and Intercable. Programming via cable shows a combination of local, Latin American and US channels, according to Bisbal (2005). An article in *El Nacional* stated there were 700,000 illegal cable subscribers in Venezuela (Alfonzo, 2008).

President Hugo Chávez versus Mass Media

The advent of Hugo Chávez to the presidency of Venezuela brought a new approach to the media. Knowing the power of electronic communication and in an attempt to counteract the influence of the private media, by 2007 the Chávez administration would own six television stations, thirty-six community television stations, three national public radio stations, four YVKE Mundial stations, 400 community radios and 100 newspapers, each medium with its own website (Bisbal, n.d.). The main television stations are VTV, Vive TV (It Lives TV), Asamblea Nacional TV (National Assembly TV), Avila TV, Telesur (Telesouth) and Televisora Venezolana Social (TVES: Social Venezuelan Television).

In 1999 President Chávez began his first term in office. This would mark a political, social and economic transformation of Venezuela as never seen before. The mass media, and especially the news media, which had enjoyed almost total freedom of the press (admittedly, with some occasional self-censoring, censoring and confiscations), would become active actors in the process of practicing somewhat a political opposition to President Chávez.

Acosta-Alzuru (2007) claims that in the beginning the Chávez–media relationship was positive, especially with the Cisneros Group (Venevisión) and the Otero family (*El Nacional*). Francisco Olivares (personal communication, March, 2008) agreed. As the investigation editor for *El Universal*, Olivares said Chávez was open to criticism. *El Universal*'s news line was objective, and even the official side of any news was reported factually, but the editorial line of the newspaper was critical of Chávez's political discourse.

Like *El Universal*, many other news media were also critical of the government, and since the opposition from the traditional parties (AD and COPEI) was weakened after the election, the private news media felt "they were unequivocally and inevitably in the opposition, and they had assumed a clear political role" (Acosta-Alzuru, 2007, p. 28).

The dissension between the news media and Chávez would continue to grow. Chávez was accused of polarizing the country, and the news media were afraid of limitations to the freedom of expression and the press. During one of his television appearances on his program *Aló Presidente* (Hello President) on May 23, 1999, Chávez said in reference to the media that some people were interested in defaming and lying about his projects (Marcano and Barrera Tyszka, 2006). But Elides Rojas, chief editor of *El Universal*, indicated that "the right to dissent is what bothered Chávez" (personal communication, March, 2008). Rojas believed the government was not interested in controlling the media but rather having them lose credibility.

The situation worsened after the ill-fated coup d'état of April 11, 2002, against Chávez, when the private media was accused of failing to provide a fair and equitable coverage of the events from different sides (Villegas Poljak, 2002). This contention is supported by Izarra (2002), who stated that he resigned his position as news production manager for Radio Caracas Televisión (RCTV) two days after the coup, because of disagreements with RCTV's general management, which directed him and his staff not to report on anything about the whereabouts of President Chávez.

From the time of this failed attempt to overthrow Chávez, the relationship between the president and the private media has been in a stalemate. Chávez continued to accuse the news media of trying to derail his plans for a new Venezuela within his "Socialism of the twenty-first century," and the media continued to denounce his plans as attempts to turn Venezuela into a communist dictatorship similar to Cuba.

However, the Cisneros Group seemed to have formed an alliance with the Chávez government. Marcano and Barrera Tiszka (2006) stated that Gustavo Cisneros and Chávez met in 2004 and reached an agreement. As a result, "the mutual aggression has ceased" (p. 197), and Venevisión decided to cancel a morning show that was critical of Chávez. Further, Raúl Sanz, a Venezuelan entrepreneur with more than 30 years of experience in the advertising and media business said (during a personal communication on September 25, 2008), that Fabiola Colmenares, a popular Venezuelan soap opera actor and a political science student was fired from Venevisión in 2007 because of her public opposition to a constitutional reform supported by Chávez.

But that was not the case for the Phelps/Granier Group. On May 14, 2007, the government cancelled the concession to RCTV, which had been in operation since its birth in 1953 (Bisbal, personal communication, March, 2008). Roberto Giusti, a journalist with *El Universal* and Globovisión, a news channel founded in 1995 in Caracas, said the reaction from viewers was overwhelming, even university students participated by organizing popular protests on the streets. The government did not back down, but "Chávez never counted on the people's rejection of the closing of RCTV" (Roberto Giusti, personal communication, March, 2008).

A final issue in this Chávez–media saga is the enacting in December 2004 of the Law of Social Responsibility in Radio and Television. Bisbal (2005) argued that although the law was supposed to regulate and improve the quality of electronic media content, it seemed to rather aim at government control of what that content must be. Bisbal also denounced the existence of a set of judicial norms aimed at controlling who, from the government side, can talk to the press (Bisbal, personal communication, March 2008). Olivares added that under these new controls, journalists have to be very careful when writing about a government official. "One can even be arrested" (Francisco Olivares, personal communication, March, 2008).

Conclusion

The confrontation between Chávez and the media continues. What is going to happen in the years to come is the subject of sheer speculation. "I don't think anybody has an accurate answer" (Catalá and Díaz Rangel, 2003, p. 195).

In the mean time, the Colegio Nacional de Periodistas (CNP: Journalists' National Guild) of Venezuela denounced publicly the physical and verbal aggressions against journalists, the government exclusion of private news media in favor of official media when news coverage is required for an official event, and the application of censorship (see more information from the Journalists' National Guild at its website www.cnp.org.ve).

Throughout its history, Venezuela's political life has always been associated with the existence of the press, which has often shown political leanings by being supportive of the president in office. Other times, it has been the watchdog of the government's actions and proceedings, but never in Venezuela's history has the press taken the primary role of the political opposition as has happened during the Chávez presidency. The loss of credibility of the traditional political parties due to years of corruption and misdeeds brought the responsibility of a democratic opposition upon the shoulders of the news media. And President Chávez, fearing the power of the mass media on the population, has been determined to confront the press by all means possible, including expanding his own media networks to promote his political agenda, trying to silence dissenting voices by way of legislative maneuvers, censorship and violence against reporters and news organizations.

This ongoing power struggle between the Venezuelan government and the news media presents to communication scholars an ample gateway for productive research in future developments and issues pertaining to the mass media in this South American country. Some of these areas of study worth considering could be the illegal use of cable television signals by a large segment of the Venezuelan population; demographics and extent of Internet access; objectives and mission of the government-owned television stations, community radios and newspapers (is it education, information and/or propaganda?); and the development of high-definition television.

In regard to the application of the Law of Social Responsibility in Radio and Television, research should look into the purpose and effectiveness of this law. The government states it is for the protection of media audiences against cultural colonialism and mediated negative influences; others see it as a way to control what the news media can report on and to punish reporters who dare to denounce government officials' misconduct.

Finally, research on the physical attacks on media workers and organizations: is this an indication of institutionalization of terrorism? And, is it self-censorship within the news media when, as a reporter once mentioned to me, a news medium is pressuring another medium not to report on a misdeed involving a member of that medium?

References

Acosta-Alzuru, C. (2007). *Venezuela es una telenovela* [Venezuela is a soap opera]. Caracas, Venezuela: Editorial Alfa.

Alfonzo A., C. S. (2008, July 29). 700.000 usuarios de TV por suscripción son ilegales [700,000 users of cable TV are illegal]. *El Nacional* [*The National*], p. 8.

Arráiz Lucca, R. (2008). *Venezuela: 1830 a nuestros días* [Venezuela: 1830 until today]. Caracas, Venezuela: Editorial Alfa.

Asociación Nacional de Anunciantes (ANDA). (2008). Comité Certificador de Medios ANDA FEVAP (ANDA FEVAP Media Certifying Committee). *Prensa (Print media)*. Retrieved September 25, 2008, from www.andaven.org/nuevo/CCMAF1.asp#Histórico.

Bisbal, M. (2005). En el aire nuestra pantalla televisiva [On the air our television screen]. In M. Bisbal (Ed.), *Televisión, pan nuestro de cada día* [Television, our daily bread] (pp. 29–88). Caracas, Venezuela: Alfa Grupo Editorial.

Bisbal, M. (n.d.). Los medios en Venezuela. ¿Dónde estamos? [Media in Venezuela: Where are we?]. Unpublished manuscript.

Botía, A. (2007). *Auge y crisis del cuarto poder: La prensa en democracia* [The rise and crisis of the fourth estate: The press in democracy]. Caracas, Venezuela: Editorial Melvin.

Catalá, J. A. & Díaz Rangel, E. (2003). *De Pérez Jiménez a Hugo Chávez: Censura y autocensura* [From Pérez Jiménez to Hugo Chávez: Censorship and self-censorship]. Caracas, Venezuela: Ediciones Centauro.

Central Intelligence Agency (CIA). (2008). *The CIA world factbook. Venezuela.* Retrieved September 14, 2008, from https://www.cia.gov/library/publications/the-world-factbook/geos/ve.html#Econ.

Colegio Nacional de Periodistas (Journalists' National Guild). (n.d.). Retrieved August 14, 2008, from www.cnp.org.ve/.

Cortina, A. (1995). *Historia de la radio en Venezuela* [History of radio in Venezuela]. Caracas, Venezuela: FUNDARTE.

Díaz Rangel, E. (2007). *La prensa venezolana en el siglo XX* [The Venezuelan press in the twentieth century]. Caracas, Venezuela: Ediciones Grupo Zeta.

Encyclopedia Britannica Online. (2006). *Venezuela.* Retrieved August 8, 2008, from http://search.eb.com/search?query=venezuela&ct=&x=14&y=15.

Izarra, A. (2002). El golpe de estado desde la cabina 12 de RCTV [The coup d'état from RCTV booth 12]. In M. Tremamunno (Ed.), *Chávez y los medios de comunicación social* [Chávez and the mass media] (pp. 81–94). Caracas, Venezuela: Alfa Grupo Editorial.

Marcano, C. & Barrera Tyszka, A. (2006). *Hugo Chávez: The definitive biography of Venezuela's controversial president.* New York: Random House.

Vanden Heuvel, J. & Dennis, E. E. (1995). *Changing patterns: Latin America's vital media.* New York: Freedom Forum Media Studies Center.

Vidal, J. (2004). *La era de la radio en Venezuela* [The age of radio in Venezuela]. Caracas, Venezuela: Alfa Grupo Editorial.

Villegas Poljak, V. (2002). Medios vs. Chávez: La lucha continua [Media vs. Chávez: the struggle continues]. In M. Tremamunno (Ed.), *Chávez y los medios de comunicación social* [Chávez and the mass media] (pp. 47–59). Caracas, Venezuela: Alfa Grupo Editorial.

7

The Mass Media in Bolivia

Gonzalo Soruco
University of Miami, USA

and Juliet Pinto
Florida International University, USA

Introduction

In 2008, the mass media of Bolivia faced significant challenges in carrying out their functions, with pressures constraining press freedom burgeoning on various fronts. By 2007, press freedom in Bolivia, Argentina, Brazil, Peru and Paraguay had worsened from the previous year, according to various watchdog groups (Freedom House, 2007; Reporters Without Borders, 2007). Legal climates have also traditionally presented difficulties: the press in Bolivia has been suppressed, censored or gagged during much of its existence by various civilian as well as military governments, but particularly by the latter. On several occasions, presses and radio and television equipment were destroyed and the buildings that housed them burned by irate mobs because of ideological reasons.[1]

The present conflict does not reflect isolated incidents, but rather the culmination of decades of ongoing transformation in relations among the media and the state, the media and their audiences, and Bolivians' experiences with their governments. In this chapter, we discuss the current snapshot of media not only within the institutional fabric of political and economic environments and societal concerns, but also as a path-dependent result of centuries of deepening cleavages along ethnic and social lines, widening inequality and tremendous poverty for indigenous populations. Present-day Bolivian media must navigate the rocky terrain of the cleavages of this country with 9.2 million inhabitants, including fractious relations between the eastern *departamentos* (states) and the central government, and the ideologies and alliances held by media organization owners and advertisers.

Perhaps the most significant variables affecting modern-day media performance have to do with the historical marginalization of a significant portion of the Bolivian population, and how the fight to change this impacts the country. Since the mid-1990s Bolivia has experienced a surge—a tsunami would be a more appropriate description—in the aspiration for recognition among its indigenous people, who constitute the majority of the country's population and who have been neglected by the ruling class for the past four centuries. It is the culmination of a struggle that started in the early 1950s. The 2006 election of Evo Morales—an indigenous man himself—with an unprecedented 53 percent of the popular vote has been a watershed in Bolivian politics as well as in race and class aspirations. Not surprisingly, it has also fed the ambitions of the indigenous people for political and social representation as well as for their share of the nation's wealth.

But finding themselves between the "rock of the state and the hard place of the market," as Waisbord (2000, p. 50) has described media systems in Latin America, is not a recent conundrum for Bolivian media professionals. Present conditions are formed by their historical trajectories and the institutional fabric in which they exist. Contentious media–state relations and exploding social unrest did not unfold overnight. We begin with a discussion of the development of Bolivian media within a context of their relations with loci of power, namely the mining, natural gas, and agricultural industries, including the vast production of coca. The richness of its natural resources catapulted Bolivia into the global environment at the turn of the twentieth century. But market instability and dependency on global commodity prices would lead to the weakening of its economy and political instability. Media had to navigate not only this instability, but also the social upheaval wrought along deep racial fractures. We then discuss the development of media technologies and media content, and the interaction of local forces with global ones. We conclude with a snapshot of worsening media–state relations under democratically elected President Evo Morales, and the significance of measures taken by his administration for press freedom.

Early Press Environment

Media in Bolivia were wrought in an environment of cyclical economic and political instability, intense competition over natural resources, and widening disparities between the wealthy ruling classes and the poor who labored for them. Indeed, the diametrically opposed extremities of poverty and wealth are exemplified in Bolivia. Foreign correspondents reporting on some event in Bolivia invariably manage to insert somewhere in the story that this country of roughly 424,000 square miles and a population of 9.2 million is the "poorest of the hemisphere, next to Haiti." It is not necessarily an inaccurate description. The country's GDP is a mere $21 billion and its population has a meager per capita income of around $1,000. By comparison, Bolivia's neighbor to the south, Paraguay, with an area of 157,000 square miles and a population of 7 million boasts an estimated GDP of $27.08 billion. The problem with the "poor country" description of Bolivia is that it hides that nation's political and economic complexities and the history behind them.

Bolivia is a country rich in natural resources, and in some ways it is handsomely so.[2] Those who know the country's history could argue that its vast natural wealth has also been at the root of many of its problems. Long before it broke its colonial chain from Spain, this region of South America began to attract adventurers searching for gold and silver. They found it soon enough. In the mid-sixteenth century, according to local lore, a young Indian shepherd searching for one of his stray llamas in a mountain near the town of Potosí serendipitously discovered the largest vein of silver in the Americas. Before long, the town of 14,000 people became the largest city in the Western hemisphere, boasting some 150,000 souls hungry to despoil the mountain of its precious metal and become a "grandee." Potosí is nestled in a plateau among the Andes mountains at an altitude of 13,000 feet—hardly a hospitable place.

This fortuitous discovery and its subsequent silver rush in a place which two centuries later would become a part of Bolivia was a harbinger of things to come. This region of the Andes turned out to be rich in precious and non-precious metals that attracted an assortment of adventurers from around the world eager to risk their lives for a chance to become wealthy. By the time Bolivia gained its independence from Spain in 1825, mining for ore around Potosí had become the country's obsession. Soon, it became its principal enterprise and its main source of revenue. At the dawn of the twentieth century, Bolivia ranked third among all the countries of the Western hemisphere in mineral wealth, "exceeded only by the United States and Mexico" (cited in Marsh, 1928, p. 34).

As proof that Bolivia was predestined by nature to remain in the grip of the Andes' charms, in 1900 some 50 miles north of Potosí in the mountain of Llallagua, a prospector by the name of Simon Patiño discovered what were then the largest deposits of tin in the world (Querejazu, 1978, p. 65). His timing was perfect. Food producers of the industrialized world had discovered that their products could retain their freshness and nutritive value almost indefinitely if they were packed in tin-plated cans. Among the other uses of tin are in toothpaste tubes, tin foil, solder, silk, and in alloys such as bronze and babbitt (white metal). World War I greatly increased the demand for this metal. By 1920, Bolivia was producing 20 percent of the world's tin. By then, Patiño was a wealthy man, and by 1927 he figured among the ten richest men in the world (Chase, 1927, p. 1). A few wealthy miners used their fortunes to enter the political arena and reach the Bolivian presidency (e.g., Gregorio Pacheco, 1884–1888; Aniceto Arce, 1888–1892; Gonzalo Sanchez de Lozada, 1993–1997 and 2002–2003) from where they molded governmental policy to make it even more favorable to mining industrialists like themselves. Others, such as Simon Patiño, shunned public office and preferred to rule discreetly from the background.[3]

Attracted by this new chance of sudden and great wealth, Bolivians and foreigners once again rushed up the harsh mountains around Llallagua to try their luck at becoming millionaires. Felix Avelino Aramayo, of French and Chilean origin, and Mauricio Hochschild, a German entrepreneur, together with Simon Patiño, were by far the most successful tin miners of Bolivia and to whom the international press referred to as the "tin barons." For half a century they controlled not only the world's tin markets, but also Bolivian politics. Bolivians referred to them disdainfully as *La Rosca* (the ring).

The mines were also a source of employment for the poor indigenous people of the Andes and the valleys of Bolivia, many of whom left the farms of the rich whites where they labored in near-slavery conditions. But none of the wealth from the mines trickled down to its workers, and little of it reached the Bolivian government's arcs.

The attitude and mentality of the miner—greed, hard work, guts, ruthlessness and the will to risk life and limb for quick wealth—would capture the national culture. It would also pervert its values. For much of the nineteenth and twentieth centuries, mine owners, who were mostly whites, constituted Bolivia's ruling class—a class imbued with economic, political and racist beliefs. Just as it was in the United States and elsewhere at the end of the nineteenth century, laissez-faire and social Darwinism were Bolivia's dominant policies and thinking.[4]

The Andean region had been divided along race lines since the arrival of the conquistadors in the early 1500s; by the 1900s the division was profound and deeply unequal. The country's population is currently composed largely of three racial groups: Indian (55 percent), mestizo or *cholo* (30 percent) and white (15 percent). The composition of the mestizo, however, is complex and correlates with social status. Persons with more Indian than white blood, for example, are more likely to be working class, poor and illiterate. Social mobility in Bolivia is almost nonexistent. The profession of journalism did not escape this racial stratification. Journalists were the white intellectuals who contributed daily with their lofty and abstract analyses. The reporters and press workers tended to be the mestizos.

Bolivian topography has also been a factor in the country's division. The Andes on the west have been a natural barrier to roads, railroads and other means of communication between urban centers of the west and those of the tropics in the east. The isolation that resulted from these natural barriers has tended to feed strong regionalist feelings. Traditionally indigenous people have preferred the settlements near the urban centers of the Andes, especially La Paz, while many whites have gravitated toward the tropics, mainly the city of Santa Cruz. Moreover, not all Bolivians speak the same language and Spanish is not the language of the majority. Aymara and Quechua are spoken by the indigenous people of the Andes and its valleys, while Guaraní is the language of an Indian nation of the tropics in southeastern Bolivia. Cultural differences are additional barriers to the integration of Bolivians. As Ramiro Beltrán, Bolivia's most eminent communications scholar, points out, "this large indigenous mass suffered until around the mid-1950s from a complete isolation of communication" (Beltrán, Suárez & Isaza, 1990, p. vi).

By and large the white minorities, together with the mestizos—particularly those with "more" white than Indian blood—shared the benefits of modernization that Bolivia could provide, such as electricity, safe water, transportation, telephony and education thanks to world demands for tin. However, the Indian workers who extracted the ore and risked their health and lives every day and every night received a small payment (between 50 cents and 1 dollar a day, in 1928 dollars) for their sacrifice, and a ration of coca leaves and alcohol to numb their hunger and pains. The women did not stay at home to take care of the children and the children did not go to school. Instead women and children worked near their husbands and fathers outside the mines, separating the ore from the rock. The average work day was between 9 and 12 hours (Marsh, 1928, p. 41).[5] Poverty and disease were endemic among mine workers and their families.

Lacking iron and coal, Bolivians could not build efficient smelters to purify their ore. They had no choice but to transport their mineral from the Andes to Chilean or Peruvian ports and from there to England and Germany, where smelters turned the ore into pure ingots. The pure metal was then transported to the United States where the factories of the United States Steel Corporation converted it into tin plate (Marsh, 1928, p. 37). Bolivia became completely dependent on the price and demand for ore in the world market and on customers who more often than not held the upper hand. It was an unhappy relationship. The country's economic stability and therefore its political stability were tied to the price that its tin or some other natural resource could fetch in the world markets. In 1920, for example, the price of a metric ton of tin sold for £296 sterling; by 1922 it had dropped to £159 sterling (Oficina Nacional de Estadística, 1929).

To avoid a serious economic recession, in 1922 the Bolivian government borrowed money from American bankers under onerous conditions. Freedman and Nearing (1925, pp. 31–32) describe that in order to obtain the $33 million loan from Stifel and Nicolaus Investment Company, Spenser Trask, and the Equitable Trust, Bolivia had to pledge most of its assets as security. The "Nicolaus Loan" became the symbol of Bolivian corruption and ineptitude as well as the rapacity of American and English bankers, whose investments in Latin America were protected by their governments' gunboats. The disastrous Great Depression in the 1930s had severe repercussions on global prices, and therefore on the industries in Bolivia. The price of a ton of tin in the world markets dropped from £226 in 1928, to £118 in 1931. During the same period, the Patiño mining enterprise reduced its workforce from 7,000 to 2,000 (Baptista, 1978, p. 22).

Bolivia's natural resources were the cause for various wars with neighboring countries, and therefore not only subsequent frosty relations with Chile and Paraguay,[6] but also greater stresses along racial and ethnic lines. In the early 1850s, Bolivians discovered that their south-west region held large deposits of nitrate and guano useful for gunpowder and fertilizer. These also caught the eye of Bolivia's neighbors. In 1879, the Chilean army occupied the region and after a brief war defeated Bolivia and annexed the territory to Chile. In that war (1879–1884), Bolivia lost not only its access to the sea coast and the rich resources it held, but also the world's largest deposits of copper in Chuquicamata. In 1899, Bolivia found itself at war again. This time it would lose almost one-third of its northern territories to Brazil, in a war over rubber. In 1932, Bolivians were once again at war, this time with Paraguay (1932–1935)—presumably aided and abetted by foreign oil companies—which had set its sights on Bolivia's oil deposits. After three years of carnage on both sides (estimated casualties 90,000 and a cost of $100 million dollars), Bolivia lost the war and a large chunk of territory known as Chaco to Paraguay, but kept its oil deposits.

Few events scar a nation's conscience as deeply as war does. Since its foundation, Bolivia has fought four of them. Historian Mariano Baptista (1978) describes the feelings of Bolivians toward these wars: "The [war with Chile]," he wrote, "was about the devil's metal; the [war with Paraguay] was about the devil's piss" (p. 83).

The war with Paraguay was an epiphany for the country's elites. For the first time the whites from La Paz, Sucre, Cochabamba, Potosí, Santa Cruz and other cities ate, slept, fought, bled and died in the trenches hand in hand and shoulder to shoulder with their Indian brothers. Bolivia's defeat in the battlefield at the hands of a presumably weak Paraguayan army also opened their eyes to the corruption of the government that put them and their Indian brothers in harm's way and to the ineptitude of the military leaders who engaged the enemy with no apparent strategy for victory. The Chaco war marked the beginning of the end of the old order, but it would be a while before the new order would take its first steps.

For the Indian recruits composing the majority of the infantry, the war was mystifying. They were told to fight an enemy they did not know, for a land that was not theirs and could own, and for reasons they did not understand. But they fought, and many died bravely in the battlefield. Their sacrifice, however, rarely made it to the front pages of a mainstream press that could publish only the field reports handed down to them by the army.

By and large, the press supported the war almost to the end with jingoistic reports. Only *La República* and *El Universal* dared to challenge the government and its conduct of the war. Their candid criticisms often resulted in censure (Knudson, 1986, pp. 7–12). In any event, in 1933, to stifle criticism on the conduct of the war by the opposition, the government of President Daniel Salamanca declared a total censorship of the media under the "Law of Social Defense" that he forced through the congress in order to control the bad news coming from the battlefield (Dunkerley, 1987, p. 150).

The rumblings of political and social revolution were rattling the trenches of the Chaco, as the seeds of social change were planted. But it would take some twenty years before veterans of that war would take the seat of power in La Paz. How the press moved toward or away from greater representation both reflected media–state relations, as well as shaped it.

The workers' demands for social and economic justice became louder in the early 1920s. It was a time when workers around the world where demanding for a more equitable treatment from their employers.[7] They formed unions, demanded higher wages, shorter hours of work and better working conditions, and organized sporadic strikes. In turn the government, obedient to the moneyed interests of *La Rosca*, sent soldiers to the mines and factories to "restore order" and compel the workers to return to their posts. In addition, the Bolivian Congress passed laws proscribing "anarcho-syndicalism" to keep unions, and especially their leaders, under control. For the emerging press, covering these events often meant taking a stand for the oppressed, seeking justice, or for the state, seeking social order.

The Press and the State

To some degree, the Bolivian press has followed the route described by Walter Lippmann (1931) and Robert Park (1967). First, it functioned as a mouthpiece for the monarchy. Then, it moved to voicing perspectives of political state parties. Next, it moved to the commercial logic of catering to mass audiences as a business model, and as democratic institutions evolved a strong advertising base developed. During the 400-year rule of Spain, the *Alto Peru* —referring to its location in the high Andes and to differentiate it from the *Bajo Peru* in the low lands—published irregularly a press known as the *gaceta* that was the official voice of the empire. On occasion colonists managed to publish their own opinions in underground newsletters that were considered "seditious" by the officials because they lacked the approval of the crown. A few of these appeared in 1780 and 1781. Presumably, they were printed in Buenos Aires but were widely distributed throughout the region. These newsletters extolled the virtues of the Indian nations and at the same time castigated the corruption and bad habits of the *Chapetones*, a colloquialism used to refer to anyone born in Spain.

Shades of the "party press" were born in the *Alto Peru*, almost two decades before Bolivia won its independence from Spain in 1825, with the publication of *El Telégrafo* (1811) which operated on and off into the twentieth century. Vicente Pazos Kanqui, himself of mixed European and indigenous heritages, published *El Censor* in which he fanned the flames of independence. The first newspaper published soon after the founding of the republic—in August of 1825—was *La Gaceta de Chuquisaca*, which produced only nine issues. It was followed by *El Condor de Bolivia* that because of its "stability" and influence many consider the first true Bolivian newspaper (Beltrán et al., 1990, p. xii).

Throughout the nineteenth century, Bolivia's party press was rich, contentious and strongly partisan. Newspapers that toed the government's line were rewarded handsomely with public monies. In 1899, La Paz's *El Radical* published a list that included a dozen newspapers around the country that for years had benefited from the government's largesse (Ocampo, 1978, p. 330).

Commercial newspapers of the twentieth century belonged to the elites and their editorial policies reflected their interests, ambitions and fears, as well as the blend of partisan views with commercial business logic. The daily *El Diario* of La Paz, for example—founded in 1903 by José Carrasco, a prestigious lawyer and expert in constitutional law, in partnership with Patiño, the mining tycoon—carried on its pages articles, essays and analyses written by the elite of La Paz.[8] Among its contributors were Federico Diez de Medina, a diplomat; Arturo Posnansky, a naturalist and explorer; Lucas Jaimes, a distinguished intellectual; and Felipe Segundo, an economist (Ocampo, 1978, pp. 347–348).

In the paper's first editorial, Carrasco described his plans: "Our objectives are broad," he wrote, "our aspiration [is] to elevate the profession of journalism; to discuss the country's problems; to favor commerce; to incentive industry; to preach peace among peoples, and fraternity among men [sic]" (Ocampo, 1978, p. 347). But also from the start the editorial policy of *El Diario* was closely identified with the political ideology of the Liberal party that ruled Bolivia at the time and would continue to do so for the next seventeen years. *El Diario* published news as well, mostly local news. But little was written about the conditions of mine workers, the farmers, the laborers, the poor in general, who were mostly Indian and mestizo and living in poverty.

In 1917, the daily *La Razón* was founded in La Paz by José Maria Escalier and mining magnate Felix Avelino Aramayo. From its earliest issues *La Razón* was a strong defender of the interests of the Republican party—which at the time was out of power—as well as those of the mining industry and would remain so until its demise thirty-five years later. Predictably, its relationship with the government and the ruling Liberal Party was rocky from the start. Soon after its first publication, the government alleged that this daily was undermining freedom of expression with its inflammatory editorials and ordered it closed. Its editors were sent into exile (Ocampo, 1978, p. 404). During the ensuing five years, *La Razón* was forced to stop its presses several times.

Between 1925 and 1952, however, this newspaper was an influential voice of the mining interests. It seized publication in 1952, after the successful revolution on April 9 by the Movimiento Nacionalista Revolucionario (MNR: Revolutionary Nationalist Movement).

Demetrio Canelas, a talented lawyer and indefatigable journalist who founded several newspapers during his lifetime, among them *La Prensa* of Cochabamba (1908), *La Patria* of Oruro (1919) and *Los Tiempos*, also of Cochabamba (1942), strived to professionalize Bolivian journalism, which he saw as pedestrian, political and biased. To this effect, he organized the First National Congress of Journalists, which took place in Oruro in August 1929. The National Congress created the Federación Boliviana de la Prensa (National Press Association), established insurance and retirement benefits for journalists and a guarantee against governmental abuse against writers; it also proposed plans to teach literacy to the indigenous people of Bolivia. *Los Tiempos* would become a thorn in the side of government—especially the MNR's—with its reports on corruption and intolerance for freedom of expression (Ocampo, 1978, p. 669).

Of concern to Bolivian journalists at the time, as well as nowadays, was the *Ley de Imprenta* (Print Law) of 1925, which not only guaranteed freedom of the press, but also stated that the journalist had a "judicial, moral, and social responsibility" toward the state. The law considered that crimes committed in printed materials (e.g., damages and libels) were crimes against public opinion. Truth was not grounds for defense. In order to judge a journalist whose article may have caused "injury," the *Ley de Imprenta* created a *Jurado de Imprenta* (Jury of Print). The jury of forty people was to be elected by local councils and composed preferably of lawyers and academicians, who would be able to judge the accused journalist objectively. To be sure, the *Ley de Imprenta* with its *Jurado* clause was part of the reigning judicial philosophy regarding freedom of expression: it was essentially "Blackstonian" philosophy with a Bolivian twist.[9] The law guaranteed freedom of expression without prior restraint, but punishment would follow any expression considered illegal, offensive, or immoral. The 1925 Print Law still is in force, and those who publish material deemed to defame, slander or insult public officials may face imprisonment, despite constitutional guarantees of freedom of speech and the press (Freedom House, 2007).

Ultima Hora, controlled by Hochschild, appeared in 1929 and became the only evening newspaper of La Paz (during its last decade of life, the paper switched to morning publication) and would form part of the mainstream media until its demise in the early 1990s. The daily *Presencia*, founded by the Catholic Church, made its debut in La Paz in 1953. *Hoy*, a daily publication founded by Alfredo Alexander in 1960, stopped publication in 1979 soon after the tragic demise of its founder. The six newspapers mentioned (*El Diario*, *La Razón*, *Los Tiempos*, *Ultima Hora* and *Presencia*) were the preeminent newspapers of Bolivia and set the national agenda for most of the twentieth century.

La Calle, which was an MNR creation of the early 1930s, was without a doubt one of Bolivia's most influential, if not contentious, newspapers of the twentieth century. Founded by leftist intellectuals Armando Arce, Carlos Montenegro and Augusto Céspedes, the paper set its sights first on the military establishment that took over the government of Bolivia after the Chaco war to cover up its shameful role in that humiliating defeat. It also attacked *La Rosca* that so often had guided the government's economic and financial policy to its own benefit. In its section "The Monkeys of Wall Street," it attacked Standard Oil and other US enterprises doing business in Bolivia. Its irreverent, sometimes humorous, but always insightful, reports of governmental corruption and its alliance with the mining interests were well received by its readers, but loathed by the authorities, which in many occasions sent the police to seal its presses and close its doors. *La Calle* stopped publishing in 1946 (Ocampo, 1978, p. 516) when a junta took over the government after a particularly bloody revolt and banned the paper.

The Movimiento Nacionalista Revolucionario and its leader, Victor Paz Estenssoro, came to power briefly in the early 1940s and became a dominant force in domestic politics (its leaders were exiled after the coup of July 1946). Initially a reformist party, the MNR showed similarities to other movements in the region, supporting military force in political processes, pursuing popular support and resisting foreign investment.[10] Notably, the MNR played the main role in the 1952 Revolution and 1953 Reform that gave widespread voting rights, especially to the disenfranchised indigenous groups, introduced land reforms and nationalized the mines, effectively reorganizing power centers of whites and indigenous populations (Yashar, 1999). Unfortunately for Bolivia, the mines were nationalized when tin was harder to extract and much of the infrastructure had fallen into disrepair. The MNR's revolution of 1952 ended the fifty-year dominance of Bolivian politics by *La Rosca*. It also harnessed the news media to its causes, utilizing dailies to garner popular support, then censoring critical voices of other news outlets or co-opting them as official voices.[11]

The MNR established a close relationship with the miners' union, the Federación Sindical de Trabajadores Mineros de Bolivia (FSTMB: Union Federation of Bolivian Mine Workers) and appointed its leader, Juan Lechín, to head the Ministry of Mines. It also opened its doors to the workers' union, the Central Obrera Bolivia (COB: Bolivian Workers' Center). More importantly, the MNR forged close relations with the indigenous groups, whom they armed and organized into militias committed to defend the Revolution. Additionally, the word "Indian" was replaced with *campesino* (peasant) in all official documents. In that climate, the press operated with caution and exercised a great deal of restraint in its coverage of the government and its indigenous policies. The MNR's fall to a military coup d'état in November of 1964 halted the incorporation, such as it was, of Bolivia's indigenous groups into the fabric of the society. It also ushered a dark period in Bolivian politics that lasted nearly twenty years during which political repression and press censorship were the rule.

Mining unions also played an important role in the formation of community radio networks in Bolivia, but the medium actually has deeper roots. According to journalist Gramunt de Moragas, Bolivians were experimenting with this medium about the same time as Marconi. The journalist points out that the first commercial radio station started in 1929, and that Radio Illimani, the official state radio, was among the first to broadcast information and propaganda during the Chaco war (as cited by Beltrán et al., 1990, p. xiv).

The invention of the transistor in the 1950s revolutionized radio. It made possible the construction of small, portable sets. People could listen to their favorite programs practically anywhere and for as long as their batteries allowed it. Radio sets became popular very quickly in Bolivia, especially among the indigenous people. Yet even nowadays, radio—long a very popular medium in a country grappling with illiteracy and poverty—continues to proliferate, particularly in terms of community media. Founded in the 1940s, community radio networks owned by the tin miners and their unions or affiliated with them have provided an alternate voice to the country's mass media (Huesca, 1995a, 1995b; O'Connor, 1990). These stations have served to communicate union messages and themes, organize political action, or form "networks of resistance" during times of political turmoil (Ferreira, 2006, p. 191; O'Connor, 1990, p. 104).

The end of the old order in 1952 should have meant a new climate for the press. After all, it saw the demise of *La Rosca* and smothered to a great degree the country's "tin mentality." The press could finally focus on reporting on the social, political and economic inequalities that had divided the country for so long. But geopolitics was about to take an important role. The relative insularity of Bolivia from much of the outside world, other than as a producer of tin, began to disappear under the forces and demands of the new doctrines of the Cold War and the growing influence of Washington on Bolivian politics.

For the press, the new doctrines meant a reaffirmation of its "responsibilities" rather than that of its "freedoms." When Nerone (1995, p. 2) argues that the "dominant way of thinking of about normative press theory in the United States has been through law," he might as well have been referring also to all of those nations in its sphere of influence, including Bolivia. "The rights of the press," he points out, "are implicitly assumed to be composed of individual rights." The Bolivian Constitution, for example, makes no direct reference to the freedom of the press. Instead, it anchors its freedom on Article 7, which guarantees the individual's freedom to express his or her opinion through any medium (Constitución Política (1967), Art. 7, Para. B). There are other freedoms that relate to the press (i.e., economic, structural) that are rarely discussed or addressed in the Bolivian public sphere. As the relationship between Bolivia and the United States drew closer, particularly in the late 1950s and early 1960, the press had greater difficulty covering issues that are normally associated with the left, such as the rights of the workers, and that of their "socialist" organizations.

After the MNR's fall, Bolivia was ruled by military dictatorships and turmoil that lasted until 1982. Ongoing censorship, harassment and aggression toward journalists and media professionals, or utilization of "official" voices would continue under the military governments. Those out of favor with the regime would be closed down or forced into exile, under President Hugo Banzer in the 1970s, or General García Meza in the early 1980s.

During the early 1980s, Bolivia became once again the victim of its rich natural resources. It was a precarious time for the country that had finally been able to contain the military and return to democracy by electing Hernan Siles, an old MNR leader (Siles had been Paz Estenssoro's vice-president and then president in the 1950s). The increasing demand of American and European markets for cocaine stimulated the production of coca leaf, which had been a staple of the indigenous diet. It took place at a time when the nation was going through the worst economic crisis in its history. The Andes region was experiencing a severe drought, and the world demand for tin was at its lowest level. Farmers and unemployed miners left their parched lands and deserted mines to settle in the Chapare region—a fertile valley between the Andes and the tropics—to produce coca. It was in the Chapare where Evo Morales began his political career as union leader. During this period, cocaine revenues became the principal source of Bolivia's foreign trade (Gamarra, 1994, p. 28). The growing salience of Bolivia as a producer of coca and cocaine ran directly against US President Ronald Reagan's "war on drugs" policies. Washington's insistence on eradication of coca crops placed the Bolivian government on a collision course with Chapare farmers' unions, which in a short time had become a force to be reckoned with. It was more than Bolivia's fragile democracy could bear (Gamarra, 1994, p. 30). Meanwhile, the press covered the issues, but from a discreet distance.

Neoliberalism, Indigenous Activism and the Media

As democratic elections returned to Bolivia in 1982, privately owned media would proliferate, but audience dynamics were changing. Indigenous demands to be allowed entry into Bolivian power centers grew as the economic and political environments transformed. Following to some degree a trend seen elsewhere in Latin America, with the shift to democratic elections in the 1980s and 1990s came neoliberal policies that deregulated and privatized swaths of industry in Bolivia, as well as opening the economy up to foreign investment again. Based on Washington Consensus policies, these measures were implemented with the so-called New Economic Policy in 1985.

Himpele (2004, p. 356) notes that something else was happening in Bolivia during this time: other reforms to incorporate indigenous population in political processes, including reformulations of political processes and rights designed to address inequalities for indigenous communities.

However, these progressive measures soon ran into the blocks of historical racial divisions, as well as new obstacles created by economic neoliberalism. As Yashar (1999, pp. 85–86) discusses, a shift toward the autonomy of the individual meant a shift away from the power of indigenous organizations, which had for decades been the avenues to any negotiations with the state. It also meant a reduction in social services, subsidies and credit programs (Yashar, 1999), and what was perceived as intense discrimination against coca growers in order to comply with terms of aid from the United States and the World Bank, something of great concern in indigenous communities (Himpele, 2004, p. 356). Increasing income inequality and rising anger at continued social, economic and political marginalization were exacerbated.

Perhaps in response, new indigenous movements mobilized in the 1990s to bring greater attention to their plight in the periphery and their demands to be brought to the core of Bolivian institutions. Networks of indigenous activist groups joined with non-governmental associations to form important alliances and gain ground (Himpele, 2004). The country had an indigenous vice-president by 1993, and by the end of the 1990s, indigenous elected officials had grown in number.[12] This opening would culminate in the election of Evo Morales in 2006.

Spurred by their slogan *ahora es cuando* (our time has come) the Indian nations of Bolivia went to the polls in mass to vote for one of their own. Before Morales, few indigenous people had played significant roles at the top of the pyramid of Bolivian political power. And those who did so were largely supporting characters to some prominent white politician. Perhaps the best example is Victor Hugo Cardenas, who served as vice-president to Gonzalo Sanchez de Lozada (1993–1997). The selection of Cardenas, an Aymara Indian, for vice-president was at that time a shrewd move by Sanchez de Lozada, who himself hailed from one of Bolivia's aristocratic white families. At the very least it showed Sanchez de Lozada's commitment to the incorporation of the Indians into the halls of power. As Carlos Mesa, journalist, historian and former president of Bolivia, points out, the inclusion of an Indian to the ticket for the second highest office in the land was a landmark, announcing that the democratic process in Bolivia had entered a new stage in the country's history (Mesa, 2006, p. 178).

Bolivia's "indigenous revolution" did not take those of European descent (or the "whites") by surprise. They knew that it would come sooner or later. They also knew they had a lot to atone for. But the tone of the demands for land reform, redistribution of wealth, and a new constitution that would guarantee greater autonomy to indigenous groups is a source of great concern to the whites, not to mention the unwavering insistence on the sharing of power. The revolution could mean a complete social, political and economic remaking of Bolivia. Morales' proposals include a new constitution which would allow his reelection (the present constitution allows one five-year term for the office of the presidency), independent courts for indigenous people, indigenous autonomy and restraints on the press. Sensing the weakness of the United States as the world's political hegemon, Morales allied himself with its enemies, such as Cuba's Fidel Castro, Venezuela's Hugo Chávez and Iran's Mahmoud Ahmadinejad. There is also a desire among some of the Movimiento al Socialismo (MAS: Movement for Socialism) leaders to change the country's name for one that reflects its indigenous origins, such as Kollasuyo—the name given to the region by the Inca rulers six hundred years ago.

To be sure, Bolivia's mainstream mass media find themselves in a difficult situation. Their owners are by and large white, yet significant portions of their audiences are indigenous. They must document the overboiling frustrations and cover the salient issues. Yet coverage can mean alienating owners and white audiences, already facing turmoil, as well as engendering the wrath of Morales' administration and his Movimiento al Socialismo followers.

Killing the messenger of unwelcome news has been practiced in Bolivia with alarming regularity throughout its history. This is the case again. Supporters of the MAS have organized civic groups that demand compliance with the "democratic" revolution of Morales, showing little tolerance for opposing views. The political opposition has blamed the government for the excesses of what it terms "MAS shock groups" and of encouraging their intimidating behavior toward those who live in the large urban centers, particularly the white population. Journalists covering confrontations between indigenous and whites have been singled out for attacks by Morales' followers (Periodistas demandan garantías, 2008). Morales himself has been engaged in an active campaign to discredit the media. He has accused journalists of taking money from the "oligarchy," of lying, of being "dirty" and has used full-page advertisements to advance his accusations (La manipulación . . ., 2008). The journalists' response to Morales' attacks was swift and forceful. In an op-ed piece published in La Paz daily *La Razón*, Humberto Vacaflor (2008), a respected journalist and one-time president of the Asociación Nacional de Periodistas (ANP: National Association of Journalists), accused Morales of lacking the moral grounds for making any accusations against anybody.[13]

The media have struggled in the midst of these transformations not only to maintain the trust and interest of their audiences, but also to compete for small advertising revenue in a fractured media environment. Public trust in the media is an issue: in 2002, the media ranked behind even the government in terms of public trust of an institution (quoted in Goldstein & Castro, 2006, p. 392) and this crisis of confidence reflects trends in other parts of Latin America (Waisbord, 2006).

The press has seen the growing influence of several dailies with national audiences (see Table 7.1), as well as increasing foreign investment in media industries. *La Razón* is a new incarnation, although in name only, of the old miner's daily. This new version is owned by Grupo Prisa of Spain. According to journalist James Breiner, the press does an excellent job covering the issues important to Bolivian society, despite the constant assaults on its journalists at the hands of Morales' followers (Breiner, 2007). At present, there are twenty newspapers that publish the news daily around Bolivia.[14]

Radio continues to be a popular medium. In 2006, Freedom House (2007) estimated that there were some 800 stations in Bolivia, with new community networks springing up, some in part with help from Venezuelan financiers.

But the richness of Bolivia's natural resources has not translated into better access to newer forms of media for many in indigenous communities. For those who have access, over-the-air

Table 7.1 Principal Newspapers of Bolivia, 2008

Newspaper	Locality	Ownership
El Diario	La Paz	Carrasco Family (Bolivian)
La Razón	La Paz	Grupo Prisma (Spanish)
La Prensa	La Paz	Canelas Group (Bolivian)
El Deber	Santa Cruz	Grupo Prisma
El Nuevo Día	Santa Cruz	Grupo Prisma
Los Tiempos	Cochabamba	Canelas Group
Opinión	Cochabamba	COBOCE
Correo del Sur	Sucre	Canelas Group

Source: Compiled by the authors from various sources

Table 7.2 Main Television Networks in Bolivia, 2008

Network name	Ownership	Location
Bolivision	Private	Based in Santa Cruz
ATB	Private	Based in La Paz
PAT	Private	National
Red Uno	Private	Based in La Paz
Televisión Boliviana (Channel 7)	State	National
TV Universitaria	State and university	Based in La Paz
Unitel	Private	Based in Santa Cruz

Source: Compiled by the authors from various sources

television is mainly privately owned, with 48 television stations and an estimated 408.4 television sets per 1,000 people. Table 7.2 shows the main television networks in Bolivia. Pay television has not penetrated to the degree seen elsewhere in South America, with only some 80,000 cable subscribers.

According to the International Telecommunication Union's World Telecommunication Development Report database, Internet use in Bolivia has increased since 2000, with approximately 6 users per 100 people in 2006, somewhat equivalent to Paraguay's estimate of 4 per 100 people.[15] However, this rate falls far below that of its neighbors, Argentina, Chile and Brazil. And with only 1.2 broadband subscribers per 1,000 people,[16] the digital divide in Bolivia is more of a gaping crevasse, as deep inequality marks who may have access to new communication technologies.

Challenges for Media in the Twenty-First Century

Clashes between Morales' supporters and his opposition highlighted divisions in Bolivia, as states contested federal decisions concerning land and resource distribution and communities clamor for political and economic recognition. While such clashes have a long history in Bolivia as discussed, the stakes were higher, as oil and natural gas revenues increased substantially, contributing to an estimated 4.2 percent increase in real GDP growth in 2007.[17]

Reforms to the chilly legal environment for press freedom could help, as they could elsewhere in Latin America (Hughes & Lawson, 2005). While mentions of freedom of the press are made in the constitution proposed by Morales and MAS, so too are chilling provisions that shrink the scope of press freedom. Chapter 7, Article 106, Section II of the proposed constitution states:

> the State guarantees freedom of expression, opinion, and information, the right to rectification and reply and the right to express free ideas through any medium without prior restraint. These rights will be exercised in accordance with the principle of responsibility.
> (Constitución Política de Bolivia, October 2008)

In other words, individuals, as well as the press, can express any opinion, or report on any event without having to seek the approval of the state, but can expect prosecution if these run afoul with the laws. Section III, of Article 109 of the proposed Constitution states that "[The State] recognizes the clause of conscience of the [people] who work in the information business." This unusual clause supports reporters' rights not to publish news, information or opinion that go against their values or beliefs.

The mass media must navigate around the Print Law of 1925, the *desacato* (insult) laws, and the laws of defamation which can land in jail any journalist who runs afoul of them. The law of *desacato* reads: "Anyone who slanders, offends, or defames a public official during the exercise of his official duties or because of them will be deprived of liberty from two months to two years" (Código Penal, Art. 162). Although truth can be a defense against slander and defamation, the burden of proof is on the reporter. Offense, on the other hand, has an unequivocal chilling effect on expression. Article 287 of the Bolivian Penal Code reads: "anybody who uses any medium and in a direct manner offends another's dignity or decorum will be deprived of liberty between thirty and 100 days." The interpretation of "offense," "dignity" and "decorum" is presumably done by the judge assigned to the case. These three articles, slander, offense and defamation, are the bases for defamation.

Beyond the animosity of the legal environment toward freedom of expression, media–state relations have become more contentious during the Morales regime. Some have charged his administration with further curtailing freedom of expression, in line with actions taken by previous regimes. In a 2008 conference in São Paulo, Brazil, Cardinal Julio Terrazas referred to the "traces of totalitarianism" in the indigenous government of Evo Morales. These comments were published in an op-ed piece by Miguel Manzanera (2008), a Jesuit priest:

> A totalitarian trace can be detected in the handling of social communication. The Government not only uses state media, radios and Channel 7, to broadcast its plans twisting objective information, but also uses large sums of money in television, radio and press in order to influence public opinion, attacking the opposition . . . The diatribes and threats to the media that do not support [its policies] complement this media dictatorship, a typical trace of the totalitarians of the right and the left.
>
> (Manzanera, 2008)

Conclusion

The historical development of Bolivian media within a fractured and deeply unequal society has provided for very difficult conditions for the exercise of an unfettered democratic press. From the time of the earliest mining companies, to the wars fought with neighboring Peru, Chile and Paraguay, through the Revolution of 1952 and subsequent military regimes, and later turn to neoliberal policies regarding the country's natural resources, tensions along ethnic, social, political and economic cleavages churned and rolled, resulting in clashes between communities, groups and sectors. Recent conflicts among Morales supporters and the opposition represent current snapshots of the bellicosity simmering along these fault lines, as groups clash in a quest for recognition, power and control.

The election of indigenous leader Evo Morales was not only a victory for communities long excluded from political power, but also a new chapter in the story of the search for press freedom and the role of the mass media in Bolivia. Federal–state clashes overlap long-simmering indigenous–white tensions, as communities grapple for control of land and natural resources, and the rules that govern them. In their assault on the political structure of Bolivia, the powerful indigenous movements have successfully vanished the political parties of the opposition. In the absence of a balancing force to counter the abuses and proposed changes of the MAS and its civic groups, the nation's minorities have turned to the mainstream media to voice their own grievances.

The impasse over constitutional reforms that would address land reform, political reorganization and term limits, among other disputed terms, revealed once again the stark polarization of modern Bolivian society, and the degree to which old cleavages continued. Media, again caught between ideologies, state interests, popular support and corporate interests, must work not only to report on those issues, but also to gain the trust and confidence of the Bolivian public they serve, as well as maintain their advertising base. Time will tell if the high drama in this highland country will result in meaningful reform, or continued polarization.

Notes

1   On several occasions during the nineteenth century, journalists were challenged to a duel by government officials or members of the military because of a critical article. In 1938, Alcides Arguedas, an influential journalist and eminent man of letters, was beaten by a mercurial President German Bush, whose prowess as a pugilist was well known (Baptista, 1978, pp. 104–105). In 1956, the partisan daily *La Nación* was burned down by an angry mob. In 1970, owners of the daily *Hoy*, Alfredo Alexander and his wife, died in a bombing of their home, a crime that remains unsolved. In March 2008, Carlos Quispe, a journalist at Radio Municipal in nearby La Paz, was beaten to death during a fracas between indigenous groups. In June 2008, in Yacuiba, a small town in southern Bolivia, the local television station was bombed. The attack has not yet been solved, but a military officer with very close ties to the office of President Morales was arrested soon after the act carrying incriminating evidence (Antezana responsabiliza, 2008).

2   A 1950 study commissioned by the United Nations described Bolivia as a country that "contained all the elements to satisfy the necessities for food, housing, clothing and electric power" of its population (cited in Baptista, 1978, p. 184).

3   According to Bedregal (1999, p. 36), Victor Paz Estenssoro—later leader of the MNR and the 1952 revolution that ended *La Rosca*'s influence in Bolivian politics—as one of Patiño's lawyers was privy to classified and secret information of the magnate's enterprises regarding not only bribes to ministers and presidents, but also of state laws and decrees written by the corporation's lawyers that were submitted to congress for their approval.

4   Bedregal argues that the "miners' mentality" fostered Bolivia's "culture of tin" which he describes as being "servile, foreign and colonial, a new true philosophy of life, norms of social interaction . . . a new way of living, a new way of dressing" (Bedregal 1999, p. 61, fn. 5).

5   Mining for gold, silver or tin—which became Bolivia's largest export during the first two decades of the twentieth century—at 13,000 feet of altitude posed formidable challenges. The ore could be found only in some of the most desolate places of the Andes and could be reached only through narrow trails. Initially tools, provisions, dynamite, management personnel and the weekly payroll had to be brought on mules from La Paz—which explains its hundred-year prominence in Bolivian politics, economy and trade—or other nearby cities, but mainly from La Paz, and at great costs. To expedite the transport of their minerals to the world markets, the miners built their own roads, their own railroads and even their own banks.

6   Recently, Bolivia began to export natural gas to Brazil and Argentina. Its deposits of gas are believed to be among the largest in South America. These deposits lay near the border with Argentina.

7   One of the most grievous attacks against the miners took place on November 21, 1942. After the miners' union's demands for higher wages and better benefits were turned down by the Patiño enterprise, a group of mine workers and their families, about 8,000 strong, marched toward the company's main office, only to be welcomed with a hail of bullets from Bolivian soldiers who had been posted in nearby hills. The government admitted only to twenty-one deaths, including that of Maria Barzola, a miner's wife who was ahead of the march carrying the Bolivian flag (Baptista, 1978, p. 147). In an attempt to cover up the attack on the defenseless miners, the government declared a state of siege and censored the media (Ocampo, 1978, p. 548). It was not the last time that soldiers would open fire on miners.

8   This newspaper continues to publish the news at the present time.

9   Sir William Blackstone (1723–1780), the English jurist who wrote *Commentaries of the Laws of England*. He asserted that people could express and publish what they wished but would be punished after the fact for "expression of criminal matter" such as blasphemy, treason or sedition.

10   From the Library of Congress Country Studies, retrieved August 10, 2008, from http://lcweb2.loc.gov/cgi-bin/query/r?frd/cstdy:@field(DOCID+bo0026).

11   Library of Congress Country Studies, retrieved August 10, 2008 http://lcweb2.loc.gov/cgi-bin/query/r?frd/cstdy:@field(DOCID+bo0108).

12   See the Ministerio de Desarrollo Humano, Secretaria Nacional de Participación Popular (cited in Yashar, 1999, p. 100).

14   Circulation figures are unreliable in the absence of an independent auditing system. They are also hard to obtain. It is accepted among the professionals that most newspapers, even those that serve the large urban centers such as La Paz and Santa Cruz, have a small circulation.

15   From Country Profile: Bolivia: retrieved August 10, 2008, from http://news.bbc.co.uk/2/hi/americas/country_profiles/1210487.stm#media.

16   Cited in the World Bank's World Development Indicators. Retrieved August 10, 2008, from http://ddp-ext.worldbank.org.

17   From the International Telecommunication Union's World Telecommunication Development Report database. Cited in the World Bank's World Development Indicators. Retrieved August 10, 2008, from http://ddp-ext.world bank.org. Also from the *CIA world factbook*, "Bolivia." Retrieved August 10, 2008, from https://www.cia.gov/library/publications/the-world-factbook/geos/bl.html.

References

Antezana responsabiliza a Evo en el caso de Yacuiba. (2008, August 20). *La Razón*.

Baptista, M. (1978). *Historia contemporanea de Bolivia, 1930–1978*. La Paz, Bolivia: Gisbert & Co.

Bedregal, G. (1999). *Victor Paz Estensoro, el político: Una semblanza crítica*. Mexico: Fondo de Cultura Económica.

Beltrán, L. R., Suárez, C. & Isaza, G. (1990). *Bibliografía de estudios sobre la comunicación en Bolivia*. La Paz, Bolivia: Empresa Editora PROINSA.

Breiner, J. (2007). *La prensa boliviana vista por un periodista norteamericano*. Retrieved October 8, 2009, from www.libertad-prensa.org/Director.aspx?P=articulo&A=259.

Chase, S. (1927, February 13). Ford's billion breaks world records. *New York Times*, p. 1.

Código Penal de Bolivia. Retrieved October 8, 2008, from www.oas.org/juridico/spanish/gapeca_sp_docs_bol1.pdf.

Constitución Política de la República de Bolivia. *Article 7, Para. B*. Retrieved October 8, 2008, from www.pdba.georgetown.edu/Constitutions/Bolivia/consboliv2005.html.

Constitución Política de la República de Bolivia. Retrieved May 22, 2009, from www.presidencia.gob.bo/download/constitution.pdf.

Dunkerley, J. (1987). *Orígenes del poder military en Bolivia: Historia del Ejército, 1879–1935*. La Paz, Bolivia: Quipus.

Ferreira, L. (2006). *Centuries of silence: The history of Latin American journalism*. Westport, CT: Praeger.

Freedman, J. & Nearing, S. (1925). *Dollar diplomacy*. New York: Monthly Review Press.

Freedom House. (2007). Bolivia, country report. In *Freedom of the press* (2007 ed.). Retrieved October 8, 2008, from www.freedomhouse.org/template.cfm?page=251&country=7139&year=2007.

Gamarra, E. (1994). *Entre la droga y la democracia*. La Paz, Bolivia: Editorial FOCET Boliviana.

Goldstein, W. & Castro, F. (2006). Creative violence: How marginal people make news in Bolivia. *Journal of Latin American Anthropology, 11*(2), 380–407.

Himpele, J. (2004). Packaging indigenous media: An interview with Ivan Sanjinés and Jésus Tapia. *American Anthropology, 106*(2), 354–363.

Huesca, R. (1995a). Subject-authored theories of media practice: The case of Bolivian tin miners' radio. *Communication Studies, 46*(3–4), 149–168.

Huesca, R. (1995b). A procedural view of participatory communication: Lessons from Bolivian tin miners' radio. *Media, Culture & Society, 17*, 101–119.

Hughes, S. & Lawson, C. (2005). The barriers to media opening in Latin America. *Political Communication, 22*, 9–25.

Knudson, J. (1986). *Bolivia: Press and revolution, 1932–1964*. Lanham, MD: University Press of America.

Lippmann, W. (1931). Two revolutions in the American press. *Yale Review, 20*(3), 433.

La manipulación informativa en los medios de comunicación. (2008, August 26). *La Prensa*.

Manzanera, M. (2008). Rasgos totalitarios del actual gobierno. *La Razón*, September 2.

Marsh, M. (1928). *The bankers in Bolivia*. New York: Vanguard Press.

Mesa, C. D. (2006). *Presidentes de Bolivia: Entre urnas y fusiles*. La Paz, Bolivia: Editorial Gisbert.

Nerone, C. (Ed.). (1995). *Last rights: Revisiting four theories of the press*. Urbana, IL: University of Illinois Press.

Ocampo, E. (1978). *Historia del periodismo boliviano*. La Paz, Bolivia: Editorial Juventud.

O'Connor, A. (1990). The miners' radio stations in Bolivia: A culture of resistance. *Journal of Communication, 40*(1), 102–110.

Oficina Nacional de Estadística Financiera. (1929). *Anuario, 2*, 47.

Park, R. E. (1967). The natural history of the newspaper. In *The city*. Chicago, IL: University of Chicago Press.

Periodistas demandan garantías (2008, March 8). *La Razón*. Retrieved October 8, 2008, from www.la-razon.com/versiones/20080308_006205/nota_247_560304.htm.

Querejazu, R. (1978). *Llallagua: Historia de una montaña*. La Paz, Bolivia: Editorial Los Amigos del Libro.

Reporters Without Borders. (2007). *Bolivia: Annual report 2007*. Retrieved October 8, 2008, from www.rsf.org/country-47.php3?id_mot=560&Valider=OK.

Vacaflor, H. (2008, August 26). Nosotros los sucios. *La Razón*. Retrieved October 8, 2008, from www.la-razon.com/versiones/20080826_006376/nota_246_658427.htm.

Waisbord, S. (2000). Media in South America: Between the rock of the state and the hard place of the market. In J. Curran & M. Park (Eds.), *De-Westernizing media studies* (pp. 50–62). New York: Routledge.

Waisbord, S. (2006). In journalism we trust: Credibility and fragmented journalism in Latin America. In K. Voltmer (Ed.), *Mass media and political communication in new democracies* (pp. 76–91). London: Routledge.

Yashar, D. (1999). Democracy, indigenous movements, and the postliberal challenge in Latin America. *World Politics, 52*(1), 76–104.

8
The Media in Ecuador

Rodrigo Jordán Tobar
Universidad de los Hemisferios, Ecuador

and Allen Panchana Macay
Universidad Católica de Guayaquil, Ecuador

Introduction

Ecuador is located in the north-east part of South America facing the Pacific Ocean. Its neighbors are Colombia to the north and Peru in the south and east. Ecuador has an area of 256,370 square kilometers and the population in 2001 was 12,479,924, projecting to increase to 14,204,900 by the year 2010 (INEC (National Institute of Statistics and Census), 2001a). The life expectancy is 72.1 years for men and 78 for women (CEPAL (Economic Commission for Latin America and the Caribbean), 2007). Ecuador is a young country: in 2001 22.99 percent of the population was between 0 and 9 years of age, and by 2010 the percentage of this age group will barely decrease (INEC, 2001b).

Ecuador is the ninth most populous country in South America, following Chile (16.4 million) and Guatemala (14.1 million) (see International Monetary Fund (IMF), 2006). In 2001, 61.1 percent of the population lived in urban areas and this percentage is expected to increase to almost 63 percent by 2010. The Ecuadorian economy is the eighth largest in Latin America. The unemployment index stands at 6.4 percent based on the economically active population (INEC, 2008a). This new index by the Corea government shows that Ecuador is one of the countries with the smallest rate of unemployment of the region, behind only Honduras (5.2 percent) and Mexico (4.6 percent) (see OIT (World Labor Organization), 2006).

The two main sources of employment are in the agricultural sector (26 percent) and the services sector (59 percent), consisting of consulting, financial, commerce, automotive and transportation.[1] Following this is the manufacturing sector (11 percent), public administration (3 percent), oil/petroleum (0.3 percent) and others (0.7 percent).

From June 2007 to July 2008 the commercial trade balance of Ecuador was positive at $2.5 billion.[2] The main exports include oil and oil products, bananas and plantains, sea products, manufactured metal products and shrimp. The key commercial partners of Ecuador are the United States, the European Union, Colombia and Russia.

A Country of High Political Instability

Ecuador has been known for a high political instability that started on February 5, 1997 when President Abdala Bucaram, the leader of the Populist Party, Partido Roldosista Ecuatorian (PRE), was thrown out of office over corruption charges. Through January 2007, the country has had a total of eleven presidents: seven elected constitutionally (due to the fact that they replaced presidents) and four factual (among them a three-member group). This instability shows indigenous groups' protests, crowded demonstrations by the middle class in Quito, betrayal of the officers of the Army and, finally, the support of the high commanders to the new president.

After the exit of Abdala Bucaram, power was in dispute between his vice-president, Rosalía Arteaga, who had the power for two days, and Fabián Alarcón, who was the last president of the Congress, and managed to have Congress to choose him on February 11, 1997 as Constitutional Interim President, a position that he held until August 10, 1998, when he handed the presidency to Jamil Mahuad Witt.

In 1998 a new Constitution was established. It was the first change since Ecuador started a new democracy era in 1979. Before that there were several dictators that ruled the country. The Constitution of 1998 was prepared by a Constituent Assembly that worked at the same time as the Congress and was ruled by the traditional parties. Jamil Mahuad was the President that finally was able to sign a peace agreement with Peru (October 26, 1998) and also took Ecuador to its worst financial crisis that ended with the bankruptcy of 17 out of 34 private banks and financial institutions in the country as 1.8 millions clients lost their deposits.[3]

Since then 1,571,450 Ecuadorians have emigrated (INEC, 2008b), mainly to the United States and Europe, due to the high unemployment rate which hit a record of 17 percent in February 2000,[4] and an inflation rate of 91 percent the same year (Naranjo & Lafuente, 2002). Due to the emergency, President Mahuad decided to use the US dollar in Ecuador beginning January 9, 2000; it was the first country in Latin America to adopt the currency solely and officially.

Due to the social and economic chaos of the Mahuad presidency, on January 21, 2000, Colonel Lucio Gutiérrez, a security officer for Abdala Bucaram, led a military and indigenous rebellion to try to remove Mahuad from office. Although Gutiérrez led the revolt, ultimately he preferred that his superior, General Carlos Mendoza, commanded the *triunvirato* or three-party council.

Mendoza, along with the president of the Indigenous Association (CONAIE) Antonio Vargas, and the president of the Court of Justice, Carlos Solórzano, signed and formed a three-party council that lasted for only four hours. At dawn on January 22, the military heads agreed to reestablish the law and named Vice-President Gustavo Noboa, a professor, as the new president. Lucio Gutiérrez and the other members spent six months in jail, until they were pardoned. Three years after that military action, in January 2003, Gutiérrez was elected president by defeating the traditional party candidates.

The Gutiérrez administration embraced corruption, nepotism, spying and repression until April 20, 2005, when thousands of people self-named the *forajidos* (a disrepectful nickname Gutiérrez called people who complain), filled the streets of Quito to demand his exit. That same day, Gutiérrez gave up power; he escaped to the Brazilian embassy in Quito before delegating the presidency. Vice-President Alfredo Palacio González assumed leadership.

On January 15, 2007, economist Rafael Correa Delgado became president. Correa is a young politician, very close to presidents Hugo Chávez of Venezuela and Evo Morales of Bolivia. Correa promotes the theory of twenty-first-century socialism. Correa promoted a new Constituent Assembly, and with the party, Movimiento País, created a new Constitution, the twentieth in Ecuador's history. It is one of the three longest Constitutions of the world with 444 articles and was approved in a referendum on September 28, 2008.

Credibility Remains an Issue

Although a decade has passed since the major financial crisis of the country, Ecuador has still not managed to heal the wounds that the massive freezing of bank deposits left. During 2008, the state intended to complete the return of deposits to all the affected bank customers. The precipice of the financial system and Jamil Mahuad's overthrow brought an irremediable loss of confidence in the democratic public and private institutions, between them, the mass media.

This phenomenon happened because the bankers who failed were owners of important channels of television, newspapers and radio stations, which never stopped reporting that these banks were enjoying good economic health.

Prior to the banking crisis, the mass media occupied the first three rankings of institutions with major credibility in Ecuador; nevertheless, after 1999 the media fell to seventh and eighth places. For the remainder of the bank crisis, Ecuadorians lived through a constant social restlessness, which turns into panic whenever rumors of closing banks are mentioned.

The State Enters the Media

Ever since the birth of the first newspaper in 1792 (a libertarian newspaper *Primicias de la Cultura de Quito*), Ecuador has been one of the few countries in Latin America with an important tradition of press, radio and television, with the private sector leading the activity. Until the late 1990s, the main government handled only three AM radio stations: Radio Nacional del Ecuador, Radio Casa de la Cultura and Radio Vigía de la Policía Nacional.

This situation changed when the government confiscated one of the main television stations and one newspaper that belonged to failed bankers; before they were owned by people whose ownership was given as payment to the customers after the financial crisis of 1999. To show that the state had no interest in controlling media, these companies were given independent administration (*El Telegrafo* newspaper) or sold to private investors (like SíTV).

The beginning of Rafael Correa's government took a radical turn and started an important state presence in the media sector, through two concrete strategies. First, the government provided institutional support of the existing state media and the creation of new entities. Specifically, the state invested almost $10 million in the reactivation and redesign of *El Telegrafo* newspaper, the creation of Ecuador TV as the first public television channel, the strengthening of Radio Nacional del Ecuador FM and the expansion of the coverage of Radio Casa de la Cultura in AM.

A second strategy was the control of twelve communication companies linked to the Isaías Group, former owners of Filanbanco,[5] through a confiscation backed in the AGD Law that protects depositors. Among the confiscated channels were Gama TV and TC Television,[6] stations that dominated 38.5 percent of the national audience of news in open VHF-TV. Also, the state now controls TVCABLE group, the biggest cable operator with 90 percent market share, Suratel and Satnet, one of the four most important suppliers of Internet and Setel, a landline telephone operator, as well as some radio stations and magazines. The state designated new managers in these media groups with the objective of supervising the contents of their news programs.[7]

This measure forced a reaction by the Inter American Press Association. Its president, Gonzalo Mallorquin, reacted on July 9, 2008, saying:

> what we cannot accept is that they put some pressure on the managers. What is not acceptable is that action had been complemented because it affects the editorial content. Maybe this action has already been complemented due to editorial policy; having appointed a press director loyal to the government ... this measure just disguises policy and censorship.[8]

This action took place two and a half months before the referendum, which was interpreted by analysts as a new hit for the government to favor a positive vote for the new constitution. In addition, the editorials of the main newspapers indicated it was questionable that the state handles seized mass media during an electoral campaign.

In less than two years, the state raised a new media group that today controls seventeen mass media: five directly and twelve by order, until those goods are sold and the money given back to the former depositors of Filanbanco. These include four VHF and UHF open television channels; two pay-television suppliers, one television station offering international television, one national newspaper, four magazines and five radio stations.

Although President Rafael Correa indicated that the media companies will not be run in the long term by the state, one of the senior ministers of the regime, Ricardo Patiño, defended the right of the government to buy seized mass media, an action that has not taken shape.

Political analysts have indicated that the sale of the companies will not be easy (see *Líderes*, a weekly magazine) because there are open legal processes against them (from the state, former proprietors and former clients of Filanbanco).[9] Also, the administration has been in state hands for several months, and by the new Constitution that defines a different legislation for the operation of the sector.

The government did not distribute a definitive timeline for selling the companies until October 2008. Government spokesmen indicate that the only clear thing in this process is that the people understand that these companies are not part of the Isaías Group, but to date, these efforts have not been successful.

The New Constitution after the "Democratization of the Media"

Since September 28, 2008, a new political Constitution has governed Ecuador. It was established by a constituent assembly chosen by popular election (and with a majority of 91 of the 130 members of the assembly). The third section is dedicated to "Communication and Information," with Article 19 marking the new vision of the government on the sector. This norm states:

> The law will regulate the prevalence of contents with informative, educative and cultural aims in the programming of mass media. The emission of publicity that it induces to the violence, the discrimination, the racism, the drug addiction, the sexism, the religious or political intolerance and all that are prohibited that attempt against the rights.[10]

For mass media directors, grouped in the Asociación Ecuatoriana de Editores de Periódicos (AEDEP: Ecuadorian Newspaper Publishers) and Asociación Ecuatoriana de Radio difusion (AER: Association of Ecuadorian Radio), Article 19 of the new Constitution implies that the state already has direct interference in the publishing line and means that law is against freedom of expression. Another key Article (16) indicates that

> all the people, in individual or collective form, have right to a free communication, intercultural, diverse and participative, in all the scopes of the social interaction, by any means and forms, in its own language and with its own symbols.

Section 2 Article 16 has a universal access to information and communication technologies and Section 3 indicates, in addition, the right to the

> social mass media creation, and to the access in equality of conditions to the use of the frequencies of the radio electric spectrum for the management of television and public,

deprived and communitarian radio stations, and to free bands for the operation of radio networks.[11]

Access to Information

Concerning information, Article 18 establishes that

all the people, in individual or collective form, have rights: To look for, to receive, to interchange, to produce and to spread truthful information, verified, opportune, plural, without previous censorship about the facts, events and processes of general interest, and with later responsibility.

According to the government, another constitutional advance is that the state specifically guarantees in Article 20

the clause of conscience to all person, and the professional secret and the reserve of the source to those who inform, they express its opinions through average or the other forms of communication, or toil in any activity of communication.

No Oligopoly, No Monopoly

The 2008 Constitution marks an important difference with respect to 1998, since it directly prevents the monopolistic handling in the sector. In this sense, Article 17 says:

The State will promote the plurality and the diversity in the communication, and to the effect it will guarantee the allocation, through transparent methods and in equality of conditions, of the frequencies of the radio electric spectrum, for the management of television and public, deprived and communitarian radio stations, as well as access to free bands for the operation of radio networks, and will prevent that in its use the collective interest prevails. The State will facilitate the creation and the mass media fortification public, deprived and communitarian, as well as the universal access to the information technologies and communication, in special for the people and collectivities' that lack this access or have it of limited form.[12]

In addition, number 3 of Article 17 says the state "will not allow oligopoly or monopoly, direct or indirect, of the property of mass media and the use of the frequencies."

Financial Groups Will Not Be Able to Own Media

A substantial change by 2010 will impact some mass media in the country. Article 312 of the new Constitution indicates that

the financial organizations or groups will not be able to have permanent participation, total or partial, in companies other people's to the financial activity. The participation in the control of the capital, the investment or the patrimony of social mass media is prohibited, to financial organizations or groups, its legal representatives, members of its directory and shareholders.[13]

This constitutional norm must be fulfilled in a term fixed to the transitory disposition number 29 of the new Magical Letter. This establishes that "the participative shareholders who have the legal people of the financial sector in companies other people's to this sector, will be alienated in the term of two years from the entrance in use of this Constitution." The document further states:

> The participative shareholders of the legal people of the financial sector, their legal representatives and members of directory and shareholders who have participation in the paid capital of social mass media, will have to be alienated in the term of two years from the entrance in use of this Constitution.

This disposition directly affects an important economic and mediatic group of the country that at the same time has interests in the television, press and banking sectors.

This situation will impact the open (free) national television channel, Teleamazonas, which first broadcast in 1974 and has bonds with Pichincha Bank, the major financial conglomerate of Ecuador. Teleamazonas became the first network to offer color TV to the country and to South America; its main studios are located in the capital, Quito. The channel was founded by the industrialist Antonio Granda Centeno and maintained under family control until 2000, when the son of the founder, Eduardo Granda Garcés, yielded the channel to Pichincha Bank, presided over by Fidel Egas Grijalva.

Group Pichincha holds forty active companies with income of $1,138,069,030 in 2007, according to the Service of Internal Rents of Ecuador (SRI). Among the most important are Pichincha Bank, General Bank Rumiñahui, Bank of Loja, House of Picaval Values, Administrator of Funds Pichincha, OPTAR (operator of credit cards, owner of Diners Club) and AIG Metropolitana Insurance. Abroad, Pichincha Bank has offices of representation and agencies in Peru, the Caribbean, Central America, the United States and Spain.

Teleamazonas is not the only mass media under industrialist Fidel Egas. Dinediciones publishes the magazine *Management*, in addition to magazines *Soho Ecuador*, *Fucsia*, *Diners World* and newspaper *Hoy*. Egas has said that he will accept the new Constitution because he is Ecuadorian. Egas will have to sell his channel at the end of the 2010, although Teleamazonas is one of the three most watched national television channels in the country and has been openly critical of the government of Rafael Correa.

The Radio Spectrum Debate

There is another article questioned by the proprietors of mass media, because it appears the state will demand part of the profits of the radio and television channels, since it was put in the Constitution that the radio electric spectrum is nonrenewable and a strategic patrimony of the state. Article 408 establishes that

> they are of inalienable property, imprescriptibly and unattachable of the State non-renewable the natural resources . . ., as well as the biodiversity and its genetic patrimony and the radio electric spectrum. These goods could only be operated in strict fulfillment of the established environmental principles in the Constitution. The State will participate in the benefits of the advantage of these resources, in an amount that will not be inferior to those of the company that operates them.

The government has reiterated, nevertheless, that when it talks about the "radio electric spectrum," it does not mean to share the gains with the mass media. That declaration, however, still leaves doubts for the industrialists because it does not have a concrete legal substance, since the new Constitution does not allow reforms in the medium term.

Little Foreign Presence

The mass media sector in Ecuador has developed mostly by national capitals, without the strong interest of foreign companies in to the country. The causes for this phenomenon are listed below:

- Ecuador is one of the three countries of South America with low advertising investment, due to the size of its market (only 13.8 million inhabitants as of September 2008).
- High political instability and legal insecurity for the foreign investments.[14]
- Ambiguity in the legislation for the sector.
- Collapse of the journalistic and entertainment during the banking and financial crisis of 1999.

The presence of foreign capital in Ecuador is very small—less than 0.5 percent from the total of mass media of the country.

Historically, television and radio were developed in Ecuador thanks to American investments made by the Christian mission organization, HCJB (Hoy Cristo Jesús Bendice, or Heralding Christ Jesus' Blessings). The group was pioneering in establishing one radio with national reach in 1933 and inaugurating the first television channel in 1959. The objective of all these actions was to propagate the Gospel from Ecuador to more than a hundred countries.

In the commercial Ecuadorian mass media sector, we can emphasize the participation of the Mexican American, Ángel González González, who according to Villarruel (2007) is one of the proprietors of Red Telesistema (RTS). RTS began in 1960, and is one of the six main VHF television stations with national reach. González is a well-known industrialist in communications, who already controls thirty television transmitters in the continent, as well as radio stations, cinemas and retail stores. González holds a monopoly on the sector in Guatemala and is known by his political influence in the region with a calculated personal fortune of $2,000 million. RTS, according to the Internal Revenues Services (SRI), registered 2007 sales of $17,855,179.

Since 2003, Editorial Televisa of Mexico has also entered the business of publishing production and broadcasts in Ecuador a local version of *Caras Magazine*, soon to be joined in the country with other titles of the group such as *Vanidades*, *TV y Novelas*, *Magazine Tu* and *Magazine Tu Hijo y Tú*, which also have local content. This publishing group offers 105 international versions of titles like *Popular Mechanics*, *Buenhogar*, *National Geographic* and *Men's Health*. Editorial Televisa of Mexico initiated commercial operations in Ecuador in the middle of 1974, through the foreign publication distribution, next to its branch.

Ecuador has international commercial agreements or franchises:

- Magazine Cosas has published in Ecuador since the 1990s thanks to a commercial agreement with Publishing Limited Present Time of Chile. The main shareholder is a well-known director of Diners Club of Egas Group.
- Radio Disney Ecuador is related to Importadora El Rosado, the second largest supermarket company of Ecuador, behind Mi Comisariato.
- Radio Exa Ecuadoris is part of an important Mexican radio station operating regionally in Radio Democracia Quito.
- Los 40 Principales Ecuador is one of the most important youthful radio services in Spain, property of Grupo Prisa. This tax exemption operates with a Radio Centro at Quito.

An Offer from the North and Spain

While the Ecuadorian sector of journalistic and entertainment companies has not been attractive to foreign investors, in the telecommunications sector there is intense competition between Telefónica of Spain and Telmex and America Movil of Mexico. Between 2007 and 2008, Telefónica of Spain invested $45 million to equip Ecuador with a new underwater cable infrastructure, harnessing the capacity of telecommunications of the country. Telmex acquired the operator of fixed telephony, Ecutel, a former Ecuadorian company that had a market share of less of 1 percent for $23 million. In addition, Telmex managed licenses to offer cable television in Quito and Guayaquil. Telmex is led by the Mexican investor tycoon, Carlos Slim, and has already initiated the local supply of "triple play" packages of Internet, fixed telephony and cable television. Telmex faces competition from the Group TV Cable, a former company of the Isaías Group, which holds a 90 percent share of the pay television market.

In Ecuador, the Telefónica Group of Spain commercializes its services through Movistar (cellular telephony and Internet) and the Telefónica International Wholesale Services (services of telecommunications by underwater cable). The group of Carlos Slim, meanwhile, is present with Porta (cellular telephony) and Telmex.

The Quito–Guayaquil Axis: A Key to Understanding Ecuador

A noticeable regional division in Ecuador influences the life of the country. This reality was incipient at the time of the Spanish colony and has its origin in the historical development of two poles of economic growth in the same country: the productive forces of the coast and those of the mountain range. This bipolarity is explained in the competitive relationship between the cities of Quito and Guayaquil.

Historically, Guayaquil, a city with more than 3 million inhabitants, has been the economic and commercial center. It has the more important seaport, an international airport and the most profitable companies. Nevertheless, Quito, with more than 2.5 million inhabitants, is the capital and the city of greater political importance. It has all of the ministries, the embassies, and the Palace of Government and the more extensive and important Historical Center of America, declared Patrimony of the Humanity in 1978.

The antagonism between both cities began when Guayaquil increased its commerce with the southern zone, that is to say, towards Peru. Quito in turn began economic interchange with Colombia toward the north. The historian, Nancy Rueda, affirms:

> Before the birth of the Republic, Guayaquil always wanted to have political protagonism, but it could not. For that reason, even, their inhabitants were against to the union that was the at the time Ecuadorian state (Real Hearing of Quito) to the Great Colombia.[15]

Quito and Guayaquil form the axis of the country, separated by only 420 kilometers.

This double-headedness has damaged other regions, whose abandonment has motivated current autonomists, as happened in 2007 with the corners, Santo Domingo of the Tsáchilas (which belonged to Pichincha with Quito as the capital) and Santa Elena (in the province of the Guayas with its Guayaquil capital). These two jurisdictions became provinces with endorsement from the government and the Congress. Thus Ecuador is known for its bicentralism: the axis of Quito–Guayaquil.

This phenomenon was reflected in the mass media, which is why less influential regions established their own informative channels. For example, the newspaper *La Hora* is considered the most important regional newspaper network of Latin America with its twelve editions, and also employs the greatest number of journalists (450) in Ecuador.

Main Media Groups

In Ecuador, the mass media sector is fragmented due to an excess of information and entertainment companies. The Supervision of Telecommunications of Ecuador (SUPERTEL) reports that a total of 652 frequencies are available to television channels (VHF, UHF, cable television) as of August 2008. There are 1,205 existing frequencies to radio stations (SUPERTEL, 2008a). The press consists of thirty-eight newspapers and thirty locally published magazines.

With the dismantling of the Isaías Group, the communications sector lost its most important protagonist involved in free-to-air television, pay television, radio and the press, whose sales in 2007 surpassed $114.5 million. The Isaías Group maintained a dominant business in telecommunications by offering Internet, data transmission, radio trunking, beeper and fixed telephony.

In Ecuador eleven concentrated social communications groups in Quito and Guayaquil exist. The largest developed from newspapers and television and are those that are leaders in information and entertainment. Based on revenues, the key groups are Isaías Group (from July 2008 when it became under control of the government), El Universo Group, Communications Group El Comercio, Fidel Egas Group and Alvarado Group, which together account for 83.79 percent of the $346,440,000 among the top nine communications groups of Ecuador in 2007 (see Table 8.1).[16]

The El Universo Group belongs to the Perez family from Guayaquil and is the publisher of *El Universo* (the number two newspaper in Ecuador), plus magazines *Sambo* and *The Magazine*. In addition, Radio City (regional) and the daily *Super* sensationalist provide national reach. El Universo is a shareholder in the pay television entity, Univisa. The El Universo Group began operations in 1921.

Communications Group El Comercio of the Mantilla family is publisher of newspaper *El Comercio* (third in national circulation) and magazines *Familia*, *Carburando* (automotive), *As Deportivo*, *Action Educativa* and *La Pandilla*. In addition, the group publishes the *Líderes* weekly magazine (businesses and entrepreneurship with national distribution), the evening paper *Ultimas Noticias* (in Pichincha), magazine *Mi Tienda*, Radio Platinum and Radio Quito (regional stations). It began its operations in 1906.

Table 8.1 Sales of the Top Nine Media Groups in Ecuador, 2007 (millions of US$)

Rank	Company	Sales
1	Grupo Isaías	114.5
2	Grupo El Universo	52.27
3	Grupo de Comunicaciones El Comercio	46.55
4	Grupo Egas	40.7
5	Alvarado-Roca Group-Ecuavisa	36.29*
6	Grupo Granasa	21.56
7	Grupo RTS	17.84
8	Grupo Rivas-Relad	14.0**
9	Grupo Eljuri-Etv Telerama	2.73

Source: Servicio de Rentas Internas (Internal Rent Services) (2008)
Notes: * Does not include income of ENSA
** Estimate

Fidel Egas is not only a major industrialist of the financial sector in Ecuador, but also the proprietor of six media companies: Teleamazonas Quito, Teleamazonas Guayaquil, Multicines, Dinediciones, Publipromueve and Planimedios. The first two operate television channels that cover Ecuador. Multicines, meanwhile, is one of the three major cinema chains of the country, with thirty theaters in Quito and Cuenca.

Dinediciones publishes the magazines *Diners* (for subscribers of that credit card) and *Management* (economic analysis), and has the Colombian franchises with local content of the magazines *Soho* and *Fucsia*.

Publipromueve is a television producer that works with Teleamazonas, and also has a unit of businesses dedicated to consulting and promoting the corporate image of companies. Planimedios is devoted to advertising planning. Egas also is tied to Delta Publicity, a promotions agency that initiated its operations in 1974.

The Alvarado-Roca Group, which began in 1957, operates TV Ecuavisa, Ecuavisa International (in Ecuador and on pay channels in Colombia, the United States and Europe) and Editores Nacionales SA Group (ENSA), which publishes the magazines *Vistazo, Estadio, Hogar, Generación XXI* and *América Economía*. The group is also a co-owner of Univisa.

The newspaper with the greatest national circulation, the *Extra*, is part of Gráficos Nacionales SA Group (Granasa). It also publishes *Expreso* and the magazine *Semana*, and participates in the political analysis magazine *Vanguardia*.

Among the smaller groups in terms of revenue and audience participation are the following:

- *Red Telesistema (RTS)* operates two pay-television channels, RTS (VHF) with national reach and Redtele Ecuador (UHF) with regional signals. It also operates four radio stations in Quito and Guayaquil and has the cellular company Interacel.
- *Relad* is controlled by the Rivas family (former executives of SíTV), which currently owns two television stations: VHF Canal 1 (national signal) and UHF Canal 1 (international), also available in Europe and the United States. In addition, it operates the radio station Sonorama, which has national reach.
- *Etv Telerama.* is owned by the Eljuri family of Cuenca (the third most important economic group of the country), who operate the first cultural and news channel of the market with national reach.
- *Group La Hora-Editorial Minotauro* publishes twelve regional newspapers; the majority shareholder is the Vivanco family from Loja.
- *Group Hoy* is publisher of the newspaper *Hoy* (national circulation) and magazines *Sí* and *Hoy Domingo*. This company is led by Jaime Mantilla, cousin of the owner of the Communications El Comercio Group, Guadalupe Mantilla. In addition, the group has TV Hoy (21 UHF in Pichincha), Hoy Radio (with two regional stations) and Edisatélite, a publisher in Guayaquil. Since 2002, Group Hoy has published the free newspapers Metrohoy (Quito) and Metroquil (Guyaquil).
- *RTU Group* has ties with politician Cesar Alarcón Costa; it operates twenty TV frequencies in several provinces, eight FM frequencies and one AM.

Multimedia Changing the Media Sector

The high penetration of the mobile phone (76 percent of the population according to official data) and increasing access to the Internet have led investors to turn their attention to the digital revolution in order to extend their businesses. In 1994, *Diario Hoy* from Quito became the first newspaper in South America to offer its content via the Internet. That same year, the main press groups opened new-media departments charged with placing the content on the web and, later, generating new online content.

As of 2008, almost 80 percent of the television channels, newspapers and magazines have Internet operations, the exception being radio. But with the digital revolution the tendency also came from traditional mass media to integrate into multimedia groups. An example is the former Isaías Group, which expanded from television and radio to pay television, the Internet, publishing, magazines and other activities online.

The same happened with the groups El Universo (which expanded with Radio City), El Comercio (Radio Platinum FM), Egas (magazines *Fucsia, Soho, Management, Multicines*), Alvarado-Roca (with Ecuavisa International and the *América Economía* magazines and *Generación XXI*). Granasa grew with magazine *Vanguardia*; RTS expanded in the radio sector and cellular contents and Relad SA with Canal 1 International. In Ecuador, the Hoy Group is the only multimedia conglomerate multimedia with a presence in radio, publishing, television and Internet. Ecuadorinmediato appeared in 2005, the first entirely digital media group that has successfully integrated the press and radio online with good advertising management.

Media Consumption

Ecuador does not have companies that research and verify data on mass media consumption (e.g., radio, television, newspaper, Internet). However, we do know the following about consumers in Ecuador:

- 87.1 percent of Ecuadorian homes have a television (INEC, 2006) and each home has an average of 1.54 sets (Ibope-Time, 2008a).
- 39.4 percent of the homes have a radio-recorder and 48.2 percent sound equipment, for a total of 87.6 percent with device to listen to broadcasting (INEC, 2006).
- 47.6 percent have a DVD, VCD or VHS (INEC, 2006).
- 17.9 percent of homes have a computer and 2.5 percent subscribe to the Internet (INEC, 2006).
- About 10 percent of population uses the Internet and has an email account (SUPERTEL, 2008b).
- Ecuador is one of six countries with a low literacy rate between Latin America students, with students reading an average of one book a year (see UNESCO, 2008).
- Every day more than 900,000 copies of newspapers are published at the local, regional and national reach, with an estimated 4.5 million people aged 10 years and older who read a newspaper, roughly 41.28 percent of the population.
- Advertising investment in Ecuador is divided as follows: television, 50.83 percent; newspapers and printed magazines, 25.59 percent; radio, 6.9 percent, Internet, 1.7 percent and others (public thoroughfare, cinema and production) 14.98 percent (Argentinian Advertising Studies (AAAP), 2006).

The consumer in Ecuador spends the most time watching television, followed by radio-listening. While Ecuadorians are not active book readers, more of the population spends time with newspapers and magazines. Internet usage is growing, especially between younger people (10–25 years of age).

In terms of content, Ecuadorians are accustomed to national and foreign programming and independent reporters in television and radio. In the press, popular news is preferred over political and economic analysis. Magazine consumption is marginal and with low penetration (this is also demonstrated in the low advertising investment in magazines). On the Internet, young people follow international tendencies and prefer social networks, music downloading, videos and games. The same is true for adults whose preference is for specialized news and multimedia.

Television

Television began in the 1950s, with stations in Quito and Guayaquil. By 1990, TV stations began to proliferate and as of 2008, there are 215 VHF and 182 UHF stations. Most stations offer news, sports and entertainment instead of cultural and educational programming. There is a state channel and one private cultural channel nationwide (Telerama-Group Eljuri). Table 8.2 lists the free television channels.

Regarding entertainment, there are national and foreign soap operas, reality shows and sports, along with movies and sitcoms. Soap operas account for 80 percent of the programming between 7 a.m. and 11 p.m. Monday through Friday. In each Ecuadorian home, the television is switched on 8 hours and 32 minutes per day, according to Ibope-Time (2008a). The same study reveals that each viewer, on average, watches 3 hours and 24 minutes of television per day.

Among the most popular programs in history are the 2006 games of the national soccer team in the World Cup in Germany, with 86 percent participating. Another landmark was the first reality show in Ecuador (Big Brother of Ecuavisa). Ecuador faces a serious problem of audience measurement, since the company of Ibope-Time uses only 550 People Meter systems installed in homes in Quito and Guayaquil, ignoring the other 218 cities of the country.

Production quality is a challenge in Ecuadorian television due to program costs, which can be as much as $2 million, an unattainable cost for a local station, whose budget is typically around $250,000. According to Ibope-Time, the highest rated channels are Ecuavisa, TC Televisión, Teleamazonas and Gama TV. Finally, Ecuador television captures about 50.8 percent (see AAAP, 2006) of the total advertising pie ($348,464,290); other studies say that this amount could rise to 69 percent.

Table 8.2 Open (Free) Television Channels in Ecuador, 2008

Station	Frequency	Group/Owner	Coverage	Category
Gama TV	VHF	Former owner Isaías Group, now state owned	National	Soaps and news
Red Telesistema (RTS)	VHF	RTS Group	National	Sports, talk shows and movies
Ecuavisa	VHF	Alvarado-Roca Group	National	Soaps and news
TC Televisión	VHF	Ex Isaías, now state owned	National	Soaps, comedies and news
Canal 1	VHF	Redal/Rivas Group	National	Sports, talk shows and news
Télérama	UHF	Eljuri Group	National	Cultural shows, music and news
RTU	UHF	RTU/Alarcón Costta. Group	National	News

Source: Compiled by the author from industry sources

Television Channel Types

According to the current Law of Broadcasting and Television created in 1975 and revised in 1995, 2001 and 2002, two types of channels exist. Private commercial channels are funded by private capital and seek to earn a profit, while public service channels provide a service to the community without commercial advertising and publicity of any nature.

There are private stations dedicated to social, educative, cultural and religious aims, also authorized by the state. The law also recognizes community stations, designed to improve local conditions. Stations are classified by their power and frequency in the following categories:

- National stations must have a minimum power of 10 kilowatts
- Regional stations have a minimum power of 3 kilowatts up to 10 kilowatt
- Local stations have a power of less than 3 kilowatts.

Regional, Local and Community Television

In Ecuador there are forty-two institutions and companies dedicated to regional, local and community television, leading to the creation of an Association of Community and Regional Channels of Ecuador (CCREA) in May 2008. This new organization was created for political reasons, as regional and community stations did not have representation in the Ecuadorian Association of Television Channels (AECTV), traditionally handled by the larger TV stations. The CCREA broadcasts over fifty-seven channels in nineteen of the twenty-four provinces in Ecuador (www.ccrea.org.ec).

Cable Television

Cable television began in 1986 with the launch of the first company dedicated to this business, TV Cable. As of June 2008, cable television reaches 7.5 percent of the population or 1,016,026 citizens (SUPERTEL, 2008c). There is increasing access to cable television, with 246 systems authorized by the National Council of Broadcasting and Television (CONARTEL). The former companies of the Isaías Group, TV Cable and Satelcom, control the business with 90 percent of the market, following by Univisa of the Group Alvarado-Roca and El Universo Group. The recent arrival of the multinational, Telmex, will mark a turn in the future of this sector (see Table 8.3).

Table 8.3 Satellite, Terrestrial and Cable Television, 2008

System	Numbers
Satellite television	26,271
Terrestrial television	73,057
Cable television	142,583

Source: SUPERTEL (2008c)

New Price Concessions and Tariffs

Ecuadorian legislation has indicated the electromagnetic spectrum is a strategic part of the state, and must pay a concession or tariff to broadcast. This has led to constant legal confrontations between the government and the media. CONARTEL, by order of President Rafael Correa, decided in May 2008, to change the system used to calculate tariffs of television and radio frequencies and radio. A VHF channel in Quito pays $4,500 for a concession of ten years and $40 for monthly use of frequencies; these costs have not been reviewed in more than ten years. The measurement will be implemented at the end of 2008 and looks to revise tariffs to reflect the current economic reality of the companies because the present ones are derisory. New demographic variables will be used, as well as advertising income, coverage, and geographic location.

Radio

With almost eighty years of existence, radio is the mass medium with greatest coverage in Ecuador. Radio began in 1929; as of 2008 there are 1,205 frequencies distributed among short wave (21), AM (271) and FM (913), with 97 percent privately held. Radio was the first mass medium available to all four Ecuadorian regions (coast, mountain range, the east and the Archipelago of Galápagos). Initially, all the stations were AM, but by 1970, FM appeared. In 1971, one government authority commented that Ecuador is a country that has the greatest number of transmitters in the world, with a total of 250 for hardly 6 million inhabitants (Rubiano, 2002, p. 20).

FM's appearance attracted new listeners because of an interactive musical content, leaving AM to air old radio and news productions. There is great fragmentation in the sector, which means there are no dominant radio groups, since very few of them provide national coverage. The regional stations have much influence.

There is no measurement of the national radio audience, but it is well known that the number of listeners is falling due to television, the Internet and video games. A few specialized studies indicate that while seven out of ten Ecuadorians declare they have listened to the radio over the past 48 hours, the medium is not very effective at positioning messages and catching consumer attention. Less than 7 percent of the advertising investment in Ecuador goes to radio.

History of Radio

The first radio station was the Prado, founded by Carlos Cordovez Borja, in 1929 in Riobamba (Bassets, 2002). Cordovez learned of this invention in the United States and brought radio to Ecuador. From the beginning the Voz de los Andes of the Worldwide Confederation of Evangelical Churches used radio. By the end of the 1940s radio reached its "Golden Era."

Commercial radio appeared with growing impact due to World War II. The news from the BBC of London and the Voice of the United States were relayed by local radio. There is an historical example of the credibility of Radio Quito that belongs to the newspaper group, El Comercio. On February 12, 1949, a Spanish version of H. G. Wells' novel *War of the Worlds* was broadcast. Listeners misinterpreted the broadcast as actual news of an extraterrestrial invasion and after realizing their misunderstanding, went to El Comercio to set the building that housed the station ablaze. Six people died in the fire. By 1980, Ecuador had granted 419 radio frequencies, most of them located in the urban centers of Quito, Guayaquil and Cuenca (De La Torre, 2008).

Commercial Radio

In Ecuador, commercial radio occupies more than 97 percent of the frequencies that cover more than 89 percent of the national territory. Nevertheless, radio faces an economic crisis due to the large number of competitors in the business and the lack of advertising revenue. In 2006, of the $685,497,220 invested in advertising, only $41,840,690 went to radio. This phenomenon has generated ferocious competition for advertising and constant reductions in the price of the spots, devaluing radio as a massive channel of communication.

The small amount of money that radio obtains has prevented important investments in renewing the sector which is increasingly dominated by formula radio (music and talk) to the extent of information (news) programming. The main radio stations in Quito and Guayaquil little by little have dismantled their teams of reporters, instead reading informative notes from newspapers. The top radio formats are listed in Table 8.4.

Almost every one of the most successful stations belongs to a great communications groups such as Tropicálida Stereo owned by Andivisión, tied to the Group RTS. Francisco Stereo belongs to the Franciscana Order of the Catholic Church and Canela Radio is owned by Jorge Yunda, current president of the National Council of Radio and Televisión (state entity that regulates radio). Zaracay radio is part of the Zaracay Group, whose home is in the newly created province of Santo Domingo in the Tsáchilas. Their proprietors are Holger and Pericles Velasteguí, who also control Zaracay TV, Activa FM and Cablezar (cable television).

Table 8.4 Radio Stations with the Highest Ratings, 2008

Quito	Guayaquil
Francisco Stereo	Canela Guayaquil
Zaracay	Fabu
Radio Disney	Galaxia
La Rumbera	Antena 3
Canela Quito	Radio Disney
La Otra	Tropicálida Stereo

Source: Mercados y Proyectos (2008)
Note: Based on all ages and social classes, from 6:30 a.m. to 9:30 p.m.

Public Radio

In Ecuador, public radio limits itself to news, music and political contents. Ecuador has thirty-eight frequencies, which is equivalent to 3.18 percent of the spectrum (CORAPE (Coordinator of Community Radio from Ecuador), 2008), less than a single deprived concessionaire, Grupo Nussbaum, which has fifty-two frequencies (4.3 percent of the spectrum).

These transmitters are part of the central state (Radio Nacional del Ecuador, Radio Casa de la Cultura and Radio Vigia of the National Police) and local and regional governments (Radio Municipal de Quito, Radio of the Provincial Council of Pichincha, Radio Municipal de Loja, Radio Municipal de Sigchos, Tarapoa Stereo (Municipality of the Cuyabeno), Radio Municipal of Cotacachi and La Voz de Imbabura of the Municipality of Ibarra). Of the total central state frequencies only seven are active.

Concentration of Frequencies

Some 20 private groups control a total of 256 frequencies, equivalent to 21.4 percent of the radio spectrum. Due to the multiplicity of frequencies assigned to the private sector, the National Council of Radio and Television (CONARTEL), the Commission of Civic Control against Corruption and the Controller of the State have initiated investigations to revert to the state some 229 frequencies believed to have illegal concessions made available to former politicians, former deputies and former state directors who regulated the sector. Table 8.5 shows the radio groups with the most frequencies.

Table 8.5 Radio Groups with the Most Frequencies, 2008

Bernardo Nussbaum	Jorge Montero	Fundación Radio María	Arroba
Lenin Andrade	Jorge Yunda	Radio Centro	Disney
Mario Canessa	BBN	Marcel Rivas	Ecuador Radio
Freddy Moreno	JC Radio	Valencia	Velasteguí
Luis Gamboa	Fundación Juan Pablo II	HCJB	

Source: CORAPE (2008)

A detailed accounting of the concessions reveals that 136 of the 1,205 frequencies are used by religious organizations, representing 11.58 percent of the total stations in the country. Universities and institutes have 10 frequencies that represent 0.84 percent of the spectrum (De La Torre, 2008).

Community Radio

In Ecuador there are twenty-six community radio stations mainly along the jungle border with Colombia, the mountain range (56 percent) and in the east (26 percent) (Carrion, 2007, p. 10). Since 1998, most of these stations are part of the Coordinator of Popular and Educative Radios of Ecuador (CORAPE) that also assigns other alternative transmitters, arriving at a total of fifty-two radios in twenty-three of the twenty-four provinces of the country. They cover 30 percent of the urban-marginal population and up to 60 percent of the total rural population. The objective of community radio in Ecuador is not commercial, but to achieve development of the rural and indigenous towns in areas of human rights, health, education, and sustainable development (see www.corape.org.ec).

Prior to 1995, Ecuadorian law did not recognize community radio, but that year Congress reformed the Law of Broadcasting and Television. That legal modification classified community ratio to restrictive parameters like a prohibition on commercial activities, to accept limits on power, and to have previous approval of the Army for reasons of "national security." CORAPE claimed this situation worked against the right to develop a more democratric radio spectrum, but that it also harmed fundamental rights like freedom of expression.

CORAPE consists of five main networks:

- The Informative Network, with mostly news programming
- Amazonian Network, promoting integration of the cultures of the Ecuadorian Amazona area for regional and national development
- Network Communicators for Teens Boys and Girls, designed to strengthen Youthful Networks of Communicators, in which 800 Ecuadorians in 15 geographic zones of the country participate
- Network Kichwa, whose aim is the indigenous empowerment of the towns and nationalities and other social actors for the construction of democracy and culture
- Network Migration, which groups specialized journalists in migratory subjects, promoting multiculture and the free mobility of people.

The indigenous organizations have nine FM, six AM and five short-wave frequencies with a total of twenty concessions, representing 1.69 percent of the radio spectrum.

The Press

With over 900,000 units published every day, newspapers in Ecuador exhibit the largest influence on public opinion. Since the return to the democracy in 1979, the proprietors of newspapers have been away from political power.

The most influential newspapers and magazines are part of the Ecuadorian Association of Newspaper Publishers (AEDEP), founded in 1985 (www.aedep.org.ec). Since 2007, AEDEP has been the target of constant attacks from the government due to its institutional official notices in defense of the freedom of expression and its calls to the president of the republic to rectify his rule of the country.

A Closer Look at the Readers

Ecuador lacks an organization for auditing newspapers, but reports from advertising and publicity agencies indicate the number of newspaper readers is falling. As of 2006, only 29.3 percent of the population aged 10 years and older read a newspaper, projected on a national scale to 3.2 million readers (*El Universo*, 2008). The lack of real data prevents an exact view, but it is known that most newspaper companies report higher circulation figures to their advertisers, as opposed to the real number that leave the presses.[17]

In 2006, several publishing groups and magazines contracted with the Kantar Average Research to conduct a study in Quito and Guayaquil on a preliminary universe of 4,006 people. Preliminary data indicate seven out of ten respondents read daily. The largest group of readers is between 25 and 44 years old and more men read newspapers (73 percent) than women (*El Universo*, 2008). In terms of time spent reading a newspaper, 44.45 percent of the sample read from 15 to 30 minutes, 29.99 percent read for between 30 minutes and 1 hour and 16.51 percent for less than 15 minutes. Only 8.3 percent of the subjects read for 1–2 hours (Ibope-Time, 2008b).

Most Read Newspapers

The most read newspaper in Ecuador is *Extra*, dedicated to news, murder, eroticism and sports (www.extra.ec). *Extra* dominates the industry with sales of more than 300,000 daily copies on a national scale, targeting people of the lower and middle classes. *El Universo* and *El Comercio* average a circulation of 136,000 daily copies (see Table 8.6). They are read in Guayaquil and Quito respectively and, therefore, are influential in the political and economic public opinion of the country.

Among regional newspapers, the leader is *La Hora*, which publishes twelve newspapers in diverse provinces of the country including *Los Andes* from Riobamba (province of Chimborazo), *Manabita* (Manabí), *Mercurio* from Manta (Manabí) and *Tiempo de Cuenca* (Azuay).

Table 8.6 Number of Printed Copies, 2007

Newspaper	Monday to Friday	Saturday	Sunday
Extra	330,000	340,000	363,000
El Universo	92,300	130,000	225,000
El Comercio	102,000	120,000	180,000
La Hora	99,000	110,000	117,640
Expreso	80,761	76,330	104,387
Hoy	42,300	52,875	52,875

Source: Ecuadorian Association of Advertising Agencies (2007)

Tendency and Challenges

The Ecuadorian press is turning towards three defined tendencies with the purpose of improving its penetration among readers. First is the free press. The first such newspaper was *Metrohoy* (Hoy

Group) which began operations in Quito in 2002. *Metrohoy* supplies an estimated 50,000 copies each day. Another successful example is *Metroquil de Guayaquil,* whose proprietor is also Hoy Group.

Second is the development of the popular press. These papers specialize in gossip and the jet set. *The Diario Super* (El Universo Group) and the *Popular* (Hoy Group) stand out in this group.

Third, most newspapers have been using their websites to offer additional information in the form of videos, photos and audio. In 2008 the Comercio Group redesigned the evening *Ultimas Noticias* to allow readers to write the news, and upload images, video and audio through www.ultimasnoticias.ec.

Magazines

The market for magazines in Ecuador is very limited due to little social demand and the difficulty in obtaining advertising. Studies by the Ecuadorian Association of Advertising Agencies (2007) indicate that the magazine industry is able to capture only about 3.5 percent of total advertising in the country. As of 2008, there are 30 locally published magazines and more than 300 international titles. *Diners, Vistazo, Cosas, Caras* and *Vanguardia* have more readers among magazines published independently.

The Internet

Ecuador is one of five countries with limited Internet penetration in Latin America and one of two nations with less money invested in the development of information and communication technologies (ITCs: Telefónica Foundation, 2007). There are approximately 290,274 (SUPERTEL, 2008d) accounts to access the Internet; of that 39.18 percent are lines with broadband potential (see Table 8.7). In August 2008 it was estimated there were 1,191,960 Internet users, equivalent to 8.6 percent of the national population.[18]

Internet access will continue to grow due to three factors: a steady reduction in the price of access, the incorporation of the Internet in education, and the growth of "cyber cafés." There are an estimated 40,000 Internet cafés in Ecuador, although only a tiny proportion have the permission of the state to operate. In these centers it costs around 60 cents for an hour of access.

In 2007, Ecuador opened a new era in telecommunications, thanks to the inauguration of a new system of the underwater cable SAm-1, a project of Group Telefónica of Spain, which invested $45 million in the project. Before this work, the companies used the capacity of Peru and Colombia at higher costs. With the arrival of SAm-1, the prices for service fell as much as 40 percent. Additionally, the government has launched campaigns to increase Internet penetration, through massive plans of connectivity with the state telecommunications companies (Andinatel and Pacifictel) targeting schools.

Table 8.7 Internet Access in Ecuador, 2008

Dial-up (dial a number for access)	176,528
Commuted users	630,532
Dedicated lines (no need to dial a number to access)	113,746
Dedicated users	501,428

Source: SUPERTEL (2008b)

The Most-Visited Internet Sites

Data from Alexa (www.alexa.com) reveals the most-visited websites are search engines, social networks, videos, academic and blogs (see Table 8.8). The typical user is a person who loves entertainment, likes to meet new people, seeks help with academic tasks, and publishes blogs; international sites are preferred. This suggests young people lead the use of the Internet. Among the most visited media sites are El Universo, El Comercio, La Hora and Diario Hoy, yet these occupy only secondary places in the rankings.

Table 8.8 Ranking of the Twenty Most Visited Websites, 2008

Rank	Website	Type of website
1	Google Ecuador	Search engine
2	Windows live	Microsoft search
3	Hi5	Social network
4	Yahoo	Search engine
5	Microsoft Network	Microsoft entertaining
6	Youtube	Videos
7	Google en español	Search engine
8	Wikipedia	Reference
9	Facebook	Social network
10	Blogger.com	Blogs
11	Mercado Libre Ecuador	Shopping
12	Rapad Share	Share content
13	Sonico	Social network
14	Microsoft Corporation	Software products
15	Google España	Search engine
16	Wamba.com	Social network
17	El Universo	Ecuadorian newspaper
18	Porta	Cell phone
19	Wordpress.com blogs	Blogs
20	Monografias.com	Reference

Source: Alexa (2008)

Conclusion

Independent and National Development

This overview of the mass media indicates the sector still maintains independence from the state, due to its historical development from private capitals, unlike some other Latin American countries. Still, as of 2007 the Correa government created a new media structure affecting radio, television and newspapers. Ecuador has little foreign investment, due to the size of the market, ambiguous legislation and legal security.

The credibility of the media is distinguished by two moments: one before the 1999 collapse of the financial system, and another one in the post-banking crisis. The old media properties owned by the broken bankers affected the trust of the journalists and their companies, and opened the door for constant attacks on the legitimacy of the press by President Rafael Correa.

The media, in addition, face the challenge to survive with the rules imposed by the new Constitution and the ideological turn of the present government towards the press. This will involve democratization of the radio spectrum, a prohibition against banks holding journalistic companies, elevating the prices of the frequencies, and other changes.

Regarding the large communications groups, the tendency is to integrate multimedia through a presence in radio, press, television and the Internet and portable devices. We found that Ecuadorians favor audiovisual media over print, and that Internet consumption is popular among young people.

Regarding challenges facing specific mediums, television faces increased competition from mobile entertainment, pay television and video games. Radio needs to restructure, due to the high fees paid for frequencies, and revalue its prices before advertisers. Newspapers need creative solutions to increase readers. The Internet is in a growth stage, but moving at marginal rates. Specialization is one route to advance the media in Ecuador.

Future Research Directions

The present investigation is this chapter is only an integral academic diagnosis of the Ecuadorian mass media sector in television, newspapers, magazines, radio and Internet. Ecuador needs organizations that prepare official, public and updated information of the total media consumption; although SUPERTEL has made an effort to spread data on television and radio frequencies. The University of the Américas of Quito created a Media Observatory addressing traditional analyses of concentration of assets following Marxist ideological currents, but lacks data with the exception of radio.

A general study of media is not conducted in Ecuador, and the media operate with limited information and data on both a regional and national scale. This situation limits any comprehensive investigation of the media, and the state does not have any organization devoted to data on media consumption. Therefore, there is much left to investigate beyond the analysis presented in this chapter.

Notes

1   Diagnosis on equity in Ecuador, Book Ecuador Sí from Diario Hoy of Quito, June 7, 2007, Industry Section.
2   Central Bank of Ecuador (BCE), Economic Statics, August 2008, Quito, 2008.
3   *Hoy* newspaper, *Special report on the 25 years*, Quito, Edimpres, June 7, 2007, Economic Section.
4   Central Bank of Ecuador (BCE), Statistics for Employment, Quito, 2003.
5   Clarifying note: according to the government, the object of the confiscation (in which 195 other companies of the Isaías Group were included) was to sell the companies as soon as possible, with the purpose of returning all the funds to the depositors of the former Filambanco clients. The confiscation was made at dawn on July 8, 2008 and at the time of writing (September 2008) the selling of the companies has not finished.
6   Among the media confiscated were: TC Televisión, Gama TV, América Visión, TV Cable and the national paid television channels CN3 y CD7, TC Radio, Radio Súper K800 and magazines *El Agro*, *La Onda*, *Valles* and *Samborondón* from Editorial Uminasa.
7   "José Toledo is in charge of the vice-presidency and the news from TC Televisión. 'The objective is to guarantee stability to all personnel, so they can cover the news the way they were supposed to be covered', said Toledo", published in *El Universo* newspaper, July 8, 2008.
8   Inter American Press Association, Institutional Communication, Miami, July 9, 2008, p. 1.
9   The French journalist Eric Samson, former president of the Foreign Press Association of Ecuador, said to the *Lideres* weekly magazine from Quito that the confiscation generates doubts abroad because of freedom of expression issues. Interview published on July 14, 2008.
10 New Constitution of Ecuador Republic, Section 3.
11 New Constitution of Ecuador Republic, p. 25.
12 New Constitution of Ecuador Republic, p. 26.
13 New Constitution of Ecuador Republic, Financial System, Section 8, p. 147.
14 According to INEC, in 2007 the country had a fall in the index of Direct Foreign Investments, having a negative amount of $300 million. The average investment in 2000 was $650 million with peaks of $1,100 million between 2001 and 2002 for the construction of the new oleoduct.

15   Interview with Nancy Rueda, historian of the Andina University Simón Bolívar, on September 20, 2008.
16   The nine biggest groups based on sales as of 2007 were Isaías, El Universo, El Comercio, Fidel Egas, Alvarado-Roca, Granasa, Red de Televisión (RTS), Relad-Canal 1-Sonorama y Eljuri-Telerama.
17   There is a rumor among advertisers that papers declare print runs of 42,000 daily issues but print only 12,000, due to the lack of demand. Papers that in the early 1990s printed 400,000 on Sunday, now print only 225,000.
18   SUPERTEL considers factors of multiplication between 3.90 and 4.5 to estimate users for each hired account in the Internet.

References

Alexa. (2008, September). *Top of Ecuador*. Retrieved March 8, 2009, from www.alexa.com/site/ds/top_sites?cc=EC&ts_mode=country&lang=none.
Argentinian Advertising Studies (AAAP). (2006). *World study 2006*. Buenos Aires: AAAP Reports.
Bassets, L. (2002). *Elements of the history of radio*. n.p.
Carrion, H. (2007). *Community radio's situation in Ecuador*. Quito: Red Infodesarrollo.
Central Bank of Ecuador (BCE). (2003). *Statistics for employment*. Quito: BCE.
Central Bank of Ecuador (BCE). (2008, August). *Economic statistics*. Quito: BCE.
CEPAL (Economic Commission for Latin America and the Caribbean). (2007). *Statistical yearbook of Latin America and the Caribbean*. Santiago: CEPAL.
Constitution of Ecuador Republic. (2008). Retrieved March 8, 2009, from www.asambleaconstituyente.gov.ec.
CORAPE. (2008, June). Coordinator of Community Radio from Ecuador (CORAPE) and World Association of Community Radio Broadcasters (AMARC). *Situation of radio and television of Ecuador*. Quito: CORAPE.
De La Torre, H. S. (2008). *The radio in Ecuador*. Quito: Central University of Ecuador.
Diagnosis on equity in Ecuador. Book Ecuador Sí. (2007, June 7). *Diario Hoy*. Retrieved March 8, 2009, from www.hoy.com.ec/temas/temas2007/ecuadorsi/industria.htm.
Ecuadorian Association of Advertising Agencies. (2007). *Report of traffic of newspapers*. Quito: Ecuadonian Association of Advertising Agencies.
El Universo. (2006, August 20). Vigente una herramienta para medir la lectonia [Tool available to measure readers. Retrieved March 8, 2009, from http://archivo.eluniverso.com/2006/08/20/0001/9/3A3BA907FF9147D1BBB86DA92620D8C4.aspx.
El Universo. (2008, July 7). José Toledo está al frente de los noticieros de TC Televisión y Gamavisión. Retrieved March 8, 2009, from www.eluniverso.com/2008/07/08/0001/9/43683565C632416486E5514305534987.html.
Hoy. (2007, June 7). *Special report of 25 years*. Retrieved March 8, 2009, from www.hoy.com.ec/temas/temas2007/aniversario25/economia1.htm.
Ibope-Time. (2008a). *Presentation of market data*. Quito: Ibope-Time.
Ibope-Time. (2008b). *Time of reading newspapers*. Quito: Ibope-Time.
International Monetary Fund (IMF). (2006). *Ranking PIB and population*. Washington, DC: IMF.
INEC (National Institute of Statistics and Census). (2001a). *Population 2001–2010: Final result of the VI census of population and housing*. Quito: INEC.
INEC. (2001b). *Ages and population: Final result of the VI census of population and housing*. Quito: INEC.
INEC. (2006). *Life condition study*. Quito: INEC.
INEC. (2008a). *Ecuador in statistics*. Quito: INEC.
INEC. (2008b). *Immigration study*. Quito: INEC.
Inter American Press Association. (2008, July 9). *Institutional communication*. Retrieved March 8, 2009, from www.sipiapa.com/espanol/pressreleases/chronologicaldetail.cfm?PressReleaseID=2146.
Líderes. (2008, July 14). *Eric Samson interview*. Retrieved March 8, 2009, from www.revistalideres.ec/solo_texto.asp?id_noticia=1482.
Mercados y Proyectos. (2008, July). *Media rating research*. Quito.
Naranjo, M. & Lafuente, D. (2002). *Central bank technical note: The initial inflation once you adopt the dollar*. Ecuador's case. Quito: Central Bank of Ecuador.
OIT (World Labor Organization). (2006). *Yearbook of labor perspective of Latin America*. Lima: OIT.
Rubiano, R. (2002). The power of radio in Ecuador. *Diners*. Retrieved March 8, 2009, from www.dinediciones.com/diners/246/desplegar.php?id=43.
Servicio de Rentas Internas (Internal Rent Services). (2008). *Report of economic groups*. Quito: Servicio de Rentas Internas.
SUPERTEL (Superintendencia de Telecomunicaciones del Ecuador). (2008a). *Statistics of the sector*. Retrieved March 8, 2009, from www.supertel.gov.ec.
SUPERTEL. (2008b). *Press release: Internet penetration*.
SUPERTEL. (2008c). *Press release: Cable TV consumers*.
SUPERTEL. (2008d). *Press release: Internet penetration*.
Telefónica Foundation. (2007). *Technologies of information and communication and health sector in Latin America*. Madrid: Telefónica Foundation.

United Nations Educational, Scientific and Cultural Organization (UNESCO). (2008). *Regional comparative and explanatory study of education.* Retrieved March 8, 2009, from http://portal.unesco.org/geography/en/ev.php-URL_ID=8259&URL_DO=DO_TOPIC&URL_SECTION=201.html.
Villarruel, M. (2007). *Monopolies and mass media in Ecuador.* Quito: Central University of Ecuador.

9

The Media in Peru

Rosa Zeta de Pozo
Universidad de Piura, Peru

Introduction

This chapter provides a consolidated and up-to-date overview of the Peruvian media. In order to meet this goal it is helpful to understand the industry situation and some general information about the country.

Peru is the third largest country in South America, with a geographical area of 1,285,215 square kilometres, and is physically divided into twenty-five departments forming regions. According to the results of the Eleventh National Population Census conducted by the Instituto Nacional de Estadística e Informática (INEI: National Institute of Statistics and Informatics), the population of Peru as of October 2007 is approximately 28 million people (INEI 2008a). Physically the coastal region is the most populated (54.6 percent), followed by the highlands (31.1 percent); the jungle is the least populated (13 percent).

The average yearly growth rate from 1993 to 2007 has been 1.6 percent, and the data confirm a decreasing tendency observed between 1961 and 2007. This declining trend in the growth of population is fundamentally explained by the reduction of fertility levels, behavior which is confirmed by the results from demographic and family health surveys conducted by the INEI.

It is important to note that Lima (capital department) has 30.8 percent of inhabitants; Lima together with four other departments—Piura (6.1 percent), La Libertad (5.9 percent), Cajamarca (5.1 percent), and Puno (4.6 percent)—constitutes 52.5 percent of the total population. The centralized system influences the concentration of information. Lima has 50 percent of the total media market in Peru. There is an equal balance among females (50.3 percent) and males (49.7 percent). The average age is 28.9 years. The population is essentially urban (76 percent), while 24 percent is rural (see Results of Eleventh Population Census: INEI 2008a).

Education levels vary in Peru. The INEI reports 7.1 percent to be illiterate, although this number is higher in rural areas (19.7 percent) than urban areas (3.7 percent). In the same period 94.9 percent of the population aged 6–11 and 88.3 percent of teenagers between the ages of 12 and 16 attend grade school, and 31.1 percent have a college or university education. The average literacy rate in Lima as of 2007 was 44.9 percent, a marginal increase from 2006 (44.8 percent). Piura (48.7 percent) is the only city which surpasses Lima. The other provinces have lower rates than those of the capital city.

The INEI reports that Peru's gross national product had an annual growth rate of 8.99 percent in 2007. The unemployment rate was 7.5 percent as of December, 2007, while inflation reached 3.93 percent (see Tables 9.1, 9.2 and 9.3).

The Press

The press industry is the largest media industry in Peru. Newspapers began in the eighteenth century, represented by the *Diario de Lima* (1790), the first Peruvian publication which contributed local information and the first participation from readers. Ideological journalism was offered under the leadership of the *Mercurio Peruano* (1791), edited by the Country Lovers' Society (Sociedad Amantes del País).

The nineteenth century essentially developed political journalism, and during that time the official newspaper *El Peruano* (1826) and *El Comercio* (1839), dean of the national press, were started. In the twentieth century *La Prensa* (1903) along with *El Comercio* placed Peruvian journalism in modern times. The most transcendental aspects of the twentieth century were the phenomenon of socialization of the press (1974–1980); the negative implications of military intervention in the exercise of free press; the difficult stage of crisis and challenges for the media during the government of Alberto Fujimori (1990–2000); and the technological revolution of the media, with electronic editions of newspapers coexisting since 1995 with the traditional paper editions.

Table 9.1 Household Media Equipment, 2005–2007 (in % of Households)

	2005	2007	Variation (%)
Number of homes	6,148,800	6,755,361	9.8
Radio	82.7	72.0	−12.2
Color TV	66.5	60.9	−9.8
Personal computer (and/or notebook)	7.8	14.8	89.0
Internet	3.5	6.0	71.0
Sound equipment	n.a.	29.3	
Cable TV	9.7	15.8	6.1
Broadband	n.a.	9.3	
Mobile phone subscribers (millions)	19.25	42.0	22.75
Fixed telephone lines (millions)	26.45	28.0	1.55

Sources: INEI (2008b, 2008c); Telefónica Press Release (August 1, 2008)

Table 9.2 Media Consumption (Lima only), 2007

Media	Time (minutes)
Newspapers	28*
Radio	168
Television	208
Internet	52

Source: Ibope-Time Peru (2007)
Note: *Kantar Media Research (2008)

Table 9.3 Media Advertising in Peru, 2007

Media	US$ millions
Television	147
Newspapers	75
Street	42
Radio	39
Cable	19
Magazines	10
Internet	7
Other (direct mailing, cinema)	5
Total	344

Source: CPI (2008)

Legal Structure

The media abide by dispositions made explicitly in the Peruvian Constitution and the penal and Civil Codes. There are no specific laws for the press, but there are general laws to which the press must abide as any other enterprise operating in free competitiveness.

Various articles within the Peruvian Constitution (1993) are related to the right to information: in Title I, From Person and the Society; in Chapter I regarding the Fundamental Rights of the Person: Article 2.3 specifies that there is no felony of opinion; Article 2.4 recognizes the right to the freedom of information, opinion, expression and diffusion of thinking through oral or written word or image, by any mean of social communication, without previous authorization nor censorship or obstacles of any kind, under the responsibilities of the law. The felonies committed through the use of books, the press and other means of social communication are typified in the Penal Code and are judged in a common forum. Any action which suspends or closes any expression or which poses an obstacle to its free circulation can be regarded as a felony. The right to inform and give an opinion include those of the founding means of communication.

Clause 2.5 recognizes access to public information with the exception of information which affects the personal privacy and those explicitly excluded by law or due to national security reasons. Clause 2.6 refers the same restrictions for information services, which whether computerized or not, public or private, should not supply information which affect personal or family privacy issues.

These proposals are complemented by Clause 2.7, which guarantees the right to "Honor and good reputation, to personal and family privacy as well as to one's own voice and self-image," and consequently has the right to be rectified in case it is affected by inaccurate information through the media (Article 2, Clause 7). Clause 2.8 guarantees the freedom of intellectual, artistic, technical and scientific creation, as well as the ownership of such creations and their products.

Clause 2.10 protects the right to secrecy and the invulnerability of its communications and private documents, and Clause 2.18 to maintain professional secrecy. The Constitution includes the media within the educational area. The last paragraph of Article 14 of Chapter II of Social and Economical Rights states that "Social media should collaborate with the State in matters related to education and the development of morals and culture." In terms of ownership, The Constitution guarantees that mass media "are not to be the object of exclusiveness, monopoly or direct or indirect takings, by the State or private entities" (Title III, Chapter I, Article 61).

Organization and Financing

There are about eighty-six newspapers distributed in the country: twenty-five in the capital and sixty-one in the provinces. Although the number of titles is higher in the provinces, the printing volume of national newspapers dominates the market. Only *El Peruano* has national distribution; it is the official newspaper and is financed by the state. The other newspapers belong to private families or are part of media groups.

Among media corporations are the following entities: The Editing Enterprise *El Comercio* SA is owned by the Miró Quesada family and has a quality newspaper, *El Comercio* (1839), a serious-economic newspaper, *Peru.21*, a popular newspaper, *Trome* (2001), an economic newspaper, *Gestión* (acquired in 2007), the website, www.elcomercioperu.com.pe, an informative channel on cable television, Canal N (1999), Uno Directo (marketing, databases), Zetta Comunicadores (pre-press), Amauta (printing) and open television with TV América (70 percent of shares). Empresa Periodística Nacional SAC (national journalistic enterprise). EPENSA is a corporate group formed by *Ojo* (1968), *El Bocón* (1994), *Ajá* (1994) and *Correo* (1962). Editora Sindesa is responsible for the publication of *Expreso* and *Extra* newspapers. The Corporación Gestión formed by *CPN* specializes in news and *Gestión Médica*. La República SA group edits *El Popular*, *Libero* and *La República* newspapers and has participation in open television with TV América (30 percent of shares). Editora Perú, a Peruvian enterprise of editiorial services, edits *El Peruano* newspaper, owns Radio Nacional, Radio Televisión Peruana and the Agencia Andina de Noticias.

According to Apoyo, an opinion research and marketing company, it can be stated that with innovations in newspapers a new classification has been adopted. Serious traditional (e.g., *El Comercio*, *La República*, *Expreso*, *El Peruano*) are quality newspapers, with years of circulation, national character and high prices. The serious economic (*Correo*, *Perú.21*), also have quality, but are more recent and have lower prices (between 50 cents and 1 sol). The tabloids (*Trome*, *Ajá*, *El Popular*, *Ojo*, *Extra*) maintain their usual features of light content at low prices (50 cents). The sports-oriented (*Libero*, *El Bocón*, *Todo Sport*) and the economic (*Gestión*) constitute specialized press areas.

Circulation and Format

In terms of circulation, newspapers adopt diverse modalities. Most national newspapers distribute most of their copies in metropolitan Lima, according to auditing studies conducted by KPMG on the main national circulation newspapers between January 1 and June 30, 2007. *El Comercio* allocates only 7.67 percent of its copies to the provinces. *Trome* sends approximately 14.46 percent and *Perú.21* 22 percent of its total number of copies. According to KPMG, *Correo* (part of the EPENSA group) has a different distribution, allocating 60 percent of its copies to the provinces and *El Popular*, belonging to the La República group, distributes almost 75 percent of its copies outside metropolitan Lima (see Table 9.4).

Most national and dailies are morning newspapers using a tabloid format, with the exception of *El Comercio* in Lima, *La Industria* in Trujillo and *El Pueblo* in Arequipa, which use Berliner or standard format. The satellite daily from Trujillo is the only evening paper.

Other notable publishing activities include *Correo* with an edition in Lima and thirteen dailies in the Peruvian coast and highland provinces, and *La Industria* in the northern coast, with two editions in Trujillo and Chimbote. *La República* has four offices, three in the provinces—Iquitos, Arequipa and Chiclayo—and one in Lima. There is no such thing as free, general information press in Peru, just newsletters and institutional magazines. The only free magazine—first among readers—is *Cable TV*, from Telefónica. Dailies are published seven days a week; some include Sunday supplements, which increase their prices.

In Lima, *Trome* has the highest circulation and reaches 13.8 percent of the population, followed by *El Comercio* (7.7 percent), *Ojo* (6.0 percent), *El Popular* (4.0 percent), *Perú.21* (3.8 percent),

Table 9.4 Top Five Dailies According to Circulation, 2007

Title	Place of publication	Type	Publisher	Average circulation
Trome	Lima	Tabloid	Empresa Editora El Comercio	228,600
Ojo	Lima	Tabloid	EPENSA	149,059
Correo	Lima/Provinces	Quality-economic	EPENSA	135,738
El Comercio	Lima	Quality	Empresa Editora El Comercio	109,982
Ajá	Lima	Tabloid	EPENSA	83,000

Source: KPMG (2007)

Ajá (3.6 percent) and *Correo* (3.4 percent) (CPI 2008). *El Comercio* is the only daily with a well-differentiated Sunday readership, which is doubled on Sundays. Sports dailies are characterized by most people reading on Mondays each week.

According to CPI (2008) the majority of readers from Lima are between 26 and 37 years old (754,600), followed by another large group between ages 38 and 50 (658,200). Also, 48 percent of the readers belong to the economically active population (EAP).

All groups are correlated to fit the three socioeconomic levels among the public. *El Comercio* addresses high and medium level readers (63 percent), *Correo* is read in all three sectors in similar proportions, and *La República* and *Perú.21* are predominantly read in the two highest sectors. *Trome*, *Ojo*, *Ajá* and *Popular* address lower-level readers (85 percent). Sports newspapers also have their greatest number of readers at this level.

Some interesting data regarding the Peruvian press as of 2007 are as follows. Advertising income increased by 10 percent. The press industry of dailies and magazines represents 24.7 percent of the advertisement market, the second largest media market in the country. The most important dailies are constantly revamping themselves, and Lima remains the most important market.

Increase in Advertising Income

Advertising in dailies grew to $75 million in 2007 (an increase of 10 percent), a smaller increase compared to 2006 (13 percent) (Zeta 2007a). Dailies still hold their position as the second-largest advertising medium capturing 21.8 percent of the total investment. Over time, the income has declined, as the industry received 28.4 percent of all advertising dollars in 2003 dropping to 21.8 percent, in 2007, indicating an overall decline in growth.

Advertising investment in supplements found within dailies is at 8 percent (CPI 2008). Magazines have grown with advertisement investment reaching $10 million in 2007, as opposed to $8 million in 2006 (Zeta 2007a). Television is the major competitor for advertising. *El Comercio* is the daily with more than 50 percent of the advertising income in the journalism market in 2007. The income of dailies in the group grew by 28 percent and its sales by 9.9 percent.

New Developments

In 2007 the most important dailies conducted several innovations including a change of owners, decentralized editions, lower prices and a subscription service. The El Comercio group acquired *Gestión*, a daily specializing in economics and businesses. The group increased its sales by subscription and started the first decentralization of its publishing house, establishing its first office in Chiclayo, in the north of the country. This decentralization will allow the group to diversify to their readers outside the capital city and to have more readers in the north of the country, where there is a predominant reading of other national dailies such as *Ajá* from EPENSA and *El Popular* from La República. *El Tiempo*, from Piura, lowered its price to 50 cents to compete with the local edition of *Correo*, a pioneer of serious-economic press in Peru.

The tabloids *Trome* from the Comercio group and *Ojo* from the EPENSA group have the highest number of copies printed in the country. *Trome* has a weekly circulation of 1,600,246 prints and *Ojo*'s circulation is 1,043,417. The quality dailies' circulation includes a weekly printing of 769,880 copies, *Correo* reaching 950,172 copies in its 13 weekly editions and *Perú.21* 500,747 in a secondary distribution.

Most dailies are distributed through individual sale, but due to the difficult situation undergone by the press, some companies have chosen subscriptions as a way of developing reader loyalty. In 2004, *El Comercio* implemented a subscription system in the city of Lima, where most of its circulation is located. In 2007 its number of subscribers grew from 40,027 to 44,701, which constitute 40.7 percent of the distribution of the paper.

As of 2008, the El Comercio group was still consolidating its subscription system. In 2007 *Gestión* distributes 31.7 percent of its copies by subscription. Subscription to the printed edition allows the reader to receive the daily first thing in the morning, Monday to Friday, within the distribution areas.

In terms of online editions, there are fifty-seven digital editions in Peru; eighteen are based in Lima and thirty-nine in the provinces. There has been an increase in the number of digital editions in the country. In summary, the Peruvian press is a growing sector, constantly innovating and continuing the transformation into the digital era which the contemporary society now requires.

Legal Structure of Broadcasting

Peruvian radio and television are governed by specialized laws. The Law for Radio and Television (2004) is the most current, with new rulings added in 2005. Work permits are issued by the Ministry of Transport and Communications—General Direction of Telecommunications. The law prevents monopolist positions. Article 22 of the norms for the holding of titles of authorizations specifies that radio and television cannot be objected to exclusiveness, monopoly or taking, whether direct or indirectly, by the State or private entities. Taking is described by the present law as a circumstance in which a natural or juridical person owns more than 30 percent of the technologically available frequencies, assigned or not, in a same frequency band within a same locality for television broadcasting and 20 percent for radio broadcasting. In regards to the counting of the number of frequencies, one juridical person is equivalent to two or more juridical people who have as common shareholders, associates, director or manager one person or relative who is within the second degree of consanguinity. Following the same objective, Articles 27 and 28 describe the transfer of titular rights and transference of shares, participations or others.

The Law of Radio and Television in Article 24 regarding Foreign Participation specifies that only people of Peruvian nationality or juridical people constituted and living in Peru can hold titles for authorizations and licenses. Participation of foreigners in juridical people who are title holders of authorizations and licenses cannot exceed 40 percent of the total number of participations or shares of social capital. Additionally these people must also be title holders or have participations or shares in broadcasting companies in their countries of origin. The foreign person, neither directly nor through a one-person company, can hold the title for authorization or license.

Article 20 of the Rules of the Law of Radio and Television (2005) allows for foreign participation in areas of geographical frontier. Juridical people with foreign participation cannot hold titles for authorizations to conduct broadcasting services, within the frontier localities of their shareholders, partners or associates' countries of origin, except in case of public necessity authorized by supreme decree approved by the Council of Ministers. This disposition is not applicable to juridical people with foreign participation who have two or more current authorizations, as long as they are within the same band of frequencies.

Article 26 of the same Rules states among the causes to deny a request failure from foreign participation to comply to the requisites established in the law that:

- Foreign participation, which directly or indirectly, exceeds 40 percent of social capital or participations of the soliciting juridical person.
- The natural or juridical foreign person is not the title holder or does not have participation in shares in broadcasting companies in his/her country of origin.

Radio

Even though Peruvians have access to new technologies, radio manages to capture a massive audience, greater than any other media. In Peru, radio is one of the most important means of communication, socially speaking, because it is easy to access and it reaches all the places with complex geography. Radio, like all media in Peru, is mostly private and offers the most complete coverage nationwide. OAX was the first radio broadcaster in Peru, in 1925.

Organization and Financing

In June 2008, the Ministry of Transport and Communications reported there were 2,229 authorized radio stations in Peru. Modulated-frequency (FM) stations are dominant (1,687) against medium-wave (AM) stations (453) and short-wave (89). Lima and Callao have 228 stations (10.2 percent). Junin and Cusco are cities with 196 and 154 stations, respectively. The number of stations has decreased since 2006, when there were 2,566. Until 1993, the number of AM stations predominated, but in 1994 the growth of FM increased, while broadcasters of medium and short wave have maintained themselves at 2001 levels.

FM transmission is dominant at 73 percent of all stations; some stations re-transmit through modulated amplitude or AM-RPP, Felicidad, Panamericana, Radiomar, Plus, La Inolvidable, CPN and Maria, with the sole purpose of better coverage of the national territory. Approximately 22 percent of the stations broadcast in AM; Del Pacífico and La Luz are among the most noted stations.

In 2007, a transition among broadcasters was observed. Radio A transformed itself into Radio Mix, and Radio Inca FM to Radio Top FM and have left their specialized genres – romantic and tropical music, respectively to transmit varied music. RPP is the radio service with the greater national audience, with 60 percent of its audience coming from outside the capital city. The same is true with Radio Moda and Radio Panamericana, with 50 percent and 56 percent audience from the provinces.

Radio is the fourth-largest medium in terms of advertising investment, reaching $39 million in 2007. The RPP group and the Peruvian Radio Corporation (Corporación Radial del Perú SAC) get almost 80 percent of the participation of the total investments. It is estimated that 10 percent of the investment in this media corresponds to local broadcasters in the provinces.

Programs and Audience Use

According to the CPI Market Report (2008), the average radio audience in the capital city reaches 14.9 percent of the people, with the largest audience from 6 a.m. to 12 noon. The same study points out stations with the most audience in Lima are RPP (news), Moda (reggae), Panamericana (salsa), Felicidad and Radio Mar Plus (salsa) (see Table 9.5).

Table 9.5 Top Radio Stations and Audience (Metropolitan Lima Only), 2008

Radio	Area of transmission	Owner or media group	Type	Market share in 2007 (%)
RPP	National	RPP	Private	1.9
Moda	National	Corporación Radial del Perú	Private	1.5
Felicidad	National	RPP	Private	1.0
Panamericana	National	Grupo Panamericana	Private	1.0
Radio Mar	National	Corporación Radial	Private	0.9

Source: Compiled by the author

Among the most important radio groups are the RPP Group (RPP noticias, Felicidad, Oxígeno, Studio 92, Corazón and La Mega) and the Peruvian Radio Corporation (Corporación Radial del Perú SAC) (La Inolvidable, Ritmo Romántica, Moda, Ñ, Radio Mar Plus, Top FM, Planeta).

Community radio also has a history in Peru. The National Radio Coordinator Coordinadora Nacional de Radio (CNR) comprises more than sixty broadcasters and production centers committed with the development and strengthening of democracy in diverse regions of Peru with a national and Latin American perspective. Another radio phenomenon is the birth of local district broadcasters. Radio stations in this category aim at being closer to their listeners, such as Radio Comas, and Radio San Borja, which try to identify themselves with people in their districts and surroundings.

Television

Television has been in Peru for over fifty years, having first appeared to a small audience in Lima on January 17, 1958. Up to 1980 there were only three channels; now there are seven open (free) channels as well as cable television.

Organization and Financing

In 2008, the Ministry of Transport and Communications reported there were 1,037 television stations, a growth of 11 percent compared to 2006. Regarding distribution as of June, 2008, 65.6 percent of the stations operated in the very high frequency (VHF) band and 34.4 percent in the ultra-high frequency (UHF) band. Lima and Callao both have 11.2 percent of the television frequencies, while Junín has 7.1 percent.

In Peru, there are several types of stations, including public service television, Channel 7—Televisión Nacional del Perú, which started in 1958. There are several free private television channels, with the date they began broadcasting listed after their names: Channel 2—Frecuencia Latina. Cia. Latinoamericana de Radiodifusión SA (1983); Channel 4—América Televisión. Cia. Peruana de Radiodifusión (1958); Channel 5—Panamericana Televisión (1958); Channel 9—Andina de Radiodifusión (1983); Channel 11—RBC Televisión; Channel 13— Red Global. All of these channels provide national coverage, except for RBC Televisión. There are regional channels such as Cia de Televisión cusqueña (Cusco), Tele San Juan, Amazonica TV (iquitos) and UCV channel 15 (Trujillo). As for pay television via cable there are two channels, Cable Mágico and Canal N.

Cable television in Peru was inaugurated in 1999. The country currently has Canal N, an informative channel and Cable Mágico, belonging to Telefónica Perú, which has a sports division Cable Mágico Deportes and another one which is more varied, Plus TV. Visión 20 is the most recent entertainment channel.

According to the Ministry of Transport and Communication, as of 2008, cable television had 722,177 subscribers, but great differences are observed between the capital (568,399 subscribers) and the provinces. The most important provinces like Arequipa and Cusco have only 28,872 and 29,980 subscribers, respectively. CPI (2008) reports that 30 percent of all households have cable nationwide; but while metropolitan Lima has 48.8 percent, the urban interior has only 18.1 percent. Similar differences can be observed among socioeconomic levels.

Television is the medium which receives the most advertising investment. In the latest available CPI Report (2008), total television advertising reached $147 million—an increase of approximately 21 percent compared to 2006. América TV is the channel which receives the largest volume of advertising, followed by ATV and Frecuencia Latina. The three channels concentrate 65 percent of the total investments in television. Cable television receives advertising investments totaling $19 million, an increase of 26.7 percent favored by advertisers to place their advertisements in more segmented spaces.

According to Apoyo (2007), almost all Peruvians aged 12 to 70 watch television at least once a week and four out of five citizens watch it every day. Television viewing is the highest in the evening hours from 8 p.m. to 12 midnight.

Programs and Audience Use

In the study of television usage in Peru conducted by the Universidad de Lima in July 2008, it is easy to see that news programs are the most watched and economics program the ones with the least audience. National television production includes news programs, journalistic programs, comic programs, sports programs and mini-series. The programs with the highest audiences are news programs, comic programs and journalistic programs (see Table 9.6). Preferences for programs are related to socioeconomic standing.

Table 9.6 Television Audience Program Habits: I Watch . . . (%), 2008

	Answer		
Programs	Yes	No	No Answer
News programs	97.4	2.3	0.3
Comedy programs	74.2	25.8	0
Movies	73.6	26.4	0
Cultural programs	70.8	28.7	0.5
Political programs	69.2	30.8	0
Documentaries	67.2	32.7	0.1
Talk shows	66	33.9	0.2
Entertainment programs	64	35.8	0.2
Quiz shows	61.4	38.2	0.5
Programs about tourism and traveling	61.1	38.5	0.4
Music programs	55.7	44.3	0
Sports programs	55.3	44.4	0.3
Cookery programs	53.3	46.7	0
Soap operas	52.8	47.2	0
Series and mini-series	48.1	51.9	0
Health programs	47.3	52.2	0.4
Noon magazines	39.7	60.2	0.2
Children's programs	39.5	60.3	0.3
Programs about economics or businesses	38.5	60.8	0.6

Source: Grupo de Opinión Publica (GOP) (2008) *Barómetro Social. La Televisión en el Perú 2, Lima y Callao 12 y 13 de julio 2008*. Lima: Universidad de Lima

New Developments

Work is being done to implement a new system of terrestrial digital television. A multi-sector commission, named in February 2007, is charged with studying the best option of standard terrestrial digital television to be used in Peru, considering technical and economic aspects as well as applicability to the reality of the situation, and to provide a recommendation to the Ministry of Transport and Communications. There are three systems or technical norms under consideration: the American ATSC, the European DVB-T and the Japanese ISDB-T. In June, 2007, a work plan was given to the Minister of Transport and Communications (see www.concortv.net/concortv/content/view/250/67).

The timetable for the definition of the system to be used has been postponed several times. The Executive Power granted an extension on September 14, 2008 of 90 days to the deadline assigned to the multi-sector commission in charge of presenting the recommendation of a standard of terrestrial digital television (TDT) to be adopted by Peru, to be computed starting in October. The Ministry of Transport and Communications explained that this decision was taken upon request by the embassies of the People's Republic of China and of Brazil in Peru, both of whom were interested in having their respective standards, DTMB and ISDB-T, considered in the evaluations by the multi-sector commission. The vice-minister of communications, Cayetana Aljovín, declared that the implementation of TDT in Peru, whose process is said to begin in 2009, will be fully established in a period between ten and fifteen years (see www.cronicaviva.com.pe/content/view/56707/36).

The Internet

Legal Structure

The Comisión multisectorial para el Desarrollo de la Sociedad de la Información (CODESI: Multi-sector Commission for the Development of the Society of Information) has developed a plan for the information society in Peru, approved through Supreme Decree no. 031-2006-PCM in 2006. The plan aims at developing five strategic objectives: infrastructure of telecommunications; development of human capacities; development and applications of information and communication technologies (ICTs) in social programs; citizen participation and development; production and electronic government (Zeta 2007b) This digital agenda will allow measureable progress as well as supervision of the proposed goals. The master plan specifies the actions, performance measures, people responsible for the execution and goals for the years 2006, 2010 and 2014.

Basic Online Data and Online Use

The introduction of the Internet in Peru happened in the early 1990s. The first network was the Peruvian Scientific Net on December 10, 1991. Internet maintains a sustained growth in Peru. According to the INEI (2008c), 6.9 percent of Peruvian households have access to Internet. In the period of January–March 2008, 26.9 percent of the population older than 6 years of age have used the Internet, 26.2 percent used the Internet daily, 55.5 percent have access to the web once a week, and 18.3 percent use the Internet once or twice a month.

Internet use is higher among males (30 percent) than females (22.85 percent), and 49.3 percent of the population between 19 and 24 are the heaviest users of the Internet, followed by young people between 12 and 18 (44.8 percent). Children aged 6 to 11 years are the next highest group of users at 18 percent, followed by adults at 4.4 percent.

In terms of where people use the Internet, 74.8 percent of users connect at an Internet café, 16.9 percent from home, 12.5 percent from work and 3.7 percent from school. The average user uses the Internet to contact other people, chatting, or by sending and receiving emails (78.5 percent). Obtaining of information ranks second (74.7 percent), followed by entertainment (42 percent), formal education (6.5 percent), banking (4.1 percent) and transactions with state organizations and public authorities (3.0 percent).

These results vary according to a user's ages and interests. People with higher education use the Internet to obtain information, while a high percentage of the population with primary education (77.9 percent) uses it for entertainment. The growth of the Internet is still very slow. The incorporation of ICT is unequal and the way to the information of society is impacted by differences within the country (Zeta 2007b). According to INEI (2008c), the ownership of computers is still low in households in Peru: approximately 15.5 percent of all Peruvian households have computers. Lima has a higher percentage (26.6 percent); in other urban areas the percentage is at 20.7 percent, while in the rural areas it is only 1.2 percent. However, 93 percent of Peruvian households have at least one computer, while 7 percent have two or more. Education, ethnicity and geographical areas are other factors that reflect differences among Internet users.

The technology with the highest penetration is the cellular telephone system; 51.5 percent of Peruvian households have access to cellular phones. As for fixed telephone lines, 30 percent of households have a fixed telephone, but the growth rate is much smaller at just 2.2 percent based on data from the first quarter of 2008. Apoyo (2007) offers some interesting information on the profile of the typical net surfer from Lima: one out of every four users access the Internet through their cell phone.

State of Convergence: The Media on the Internet

The convergence of the media started in Peru in 1995. The press was the first pioneer, and as of 2008 all traditional media can be found on the Internet (see Figure 9.1).

The Press

The traditional press adopted technical support and is present on the Internet. *Caretas* was the first magazine to appear on the Internet in 1995. *La Encuesta* was the first electronic daily in Peru to appear in 1996. *La República*, *El Peruano* and *Gestión* were the first traditional dailies to have

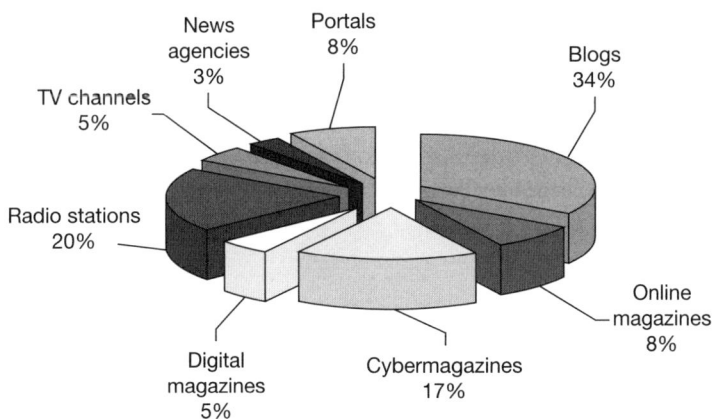

Figure 9.1 Presence of Peruvian Media on the Internet, 2006

Source: Yezers'ka (2006)

136 • Rosa Zeta de Pozo

Table 9.7 Growth of Press on the Internet and Cybermedia, 1997–2004

Year	1997	1998	1999	2000	2001	2003	2004
Number of dailies	11	19	24	25	28	30	38

Source: Yezers'ka (2006)

an electronic edition, also in 1996. *Expreso, Ajá, Ojo, Correo, El Bocón, La Razón* and *El Chino* all began in 1998 (see Table 9.7).

El Tiempo, a daily from Piura, was the first provincial newspaper on the Internet in 1997. Other provincial dailies which later entered the Internet are *Arequipa al Día* (2000) and *Satélite* and *La Industria*, from Trujillo in 2001. Andina, the online news agency, has been on the Internet since the year 2000, and news agency Perú.com since 2002. La Red, from the Peruvian Scientific Net, appeared in 1996, and Peru.com, made its appearance in 2007.

Although the fact that they are free constitutes the predominant feature of online editions in Peruvian dailies, some Peruvian dailies and magazines maintain paid subscriptions: *Perú.21, Gestión, Etiqueta Negra* and *Caretas* in Lima, and *Hoy*, a daily in Huánuco. By 2007, fifty-seven digital editions of Peruvian dailies were to be found on the net, eighteen in Lima and thirty-nine in the provinces. There has been an increase in the number of digital editions in the inner parts of the country.

Regarding online journalism, the progress of existing editions is more important than the increment of editions in provinces. *El Comercio* and *Perú.21* have incorporated blogs in their editions, and have implemented news sharing. *La República* has included video and other multimedia sections. The insertion of online advertising began timidly with *El Comercio* and *Correo*. Dailies of both groups have increased their time-spent-reading rates. *El Comercio* scored a monthly average of 1,099,280 readers in 2007. *Correo* registered an average of 374,480 readers as of February 2008.

Radio

Radio is also on the Internet. Lyudmyla Yezers'ka (2006) points out the existence of twenty-three services in 2004, of which only thirteen (56 percent) offer programming through Real Player. The most complete service is Radio Programas del Perú (RPP), on the Internet since 1996 (see www.rpp.com.pe) and also available via cable (Channel 6).

Television

The five open national channels are available on the Internet: Channel 7, Televisión Nacional del Perú; Channel 2, Frecuencia Latina; Cia, Latinoamericana de Radiodifusión SA (2002); Channel 4, América Televisión (1998); Cia, Peruana de Radiodifusión; Channel 5, Panamericana Televisión (2001); and Channel 9, Andina de Radiodifusión.

Conclusion

The media in Peru are in the process of continuing development. The press is innovating itself; editions are decentralized, prices are reduced, and subscriptions are seen as a system of distribution. The press groups among which there is more competition (Grupo El Comercio, EPENSA, Grupo La República) are strengthened and have newspapers of quality, popular and specialized for all sectors. Publishers are working to increase the number of readers of their digital editions and are starting to take advantage of online advertising.

Digital radio is increasing the system of real audio and continues to be the top free media, while traditional television is diversified as pay per view through cable and satellite. Terrestrial digital television will begin distribution in 2009 and should be completed by 2015.

Directions for Future Research

There are four important areas for future research on Peruvian media:

1. The media must take better advantage of the possibilities afforded by new technologies. There are many opportunities for development including: interactivity, for the knowledge of the public and the generating of new content; hypertextuality, for in-depth information; real-time, ubiquity, greater access to sources, multimediality, etc.
2. Generation of quality content for a multiplicity of supports. We need quality content for terrestrial digital television, mobile applications, and future integrated systems.
3. Training of professionals for the era of knowledge is needed. Peru needs professionals who can handle technology, are analytical, and have the criteria to evaluate information and entertainment products for both local and national distribution. Products that are both relevant and attractive are needed for all types of support, essentially for Internet and mobile applications. In Peru there is a 16 percent penetration in Internet and more than 50 percent of the population has access to mobile telephones, so there is much potential to be realized.
4. In the midst of globalization, the local context cannot be neglected. Local aspects remain important, and deserve more study.

References

ANDA News. (2007). *Revista no. 69, diciembre 2007*. Lima: Asociación Nacional de Anunciantes (ANDA).

Apoyo. (2007). *Marketing Data no. 94*: Perfil del Internauta Limeño 2007. *Marketing Data no, 101*: IGM Hábitos y Actitudes hacia la TV 2007. Lima: Apoyo.

El Comercio. (2008). *Informe de los directivos del Grupo El Comercio*. Lima: El Comercio.

Consejo Consultivo de Radio y Televisión. (2008). *Especiales, TV digital terrestre*. Retrieved October 15, 2008 from www.concortv.gob.pe/es/index.php?option=com_content&view=article&id=153&Itemid=48.

CPI (Compañía peruana de estudios de mercados y opinión pública). (2008). Market Report. Tendencias de los Medios en el 2007. Lima: CPI.

EPENSA. (2008). *Informe de los directivos del Grupo Epensa*. Lima: EPENSA.

Grupo de Opinión Publica (GOP). (2008). *Barómetro social. La televisión en el Perú 2, Lima y callao 12 y 13 de julio 2008*. Lima: Universidad de Lima.

Ibope-Time Peru. (2007). *Consumo de medios*. Lima: Ibope.

INEI (Instituto Nacional de Estadística e Informática). (2008a). Press release. Resultados del XI Censo nacional de Población, no 77, June, 2008. Lima: INEI.

INEI. (2008b). *Perú compendio estadístico 2007*. Lima: INEI.

INEI. (2008c). *Las tecnologías de la información y la comunicación en los hogares enero-marzo 2008. National households survey—Technical Report no. 02*. Lima: INEI.

Kantar Media Research. (2008). Data collected by the World Association of Newspapers (WAN).

KPMG. (2007). *Resultados de Auditoría de Tiraje, presentados en Reunión convocada por la Sociedad de Empresas Periodísticas del Perú (SEPP), el Consejo de Usuarios de Medios Impresos (CUSEMI) y la Asociación Nacional de Anunciantes (ANDA)*.

Ministerio de Transportes y Comunicaciones. (2004). Ley de Radio y Televisión.

Ministerio de Transportes y Comunicaciones. (2005). Reglamento de la ley de Radio y Televisión.

Ministerio de Transportes y Comunicaciones. (2007). Plan de trabajo de la Comisión Multisectorial TV Digital Terrestre. Retrieved October 15, 2008 from www.mtc.gob.pe/portal/tdt/plan.html.

Ministerio de Transportes y Comunicaciones. (2008). *Estadísticas de los servicios públicos de telecomunicaciones, 2T2008*. Lima: Ministerio de de Transportes y Comunicaciones.

Perú. (1993). *Constitución Política 1993.* Lima: El Peruano.

Yezers'ka, L. (2006). The cybermedia in Peru (Los Cibermedios en Perú). *En Revista Latina de Comunicación Social, 61,* 1–19. Retrieved July 10, 2006 from www.ull.es/publicaciones/latina/200606Lyudmyla.pdf.

Zeta, R. (2002). Los medios de Comunicación en el Perú. *Comunicación.* Piura: School of Communication, Universidad de Piura, 67–95.

Zeta, R. (2007a). Peru. In WAN, *World press trends 2007* (pp. 564–572). Paris: ZenithOptimedia.

Zeta, R. (2007b). *El Perú en el marco de la sociedad mundial de la información. EPTIC online from Brasil.* Vol. 9, no. 1. (January–April 2007). Retrieved October 7, 2008, from www2.eptic.com.br/arquivos/Revistas/v.%20IX,n. percent201,2007/4 percent20RosaPozo.pdf.

Zeta, R. (2008). Peru. In WAN, *World press trends 2008* (pp. 680–690). Paris: ZenithOptimedia.

10
The Chilean Media Landscape

Cristóbal Benavides
Universidad de los Andes, Santiago, Chile

Maria Ignacia Errázuriz
Universidad de los Andes, Santiago, Chile

David Kimber
Universidad de los Andes, Santiago, Chile

Isabel Santa María
Universidad de los Andes, Santiago, Chile

and Aldo van Weezel
Jönköping International Business School, Sweden

Introduction

Chile is one of the leading countries in Latin America. Although its population of 16.4 million is small compared to other countries in the region, its economy is strong and moves rapidly in the direction of that of developed countries. Per capita GDP was $8,875 in 2006 and inflation levels are low. Real GDP growth has fluctuated between 4 percent and 6 percent in the period 2003–2006. (Information obtained from *The Economist*, 2008.)

After seventeen years under a military regime, Chile returned to democracy in 1990 and now has a presidential system. Since then, the country has been ruled by a center-left coalition, which has continued implementing the liberal economy initially introduced by the military government in the 1980s. Since the late 1990s, Chile has become one of the most stable democracies in the region.

Chile has opened its economy via free trade agreements with the United States, the European Union, Canada, Mexico, South Korea and China. It is one of the main copper producers in the world, with copper representing over 55 percent of total Chilean exports. Fresh fruit, accounting for only 4.1 percent of the total, ranks second. Other export products are salmon and wine, the latter well known all over the world. The most important markets for Chilean products are the United States, Japan and China, while the country's main suppliers are the United States, Argentina, Brazil and China.

Television

Television is the most important mass medium in Chile in terms of consumption and advertising expenditure. The penetration rate of free-to-air (FTA) television reaches almost 100 percent and the average number of television sets per home is 2.3 (Consejo Nacional de Televisión (CNTV), 2005). Television sets are located mainly in the living and dining areas and the master bedroom. The average consumption time of television programs is 3 hours and 4 minutes per day (CNTV, 2005). In terms of advertising, FTA television had 48.2 percent of the advertising market share ($458 million) in 2007. Of this amount, 27 percent corresponds to product placement and other kinds of non-traditional advertising.

Television is available on different distribution platforms. Free-to-air television is the most common platform. Cable television and direct broadcast satellite (DBS) has a penetration rate of 29.5 percent. Finally, new distribution technologies such as Internet Protocol Television (IPTV) have launched in the country in recent years.

The majority of television networks broadcast in the VHF band, which has room for eight channels. The UHF band fits forty channels, but at present there are about fifteen UHF stations throughout Chile because of the small size of the market. There are no legal restrictions regarding ownership of television stations, but the company must be based in Chile and its top executives must be Chilean nationals (Law 19,277 of 1994).

The universities were the first to obtain VHF spectrum licenses for television broadcasting. These licenses were granted for an unlimited period of time. The Pontificia Universidad Católica de Valparaíso was assigned Channel 5 (UCV) in 1957; the Pontificia Universidad Católica de Chile received Channel 13 (UCTV) in 1959; and the Universidad de Chile was assigned Channel 11 in 1960. Although Universidad de Chile still owns the license for Channel 11, the well-known businessman and leader of the center-right coalition, Sebastián Piñera, leased the license. The public service television—Televisión Nacional de Chile (TVN)—on Channel 7 did not appear until 1969. Currently, TVN and UCTV are the market leaders.

The military government passed a law in 1989 allowing the creation of private television networks that could apply for twenty-five years of renewable VHF and UHF licenses (Law 18,838 of 1989). Channel 9 was awarded to the Claro Group (Mega), Channel 4 belongs to the Mexican businessman Ángel González González (La Red) and Jaime Cuadrado, a former Channel 13 executive, acquired Channel 2 in 2005 (Telecanal). So far, Mega is the only private channel that has reached a level of rating similar to that of TVN and UCTV. The other channels usually average single-digit rating levels.

After the merger in 2005 of the two main cable operator systems—VTR and Metropolis Intercom—the largest share of the cable market is now concentrated in VTR, a single company. VTR specializes in offering the attractive 'triple play' package that includes television, telephony and broadband Internet. In December 2007, VTR's market share was 68.38 percent (848,803 subscribers). The second cable operator is Telefónica with 17.53 percent of the market (217,590 subscribers). Satellite television is in a distant third place. DirectTV, owned by Liberty Media, which also has a controlling share in VTR, has 8.21 percent of the market (101,916 subscribers). In fourth place is the DBS provider Telmex. In 2007 it acquired the Chilean company ZAP TV, which has 4.13 percent of the market (51,212 subscribers) (Subsecretaría de Telecomunicaciones (SUBTEL), 2008).

Television Programming and Consumption

The most viewed blocks of programming from Monday through Friday are before 9 a.m., between 3 and 7 p.m., and between 8 p.m. and 12 midnight—the last period being prime time. These blocks concentrate the largest share of advertising expenditure, which peaks at 9 p.m. when the main news broadcasts start (CNTV, 2005).

Although FTA television is considered the most important source of entertainment and information, the level of dissatisfaction has risen: 48.5 percent of respondents claim they are little satisfied, while 10.3 percent say they are not satisfied at all (CNTV, 2005). The TV Quality Index developed by Mir, Errázuriz, Santa María and Kimber (2006) confirmed these initial findings. Based on rating and content analysis, the authors found that Chilean television is mediocre when assessed by quality standards. Whereas talk shows and late-night shows are the worst-rated programs of all, journalistic programs are usually well evaluated (Mir et al., 2006). The latter include the main news broadcasts of UCTV and TVN, and special in-depth reports in the style of CBS's *60 Minutes* or BBC's *Panorama*—*Contacto* on UCTV and *Informe Especial* on TVN.

Telenovelas have a longstanding tradition on Chilean television. A *telenovela* usually lasts five months, which accounts for the fact that twice a year TVN and UCTV wage war over the *telenovelas*. The network that wins the battle for 8 p.m. is the one that usually leads the rating for the rest of the prime-time slot. However, from 2007, this situation seems to have changed since Mega and Chilevision began to produce their own *telenovelas*. Furthermore, Mega has also started to show local adaptations of US sitcoms such as *Married with Children* with remarkable success. Finally, a host of reality shows have become popular, as has happened in the rest of the world.

Paid television, which includes cable and DBS, shows mainly foreign programs, reaching its maximum audience during the week between 9 a.m. and 12 noon, between 3 and 7 p.m. and between 10 p.m. and midnight. In contrast to FTA television, the levels of satisfaction generated by paid television in the last few years have gone up from 59.1 percent to 69.3 percent (CNTV, 2005).

The Press

Newspapers

According to a report by the Asociación Nacional de la Prensa (2007) there are ninety-six newspapers in Chile, including dailies, periodicals and Sunday newspapers. The total daily circulation reaches 1.1 million, which corresponds to an average of 49.3 newspapers per thousand inhabitants. This is a low reach index albeit close to the average of the region.

Despite their low circulation and reach, newspaper brands seem to be fairly strong and keep the business profitable. Furthermore, 29.4 percent of advertising expenditure goes to this medium given that readers spend 30 minutes per day on newspapers. Figures for readership and circulation of some of the most important newspapers are shown in Table 10.1. Unfortunately the circulation of regional newspapers has not been audited.

El Mercurio has the highest circulation in Chile although it is the fourth newspaper in terms of readership. It is a traditional and conservative national newspaper and also the most prestigious and influential. It targets well-educated people and reaches a subscription level of 80 percent. Its main competitor is *La Tercera*, which has been trying to reposition itself from middle-market to up-market reader segments. Its focus is on political news, with a permanent search for journalistic scoops. *La Tercera*'s readers are usually younger than *El Mercurio*'s, and its efforts in recent years

Table 10.1 Readership and Circulation of Newspapers, January–June 2007

Newspaper	Readership	Circulation	Percentage of total circulation	Ownership
La Cuarta	510,325	146,615	17.41	Copesa
Las Últimas Noticias	423,984	144,320	17.14	El Mercurio
Publimetro	400,928	108,934	12.94	MTG (Sweden)
El Mercurio	372,475	166,698	19.8	El Mercurio
La Tercera	367,017	137,179	16.29	Copesa
La Hora	266,006	96,213	11.43	Copesa
La Segunda	74,687	32,000	3.8	El Mercurio
La Nación	31,520	10,000	1.19	Chilean State
Total	2,446,942	841,959	100	

Source: Asociación Nacional de la Prensa (2007)
Note: Readership and circulation reflect weekly averages

have concentrated on increasing subscription by offering very flexible schemes (e.g. weekend subscriptions).

The most-read newspapers are *La Cuarta* and *Las Últimas Noticias*. These are popular tabloids addressing a down-market audience. The former aims at low-income readers and uses colloquial and picaresque language; its cover pages usually highlight crime stories and sports news. *Las Últimas Noticias* centers on television celebrities and gossip.

La Segunda is the only newspaper in Chile published in the afternoon on weekdays. It covers mainly politics and business events. Its readers are well educated and usually upper-middle class. *Publimetro* and *La Hora* are free daily newspapers. The former belongs to the Swedish publishing company Metro.

Finally, there are two daily financial newspapers. *Estrategia*, founded in 1978, was the leader for many years, but the *Diario Financiero*, founded in 1988, has successfully displaced it in the last few years. The *Diario Financiero* readership was 70,300 in 2006 compared with *Estrategia*'s 52,000.

Magazines

The magazine market in Chile is fairly small, underdeveloped and data are scarce. The market share for the most popular magazines is shown in Table 10.2.

Editorial Televisa publishes *Caras*—the bimonthly magazine with the highest circulation in the country. This publishing company is part of the Mexican media conglomerate Televisa and started after the parent company bought Editorial América in 1992. Its titles include *Vanidades*,

Table 10.2 Market Share of Magazines, 2007

Magazine	Market share (%)	Ownership
Caras	20.4	Televisa
Cosas	16.5	Tiempo Presente
TV Grama	8.5	Holanda Comunicaciones
Paula	6.9	Copesa
Qué Pasa	5.3	Copesa
Vanidades	4.6	Televisa
Vea	3.1	Holanda Comunicaciones

Source: I. Muñoz, Research Director of ANP, personal communication (January 8, 2008)

Cosmopolitan, PC Magazine, Conozca Más, Buen Hogar, Condorito, TV y Novelas, Popular Mechanics and *National Geographic*.

Editorial Tiempo Presente publishes *Cosas*. This magazine, founded in 1976, is also published in Peru, Ecuador and Bolivia. Its topics are similar to those of *Caras*, with an emphasis on social life and events, socialites, European royalty and the like. *Caras* usually includes interviews with Chilean politicians. It also publishes *Casas*, a monthly magazine dedicated to avant-garde decoration and house design.

Copesa publishes the magazines *Paula* and *Qué Pasa*. The former is a bimonthly magazine with a female, young-adult target. *Qué Pasa* is a current affairs weekly magazine with an emphasis on contingent Chilean politics. These magazines are both offered free to subscribers of the newspaper *La Tercera*.

TV Grama is published by Holanda Comunicaciones. This magazine centers on television celebrities and gossip. Holanda Comunicaciones also publishes *Ercilla, Publimark, Look, Miss 17, Elle* and *Cine-Grama*.

Radio

Radio is one of the largest media in Chile. There are about 175 AM stations and 1,319 FM stations. The number of radio stations on the AM band has been declining since the 1970s. Some 48 radio stations are based in Santiago and they are usually part of a country network. In addition, many of these are small community stations located throughout the country. Table 10.3 shows the main radio networks in Chile.

Audiences usually assess radio as being close to them and also very credible. Programs are very segmented and target specific interest groups. The daily reach of radio exceeds 85 percent (L. Pardo, President of Asociación de Radiodifusores de Chile, personal communication, January 10, 2008). Nearly all households have at least one radio receiver, and radio consumption is high in all income groups, reaching an average of 5 hours a day during weekdays. Daily reach is slightly higher for women (85.1 percent) than for men (81.9 percent), particularly in the morning. Also, the most important group for radio broadcasters is working-class people between the ages of 25 and 35. Peak time for radio consumption is around 1.30 p.m. and 9 p.m. during weekdays. After 9 p.m. radio audiences turn to television.

Table 10.3 Main Radio Networks in Chile, 2008

Radio networks	Ownership
Radio Play	UCTV (Channel 13)
Digital FM	El Mercurio
Zero, Duna, Carolina, Paula FM and Carino	Dial Group (Copesa)
Imagina, Rock & Pop, Concierto, Future, FM Dos, Corazón, Pudahuel, ADN, FM Hit and others	GLR Networks (PRISA, Spain)
Cooperativa and Universo	Compañía Chilena de Comunicaciones
Infinita, Tiempo, Romántica and Amadeus	Bezanilla Family
El Conquistador and Radio X	Molfino Group
Horizonte and Oasis	Julián García Reyes
Agricultura	Sociedad Nacional de Agricultura
Radio Bio-Bio	Mosciatti Family

Source: Compiled by the authors from public information

The Internet

Internet penetration has grown steadily in recent years (see Table 10.4). In 2007, the Internet penetration rate was almost double relative to 2000 with a total of 1.17 million connections. Telephone access has been replaced by broadband connections, which now account for 90 percent of the total. The growth of the market will be fueled by the decision of the two main Internet providers of tripling the bandwidth for their customers without increasing prices (Hrepich, 2008).

Two companies dominate the market for Internet service providers (ISPs) in Chile (SUBTEL, 2007a). Telefónica Internet offers DSL service and has a market share of 47.6 percent, followed by VTR, which offers Internet via cable with a market share of 29.9 percent. Other ISPs include Terra (6.9 percent), Telefónica del Sur (5.3 percent), Entel (4.3 percent) and Complejo Manufacturero de Equipos Telefónicos CMET (1.7 percent).

The Chilean version of the World Internet Project is one of the few studies available in Chile addressing Internet consumption and behavior (World Internet Project—Chile (WIP-Chile), 2006). According to this study, 40.2 percent of the population over 6 years of age uses the Internet. The average consumption time is 19.8 hours a week, up 5 hours more from 2003. The main reasons that users access the Internet have to do with personal hobbies, visiting public or state services websites, reading newspapers online, visiting company websites, listening to music and downloading MP3 files. Only 26.7 percent of users have bought something on the Internet and the main concerns regarding e-commerce are information privacy and security of the transactions. Finally, most Internet users spend less time watching television and more time reading newspapers.

The Asociación de Medios de Internet (AMI: Internet Media Association), a trade association founded in 2001 and now part of the Internet Advertising Board based in the United States, measures the online activities of its members. Table 10.5 summarizes the statistics of the most visited sites during January 2008 according to AMI.

Advertising

Advertising expenditures totaled $951 million in 2007, equivalent to 0.6 percent of Chile's GDP. Between the years 1995 and 2007, advertising expenditures grew at a compound annual growth rate (CAGR) of 1.9 percent (Table 10.6).

Despite the positive trend, advertising expenditures started to decline in 1998 reaching its lowest level in 2001. This situation was the result of the Asian crisis, which strongly affected the country in that period and had a deep impact on consumption. Since 2001 the advertising industry has been recovering, but growth rates have not yet reached their pre-crisis levels. At the end of 2006 the industry reached an expenditure level similar to that of 1997. The negative effects of the recession can also be seen when comparing the growth rate of advertising expenditure to the GDP growth rate between 1997 and 2004, where the former is consistently lower that the latter with the exception of 2002 (see Table 10.6). The situation appears to change in 2005.

Television and newspapers have traditionally attracted the largest share of advertising expenditure with an average of 46 percent and 32 percent between 1995 and 2007, respectively (see Table 10.7). By the end of the 1990s television was having problems attracting advertising, newspapers and radio increased its share of the advertising market. However, as from 2001 television recovered its pre-crisis levels whereas newspapers and radio are now in a worse position than before the crisis. This seems to point that the changes in advertising share are not only due to the crisis but also to increased media competition and changes in consumer behavior.

Table 10.4 Internet Access Statistics in Chile, 2000–2007

	Telephone access	Broadband	Total	Annual growth (%)	Penetration rate (%)
2000	577,809	7,680	585,489	n.a.	15.01
2001	631,404	66,723	698,127	19.24	17.69
2002	569,306	188,454	757,760	8.54	18.99
2003	483,773	352,234	836,007	10.33	20.24
2004	326,432	478,883	805,315	−3.67	19.29
2005	197,515	708,564	906,079	12.51	21.47
2006	115,436	979,012	1,094,448	20.79	25.67
2007*	112,922	1,054,489	1,167,411	n.a.	27.11

Source: SUBTEL (2007b)
Note: * As of second quarter.

Table 10.5 Top Fifteen Chilean Websites Ranked by Unique Visitors, January 2008

Ranking	Website	Page views	Unique visitors ('000)
1	Emol (El Mercurio)	269,677	5,130
2	Terra	247,804	3,986
3	123 (Entel)	38,246	1,278
4	UCTV (Canal 13)	52,216	1,269
5	VTR	9,303	980
6	Radio Cooperativa	9,511	877
7	TVN	23,905	828
8	Publiguías	13,119	787
9	Chilevisión	17,451	659
10	La Nación	5,228	649
11	Chile.com	6,362	576
12	Ibero American Radio Chile	6,201	531
13	Megavisión	2,145	221
14	Diario Financiero	1,220	121
15	Salo	2,813	104

Source: Asociación de Medios de Internet (2008)

Table 10.6 Advertising Expenditure in Chile, 1995–2006 (US$ millions) (constant 2007 prices)

	1995	1996	1997	1998	1999	2000	2001	2002	2003	2004	2005	2006	2007
TV	345	366	372	332	315	315	331	360	365	384	403	426	458
Newspapers	263	286	306	270	259	254	213	218	210	229	250	259	272
Radio	59	96	98	85	70	77	71	69	68	64	70	66	66
Magazines	26	47	39	35	26	37	31	30	29	27	27	27	30
Outdoors	50	50	56	49	47	49	47	46	49	60	72	78	90
Cinema	1	2	2	2	3	3	3	3	3	3	3	3	3
Cable TV									12	13	15	15	18
Internet									7	7	9	12	15
Total	745	848	873	773	720	735	695	727	742	787	848	886	951
ΔTotal (%)	10	14	2.5	−11.5	−6.9	2.1	−5.4	4.5	−0.5	4.9	7.8	4.5	7.3
ΔGDP (%)	11	7	7	3	−1	5	3	2	4	6	6	4	5

Source: Asociación Chilena de Agencias de Publicidad (2008)

Table 10.7 Advertising Expenditure by Medium, 1995–2007

	1995 (%)	1996 (%)	1997 (%)	1998 (%)	1999 (%)	2000 (%)	2001 (%)	2002 (%)	2003 (%)	2004 (%)	2005 (%)	2006 (%)	2007 (%)
Television	46	43	43	43	44	43	48	50	49	49	48	48	48
Newspapers	35	34	35	35	36	34	31	30	28	29	30	29	29
Radio	8	11	11	11	10	11	10	9	9	8	8	7	7
Outdoors	7	6	6	6	6	7	7	6	7	8	9	9	9
Magazines	4	6	4	5	4	5	5	4	4	4	3	3	3
Cable TV	n.a.	n.a.	n.a.	n.a.	n.a.	n.a.	n.a.	n.a.	2	2	2	2	2
Internet	n.a.	n.a.	n.a.	n.a.	n.a.	n.a.	n.a.	n.a.	1	1	1	1	1.6
Cinema	0.1	0.2	0.2	0.3	0.4	0.4	0.5	0.3	0.3	0.3	0.4	0.2	0.3

Source: Asociación Chilena de Agencias de Publicidad (2008)

Advertising is very concentrated in Chile: 80 percent of the expenditures are concentrated among ten specific media outlets; 47 percent in just three. In television, 66 percent of expenditure goes to the two main networks, i.e. TVN and UCTV. In newspapers, 52 percent goes to *El Mercurio*. In magazines, 56 percent is spent on five publications, i.e. *Caras, Cosas, TV Grama, Paula* and *Qué Pasa*. In radio, 55 percent goes to the former Iberoamerican Group (now GLR Networks), the most important holding in this sector.

The only exception to expenditure concentration appears to be the Internet. According to the IAB, there are 7 million users in the country, 33.74 percent of whom are over 35 years of age and make around 162 million visits (Netcraft Ltd., 2008). Internet shows the greater growth rate in the period 2003–2006. Due to the nature of this medium, advertising expenditure is aggregated by industrial sector.

Advertising Agencies

There are some thirty-seven advertising agencies that are members of the Asociación Chilena de Agencias de Publicidad (ACHAP: Chilean Advertising Agencies Association, 2008). Most of them operate their own media agency, research company and/or specialized services company, such as direct marketing. The most important advertising companies in the world operate in Chile— either with their own agencies or in association with local partners.

In 2006, the top ten advertising agencies in the country in terms of revenue were McCann Erickson, BBDO, Prolam Y&R, Lowe Porta Partners, Dittborn Unzueta, IDB/FCB SA, J. Walter Thomson, Leo Burnett Chile, 180 Grados and Zegers DDB (Triangulo Media Agency, 2008).

The most common sources of standardized information used by advertising and media agencies are Time Ibope (TV ratings measurements); Kantar Media Research (media audience and consumer behavior); Megatime (advertising expenditure on media); Search Marketing (data on radio/newspaper audience and consumer behavior); Interactive Advertising Bureau for Internet; and ACHAP. It is important to mention that, in the case of outdoor advertising, there is no standardized system to measure audience numbers, just information about vehicle circulation.

Media Conglomerates

Chile is a relatively small country and a handful of media conglomerates own most of the media outlets. In fact, 80 percent of advertising expenditure goes to no more than ten media groups, the most relevant of which will be briefly described below.

Catholic Church

The Catholic Church is an important player in the Chilean media market. It owns the national network Channel 13 (UCTV) and Channel 5 in Valparaíso. Channel 13 (UCTV) has been the market leader for many years and is controlled by the Pontificia Universidad Católica de Chile. Channel 5 (UCV) is a regional television station controlled by the Pontificia Universidad Católica de Valparaíso and available on cable television in the rest of the country.

Channel 13 launched a national radio network on February 27, 2006—Radio Play FM. It broadcasts in the frequencies of a defunct radio station, Radio Chilena, owned by the Archdiocese of Santiago. The radio's main target group is that of upper-middle-class young-adult women between 25 and 44 years old. Other holdings include Channel 13 Cable, available only via cable; its website, www.canal13.cl; a magazine, D13; and a film production unit.

Claro Group

Ricardo Claro is a well-known businessman in Chile. He is an important stakeholder in a number of large companies in the country, including a shipping company, Sudamericana de Vapores, Santa Rita Vineyards, Cristalerías Chile and Elecmetal. He also owns Mega, a national television network, a financial newspaper, *Diario Financiero*, and owns a 20 percent interest in a cable television system, VTR. The group recently bought *Revista Capital*, a business and lifestyle magazine.

Mega (Channel 9) was the first private television company in Chile. It started operating on October 23, 1990 after Claro won the bid for the frequency. Mega partnered with Televisa Mexico in 1991, but nine years later Televisa agreed to pull out of the joint venture and Claro regained total control.

The Claro Group owned a cable system operator, Metropolis-Intercom, until it merged with its main competitor and market leader, VTR, in April 2005. The resulting company kept the name VTR and is owned by Claro (20 percent) and Liberty Global (80 percent). VTR serves forty-nine cities across the country, and also offers telephone and broadband Internet services.

The financial newspaper *Diario Financiero* was founded in 1988. The Claro Group bought the newspaper in 1995 and entered into a joint venture with the Spanish publishing group Recoletos. In 2005 Recoletos sold its stake in *Diario Financiero* for €2.5 billion, leaving Claro as sole owner.

Edwards Family

The newspaper *El Mercurio* was founded in Valparaíso on September 12, 1827. It is the oldest Spanish-speaking newspaper currently published in the world. After changing publishers and owners on several occasions, it was acquired by Agustin Edwards in 1880. *El Mercurio* of Santiago was founded on June 1, 1900. This edition became the national newspaper while Valparaíso still publishes its own regional edition.

Agustin Edwards Eastman, great-grandson of the Edwards who bought the newspaper, is currently leading the company. El Mercurio Group owns now sixteen newspapers, three of them published in Santiago—*El Mercurio*, *La Segunda* and *Las Últimas Noticias*—and the rest in various regions of the country.

El Mercurio owns Editorial Lo Castillo, which publishes the magazine *DatoAvisos* (sales, discounts, etc.). It also produces customized magazines and catalogs for companies from different sectors. In addition, El Mercurio Group has a production department for events and fairs.

El Mercurio-Aguilar is a joint venture created in late 2000 by El Mercurio and the publishing house Aguilar of the Spanish group Prisa. It has published a wide range of books, including topics such as food, gardening, photography, self-help, city guides, psychology, etc.

Emol, which stands for *El Mercurio Online*, is the Internet portal for the group's media. Digital FM is a regional network of the group. It operates in more than forty cities offering content specific to each city. Its goal is to provide entertainment, information, music, community service and culture.

Saieh Family

The Saieh family, a major economic group in the country, has been the main shareholder of the media company Copesa since 2000. Copesa publishes two daily newspapers, *La Tercera* and *La Cuarta*; a freesheet, *La Hora*; a news magazine, *Qué Pasa*; a women's magazine, *Paula*; and an annual tourist guide, *Turistel*. The group also owns a number of other media companies: Dial is the parent company of six radio stations, Beethoven, Carolina, Zero, Duna, Paula FM and Cariño; the printing company Prosa; the distribution company Meta; and Promoservice for managing subscriptions and promotions. The Copesa Group announced in January 2007 the purchase of the website www.laborum.com, one of the major job search portals in Chile.

The State

The State of Chile owns one of the leading national television networks, TVN, and a newspaper, *La Nación*. TVN, which stands for Televisión Nacional de Chile, began operations in 1969 and aims at offering public service television. Nevertheless, its sole source of funding is advertising and thus its programs are fairly similar to those of commercial television. Furthermore, it is supposed to be neutral in political terms but has traditionally—although not openly—served the interests of the ruling parties. The chairman of the board of directors is appointed by the president of Chile and the remaining board members must be approved by the Senate.

La Nación is a small daily newspaper with national coverage. In contrast to TVN, *La Nación* openly promotes the government; 31 percent of its property is in private hands. Besides the newspaper, the company also owns the *Diario Oficial*, the periodical that publishes laws, resolutions and other official information, the printing company Gráfica Puerto Madero, and the distribution company Vía Directa.

GLR Networks

GLR (Grupo Latino de Radio) is the international subsidiary of Prisa's radio division, Unión Radio. Unión Radio is one of the largest radio companies in the Spanish-speaking markets, with more than 1,200 stations in all, including its own and those of partners, and some 28 million listeners. It bought Iberoamerican Radio Chile from the Claxson Group in 2007, gaining control of eighty-nine radio broadcasting licenses, two of which are national networks. The stations include Los 40 Principales Chile, Bésame, Radioactiva, Imagina, Rock & Pop, Concierto, Futuro, FM Dos, Corazón, Pudahuel, ADN and FM Hit. All these ownership stakes give GLR a 37 percent share of the radio advertising market in Chile.

Media Policy

The Constitution of Chile guarantees freedom of speech. The details are specified in the Law on Freedom of Expression and Information—also known as the Law of the Press—which asserts the freedom to express an opinion and to inform, with no previous censorship, as a fundamental right of all persons (Law 19.733: Ley de Libertad de Opinión e Información, 2001). It also states the right of any person, natural or legal, to found, edit, establish, operate and maintain a mass media company with no other conditions than the ones stipulated by law. These required conditions make it mandatory that the chief executives of television must be Chilean and not have been convicted of a felony or crime.

Besides the aforementioned legislation, Chile has two other statutory laws dealing with aspects specific to mass media. The General Law on Telecommunications states that the use and benefits of broadcasting frequencies will have free and equal access by means of the allocation of temporal concessions or licenses by the State (Law 18.168: Ley General de Telecomunicaciones, 1982).

Law 18.838 created the Consejo Nacional de Televisión (CNTV: National Television Council). The CNTV is closely related to the government and specifically to the president of the republic. On the one hand, the CNTV is responsible for assigning licenses to television broadcasters applying for a concession. On the other, the CNTV must supervise all television services, particularly vis-à-vis respect for moral and cultural values, personal dignity, family, pluralism, democracy, peace and the environment. It must also make sure that these moral values are incorporated into the program grid and contribute to the intellectual and spiritual education of children. In recent years, the CNTV has promoted quality cultural programs by means of financing new innovative ideas.

There are no specific laws dealing with media concentration issues. Until recently concentration had not been a problem because media companies in Chile had been mainly single-medium companies. Nevertheless, the convergence process is turning these single-medium companies into multimedia companies. The only laws that may be applied in cases of media concentration are antitrust laws, which are enforced by the Tribunal de Defensa de la Libre Competencia (Free Competition Defense Tribunal). In 2005, this tribunal had to deal with the merger of the two main cable system operators. The ruling of the tribunal approved the merger with a series of restrictions such as not increasing prices for several years and fair access to third-party cable channels wanting to distribute their content.

Digital Terrestrial Television

The debate on digital terrestrial television began in Chile in the late 1990s. However, the decision on which technology will be adopted—ATSC, DVB or ISDB—is just the first step. Two issues need to be addressed as well. First, the *simulcasting* period in which television stations broadcast both in analog and digital modes at the same time will require that the regulatory authority allocates extra spectrum to existing television stations. This would imply a change in the law that prohibits companies to have more than one television license (Law 19.131 modifies Law 18.838: Ley que modifica la Ley no. 18.838, 1992). Second, there is some dispute over the extent of the right of the licensees. Already established television license holders claim they have the right to the spectrum they were originally awarded, i.e. 6 megahertz, regardless of the number of channels that can be broadcast in that space. It remains to be seen whether the regulating authority will adhere to that reasoning or will reallocate the freed VHF spectrum to new entrants leaving existent license holders with a fraction of the space they currently use to broadcast in analog.

References

Asociación Chilena de Agencias de Publicidad (ACHAP). (2008). *Estadísticas de inversión publicitaria* [Advertising expenditure statistics]. Retrieved February 15, 2008, from www.achap.cl/estudios/inversion/index.php.

Asociación de Medios en Internet. (2008). *Estadísticas generales en enero* [General statistics in January]. Retrieved February 15, 2008, from www.iab.cl/estadisticas-generales/index.php.

Asociación Nacional de la Prensa. (2007). *Estadísticas del sector* [Sector statistics]. Retrieved January 8, 2008, from www.anp.cl/p4_anp/stat/fset/estadisticas/index.html.

Consejo Nacional de Televisión (CNTV). (2005). *V Encuesta nacional de Televisión* [Fifth national television survey]. Santiago, Chile: Departamento de Estudios CNTV.

The Economist. (2008). *Country Briefings: Chile. The Economist.* Retrieved March 11, 2008, from www.economist.com/countries/Chile/.

Hrepich, B. A. (2008, February 29). Las compañías despiden a los planes de banda ancha en kilobits: Desde ahora sólo mbps [Companies say goodbye to broadband plans in kilobits: From now on, only mbps]. *El Mercurio Online.* Retrieved March 11, 2008, from www.emol.com/noticias/tecnologia/detalle/detallenoticias.asp?idnoticia=294501.

Interactive Advertising Bureau. (2006). *El poder de Internet* [The power of the Internet]. Retrieved February 15, 2008, from www.ami.cl/publicidad/elpoderdeinternet/index.htm.

Ley de libertad de opinión e información [Law on freedom of expression and information], no. 19.733, Chile. (2001).

Ley general de telecomunicaciones [General law on telecommunications], no. 18.168, Chile. (1982).

Ley para la creación del Consejo Nacional de Televisión [Law for the establishment of the National Television Council], no. 18.838, Chile. (1989).

Ley que modifica la Ley no. 18.838 [Law amending Law no. 18.838], no. 19.131, Chile. (1992).

Mir, M. A., Errázuriz, M. I., Santa María, I. and Kimber, D. (2006). *Índice de calidad en la televisión abierta chilena* [Quality Index of Chilean Television]. Santiago, Chile: Ediciones Cimas.

Netcraft Ltd. (2008). *Netcraft web server survey.* Retrieved April 7, 2008, from http://news.netcraft.com/.

Subsecretaría de Telecomunicaciones (SUBTEL). (2007a). *Encuesta de satisfacción de usuarios de servicios de telecomunicaciones: Informe final* [Satisfaction survey of users of telecommunication services: Final report]. Santiago, Chile: Departamento de Economía Universidad de Chile.

Subsecretaría de Telecomunicaciones (SUBTEL). (2007b). *Series conexiones Internet (Enero 2000-Junio 2007)* [Series of Internet access (January 2000–June 2007)]. Retrieved April 1, 2008, from www.subtel.cl/prontus_subtel/site/artic/20070212/asocfile/20070212182348/1_series_conexiones_internet_07.xls.

Subsecretaría de Telecomunicaciones (SUBTEL). (2008). *Indicadores de industria suscriptores televisión de pago a Diciembre 2007* [Subscription indicators for the paid television industry as of December 2007]. Retrieved April 1, 2008, from www.subtel.cl/prontus_subtel/site/artic/20070212/asocfile/20070212182348/3_indicadores_industria_tvdic07.xls.

Triangulo Media Agency. (2008). *Panorama de Medios en Chile: Presentación en powerpoint de la compañía* [Chilean media landscape: Company's powerpoint presentation]. Created on January 2, 2008.

World Internet Project—Chile. (2006). *Monitoreando el futuro digital: Resultados encuesta WIP-Chile 2006* [Monitoring the digital future: Results of the WIP-Chile 2006 survey]. Pontificia Universidad Católica de Chile/Cámara de Comercio de Santiago. Retrieved March 11, 2008, from www.wipchile.cl/estudios/WIP_Chile_2006___informe.pdf.

11

Media and Entertainment in Argentina
Doing Business in a Fragmented Society

Luciana Silvestri and Roberto S. Vassolo
IAE Business School, Buenos Aires, Argentina

Introduction

We explore the issues of vertical and horizontal fragmentation in Argentina by examining how consumers relate to media and entertainment (M&E) content and technologies. We focus on middle-market consumers (the most affluent at the bottom of the pyramid) and observe the way they relate to products and services, move to acquire them, and build aspirations and dreams. Subsequently, we compare their behavior with that of high- and low-income consumers. Results show that both vertical and horizontal fragmentation are prevalent: middle-market consumers differ not only in their behavior with individuals of different socioeconomic characteristics, but also (quite strongly) among themselves. Fragmentation seems to be tied to four distinct factors: consumers' lifecycle stage, gender, income level and degree of social embeddedness. Our findings have important implications for companies doing business in fragmented societies where the M&E industry is still awaiting major changes in structure, technology and market offerings.

Over the past hundred years, Argentina has struggled to bring stability and consistence to its process of economic and social development. Like many emerging economies, the country is prone to sudden stops (sharp falls in capital inflows that produce violent contractions in the country's GDP) and phoenix miracles (relatively quick recoveries in GPD levels after these sharp contractions) that routinely mar and boost its economy (Calvo, Izquierdo & Talvi, 2006). At the beginning of the twentieth century, Argentina was the seventh-richest nation worldwide, thanks largely to a successful agriculture-based export model. In 1913, the country's per capita income mirrored that of France and Germany, and was far ahead of that of Italy or Spain (*The Economist*, 2004). From 1930 onwards, the country was plagued by a series of political and financial roller-coasters that included several coups d'état, numerous default instances, and two hyperinflation episodes. As a result, Argentina's GDP per capita ranking plummeted to the forty-eighth position (International Monetary Fund (IMF), 2007). The latest and potentially most damaging crisis in the country's history began in December 2001 and extended throughout most of 2002. The economy shrank by 15 percent in the year to March 2002, poverty—according to the national poverty line—rose from 38 percent to 56 percent, and unemployment climbed to 21 percent (*The Economist*, 2006). This crisis came after a decade of monetary stability (with the peso pegged one-to-one to the US dollar throughout most of the 1990s), market liberalization and dynamism. The Argentine economy has since recovered, matching or surpassing pre-crisis activity levels and growing approximately 8 percent annually over the period 2003–2006 (IMF, 2007). Since then, inflation, conflicts between the government and key productive sectors, and the virtual lack of external financing raise questions about future growth perspectives (*The Economist*, 2009). Table 11.1 summarizes key facts about Argentina (CIA 2008).

Table 11.1 A Socioeconomic Portrait of Argentina, 2008

Location	Southern tip of Latin America
Area	2,766,890 sq km
Population	40,677,348 (July 2008 est.)
Ethnicity	White (mostly Spanish and Italian) 97%; mestizo (mixed white and Amerindian ancestry), Amerindian, or other non-white groups 3%
Literacy	97.2%
GDP 2008 (official exchange rate)	US$181.9 billion (2008 est.)
GDP real growth rate	7.1% (2008 est.)
Labor force	16.27 million
	note: urban areas only (2008 est.)
Unemployment rate	7.8% (September 2008)
Population below poverty line	23.4% (January–June 2007)

Source: CIA (2008, 2009)

Media and Entertainment Industry

Argentina was one of Latin America's pioneers in M&E. Traditional media such as newspapers, radio, broadcast television and the cinema were launched in the country shortly after being introduced in Europe or the United States. After a booming period at the beginning of the twentieth century, the industry faced severe restrictions between the 1930s and 1980s, due to Argentina's fluctuation between democratic and military governments. Since the 1990s, the industry has experienced significant growth and consolidation. Two major players dominate the scene: Grupo Clarín, a local multimedia holding, and Grupo Telefónica, a subsidiary of Telefónica de España. Other smaller groups complete the picture: América Medios, T&C, Hadad and Liberty Media/Global, among the content providers, and Telmex and Telecom Argentina among the connectivity providers (Convergencia, 2007).

Despite this recent advancement, certain industrial domains remain highly regulated, with numerous taxes and ownership restrictions. For instance, in pay-television foreign investors have an ownership cap of 30 percent. There is also a prohibition to provide telecommunications services simultaneously with cable television and Internet connections. Following a decade of intense lobbying in favor of triple- and multiple-play services, both incumbent media companies and telecommunications carriers expect the market to be deregulated in the near future. The conditions for this deregulation are still being discussed. One of the main points of discussion is the norm to adopt for digital television and convergence services; carriers vie for the European norm, Grupo Clarín for the US norm, and other players for the Japanese norm, which was adopted in Brazil. While waiting for these developments—which should trigger investments in modern technologies—the industry remains overwhelmingly analog. Both competitors and consumers are, arguably, missing out on services and opportunities already enjoyed by their counterparts in several Latin American countries.

Newspapers

Gazetas (single-sheet summaries of relevant news) began circulating in the territory later known as Argentina as early as 1764. In 1867, after Argentina established its independence from Spain and drew up its constitution, *La Capital*, the first newspaper per se, was launched, followed some years later by many others such as *La Prensa*, *La Nación* and *La Razón*. At the time, newspapers were seen as a practical way to disseminate political ideas. The line between a journalist and a politician was rather blurred (Ulanovsky, 2005). In 1900, Saporiti, the first news agency in Argentina and the sixth worldwide, was founded. In 1908, *El Cronista Comercial*, a newspaper exclusively dedicated to financial and commercial issues, was created.

Today, no newspaper in Argentina boasts national coverage. Readership is closely tied to print location. Approximately 58 percent of all newspapers are edited in Buenos Aires and the rest in other Argentine provinces. Only 10 percent of sales in these provinces correspond to newspapers edited in Buenos Aires (Asociación de Diarios del Interior de la República Argentina (ADIRA: Association of Regionally and Locally Edited Newspapers of Argentina), 2008).

Newspapers have seen their revenues diminish consistently, with consumers favoring the free-access online version instead of the paid print version. The circulation of leading newspaper *Diario Clarín* has fallen by 30 percent since the late 1990s while that of rival *La Nación* (targeted mostly at high-income consumers) fell by 7 percent (*La Nación*, 2007). Combined, they did not print more than 600,000 issues a month, Monday to Sunday, over the period 2004–2007 (Instituto Verificador de Circulaciones (IVC: Institute for the Verification of Newspaper Circulation, 2007). Advertising revenues are still strong in the paper version and incipient online, a relationship which will have to be altered if the newspaper business is to remain profitable.

Magazines

Launched in 1863, *El Mosquito* was Argentina's first political humor magazine. Others such as *Don Quijote* and *Caras y Caretas* would soon follow. In 1904, *El Hogar Argentino* would become the first magazine dedicated to social issues such as fashion, housekeeping and culture for the rising middle class. *PBT* was the first magazine dedicated to children, followed by *Billiken*. *El Gráfico*, one of Argentina's most influential sports magazines, appeared in 1919. *Sur*, first edited in 1931, was Argentina's quintessential literary journal. Launched in 1935, *Radiolandia* chronicled relevant news from the world of show business.

There are approximately 1,405 magazines in Argentina as of 2008. In 1998, almost 207 million issues were sold among the categories of technology; women's and housekeeping; comics; sports; show business and art; current events; and do-it-yourself. In 2002, circulation diminished abruptly due to Argentina's economic crisis, dragging sales to a mere 64 million issues. Sales picked up to 114 million issues in 2007. Sales of foreign magazines have represented a fairly stable 10 percent over the period 1998–2007 (Asociación Argentina de Editores de Revistas (AAER: Argentine Association of Magazine Editors), 2008).

Radio

The first radio transmission took place in 1920. By the 1940s, the technology had disseminated widely and radio broadcasts were at the center of family life (Matallana, 2006). Radio soap operas and shows broadcast before a live audience were in high fashion. Between the 1960s and 1980s, radio underwent an impasse due to the appearance of television. Talent and audiences migrated from the microphone to the screen. As of the 1980s, the radio industry redefined its social function and positioned itself as the quintessential medium to shape public opinion and social interaction. It reconverted its programming to include information, talk shows and music in a highly interactive setting. The traditional advertising-based business model migrated to dual partnerships between the network and the talent, who are now partners sharing both risk and profits (Ulanovsky, 2007).

Television

In 1951, Canal 7, Argentina's first state-owned broadcast television channel, was launched. Throughout the 1960s and beyond, four other channels were licensed as private enterprises. These networks had agreements with their US counterparts ABC, CBS and NBC for the provision of technology and content (Buero, 1999). Local content was produced live, without resorting to videotape. Entertainment rather than critical analysis was the key to programming. Local television networks in cities other than Buenos Aires "repeated" the leading networks' programming. The 1970s were a bittersweet decade for Argentine television. In 1974, private channels were expropriated by the government; in 1976, the last coup d'état was perpetrated by the military junta; and in 1978, the first color transmission was broadcast. Upon the return of democracy in 1983, during the 1990s most television channels returned to private hands.

Cable Television

Argentina is Latin America's most developed pay-television market. Pay-television started in the 1980s but it was not until the 1990s that it became widespread. Penetration is considerably high, reaching 62 percent of households in Buenos Aires and other major cities (Ipsos, 2007) and almost 50 percent in the country as a whole (Informa Telecoms & Media, 2007). In addition, the number of illegal connections is estimated at 1 million or 20 percent of users (Infobrand, 2008). In most Argentine provinces, even in those where pay-television penetration is lower than the country average, a higher number of households have pay-television Cable connections than landline telephone connections (Asociación Argentina de Televisión por Cable (ATVC), 2006). Three providers (Grupo Clarín-owned Cablevision and Multicanal, and Supercanal) account for over 50 percent of subscribers. About 700 local providers cover the rest; 8 percent of the market is held by the only digital provider, DirecTV (Informa Telecoms & Media, 2007).

The Internet

Introduced in the late 1990s, broadband services have been increasing their penetration at staggering rates. The business grew 72 percent over the period 2004–2005 and 71 percent over the period 2005–2006 (Convergencia Latina, 2006) and is expected to sustain these growth rates in the near future. In mid-2008, 2.5 million connections were in place (Cisco, 2008). The dispute for market leadership has been reduced to three players: Grupo Clarín's Fibertel, Telefonica's Speedy and Telecom's Arnet. Still, about 50 percent of all broadband connections are located in the city of Buenos Aires. Local pay-television providers in small cities are expected to act as broadband Internet providers as well (ATVC, 2006).

Mobile Communications

Mobile technologies have also experienced high growth since the late 1990s thanks to the implementation of pre-paid cards. Penetration reached 80 percent in 2006 and is expected to expand in single digits in the near future (Convergencia Latina, 2006). Wireless broadband services are expected to take off with the launch of 3G networks by incumbents Movistar (a subsidiary of Grupo Telefónica), Personal (a subsidiary of Telecom) and Claro (Telmex's recently rebranded wireless division).

Media and Entertainment in a Fragmented Society

Throughout the twentieth century, Argentina prided itself on having a large and relatively strong middle class. That pride subsided somewhat after the 2001 crisis, when Argentine society started showing signs of severe fragmentation between high-income consumers (many of whom had managed to elude the crisis by taking their wealth out of the country) and low-income consumers (many of whom lost their life savings and were forced to descend from the middle to the lower segments of the pyramid). Despite the country's speedy recovery in subsequent years, a devalued peso, rising inflation and drastic changes in income distribution determined that former levels of wealth would be difficult to reach again. Inequality escalated. In greater Buenos Aires, the Gini coefficient rose from around 0.38 in 1980 to nearly 0.53 in 2002 (Perry, Arias, Lopez, Maloney & Serven, 2006). In 2005, approximately 20 percent of the population still lived under the $2 poverty threshold (Gasparini, Gutiérrez, & Tornarolli, 2005).

This altered societal structure has presented opportunities and challenges for companies operating in the country. M&E companies, in particular, faced double jeopardy. On a global scale, their business has been converging and evolving thanks to forces not entirely within their control; on a local scale, their business remains closely tied to consumers' willingness to pay for content and technology. Both purchasing power and cultural engagement have suffered since the Argentine crisis, and the gap between more and less affluent consumers has only widened.

Like many emerging markets, Argentine society is showing evidence of *vertical fragmentation*. The socioeconomic pyramid is dramatically narrow at the top, where high-income consumers reside, and wide at the center and bottom, where mid- and low-income consumers reside. In comparison, societies with little vertical fragmentation boast smoother pyramids. Figure 11.1 (overleaf) provides a conceptual image.

The effects of vertical fragmentation on a society have been thoroughly explored by Prahalad (2004) in a seminal work on bottom of the pyramid (BOP) consumers. An immediate consequence of vertical fragmentation is that it leads products and services that are considered standard in developed countries to be viewed as premium in emerging ones. This is often the case with M&E content and technologies. Price–performance relationships render these products affordable for only a reduced number of consumers. Attempting to market a product or service across the entire pyramid, from its relatively more affluent section to the relatively less affluent, is a radical endeavor. The distance that separates consumers at the top and bottom of the pyramid, measured mostly in terms of budget, may be qualified as staggering.

Another consequence of vertical fragmentation is that organizational capabilities developed to serve affluent consumers may not be fit to serve consumers positioned further down the pyramid. In this scenario, companies are faced with the need to rethink their operations before entering the BOP playing field. Scholars have urged companies to redefine their value chains, business models, product functionalities and performance metrics (Prahalad, 2004). They have also warned companies that BOP market penetration would largely depend on their ability to establish

Developed markets
Moving down the
pyramid involves a
smooth transition

Emerging markets
Moving down the
pyramid involves
overcoming vertical
fragmentation

Top of the
pyramid

Middle market and
bottom of the pyramid

■ High income
▨ Middle income
☐ Low income

■ High-middle income
▨ Lower-middle income
☐ Low income
☐ Indigents

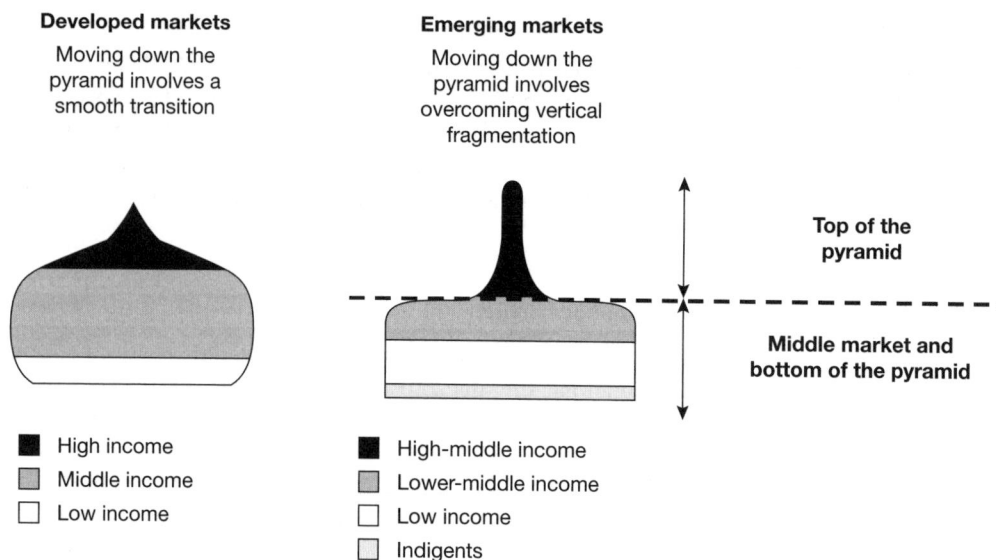

Figure 11.1 Socioeconomic Pyramids in Developed Markets and Emerging Markets: An Illustration of Vertical Fragmentation

adequate partnerships (London & Hart, 2004). These warnings are not without merit. Still, they may lead companies to approach BOP markets strictly with a business-centric perspective. In the process of generating the necessary capabilities to compete in BOP markets, this perspective is putting companies at risk of focusing excessively on what needs to be done internally and not enough on the consumer.

An adequate look at consumers in a fragmented society entails an analysis not only of the degree of vertical fragmentation present, but also that of *horizontal fragmentation*. This is especially true in cultural industries such as M&E. Entertainment is a relevant part of life at all stages of life; however, it is also an intensely personal experience subject to special significance. Entertainment triggers powerful psychological and emotional effects (Vogel, 2007) that render an opening into an individual's very being (Marano, 1999). M&E content and technologies are therefore of special interest to consumers. Choices in these matters have come to be regarded as personal statements, that is, forms of self-expression and self-affirmation. Choices also help make consumers' identities known to others and communicate aspects of their selves that could not be immediately evidenced otherwise (see e.g. Boyd's (2007) account of identity formation on social networking sites). Choices thus lead to bonds among consumers, content and technology.

Consumers' keen interest in content and technologies is mirrored by M&E products and services' relatively high degree of social permeability. Specifically in emerging markets, innovative products and services are introduced at the top of the socioeconomic pyramid, where most early adopting consumers reside. However, they tend to reach lower levels of the pyramid with considerable speed. Rapid spillovers in knowledge and technology development (Steiner, 2004) and increased commitment of retailers (D'Andrea, Costa, Fernandes & Fossen, 2007) and financing entities grant low-income consumers easier access to M&E offerings than they had in the past. Access breeds permeability through purchase. Worldwide, entertainment is the second destination for disposable income, after adding to family savings. In Latin America in general and in Argentina in particular, it is the first (Nielsen, 2006).

By emphasizing experience, choice and access, empirical studies on horizontal fragmentation may shed light on the problematic issue of *how*, rather than *if*, less affluent consumers should be approached (Seelos & Mair, 2007). (See D'Andrea, Stengel & Goebel-Krstelj (2003) for an example set in the Latin American retail industry.) Our study responds to this demand by exploring the extent to which horizontal and vertical fragmentation prevail Argentina's media and entertainment industry. To that end, we attempted to identify structural differences in the way groups of high-, middle- and low-income consumers relate to M&E content and technologies. We also sought to identify the factors upon which these structural differences hinge, and to examine their interrelations.

Results revealed that fragmentation is tied to four distinct factors. Consumers' lifecycle stage and gender contribute mainly to horizontal fragmentation. Conversely, consumers' income level and their degree of social embeddedness (i.e. consumers' positioning within social networks) contribute mainly to vertical fragmentation. Combinations of these factors generate structural differences in the way consumers relate to similar product offerings. Fragmentation is evidenced in divergent consumer behavior as regards the relationships consumers build with devices, content and fellow consumers, the way they identify purchasing opportunities and carry out the purchasing process, and the aspirations they create vis-à-vis M&E content and technologies.

Results also indicate that consumers at the BOP are complex rather than simple individuals. Reduced budgets are no indication of reduced expectations over products and services consumers know and demand actively. However, most consumers require coaching in order to incorporate novel offerings into their lives, especially technology-related ones. Understanding the person beneath the consumer emerges as a strategic imperative for companies that wish to convey effective messages to the BOP. Recognizing consumer heterogeneity should have significant implications for companies in the areas of strategic planning, resource allocation, capability development, and business model design and implementation in emerging markets.

Research Design

In order to explore the issue of fragmentation, we focused our research on Argentina's lower-middle-income consumers and upper-low-income consumers, that is, the least affluent among the middle class and the most affluent among the lower class. These consumers, positioned at the middle of the market, may be considered M&E companies' next consumers moving downwards in the socioeconomic pyramid. Jointly, these segments cover 44 percent of the country's population. We will address horizontal fragmentation by looking for structural differences among groups of consumers within this large group. Conversely, we will address vertical fragmentation by looking for structural differences among groups of middle-market consumers and their high-income and low-income counterparts. High-income consumers represent 10 percent of the country's population, while low-income consumers represent 31 percent. We have purposefully excluded two segments from our study: middle-income consumers and the lowest income consumers, that is, the indigent population. The former, which represent 11 percent of the population, were excluded because the vertical contrast with our target middle-market consumers would not have been rich enough to draw significant conclusions about fragmentation. The latter, which represent 4 percent, were excluded because, due to severe budget constraints, they remain largely oblivious to advances in M&E content and technologies. Figure 11.2 illustrates the significance of different consumer segments in Argentina and their role in our study.

High-income consumers' habits and expectations vis-à-vis M&E content and technology have been thoroughly researched. However, little is known about the habits and expectations of

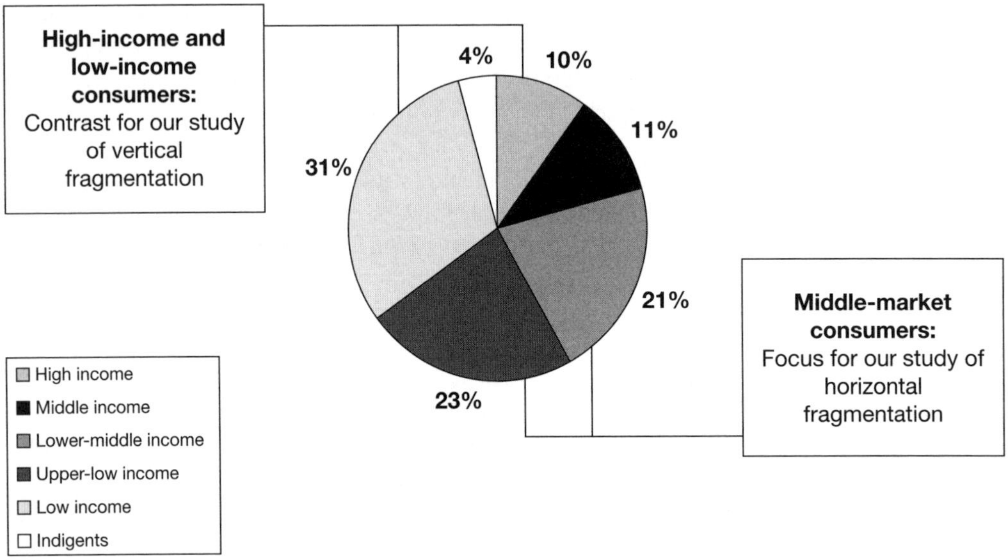

High-income and low-income consumers:
Contrast for our study of vertical fragmentation

4% 10%

11%

31%

21%

Middle-market consumers:
Focus for our study of horizontal fragmentation

23%

☐ High income
■ Middle income
☐ Lower-middle income
■ Upper-low income
☐ Low income
☐ Indigents

Figure 11.2 Socioeconomic Segments in Argentina as Considered in Our Study

Source: Asociación Argentina de Marketing (Argentine Marketing Association)
Note: Segment size shown as a percentage of total population

middle-market consumers. It therefore seemed inappropriate to perform a quantitative study where distance across several dimensions could be measured. Instead, we used a qualitative, exploratory approach which allowed us to identify relevant factors that lead to structural differences among groups of consumers and to explore their interrelations. This methodology worked by allowing us to gather insights from consumers until saturation (i.e. redundancy in consumers' replies) was reached (Lincoln & Guba, 1985).

Exploring Horizontal Fragmentation

In order to explore the issue of horizontal fragmentation, we performed six focus groups with approximately eight participants each in our target audience of middle-market consumers. As we intended to cover different stages in a person's lifecycle, we summoned individuals (separated by gender) with the following characteristics: young, single men and women between 18 and 25 years of age, young and middle-aged parents with children of up to 12 years of age, and middle-aged parents with children between 12 and 20 years of age. Not mere wages but a comprehensive idea of lifestyle was the main determinant for selection. Table 11.2 lists the participants' profiles.

Focus groups were conducted by a professional trained in psychology and anthropology, and observed in real time by the authors. The conductor was instructed to progressively introduce a series of triggers for discussion, gather all spontaneous answers by the participants that might arise and, if the situation warranted, pointedly ask questions to obtain further insight. Participants were prompted to discuss issues related to (1) the meaning of entertainment in life, (2) the restrictions (such as time and money) they face when seeking entertainment options, (3) the relationships they have built with particular forms of entertainment, and (4) their aspirations. Specifically, we aimed to gather evidence of participant's familiarity with and frequency of use of M&E content and technologies. We expected participants to express their views on entertainment options such as feature films, DVD/VHS content, cable and broadcast television, music, reading materials (e.g.

Table 11.2 Focus Group Participants: Middle-Market Consumers (Profiles and Demographic Data)

Demographics	Participants	Gender	Occupation
Single men and women between 18 and 25 years of age	8	Female	• Babysitter • Employee at children's entertainment venue • Business administration student, employee at social security office • Hotel management student, secretary • Waitress • Graphic design student • Physical education student • Japanese tutor, babysitter
	7	Male	• High school student, delayed • Business administration student, works at accountant's office • Business administration student, intern at university • Carpenter • Employee at furniture upholstering business • Gofer • English student, does not work
Young and middle-aged parents with young children of up to 12 years of age	8	Female	• Emergency line operator • Employee at drugstore • Call center representative • Occasional waitress at functions and events • Employee at cultural center • Make-up artist • Artist, works at home • Employee at recovery center for handicapped adults
	8	Male	• Store owner • Store employee • Driver • Bicycle repair man • Elevator repair man, technician • Shoe repair man • Independent salesman (wine) • Postman
Middle-aged parents with children between 12 and 20 years of age	8	Female	• Housewife (4) • Babysitter • Employee at public hospital (2) • Baker
	8	Male	• Unemployed • Taxi driver • Driver • Delivery man, dairy products • Employee at poultry business • Employee at hardware store • Maintenance worker at hospital • Drugstore owner

books, periodicals), games and digital content accessible on the Internet via personal computers and mobile phones.

Since M&E content and technologies are but a part of the entertainment universe, we allowed for participants' mentioning other forms of entertainment less dependent on content and/or technology, such as camping, sports, card-playing, dancing, etc. This served as a sort of proxy for the degree of technical sophistication inherent to their chosen forms of entertainment. Regarding frequency and opportunity of use or purchase, we aimed to understand on which occasions (e.g. alone, with others, at home, during vacations, while commuting, during free time) participants preferred engaging in each form of entertainment. Light was thus shed on the purchasing process followed by consumers. Finally, we prompted participants to describe an ideal entertainment experience given unlimited availability of resources. This question was designed to tap into participants' dreams, aspirations and desires regarding entertainment. Participants were also asked to reflect on what would constitute an ideal entertainment experience for their parents or children. A summarized version of the list of guidelines followed by the conductor can be found in Table 11.3.

Table 11.3 Focus Group Interview Guidelines

Focus point	Discussion triggers
The concept of entertainment and its meanings	• What comes to your mind when you think of the word "entertainment"? • Is entertainment important in life? Why?
Restrictions to entertainment	
Time	• How much time do you devote to entertaining yourself on weekdays? • What about on the weekend? • Is Saturday different from Sunday when it comes to entertainment?
Financial resources	• Do you set aside a certain amount of money per month/week to spend on entertainment or do you spend on the go? • How do you prioritize among entertainment options when money is tight?
Forms of entertainment	
Broadcast and cable television	• Do you watch TV? • What kinds of shows do you watch? • Do you have a schedule of shows to watch or do you watch spontaneously? • Do you watch alone / with others (friends, family)? • Who at home decides which show to watch? • How many TV sets are there in your home? • Do you own any plasma / HD TV sets?
VHS/DVD	• Do you own a VHS/DVD player? • Do you rent/buy/download films? • Who at home decides which film to rent/see? • How often do you rent/buy/download films?
Music	• Do you listen to music? • Which device do you frequently use to play music (radio, CD, PC, MP3 player, mobile phone)? • Regardless of whether you use it or not, what other devices are there in your home? • How do you acquire new music? • Do you play any instruments?
Feature films	• Do you go to the cinema? • Do you go alone or with others? • Who at home decides which film to see?
Video games	• Do you own or have access to a videogame console? • How do you acquire games? • Do you play alone or with others?
Digital content	• Do you own or have access to a personal computer? • If you own one, how and why did you decide to acquire it? • Do you have an Internet connection for your computer? • Do you use the Internet? What for? How often? • If you do not use the Internet, would you like to? What would you do?

Exploring Vertical Fragmentation

In order to explore the issue of vertical fragmentation, we compared middle-market consumers with high-income consumers and low-income consumers in their approach to M&E content and technologies. We performed twelve in-depth personal interviews with high-income and low-income individuals mirroring the demographics selected for the focus groups, that is, young, single men and women aged between 18 and 25 years of age, young and middle-aged parents with children of up to 12 years of age, and middle-aged parents with children between 12 and 20 years of age. These interviews followed the same discussion triggers as the focus groups. Table 11.4 lists the participants' profiles.

Table 11.4 Participants of Personalized, Semi-Structured Interviews: High-Income and Low-Income Consumers (Profiles and Demographic Data)

Demographics	Participants	Gender	Occupation
Single men and women between 18 and 25 years of age	2	Female	High income • CPA student, works at her father's accountancy firm Low income • Student
	2	Male	High income • Law student, works at public defendent's office Low income • Pizza delivery man
Young and middle-aged parents with young children of up to 12 years of age	2	Female	High income • Architect, works in city planning Low income • Housewife
	2	Male	High income • Attorney at law Low income • Taxi service telephone operator
Middle-aged parents with children between 12 and 20 years of age	2	Female	High income • Saleswoman at pharmaceutical company Low income • Part-time cleaning lady
	2	Male	High income • CPA, manages agricultural businesses Low income • Postman

Results

The study produced a series of dimensions that help explain structural differences among groups of consumers. Figure 11.3 presents these dimensions in an organizing framework.

The first section of the framework in Figure 11.3 illustrates how consumers in Argentina conceptualize entertainment. When asked about the meaning and value of entertainment in daily life, consumers tended to refer to concrete activities that gave them pleasure rather than to a particular feeling, emotion or state of mind. This suggests that consumers associate the concept of entertainment to a tangible universe instead of an abstract universe. Activities mentioned spontaneously by focus group and interview participants could be classified as (1) technology related (i.e., forms of entertainment that are heavily dependent on a high-tech device and where

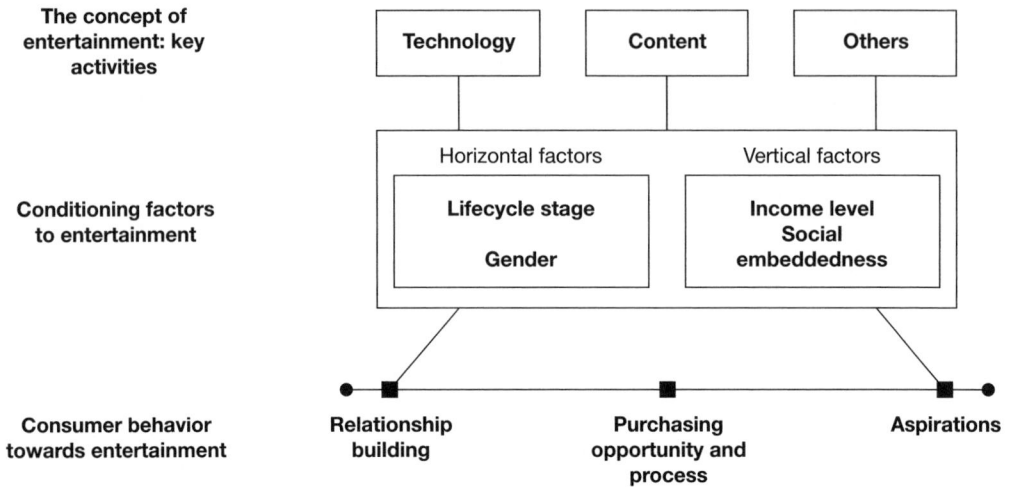

Figure 11.3 Emerging Framework: Dimensions Generating Structural Differences among Groups of Consumers

content tends to be of a digital nature; examples include the use of Internet-enabled personal computers, mobile phones, game consoles); (2) content related (i.e. forms of entertainment that do not rely on sophisticated devices and where content rather than technology plays a major part; examples include listening to the radio, watching television, going to the cinema, reading); and (3) others (i.e. all forms of entertainment that do not rely on technology or content in ways similar to those explained above; examples include exercising, playing cards, meeting friends, sewing, knitting, cooking).

Despite the pervasiveness of this definition of entertainment in all social segments studied, not all consumers sought technology, content or other entertainment options in the same way. Conditioning factors moderated the availability and/or the attractiveness of each form of entertainment. Horizontal conditioning factors, that is, those that generate structural differences among middle-market consumers, include lifecycle stage and gender. Vertical conditioning factors, that is, those that generate structural differences between consumers at different levels of the socioeconomic pyramid, include social embeddedness or the depth and breadth of social networks to which consumers are associated and—naturally—income.

Given the existence of an entertainment universe composed of technology, content and other options and the mediating effect of horizontal and vertical conditioning factors, our study shows that fragmentation is evidenced in consumer behavior regarding the relationships consumers build with devices, content and fellow consumers, the way they identify purchasing opportunities and carry out the purchasing process, and the aspirations they create vis-à-vis M&E content and technologies.

Evidence of Horizontal Fragmentation

The effects of gender
The study showed that middle-market men and women took different approaches to entertainment. These diverging approaches were most evident in the process of relationship building. Men showed a keen interest in pursuing entertainment options that connected them with the world around them, while women preferred entertainment options that would nurture them

internally. Men appeared eager to connect themselves with nature and other people. Preferred activities included meeting friends for a beer, playing soccer, camping and fishing. Women, on the other hand, seemed hungry for self-development. The possibility of taking a course in anything that may broaden their horizons (e.g. a foreign language, cooking or sewing) was viewed as a possibility for entertainment. This may be so because most middle-market women in Argentina have not attended a university nor built significant careers; a good number are housewives working part time or not at all.

In parallel, the women's entertainment universe showed more variety than men's. Women presented an ample array of activities that interested and engaged them, while men tended to focus on a few favorite activities. Women also seemed more prepared to integrate entertainment to their daily life and responsibilities. A participant stated: "If I am at home making the bed and a good song comes up on the radio, I stop, dance around, and then continue making the bed." For men, personal spaces of entertainment tended to be separated from the home. A participant with young children said: "Since I was 15, every Monday and Wednesday I play racquetball—for me this is sacred." This distinction extended to the aspirational universe, where women included entertainment forms that could be shared among family members (a comfortable home with all amenities or an amusement park) while men included entertainment forms that stressed masculinity and individuality (a sports car, a motorcycle, or a private soccer field).

Finally, men showed more familiarity and easiness around technology than did women. Men seemed more willing to experiment with new devices and to learn from trial and error. Given a specific device (e.g. a mobile phone) men also seemed more comfortable using sophisticated functionalities than did women. Women showed considerable doses of fear and apprehension when it came to interacting with technology. This attitude extended from approaching technology to actually using it. In reference to computer-based entertainment, female participants stated: "The computer is there, always turned off." "All I know about computers is that they are shaped like cubes." "I always follow the same routine when I use the computer." Some who have gone beyond the obvious in their use of technology received unpleasant surprises and never tried again: "I bought a pre-paid card for my mobile phone for 35 pesos, I accessed the Internet, listened to a few ringtones to see if I liked them, downloaded one, and the credit was gone." This relationship with technology remained thus in men's and women's aspirations regarding entertainment. Men's ideal entertainment universe entailed many more technical devices than did women's.

The effects of lifecycle stage

Consumers' disposition towards entertainment presented differences according to their lifecycle stage. Creativity, curiosity and proactivity were prevalent among young, single consumers; however, consumers with established families were markedly less creative or curious. We infer that this loss of creativity and dreams could be, in part, an unwanted consequence of the severe economic crises Argentina has undergone since the late 1980s. A significant proportion of the consumers under study used to be mid-income consumers whose lifestyles were negatively affected.

Lifecycle stage was also a relevant factor affecting consumers' conceptualization of entertainment. Young single people stressed the connection between entertainment, fun and immediate pleasure. They also associated entertainment with breaking away from daily routines and "killing time." Entertainment was also strongly connected to friends but not so much to family, a condition which evidenced young consumers' desire to assert their individuality among peers. Parents of young and older children coincided in referring to entertainment as a space for relaxing, evading oneself from daily responsibilities, and leaving problems behind. One female participant referred to entertainment as "a necessary element to regaining one's mental health."

Parents of young children, in particular, tended to integrate the notion of personal entertainment with that of family entertainment. One participant conceded: "The best entertainment option for me and my husband is watching our son play little league soccer." Another participant replied: "I cannot go out alone, my children are always in tow: I go shopping with them, cook with them, play with them." Conversely, parents of older children seemed to be rediscovering personal spaces of entertainment they had previously neglected. A participant stated: "I am no slave to my home—I make my own time for entertainment. If I have clothes to iron and cannot finish in one go, I'll leave some items for the next day." They also took pleasure in joining their children in entertainment activities that brought them together, such as Internet surfing.

In terms of relationship building, lifecycle stage drew significant differences among consumers. The first such difference was seen in consumers' approach to technology. Figure 11.4 provides a conceptual image.

Young, single consumers seemed much more comfortable around technology than did parents of young and older children. Young consumers were significantly aware of what was going on in entertainment technology; at home, they were the driving force behind the purchase of advanced mobile phones and personal computers. Parents with young children were the least technology-oriented segment in our study. They were born in and around the 1970s, the last generation in Argentina to grow up without a computer. Because their children did not yet demand technology, and they tended not to encounter technology in the workplace, they seemed to lack the motivation to incorporate it to their entertainment universe in particular and their lives in general—at least "until the children ask for it." Parents of older children found a way to technology through their children. While not proficient, many participants conceded that their children had been a major influence in their becoming familiar with technology, for example by showing them how to use their mobile phones or by helping them download music of their preference.

The second difference was seen in the consumers' approach to content. Figure 11.5 provides a conceptual image.

Young, single consumers showed a marked preference for digital content. They relied heavily on the Internet, their mobile phones and MP3 players as entertainment platforms, shunning broadcast and cable television. They resorted to television only to watch content that was not available on any other medium, especially weekly shows featuring irreverent hosts. Young, single

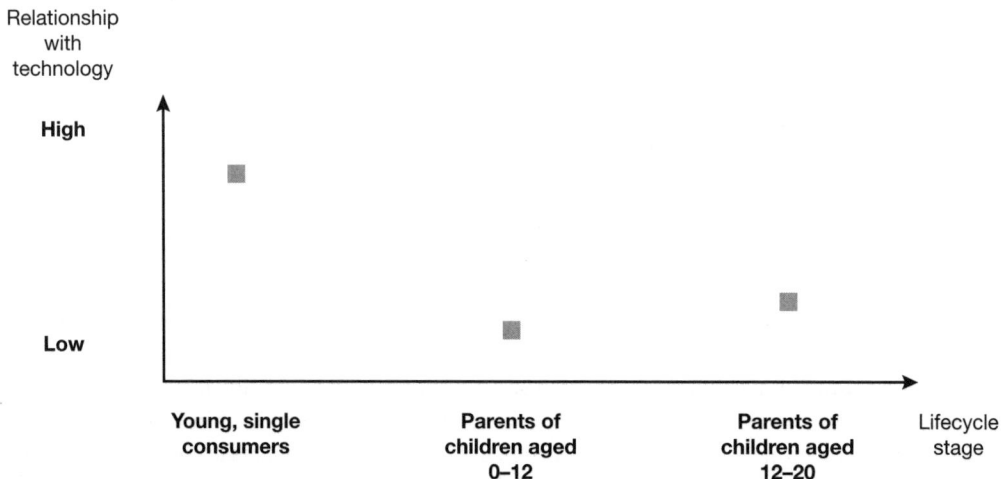

Figure 11.4 Middle-Market Consumers: Relationship Building with Technology According to Lifecycle Stage

Platforms

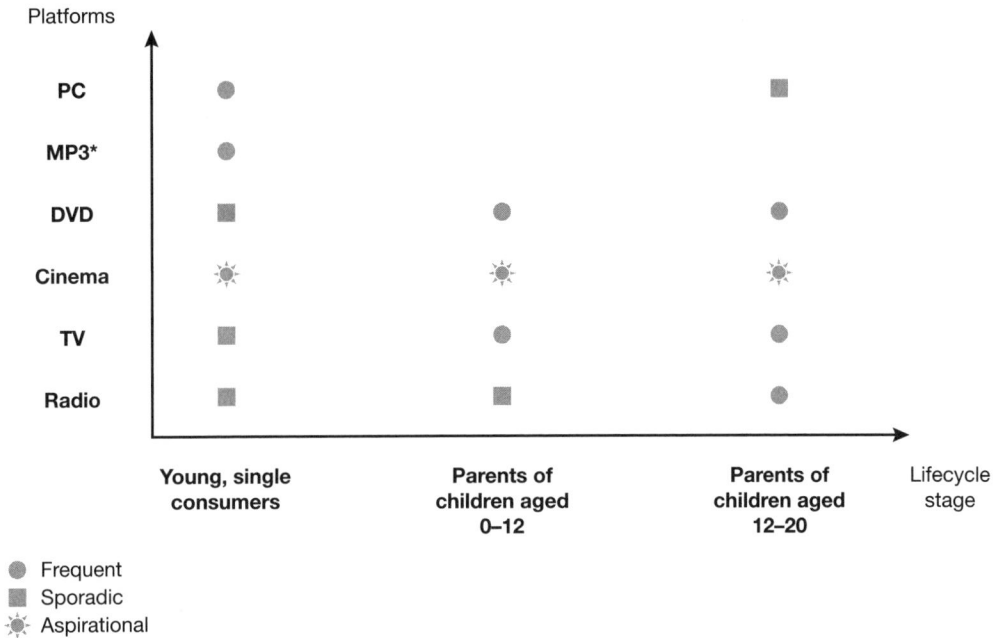

Frequent
Sporadic
Aspirational

*Both stand-alone and embedded in mobile phones

Figure 11.5 Middle-Market Consumers: Relationship Building with Content and Preferred Platforms According to Lifecycle Stage

consumers thus tended to experience content alone or with others located remotely. Conversely, parents of young and older children tended to prefer content available through simple outlets such as television, CDs, DVDs and the radio, and to enjoy it in social settings. Parents of young children often relinquished their preferred content in favor of their children's. A participant stated: "If I am listening to music and my daughter asks for Barney, I have to turn off the music and turn on the TV." Another participant echoed: "I cannot remember what it was like to watch a movie from beginning to end." These consumers seemed disconnected from the newest and latest offerings in content: they paid no attention to new releases and were oblivious to the recommendations on their television guides. Because children aged 12–20 are more independent, their parents seemed to have more time to enjoy their preferred content. Still, they cherished the moments when the family could come together for a television show or a football match. These consumers were also considerably attached to the radio and had generated strong emotional ties with specific broadcasters.

The aspirations of consumers in different lifecycle stages mirrored, to some extent, their current choices in technology and content. Young, single consumers focused on the element of fun, the latest technology, their friends, and live entertainment, especially concerts. Parents of young and older children filled their ideal entertainment universe with options that marked radical differences with their financial reality. They dreamed of providing their families with a beach house, a boat, a better car, open-air entertainment, nature and unlimited shopping. Perhaps not surprisingly, the cinema appeared to be an aspirational entertainment form for all consumers, regardless of lifecycle stage. The movie theatre experience changed significantly in Argentina since the arrival of the multiplex—higher sophistication has brought along higher ticket prices. Parents of young and older children seemed nostalgic for the old days when one could pay for a movie and see a three-feature show.

Evidence of Vertical Fragmentation

The effects of income

Income level drew significant differences among consumers in their conceptualization of entertainment. As mentioned earlier, middle-market consumers associated entertainment with concrete activities performed in relaxed or fun-filled environments. For high-income consumers, entertainment equaled emotion and motivation. Any activity opposed to boredom or work could be deemed entertaining. In this respect, diversity of choice was paramount. Entertainment also entailed a personal care or "pampering" dimension associated with doing things that are good for the mind and body such as cultural activities, sports and traveling. At the other end of the continuum, low-income consumers conceptualized entertainment as any opportunity to alter their routines. The mere act of "going out" signified an opportunity for entertainment. Simple tasks connected to an entertainment experience were viewed as an integral part of that experience.

Income level also had an influence over the amount of free time available for entertainment. While Argentine consumers in all socioeconomic segments endure long working hours—they work an average of 2,053 hours a year and enjoy 18 vacation days, compared to global averages of 1,844 and 20, respectively (UBS (Union Bank of Switzerland), 2006)—our study showed that middle-market and low-income consumers had less disposition and/or possibility of fully devoting that free time to entertainment, compared with high-income consumers. For middle-market and low-income consumers, working hours and commuting times were long. Most of them made it home just in time to take care of the essentials before beginning a new day. Since little room remained for entertainment during the week, most consumers in this segment tended to focus on the weekend. A participant stated: "To me, the weekend equals entertainment." Another echoed: "The only day when none of my friends work and I can meet them is on Sunday." A "weekend feeling" extended to those consumers who worked on Saturday and Sunday but had time off on other days of the week. Conversely, high-income consumers tended to make entertainment plans all week long. On weekdays, consumers chose entertainment options that could be shared with friends; on the weekend, they seemed to concentrate more on family and on themselves.

Income level also influenced the way customers approached entertainment spending. Contrary to what may be expected, middle-market consumers did not seem to monitor entertainment spending closely. They set no specific budget aside for entertainment purposes. Rather, they were very much aware of their financial obligations in other realms (e.g. rent, family consumption) and estimated how much they could spend on entertainment by deducting that from their income. Since income may vary—as it usually does for part-time or independent workers—consumers have varying degrees of freedom to spend on entertainment from week to week. A participant stated: "If I have the money, I'll spend it [on entertainment]. If I don't, then I won't." Another participant echoed: "I can feel the limit." High-income consumers worried about budget only when the purchase of luxury goods and services was involved. No specific calculations were made for what was considered regular entertainment. Low-income consumers were so financially constrained that they could partake of paid entertainment activities only sporadically. Consumers opted for free or low-cost options such as meeting friends, watching television or simply resting. In light of these differences, consumers' approach to open-to-the-public entertainment options (i.e. options offering free admission) was somewhat puzzling. High-income consumers showed a guilt-free attitude towards any such option, such as museums and art galleries. Middle-market consumers had mixed feelings: the perceived quality of free entertainment options such as community theatre plays was heterogeneous.

Dubious quality, matched by sure costs such as transportation and food, turned open-to-the-public options into a risk. A participant stated: "What if I go through all that trouble and my child does not like [the play]? Low-income consumers, on their part, viewed free options as "hand-me-downs" and tended to shun them.

Finally, income level determined the degree of involvement with technology at each stage of a consumer's lifecycle. Young, single consumers were relatively close in their familiarity with technology, regardless of their socioeconomic standing. A specific trait stood out: while high-income consumers focused on design and brands (e.g. referring to the "iPod"), middle-market and low-income consumers focused on the underlying functionality (e.g. referring to the "MP3 player"). Socialization of technology was also another difference: while middle-market consumers seemed prone to share technology with others (e.g. lending a videogame console to a cousin or friend), low-income consumers tended to restrict access to devices they had purchased with their own hard-earned money.

Parents of children aged 0–12 showed the most significant distance, according to income level, in their familiarity with technology. High-income parents, who often had access to technology through their work, could easily relate to technology in other areas of life. Conversely, low-income parents resembled middle-market parents in that they remained distanced from technology. Low-income women, especially, tended to shun technology: many did not own mobile phones for lack of interest and/or a clear notion of their usefulness; few homes had computers or Internet access.

Distance across socioeconomic segments decreased for parents of children aged 12–20. While all parents seemed to learn about technology from their adolescent children, high-income parents tended to proactively demand technology, turning to their children in matters of functionality and brand. Low-income parents again resembled middle-market parents in that they tended to incorporate technology in their lives through their children, e.g. "inheriting" an old mobile phone, albeit to a lesser extent. Figure 11.6 provides a conceptual image.

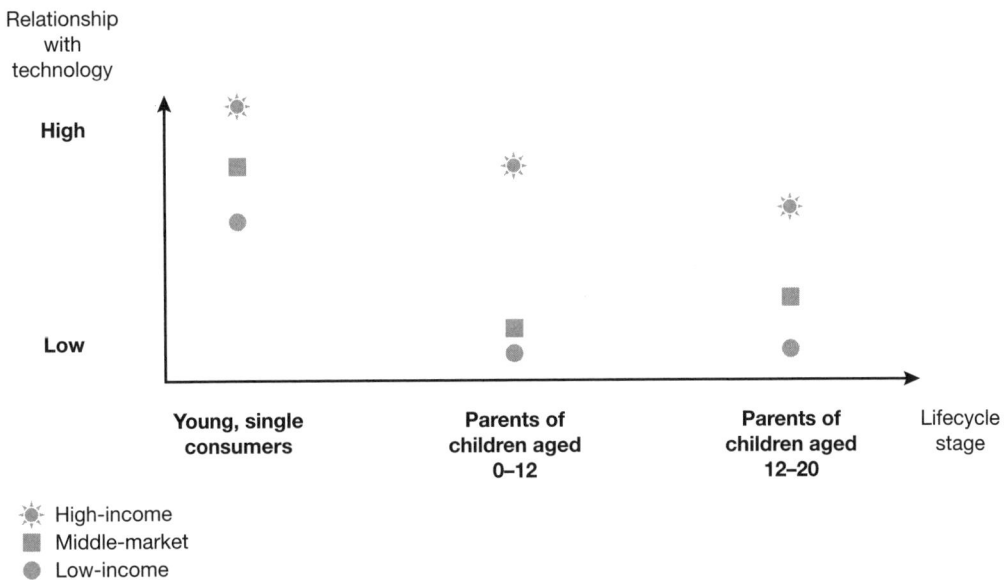

Figure 11.6 Middle-Market Consumers vis-à-vis High-Income and Low-Income Consumers: Relationship Building with Technology According to Lifecycle Stage

The effects of social embeddedness

Burt (2004) proposed that ways of thinking and behaving are more homogeneous within than between social groups. In agreement with this proposition, our study showed that consumers' awareness of and access to entertainment options hinged significantly on the variety and size of the social networks they belong to.

Low-income consumers tended to be deeply ingrained in their local communities. Their social universe was mainly composed of neighbors and family members living close by. The close-knit nature of these consumers' social networks had an evident consequence: consumers tended to always entertain themselves in the same way. Access to other entertainment possibilities—even those potentially within their reach—were rarely experimented with. Endogamic social networks also led to spontaneity in entertainment planning; get-togethers with neighbors emerged on impulse from a chance encounter on the street.

Middle-market consumers were connected not only to family and neighbors but also to some circles of friends. These friends tended to share consumers' circumstances in life; for example, parents of children aged 0–12 tended to bond with other such parents as this tended to simplify the process of getting together. While there was some spontaneity in entertainment planning, most get-togethers were planned by phone or text message. Many consumers had fallen into a routine. A married man stated: "I have lived in the same neighborhood for forty-five years. [A friend] barbecues every Friday night. Eight or nine of us will surely go over for dinner. We do not even exchange phone calls, we just drop by." A young single man echoed: "On Saturday night, we always gather in the same corner. I know I can find everybody there, even when we have no specific plan."

High-income consumers lived at the intersection of many social worlds. They were involved in a variety of networks based not only on geographic proximity and blood ties but also on shared interests, experiences and goals. To family and neighbors they added friends from university, work, country clubs and sports clubs, among other venues. From each group, consumers seemed to derive different entertainment possibilities. Consumers were thus aware of a myriad of entertainment options and tended to plan their schedules carefully in order to fit in all activities of interest.

Conclusion

This study of vertical and horizontal fragmentation among consumers in Argentina's M&E industry sheds light on several aspects of doing business at the bottom of the pyramid. First, results point to important differences not only between middle-market consumers and their high-income and low-income counterparts but also among middle-market consumers themselves. Lifecycle stage, gender, income level and degree of social embeddedness were identified as factors that lead to fragmentation by conditioning the way consumers relate to products and services, move to acquire them, and build aspirations and dreams.

Second, results indicate that BOP consumers are more sophisticated in their interests, tastes and expectations, than portrayed in earlier research. Consumers in our study evidenced a high degree of complexity in their attitudes and behavior vis-à-vis M&E content and technologies. Part of this complexity appears to be rooted in economic, social and psychological barriers that affect consumers' ability to dream, to desire and to experiment. The significance of these barriers for each group of consumers determines the degree of difficulty they find when trying to adopt new, technologically advanced products and services. In this vein, results support the notion that, even when middle-market consumers manage to increase their real income level—as is happening in most of Latin America (*The Economist*, 2007)—consumption of advanced M&E products and services would still be marred by these barriers.

Finally, results suggest that companies doing business in emerging markets should not overlook the importance of properly scanning and segmenting the bottom of the pyramid *before* effecting change in high-impact organizational functions such as product design, production and marketing. Considering the significant changes in industry structure, technology and offerings that lie in store for M&E companies in Argentina, an adequate knowledge of the consumer as an individual (along dimensions that exceed the merely economic) emerges as a necessary antecedent to strategic action.

References

Asociación Argentina de Editores de Revistas (AAER). (2008). *Annual statistics bulletin 2007*. Retrieved September 1, 2008, from www.learevistas.com/editoresrevistas/estadisticas/2007/.

Asociación Argentina de Televisión por Cable (ATVC). (2006). *Cable television is a bridge towards the future*. Buenos Aires: ATVC.

Asociación de Diarios del Interior de la Republica Argentina (ADIRA). (2008). *Regional press*. Retrieved September 1, 2008, from www.adira.org.ar/regional.asp.

Boyd, D. (2007). Why youth (heart) social network sites: The role of networked publics in teenage social life. In D. Buckingham (Ed.), *MacArthur Foundation series on digital learning: Youth, identity, and digital media volume* (pp. 119–142). Cambridge, MA: MIT Press.

Buero, L. (1999). *A history of Argentine television told by its protagonists: 1951–96*. Buenos Aires: Universidad de Morón.

Burt, R. (2004). Structural holes and good ideas. *American Journal of Sociology, 110*(2), 349–399.

Calvo, G. A., Izquierdo, A. & Talvi, E. (2006). *Phoenix miracles in emerging markets: Recovering without credit from systemic financial crises*. Washington, DC: Inter-American Development Bank.

Central Intelligence Agency (CIA). (2008). *The CIA world factbook*. Retrieved September 1, 2008, from https://www.cia.gov/library/publications/the-world-factbook/.

Cisco. (2008). *Cisco broadband barometer* (5th ed.). Brazil: Cisco.

Convergencia. (2007). *Map of communications alliances in Argentina*. Buenos Aires: Grupo Convergencia.

Convergencia Latina. (2006). *Latin American yearbook: Broadband scenarios and market trends*. Buenos Aires: Convergencia Latina.

D'Andrea, G., Costa, L., Fernandes, F. & Fossen, F. (2007). Three ways to seduce emerging consumers. *Harvard business review América Latina*, (May), 40–49.

D'Andrea, G., Stengel, E. A. & Goebel-Krstelj, A. (2003). Creating value for emerging consumers. *Harvard business review América Latina*, (November), 112–119.

The Economist. (2004). Becoming a serious country. *The Economist, 371* (8378), June 3, 3–5.

The Economist. (2006). Tucking in to the good times. *The Economist, 381* (8509), December 19, 51–52.

The Economist. (2007). Adiós to poverty, hola to consumption. *The Economist, 384* (8542), August 16, 21–23.

The Economist. (2009). The Kirchners make a dash for it. *The Economist, 390* (8624), March 28, 43.

Gasparini, L., Gutiérrez, F. & Tornarolli, L. (2005). Growth and income poverty in Latin America and the Caribbean: Evidence from household surveys. *Review of Income and Wealth, 53*(2), 209–245.

Infobrand. (2008). Illegal cable connections make an appearance in advertising. *Infobrand, 214*, March 10.

Informa Telecoms & Media. (2007). *Cable and satellite yearbook 2008*. London: Informa.

Instituto Verificcador de Circulaciones (IVC). (2007). *Monthly bulletin*. January–December issues.

International Monetary Fund (IMF). (2007). *World economic outlook database—October 2007*. Retrieved September 1, 2008, from www.imf.org/external/pubs/ft/weo/2007/02/weodata/index.aspx.

Ipsos. (2007). *General media study*. A database accessible by subscription only.

Lincoln, Y. S. & Guba, E. G. (1985). *Naturalistic inquiry*. Newbury Park, CA: Sage.

London, T. & Hart, S. L. (2004). Reinventing strategies for emerging markets: Beyond the transnational model. *Journal of International Business Studies, 35*(5), 350–370.

Marano, H. E. (1999). The power of play. *Psychology today, 32*(4), 36–40, 68–69.

Matallana, A. (2006). *Crazy about radio: A social history of radio broadcasting in Argentina, 1923–1947*. Buenos Aires: Prometeo.

La Nación. (2007). Goodbye to paper? Newspapers before the digital challenge. *La Nación*, February 25. Retrieved September 1, 2008, from www.lanacion.com.ar/886315.

Nielsen. (2006). *Survey on consumer opinion and confidence*. Retrieved September 1, 2008, from www.amai.org/datos_files/ACNIELSEN_Estudio_mundial_confianza_del_consumidor.pdf.

Perry, G. E., Arias, O. S., Lopez, J. H., Maloney, W. F. & Serven, L. (2006). *Poverty reduction and growth: Virtuous and vicious circles*. Washington, DC: World Bank.

Prahalad, C. K. (2004). *The fortune at the bottom of the pyramid: Eradicating poverty through profits*. Upper Saddle River, NJ: Wharton School.

Seelos, C. & Mair, J. (2007). Profitable business models and market creation in the context of deep poverty: A strategic view. *The Academy of Management Perspectives, 21*(4), 49–63.

Steiner, M. (2004). Knowledge network as institutions for technology management. In C. Karlsson, P. Flensburg & S.-A. Hörte (Eds.), *Knowledge spillovers and knowledge management* (pp. 373–395). Cheltenham, UK: Edward Elgar.

UBS (Union Bank of Switzerland). (2006). *Prices and earnings: A comparison of purchasing power around the globe* (2006 ed.). Retrieved September 1, 2008, from www.ubs.com/1/e/ubs_ch/wealth_mgmt_ch/research.html.

Ulanovsky, C. (2005). *Stop the presses: Newspapers, magazines, and journalists (1920–1969)*. Buenos Aires: Emecé.

Ulanovsky, C. (2007). *I always listen to you: Portraits of Argentine radio in the twenty-first century*. Buenos Aires: Emecé.

Vogel, H. L. (2007). *Entertainment industry economics: A guide for financial analysis* (7th ed.). New York: Cambridge University Press.

12
The Media in Uruguay

Eileen Hudson, Fernando Salas, Lucila Carbajal and Florencia Traibel
University of Montevideo, Uruguay

Introduction: Half a Century of Transformation in Uruguayan Society

Celedonio Nin y Silva describes Uruguay as "the smallest of South American countries, 15 times smaller than Argentina and 45 times smaller than Brazil." However, "comparing its area with that of some European countries, one can see that it is larger than Switzerland, Denmark, Belgium, Holland, Luxembourg and Albania put together" (Nin y Silva, 1930, p. 2).

During the first half of the twentieth century Uruguay felt like a great little country. President Luis Batlle Berres wrote in 1948 in an editorial in the dialy newspaper *Acción*:

> Ours is a great little country. If once it could rightly be called a laboratory in labor rights experimentation, nowadays it can be called, just as rightly, a small oasis of peace, freedom and justice, in a world upset by tragic realities or compromising prospects. Let us be clearly conscious that Uruguay is a country of exception.
>
> (Batlle Berres, 1948, p. 2)

"Social laboratory," "Switzerland of South America," "Athens of the River Plate," "oasis of peace and freedom" were all descriptions alluding to a country exceptional in Latin America due to its economic, political and social development. However, the latter half of the twentieth century seems to have led it, as Carlos and Fernando Filgueira said in the title of their book, through a "long goodbye to the model-country" (Filgueira and Filgueira, 1994, p. 305).

Economic Transformation: Evolution of the Gross Domestic Product

The dynamic Uruguayan economy during the first half of the twentieth century (a yearly 3.3 percent growth between 1900 and 1957) contrasts with its modest growth in the second half (1.7 percent growth between 1957 and 2000), ending in one of the most serious economic crises in the twentieth century (1999–2002). By the end of that crisis, the GDP had shrunk 18 percent, a drop surpassed in the twentieth century only by the aftermath of the 1929 crisis (Bértola & Bittencourt, 2005).

Starting in 2003, Uruguay recovered in great stride with a 7 percent average annual growth which continued until 2007 and in 2005 allowed for the recovery of the GDP previous to the crisis.

This growth is significant in comparative terms and placed the country in thirty-eighth place worldwide and in fifth place in Latin America regarding growth rates in 2007.

However, the Uruguayan economy's absolute numbers are not that impressive. While the average GDP of the world's countries amounts to $286 billion and that of the Mercosur group to $606 billion, Uruguay's GDP is barely $37 billion, which in 2007 ranks it in ninety-eighth place worldwide and in fifteenth place in Latin America.

The situation improves when one considers GDP per capita ($10,700) in which Uruguay ranks only slightly above the world average ($10,000) and that of Latin America ($8,815). The country is ranked ninety-third globally and seventh in the region (Central Intelligence Agency (CIA), 2008).

Economic differences with the West have expanded throughout the years. In 1957, the Uruguayan GDP per capita amounted to 65 percent of the average GDP of Germany, United States, France and Great Britain. In 2007 it was equal to 29 percent of the GDP of these countries.

Political Transformation: Governance

Uruguay is a democratic republic, with a two-chamber Parliament, within a pluralistic political context that respects civil and political rights and liberties. Uruguay has stood out in the region for its strong democratic commitment during the twentieth century. This does not mean that non-democratic governments did not exist. In fact, for every six years in the twentieth century, one was spent under an authoritarian government, although these were less frequent than in neighboring countries. Except for these periods, political parties have been the key players in government.

Since the beginning of constitutional life until 2005, the executive branch was held by two parties: the Colorado Party and the Nacional Party. The left-wing coalition Encuentro Progresista–Frente Amplio–Nueva Mayoría (Progressive Encounter–Broad Front–New Majority) won the national elections in 2004.

Lobby groups also have significant activity in the government, especially those that represent workers and businessmen. They take part in corporate institutions such as wage councils, the National Employment Board and the board of directors of the Banco de Previsión Social (BPS: Social Insurance Bank).

Population Trends

If we compare Uruguay's demographic density with the European Union countries, one can conclude that this country is deserted. Only nineteen inhabitants per square kilometer live in Uruguay compared to eighty in Mediterranean European countries with the lowest population density.

Twenty years after its independence, Uruguay had a population of 131,969 people. In 2008 there were 3,460,607 people, but Uruguay continues to be the least inhabited country in Latin America, after Panama.

It is a desert that is becoming more and more insignificant in comparative terms. While the average growth of the world's population reaches an annual 1.3 percent, in Uruguay it reaches only 0.5 percent a year (CIA, 2008). In Latin America, only Cuba, Puerto Rico and Nicaragua have such a low growth rate.

The scarce population growth is due to Uruguayans' low birth rate as well as to their willingness to emigrate. Uruguay reduced its birth rate at the same time as European countries did, and before any other Latin American country. That progress has led nowadays to a birth rate of 1.97 children per woman, a figure below that needed to reproduce the number of inhabitants. Only Chile, Brazil and Cuba have similar or lower rates in Latin America.

Even worse, Uruguayans waste no time in packing their luggage. The nation was built with a strong European immigration who had fled wars and economic crises. In the 1970s the country was hit by a major economic crisis, a guerrilla movement (Tupamaros) and military brass willing to stage a coup d'état. In this context, 580,000 people (approximately 17 percent of the current Uruguayan population) left the country.

Population distribution within the territory is also peculiar. Montevideo, the capital, is the smallest of Uruguay's political districts. However, it holds more than 40 percent of the total population. Also, Uruguayans prefer living in cities instead of rural areas. While worldwide, one in two people live in cities, in Uruguay 92 percent live in urban areas. Only thirteen countries are more urbanized than Uruguay.

About 13.4 percent of Uruguayans are over 65, while 100 years ago, this age group amounted to only 2 percent of the population. Meanwhile, children are a shrinking group, from 41 percent to 23.4 percent of the population in the same period. These trends have led Uruguay to become the country with the oldest population in Latin America.

Radio

Birth of Radio

Radio was launched in Uruguay in 1922, although the first broadcasting attempts were made a year earlier by Sebastián Paradizábal, from the rooftop of the Florida Hotel (then located in the historic center of Montevideo). It was also Paradizábal who on November 6, 1922, founded the first commercial radio transmitter in Uruguay, called Radio Paradizábal. Six days after it was launched, it was used for the first time to deliver a speech by a politician, José Batlle y Ordóñez, the two-time constitutional president of the country.

Radio and Other Media

In contrast with the press, radio demands fewer expenses and is more economic for the user. The reception of its messages does not face cultural limitations, since it reaches both illiterates and those who are not everyday readers of newspapers. This is a trait that radio in Uruguay shares with television.

In the 1940s, radio was at its height, becoming the first-choice medium for information. It became the centre of family life. In politics it held an important place, not only because political leaders used it frequently and efficiently, but also because it bore concrete good results.

With the emergence of a new medium began a period in which political leaders sooner or later adapted to. Historian José Rilla believes the phenomenon by which political leaders adapted to radio is comparable to the one that happened with television a few years later. "Politicians took time to learn to use the radio, as one can still see them doing with television" (Rilla and Caetano, 2005, p. 310). One of the first to learn about the use that could be made of radio was political leader Benito Nardone, with his *ruralism* movement,

> because he had managed to take advantage of that conversational thing, which mixes anecdote with politics. It was a language of conversation, not of speeches in a rally, which also existed; there were people who used the microphone as if they were in front of 50 thousand people. But slowly political leaders began to understand.
>
> (Rilla and Caetano, 2005, p. 310)

With the invention of transistors a portable receiver was made possible, which coincided with the appearance of television. Although radio suffered from the impact of the latter, it benefited from being the more economic medium and, by being portable, it could be taken anywhere, even to work.

Although radio grew similarly to other media and had no major technological flaws, it was the gap between the launching of FM technology and its introduction in Uruguay which caused a domestic quality difference in radio. FM appeared in 1938, but in Uruguay it emerged twenty years later. This led to an uneven growth between both radio bandwidths as tools of the same medium. Only in the 1990s would AM and FM no longer have differences in terms of technology or contents.

With the emergence of the Internet, radio had another ally: most of the country's radio stations have their own website. The first Uruguayan radio station to become part of the web was El Espectador, which launched its site in 1996, also being one of the first in Latin America to do so.

Thousands of Uruguayans connect to Uruguayan radios from abroad. One should remember that some half a million Uruguayans live abroad, mostly in the United States, Spain and Argentina.

Radio as an Element of Resistance

The last military dictatorship in Uruguay (1973–1984) used communications media with propaganda purposes, and also applied severe censorship to journalists and media owners. Public announcements, music and public figures which attended the shows had to pass through the military censorship filter. Radio, although not exempted from this censorship on freedom of speech, also enabled in a clandestine way resistance to the status quo. The silences, intonation, the way things were read, and coded messages for attentive ears turned out to be key weapons in this sense.

It was natural to listen to journalists who opposed the regime and who said so without saying. For example, at the beginning of the period, journalist Ruben Castillo, with his show *Discodromo* on Radio Sarandí, announced in a very particular way that a public demonstration against the dictatorship was to take place. Each time he came on after commercials, using a García Lorca poem and tricking the censors, Castillo simply said: "At five in the afternoon." Thus he communicated the time of what turned out to be a massive rally on 18 de Julio Avenue, with thousands of people from various political parties. Democracy brought with it a lot of information and journalistic shows became key players of national reality at a time where society was undergoing a true renaissance.

Currently, Uruguay has a very strong legal framework which seeks to preserve freedom of speech for the media. Section 29 in the Constitution of the Republic enshrines freedom of thought, of word, private or public texts in the press, with no need of censorship. There is also a national Radio Broadcasting Act (14.670) and a state agency regulating the concession made by the government of radio waves to private parties. According to the law, the state owns all radio and television frequencies, and runs only some as official stations joined in an agency called SODRE, and granting the rest to private parties, albeit irrevocable and non-permanently.

Radio at the Present Time

Uruguay has more than 160 AM, FM and short-wave radio stations operating in the capital and the interior. Uruguayan radio broadcasting is dense in radio stations, compared to its slightly more than 3 million people and less than 176,000 square kilometers (approximately one station for every 26,000 inhabitants, a number equal or higher to that of developed countries).

It is quite common for the average Uruguayan to tune in to a favorite radio station for the whole day. That is why dial surfing is not as extensive in radio as it is in television.

Radio broadcasting in Uruguay can be described—although with exceptions in every case—as follows: stations are not run in isolation; they are part of radio-television or radio network conglomerates. They have transmission and taping studios and broadcast stations, most of them set up with low technical infrastructures. The stations transmit with low output power, which lowers costs between 10 and 0.25 kilowatts. If we consider that some 40 kilowatts are needed as output to cover the whole country, there are very few stations with such coverage. In the interior there are no transmitters with nationwide coverage. They exist in Montevideo, although due to various technical reasons, not all of them can be heard nationwide. They are CX4 Radio Rural, CX6 Sodre, CX 12 Oriental, CX14 El Espectador, CX16 Carve and CX38 Sodre. Only six stations cover the whole nation.

Regarding programming, quality in radio is comparatively higher than that of television. There are several stations in Uruguay with an extensive journalistic tradition and shows of great quality on the air. However, radio also faces problems regarding availability and economic investment. This forces several radios to base their programming on music, which is considerably less costly than offering a journalistic product.

As to the quality of broadcasts, technological dynamism has raised competitiveness among radios to a good degree. The use of laser sound, as well as digital systems and archives, are now key factors for any station that seeks to offer good audio quality. Nowadays there is almost no difference between the technology used by an AM or FM station.

Another distinction among Uruguayan radios can be found between the Montevideo and interior stations. Each one of the regions comes from different economic and cultural scenarios, with their own cultural identity, specified by the type of use of the primary sector, and by demographic structure and population distribution among urban and rural areas. Among the interior provinces there are stations that play more of a social than an informational role and cover services which Montevideo stations do not offer. The information varies according to the location. News has a nationwide nature that, once it passes through the local filter, loses importance. International news depends not only on the province, but also on the relation it may have with other countries. Thus, the provinces that have borders with Argentina or Brazil have a large influence from these countries and also many in its audience listen to their radios.

The radio audience is not merely a receptive and passive mass; it tends to be highly involved and demands various styles on the Uruguayan dial. Localism is very important for cities in the interior, and even in the capital this practice is reproduced in the so-called community radio stations. Communication from these stations that are not regulated by the government, and are therefore illegal, is much more segmented than national services. Information, mixed with daily life and things close to home, and what is happening where one lives, makes a difference for listeners. At present, the regulation of these low-range radios is being discussed by the Uruguayan Parliament.

There is a wide range of radio stations: journalistic, religious (which play a social role for their followers), stations that have interactive shows with the audience, radios that have only music, and sports (in a country that is highly fanatical about sports, where sports history is very linked to radio and television, and where radio commentators have not lost their place with the appearance of television and cable). There are formats with other profiles, mostly political where leaders have their own space, or those that are more pluralistic than others, depending on the objectivity the medium gives to its product.

In short, radio in Uruguay is a very extended communication medium. The country has several stations with a significant informative tradition, such as El Espectador, which has been on the air for eighty-five years, and Radio Sarandí, which produces renowned journalistic shows and figures. Many stations use all of the radiophonic formats. Apart from using advanced technological elements, they use the services of international agencies, reporters from the interior and abroad, mobile units and the audience itself.

In contrast, radio stations need to improve their investment potential. The advertising pie is very limited and this is a hard obstacle to overcome, which is further stressed by the number of stations operating in Uruguay. Also, people working in radio should be professionals. Many lack professional training, in part because university communication studies are a relatively recent phenomenon in Uruguay.

The medium enjoys freedom of speech in its widest sense, which can be seen in how carefully content is handled in order not to harm anybody in the community. For public opinion, radio is not a mere companion, its power as a medium and its importance to reaching more people is critical. Radio continues to be the mass medium that fosters the imagination.

The Press

Press Landmarks throughout the Twentieth Century

Uruguay's press developed two traits throughout the twentieth century. The first is that dailies were born and developed as vehicles for political parties. This is detailed in *Crónica del Periodismo en el Uruguay* (A Chronicle of Journalism in Uruguay) by Álvarez Ferretjans (1980), which reproduces the editorials of all of the Uruguayan press since 1807. Second, since the late 1980s, Uruguayan dailies did not publish news, except in the case of the weekly *Búsqueda*.

El Día was published for the first time on July 16, 1886, as an opposition vehicle to the dictatorship of General Máximo Santos. In 1903, José Batlle y Ordóñez, its founder, was elected president of the republic and the daily became the Batllismo's party vehicle. In the 1920s, political leaders thought that the shortest path for political proselytism was launching a daily. When nationalist daily *La Democracia* closed in late 1917, the Nacional Party "was seeking a press organ that reflected its aspirations, demands and points of view on the varied problems of national reality" (Álvarez Ferretjans, 1980, p. 313). Thus, on September 14, 1918 three Nacional Party activists founded *El País* daily. Also in 1917 appeared *La Mañana*, founded by two Colorado politicians, who had left Batllismo. On July 6, 1923 the first issue of *El Diario* was published by Sociedad Editora Uruguay, owner of *La Mañana*, and therefore, close to the Colorado Party. According to Álvarez Ferretjans (1980, p. 321), *El Diario* was the first newspaper to design a front page only with one title and a large photograph, "in the best style of North American dailies".

During the electoral campaign of 1966 the golden rule was applied and every candidate wanted to have their own daily. The dailies were the primary tools of the political work of politicians. Readers were not expecting to find independent information but the confrontation of political ideas. This trend was maintained until the late 1980s.

The military dictatorship which ruled Uruguay from June 27, 1973 until March 1, 1985 worsened the situation, and the media's political dialog was replaced by "homogenized and monotonous information, determined in its major and also its minor lines by the military regime" (Álvarez Ferretjans, 1980, p. 374). According to Álvarez Ferretjans (1980), the military government was a setback for Uruguayan journalism since informative journalism limited itself to the information allowed according to new national security criteria. Also, the reversal of the democratic principle that says there should be minimum secrecy and maximum information has led to ludicrous extremes such as considering State secrets common activities of the industrial agencies or public utilities. The fall in sales during the dictatorship was estimated at 75 percent.

(Álvarez Ferretjans, 1980, p. 375)

Just before 1973, the Uruguayan press sold 500,000 newspapers per day.

In 1981, four years before the end of the dictatorship, the afternoon daily *Últimas Noticias* began. The newspaper was presented as "an opposition to Marxism-Leninism and Communist political leaders, whichever may be the mode of their presence, tactics and fellow companions" (Álvarez Ferretjans, 1980, p. 2).

Among non-daily publications was *Búsqueda*, a monthly magazine founded in 1971 by Ramón Díaz, a distinguished Uruguayan economist and lawyer. *Búsqueda* specialized in economic policy and its target audience was the sector made up by leaders.

In 1990 the top-selling dailies were *El País* and *La República*. *La República* was launched in April, 1988, founded by Federico Fassano. Both treated information with substantial differences.

Typically, *El País* has handled everyday information through the particular sympathies of its numerous editorial board, which has notoriously affected the credibility of its contents. We should add to this circumstance the evident lack of professionalism in the handling of information, whose titling and writing deviates from the basic style rules taught in manuals for beginner journalists.

(Research Internacional, 1991, p. 31)

La República based its success on

a curious mix of sensationalism and a certain dose of professionalism in its treatment of information. Its model panders with intelligence to Uruguayan society's hyper-politicism; a defect which turns political issues into the main core of its concerns.

(Research Internacional, 1991, p. 33)

Meanwhile, *El País* and *La República* developed very different commercial policies. *El País* based its growth on a classified ads supplement which, apart from attracting advertisers, was key to the growth of the daily in the 1980s. In 1991, three years after it was launched, *La República* lacked advertisers but had developed a niche of readers made up by those who did not want to read *El País* and those who bought it as their second daily newspaper.

Búsqueda's situation was unique. The weekly's readers belonged to the upper and upper-middle social and economic levels, and although it sold only 18,000 copies per week, it competed in the advertising market with *El País*. *El Observador* was published on October 22, 1991. The daily was founded by Dr Ricardo Peirano, a lawyer and businessman. The idea was to create a publication that informed and interpreted news and attracted the upper and middle social and economic readers' market. *La Diaria* was founded in 2006; it is published from Monday to Friday and also specializes in interpretative journalism.

Transformation of the Press during the 1990s

In 1991, motivation to purchase and read dailies was very determined by "the tradition value, a value which grants newspapers a very high margin of credibility and confidence" (Research Internacional, 1991, p. 5). The second motivation was "habit, an aspect which strengthens the daily's affective significance" (p. 13). The confidence that comes with something one already knows was so decisive it even neutralized the non-conformance caused by the approach, style or depth of some of the publications (Research Internacional, 1991).

In 1991 El País was the most traditional daily and held 49 percent of the market. The rest of the market was shared by six dailies being published in Montevideo.

One of the journalistic landmarks of the decade was the coverage of the referendum on the Public Utilities Act, in December 1992, in which El Observador gave priority to its independence, even going against its corporate interests, while El País continued its tradition of partisan journalism.[1]

Starting in 1993, El País and El Observador became the two Uruguayan dailies with the largest distribution and highest penetration in the country. Both began processes to redesign their papers and redefine their contents. The companies also worked with expert international consultants.

The aim of the journalistic firms' management in the following years was to professionalize their staff, which had worked up to then in hierarchic, closed compartments. Both El País and El Observador launched newsrooms. Their aim was to eliminate the spirit of the assembly line and strengthen the teamwork of their journalists.

Even so, in 1996 the market for dailies kept shrinking. In 1992, an average of 51,365 daily newspapers was sold in Montevideo. In 1994 it fell to 50,238, and in 1995 to 44,921 (Research Internacional, 1997).

For this reason, and although they were managing different processes and experiences, as well as consultants, both companies defined their growth strategy increasing the readership among their target audience and also strengthening the identity and image of each medium. According to the market studies at the time, credibility was the quality best valued by readers. The newspapers sought to follow the advice that Carl Sessions Stepp published in 1997: "dailies that wish to survive must invest in human resources and take long term decisions that impact the informative quality of their contents" (Stepp, 1997, p. 31).

In April 1996, the market for the Uruguayan press continued to drop. El País, El Observador and La República, the three top-selling dailies, barely reached average sales of 21,786 copies per day.

Journalistic companies then redoubled the effort to strengthen their daily contents and also began a battle to hold on to their best journalists. If they offered better contents, they thought, they would keep their readers, even if they belonged to an elite sector, and later on would have the chance to try to develop massive growth strategies.

Meanwhile, both invested in the development of their websites. Between 1995 and 2005 El Observador redesigned its website four times; El País, twice. The former worked with the help of the Catalonian company Sol90; the latter, with Mario Tascón, from El País of Madrid. Although the number of daily visitors has been a success, they still have not managed to attract advertising investors. Therefore, this success does not reflect in the salaries of their web journalists.

Primary elections prior to the general elections of November took place in April 26, 1999. El Observador and El País launched special sections to cover the elections. Thus the work routine was drastically modified and 'he said – she said' journalism, at least during election time, was history. In 1999, political journalism produced by El Observador and El País was very little like the content published in 1991.

Even though the sale of dailies was sustained throughout the first decade of the twenty-first century, both companies resorted to promotional products such as history and sports books in order to increase their readers. In the case of El Observador, investment in this type of product grew 96 percent.

The Argentine crisis in 2001 and the unprecedented Uruguayan crisis in 2002 affected the national press in a considerable way. Earnings from advertising and sales fell, and therefore many journalists lost their jobs.

Television

Since 2000, Uruguayan television has completely changed. As in other Latin American countries, the broadcasting market has grown enormously in a very short period of time. Since the arrival of television in 1956, the spectators have gone through a lot of new possibilities in the televion market. But some of the most important possibilities are on the way.

"Ladies and gentleman, from this moment, CXATV Channel 10, Saeta, is on air to all over Uruguay." These were the first words transmitted by television in Uruguay on December 7, 1956. This year the family group Fontaina-De Feo, founded Channel 10-Saeta TV and made the first telecast. Raul Fontaina welcomed Uruguayans to the "media revolution." That was the beginning of television in Uruguay. In that first broadcast Fontaina interviewed some personalities and an American newscast was put on air. At that time no more than 500 people owned a television receiver. The telecast was from 8:30 p.m. to 12 midnight. Five years later, Channel 4-Montecarlo TV, owned by the group Romay Salvo, was inaugurated, and in 1962 Channel 12-Teledoce entered in the business managed by the family Giampietro Scheck. The three economic groups were also involved in other media business such as newspapers and radios (Rubio, 1995).

Since then, the television market has become more competitive. From 1962 to 2002, the same families run the channels. The Over the View TV in Uruguay was born as an oligopoly of family business. Some years later, the television groups also began to operate in the cable television business. This reality defined the sense and contents of Uruguayan television until the present day (Rubio, 1998).

The 2002 economic crisis left the broadcasting firms in need of money and this became an opportunity for other national groups to invest in the television channels. Some of the most important economics groups entered the business. The market became more professional and began to require trained professionals. Despite that, the three families maintained a large share of the enterprise and still have influence in the management of the channels.

Located in the capital of Uruguay, television took a few years to reach the rest of the country. In 1981, three channels founded the Red Uruguaya de Televisión, an association for broadcasting to the rest of the country through seventeen television stations. Due to the creation of the Red (network), they had absolute control of private television in Montevideo and guaranteed a strong presence in the rest of Uruguay. In 1981, color television arrived, but it was not until 1984 that the public television channel began to telecast in color. Nowadays the private television system includes sixty-one channels all over Uruguay, with three main channels located in Montevideo and fifty-eight in the rest of the states (Da Rosa, 2004).

Cable Television

The arrival of cable television in the early 1990s changed the Uruguayan system. As Carlos García Rubio notes, "pay TV created an enormous market involving millions of dollars per year in a short period of time" (Rubio, 1998, p. 34). Cable television "woke up" the local market and pushed the private channels to put more efforts into programming. It also created a new kind of consumer, one more demanding of good service. The consumers were paying to watch television, because they wanted variety and less advertising time, as well as 24/7 service. This demand forced the private television channels to change. But the arrival did not bring a public and serious debate on the new television system. According to García Rubio: "neither the mass media nor the policy leaders discussed the importance of cable television in Uruguay. This matter was not treated with transparency" (Rubio, 1998, p. 45).

In 1993 the Uruguayan government opened the cable television market for operators. A total of thirteen companies applied to supply the service, but only five were selected. The oligopoly of the family companies remained. Three licenses to develop cable services in Uruguay were given to three companies linked to the TV Channels: Nuevo Siglo Cable TV belongs to Channel 12, Televisión Cable Color to Channel 10 and Montecable to Channel 4. The government also sold the license of "Codified TV" (UHF) to two companies: Multiseñal (currently, Multicanal, owned by Equital) and TVC (national economics groups). Equital SA was created by the television channels to advise legally and financially to other companies interested in providing cable television in other states outside Montevideo.

Years later, the television firms arranged with the capital state government to broadcast a public channel in their programming to promote culture and entertainment in Montevideo. They also made an arrangement with Tenfield SA, the company that owns the rights for soccer match telecast in Uruguay. Federico Fasano, the owner of *La República*, arranged with Multicanal to have a news and entertainment channel, called VTV.

The way the government awarded the cable systems limited the possibility of having more variety and opportunities available to the audience. If the market had been opened to other companies (instead of the ones which already held the oligopoly on private television) there would have been more competition and more opportunities to create and develop television programming. It must be stated that the international legislation considers this matter as an important issue and forbids a company to operate both television stations and cable television in the same area (Lieber & Luzardo, 2002).

The Arrival of DBS (Direct Broadcast Satellites)

In 1996, Latin American welcomed "Direct To Home" (DTH) broadcasting. Direct TV (Echo Star Communications in association with Editorial Abril from Brazil, MVS Multivision of Mexico and Grupo Cisneros from Venezuela, Multivision Chile and Grupo Clarín from Argentina) was the first company to provide satellite television to the region. One year later, Sky Latin American (owned by Rupert Murdoch) arrived in the market and built a partnership with Globo Brazil and Televisa Mexico (Lieber & Luzardo, 2002).

According to García Rubio, television companies put pressure on the government to avoid the arrival of Direct TV (Rubio, 1998). On February 10, 2000, the administration of President Julio María Sanguinetti ordered that satellite television could provide only sixteen channels, a lower number in comparison with those offered by Direct TV. A few months later, the new government, headed by Jorge Batlle, annulled the decree and in 2001 Direct TV finally began operating in Uruguay.

Nowadays there are more than 250 television operators including OVTV (over-the-air) channels, cable and satellite television. Only 2 percent of the companies are in Montevideo. In the rest of the country, Direct TV and cable reach more people than terrestrial television. The channels include basically the same television networks. Uruguayans pay an average of $30 dollars per month for cable television or Direct TV. According to the rating system, cable has almost the same number of viewers as regular TV. The public exhibits the same behaviors; they watch the most television or cable during prime time. By 2007 almost 390,000 homes in Uruguay subscribed to cable television (66 percent). If the crisis of 2002 had not happened, the number would have been larger.

Trying to Enter into the World

With the competition of cable and Direct TV, the OVTV channels adopted new strategies. With globalization, the arrival of many television productions from Argentina, Brazil and the United States forced producers to adapt to a new reality. The Uruguayan audience became a more demanding public. Broadcast producers found themselves forced to reach a higher level of quality in order to compete with foreign programs.

In 1990, Argentine television began to have a great influence in Uruguay. The channels purchased more foreign programs and gave the public more variety. Presently, each channel has an Argentine partner. Channel 4 is associated with Telefé (Channel 11), Channel 12 Teledoce is associated with Canal 13 (Artear Argentina) and Channel 10 Saeta buys some programs from Channel 9. They also have particular arrangements with global news agencies and news networks from other countries. Uruguayan television does not itself contribute to the global market.

In terms of a digital television standard, Uruguay ended the internal debate on which system to implement. It took the government and the Asociación Nacional de Broadcasters Uruguayos (ANDEBU: Association of Uruguayan Broadcasters) almost a year to reach the conclusion that the European set DVB-T/DVB.H was best for the Uruguayan television system.

Now television operators must take on the challenge of converting to digital and accelerate the process of updating their stations. Some have already started. The OVTV channels decided to embark on globalization by hiring experts to tell them how to invest in technology and intending to professionalize a business that was traditionally associated with family issues.

But other segments of the market are being discovered. Uruguay began to study the possibility of combining television with Internet and mobile telephony. In January 2008, Ancel, the state-owned telephone company, announced a new service for its clients: the possibility to access pay-per-view television on mobile phones. Initially only four channels are included.

The process of entering the global television market has not been easy for the Uruguayan companies. It will take a few years to reach the quality expected to compete with other global companies. But they are urged to be ready to face the revolution that will come with the advent of digital television.

Note

1   *El País* and *El Observador* supported the law that privatized public utilities. Two days before the referendum, *El Observador* issued headlines with the results of surveys that forecast the death of the bill, while *El País* ignored reality and chose a headline from a society section news instead.

References

Alvarez Ferretjans, A. (1980). *Crónica del periodismo en el Uruguay, Montevideo, Uruguay*. Fundación: Hans Seidel.
Batlle Berres, L. (1948, October 22). Editorial page published on the first edition of the newspaper *Acción*.
Bértola, L. & Bittencourt, G. (2005). Veinte años de democracia sin desarrollo económico. In G. Caetano (Ed.), *Veinte años de democracia* (pp. 305–330). Montevideo, Uruguay: Taurus.
Caetano, G. & Porzekanski, T. (1997). *Historia de la vida privada en el Uruguay, individuo y soledades 1920–1990*. Montevideo, Uruguay: Taurus.
Central Intelligence Agency (CIA). (2008). *The CIA world factbook*. Retrieved June 4, 2008, from https://www.cia.gov/library/publications/the-world-factbook/.
Da Rosa, J. (2004, July). *Informe Seminario públicos: Públicos, medios y calidad*. Seminar held in Montevideo.
Diario Ultimas Noticias. (1981, September 18). Editorial page published on the first edition of the newspaper.
Filgueira, C. & Filgueira F. (1994). *El largo adió al país modelo: Políticas sociales y pobreza en Uruguay*. Editorial Arca y Kellog.
Lieber, E. & Luzardo. V. (2002). La televisión Uruguaya. Unpublished graduate thesis. Montevideo, Uruguay: Universidad Católica del Uruguay.

Nin y Silva, C. (1930). *La República del Uruguay en su primer centenario, 1830–1930*. Montevideo, Uruguay: Ministerio de Relaciones Exteriores.

Research Internacional. (1991). *Informe sobre el mercado de la prensa escrita, una investigación previa al lanzamiento de El Observador*. Montevideo, Uruguay: Archivo del diario El Observador.

Research Internacional. (1997). *Informe sobre la evolución del mercado total de diarios en Montevideo para El Observador*. Montevideo, Uruguay: Archivo del diario *El Observador*.

Rilla, J. & Caetano, J. (2005). *Historia contemporánea de Uruguay: De la colonia al siglo XX*. Montevideo, Uruguay: Fin de Siglo y Claeh.

Rubio, C. G. (1995). *Lo que el cable no dejó: Televisión para abonados. Comunicación y democracia en el Uruguay*. Montevideo, Uruguay: La pluma de Montevideo.

Rubio, C. G. (1998). *El Uruguay cableado: Actualidad de la televisión de pago*. Montevideo, Uruguay: Zeitgeist.

Stepp, C. S. (1997). Firing up the newsroom. *American Journalism Review, 19*(10), 28–33.

13

The Media in Paraguay

A Locked Nation in Times of Change

Ligia García Béjar

Universidad Panamericana, Guadalajara, Mexico

Introduction

Understanding the media system in Paraguay starts with a crucial obstacle: poor reliable sources and deficient research on media companies and audiences in that country. Paraguay is actually long overlooked and in some ways a locked country among stronger neighbors. Nevertheless, the last pages of Paraguayan history have placed the country on the verge of new political times. In early 2008, a 57-year-old former Roman Catholic priest, Fernando Lugo, won presidential elections, and finally gave birth to the left in a nation historically dominated by conservative political parties and long-term authoritarian governments, breaking down with this historical fact the iron grip of the world's longest-ruling political party (McDermott, 2008).

Moreover, this nation has been burdened with a reputation for corruption. Additionally, Paraguay has been considered a major illicit producer of cannabis, much of which is distributed and consumed in the regional South American market (mostly in Brazil) and Europe. These political facts, among other elements, place Paraguay in a remote position compared with some of its closest neighbors. Nonetheless, Paraguay is increasingly getting involved with its neighbors, especially thanks to the help of Mercado Común del Sur (MERCOSUR: Common Market of the South), which might be useful for a country trying to slowly tackle political and economical underdevelopment and isolation.

With a population that barely passes 6 million (Dirección General de Estadísticas, Encuestas y Censos (DGEEC: Directorate General of Statistics, Surveys and Censuses), 2006), Paraguay has an economy marked by agriculture, industry and commerce along with a significant informal and underground market economy, primarily in electronics and liquor. In addition, it is the country in Latin America with the lowest penetration of the Spanish language; its more widespread Indian tongue, Guaraní, is used by 29 percent of Paraguayans, who do not speak Spanish on a daily basis (Fundación Telefónica, 2007).

Paraguayan wealth is highly concentrated, as approximately 60 percent of urban and 80 percent of rural Paraguayans live in poverty, with a per capita income of $1,700 dollars (Press Reference n.d.).

Media companies are highly concentrated, primarily in the capital of Asunción, which has a population of 519,000 (DGEEC, 2006). There are no relevant multimedia companies domiciled in Paraguay. The largest media group until 2000 was Red Privada de Comunicación (Communication Private Network), which owned the daily newspaper *Noticias*, and several radio and television stations, but after a long feud among its owners the company split up (Press Reference, n.d.). Furthermore, since Paraguay is a small country it is not difficult for media companies to have a national reach, without having to hold numerous types of media outlets.

Table 13.1 illustrates the tremendous differences in technology that exist in the country's urban and rural regions. The low penetration of cable, satellite and computers (with and without Internet) among Paraguayans is notable in rural areas. The overview of the media industry in Paraguay will be presented by examining individual sectors in the following sections.

Table 13.1 Total Number of Users and Percentage of Media Products, 2005

Media sector	Total users	Urban	Rural
Total users	1,288,717	765,308	523,409
Television	76.1%	85.9%	61.7%
Fixed telephone lines	16.3%	26.3%	1.7%
Mobile telephone lines	36.0%	46.1%	21.1%
Video/DVD	15.2%	21.9%	5.3%
Satellite television	3.8%	2.5%	5.7%
Cable television	10.2%	16.7%	0.8%
Computers	6.4%	10.0%	1.2%
Computer access with Internet	1.4%	2.2%	0.2%

Source: Compiled by the author from several sources including DGEEC (2005)

The Press

With a literacy rate of approximately 94 percent (Central Intelligence Agency (CIA) 2008), one might reason that Paraguay would have a lot of readers, but the situation is very unusual. The capital of Paraguay features the main market of press and magazine readers, which includes six newspapers: *ABC Color, Crónica* (Report), *El Diario Popular* (The Popular Daily), *La Nación* (The Nation), *Noticias* (News) and *Última Hora* (Last Hour) (Press Reference, n.d.).

Newspaper readers in Paraguay are limited by a significant number of people who do not read Spanish. The circulation estimates among the six newspapers indicate only 179 issues per 1,000 residents of the city. In fact, the main newspaper in Paraguay, *ABC Color*, has a weekday circulation of 45,000, followed by *Última Hora* with a circulation of about 35,000, while *Noticias* has a daily circulation of about 30,000 (Fundación Telefónica, 2007).

Circulation rates for magazines were not identifiable, but *Paraguay Ahora* (Paraguay Now), a political specialized magazine, appears to be the most relevant magazine in the country. The digital transition of all newspaper has already begun, although Internet penetration is one of the lowest in Latin America, estimated at just 3.6 percent of the total population (Fundación Telefónica, 2007). It is important to mention that in rural areas where Spanish is not the dominant language, radio is the central means to get information and entertainment.

Radio

Radio is one of the chief sources of entertainment and information in Paraguay. In a country with two official languages (Spanish and Guaraní) and a low penetration of printed options in the media market, radio plays a significant social relevance role, especially in rural areas. According to the Comisión Nacional de Telecomunicaciones (CONATEL: National Commission of Telecommunications, 2008) there are around 200 radio stations in the country. There are two organizations that regulate the radio industry in Paraguay, one is the Asociación Paraguaya de Radiodifusión (APRAP: Paraguayan Association of Radio Broadcasting) and the Administración Nacional de Telecomunicaciones (ANTEL: National Management of Telecommunications). However, these bodies do not provide updated data on the radio industry in the country.

The most important nationwide radio stations are Holding Radio, Canal 100 (Channel 100), Radio Cardinal and Radio Conquistador, primarily offering Latin music and domestic information. There is one public broadcast station, Radio Nacional de Paraguay (National Radio of Paraguay), under the ownership of the government and used essentially for political propaganda.

Community radio in Latin America reaches special significance in Paraguay, all gathered in the Asociación Mundial de Radios Comunitarias (AMARC: World Association of Community Radio Broadcasters). These groups of radio stations have taken a lead role in the democratization process of the country. They have contributed to promote and protect free expression among different social groups, and to support different kinds of social initiatives encouraging education, health prevention and community development (Fundación Telefónica, 2007).

One example is FM 95.1 Trinidad, La Voz de la Gente (Trinity, the Voice of the People). One of the most popular in the region, for over twenty years the station has promoted socioeconomic development in rural communities. Most of these stations do not operate under a commercial structure, so they survive economically by promoting cultural activities (e.g., concerts, festivals, religious celebration) to finance their operations. Paraguay is probably the only country in Latin America that produces more talk radio programming in Indian languages (Ayoreo and Guaraní) than in Spanish, and this is possible thanks to community radio.

When Fernando Lugo, the new president of Paraguay, was elected in August 2008, he officially announced that under his government, the situation of community radio stations will be completely regulated, given the fact most of the fifty community radio stations in Paraguay broadcast illegally (AMARC, 2008).

Television

Television was first broadcast in Paraguay in 1965, through Canal 9 (Channel 9). As of 2008, there are five national broadcast networks: EL TRECE (Canal 13), SNT Cerro Corá (Canal 9), Telefuturo (Canal 4), Red Guaraní (Canal 2) and Paravisión (Canal 5), all of which are privately owned. Television is the medium with the most penetration in the country. Approximately 76 percent of Paraguayan households have at least one television; however, Asunción and Central are regions with a higher penetration, at 93 percent and 87 percent respectively. In urban areas, nine out of ten households have television, while in rural areas the number falls to six out of ten (MERCOSUR, 2005). The Metropolitan area of Asunción is Paraguay's principal advertising center, with television the primary media for advertising. Government advertising represents a lot of revenue for television stations in Asunción, the capital of the country.

Regarding the cable industry, there is little information or updated data, but according to MERCOSUR, on average 10 percent of homes in Paraguay had a cable subscription in 2005. Despite the media concentration in the country, some cities along the Brazilian border, like Canindeyú, have a considerable higher penetration of cable and satellite services, with more than 21.7 percent subscribers (MERCOSUR, 2005).

Telecommunications

Paraguay's state-owned telecommunications operator COPACO SA has approximately 280,000 lines in service out of a total installed capacity of 320,000 lines. COPACO enjoys a monopoly among both fixed-line and long-distance telephony services nationwide (Compañia Nacional de Comunicaciones, 2008).

Around 80 percent of the total population in Paraguay has a cell phone (Ad Latina, 2008). This market has registered a rapid increase in users. According to CONATEL, in 2005 there were 4 million registered cell phones in the country; new data suggest that by the first quarter of 2008 the number surpassed 5 million users (CONATEL, 2008).

According to the Subsecretaría de Economía e Integración (Under-Secretary of Economy and Integration) and the Ministerio de Hacienda de Paraguay (Treasury Department of Paraguay) there are four cell-phone operators in Paraguay: Claro and Personal (property of Mexico), América Móvil (controlled by Carso Global Telecomm SA), Vox (a subsidiary of KDDI Corp.) and Tigo (Millicom International Cellular SA). Mobile phones have already overtaken fixed lines in Paraguay. Paraguayan mobile-phone firms, mostly private and backed by foreign investment, have benefited from the inefficiency of the state-owned fixed-line operator (López, n.d.).

Unlike most of its neighbors, Paraguay has not privatized its telecommunications operator, and basically it has done poorly in providing fixed-line services. Under this state of telecommunication services, and the fierce competition between operators, mobile phone rates remain low and explain the current growth of this mass market, which is largely due to prepaid call schemes. In Paraguay, as in many countries in Latin America, prepaid plans are more common that monthly plans. Users charge their cell phones through prepaid cards.

Film

Cinema in Paraguay has barely had the attention of closer and distant spectators. Paraguay is still a nation without moving images (Gamarra, 2002). The filmmaking industry in Paraguay has struggled over the years for many reasons, the main one being the fact that Paraguay has lacked a cinematographic tradition. There have been sporadic co-productions on location in Paraguay, but none of them have been 100 percent Paraguayan productions. The first steps in filmmaking production in Paraguay were taken by Cero Corá (Television Network) and were made for political propaganda (Gamarra, 2002).

Fundación Cinemateca (Cinematique Foundation) and Archivo Visual del Paraguay (Paraguayan Visual Archives) are the only two organizations dedicated to the promotion, research and defense of film culture in the country. Both were established in 1990 without state funding, and only minimal municipal subsidy. Probably, the only possibility for Paraguay, as with other small Latin American countries, in developing a motion-picture industry is to give an incentive of international co-production in collaboration with neighboring countries and especially members of MERCOSUR. In fact, this trade organization has, among its purposes, the promotion of arts among its members (Argentina, Brazil, Chile, Uruguay and Paraguay). The challenge for the nascent Paraguay film industry could be to take advantage of MERCOSUR's efforts, private companies' funding and diplomatic missions in order to move toward a new era of film in the country.

At least, since the late 1990s, national consciousness and appreciation of motion pictures has grown significantly. Since 1998, three Paraguayan feature films have achieved significant attention in international film venues: *The Call of Oboe* (Paraguay–Brazil, 1998), *The Gate of Dreams*

(Paraguay, 1998) and *María Escobar* (Paraguay, 2001). Since 1999, Paraguay has organized the Asunción International Film Festival with an eclectic program which has boosted interest in independent films. Digital technology and the presence of highly motivated and young talent might suggest a promising future for Paraguayan film production (Gamarra, 2002).

In terms of exhibition, there were, twenty cinemas operating in shopping centers in the capital, Asunción, and four in other medium-sized cities of Paraguay (Getino, 2001). Over 90 percent of films shown in movie theaters are mostly from American major distribution companies, and the remaining 10 percent are European or independent American films that come from small independent distributors in Argentina. Because of its proximity in the region, Paraguay is included in the exhibition rights of Argentina (Getino, 2001).

The creation of entities such as Cámara Paraguaya de Compañías Audiovisuales (Paraguayan Chamber of Audiovisual Production Companies) and Fondo National de Cultura (FONDEC: National Fund for Culture), and the opening of university programs and formal degrees in audiovisual studies are formal mechanisms to aid the future production and promotion of Paraguayan films.

The Internet

Only the most educated Paraguayans are likely to use the Internet. According to data offered by MERCOSUR in 2005, there were, at that time, 9.6 personal computers per 1,000 people. From another perspective, approximately 260,000 people in Paraguay are regular Internet users, located primarily in urban areas. In Paraguay the numbers are still way below average compared with other Latin American countries. Paraguay has one of the lowest Internet penetration rates in the continent, as just 3.6 percent of all Paraguayans use the Internet (Fundación Telefónica, 2007).

Conclusion

Paraguay's relatively weak economy helps to explain its equally weak communication industry. With around 300 televisions and 300 radios per 1,000 adults, Paraguayans rely on the electronic media for their news and entertainment, rather than upon the written press (MERCOSUR, 2005). Total advertising spending including newspapers, magazines, radio, broadcast television, cable television, direct mail, billboards and displays, Internet and other forms comprises $50 million per year (Fundación Telefónica, 2007).

The sound recording and music publishing industries are two other sectors that are negatively impacted in Paraguay. The industry estimates that trade losses in 2006 due to music and record piracy remain at approximately $128 million annually, with a 99 percent piracy level in the country. The levels of pirate products offered in the main cities of Asunción and Ciudad del Este are extremely large compared to the very few stores with legal products that exist in the country (International Intellectual Property Alliance, 2007).

The entertainment software industry suffers similarly. Counterfeit and pirated material continues to be imported, largely from Asia, to be distributed nationally and exported to neighboring countries. Unfortunately, Paraguayan authorities do little to combat them.

When and if the democratic state of Paraguay ever stabilizes, which will require a significant economic recovery, there might be a great opportunity for growth in the media industry in this southern Latin American country. In addition, the expectation generated with Fernando Lugo assuming the presidency of Paraguay comes with the hope that the government will undertake several important steps in trying to address the development of media industry, to strength macroeconomic conditions, and address piracy issues that directly affect the media sector. Paraguay is at the crossroads of several transformations. Time will determine if the new government and a more developed democracy will be enough to produce relevant changes in the country and its media sector.

It will be important to see if media companies in Paraguay redefine their basic operations thanks to the technological changes with digital television, the Internet and convergence, although Paraguay might be facing these changes slowly. Undoubtedly, the struggle of the Paraguayan media industry to develop itself in spite of domestic issues will depend on the shared vision among entrepreneurs, professionals and citizens truly committed to structural changes for the advance of true democracy, and as a side effect, of the country's media system.

References

Ad Latina. (2008). El portal de la comunicación Latina, July 14. *Las operadoras de celulares son los principales anunciantes.* Retrieved July 28, 2008, from www.adlatina.com/notas/noticia.php?id_noticia=28150.

Asociación Mundial de Radios Comunitarias (AMARC). (2008). Programa de legislaciones y derecho de las comunicaciones, América Latina, July 11. *Fernando Lugo legalizará radios comunitarias.* Retrieved July 22, 2008, from http://legislaciones.item.org.uy/index?q=node/687.

Central Intelligence Agency (CIA). (2008). *The CIA world factbook.* Retrieved March 8, 2009, from www.cia.gov/library/publications/the-world-factbook/.

Compañia Nacional de Comunicaciones. (2008). *S. A. Company profile business news Américas,* June 4. Retrieved July 29, 2008, from www.bnamericas.com/.

CONATEL. (2008). *Informaciones generales: Consejo Nacional de Telecomunicaciones.* Retrieved August 6, 2008, from www.conatel.gov.py/INFORMACIONESGENERALES.htm.

Dirección General de Estadística, Encuesta y Censos (DGEEC). (2005). *Encuesta permanente de hogares.* Retrieved March 8, 2009, from www.dgeec.gov.py.

Dirección General de Estadística, Encuesta y Censos (DGEEC). (2006). *Anuario estadístico.* Retrieved July 18, 2008, from www.dgeec.gov.py.

Fundación Telefónica. (2007). *Medios de comunicación, el escenario Iberoamericano.* Madrid: Ariel.

Gamarra, H. (2002). What does cinema mean for Paraguay? *Sense of Cinema.* Retrieved July 14, 2008, from www.sensesofcinema.com/contents/02/21/paraguay.html.

Getino, O. (Coord.). (2001). Las industrias culturales en el MERCOSUR. *Observatorio de las industrias culturales OIC,* Secretaría de Cultura y Medios de Comunicación-OEA, Buenos Aires. Retrieved July 22, 2008, from www.buenosaires.gov.ar/areas/produccion/industrias/observatorio/documentos/ind_cult_en_el_mercosur.pdf.

International Intellectual Property Alliance. (2007). *Special Report on Paraguay.* Retrieved July 22, 2008, from www.iipa.com/rbc/2007/2007SPEC301PARAGUAY.pdf.

López, A. (n.d.). *South goes mobile.* Retrieved August 15, 2008, from www.unesco.org/courier/2000_07/uk/connex.htm.

McDermott, J. (2008). Ex-bishop becomes President of Paraguay. *Telegraph.* August 15. Retrieved August 17, 2008, from www.telegraph.co.uk/news/worldnews/southamerica/paraguay/2566681/Ex-bishop-becomes-President-of-Paraguay.html.

MERCOSUR (Mercado Común del Sur). (2005). Reunión especializada de ciencia y tecnología del MERCOSUR, *Indicadores de TIC's en Paraguay,* Anexo XV.

Press Reference. (n.d.). *Paraguay press, media, TV, radio,newspapers.* Retrieved July 13, 2008, from www.press reference.com/No-Sa/Paraguay.html.

14

The Media in Cuba, the Dominican Republic and Puerto Rico

Juan Pablo Artero
University of Navarra, Spain

Introduction

Media systems among Latin American countries differ largely in terms of development of different industries, presence of international investors and legal framework, among other aspects. In this chapter, three Caribbean countries (Cuba, the Dominican Republic and Puerto Rico) will be examined.

All three countries share certain aspects in terms of cultural background and historical roots: their official language is Spanish and they are part of the Hispanic universe, even though they have all had certain periods of some or strong American influence. But at the same time, history has put them in different stages at the moment. This fact will be reflected in the structure of the media too.

As far as this chapter is concerned, the situation of media industries in these countries is largely different, as it will be seen. Apart from this, there is a common point in terms of the difficulty to obtain reliable and comparable data about media industries within these countries. Moreover, little academic research is available from the economic and business point of view of the media. In the existing literature, one generally finds a great deal in accessing international environments and academic publications. This is a common situation for Latin American scholars in media and communication studies, as well as other fields of scientific knowledge. That is why very little research on these countries can be found in international journals and publishing houses.

Cuba

Cuba is a socialist republic, led by the Communist Party of Cuba, with a population of 11,423,952 inhabitants. The estimated GDP per capita in 2007 was $4,500 (Central Intelligence Agency (CIA), 2008). Similarly as communications made feasible the formation of a national identity in nineteenth-century Cuba (García-Montón, 1993), in the second half of the twentieth century the media were a crucial factor for the consolidation of the authoritarian regime of Fidel Castro.

The one-party dictatorship defines not only the country's life but also the legal framework in which the media develop. While the Cuban constitution contains elements pertaining to freedom of speech, rights are limited by Article 62, which states that none of the freedoms which are recognized for citizens can be exercised contrary to the existence and objectives of the socialist state.

The Cuban government adheres to socialist principles in organizing its largely state-controlled planned economy. Most of these means of production are owned and run by the government and most of the labor force is employed by the state. There has been a trend towards more private sector employment. By the year 2006, public sector employment was 78 percent and the private sector at 22 percent compared to the 1981 where public sector employment was 91.8 percent compared to only 8.2 percent in the private sector.

In the absence of any freedoms of speech and press, domestic media must operate under party guidelines and reflect official government views. The state owns and operates all mass media except for publications of the Roman Catholic Church. The Cuban government and Partido Comunista de Cuba (PCC: Communist Party of Cuba) strictly censor news, information and commentary and restrict dissemination of foreign publications to tourist hotels. Laws against disseminating anti-government propaganda, graffiti and disrespect of officials carry prison penalties.

According to Cepero (2007), all media in Cuba are owned by the government, which controls editorial positioning as well as appointment of managers. Since 1959, the Communist Party has determined the public issues to be displayed in the media, applying rigid censorship policies when necessary. The media in Cuba are understood just as a tool for political and ideological control of society. In fact, journalists are considered to be political-ideological workers and receive an authoritarian education. Censorship is applied to any piece of news coming from abroad the country.

The Internet is forbidden for the population and only some professionals have limited access to the web. The only accessible free press occurs when Cubans or their friends bring publications illegally from outside the country. Cubans receive some radio and television channels from the United States, but periodically the government launches a campaign to electronically jam the signal receivers, especially in larger cities. With such a situation, in a future transition to democracy, the media system is not likely to adopt easily a Western free-speech model, but one very similar to that prevailing in Russia or China (Cepero, 2007).

Newspapers

The first newspaper appeared in Cuba as early as 1790. The so-called *Papel Periódico de la Habana* was then published on a weekly basis. Many others followed this first experience, like *Prensa Libre*, *The Havana Post*, *Excelsior* or *Patria*, founded by José Martí. But the Castro regime changed the landscape of newspapers. Table 14.1 shows basic data about the current newspapers in Cuba.

The only national daily paper is *Granma*, the official organ of the PCC. A weekly version, *Granma International*, is published in English, Spanish, French, Portuguese and German, and is available online. Havana residents also have their own newspaper, the Havana-oriented paper *Tribuna de La Habana*. The weekly *Juventud Rebelde* is the official organ of the Communist Youth Union. Cuba has several dozen online regional newspapers.

Magazines

The biweekly *Bohemia* is the country's only general-interest newsmagazine. Cuba's official news agency is Prensa Latina, which publishes several magazines, including *Cuba Internacional*, directed at foreign audiences. Table 14.2 lists the main magazines in Cuba.

Table 14.1 Main Newspapers in Cuba, 2008

Newspaper	Frequency	Owner	URL	Content
Granma	Daily	State	www.granma.cu	General
Granma Internacional	Weekly	State	www.granma.cu	General
Juventud Rebelde	Weekly	State	www.juventudrebelde.cu	Youth
Trabajadores	Weekly	State	www.trabajadores.cu	General
Tribuna de La Habana	Daily	State	www.tribuna.co.cu	General
Adelante	Weekly	State	www.adelante.cu	General
El Habanero		State	www.elhabanero.cubaweb.cu	General
Venceremos	Weekly	State	www.venceremos.co.cu	General
El Economista de Cuba	Quarterly	State	www.eleconomista.cubaweb.cu	Economics and business
Opciones	Weekly	Juventud Rebelde	www.opciones.cu	Economics and tourism
Negocios En Cuba	Weekly	Prensa Latina SA	www.prensa-latina.cu	Business

Source: Compiled by the author from country and media websites

Table 14.2 Main Magazines in Cuba, 2008

Magazine	Frequency	Owner	URL	Content
Bohemia	Weekly	State		Art, sport and technology
Revolución Y Cultura	Quarterly	State	www.ryc.cult.cu	Art and literature
Prisma	Bimonthly	Prensa Latina SA		Tourism
Record	Irregular	State		Sport
Tricontinental	Quarterly	OSPAAL	www.tricontinental.cubaweb.cu	Ideological
Alma Mater	Monthly	Casa Editora Abril	www.almamater.cu	Culture, science and sport
Cuba Socialista	Quarterly	State	www.cubasocialista.cu	Political
Revista Cub. De Medicina		SCIELO	www.scielo.sld.cu	Medicine
Cuba Internacional	Bimonthly	Prensa Latina SA		
Temas	Quarterly	State	www.temas.cult.cu	Critical thinking
La Jiribilla de Papel	Monthly	State	www.lajiribilla.co.cu	Cuban culture
Pionero	Monthly	State	www.pionero.cu	Education ideology for youth

Source: Compiled by the author from country and media websites

Radio

Regarding radio, in 2005 Cubans had at least 3.9 million radio receivers, and the country had 169 AM and 55 FM stations. Of the six national FM radio stations, the top three are Radio Progreso, Radio Reloj and Radio Rebelde, in that order. Two other national radio networks that also provide news and entertainment are Radio Musical Nacional (CMBF) and Radio Enciclopedia. Another station, Radio Taíno, promotes tourism (see Table 14.3). The Cuban government also operates Radio Havana, the official Cuban international short-wave radio service. More than ninety municipalities have their own locally run radio stations.

All of the radio stations are owned by the state-owned Instituto Cubano de Radio y Televisión (ICRT: Cuban Institute of Radio and Television), which manages Radio Rebelde, the largest AM network, and the SW service Radio Habana Cuba (World Radio TV Handbook (WRTH), 2005).

Table 14.3 Main Radio Stations in Cuba, 2008

Radio	Operation	Owner	Coverage	URL	Content
Radio Taíno	24 hours	State	National	www.radiotaino.cubasi.cu	Music and tourist information
Radio Progreso	24 hours	State	National	www.radioprogreso.cu	Entertainment
Radio Rebelde	24 hours	State	National	www.radiorebelde.com.cu	Sport
Radio Enciclopedia	24 hours	State	National	www.radioenciclopedia.cu	Cultural
Radio Reloj	24 hours	State	National	www.radioreloj.cu	Information
CMBF	24 hours	State	National	www.cmbfradio.cu	Music and culture
Radio Habana Cuba information	Irregular hours	State	International	www.radiohc.cu	Music and tourist

Source: Compiled by the author from country and media websites

Television

Television began in Cuba in 1950. In the early stages of development, Cuban television was recognized as the best of Latin America, and even as good as that in the United States. This new communication medium was understood as a sign and as a tool for Cuban modernization (Rivero, 2007). Nowadays the industry is small and devoted to communicating the views of the official party and the government. Table 14.4 lists the most important television channels.

Table 14.4 Main Television Channels in Cuba, 2008

Television channel	Hours	Owner	Coverage	Content
Cubavisión (Canal 6)	24 hours	State	National	Information and entertainment
Cubavisión Internacional	24 hours	State	International	Information and entertainment
Telerebelde (Canal 2)	12 hours Mon–Fri	State	National	Information and entertainment
Canal Educativo 1	15 hours Mon–Sat	State	National	Educational
Canal Educativo 2	85 hours/week	State	National	Educational
Television Serrana	86 hours/week	State	Local	Educational

Source: Compiled by the author from country and media websites

In 2005, Cubans had 3 million television sets and fifty-eight TV broadcasting stations. The Cuban Institute of Radio and Television serves as the government's administrative outlet for broadcasting. The Cuban television system is made up of two networks: Cubavisión and Tele Rebelde. Cuba's restriction of foreign broadcast media is one reason the US government has sponsored radio and television broadcasting into Cuba through Radio and TV Martí, much of which is jammed.

There are five national channels: Cubavisión, Tele Rebelde, Canal Educativo, Canal Educativo 2 and the newest entry, Multivisión. Additionally each province has a local television channel. Television Serrana can be considered a special case as it is a community medium financed and controlled by the government than directly an official station (Gumucio, 2001).

The Internet

Access to the Internet is forbidden for most of the population and only a few professionals (some government officials, medical doctors or college professors) can use a limited version of the web. Private citizens are prohibited from buying computers or accessing the Internet without special authorization. The country has only 3,388 Internet hosts in 2007 and five Internet service providers in 2001 (CIA, 2008). The most popular websites are those of the main media in the country as well as Cubasí.

Summary

The current situation for Cuban media is basically limited for political and economic reasons. Some authors argue that Cuba nowadays finds itself in a new form of colonialism, with tourist dollars coming at the expense of underdeveloping other parts of its economy. So that, to some extent, the same factor that nowadays can be sustaining the economic side of the regimen would be destroying its future perspectives (Roberg & Kuttruff, 2007).

The rise of Raul Castro to power as the new president has meant a certain openness in terms of technology acquisition by the population (such as consumer electronics or cell phones), but no significant changes in the authoritarian media system have been made.

Dominican Republic

The Dominican Republic is a presidential democratic republic with a population of 9,507,133 (July 2008 est.) and a GDP per capita in 2007 of $7,000 (CIA, 2008). It shares Hispaniola island with Haiti and is located in the central Caribbean Sea just between Cuba and Puerto Rico. All three islands are known as the Greater Antilles.

The development of the media in the Dominican Republic has been deeply related to the political and economic history of the country. Cruz (1994) identifies ten periods in the history of the media from 1800. The three last periods cover the US military occupation (1916–1924), the dictatorship of Rafael Leónidas Trujillo (1930–1961) and contemporary times (1961–1993). Common issues that overlap this process are the creation of national identity, political consolidation, censorship and the emergence of different media arts (Cruz, 1994).

The Dominican Republic has enjoyed strong GDP growth since 2005. Although the country has long been viewed primarily as an exporter of sugar, coffee and tobacco, in recent years the service sector has overtaken agriculture as the economy's larger employer due to growth in tourism and free-trade zones. The economy is highly dependent upon the United States, the source of nearly three-quarters of exports (CIA, 2008).

Newspapers

The development of the newspaper industry in the country has been very recent. When the dictator Rafael Trujillo was executed in 1961, there were only three daily newspapers in the Dominican Republic. Table 14.5 (p. 194) contains some data about the current main newspapers in the country. *Listin Diario* is the main newspaper in the country, jointly with others such as *El Caribe*, *El nacional* or *El Nuevo Diario*.

Magazines

Among magazines, *Ahora* and *Clave* can be highlighted. The former has experienced diverse formats: online, weekly publication and even free paper. *Revista Dominicana* contains information on the economy, politics and sports in the country. *Dominican Times* is a news magazine published in English on the east coast of the United States.

Table 14.5 Main Newspapers in Dominican Republic, 2008

Newspapers	Circulation	Owner	Coverage	URL
Listin Diario	Daily	Listin Diario	National	www.listin.com.do
El Caribe	Daily	Multimedios Del Caribe	National	www.elcaribecdn.com.do
El Nacional	Daily	Grupo Corripio	National	www.elnacional.com.do
El Nuevo Diario	Daily	Editora El Nuevo Diario	National	www.elnuevodiario.com.do
Hoy	Daily	Grupo Corripio	National	www.hoy.com.do
La Información	Daily	Nueva Editora La Informacion	National	www.lainformacionrd.net
Diario Libre	Daily	Grupo Omnimedia	National	www.diariolibre.com
El Dia	Daily	Grupo Corripio	National	www.eldia.com.do

Source: Compiled by the author from country and media websites

Radio

Radio is a well-developed and popular medium in the country. In fact, until the 1970s radio was the most important industry, because most of the population lived in rural areas where television was difficult to access. In 1998, the country had 120 AM stations, 56 FM stations and 4 short wave signals, as well as 1.44 million receivers (CIA, 2008). Nowadays, the most popular radio stations are devoted to music (see Table 14.6).

Television

Television broadcasting is a popular industry in the Dominican Republic. Most of the content is distributed in Spanish, even though an important portion of content in English is maintained. Data are scarce; the country had fifty-three television broadcast stations in 2003 and 770,000 television sets in 1997 (CIA, 2008). It has a wide range of general television networks (Table 14.7).

Table 14.6 Main Radio Stations in Dominican Republic, 2008

Radio*	Owner	URL	Content
Merengue	Circuito Merengue	www.circuitomerengue.com	Information
Noticias De Radio	Multimedios Del Caribe	www.elcaribecdn.com/cdnradio	Information
Radio Universal	Radio Universal	www.radiouniversalfm.com	Music
Raíces	Centro Cultural E. L. Jimenez	www.raicesradio.org.do	Culture and music
Kiss FM 95	Kiss95 FM	www.kiss95.com	English, music and information
91 FM	La 91 FM SA		Music
La Nota Diferente			Music
Z101			Music
Primera FM			Music
Radio Listin	Radio Listin	www.radiolistin.com	Rock and pop
Amor FM		www.amorfm91.com	Music
Monumental		www.monumentalfm.com	Music
La Nueva 106 FM	La Nueva 106 FM	www.lanueva106fm.com	Music

Source: Compiled by the author from country and media websites
Note: * All stations have national coverage of the country

Table 14.7 Main Television Channels in Dominican Republic, 2008

Television	Owner	Coverage	Language	URL
Colorvision (Channel 9)	Color Vision	National	Spanish	www.colorvision.com.do
Super Canal 33/Caribe	Super Canal	National and international	Spanish and English	www.supercanal.com
Telemicro (Channel 5)	Medios Telemicro	National and international	Spanish and English	www.telemicro.com.do
Telemedios TV (Channel 25)	Telemedios Dominicanos	National	Spanish and English	www.canal25.net.tv
Cdn (Channel 37)	Multimedios Del Caribe	National	Spanish	www.elcaribecdn.com
Teleantillas (Channel 2)	Corripio	National	Spanish	www.tele-antillas.tv
Certv (Channel 4)	State	National	Spanish	www.certvdominicana.com
Teleuniverso (Channel 29)	Teleuniverso	National and international	Spanish and English	www.teleuniversocanal29.com
Digital 15	Medios Telemicro	Local	Spanish	www.digital15.com.do
Antena Latina (Channel 7)	Antena Latina	National	Spanish	www.antenalatina7.com
Telesistema (Channel 11)	Telesistema	National	Spanish	
Televisión Dominicana	Television Dominicana	National	Spanish	www.televisiondominicana.tv

Source: Compiled by the author from country and media websites

The Internet

The Internet is well developed in the Dominican Republic, with a good telecommunications infrastructure and an increasing number of Dominicans participating in the digital age: in 2006 1,232 million were Internet users. The country had 81,218 Internet hosts in 2007 and 24 Internet service providers in 2000 (CIA, 2008). The country has an important industry of popular news websites, apart from that of the traditional media (see Table 14.8).

Table 14.8 Main News Websites in Dominican Republic, 2008

Internet	Owner	Coverage	URL
Clavedigital	Media Team Dominicana	National	www.clavwww.clavedigital.com.do
Diario Digital Rd	Grupo Imagen 2000	National	www.diariodigitalrd.com
Elcaribecdn.Com	Multimedios El Caribe	National	www.elcaribecdn.com
7 Días	Fundación Macroeconodata	National	www.7dias.com.do
Dominican Today	Dominican Today	National	www.dominicantoday.com
Dominicana Online	Funglode	National	www.dominicanaonlie.org
Noticias Sin	Antena Latina	National	www.antena-sin.com
Barriga Verde	Editora Barrigaverde	Local	www.barrigaverde.net
Las Principales	Las Principales	National	www.lasprincipales.com

Source: Compiled by the author from country and media websites

Summary

The structure of the media industry in the Dominican Republic is very similar to that dominating in most small and medium-sized Latin American nations. There are few media concentrated in few geographical markets and controlled by a small number of traditional families. The weight of Santo Domingo as the capital of the country and the center of the media system is very important, as well as the presence of some industrial families in the media ownership, even though they are involved in other sectors of the economy. This aspect does not help the development of an independent media market, but in terms of political restrictions, the Dominican Republic does not limit free speech and free enterprise in the media arena.

Puerto Rico

The Commonwealth of Puerto Rico has a republican government, in which the head of state is that of the United States and the head of government is popularly elected. The country has a population of 3,958,128 (July 2008 est.) and an estimated 2007 GDP per capita of $19,600 (CIA, 2008).

Puerto Rico's particular status of association to the United States since its independence from Spain in the late nineteenth century has given the island its own development model, different from the rest of the Caribbean and Latin American republics. To some extent, Puerto Rico is in part an independent republic, but at the same time part of the United States. In terms of the media industry, it maintains some similarities to the United States, especially in broadcasting industries, as far as the regulation and market structure can be defined it is similar to those in any US state with a high proportion of Latino population.

Newspapers

The first newspaper in the country, *La Gaceta de Puerto Rico*, was published for the fist time in December 1806. It turned into daily circulation in 1823 and it lasted till the end of Spanish rule of the island in 1898. In the twentieth century, the newspaper industry was moderately developed in Puerto Rico. Table 14.9 (opposite) contains basic data about the main newspapers in the country.

The leading newspaper in Puerto Rico is *El Nuevo Día*, with more than 1 million readers per day. *Primera Hora* and *El Vocero de Puerto Rico* are important as well. *San Juan Star* is published in the capital in English language.

Magazines

Among magazines, *Claridad* and other non-daily free publications such as *El Expreso de Puerto Rico* are notable. The women's and family lifestyle magazine *Imagen* has nearly 400,000 readers. The weekly *Caribbean Business* has more than 200,000 readers for each issue. In addition, many popular magazines published in the United States and written in English are distributed in Puerto Rico too.

Radio

Sabés (2005) reports there are 135 radio stations in Puerto Rico as of 2005, of which 52.6 percent are commercial musical ones, 21.5 percent are religious channels, 22.9 percent are devoted to news and talk radio, and only 2.9 percent public service broadcasters. The number of AM and FM

Table 14.9 Main Newspapers in Puerto Rico, 2008

Newspaper	Circulation	Owner	Cost	Coverage	URL
El Nuevo Día	Daily	El Nuevo Día	Paid	National	www.elnuevodia.net
Primera Hora	Daily	Grupo Ferré Rangel	Paid	National	www.primerahora.com
El Vocero de Puerto Rico	Daily	El Vocero de Puerto Rico	Paid	National	www.vocero.com
San Juan Star	Daily	Star Media Network	Paid	National	www.thesanjuanstar.com
Claridad	Weekly	El Periodico de la Nacion Puertoriqueña	Paid	National	www.claridadpuertorico.com
El Expresso de Puerto Rico	Weekly	El Expresso	Free	Local	www.elexpresso.com
Bandera Roja	Monthly	Mov.Socialista de Trabajadores	Free	International	www.bandera.org
La Estrella de Puerto Rico	Weekly	Periodico La Estrella	Paid	Local	www.periodicolaestrella.com
La Semana	Weekly	La Semana	Free	Local	www.lasemana.com
La Esquina	Weekly	La Esquina	Free	Local	www.laesquina,com

Source: Compiled by the author from country and media websites

stations is almost equal, distributed among the three geographic areas of San Juan, Ponce and Mayagüez. This author identified several trends in Puerto Rican radio: the dominance of music radio, the increasing presence of religious stations, the change of news stations to more entertainment content, and the irrelevance of public service broadcasters.

Some of the main radio networks are Cadena Radio Puerto Rico, NotiUno, Radio Reloj and Radio Isla; in San Juan Emisora de Radio WEXS "X-61 am" and WAPA; in Mayagüez, WAEL FM96 and WERR "Redentor 104 FM"; in Ponce, WKCK "Cumbre 1470 AM" and WPUC "Católica Radio 88.9 FM". Table 14.10 contains a ranking of radio stations in the country, according to Arbitron data in Spring 2004. It is important to highlight that both Univision and SBS are based in the United States.

Table 14.10 Main Radio Stations in Puerto Rico, 2008

Radio	Format	Owner
WPRM – Salsoul	Tropical	Uno Radio Group
WVOZ FM	Adult contemporary	International Broadcasting Corporation
WKAQ FM Kq	Pop contemporary	Univision Communications
WZNT – Cadena Z	Tropical	Wznt Inc.
WKAG-Om Radio Reloj	Talk and news	Univision Communications
WFID FM Fidelity	Adult contemporary	Uno Radio Group
WBRQ FM Nueva Vida	Christian cont.	New Life Broadcasting
WORO FM Radio Oro	Easy listening 3	Catholic Church
WUNO Om Notiuno	Talk and news	Uno Radio Group
WIOA FM Estereotempo	Contemporary music	Spanish Broadcasting System (SBS)

Source: Compiled by the author from country and media websites

Television

In television, the main networks are Univision and Telemundo, the main Spanish language channels in the United States. Additionally, in Puerto Rico is the very popular Wapa TV (Table 14.11).

The network system is clearly similar to that in the United States. Some of the main stations are WKAQ-TV, Channel 2 in San Juan (Telemundo), with WOLE-TV, Channel 12 in Aguadilla; WAPA-TV, Channel 4 in San Juan (Independent), with WTIN, Channel 14 in Ponce and WNJX-TV, Channel 22 in Mayagüez; WIPR-TV, Channel 6 in San Juan (PBS), with WIPM-TV, Channel 3 in Mayagüez; WSTE, Channel 7 in Ponce (Independent); WLII, Channel 11 in Caguas (Univision), with WSUR-TV, Channel 9 in Ponce and WORA-TV, Channel 5 in Mayagüez; WPRU-LP, Channel 20 in Aguadilla (ABC); WSJX-LP, Channel 24 in Aguadilla (FOX); WSJP-LP, Channel 30 in Aguadilla (CW); WMTJ, Channel 40 in Rio Piedras (PBS). Most Puerto Rican stations are affiliated with an American network, including not only Univision and Telemundo, but also ABC, FOX, CW and PBS, among others.

Table 14.11 Main Television Channels in Puerto Rico, 2008

Television	Owner	Cost	Coverage	URL
WAPA-TV	Televicentro	Free	National	www.wapa.tv
Telemundo (WKAQ-TV)	NBC Universal	Free	International	www.telemundo.yahoo.com
Univisión Puerto Rico	Univision Communications	Free	National	www.univision.com
TU TV (WIPR-TV)	Puerto Rico Public Broadcasting Corporation	Free	National	www.tutv.puertorico.pr
Caribevisión (WJPX)	Caribevision Station Group	Free	International	www.caribevision.com
Direct TV	DirecTV	Pay	National	www.directvwebpr.com
Telefutura	Univision Communications	Free	Puerto Rico and United States	www.telefutura.com
Galavisión	Univision Communications	Free	Puerto Rico and United States	
Supersiete (WSTE)	Univision Communications	Free	Local (Ponce)	

Source: Compiled by the author from country and media websites

The Internet

Puerto Rico had 413 Internet hosts in 2007 and 76 service providers as of 2000 (CIA, 2008), which reflects the high dependence of this industry on the United States. Approximately 915,600 Puerto Ricans were Internet users in 2005. The main news websites are those of the traditional media, as well as the local site Notiemail.

Summary

Puerto Rico's media system is highly dependent on the United States, especially in some industries like radio, television and the Internet. In terms of free speech and free enterprise, the country enjoys Western standards similar to those that can be found in other American states. Additionally, the country maintains the Latino heritage which results in a mixed media system, with common elements from the United States and other Latin American countries.

Conclusion

Three different media systems have been compared in this chapter on Cuba, the Dominican Republic and Puerto Rico. From an economic point of view, Puerto Rico has a GDP per capita two times bigger than the Dominican Republic and four times that of Cuba. Its translation into the media economy of the country can be stated as almost direct: Puerto Rico has a much stronger media system than the Dominican Republic and, similarly, this country is more highly developed than Cuba both in general economic and media terms.

Additionally, in terms of a political framework, the differences are also important. Cuba is a socialist dictatorship where free speech and enterprise are seriously limited. The Dominican Republic is an independent Latin American republic with constitutional rights in terms of flow of information and creation of media companies. Puerto Rico has a democratic government maintaining an association with the United States, which assures a similar legal environment to that ruling in any other state of the union.

In conclusion, Cuba has a non-democratic media system largely controlled by the government with little development of the industry and no guarantees in terms of basic rights. The Dominican Republic has a developing media industry, especially strong in broadcasting and ruling free speech and enterprise. Puerto Rico maintains a more developed media industry, with higher investments, more presence of US investors, and full legal guarantees in terms of free speech, creation of news firms and democratic respect of the law in the media market.

The importance of these countries in the overall growth and development of Spanish language media is expected to be different. If democracy and capitalism finally arrive in Cuba, strong changes can be expected in the Cuban media system. The Dominican Republic is expected to increase significantly the weight of its media system as tourism and services sector continues to grow in the country. Finally, Puerto Rico has a solid market, mostly integrated in the United States, but the relevance of Spanish language media is expected to decrease due to the ongoing Americanization of new generations and the adoption of English as a daily language in the island. Scholars need to pay more attention to the future development of media industries in these countries as good examples of different approaches and models to the public issue of satisfying the needs of any population for information, advertising and entertainment content.

References

Central Intelligence Agency (CIA). (2008). *The CIA world factbook*. Retrieved March 8, 2009, from www.cia.gov/library/publications/the-world-factbook/.

Cepero, I. (2007). *Los medios de comunicación en la cuba post-Castro*. [The media in post-Castro Cuba]. *ARI 42/2007*. Madrid: Real Instituto Elcano.

Cruz, F. (1994). *History of the mass media in the Dominican Republic*. Santo Domingo, DR: Editora El Nuevo Diario.

García-Montón, I. (1993). Los medios de comunicación en la formación de una conciencia nacional: Cuba a mediados del siglo XIX [The media in the creation of a national identity: Cuba in the middle of the eighteenth century]. *Revista Complutense de Historia de América, 19*, 293–307.

Gumucio, A. (2001). *Arte de equilibristas: La sostenibilidad de los medios de comunicación comunitarios* [Acrobat arts: The sustainability of community media]. New York: Rockefeller Foundation.

Rivero, Y. M. (2007). Broadcasting modernity: Cuban television, 1950–1953. *Cinema Journal, 43*(3) 3–25.

Roberg, J. & Kuttruff, A. (2007). Cuba: Ideological success or ideological failure? *Human Rights Quarterly, 29*, 779–795.

Sabés, F. (2005). La radio en Puerto Rico: Emisoras musicales, religiosas, generalistas y el sector público alternativo [Radio in Puerto Rico: Music, religious, general informtion and alternative public service stations]. *Ámbitos, 13–14*, 331–348.

World Radio TV Handbook (WRTH). (2005). *World radio TV handbook*. Retrieved March 8, 2009, from www.wrth.com.

II
Topics and Issues in Spanish Language Media

15
Growth and Trends in Spanish Language Television in the United States

Amy Jo Coffey
University of Florida, USA

Introduction

Each media industry experiences its own lifecycle, and Spanish language media are no exception. Newspaper and print media have served Spanish-speaking audiences in the United States for some time, but quickly made room for Spanish language radio, which continues to be a growth area. In the late twentieth century, Spanish language television emerged. While it began slowly with a few pioneers such as Spanish International Network (later to become Univision), the industry growth would explode in the 1990s and early 2000s. This chapter examines the growth of Spanish language television in the United States for a twenty-year period spanning 1986–2005 and the factors most likely to have contributed to this growth. Some of these factors include a growing Spanish-speaking population with demand for such content, US Census data revealing the increasing size of the Spanish-speaking audience, and the subsequent reaction by advertisers desiring new audiences and revenue streams. In fact, the growth in the United States' Hispanic population and the number of Spanish language networks lends itself to a classic supply and demand illustration. In order to understand the extent of this supply and demand, the growth of key variables—Hispanic population, Spanish language networks and advertising revenues—is examined and compared.

Growth Areas

To measure the extent of the recent growth in Spanish language television in the United States, a secondary data analysis was conducted using data supplied by TNS (Taylor, Nelson, Sofres) Media Intelligence and the US Census Bureau. Trends in population, income, television advertising revenues and television network and local station expansion were tracked to identify trends and patterns among these variables in order to understand the variables' growth and the conditions surrounding this growth.

US Hispanic Population versus Television Network Growth

This first descriptive analysis was conducted for the years 1986–2004 (see Figures 15.1 and 15.2). Separate analyses were conducted at both the network level and the local (spot advertising) level for Spanish language television, using the Top 75 markets monitored by TNS in order to identify trends, with the local level analysis encompassing a shorter time frame due to data availability. Both analyses utilized the same census population data. The data showed correlated growth (see Figures 15.1 and 15.2). However, while growth of the US Hispanic population was fairly steady at 3–4 percent for the period, the number of Hispanic-targeted networks saw much greater growth rates during this same period, usually in double digits.[1] The rapid population growth of the Hispanic demographic compared to other ethnic demographics is also documented.

The shape of the correlation between the growth of the United States' Hispanic population and the number of Hispanic networks suggests that the population and number of networks maintained a steady and parallel path until the mid-1990s (see Figure 15.1). However, the number of Hispanic networks sharply increased after this point, when their growth began outpacing that of the Hispanic population. While the Hispanic population grew steadily at 3–4 percent annually through the 1990s, the number of new Hispanic networks grew by anywhere from 20 to 55 percent during a given year beginning in 1995. More revealing is the percentage change in growth over the 1986–2004 period. While the Hispanic population grew by nearly 116 percent (from 19 million to 41 million), the number of Hispanic networks grew even faster— by 2,400 percent—during the same period (from three to seventy-five). It is important to acknowledge that the percentage change is likely to be large when the base number is small (such as three networks), and rapid growth during the initial stage of an industry is not uncommon. Nevertheless, the 2,400 percent growth rate in the number of networks for the period 1986–2004 far outpaces the growth rate of the Hispanic population (116 percent) for that period. A listing of the Hispanic networks and their respective launch dates can be found in Table 15.1. This latest accounting finds 102 Hispanic-targeted networks in the United States, with all but four broadcasting in Spanish.

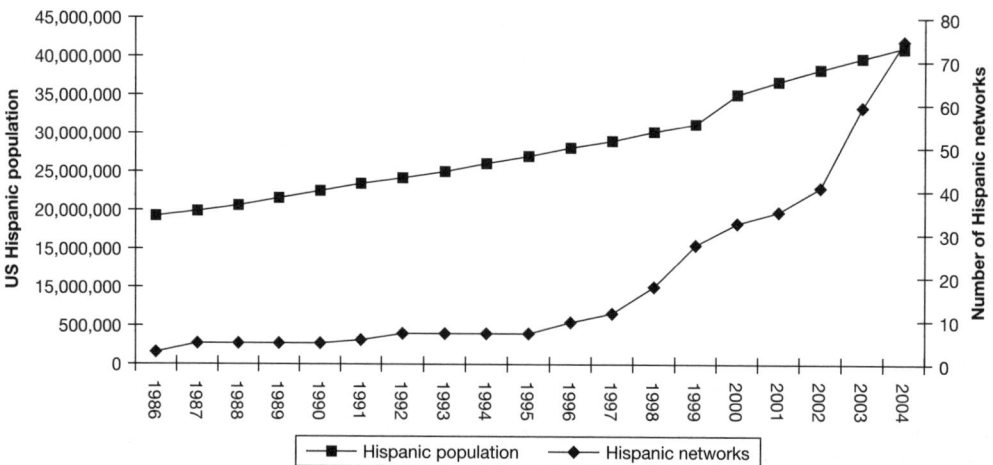

Figure 15.1 US Hispanic Population versus Number of Hispanic Networks, 1986–2004

Sources: Multichannel News, DirecTV, Echostar, US Census Bureau

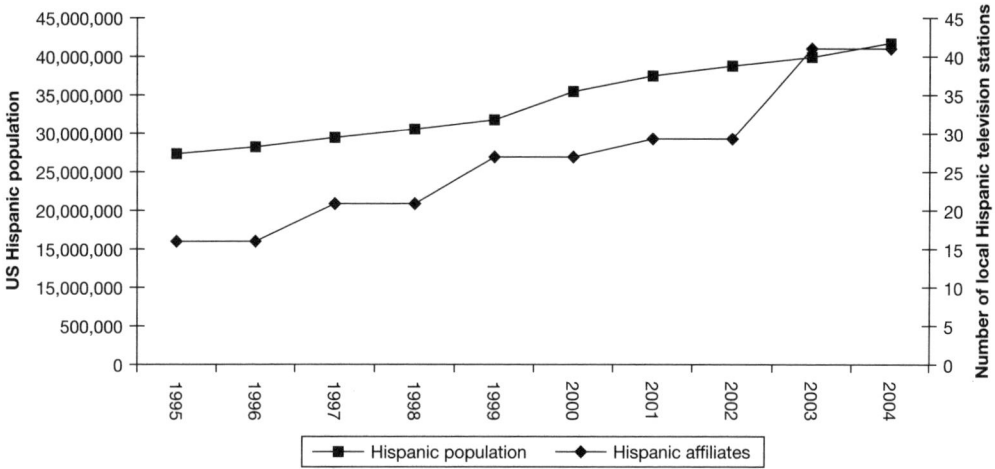

Figure 15.2 US Hispanic Population versus Number of Local Hispanic Television Stations, 1995–2004

Sources: TNS Media Intelligence, US Census Bureau

Table 15.1 Hispanic Networks and Launch Dates, 1961–2008

Order	Network	US launch date	Headquarters
1	Univision	1961	USA
2	Galavisión	1979	USA
3	HITN	1983	USA
4	Hispanic Information and Telecommunications Network	1987	USA
5	Telemundo	1987	USA
6	Canal Sur	1991	USA
7	Cartoon Network (SAP)	1992	USA
8	Antena 3	1996	Spain
9	Fox Sports en Español	1996	USA
10	Utilissima	1996	Argentina
11	CNN en Español	1996	USA
12	Fashion TV	1997	Not available
13	Discovery en Español	1998	USA
14	Latin TV (LTV)	1998	USA
15	Más Música TeVe Network	1998	USA
16	Tr3s (MTV Español)*	1998	USA
17	Olé TV	1998	USA
18	Toon Disney (SAP)	1998	USA
19	Canal 52 MX	1999	Mexico
20	Cine Latino	1999	Mexico
21	CNC Colombia	1999	Colombia
22	EWTN Español	1999	USA
23	docTVE (Grandes Documentales)	1999	Spain
24	HTV	1999	USA
25	Puma TV	1999	Venezuela
26	TV Chile	1999	Chile
27	TVE Internacional	1999	Spain
28	VHUno	1999	USA
29	Boomerang (SAP)	2000	USA
30	Canal 24 Horas	2000	Spain
31	HBO Latino	2000	USA

Table 15.1 Continued

Order	Network	US launch date	Headquarters
32	Playboy en Español	2000	USA
33	Video Rola	2000	Mexico
34	Azteca America	2001	USA
35	mun2*	2001	USA
36	Telefe International	2001	Argentina
37	Infinito	2002	USA
38	La Familia Cosmovision	2002	USA
39	TBN Enlace USA	2002	USA
40	TeleFórmula	2002	Mexico
41	TeleFutura	2002	USA
42	Nicktoons Network (SAP)	2002	USA
43	Bandamax	2003	USA
44	Canal (á)	2003	Argentina
45	Caracol TV Internacional	2003	Colombia
46	Casa Club TV	2003	USA
47	De Película	2003	USA
48	De Película Clasico	2003	USA
49	elgourmet.com	2003	Argentina
50	Family Christian Network	2003	Costa Rica
51	Gol TV	2003	USA
52	LATV*	2003	USA
53	MariaVision	2003	Mexico
54	MomentumTV	2003	Mexico
55	MovieWorld	2003	Mexico
56	Ritmoson Latino	2003	USA
57	Sorpresa	2003	USA
58	Telehit	2003	USA
59	TV Colombia	2003	USA
60	TyC Sports Channel	2003	Argentina
61	World Picks Latino on Demand	2003	USA
62	CB TV Televisión Michoacán	2004	Mexico
63	Centroamerica TV	2004	USA
64	Cine Mexicano	2004	USA
65	Ecuavisa Internacional	2004	Ecuador
66	ESPN Deportes	2004	USA
67	The History Channel en Español	2004	USA
68	Latinoamérica TV	2004	Uruguay
69	Mexico 22	2004	Mexico
70	NDTV Color Visión (The Dominican Channel)	2004	Dominican Republic
71	Nicktoons (SAP)	2004	USA
72	Nueva Vida Vision	2004	USA
73	Once Mexico	2004	Mexico
74	SíTV*	2004	USA
75	WAPA-America	2004	USA
76	Discovery Kids En Español	2005	USA
77	Discovery Travel and Living (Viajar y Vivir)	2005	USA
78	DocuTVE	2005	Not available
79	El Garage TV	2005	Argentina
80	LN: Latele Novela Network	2005	USA
81	Mexicanal	2005	USA
82	Sol VOD	2005	USA
83	SUR MEX	2005	USA
84	SUR Perú	2005	USA
85	SUR Venezuela Globovision	2005	USA

Table 15.1 Continued

Order	Network	US launch date	Headquarters
86	Telemundo Puerto Rico	2005	USA
87	TV Venezuela	2005	USA
88	SuperCanal Caribe	2006	Dominican Republic
89	AYM Sports	2006	Mexico
90	BarcaTV S-VOD	2006	USA
91	Ecua-TV	2006	Ecuador
92	VeneMovies	2006	USA
93	MEGA TV	2006	USA
94	V-Me	2007	USA
95	BullaTV	2007	USA
96	Discovery Familia	2007	USA
97	TuVisión	2007	USA
98	Real Madrid TV	2008	USA
99	MI CINE	Not available	USA
100	ochoTV	Not available	Mexico
101	Teve-de-mente	Not available	Mexico
102	VOY Network	Not available	USA

Sources: *Multichannel News* (October 17, 2005; October 1, 2007); Television and Cable Factbook Online, DirecTV and Echostar
Notes: * These networks air bilingual or English language programming

Factors Contributing to Network Growth

Language and culture are valuable to advertisers as market segmenters (Coffey, 2008). While household income and size have been known to be traditional predictors of audience value, advertisers have indicated that there is value in reaching audiences via language and culture. Moreover, these factors were found to be more important than household income and size, once an advertiser has determined to target a foreign language audience (Coffey, 2008). This phenomenon can be observed by the fact that, while African Americans have higher median household income than Hispanics in the United States, the African American audience does not speak a foreign language and has not enjoyed a comparable number of networks targeting them as a group (Coffey, 2007). "Nearly one-quarter of all cable revenue comes from African-American homes, according to BET, and yet less than 1 percent of the industry's video channels target that audience," according to Umstead (2007a). In fact, the most recent cable network seeking to reach African Americans in the United States has failed, due to lack of carriage and low advertiser investment (Umstead, 2007b).

Major events in the Hispanic programming industry and in the United States during this time period offer likely reasons for the differences in growth rate between the Hispanic population and networks, all of which point to the high value placed on language and culture as foundational segmentation strategies. In late 1992, Nielsen Media Research began measuring Hispanic audiences, introducing its Nielsen Hispanic Television Index (NHTI), which provided separate measurement of Spanish language television and Spanish language audience viewing habits in the United States (Nielsen Media Research, 2006). Since research indicates that advertisers and programmers value accurate measurement, it would follow that this new measurement tool would have helped legitimize Spanish language programming to would-be investors, whether they were programmers or the advertisers necessary to support such programming. Since the steady growth in the number of Hispanics began in 1996, this four-year period following the NHTI's introduction would have been adequate time for media managers to recognize the value of a separate ratings index for Hispanic audiences and to launch new networks in response. Consistent with the growth patterns above, reports from the 2000 Census on language use painted a new linguistic landscape of the United States for many in the media industry. Once tabulated, the sheer number of Spanish speakers in the United States provided national recognition of the size of the Spanish-speaking demographic—a surprise for many programmers and advertisers. As seen in Figure 15.1, the growth in Hispanic networks was steady, with the largest gains occurring in the years just prior to 2004.

While a couple of networks launched in the early 1990s, the first growth spurt seems to have arrived in 1996. From that year forward, sustained growth was observed at the rate of two, six and even ten new Hispanic networks per year through 2000. It may be that the brand recognition of some of the new networks' parent companies influenced other programmers and advertisers to test the waters. The debut of CNN en Español, FOX Sports en Español and Discovery en Español from 1996 to 1998 likely signaled to other programmers that Spanish language television was a safe move, that it had been officially embraced and validated by leaders in the multichannel industry.

Finally, the release of 2000 US Census data indicating that Hispanics had surpassed African Americans as the largest minority group in the United States undoubtedly served as a wake-up call to advertisers and programmers, particularly those not yet actively marketing to or doing business with Hispanics. This news was released in 2002, the same year in which there was a second sharp upturn in the number of new Spanish language networks (see Figure 15.1). While in 2002 there were forty-one Hispanic-targeted networks, two years later in 2004, there were seventy-five, an increase of 83 percent. Local Hispanic station growth experienced a similar spike in 2002 (see Figure 15.2). The US Census Bureau news release serves as a possible explanation for this sharp growth. As Cartagena (2005, p. xiii) notes, this demographic event "caused many in the business world to rethink their attitudes toward the Latino community." While a causal relationship cannot be proven without asking advertisers directly why they invested in 2003, the census news seems a likely explanation for the phenomenon, given the timing.

It is worth mentioning one of the commonly overlooked reasons for the growth rate of the US Hispanic population—3.3 percent annually, compared to just 1.0 percent for the general population of the United States—a demographic group projected to be nearly 25 percent of the population by the year 2050 (US Census Bureau, 2006a, 2006b). In addition to immigration, which provides much of the demand for Spanish language programming, the greatest driver of US Hispanic population growth is a high birth rate (Passel & Edmonston, 1994). While Hispanics made up 14.8 percent of the US population in 2006, they contributed to 22 percent of the births (US Census Bureau, 2006b). This also makes the US Hispanic audience younger, on average, than any other demographic group in the country, with a median age of 25 (Pew Hispanic Center, 2005)—a boon to advertisers who value the disposable income and impressionable minds of young people, and who have the potential to win hearts, pocketbooks, and a stable consumer base for a lifetime.

Hispanic Population and Spanish Language Station Growth

The relationship between the US Hispanic population and local Spanish language stations was also examined, but for the period 1995–2004, since 1995 was the earliest date TNS affiliate data were measured and available for analysis. However, data points were used every other year (1995, 1997, 1999, 2001 and 2003) because this was the frequency with which TNS noted new stations. A slight uptick in local Spanish language station growth is observed in 1998 and again in 2002 (see

Figure 15.2). In these years, the number of local Hispanic stations grew by six and twelve stations, respectively. It is important to note one additional factor regarding the local stations. Not only did new local Spanish language stations enter the marketplace, but also existing local stations changed their language formats from English to Spanish. This is referred to as "organic growth" (M. Ray, personal communication, July 14, 2006), although it is worth mentioning that the TNS data set did not distinguish between organic station growth and new station growth. Again, post-2002 growth may be a response to the release of the US Census data, which seems to be confirmed by the advertisers' own responses in terms of timing.

There is a clear correlation between Hispanic population size and the number of Hispanic networks. For context, it is important to note that there was also a large increase in the number of new networks *in general* for the period studied. However, closer inspection reveals a *faster* rate of growth for Hispanic networks, and for good reason. For comparison purposes, the US White (non-Hispanic) population was analyzed for the years 1994–2004, along with the total number of television networks within the US market. Because there are no known "White-targeted" networks, the total number of US networks was used as a surrogate measure. These network figures were compiled from the annual video competition reports of the Federal Communications Commission (FCC) from 1994 to 2004, the years for which comparable data were available. The figures included all networks that were available via satellite delivery.

While the White population remained fairly stable, the total number of US television networks exploded between 1995 and 1996, likely due to enhanced technologies and additional cable system channel capacity. While the number of general market networks certainly outpaced the number of Hispanic networks, it was the rate of growth on the Hispanic networks that beat out the general market. While the total number of cable networks grew 266 percent from 1994–2004 (from 106 to 388), the number of Hispanic networks soared 971 percent (from 7 to 75) for the same period (Federal Communications Commission, 1995, 1996, 1997, 1998, 1999, 2001a, 2001b, 2002, 2004, 2005). This suggests that while size of a demographic is related to network growth, there must be other factors that help to explain such a phenomenon as the Hispanic network growth rate—likely the segmentation value and power that language and culture deliver to programmers and advertisers, a topic to be discussed shortly.

In sum, the size or population of the US Hispanic population and the number of Hispanic networks in the United States are related. This relationship also holds true between the US Hispanic population and local Hispanic station growth. The shape of Figure 15.1 does suggest, however, that the population was growing at a slightly greater rate than the networks, at least initially. This is logical in that it is important to recognize a potential audience or consumer base before creating television networks that target it. Figure 15.1 shows that the Hispanic population was growing steadily, and Hispanic network growth accelerated later (around 1995–1996). This steady population growth followed by rapid media product development is also indicative of a latent demand among advertisers for the new Hispanic audience. Programmers must have sensed this latent demand before taking the initial risk of creating Hispanic-targeted programming.

Hispanic Population and Hispanic Advertising Expenditures

This second analysis examined the relationship between the growth of the US Hispanic population and the growth of advertising expenditures for Hispanic television. As noted in the beginning of this section, the Top 75 Designated Market Areas were analyzed. The analysis was conducted for broadcast television on three levels for the period 1997–2004, in order to have parallel data sets for both the network and local levels. It first examined the relationship between population and

(a) total Hispanic advertising revenue, (b) spot advertising revenue, and (c) network advertising revenue.

Advertising data reveal rapid revenue growth for the period in comparison to the growth rate of the US Hispanic population (see Figure 15.3). At all time points within the period measured, total Hispanic advertising expenditures grew at a much greater rate than did the Hispanic population. Percentage growth for total advertising revenue for all years except one was in the double digits, for instance 14 percent or 29 percent annual growth.

Advertising revenue growth rates at the spot and network levels showed similar patterns.[2] While the US Hispanic population grew 41.6 percent from 1997 to 2004, Hispanic spot television advertising revenue grew 124.5 percent and Hispanic network television advertising grew 205.5 percent (see Figures 15.4 and 15.5). These high growth rates in advertising revenue are likely related to the growth in the number of Spanish language affiliates and networks for the same period; more stations and networks mean more advertising inventory available for purchase. In both cases but particularly the network advertising revenue comparison, Hispanic revenue experienced a steady climb, whereas the general market revenue performance was more volatile (see Figure 15.6).

The shape of the growth curves in Figures 15.3, 15.4 and 15.5 are similar to the shape of Figures 15.1 and 15.2, and for good reason. Programmers are dependent upon advertisers to support new programming ventures. If new programming has launched, it has launched because its studio and producers feel secure in the potential income from advertising inventory offered within that programming. Without sufficient levels of advertising revenue, a given program cannot survive in the dual product marketplace. As discussed earlier, one likely catalyst for advertiser confidence was the 2000 Census data, which indicated that Hispanics had surpassed African Americans as the largest minority group in the United States. When this milestone occurred in 2002, it received substantial press coverage. This news gave Hispanics greater visibility and consumer clout than they had previously enjoyed, and they began receiving more attention from advertisers (Cartagena, 2005).

Finally, Hispanic television advertising data were compared with general market television advertising data for the same time period, 1997–2004 (see Figures 15.6, 15.7 and 15.8). Hispanic

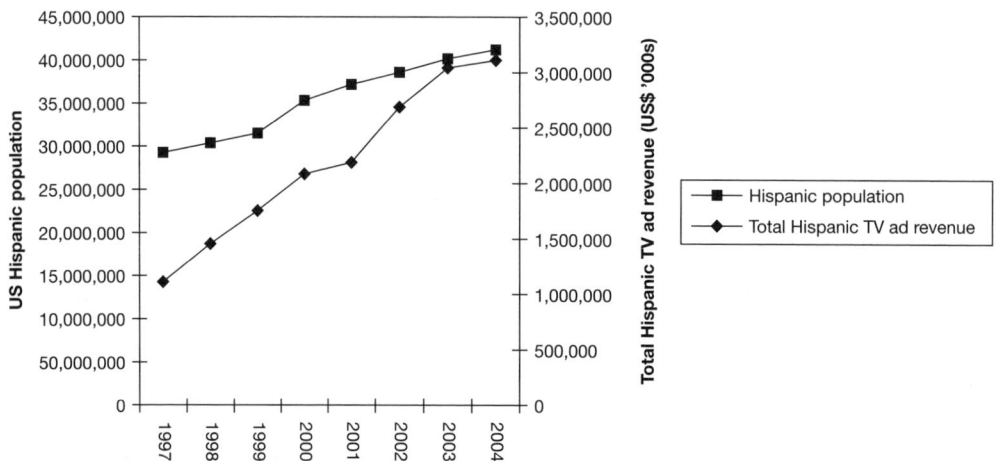

Figure 15.3 US Hispanic Population versus Total Hispanic Television Advertising Revenue, 1997–2004

Sources: TNS Media Intelligence, US Census Bureau

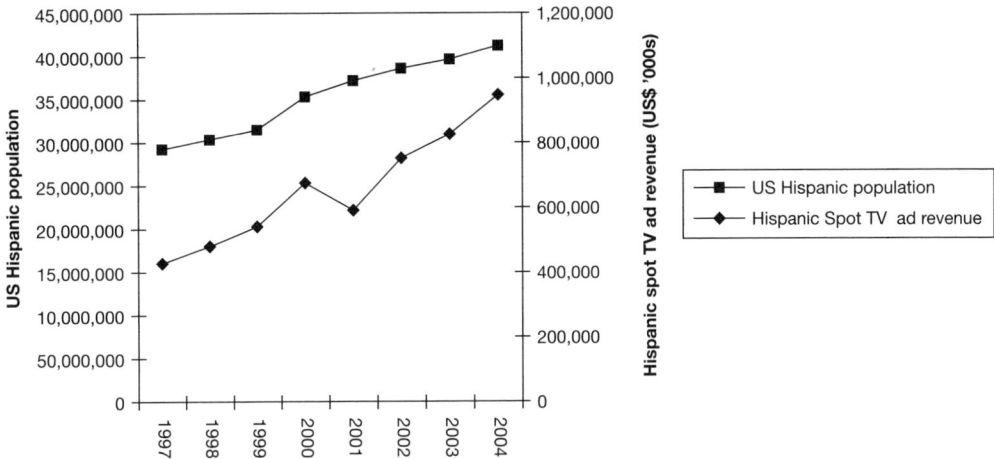

Figure 15.4 US Hispanic Population versus Total Hispanic Spot TV Advertising Revenue, 1997–2004

Sources: TNS Media Intelligence, US Census Bureau

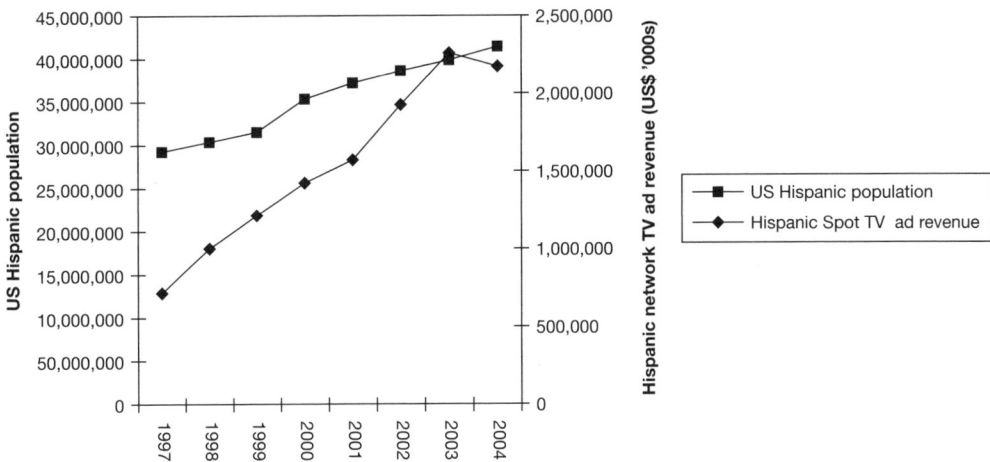

Figure 15.5 US Hispanic Population versus Total Hispanic Network TV Advertising Revenue, 1997–2004

Sources: TNS Media Intelligence, US Census Bureau

television revenues grew at a more rapid pace than the general television market revenues at all three levels of comparison: total broadcast television revenue, spot television revenue and network television revenue. While Hispanic spot TV advertising revenue increased 124.5 percent from 1997 to 2004, the general market spot TV category decreased 1.5 percent (see Figure 15.7). Similarly, while Hispanic network TV advertising grew 205.5 percent for that period, general market network TV advertising revenue grew just 24.8 percent (see Figure 15.8). Finally, total Hispanic TV advertising revenue grew 175 percent for the period 1997–2004, while total general market advertising revenue grew just 12.2 percent (see Figure 15.6).

A few observations are worth noting when comparing the Hispanic and general television markets for the period studied.[3] First, while network and total broadcast television revenue in the

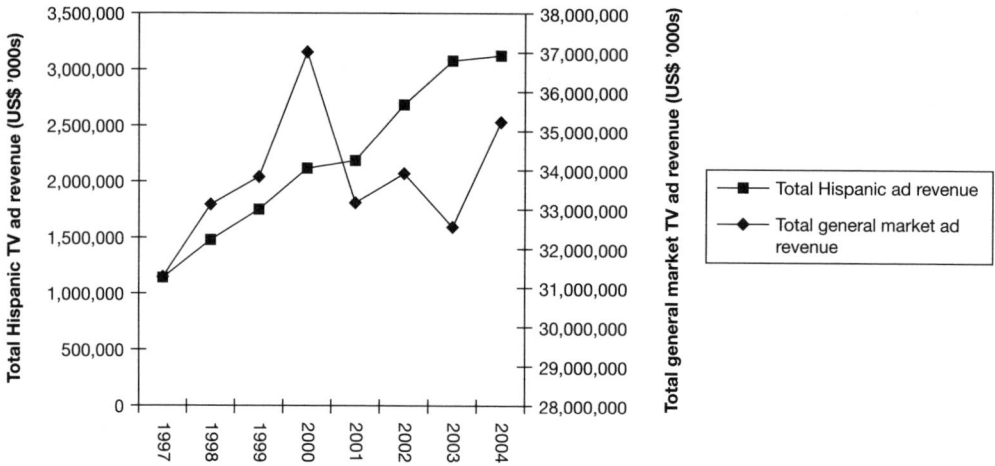

Figure 15.6 Hispanic versus General Market Total Broadcast Television Advertising Revenue, 1997–2004

Source: TNS Media Intelligence

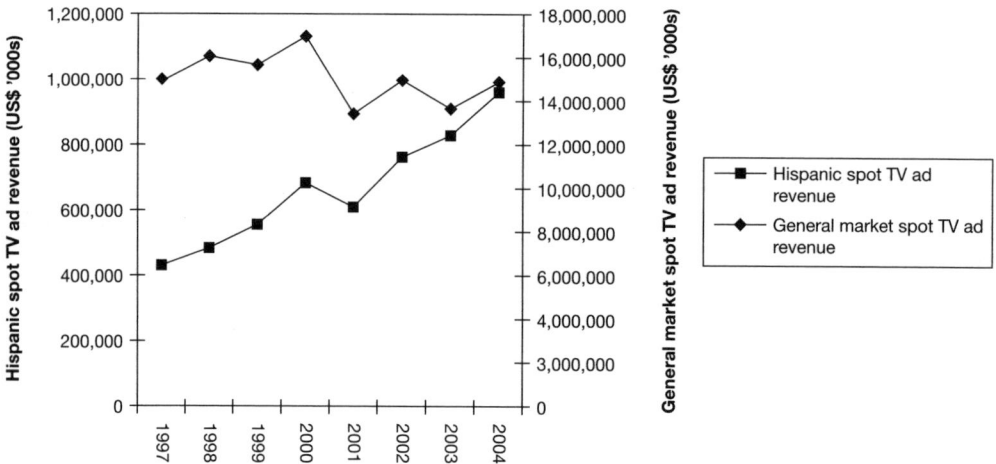

Figure 15.7 Hispanic Spot versus General Market Spot TV Advertising Revenue, 1997–2004

Source: TNS Media Intelligence

general market slipped in 2001 due to 9/11, Hispanic television revenue continued to grow steadily (see Figures 15.6 and 15.8). Second, while total Hispanic television revenue and total Hispanic network revenue grew steadily from 1997 to 2004 and did not seem to have been affected by the general advertising drop-off of 2001, Hispanic spot revenue *did* experience a drop-off similar to that of the general market (see Figure 15.7). However, after this decline for 2001, Hispanic spot market revenue quickly recovered and in fact grew at a sharper rate than did general market spot revenues.

Third, a slightly higher rate of growth can be observed for Hispanic advertising revenues at all levels of analysis (total revenue, spot revenue and network revenue) compared to the general market during 2001–2004 (see Figures 15.6, 15.7 and 15.8). This is due to two factors. First, as

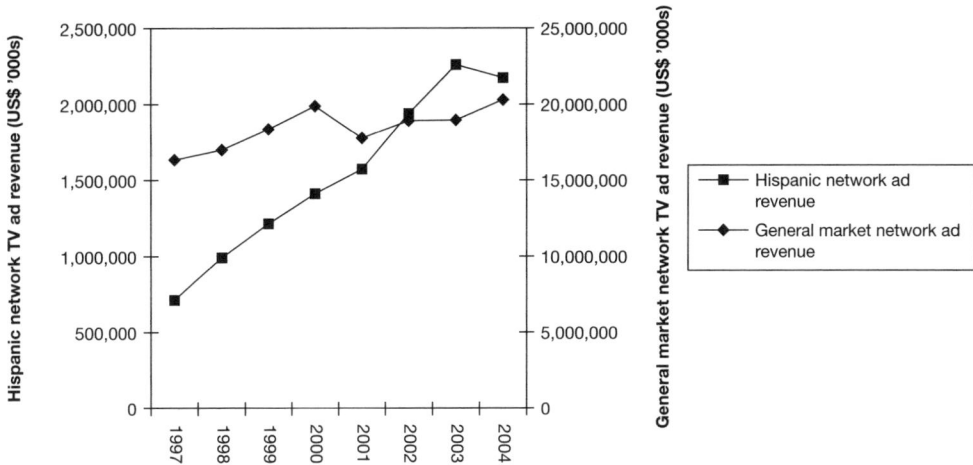

Figure 15.8 Hispanic versus General Market Broadcast Network TV Advertising Revenue, 1997–2004

Source: TNS Media Intelligence

previously noted, the release of US Census figures in 2002 probably played a role in this growth. News of this consumer group's size, combined with media coverage, spawned even more advertiser interest and stimulated further advertising sales. This is not an effect that would have occurred immediately, but one that would have gained momentum as news of the Census data spread, causing advertisers to process the information and gradually make advertising investment decisions. Second, the sharp increase in revenue growth coincided with the sharp increase in Hispanic network growth from 2002 onward, as previously noted. The increased Hispanic advertising inventory for those years made greater investment levels possible, again suggestive of latent demand that could finally be satisfied with the arrival of Hispanic television vehicles.

Networks

The top four Spanish language television networks in the US include broadcasters Univision (privately owned), Telemundo (owned by NBC Universal), Telefutura (owned by Univision) and Azteca America (owned by TV Azteca). Growth of Spanish language networks continues, but so does the growth of networks seeking to reach Hispanics in English or bilingually. As of early 2008, there were 102 Hispanic-targeted networks available in the United States, with all but four broadcasting in Spanish (see Table 15.1). Newcomer LATV rounds out the networks that have chosen to reach the young Hispanic demographic in English or bilingually; it is distributed as a digital subchannel. SíTV, mun2 and MTV Tr3s are three networks that embraced the English and bilingual approaches in the early 2000s.

Viewership on the principal networks has also grown. Larger audiences on more networks have resulted in increased ratings, which have captured advertisers' attention and investment dollars. Univision has long held the top spot in Nielsen ratings among all of the Spanish language broadcast networks. However, when the NHTI gave way to the national People Meter sample in fall 2007—in which English and Spanish language networks were measured together in the same sample—Univision's market share was evident. Moreover, advertisers and programmers alike were able to clearly see the consistently high 18–34 ratings held by Univision nationally, and not just among Hispanics (Univision, 2007). Various Spanish language affiliates in markets across the country have also enjoyed ratings bragging rights. When compared side by side, the size and value of the Spanish language television audience is undeniable—and difficult for advertisers to ignore.

Advertiser Investment

While advertiser investment has certainly increased, investment levels are still below what would be expected given the relative size of the US Spanish-speaking population. The Association of Hispanic Advertising Agencies (AHAA) noted this disparity in its report, *Missed Opportunities*, stating that "while Hispanics respresent[ed] about 13 percent of the population [in 2003], in aggregate America's leading advertisers are allocating an average of 2.4 percent of their measured media advertising resources targeting Hispanics" and noted that it takes at least 8 percent revenue allocation to be effective in reaching the demographic (AHAA, 2003). So while many major US companies have taken notice and invested in the US Hispanic population, others have yet to commit their resources. Even those companies investing in the Hispanic and Spanish-speaking populations are sometimes doing so at very low rates. Reasons US advertisers provide for not investing in the Spanish-speaking population are many and varied, but cost is the most commonly stated reason, followed by a lack of staffing or creative resources (Coffey, 2007).

Spanish Language Metrics

Much of the value of advertisers targeting Spanish language audiences comes, not surprisingly, from the segmentation power of language (Coffey, 2008). Accurate metrics that can measure the extent to which households are watching in a given language, then, are of utmost value to advertisers who want not only to be certain of the households they are reaching, but also to plan for future investment in Spanish language audiences. The demand for specific metrics for Hispanic and Spanish-speaking audiences is felt by Hispanic media companies and ad agencies who say they are always being "put to the test" to "prove that [their] viewer is viable" (Rodriguez, 1997, p. 286).

In 1992, Univision and Telemundo recognized a need for metric quantification of Spanish language viewing, and lobbied Nielsen Media Research for a separate ratings index that would more accurately count Hispanic households (Rodriguez, 1997). The networks financially supported the development of the National Hispanic Television Index (NHTI), which did result in higher counts of Hispanic households and advertiser investment, but not comparable advertising rates to English language television (Coffey, 2007; Rodriguez, 1997). The NHTI continued until late 2007, at which time Univision and Telemundo determined that their networks' growth, and that of the Hispanic audience, would be better recognized if measured alongside English language networks in the Nielsen Television Index (NTI). The 2007 upfront negotiations were based on the mainstream metric. The move also indicates, say some, the evolution of Spanish language programming to mainstream status (Tiegel, 2007). As noted above, advertisers did notice Hispanic growth and networks more. Whether or not a direct result of using the NTI, television advertisements targeting Hispanics on the mainstream English networks have become more common, as have bilingual and even Spanish language advertisements.

Market Maturation and Trends

As with any other media industry, growth and expansion are followed by competition, consolidation and concentration. The last few years have brought a fourth Spanish broadcaster, Azteca America, as well as more Hispanic-targeted cable networks, including MegaTV, LATV,

SíTV, mun2 (owned by NBC Universal), and V-Me. Some of the networks have achieved or seek cable and satellite distribution, while others are marketing themselves as digital subchannel services that can assist broadcasters with programming options following the digital conversion. Consolidation has been most pronounced with industry leader Univision, which has acquired other Spanish language properties, most notably the top Spanish language radio broadcaster in the United States, Hispanic Broadcasting Corp (HBC), with a controversial merger in 2003 (Coffey, 2005). Telemundo became a subsidiary of NBC Universal in 2002 as well (NBC Universal, 2008) and MegaTV is a subsidiary of Spanish Broadcasting System (SBS). Spanish language television may be a market segment, but it is one that has evolved and matured as many other media industries have before it.

The Future

As noted earlier, Spanish language television has and will continue to follow the lifecycle just as other media industries have done. The emerging industry has become mainstream, competition is being followed by consolidation and concentration, and this will soon be followed by fragmentation once again. It is a lifecycle noted by McQuail (2000), who described the evolutionary phases of the television industry as the number of choices increases. This lifecycle will repeat itself as the Hispanic and Spanish language television industry matures. That is, what was once a market segment—the Spanish language or Hispanic market—will cease to be one large market segment. Instead, further fragmentation will produce microsegments or microniches to serve the various demographics and psychographics within the Hispanic market.

Such fragmentation is already being witnessed with the emergence of bilingual and English language networks to serve second- and third-generation Hispanics, and millenials in particular. Toward this end, broadband video networks have emerged to serve Hispanic millenials, and other Hispanics, who overindex on some new media platforms when compared to non-Hispanics (Boyle, 2007). Spanish language sports programming and film networks have arisen to fill the niche for specific content, as have online social networking sites.

Valuation of foreign language audiences will continue to be a matter of concern and debate as the number of US non-English speakers continues to increase. The National Association of Broadcasters (NAB) has made its position clear on what appears to be a continuing practice of "dictates"—media buyers being instructed not to purchase advertising inventory on minority (e.g. Hispanic or urban) stations (National Association of Broadcasters, 2008). When advertising buys are made, lower valuation of minority audiences, even on a CPM basis, also continues to be problematic (Coffey, 2007; Napoli, 2002; Ofori, 1999; Webster & Phalen, 1997). It seems that while advertiser recognition of the Spanish language audience has arrived (though the task is far from over, given the large number of non-investors), the valuation of Spanish language audiences has lagged. Language will continue to be a focus of Hispanic media in general, as the number of second- and third-generation US Hispanics grows. This group of Hispanics tends to be English-only, bilingual or less reliant on Spanish overall. However, growth trends are likely to continue upward for Spanish language television as long as immigration rates remain steady, as long as bilingual Hispanics prefer watching some programs in Spanish, and as long as there continues to be multigenerational viewing in which older Spanish-dominant members of the family exercise group program preferences. Demand for Spanish language programming will be fueled by such factors, and will shape the lifecycle of Spanish language television in the United States.

216 • Amy Jo Coffey

Notes

1 The term "Hispanic-targeted networks" is used instead of "Spanish language networks" in this chapter because there are four networks (of 102) that target Hispanics in English or are bilingual. The majority of Hispanic networks are Spanish language (see Table 15.1), and the reader may wish to substitute these terms. However, Hispanic networks is a more accurate term since it includes all Hispanic-targeted networks regardless of language.

2 One exception occurred in the spot revenue category in 2001, when it registered a 12.2 percent drop. A slowing was noticeable in the total advertising revenue as well. Both are likely due to the advertising revenue drop-off from the economic recession (Hall, 2003) and 9/11. Most advertisers in 2001 experienced a drop in 2001 revenue for this reason. However, Hispanic network television advertising revenue held steady throughout the 9/11 drop-off experienced by so many others; it appears that the strong growth in this area was enough to cushion Hispanic networks from the fall-off.

3 Because insufficient data existed to perform comparable analyses with Hispanic cable television, these secondary data analyses focus solely on Hispanic broadcast television. Most Hispanic television revenue is actually within broadcast television (mainly Univision and its properties).

References

Association of Hispanic Advertising Agencies. (2003). *Missed opportunities.* Retrieved May 13, 2008, from www.ahaa.org/research/Missedopportunities.pdf.

Boyle, L. (2007). *Beyond traditional Spanish language media: Alternative methods in creating integration in a mature U.S. Hispanic market.* Retrieved May 13, 2008, from www.spanishmedia.unt.edu/Vol.%201%202008%20%282%29.pdf.

Cartagena, C. (2005). *Latino boom!* New York: Ballantine.

Coffey, A. J. (2005, May). Defining a product market for Spanish language media: Lessons learned from Univision Communications Inc. & Hispanic Broadcasting Corp. Paper presented at the International Communication Association, New York.

Coffey, A. J. (2007). Linguistic market segmentation and audience valuation by U.S. television advertisers. Unpublished doctoral dissertation, University of Georgia, Athens.

Coffey, A. J. (2008). The case for audience isolation: Language and culture as predictors of advertiser investment. *International Journal on Media Management, 10*(2), 81–90.

Federal Communications Commission (FCC). (1995). *Second annual video competition report.* Retrieved May 7, 2006, from www.fcc.gov/mb/csrptpg.html.

Federal Communications Commission. (1996). *Third annual MVPD competition report.* Retrieved May 7, 2006, from www.fcc.gov/Bureaus/Cable/Reports/fcc96496.txt.

Federal Communications Commission. (1997). *Fourth annual MVPD competition report.* Retrieved May 7, 2006, from www.fcc.gov/Bureaus/Cable/Reports/fcc97423.pdf.

Federal Communications Commission. (1998). *Fifth annual MVPD competition report.* Retrieved May 7, 2006, from www.fcc.gov/Bureaus/Cable/Reports/fcc98335.pdf.

Federal Communications Commission. (1999). *Sixth annual MVPD competition report.* Retrieved May 7, 2006, from www.fcc.gov/Bureaus/Cable/Reports/fcc99418.doc.

Federal Communications Commission. (2001a). *Seventh annual MVPD competition report.* Retrieved May 7, 2006, from www.fcc.gov/Bureaus/Cable/Reports/fcc01001.pdf.

Federal Communications Commission. (2001b). *Eighth annual MVPD competition report.* Retrieved May 7, 2006, from http://hraunfoss.fcc.gov/edocs_public/attachmatch/FCC-01-389A1.pdf.

Federal Communications Commission. (2002). *Ninth annual MVPD competition report.* Retrieved May 7, 2006, from http://hraunfoss.fcc.gov/edocs_public/attachmatch/FCC-02-338A1.doc.

Federal Communications Commission. (2004). *Tenth annual MVPD competition report.* Retrieved May 7, 2006, from http://hraunfoss.fcc.gov/edocs_public/attachmatch/FCC-04-5A1.doc.

Federal Communications Commission. (2005). *Eleventh annual MVPD competition report.* Retrieved May 7, 2006, from attachmatch/FCC-05-13A1.doc.

Hall, R. E. (2003, Fall). Economic fluctuations and growth. *NBER Reporter,* 1–8. Retrieved April 11, 2007, from www.nber.org/reporter/fall03/fall03.pdf.

McQuail, D. (2000). *McQuail's mass communication theory* (4th ed.). Thousand Oaks, CA: Sage.

Napoli, P. M. (2002). Audience valuation and minority media: An analysis of the determinants of the value of radio audiences. *Journal of Broadcasting & Electronic Media, 46*(2), 169–178.

National Association of Broadcasters. (2008, March 31). *Broadcasters urge end to advertising "dictates."* Retrieved April 11, 2008, from www.nab.org/AM/Template.cfm?Section=Press_Releases1&TEMPLATE=/CM/ContentDisplay.cfm&CONTENTID=11963.

NBC Universal. (2008). *NBC milestones.* Retrieved May 13, 2008, from www.nbcuni.com/About_NBC_Universal/Company_Overview/overview09.shtml.

Nielsen Media Research. (2006). NHTI TV audience report: Hispanic report. Retrieved September 9, 2006, from www.nielsenmedia.com/nc/portal/site/Public/menuitem.d7deb7344c5a8ffe818e6c1047a062a0/?vgnextoid=7fd12417f58f4010VgnVCM100000880a260aRCRD.

Ofori, K.A. (1999). *When being no. 1 is not enough: The impact of advertising practices on minority-owned & minority-formatted broadcast stations.* Washington, DC: Civil Rights Forum on Communications Policy.

Passel, J. S. & Edmonston, B. (1994). Immigration and race: Recent trends in immigration to the United States. In J. S. Passel & B. Edmonston (Eds.), *Immigration and ethnicity: The integration of America's newest arrivals* (pp. 31–72). Washington, DC: Urban Institute Press.

Pew Hispanic Center. (2005). *Hispanics: A people in motion.* Washington, DC: Pew Hispanic Center.

Rodriguez, A. (1997). Commercial ethnicity: Language, class and race in the marketing of the Hispanic audience. *Communication Review, 2*(3), 283–309.

Tiegel, E. (2007, March 26). Leveling field in ratings game. *Television Week, 26*(13), 15.

Umstead, R. T. (2007a, May 16). Black Family Channel: Big loss. Retrieved May 14, 2008, from www.multichannel.com/blog/1800000180/post/730009473.html.

Umstead, R. T. (2007b, April 30). Black Family irons out details of move to web. Retrieved May 14, 2008, from www.multichannel.com/article/CA6437756.html.

Univision. (2007, September 6). *Univision #1 network for entire week beating ABC, CBS, NBC, FOX and CW.* Retrieved May 13, 2008, from www.univision.net/corp/en/pr/Miami_06092007-1_print.html.

US Census Bureau. (2006a). *Nation's population one-third minority.* Retrieved July 14, 2006, from www.census.gov/Press-Release/www/releases/archives/population/006808.html.

US Census Bureau. (2006b). *Hispanics in the United States.* Retrieved May 13, 2008, from www.census.gov/population/www/socdemo/hispanic/files/Internet_Hispanic_in_US_2006.pdf.

Webster, J. G. & Phalen, P. F. (1997). *The mass audience: Rediscovering the dominant model.* Mahwah, NJ: Lawrence Erlbaum Associates.

Winston, G. (2007, October 1). Guide to Hispanic TV networks. *Multichannel News.* Retrieved April 11, 2008, from www.multichannel.com/article/CA6485543.html.

16

Television News
Spain, Mexico, Colombia and the United States

Phyllis Slocum
University of North Texas, USA

Introduction

This chapter looks at the models of television news in three Spanish-speaking countries and in the United States where Spanish language television news is a well-established facet of the information media landscape. Spain, Mexico and Colombia represent television news models with individual characteristics evolving from their national development but which also share common elements that can be considered when looking at other Spanish language media models. However, Spanish language media developed from very different circumstances in the United States. Among the elements that distinguish the US model from the three other countries are the government and press historical development and economic climate. Because Spanish language media in the United States evolved in that climate, it forms a different television news model and will be reviewed last.

The Growing Impact of Television News

Television news has become a global communications staple. Where radio first transmitted words and ideas across borders, television adds the impact of pictures. Advancing Internet technology allows video to be sent worldwide literally with the click of a button. In terms of journalism, the audio–video combination makes television news a potent and easily understandable communication medium.

In the United States, the first decade of the twenty-first century shows continuing television news audience realignment influenced by such issues as developing technology, lifestyle change and increased availability of information sources. But despite these shifts, the various forms of television news such as broadcast network, cable news networks and local station newscasts continue as a primary source of information (*Wall Street Journal*, 2008). Add to that the television-style information provided by network and local station websites and the impact of television news is even more pronounced. Globally the importance of television is also growing to the extent that, despite geographic, political or economic obstacles, it has become a key if not major source of information for populations.

Television in Spain has developed significantly in recent years with a number of new commercial operators as well as the debut of digital services (BBC, 2008b). Spain is scheduled to make the monumental technology shift from analog to digital television in April, 2010. But because there are so many television channels (both commercial and public at both national and regional levels), the Spanish government may allot the new digital bandwidth opened up by the transition to television entities rather distribute it among other media sources like telephone and broadband (West, 2008).

More than 90 percent of all Mexican households have a television set (BUYUSA, 2008). International media consulting firm Carat has identified Mexico as a fast-growing, emerging economy and estimates its television advertising revenue to grow 20 percent over 2007 into 2008 (Carat, 2008).

As of 2008, Grupo Televisa was the number one Spanish language media company in the world (Bramhall, 2008). Additionally, Mexican television and media companies such as Televisa and TV Azteca are major content providers to the burgeoning Hispanic population in the United States where Spanish language television has emerged as a major player.

The Colombian television industry is also experiencing an unparalleled level of growth. While estimates vary, between 94 percent and 98 percent of the population has access to television programming from a variety of television operators recognized by the Comision Nacional de Television, the Colombian television regulatory body which establishes the procedures and rules by which the industry operates (BBC, 2008a; see also Chapter 5 in this handbook).

With the growth of television in these countries, the importance of television news has also increased. In Latin America, for example, as early as 1993, Perez-Linan (2002) reports the impact of television and the broadcast media was so great that they were considered more powerful than contemporary political parties by some observers. Executive Director of the Center for Media Freedom and Responsibility Melinda Quintos de Jesus cites the critical importance of journalism in today's world.

> we have moved through historic ages defined by advances in communication technology—from electronic to satellite to digital. These systems . . . have transformed the conduct of politics, business, and human relationships. Mass media opened up for the public unprecedented levels of access to information [empowering] ordinary people to seek and to search out the knowledge and information they need.
>
> (Quintos de Jesus, 2002, p. 2)

Television news developed in different ways around the globe depending on circumstances in each country. In 2004, Hallin and Mancini developed three media models to help put those differences into context and provide a basis for analyzing news media in global circumstances. They defined them as the Liberal or North Atlantic model, the Democratic Corporatist or Northern European model and the Polarized Pluralism or Mediterranean model. The first model is characterized by a strong commercial media and general market influences resulting in less government influence. The second is a combination where historically both commercial media and media with social and political ties coexist. In this instance, there is active but legally restricted governmental influence. The third model is characterized by media being part of party politics, a weaker history of commercial media development, and significant influence by the government in media issues (Hallin & Mancini, 2004).

It is in this context that we will look at the four countries already identified and how their individual television news models developed; what long-term issues may affect the models; and consider what differences and/or similarities exist. While Spain, Mexico and Colombia reflect unique circumstances in their television news growth, there are aspects in each case that are relevant to the development of television news in other Spanish language nations. The United States presents a news model distinct from these three and will be reviewed as the last of the four countries.

Spain

The end of the first decade of the twenty-first century saw a global economic slowdown. However, because of Spain's strong economic growth in previous years, the country had established itself as one of the world's most competitive economies (Fishbein, 2008). That aside, using the Hallin and Mancini (2004) definition of media models, Spain can still be described as a Polarized Pluralist model which is characterized by political party influence on the media, a weaker development of commercial media and a strong governmental role in media development. However, it is also important to note that Spain is on the verge of breaking out and moving into a more Democratic Corporatist model where commercial media and social/political groups coexist and the government influence on journalists is limited. But to understand the transition that appears to be coming in Spanish television it is helpful to look at the current model and how it developed.

Historical Context

Spanish media have a long and volatile history. To understand the changes taking place in twenty-first-century television news it is helpful to offer some context. Print media began in the 1600s with pamphlets or gazettes coming into Spain from France and were regularly published as early as 1641 (Chabran, n.d.). Although for several decades in the 1700s the Spanish monarchy limited newspaper publication, by 1792 it was restored. This continued well into the nineteenth century when transportation issues inside the country made newspaper distribution on a national level difficult although continuing governmental restrictions as well as low literacy rates limited readership. At the same time, a strong literary movement known as Costumbrismo was drawing attention to Spanish authors (Chabran, n.d.). Although efforts to provide a freer press occurred in the late nineteenth century, political circumstances leading into the twentieth century resulted in many of the print media becoming closely tied to political parties. Then, at the beginning of the twentieth century, broadcast media—first, of course with radio—became a part of the nation's media landscape and with it governmental control continued.

From the beginning, electronic media has been recognized as a highly effective and valuable resource for political authorities. In 1908 the government passed a law giving it the right to regulate and control the current radio/telegraphy systems in use as well as those that would be invented in the future (Maxwell, n.d.). Despite that decree, experimental radio stations did spring up funded by private, profit-oriented companies and the first official license for radio was granted in 1924. However, in 1934 the government further tightened its hold on the broadcast media. It declared radio to be essential to the government and a year later tacitly acknowledged the growth of visual media by stating that, in addition to the audio systems for broadcast communications that were then available, all systems that produced pictures then and in the future were to also be controlled by the state (Maxwell, n.d.). With the outbreak of the Spanish Civil War in 1936 and the subsequent rise to power of General Francisco Franco, freedom of the press was stifled. The broadcast industry, still only radio, was nationalized and all radio stations were put under the direction of the Franco government. Further, the government outlawed broadcasting in any language except Spanish as well as any reports or programs that were perceived to be negative toward the government (Maxwell, n.d.). This issue of language is important in Spanish media, especially television, because there are multiple languages in that country and the impact will be considered later in this section. Spanish journalists continued to be tightly regulated in those decades before and during the political administration of General Francisco Franco. The impact of nearly forty years under an authoritarian government meant little or no freedom of the press. The result was that journalism as a profession began to emerge later than in other Western democracies (Stromback & Garcia-Luengo, 2007).

Television did not make its appearance until 1948 with a public demonstration of the device and it was not until 1957 that the first television news program went on air. Television growth continued slowly over the years, confined to cities and remained under the control of the state even though private companies did emerge (Chabran, n.d.). When Franco died in 1975 a transition toward a more open, liberal media began and since then Spanish media has been caught up in change (Stromback & Garcia-Luengo, 2007). During the years after Franco and into the twenty-first century, television surpassed newspapers becoming the news medium of choice for most people (Chabran, n.d.). The Constitution of 1978 guaranteed a free press and outlawed prior censorship. Spanish television developed from a state-controlled system to a regulated one that combined public and privately owned TV stations and channels competing for advertising revenue (Maxwell, n.d.). Also important was the now-legal right to broadcast in other languages.

Television News Issues

As television moved to a more liberal environment, one of the most important now-legal rights was to broadcast in languages other than just Spanish. Historically, the Basque, Catalan and Galician regions of Spain have valued their independence and certainly their regional identities. They also have their own languages, which were repressed under the Franco government. As broadcast freedoms grew, television channels developed in the Basque, Catalan and Galician regions of Spain and programming emerged in these languages as well as Spanish. Thus, while Spanish is the universally understood language of Spain, these three languages are part of the television (and radio) media with some news reports and programs broadcast in those languages (Chabran, n.d.).

The situation has become more complex with the transition to digital. The many small television stations (regional/local) now broadcasting via analog are guaranteed by the government the right to continue broadcasting when the switch to digital is complete. But there may not be enough channels to fulfill that commitment (Ferreras, 2008) and this circumstance should be studied for any long-term impact on non-Spanish language stations and their role as journalists in their communities.

The Spanish media industry shares a trait with many other nations that of media trade unions—a tradition of labor organization among journalists. One of the most important associations for television is the Union de Televisiones Comerciales Asociadas (UTECA: Associated Commercial Televisions Union). While there are numerous professional media organizations, the level of participation by Spanish journalists is low (Salaverria, 2006). There are several trade unions whose goal is to improve working conditions for journalists and they are all part of a larger group called the Federation of Journalist Trade Unions (Salaverria, 2006). Additionally, journalists of all types are registered by the government (Chabran, n.d.).

Issues Affecting Working Journalists

Television reporting in Spain is undergoing major changes due to advancing technology and the growing trend of traditional television or broadcast journalists becoming the "converged" journalist.[1] However, the transition is also having some negative reactions because of additional job responsibilities and the expectations of increased production of content (Scolari, Navarro & Pardo, 2007).

Impact of Technology

In 2000, a study revealed that nearly 70 percent of Spanish journalists have considered changing professions. Issues of professionalism, long working days and low pay were key concerns (Rodriguez Andres, 2000, as cited in Gill, Blanco & Arroyave, 2006). The trend of the television journalist performing multiple tasks is not atypical and is a major element of American television newsrooms, especially in smaller markets.

Increasingly, Spain's television stations expect reporters to be involved in all aspects of news production because of expanding technology. Scolari et al. (2007) report the impact on television news personnel seems to be related to the size of the operation. New or smaller television news organizations have little trouble adapting since most personnel (often university trained and younger in the profession) have always worked in a multi-task or technology-oriented environment. Some larger television operations with older personnel trained in more traditional journalistic processes report the transition "often proved traumatic" (Scolari et al., 2007, p. 9).

As already noted, television rather than the print media serves as the primary news source for most of the Spanish public (Chabran, n.d.). That situation, in conjunction with the liberalization of the media from government control and influence, and the role of technology are keys to Spain's transition from a Polarized Pluralist media model to the Democratic Corporatist model.

In fact, there are striking similarities in working models between many US television reporters and television reporters with TV3, a large publicly owned television company in Catalunya. In an interview, a Spanish television reporter describes job requirements as needing

> to have, at the very least, knowledge about how to film, a capacity to write the story, and a knowledge of editing processes. With time [reporters] will need to have knowledge of infographics and technical skills in telecommunications, so that they will be able, at a given moment, to connect up to a fibre optic network.
>
> (Scolari et al., 2007, pp. 9–10)

Dangerous Work

However, Spanish news personnel face another reality—potential physical danger, particularly from terrorist or national separatist activities. In March 2004 Spain suffered the worst terrorist attack in European history. Bombs exploded in four commuter trains in Madrid, killing 119 people. It was later proven at the trial that the perpetrators were inspired by al-Qaeda and were not part of a well-established domestic separatist organization. But, it is this organization, the militant Basque separatist group ETA (Euskadi ta Askatasuna) that continues to be a threat and has targeted journalists (Reporters Without Borders, 2008a).

ETA has been a dangerous part of Spanish society for more than forty years and is held responsible for the deaths of over 800 people, politicians, police officers, civilians and journalists through bombings and other violent attacks. The Council on Foreign Relations reports that journalists have been ETA targets (Hanson, 2008). According to the organization Reporters Without Borders (2008a), ETA has targeted reporters working the Basque Country or reporting on regional issues. The journalists have used bodyguards and even traveled in armored vehicles in efforts to protect themselves from attacks. Prime Minister Jose Luis Rodriguez Zapatero began efforts to negotiate with ETA establishing a ceasefire in early 2006. But in 2007 ETA placed a bomb in a Madrid airport, ending the ceasefire (BBC, 2008b). New restrictions on freedom of the press have also been part of the Zapatero government, among them stricter enforcement of defamation laws with a new law aimed at protecting the public image of the Spanish monarchy. A major political party called for a boycott against a media group which includes a major television station because of an editorial stance, and in Valencia (which has an autonomous regional government) one of three TV transmitters was shut down belonging to ACPV (Acció Cultural del País Valencià), which broadcast TV3, a regional public station on air for twenty years. Negotiations to resolve the issue have been ongoing (Reporters Without Borders, 2008a).

Global Impact

Spain also has a major impact on international television. The news agency EFE, founded in 1939, is the fourth-largest global news-gathering agency and the largest Spanish language news organization. It provides news across multiple platforms to Spanish language media outlets worldwide. EFE operates in 120 countries with a staff of more than 3,000. Its operations include four major information hubs, including one in Miami, Florida, and the company began service to Arabic nations in 2006. EFE claims to provide more than 40 percent of international news broadcast or published in Latin America (Agencia EFE, n.d.).

Summary

Despite the issues still facing Spain that inhibit television news and its associated broadcast and other journalist partners, it appears that the nation is on the path toward a new media model. If government restrictions continue to be relaxed at both the federal and regional levels, the overall working environment for reporters will continue to improve, and with the expansion of digital technology, Spanish television news and its media model should move into another even more influential era of journalism.

Mexico

In looking at the development of news media and television news in Mexico, it is important to review the fundamentals of the Hallin and Mancini media model. The Polarized Pluralist model is characterized by a strong relationship between media and political parties, strong involvement by the state in journalism and media, and a weaker historic development of commercial media. There is one significant and distinguishing aspect of Mexican media that may signal the beginning of a transition from this model to another, and that is the growth of commercial media and advertising (Gutierrez, 2008). However, when considering news media, government controls and other roadblocks exist.

Unique Case

Mexico's overall television industry shares certain characteristics with some other Latin American nations, such as the influence of Spain, but there is one that is unique—the proximity of Mexico to the United States. In 2007 the US Hispanic population (45.5 million) was greater than any other nation in the world except Mexico and, of that population, 64 percent were of Mexican heritage (US Census, 2008). The United States and Mexico share another common trait. The two nations are among the greatest users of television in the world (Gutierrez, 2008). But the focus of this commonality tends more toward entertainment rather than news.

When it comes to television news and the issues of journalism, the media models for Mexico and the United States developed along very different lines. The Mexican television (and media) situation, early in the twenty-first century, is complicated, volatile and in a state of change.

Historical Context

From the time the Spanish explorer Hernando Cortes conquered the Aztecs in 1521 until the Treaty of Cordoba in 1821, Spain ruled Mexico. With that long occupation Mexico inherited many traditions including the Spanish belief in government or state control of the press (McPhail, n.d.). During the remainder of the nineteenth century and even into the twentieth century limited freedom of the press and significant political influence over the news media were major factors. During those years, while many Mexican journalists lobbied for practices like those in the United States, the reality was quite different. Laws limited criticism of the government and some Mexican presidents closed down newspapers, jailing their employees. Bribery by officials, or coverage for cash, was not uncommon because reporters made so little money (McPhail, n.d.). The advent of radio and television did nothing to change that. Efforts to influence the media continued as the opportunity to reach large populations was obvious.

Media Families, Political and Economic Ties

Mexico's first experimental television transmission occurred in 1931—funded by the political party then in power, the Partido Revolucionairo Mexicano. That party later became the Partido Revolucionario Institucional (PRI) and remained in control for the next seventy years (Barerra, n.d.). Then, in 2000, a different party, Partido Acción Nacional (PAN), was voted into office.

The power of television was clearly understood by Mexican government officials. During years the PRI was in power, journalists were often spied on by the government's intelligence agency, the Center for Information and National Security (McPhail, n.d.). Television was regulated by Article 42 of the Mexican Constitution which claimed ownership of the territory above the nation, translating that into ownership of the airwaves (Facts About Mexico, n.d.). Government licenses for television stations were initially given to friends or powerful families associated with media ownership and over the years the broadcasting rights have remained closely tied to those families.

In their study of media practices in Latin American countries, Spencer and Straubhaar (2006) report a pattern of governments awarding media licenses to families already in the industry, favored businesspeople, and even political allies. In one case, the president of Mexico, Miguel Aleman Valdes, who had the authority to give out television concessions (essentially licenses to operate), awarded three, one to his own family. The concessions went to the Azcarraga, Aleman and O'Farrill families. They ultimately merged into one network (Telesistema Mexico) which eventually became Grupo Televisa in 1972 and then a final merger with Television Independiente de Mexico (FundingUniverse, n.d.).

The result in Mexico's case was a near monopoly on television by one company now known as Televisa. Over a period of forty years, it became an international media empire comprising dozens of radio and television stations and developed strong economic ties inside the United States, specifically with the Univision chain (Ferreira, 2006). Televisa labels itself the world's foremost Spanish language media corporation and reported an average sign-on to sign-off audience in 2007 of more than 70 percent and forty-five of the top fifty programs seen on Mexican television (Grupo Televisa, 2007). But with strong economic growth in Mexico during the latter part of the twentieth century, Televisa was challenged by a number of other television companies, most notably TV Azteca. Created in 1968, it is the number two television company in Mexico (Reuters, 2008).

The growth of television benefits the national economy and provides an important social link making it the country's most important communications medium (Gutierrez, 2008; see also Chapter 3 in this handbook). However, the Mexican media model is still closely aligned with government and the broadcast media is concentrated in only a few companies. Televisa controls three-quarters of the advertising revenue (Winseck, 2008) and Televisa and TV Azteca together control 95 percent of Mexico's television stations (Dickerson, 2005). Seven out of ten television viewers watch channels that belong to Televisa and two out of ten watch TV Azteca stations (Cevallos, 2008).

News Media: Impact of Government and Economics

For reporters the early twenty-first century has not necessarily meant freedom of the press, less impact by government on broadcasting or personal safety in covering the news. However, legislation to confirm press freedom and limit influence by government has been passed. The economics of the television industry also have an impact on reporters, especially in an environment where only a few companies control potential jobs.

A move beginning in the 1970s to amend the Mexican Constitution which would formalize the rights of the public to get information concluded in 2002 with passage of federal and state freedom of information acts (Doyle, 2002). In November 2007 a controversial election reform law went into effect banning political parties from buying advertising time on television and radio stations. The law was a response to the contentious and expensive 2006 presidential election. The Mexican Federal Elections Board reported the amount of money spent on television advertising in that one election totaled $130 million (Young, 2008). While the new law was presented as an effort protect the media from undue political and economic influences relating to elections, (McKinley, 2007), television and other media claimed it would hurt their profits, put some stations out of business, and limit free speech over broadcast media. The law limited political advertising to 48 minutes per day, which was provided free to candidates, and made it illegal for candidates to buy their own airtime. In the past, there had been no limit on how much airtime candidates could buy (*International Herald Tribune*, 2007). In May 2008 TV Azteca was hit with a $500,000 judgment for breaking the new law. Mexico's Federal Election Board levied the fine because the network ran a series of spots advertising a demonstration by a former Mexican presidential candidate (Young, 2008).

Another move challenging the near monopoly by Televisa and TV Azteca is under consideration, allowing US-based Telemundo network (owned by NBC Universal and its parent, General Electric) to become a third major television player in Mexico. Economists believe a third broadcaster would not only benefit the economy of Mexico by providing new competition but also increase information sources to audiences (Llana, 2007).

New legislation signed into law in April 2008 ended federal criminal penalties for defamation (Reporters Without Borders, 2008c). In June 2008, after a surge of violence against reporters, Mexican President Felipe Calderon announced support for new legislation to federalize crimes against freedom of expression saying: "The most important threat to independent journalists in Mexico is the same threat faced by society as a whole—organized crime" (Committee to Protect Journalists, 2008, para. 5). Two years earlier, in 2006, a special federal prosecutor's office was created to investigate crimes against journalists (Ellingwood, 2008) but that danger continues. Physical violence against reporters, especially those covering organized crime and drug trafficking, made Mexico the most dangerous place in the world for journalists (Reporters Without Borders, 2008c).

Dangerous Work

Reporting news, whether on television, radio, newspaper or the Internet, remains a dangerous profession. The numbers vary: Reporters Without Borders say that in 2007 five journalists and media assistants were killed and another three went missing (Reporters Without Borders, 2008c). The Inter American Press Association (2007) calls journalism in Mexico a "highly risky activity" with thirty-one professionals murdered during the six-year administration of Vincente Fox (2000–2006). In that same mid-year review, the organization reports that another seven journalists died between October 2006 and February 2007. Another count suggests thirty-five journalists killed and six missing from 2000 through the end of 2007 (Cevallos, 2008). The missing included a TV Azteca news crew (Committee to Protect Journalists, 2007), while those murdered included a Televisa reporter whose body was found in December 2007 and an American TV cameraman for Indymedia, shot to death in 2006 covering a demonstration.

These are just a few examples of the obstacles facing reporters in twenty-first-century Mexico. Violence and threats against reporters are associated with their assignments covering drug traffickers, organized crime and potential government corruption (Reporters Without Borders, 2008c). Because of the ongoing danger, many reporters and news operation managers say they self-censor their work. Ellingwood (2008) reports that journalists held off reporting details about crimes or mentioning drug trafficking groups by name because of the potential danger to both reporters and the media outlet itself.

Summary

The situation facing Mexican journalism in the first decade of the twenty-first century is complicated. From a television perspective there remain economic and political influences that have an impact on the way in which broadcast journalists can function. The very dangerous working conditions also have a tangible impact on how Mexican reporters do their job. These fundamental influences also affect all other news media reporting organizations. The Committee to Protect Journalists states that regardless of what medium journalists are using, the fear of violence and resulting use of self-censorship mean the real losers are the citizens because issues are not being properly covered (Committee to Protect Journalists, 2008).

Although the nation continues to grow in global importance, the concerns centering on freedom of the press, the impact of crime and the still-existing influence of government over independent media keep Mexico in the Hallin and Mancini Polarized Pluralist media model.

Colombia

While Spain may be close to moving from one media model to another, Mexico still has issues it must resolve. For Colombia, however, the move from the Hallin and Mancini media model of Polarized Pluralist may be an even more daunting task.

Colombia is a complex mix of theoretical and even constitutional support for an open, free press but in daily practice it is a difficult, even deadly environment for working journalists. Drug trafficking, guerrilla fighting and paramilitary groups all operate in various parts of the country and make Colombia one of the world's most dangerous places to work (BBC, 2008a). The media model for this country follows a pattern of ownership and control by wealthy and politically connected concerns. When dealing with news, the media model is heavily effected by the violence and pervasive influence exercised by the drug cartels, organized crime and some degree of government corruption.

Historical Context

Colombia's colonization by Spain brought with it a history of controlling the media. But after winning its war for independence in 1819, Colombia established its first constitution which included a guaranteed freedom of the press. That promise was reaffirmed and expanded in 1991 when the constitution was rewritten supporting freedom of expression and freedom of the press (Corporación Transparencia por Colombia, 2001). On paper, Colombia's press laws were very supportive of a free media such as freedom of expression and the right of journalists to protect the identity of their sources (Ginsberg, 2003). There were standards set under the Law of the Journalist Act which required new professionals to have a university degree. However, those regulations were abolished in 1998 (Ginsberg, 2003).

During the twentieth century, the nation experienced turbulent times with conflict between rival political parties. For example, in the "War of the Thousand Days" (1899–1903) an estimated 120,000 people were killed. Between 1948 and 1957 yet another civil war erupted and more than a quarter of a million people died in the political fighting. The 1960s brought a different violence from various rebel or guerrilla groups fighting the government and each other for control of the country (BBC, 2008a).

Two of the most prominent groups are Fuerzas Armadas Revolucionarias de Colombia (FARC: Revolutionary Armed Forces of Colombia) and Ejército de Liberación Nacional (ELN: National Liberation Army) who had, at various times, both cooperated with each other and fought each other. In many cases funding for the various paramilitary groups came from the drug traffickers (Hanson, 2008). An effort by the government to crack down on the drug trade began in earnest in 1978 and the struggle has continued ever since. For reporters it was the beginning of what remains a dangerous assignment. Although the numbers vary, the BBC reports that more than 120 journalists were killed in the 1990s; many were associated with stories connected to the drug trade and corruption (BBC, 2008a). But changing attitudes among the people began to surface. In early February 2008, hundreds of thousands of Colombians demonstrated in cities across the country protesting abductions and killings by FARC, the largest rebel group (Gonzalez & Romero, 2008). This growing civil agitation across the country against the violence and its impact on the lives of the people perhaps signaled some small positive movement by official forces against the worst of that violence and may also have an impact on reporters as they go about their daily professional lives.

The Business of Media

Colombia's media history is an active one. Newspapers served as a key source of information when as many as fifty-five generally independent daily newspapers per thousand people available in the early 2000s (Ginsberg, 2003). However, papers also reflected a political tone and had to rely on extensive advertising revenue from government sources. Many of the papers were owned by wealthy people and that pattern became typical of television companies as well (Ginsberg, 2003).

Impact of Television

Colombian television is regulated by the National Commission for Television (CNTV) and the Ministry of Communications. It is the primary communications medium for this nation of 44 million people and about 98 percent of all homes have television (Colombia Reports, 2008). But nearly universal coverage has not led to multiple television companies.

Essentially Colombian television is a duopoly in the private sector with the government controlling a few additional educational outlets. There are two primary television networks.

Caracol TV is owned by the Santo Domingo family and was started in the mid-1950s as a production company within a radio network. It offered financial support to the government by paying for exclusive commercial time and that developed into a company called TVC (Television Comercial Ltda). Then, in 1998 the government gave Caracol one of two licenses to begin a national television network. Since then Caracol Television has become one of the two most watched networks in Colombia (NationMaster.com, n.d.a). Among its holdings is ownership of WGENTV, Channel 8 in Miami (Florida) which is also one of two operational hubs for Caracol International, the other hub located in Bogotá, Colombia (Hispanic PR Wire, 2007). The main shareholder in Caracol Television is Julio Mario Santo Domingo listed by *Forbes Magazine* as 132 in the world listing of billionaires (Forbes, 2007).

The other major private television network in Colombia is RCN TV, which is controlled by the Ardila Lulle beer company (Ginsberg, 2003). RCN (Radio Cadena Nacional) also began as a production company in 1967. In 1998 it was awarded the second of two television network licenses by the Colombian government (NationMaster.com, n.d.b). RCN TV, like its rival Caracol Television, has growing international ties. For example, in 2008, the US media corporation Disney completed a deal with RCN to produce a Spanish language version of two ABC network series, *Grey's Anatomy* and *Brothers and Sisters* (Jaafar & Hopewell, 2008). Disney owns ABC. As for private television expansion, a third license offering is under consideration by the Colombian government and a number of foreign media groups have indicated they would be interested (*The Economist*, 2008).

On the Job: Daily Media Issues

Over the years, media companies that used to be family businesses with specific political and economic ties have developed into primarily commercial corporations (*The Economist*, 2008). This trend of a few media conglomerates controlling multiple media sources has consequences for journalists. According to Arroyave and Barrios (2007, p. 18), it "allows them [companies] to impose their own rules regarding the commercial conditions" on their employees. The impact on the daily lives of reporters is tangible.

In 2004 a major study focused specifically on Colombian news media. Cardona (cited in Gill et al., 2006) looked specifically at labor conditions among Colombian journalists across various media platforms and concluded they were generally young, with little professional experience, and underpaid (cited in Gill et al., 2006). The issue of low pay is one that has potentially far-reaching implications for the quality of reporting especially in a country where many journalists already face other obstacles to their work. Media concentrated in the hands of a few companies result in economic pressures on reporters relating to their salaries. For example, a number of television and radio stations require employees to sell advertising to supplement their low pay. According to Arroyave and Barrios (2007) some companies pay reporters in two ways—the company pays a minimum wage but then requires reporters to sell commercial spots. Part of that advertising revenue becomes part of their salary. In some cases, salaries are based entirely on advertising sales.

The ethical implications are obvious. One reporter said it was a shock to leave college as journalism professional and find that he was working as a salesman. Another reporter said this situation limits professional independence since "one cannot speak evil about [a] company because they provide us with our supper" (Arroyave & Barrios, 2007, p. 11).

Colombian journalists remain motivated despite this situation coupled with long hours and potential danger in simply doing their job. It is important to understand Colombian media hold the idea of serving society or civic journalism as an important tenet of their profession. Interviews with reporters underscore that motivation. One reporter described his work as being a "bridge between the communities and the public authorities" (Arroyave & Barrios, 2007, p. 12), acting as almost a go-between to help to individual people or address social issues.

But helping society by doing their job can be dangerous. This reality has created an unusual undercurrent in Colombian journalism, which includes such practices as seeking anonymity, not appearing on camera, not signing written reports, and working together on stories even if employed by competing news organizations.

Dangerous Work and its Impact on Reporting the News

In the United States, the concept of an exclusive story is a positive goal for all news people. For television reporters, being able to associate themselves with a big story that is researched and broadcast before their competition, can result in awards, local or even national recognition, and help pave the way for a promotion, higher salary, or move to another television market. Skilled American reporters work hard to develop contacts that other journalists do not have, thus getting in-depth information, new details or even breaking stories about important issues to their audience. The technique of the "standup" in which the reporter is visually in the story is a standard approach to storytelling whether on the local or national level. For viewers, seeing the reporter doing his or her job is part of the subtext of credibility: the reporter is actually on the scene of the story or event. But that is not necessarily the case in twenty-first-century Colombia and it has nothing to do with the quality of the reporters or their commitment to their assignments; it has to do with safety.

Self-censorship is not unusual and may be considered necessary for the well-being of the reporter depending on the content of the story. Ginsberg (2003) makes the observation that while Colombia's free press laws are in place, the practical aspects of doing the job actually restrict the press. Reporters have been kidnapped, tortured, even killed by various rebel, drug and paramilitary groups, while television and radio stations and newspapers have been bombed by these same kinds of organizations (Arroyave & Barrios, 2007).

So, how do many reporters cope? One approach is to develop a type of partnership. By working in pairs or even groups, reporters look at the importance of the story or information first and then consider the potential danger to each other. The concept of exclusive or breaking news is not a central issue (Arroyave & Barrios, 2007). Working in groups and refusing to report in what they consider dangerous conditions is a way to ensure survival.

Summary

Violence against the press actually abated somewhat during 2007 and early 2008. Six reporters were murdered in 2007 but only one case was considered to be job related (Reporters Without Borders, 2008b).

According to Reporters Without Borders (2008b), reporters and their families instead have begun to leave the country or the region in which they live when threatened with violence. This reporter watchdog organization reports that the illegal drug industry remains the most dangerous subject for reporters to cover. However, increasing efforts by the Colombian government to blunt drug trafficking may be having some positive effects. The already mentioned nationwide demonstration against the rebel and paramilitary groups and drug cartels is one example and a July 2, 2008 successful rescue by the Colombian military of a group of hostages is yet another (Romero & Cave, 2008).

The complexity of working as a journalist in twenty-first-century Colombia is created in part by the impact of still extensive violence (especially in the rural areas), the control by drug cartels and paramilitary groups in those rural and poor areas (Romero, 2008), and the extraordinary economic impact of the illegal drug trade on the nation's economy. Although difficult to calculate, one estimate of the commercial value of illegal drugs is between 5 and 10 percent of the nation's gross domestic product (Department of Foreign Affairs and Trade, Australia, 2008).

While considered to have a high-quality press overall, the limitations resulting from such an unstable working environment have an impact on how reporters can perform their daily jobs. Until there is significant improvement in the nation's social, economic, and political environment, it will be difficult for Colombia to redefine its position in the Hallin and Mancini media model.

The United States

Spanish language media in United States is, in one sense, no different from its counterparts in other countries. Latin American media was influenced by the attitudes and practices of Spain which colonized many nations. In the United States, Spanish language media has followed the model and influences of American media development complete with protection of constitutional guarantees as well as experiencing the impact of a commercial rather than a government-controlled or -funded environment. In considering the Hallin and Mancini approach it is easy to apply the characteristics of the Liberal model to the United States: market mechanisms and commercial media tend to dominate with no mention of interference by the government.

Historical Context

The First Amendment to the United States Constitution states the government cannot enact any law against freedom of speech or of the press. The US legal system is based on a series of checks and balances and the federal courts, including the Supreme Court, can determine or interpret laws based on the circumstances of the time. Nevertheless, the freedoms of speech and the press are two of the most highly regarded rights given to American media and the public. In addition, the role of the US news media regardless of the medium has always been that of a government watchdog. A common nickname for the news media is the Fourth Estate, meaning its role in the tri-part US governmental system of Executive, Judicial and Legislative has been to hold these entities accountable to the people. The result is, for the most part, a somewhat skeptical eye by reporters looking at government and social issues in their daily work assignments. Investigative journalism for example has a strong tradition in the United States.

Media and Economics

In the United States ownership and operation of television and radio stations is driven not so much by family or political ties but rather by economics—being able to afford the property and hire the legal staff to execute the extensive documentation required by the Federal Communications Commission (FCC) in order to obtain a license. Spanish language media follows this system as well.

In 1961 the Spanish International Network (SIN) began broadcasting in San Antonio, Texas. It ultimately became Univision (Univision, n.d.), the largest Spanish language media company in the United States. Univision reaches nearly all US Hispanic television households. Together with its sister network TeleFutura and cable channel Galavision, the company owns and operates sixty-three stations in both the United States and Puerto Rico (Investor Relations, 2008) as well as supplying programming to affiliates owned by other companies such as Fisher Communications or LIN Communications (Fisher Communications, n.d.; LIN, n.d.). What further tempers the power of this one company is the lucrative US media market itself. Between 1990 and 2008 many established networks and television groups began producing local Spanish language news and information shows as well as broadcasting Spanish entertainment. Among the big players in the US market are Telemundo (owned by NBC), Azteca America, TuVision and LAT TV, to name just a few. Other entrants in this area include CNN en Español, MTV Tr3s and FOX Sports en Español, which all produce shows in Spanish.

While language identifies Spanish media as a specific, growing market, the revenue produced by these stations and networks is significant. The media model for the United States is based on selling advertising for programs that audiences at the local and national level want to watch, whether content is news or entertainment. For broadcasters and advertisers, the growing Hispanic population means an increasing value to the Spanish-speaking audience. By 2010 Spanish language media are expected to pull in $5.5 billion (Tekrati, 2007).

Television News and the US Model

In the United States, television news at the local level serves as a link between the audience and the station. The on-air personnel give a face to the station which provides the service, the information and the local coverage needed by the specific market audience. Spanish language stations and their newscasts are no different. At the local level, they too provide a service unique to their audience and link the community to the station (Slocum, 2008). What makes the US model different from the Latin American models is the content. Reporters in Spanish language US stations are generally free from concerns over low pay or ethical dilemmas about selling advertising while covering the news, dealing with near-monopoly ownership or government restrictions on content, or fear of physical violence in covering stories. However, they do share a defined commitment with Latin American journalists about responsibilities to their communities. For Hispanic viewers in the United States, especially those new to the country, local television newscasts provide information access to important issues such as health and education (Slocum, 2008). This approach to news coverage at both the local and national level is a common thread among US Spanish broadcasters. The former head of the National Association of Hispanic Journalists Veronic Villafane suggests these newscasts actually serve an educational purpose by helping the audience to acclimate to a new environment and learn about issues and services available to them (Arnoldy, 2007). Local newscast focus groups (a form of media research) support this observation. That research showed Hispanic viewers (especially those with limited English skills or new to the country) considered the local news as guide to understanding daily issues, especially health or education news (J. Aviles, personal communication, October 21, 2007). Overall, Spanish language broadcast news contributes to the large US Hispanic population with opinions about the role news media should play:

> The vast majority of Latinos, including those who only get news in English, view the Spanish language media as an important institution for the economic and political development of the Hispanic population.
>
> (Pew Hispanic Center, 2004)

Another aspect of Spanish television news in the United States is competition. Spanish language and English language media both compete for employees on an equal footing, in many cases—especially news and on-air talent—for the same personnel. That means television and radio journalists in the United States work in an environment that is judged on the same scale—ratings and quality of content.

Summary: A Change in the Model?

The current media model in the United States has produced a television news media with a record of excellence and service, whether it is Spanish or English language. The historic environment for the press in the United States supported Spanish language television news to become a strong partner in a free press. However, what is unknown is how the commercially supported model of television media in the United States may change given the increasingly volatile world economy in the twenty-first century.

Already there are some changes in the Spanish television media that reflect this development. The growing Hispanic audience in the United States has spawned a new 24-hour satellite network broadcast by DirecTV through its DirecTV Mas. Called Azteca Mexico, its programming will come from TV Azteca's three Mexican networks—different programming from the offerings on Azteca America. What makes this worth understanding is that it puts viewers in Mexico and the United States in the same audience and according to one DirecTV executive, watching those shows at the same time (Hispanic PR Wire, 2008). But while the Spanish language market is expanding, the economic realities of the US media industry have resulted in cutbacks by some companies.

In May 2006, Telemundo eliminated numerous television news jobs as a cost-saving measure. A new production center was established in Dallas, Texas serving as a local, regional and national news hub (Zaragoza, 2006). In June 2008, Equity Media Holdings Corp. shut down six of its Univision affiliates in five states including two stations in Fayetteville and Fort Smith, Arkansas. The company said the move was caused by economic problems (Bradford, 2008). Although local news is one key way for stations to stay competitive in a market, it is expensive because it is both personnel and technology heavy. Another example of the impact economic issues have on the Spanish–US media model is TV Azteca's move from Los Angeles to Mexico City. The network Azteca America laid off nearly twenty people in its news division and moved production of the US national newscast and the Los Angeles newscasts to its Mexico City facilities. According to Azteca America's chief executive Adrian Steckel, it was economics, describing news as no longer a profitable activity and the cuts were both a cost and efficiency issue (James, 2008).

Despite the economic issues facing all US television news media in the twenty-first century, the overall strength of the nation's economy and its equally strong history of a free press separate from government interference should guarantee the United States remains solidly defined by the Liberal media model.

Conclusion

The global impact of television as a medium for information, entertainment and social communication shows no sign of weakening. If anything, television appears to be a growing communications medium in many countries. This chapter has used the Hallin and Mancini (2004) model to consider the media models of four nations. Three countries, Spain, Mexico and Colombia, share Spanish as a common language as well as some common elements contributing to the development of their news media. The fourth country, the United States, has a distinctly different basis for its media model and that has provided the foundation for Spanish language media to grow in a unique environment.

The international television world is changing rapidly. The volatile global economy, advancing technology and changing political climates are all significantly influencing the direction of television, especially news. Freedom of the press is a fragile concept even when deeply rooted in a nation's fabric. When freedom of the press and the role of reporters are hampered by government influence, social problems and military or criminal elements, that concept weakens even more.

Spain appears to be on a strong, positive path toward developing a more open and independent media. There are still lingering issues to be resolved, including governmental efforts to influence the media, some physically dangerous work environments, and the impact of technology. Will Spanish media companies tackle these issues and will the government willingly relax more control to allow greater freedom for journalists? These two questions appear to form the basis for Spanish media's future growth and should be targeted for future study.

Mexico's media and governmental efforts in the recent years suggest some positive movement in the Hallin and Mancini model toward a more open press environment. However, the national economic situation coupled with a dangerous and economically powerful narcotics underworld pose clear problems for growing freedom of the press. One of the most important positive influences for Mexican television and news development may be its relationship with the United States. Its proximity and history could create a fundamental change in the balance of television power in Mexico especially if a United States based broadcaster becomes a player on a national scale. How media power is redistributed in the coming years is an important issue for scholars studying the Mexican television environment.

Colombia poses many questions. The history of strong support for press freedoms but practical limitations, a near duopoly of commercial media limiting competition, and the ongoing struggle by the government with social issues such as narcotics dealers and paramilitary organizations make journalism a difficult profession. Nevertheless, strong commitments by Colombian journalists in all mediums as well as the potential changing attitudes of ordinary citizens offer optimism for the future. However, media companies and political party coexistence based on economics and control will need to change. Reporters will need to feel both safe and supported by their media employers. Studies of how Colombian media companies react to technological and global economic changes are essential. In addition, how the government awards the valuable television licenses to potentially new operators will have a significant impact on Colombia's television future.

As for the United States, it is one of the most studied media markets in the world. The overriding issue facing US broadcasters at all levels is the economic situation. While Spanish language media enjoys a solid and strong economic position, it too is faced with the same issues as its English counterpart. How can they survive in an environment of escalating technological costs, falling audience levels and competition from the Internet and other media sources? Especially for television news, this is the area that requires excellent research with a goal of providing guidance to the industry.

Note

1   For this chapter, the author uses "convergence" to refer to journalists who not only shoot, edit, write and may voice broadcast pieces but also provide content for news websites, radio, and perhaps newspapers or other regional/national media outlets.

References

Agencia EFE. (n.d.). *Companies.* Retrieved June 23, 2008, from www.efe.com/empresas/principal.asp?opcion=8&idioma=INGLES.

Arnoldy, B. (2007, September 17). Among networks, Spanish language Univision is now a top contender. *csmonitor.com.* Retrieved October 27, 2007, from www.csmonitor.com/2007/0917/p01s03-ussc.html.

Arroyave, J. & Barrios, M. (2007). A sociological profile of Colombian journalists. *Conference Papers, International Communication Association, 2007 Annual Meeting,* p. 1. Unpublished manuscript. Retrieved June 15, 2008, from http://libproxy.library.unt.edu:2055/ehost/pdf?vid=21&hid=21&sid=a69da22f-e250-4328-aeb7-a4767b42e452%40SRCSM2.

Barrera, E. (n.d.). *Mexico: The Museum of Broadcast Communications*. Retrieved May 15, 2008, from www.museum.tv/archives/etv/M/htmlM/mexico/mexico.htm.

BBC. (2008a). Country profile: Colombia, July 19. Media. *BBC News*. Retrieved July 26, 2008, from http://news.bbc.co.uk/1/hi/world/americas/country_profiles/1212798.stm.

BBC. (2008b). Country Profile: Spain, July 8. Media. *BBC News*. Retrieved July 10, 2008, from http://news.bbc.co.uk/1/hi/world/europe/country_profiles/991960.stm#media.

Bradford, M. (2008, June 22). Univision eliminates local news segments. *Arkansas Democrat-Gazette*. Retrieved August 1, 2008, from www.nwanews.com/adg/News/229339/.

Bramhall, J. (2008). *Grupo Televisa, S. A*. Retrieved August 3, 2008, from www.hoovers.com/televisa/—ID__51043—/free-co-profile.xhtml.

BUYUSA. (2008, April 16). *Pay-TV in Mexico, U.S. Commercial Service, United States of America Department of Commerce*. Retrieved July 13, 2008, from www.buyusa.gov/mexico/en/telecom.html#_section1.

Carat. (2008). Carat revises global ad spend growth forecasts. *MC Marketing Charts*. Retrieved September 21, 2008, from www.marketingcharts.com/television/carat-revises-global-ad-spend-growth-forecasts-5838/.

Central Intelligence Agency (CIA). (2008). *The CIA world factbook*. Retrieved July 15, 2008, from www.cia.gov/library/publications/the-world-factbook/geos/sp.html#Econ.

Cevallos, D. (2008, January 7). Media-Mexico: Freedom of the press? *Inter Press Service News Agency*. Retrieved July 22, 2008, from http://ipsnews.net/news.asp?idnews=40698.

Chabran, R. (n.d.). Spain press, media, TV, newspapers forum. Retrieved June 12, 2008, from www.pressreference.com/Sa-Sw/Spain.html.

Colombia Reports. (2008, August 28). Colombia chooses European digital TV Standard. *Reuters*. Retrieved September 7, 2008, from http://colombiareports.com/2008/08/28/colombia-chooses-european-digital-tv-standard/.

Committee to Protect Journalists. (2007, May 14). *Mexican TV news crew missing since Thursday*. Retrieved July 19, 2008, from www.cpj.org/news/2007/americas/mexico14may07na.html.

Committee to Protect Journalists. (2008, June 8). *Calderon endorses federalization of crimes against freedom of expression*. Retrieved July 23, 2008, from www.cpj.org/news/2008/americas/mexico09jun08na.html.

Corporación Transparencia por Colombia. (2001). Integrity systems country report, Colombia. Retrieved July 26, 2008, from http://info.worldbank.org/etools/ANTIC/docs/Resources/Country%20Profiles/Colombia/TransparencyInternational_NIS_Colombia.pdf.

Department of Foreign Affairs and Trade, Australia (2008, May). Colombia country brief. *Department of Foreign Affairs and Trade*, Australian Government. Retrieved July 27, 2008, from www.dfat.gov.au/GEO/colombia/colombia_brief.html.

Dickerson, M. (2005, January 17). Battle intensifies over control of Mexican TV. *Los Angeles Times*. Retrieved August 31, 2008, from http://articles.latimes.com/2005/jan/17/business/fi-mextv17.

Doyle, K. (2002, June 10). Mexico's new freedom of information law. *National Security Archive*. Retrieved July 22, 2008, from www.gwu.edu/~nsarchiv/NSAEBB/NSAEBB68/.

The Economist. (2007). Emerging journalism. *The Economist, 384*, (8546), September 15, p. 75, Retrieved June 15, 2008, from http://libproxy.library.unt.edu:2055/ehost/detail?vid=7&hid=22&sid=56c52b1d-c0da-4f17-a3d5-a26478a243f2%40sessionmgr9.

The Economist. (2008, May 22). An icon reborn. *Economist.com, the Americas*. Retrieved September 6, 2008, from www.economist.com/PrinterFriendly.cfm?story_id=11412791.

Ellingwood, K. (2008, July 6). Reporters covering Mexico drug wars risk their lives. *Los Angeles Times*. Retrieved July 23, 2008, from www.latimes.com/news/nationworld/world/la-fg-journalists6-2008jul06,0,6443496.story?track=rss.

Facts About Mexico. (n.d.). *Location and area*. Retrieved July 22, 2008, from www.mexican-embassy.org.yu/AboutMexico.html.

Ferreira, L. (2006). *Centuries of silence: The story of Latin American journalism*. Westport, CT: Praeger.

Ferreras, I. (2008, June 8). Spain: All spectrum for TV. *Rapid TV News*. Retrieved June 16, 2008, from http://rapidtvnews.com/index.php/200806081373/spain-all-spectrum-for-tv.html.

Fishbein, J. (2008, May 16). The world's most competitive countries *BusinessWeek*. Retrieved September 20, 2008, from http://bwnt.businessweek.com/interactive_reports/competitive_countries_2008/.

Fisher Communications. (n.d.). *Stations and markets*. Retrieved September 6, 2008, from www.fsci.com/markets.html.

Forbes (2007, March 8). #132 Julio Mario Santo Domingo. *Forbes*. Retrieved September 7, 2008, from www.forbes.com/lists/2007/10/07billionaires_Julio-Mario-Santo-Domingo_YNZG.html.

FundingUniverse. (n.d.). *Grupo Televisa, S.A*. Retrieved August 30, 2008 from www.fundinguniverse.com/company-histories/Grupo-Televisa-SA-Company-History.html.

Gill, J., Blanco, I. & Arroyave, J. (2006). Latin American journalists' perceptions of the profession: Between exhaustion and fascination. *Conference Papers, International Communication Association*. Retrieved June 15, 2008, from http://libproxy.library.unt.edu:2055/ehost/pdf?vid=8&hid=13&sid=ea3f59de-5a89-4594-851e-3f87b27dc988%40SRCSM1.

Ginsberg, L. (2003). Colombia. *World press encyclopedia*. Retrieved August 31, 2008, from http://findarticles.com/p/articles/mi_gx5223/is_2003/ai_n19143069/pg_1?.

Goetz, D. (2008, March 3). Reaching a mass audience. *Broadcasting & Cable*. Retrieved June 23, 2008, from www.broadcastingcable.com/article/CA6537170.html.

Gonzalez, J. C. & Romero, S. (2008, February 5). Marches show disgust with a Colombian rebel group. *New York Times*. Retrieved July 26, 2008, from www.nytimes.com/2008/02/05/world/americas/05colombia.html?_r=1&oref=s login.

Grupo Televisa. (2007). *Investor relations annual report: business description*. Retrieved August 31, 2008, from www.esmas.com/documento/0/000/002/030/Business_Eng.pdf.

Gutierrez, M. E. (2008, April 10). Media issues in Mexico. Presentation at the University of North Texas, Center for Spanish Language Media, Denton, TX.

Hallin, D. & Mancini, P. (2004). *Comparing media systems: Three models of media and politics*. Cambridge: Cambridge University Press.

Hanson, S. (2008, March 11). FARC, ELN: Colombia's left-wing guerrillas. *Council on Foreign Relations*. Retrieved August 31, 2008, from www.cfr.org/publication/9272/#4.

Hispanic PR Wire. (2007). GENTV channel 8 launches Groundbreaking new program *La boca loca de Paul*. Retrieved September 7, 2008, from www.hispanicprwire.com/news.php?l=in&id=9405&cha=7.

Hispanic PR Wire. (2008, June 5). DIRECTV to launch Azteca Mexico: Exclusive channel will air nationally on DIRECTV MAS channel 442. Retrieved September 6, 2008, from www.hispanicprwire.com/news.php?l=in&id=11668&cha=7.

Hughes, S. (2006). *Newsrooms in conflict: Journalism and the democratization of Mexico*. Pittsburgh, PA: University of Pittsburgh Press.

Inter American Press Association. (2007, March 16–19). Mexico. *Inter American Press Association*. Retrieved July 23, 2008, from www.sipiapa.com/pulications/informe_mexico2007ca.cfm.

International Herald Tribune (2007, November 13). Mexican electoral reform becomes law, bans paid TV and radio advertisements. *International Herald Tribune*. Retrieved August 31, 2008, from www.iht.com/articles/ap/2007/11/14/america/LA-GEN-Mexico-Electoral-Reform.php.

Investor Relations. (2008, August 8). *Univision announces 2008 second quarter results*. Retrieved September 6, 2008, from http://ir.univision.net/.

Jaafar, A. & Hopewell, J. (2008, April 7). Disney racks up Mip TV deals. *Variety TV*. Retrieved September 7, 2008, from www.variety.com/article/VR1117983608.html?categoryid=14&cs=1&query=RCN+Television+Colombia.

James, M. (2008, May 29). Azteca shifts production of U.S. newscasts to Mexico. *Los Angeles Times*. Retrieved August 1, 2008, from http://articles.latimes.com/2008/may/29/business/fi-azteca29.

LIN. (n.d.). *Television*. Retrieved September 6, 2008, from www.lintv.com/about/television.html.

Llana, S. M. (2007, January 23). Calderon's challenge: Confronting monopolies. *Christian Science Monitor*. Retrieved July 23, 2008, from www.csmonitor.com/2007/0123/p12s01-woam.html.

Mavise. (2007, December 13). Spain: National TV market description. *Mavise Country Profile: ES—Spain*. Retrieved June 16, 2008, from http://mavise.obs.coe.int/documents/countries/ES/country_description.html.

Maxwell, R. (n.d.). *Spain: The Museum of Broadcast Communications*. Retrieved on June 30, 2008, from www.museum.tv/archives/etv/S/htmlS/spain/spain.htm.

McKinley, J. C. Jr. (2007, September 14). Mexico's congress considers proposals to change election laws. *New York Times*. Retrieved July 23, 2008, from www.nytimes.com/2007/09/14/world/americas/14mexico.html?fta=y.

McPhail, T. (n.d.). *Mexico press, media, TV, newspapers forum*. Retrieved June 12, 2008, from www.pressreference.com/Ma-No/Mexico.html.

NationMaster.com (n.d.a). *Encyclopedia Canal Caracol*. Retrieved September 7, 2008, from www.nationmaster.com/encyclopedia/Canal-Caracol.

NationMaster.com (n.d.b). *Encyclopedia RCN TV*. Retrieved September 7, 2008, from www.nationmaster.com/encyclopedia/RCN-TV.

Perez-Linan, A. (2002, September). Television news and political partisanship in Latin America. *Political Research Quarterly*, 55(3), 571–588.

Pew Hispanic Center. (2004, April 19). *Latinos' choices in news media are shaping their views of their communities, the nation and the world*. Retrieved October 11, 2007, from http://pewhispanic.org/newsroom/releases/print.php?ReleaseID=10.

Quintos de Jesus, M. (2002, July). *Information literacy and the changing role of the press*. Retrieved August 11, 2004, from www.nclis.gov/libinter/infolitconf&meet/papers/dejesus-fullpaper.pdf.

Reporters Without Borders. (2008a). Spain annual report 2008. *Reporters Without Borders*. Retrieved July 2, 2008, from www.rsf.org/article.php3?id_article=25581.

Reporters Without Borders. (2008b). Colombia annual report 2008. *Reporters Without Borders*. Retrieved July 30, 2008, from www.rsf.org/article.php3?id_article=25586.

Reporters Without Borders. (2008c). Mexico annual report 2008. *Reporters Without Borders*. Retrieved July 20, 2008, from www.rsf.org/article.php3?id_article=25592.

Reuters. (2008, July 22). Mexico's TV Azteca sees second-quarter profit up 48 pct. *Reuters UK*. Retrieved July 23, 2008 from http://uk.reuters.com/article/governmentFilingsNews/idUKN2232045020080722.

Romero, S. (2008, July 27). Despite rebel losses, cocaine sustains war in rural Colombia. *New York Times*, pp. 1 and 8.

Romero, S. & Cave, D. (2008, July 4). Bold Colombia rescue built on rebel group's disarray. *New York Times, Americas*. Retrieved July 25, 2008, from www.nytimes.com/2008/07/04/world/americas/04rescue.html?pagewanted=1&_r=1.

Salaverria, R. (2006). *Media landscape—Spain, European Journalism Centre*. Retrieved June 16, 2008, from www.ejc.net/media_landscape/article/spain/.

Scolari, C., Navarro, H. & Pardo, H. (2007). The digitalizing of the media. New competences, polyvalence and professional skills in Catalan journalism. *Conference Papers, International Communication Association, Annual Meeting*. Retrieved

June 15, 2008, from http://libproxy.library.unt.edu:2055/ehost/pdf?vid=2&hid=12&sid=b4e8edc4-e040-4d75-928d-2f7026f41efb%40sessionmgr3.

Slocum, P. (2008). Attitudinal changes toward electronic news consumption by the US Hispanic audience. *Journal of Spanish Language Media, 1,* 150–167. Retrieved June 12, 2008, from www.spanishmedia.unt.edu/Vol.%201%20 2008%20%282%29.pdf.

Spencer, D. & Straubhaar, J. (2006, September). Broadcast research in the Americas: Revisiting the past and looking to the future. *Journal of Broadcasting & Electronic Media, 50*(3), 368–382. Retrieved June 23, 2008 from http://libproxy. library.unt.edu:2055/ehost/pdf?vid=13&hid=112&sid=76731191-9d94-4970-883d-d227a2036afd%40sessionmgr3.

Stromback, J. & Garcia-Luengo, O. (2007). Polarized pluralist and democratic corporatist models: Electoral campaign news coverage in Spain and Sweden. *Conference Papers, International Communication Association.* Retrieved June 15, 2008, from http://libproxy.library.unt.edu:2055/ehost/pdf?vid=17&hid=21&sid=a69da22f-e250-4328-aeb7-a4767b42e452%40SRCSM2.

Tekrati (2007, February 21). Hispanic radio and TV ad revenue to reach $5.5.billion by 2010, says Kagan Research. *Tekrati.* Retrieved September 6, 2008, from http://industry.tekrati.com/research/8528/.

Univision. (n.d.). *History.* Retrieved October 20, 2007, from www.univision.net/corp/en/history.jsp.

US Census. (2008, July 9). *Facts for features.* Retrieved July 21, 2008, from www.census.gov/Press-Release/www/releases/ archives/facts_for_features_special_editions/012245.html.

Wall Street Journal. (2008, August 18). Survey shows TV is still the main news source. *Wall Street Journal.* Retrieved August 19, 2008, from http://online.wsj.com/article/SB121902509874048617.html?mod=todays_us_marketplace.

West, D. (2008, June 10). Spain keeps all analogue spectrum for TV. *Digital Spy.* Retrieved June 12, 2008, from www.digitalspy.co.uk/digitaltv/a98560/spain-keeps-all-analogue-spectrum-for-tv.html.

Winseck, D. (2008, January 14). The state of media ownership and media markets: Competition or concentration and why should we care? *Sociology Compass, 2*(1), 34–47. Retrieved August 31, 2008, from www3.interscience.wiley.com/ cgi-bin/fulltext/120185418/HTMLSTART.

Young, J. (2008, May 4). TV Azteca fined over ads. *Variety.* Retrieved July 23, 2008, from www.variety.com/article/ VR1117985064.html?categoryid=1236&cs=1.

Zaragoza, S. (2006, October 20). Telemundo to cut Texas staff. *Dallas business journal.* Retrieved September 6, 2008, from http://dallas.bizjournals.com/dallas/stories/2006/10/16/daily45.html.

17

Univision and Telemundo
Spanish Language Television Leaders in the United States

Guillermo Gibens
William Penn University, Iowa, USA

Introduction

Univision and Telemundo have been competing for the Latino market for many years, and both have consolidated their relative positions within Hispanic audiences in the United States. According to Univision (2008a), the network reaches 99 percent of Spanish-speaking audiences, and Telemundo 93 percent (NBC Universal, 2008).

Univision is the largest Spanish language television network in the United States with headquarters located in Miami, Florida. It owns and operates nineteen full-power and eight low-power television stations. Univision also owns Telefutura and the satellite network, Galavisión. The Telefutura network operates eighteen full-power and thirteen low-power television stations. Additionally, Univision Radio includes seventy radio stations in the United States and four stations in Puerto Rico. Univision Online is the Internet portal of Univision Communications Inc. Campbell, Martin and Fabos (2009) add that Univision also owns Univision Records, La Calle Records, Fonovisa Records and Disa Records of Mexico.

Telemundo, meanwhile, is the second largest Spanish language television network in the United States; it is headquartered in Hialeah, Florida, and owned by NBC Universal and parent General Electric.

Telemundo owns fifteen full-power stations and nine low-power stations in the United States, in addition to one full-power station in Puerto Rico. There are also thirty-six network affiliates and about 684 cable and wireless systems that carry the network (Yahoo!, para. 2–3). The Telemundo Communications Group is also the owner of Mun2 (Mundos) in the United States and Telemundo Internacional (Telemundo International) for Latin America.

Spanish Language Television History

From a socio-cultural standpoint, the establishment of Spanish language television in the United States is a combination of three factors:

- The Hispanic community in the United States has been looking constantly for ways to express its own identity, and Spanish language television provides an excellent channel for that purpose.

- The apathy shown by commercial networks (e.g., ABC, CBS, NBC) toward the need to include more positive and important Hispanic role models in their programming.
- A need to provide more information, beyond earthquakes and revolutions, from Latin American countries for a Hispanic audience that originates from many Central and South American nations.

When one looks into the history of Spanish language television in the United States, it is unmistakably linked to that of Univision. According to Subervi-Vélez et al. (1993), KCOR-TV began broadcasting in Spanish in 1955 on Channel 41 in San Antonio, Texas. Emilio Nicolás, one of the first general managers of KCOR-TV, said that about 50 percent of the programs broadcast were "live variety and entertainment shows that featured a host of the best available talent from Mexico" (Subervi-Vélez, 1993, p. 653). The other half was composed of movies and other pre-recorded material also imported from Mexico.

Prior to KCOR-TV, there was some time brokered for Spanish programs on English language stations in San Antonio and New York. One of the earliest of these Spanish programs was *Buscando Estrellas* (Looking for the Stars), which began in 1951 produced and hosted by José Pérez (Pepe) del Río, a citizen of Mexico (Subervi-Vélez et al., 1993). Del Río's work in the early 1950s is an indication of the influential role that Mexican citizens and organizations have had in the development of Hispanic television in the United States since the beginning, and contemporary Spanish language television still shows that influence in programming, commercials and even the use of the Spanish language. *Buscando Estrellas* was broadcast live on KERN Channel 5, an English language station in San Antonio. It was a talent-search show that lasted for three years. The program looked for talent in Mexico, and also gave local amateurs the opportunity to show their flair for the entertainment business (Subervi-Vélez et al., 1993). Local talent was most likely of Mexican origin since San Antonio's population traditionally has been Mexican American. Further, from 1956 to 1961, del Río hosted another popular Spanish language program in San Antonio, *Cine en español* (Movies in Spanish). Most movies were old and imported from Mexico, Spain and Argentina.

In New York City, Spanish language television may have started in the late 1940s, according to some anecdotal references found by Subervi-Vélez et al. (1993). Some Spanish entertainment programs were broadcast on English language stations. Subervi-Vélez et al. (1993) also found evidence of *El Show Hispano* (The Hispanic Show), which began in 1952 and lasted for two years. This program contained music and comic segments and what probably could be considered the first Spanish language news section.

Spanish language programs on English language stations began to proliferate during the 1960s in cities with large Latino populations (Subervi-Vélez et al., 1993). With the exception of Miami and Chicago, most of these cities (Los Angeles, Houston, Phoenix and Tucson) were located in south-western states. Thus, most Hispanics living in these cities historically have been Mexican immigrants or Mexican Americans. This observation is supported by Veciana-Suárez (1990). Using 1988 population reports from the Bureau of the Census, Veciana-Suárez (1990) stated that most of the Hispanics living in the United States were of Mexican origin (about 12.1 million people or 62 percent). California, Texas, Arizona, New Mexico and Colorado were home for 63 percent of the Hispanic population in 1988. Furthermore, Hispanics tended to concentrate geographically by country of origin with Puerto Ricans in New York, Cubans in southern Florida and Mexicans in the south-west.

The fact that the largest Hispanic group living in the United States is of Mexican origin is also confirmed by figures from the Bureau of the Census for 2002, which showed that Mexicans constituted 66 percent of the total Hispanic population in the United States, followed by Central and South Americans with 14 percent, Puerto Ricans 9 percent, Cubans 4 percent and the category "Other Hispanic" 6 percent (Israel & Nelson, 2005) Because the Mexican culture has been dominant in the south-west for more than a hundred years, it is not surprising that this Hispanic group has had so much influence in the development of Spanish language television and its programming.

In the 1960s, the Hispanic market was not recognized as being important enough to be a target for marketing by mainstream corporate America. In economic terms, Hispanics in the United States did not have consumer power. Consequently, financial support was lacking, and the San Antonio station was eventually sold. The station continued operating with English language programming and some Spanish language programs until 1961, when the station, under the new call letters KWEX, was again sold, this time to Emilio Azcárraga, a Mexican media magnate who owned Telesistema Mexicano S.A., a Mexican broadcasting empire which would become known as Televisa (Subervi-Vélez et al., 1993).

From this moment on, Televisa would play a key role in the direction of Spanish language television in the United States. Televisa was, and remains, the power behind the finances and program production of Univision.

In 1961, the acquisition of Channel 41 in San Antonio was a significant step taken by Azcárraga and his son to enter the US media market. Their ultimate goal was to establish the largest and most culturally influential Spanish language television network in the United States (Fernandez & Paxman, 2000).

Univision History

Subervi-Vélez et al. (1993) state that Azcárraga and other American citizens went into a partnership and founded Spanish International Communications Corporation (SICC), later known as Spanish International Broadcasting Corporation (SIBC). Azcárraga needed American citizens as partners in order to conform to Federal Communications Commission (FCC) regulations that prohibit issuing broadcast licenses to aliens when they control more than one-fifth of the stock. Although Azcárraga owned only 20 percent of the company, his influence in the organization was keenly felt, especially through his main media partner Reynold Anselmo, a US citizen.

The Rise of Univision

In 1961, Azcárraga and Anselmo established what was to later become the home company for Univision. Spanish International Network (SIN) brought programming from Mexico's Televisa to SICC, which continued to expand its Spanish broadcasts by purchasing more television stations. SIN bought Channel 34 in Los Angeles in 1962, Channel 41 in New York in 1968, Channel 23 in Miami in 1971, Channel 21 in Fresno/Hanford in 1972, Channel 14 in San Francisco in 1974 and Channel 33 in Phoenix in 1976. Additionally, affiliated stations were operating in Albuquerque, Chicago, Corpus Christi, Houston and Sacramento. Meanwhile, Televisa operated stations in Ciudad Juárez, Mexicali, Nuevo Laredo and Tijuana to serve the Spanish population in US cities adjacent to the Mexican border towns of El Paso, El Centro, Laredo and San Diego, respectively.

Azcárraga's initial plans, however, were not to buy stations in the United States and found a Spanish language network. In the early years, he wanted to sell Mexican television programs to US networks the same way that US networks sold US television programs to Mexican networks. Spanish language programs would have been dubbed into English as English language programs were dubbed into Spanish before being imported into Mexico (Gutiérrez & Schement, 1984).

However, this goal was unattainable as the three major American networks saw the Latino market of little value to advertisers. Consequently, Azcárraga's effort failed. This situation and a small flaw in the FCC rules opened the door for Mexican television to penetrate the Latino market in the United States. In order to protect US national media's interests from intervention of foreign power, FCC regulations prohibit any foreign individual or organization to obtain broadcast licenses in the United States when they own more than one-fifth of the stock. However, "federal law regarding ownership applies only to television stations and not to television networks" (Gutiérrez & Schement, 1984, p. 244). This loophole in the law allowed Azcárraga to bypass the government's ownership policies and to expand the SIN network in the United States.

Although the prime source of programming for the SIN network continued to be Televisa, Azcárraga sold his 75 percent holdings in SIN to Televisa in 1975 (Gutiérrez & Schement, 1984). This move meant that Azcárraga's money just went from his right hand to his left because he remained Televisa's owner. SIN continued to expand its outlets, including the buying of low-power television stations. By 1983, SIN/SICC was reaching about 3.3 million Hispanic households in the United States (Subervi-Vélez et al., 1993).

After a period of financial turmoil that included lawsuits and a bidding war between SIN/SICC stockholders, Hallmark Cards acquired SICC properties in 1986. Rumors were that Televisa was losing money with SIN, and Azcárraga wanted to get rid of it, but Fisher (1992) indicated that Azcárraga was in violation of foreign ownership policies of media companies in the United States and was ordered to divest his ten US Hispanic stations. In 1987, SIN and SICC merged, and the newly formed enterprise was renamed Univision. In February 1988, Univision was purchased by Hallmark for $565 million (Dolan, 1996).

The success in horizontal concentration enabled Hallmark to expand its economic influence from the publishing sector to the television sector. However, Hallmark realized that managing a television network was different than handling the business of greeting cards. On the positive side, Hallmark tried to provide audiences with more locally produced programs, but costs began to soar and revenues plunged. To balance its cash flow, Hallmark had to deal with Televisa for production of shows. This decision put Televisa back in control of Univision as most of the programs broadcast by Univision were produced in Mexico by Televisa.

In 1992, Hallmark sold Univision to US media entrepreneur Jerrold Perenchio, Televisa of Mexico and Venevisión of Venezuela (Fisher, 1993). This time, Azcárraga did not have any problems with FCC rules regarding foreign ownership. According to Dolan (1996), changes in the government's communication policies and a complicated legal solution provided a managerial structure wherein Perenchio emerged as chief executive, with a large interest in the network, and Televisa and Venevisión each had a minority interest.

From the beginning, Univision had been operating with a deficit. Lack of advertisers had made life difficult for this Hispanic network. However, economic support was available from powerful Televisa, Venevisión and Perenchio. This made it possible for this network to remain on the air as it struggled to become self-sustaining. Gutiérrez and Schement (1984, p. 246) noted that SIN (Univision's predecessor) "was subsidized by Mexican television in the form of capital loans, program subsidies and of providing personnel."

Through the years Univision became self-sustained, with total revenues of $121 million in 1996 (Dolan, 1996) and $197 million in 1999 (Grover, 2000). In 2000, the network posted sales totaling

$501 million (Wentz, 2001). In the mid-1990s, the network claimed to reach about three-quarters of the country's 28 million Hispanics through its eleven full-power and seven low-power stations, twenty-one affiliates and 740 cable affiliates (Green, 1996).

Nevertheless, one fact that has not changed is the power of Televisa behind Univision. As one examines Univision's program schedule, one can see the influence of Televisa is still prevalent. Its power is evident at all times, and this supremacy is expected to continue through 2017 due to an agreement signed by Televisa, Venevisión and Univision in December 2001. This alliance gives Univision exclusive broadcast rights and access to Televisa programming, along with that of Venevisión (Univision, 2008a, para. 8), even if Univision changes ownership as happened in June 2006, when the network was bought by Broadcasting Media Partners (Univision, 2008a, para. 10).

In summary, Univision's birth and development have traditionally been linked to Televisa of Mexico. This situation has brought about some discussion on the issues of national identity and cultural hegemony. However, despite its somewhat troublesome past, Univision continues as the largest and most powerful Spanish language television network in the United States. Its influence on Spanish-speaking audiences cannot and should not be overlooked. Univision is being watched by Hispanics, Latinos and some non-Hispanics of different origins, and the predominance of Mexican symbols and values is conspicuous.

Telemundo History

Telemundo is Univision's strongest competitor in the United States. Telemundo was founded in 1986 by Reliance Group and was interested in entering the Spanish language television market to compete with Univision for attention from the Spanish-speaking audiences (Constantakis-Valdés, 2008).

Telemundo's early years can be traced back to Puerto Rico. In 1954, Angel Ramos founded a television station (WKAQ), which throughout the upcoming years would become "the foundation of Telemundo's legacy and tradition" (Yahoo!, n.d., para. 1).

John Blair & Company had acquired Channel 51 (WSCV) in Miami and Channel 2 (WKAQ) in San Juan, Puerto Rico, which was Ramos' television station. The Telemundo Group began in May, 1986, when Reliance Capital Group bought Blair's stock for $325 million. The official name change to the Telemundo Group occurred on April 10, 1987.

The Reliance Group already had interests in the Hispanic market since 1985, when it owned Estrella Communications (Star Communications), a company formed to buy Channel 52 (KBSC) in Los Angeles. This station was owned by Columbia Pictures and A. Jerrold Perenchio. Perenchio, who would become one of Univision's shareholders in 1992, had established the station in the 1970s to compete with Univision's KMEX in Los Angeles (Subervi-Vélez et al., 1993)

Key figures in the founding of Telemundo were Saúl Steinberg (chief executive of Reliance) and Henry Silverman, who in time would become Telemundo's president, chief executive and director. But another key player in the foundation of Telemundo was WNJU Channel 47 in New Jersey. In 1965, the station broadcast some Spanish language programs, along with its regular English language shows, for the Hispanic audiences of New Jersey and New York City. In 1971, according to Subervi-Vélez et al. (1993), Columbia Pictures (which owned WAPA of Puerto Rico) bought WNJU. This purchase provided the opportunity for the New Jersey station to have access to a variety of Spanish language shows from the Puerto Rican station, and a number of Columbia Pictures films marketed to Latin America. By then, 60 percent of WNJU programming was in Spanish and included novelas (soap operas), musical shows, sports, news and public affairs.

In 1986, following the success of the station within the Hispanic market, Reliance Group bought the station for $75 million from a group of investors that included Perenchio, Norman Lear and Spanish-American Communications Corporation (SACC). These investors acquired the station from Columbia Pictures in 1980 (Subervi-Vélez et al., 1993).

The expansion of Telemundo continued, and in 1987 the company acquired KSTS, Channel 48, which served the San Francisco and San Jose market. In the Houston and Galveston area, in Texas, it acquired KTMD Channel 48 in 1988, and in Chicago, WSNS Channel 26. In San Antonio, Texas, another affiliate, KVDA Channel 60 in 1989, and then in 1990 it bought KVDA (Subervi-Vélez et al., 1993). With all these television stations, according to Subervi-Vélez et al. (1993, p. 659), Telemundo "was firmly established and potentially available to over 80 percent of Hispanic households in the United States."

Unlike Univision, which imported most of its programs from Mexico's Televisa, Telemundo tried to maintain a large proportion of locally produced programs, like *MTV Internacional* (MTV International), a one-hour program in Spanish similar to programming offered on MTV network. But Telemundo still imported many novelas from Brazil, Venezuela, Mexico, Argentina and Spain (Subervi-Vélez et al., 1993). By 1995, Telemundo produced half of its programs in the United States from its facilities in Hialeah, Los Angeles and Puerto Rico (Constantakis-Valdés, n.d., para. 5). However, thirteen years later, Bednarski and Marich (2008) stated that Telemundo was producing more than a thousand hours of programming for prime time in Miami, Mexico City and Bogotá, Colombia.

Other important developments in the history of Telemundo include the acquisition of the group by NBC Universal in 2001 for $2.7 billion and the launching of Mun2. In 2004, Telemundo became the first Spanish language network in the United States to broadcast the Olympic Games from Athens, Greece, in Spanish. In 2006, Telemundo founded Estudios Mexicanos Telemundo (Mexican Studios Telemundo) to produce television content, and in May, it entered into a partnership with Yahoo! and NBCU to form a new website (telemundo.yahoo.com). The same year, Telemundo stated it had plans for a new Telemundo Mexico headquarters in Mexico City, and it created Telemundo Internacional (MediaWeek). In 2008, Telemundo broadcast the Olympic Games in Beijing, China, in Spanish, while its partner NBC was doing the same in English.

Conclusion

The growth of Spanish language media will continue in the United States, with a Latino population that is expected to increase to 132.8 million by 2050 (Overberg, 2008). Spanish language television is an invaluable tool for advertisers. An example of this trend is the existence of new networks like Azteca America and La Mega. But aside from the marketing standpoint, there is a cultural facet that should not be ignored by television networks. Tunstall (2008, p. 409) argues that Hispanic audiences are "highly fragmented" because they represent different social classes, incomes, countries of origin and (I may add) different Spanish accents. These variations proclaim the need for US Spanish language television to be more assertive in the selection and production of programs that will be representative of this rich and varied cultural heritage. Networks are probably aware of this reality as it is attested by Univision asking Jorge Ramos, a leading news anchor with Noticiero Univisión (Univision Newscast), to try to drop his Mexican accent and use a more standardized Spanish accent (Tunstall, 2008). But there is still room for improvement, including more domestic productions and programs of higher quality. In regard to imports, viewers will expect to see not only Mexican soap operas, game shows and musicals, but also an assortment of programs from Central and South America.

The networks need to listen to their audiences by careful research and analysis of viewers' likes and dislikes about Spanish language television. Studies of this kind should always be on the agenda. In one qualitative study, Univision viewers, gathered in focus group sessions, expressed their desire for more educational programs, high quality productions, more variety and fewer soap operas during prime time (Gibens, 2003).

Further, the future expansion of these two networks should open new opportunities for research and development in multimedia platforms. For example, are Latinos and Hispanics willing to use Univision or Telemundo for their Internet communication needs beyond the act of watching television? Would there be English–Spanish programming for bilingual audiences? Are these networks attracting the attention of members of other minority groups who do not speak Spanish? Univision and Telemundo are reaching audiences beyond the United States. What consequences does this have in terms of cultural imperialism? Would they be able to survive competition from an increasing number of new Spanish language networks which may target specific Hispanic subgroups (Cubans, Venezuelans, etc.)? These are just a few areas in the Spanish language television market that will be a fertile ground for those interested in conducting more research in the field.

References

Bednarski, P. J. & Marich, R. (2008). Univision, Telemundo ramping up product placement projects [Electronic version]. *Broadcasting & Cable*, May 19, p. 16.

Campbell, R., Martin, C. R. & Fabos, B. (2009). *Media & culture: An introduction to mass communication* (5th ed.). Boston, MA: Bedford/St Martin's.

Constantakis-Valdés, P. (2008). Univision and Telemundo on the campaign trail: 1988. In F. A. Subervi-Vélez (Ed.), *The mass media and Latino politics* (pp. 131–153). New York: Routledge.

Constantakis-Valdés, P. (n.d.). *Telemundo*. Retrieved August 18, 2008, from www.museum.tv/archives/etv/htmlT/telemundo/telemundo.htm.

Dolan, K. A. (1996). Muchas gracias, Congress. *Forbes*, 15 (October 7), 46–47.

Fernandez, C. & Paxman, A. (2000). *El Tigre: Emilio Azcárraga y su imperio Televisa* [The tiger: Emilio Azcárraga and his Televisa empire]. Mexico, D.F.: Grijalbo.

Fisher, C. (1992). Turmoil in wake of Univision sale. *Advertising Age*, June 8, 63.

Fisher, C. (1993). Hispanic TV networks take the gloves off; Blaya leads Telemundo against ex-employer Univision. *Advertising Age*, November 8, 44.

Gibens, G. (2003). *Audience perceptions of Univision: Three Hispanic groups*. Unpublished doctoral dissertation. Bowling Green State University, Bowling Green, OH.

Green, M. Y. (1996). Spanish battle lines drawn. *Broadcasting & Cable*, November 18, 126, 50–54.

Grover, R. (2000). Can the Hispanic TV giant transfer its clout to the Web? *Business Week*, January 17, 74–76.

Gutiérrez, F. F. & Schement, J. R. (1984). Spanish International Network: The flow of television from Mexico to the United States. *Communication Research, 11*, 241–258.

Israel, R. & Nelson, C. (2005). Marketing to U.S. Hispanics online. In E. del Valle (Ed.), *Hispanic marketing and public relations* (pp. 195–231). Boca Raton, FL: Poyeen.

MediaWeek. (2007, October 22). *Tracking Telemundo*. Retrieved August 7, 2008, from Communication and Mass Media Complete database.

NBC Universal. (2008). *Telemundo networks and stations*. Retrieved September 30, 2008, from www.nbcuni.com/About_NBC_Universal/Company_Overview/overview02.shtml.

Overberg, P. (2008). America's face evolves, blurs, ages. *USA Today*, August 14, p. 1A.

Subervi-Vélez, F. A., Ramírez Berg, C., Constantakis-Valdés, P., Noriega, C., Ríos, D. & Wilkinson, K. (1993). Media. In N. Kanellos (Ed.), *The Hispanic American almanac: A reference work on Hispanics in the United States*. (pp. 621–674). Detroit, MI: Gale Research Inc.

Tunstall, J. (2008). *The media were American: U.S. mass media in decline*. New York: Oxford University Press.

Univision (2008a) *Company overview*. Retrieved August 17, 2008, from www.univision.net/corp/en/history.jsp.

Univision (2008b) *Media properties*. Retrieved August 17, 2008, from www.univision.net/corp/en/mp.jsp.

Univision (2008c). *Business description.* Retrieved September 28, 2008, from www.univision.net/corp/en/business.jsp.

Veciana-Suárez, A. (1990). *Hispanic media: Impact and influence.* Washington, DC: Media Institute.

Wentz, L. (2001). Univision steps up at upfront. *Advertising Age,* May 21, 72.

Yahoo! (n.d.). *Hecho para ti: Información corporativa* [Made for you: Corporate information]. Retrieved August 17, 2008, from http://tv.telemundo.yahoo.com/corporativo/articulo/29092006/71/corporativo-corporate-information-english.html.

18

The Latinos and Media Project

Federico Subervi
Texas State University-San Marcos, USA

Introduction

The Latinos and Media Project (LAMP) is a web-centered organization that seeks to serve as a guiding light for information and resources about a variety of issues related to Latinos and the media. The website (www.latinosandmedia.org) aims to highlight people, publications, media, organizations, institutions and events that illustrate the growth of Latinos in various communication arenas in the United States, Latin America and other parts of the world.

History of LaMP

The seeds for LaMP were sown in 1995–1996 at the University of Texas at Austin under the stewardship of Dr. Federico Subervi, who at the time was associate professor at the Department of Radio-TV-Film. That year, Subervi had already compiled dozens of sources for the seminal chapter "Mass Communication and Hispanics" (co-authored with Charles R. Berg, Patricia Constantakis-Valdés, Chon Noriega, Diana I. Ríos and Kenton T. Wilkinson), and published in the *Sociology* volume of the *Handbook of Hispanic Cultures in the United States* (Padilla, 1994). Given his membership and collaborations with the National Association of Hispanic Journalists (NAHJ), Subervi had been learning about the many Latinos who had won journalism prizes, yet whose journalistic works were not easily found. Subervi had also been responding to numerous telephone calls and letters from journalists, scholars and students requesting guidance for stories and research related to a variety of topics about Latinos and media.

Recognizing the need and value of a centralized and public space from which to share the rapidly growing information and resources about the subject, he explored options that would make that possible. In 1997, upon obtaining a grant from the National Association of Hispanic Journalists and the National Council of La Raza, Subervi hired graduate students and assigned them the task of systematically searching for, compiling and organizing data and resources to be featured on what was then an emergent Internet site. His undergraduate students (especially those enrolled in his Latinos and Media classes) were also engaged in the project by replacing the traditional term-paper assignments with legacy research endeavors that would enhance the LaMP website. Some students were assigned the task of gathering information while others took the lead in developing the design and structure of the website. (The names of all the contributors are listed in the "Thanks" section on the website.)

The students' searches focused on the following. First, award-winning Latino journalists and their professional work were sought. Second, all forms of publications (books, book chapters, dissertations, master's theses, journal articles, reports, etc.) on the subject of Latinos and the news media. Third, names, addresses and the corresponding web links of Latino-oriented newspapers, magazines, and television and radio networks and stations, as well as of different types of organizations whose operations center on Latino journalism and communication issues. Also gathered were the names, contact information and writings of Latinos and non-Latino communication scholars whose research and teaching centered on Latino communication issues. Early in the process, the website additionally sought a variety of information related to Latinos in the entertainment industry, for example Latino actors and actresses, Latino-themed or produced films, and Latino film festivals. But that part of the project was not continued as information on each of those topics became increasingly available in numerous web sites.

All the gathered information was then organized into the current categories featured in the LaMP website: Resources and Research, which includes the searchable Latinos and News Media Database and the listing of professors whose expertise is in Latinos and media; Journalism Award Winners, which contains a (still incomplete) list of Latino journalists who have won Pulitzer, NAHJ and other types of prizes; a list of organizations whose members and mission intersect with Latinos in media and communication professions, or who advocate for improving the portrayals and employment of Latinos in the media.

The Latinos and Media Project went through a hiatus phase when in 2002, Subervi left the University of Texas to take an administrative academic job in New York City. He returned to academia and to the project again upon joining the School of Journalism and Mass Communication at Texas State University-San Marcos. In 2006, thanks to a $30,000 grant from the Ford Foundation, the project began its new revitalizing phase, which continues to date.

Complementary Research Endeavors

Conducting research about a variety of issues related to Latinos and the media are the central axis of Subervi's academic endeavor. Thus, his expertise in this arena and the LaMP effort, and the establishment of a research facility at the University of Texas, contributed to his obtaining in 1997 a $103,000 grant from the Kaiser Family Foundation (KFF) to assess the portrayals of health issues in US Latino-oriented media. The findings from that study were reported by the KFF (Subervi-Vélez, Vargas & Brady, 1998) and then summarized and subsequently published in a special issue of the *Howard Journal of Communications* (Subervi-Vélez, 1999). Another complementary research was the news and race models of excellence study. With a $223,000 grant from the Ford Foundation and support by the Poynter Institute, Federico Subervi, Ted Pease, Erna Smith and their assistants assessed during 1999–2001 newsroom attitudes about race and ethnicity to the publication and broadcasting of news content about ethnic minorities (Pease, Smith & Subervi-Vélez, 2001).

During the years 2003–2005, while no longer affiliated with the University of Texas but still directing LaMP, Subervi conducted three research projects funded by the National Association of Hispanic Journalists. Two of those studies assessed the portrayals of Latinos in network news (Subervi, Torres & Montalvo, 2004, 2005); the other was a survey of attitudes and working conditions of journalists employed by Spanish language media in the United States (Subervi, 2004). In 2006, Subervi and the Latinos and Media Project were recipients of a Social Science

Research Council grant to analyze the diversity of voices in the Latino media in Central Texas (Correa & Subervi, 2008). And at the time of this writing, a $30,000 grant from the McCormick Foundation is enabling Subervi to analyze the policies and practices of the states of Texas and Illinois to communicate during emergencies with non-English-speaking populations.

Future of LaMP

The revitalization and development of the Latinos and Media Project is scheduled to continue under the guidance of Federico Subervi and auspices of the Center for the Study of Latino Media and Markets, which was established at Texas State in 2008. New annotated bibliographic notations about Latinos and the news media, about Latinos, media and politics, and related to Latinos and Latino-oriented companies involved in advertising, marketing, entertainment and public relations will be added to the resources and research section of the website. The other major sections of the LaMP site will also be updated.

The process of enhancing the information on the site will be facilitated and complemented by other websites that have been developed recently and that overlap with components of LaMP. For example, the Center for Spanish Language Media inaugurated in 2006 at the University of North Texas, has a website that includes a section on resources and research (www.spanishmedia.unt. edu/index.php?option=com_content&task=section&id=13&Itemid=51) that lists Spanish language media and annotated bibliographies on the subject. Two other complementary sources are the Race and Media Diversity Database (www.stjohns.edu/demo/baynes/baynes.sju) initiated in 2006 at the St John's University's Ronald H. Brown Center for Civil Rights and Economic Development, and the annotated bibliography of the Forum on Media Diversity (www.mass communicating.lsu.edu) established in 2004 at the Manship School of Journalism and Mass Communication at Louisiana State University. Collaborative and exchange agreements are in effect between LaMP and these three other entities. However, it should be noted that the latter two databases are broader in their inclusion of diversity references, of which Latino bibliographies are one of the topics covered.

Future Research Directions

As the Latinos and Media Project continues to evolve—and as the aforementioned and other centers, programs and websites also develop—it is hoped that scholars, students and media professionals seeking information about issues related to Latinos and media will find the guides they need to contribute to the better understanding of this dynamic topic.

However, much more research about Latinos and media issues is still needed in all areas of the field. For example, political communication research focused on Latinos and Latino-oriented media is imperative, especially as this population and Latino-oriented media expand their roles in American politics. The 2008 presidential elections are testimony to the fact that Latinos and Latino issues (e.g., immigration) are no longer just in the periphery of political campaigns. Yet assessments of how the media, including Latino-oriented media cover and affect Latinos are lacking.

Also needed are inquiries about telecommunication policies that affect Latinos and Latino-oriented media. While new media technologies are impacting society at large, little is known about how Latino-oriented media and their audiences have voices in the establishment and implementation of such policies, much less regarding the outcomes of the new rules and regulations concerning the new media.

Of particular concern is the influence of old and new media on Latino children. The surge of young Latinos is well known, especially in states such as California, where in 2003 there were more births to Latino families than to any other ethnic group. But just how do the traditional media (e.g., television) as well as the newer outlets (e.g., iPods, computers) affect the socialization of this diverse group that includes recent immigrants, first- and second-generation offspring, and even children of mixed racial heritage of divergent social backgrounds and language abilities?

Assessments of the marketing efforts directed to Latinos and of Latinos' consumer behaviors are likewise lacking comprehensive social-science-based research. Yet millions of dollars are being directed at reaching out specifically to Latinos, and even more so to the younger generations. How effective are those efforts? What works best or not at all? On the other side of the marketing and advertising equation, research is sorely lacking that could help Latinos become more media literate and consumer savvy—be it regarding commercial products or health-related behaviors. In fact, health communication research pertinent to Latinos is also a growing need given the particular health problems faced by this population and their distinct patterns in interpersonal communication and mass-media uses.

Last, but not least, there are still limited inquiries about the representations and portrayals of Latinos in general market media as well as in Latino-oriented media. The areas that need additional research span from news, entertainment, commercial advertisements and even public service announcements. While various content analyses of media representations of Latinos have been conducted over the years, the research has been mostly descriptive with little or no complementary studies about if and how those (still too often stereotyped) portrayals of Latinos *affect* the social, cultural, psychological and political knowledge, attitudes and behaviors of either Latinos or on non-Latinos who are exposed to such images.

This brief overview of future research directions is a partial sample of the work that will continue as part of the mission of the Latinos and Media Project, as well as the Center for the Study of Latino Media and Markets at the School of Journalism and Mass Communication at Texas State University, along with the collaboration with of scholars, students and even media professionals who seek to continue serving together as guiding lights for information and resources about a variety of issues related to Latinos and the media.

References

Correa, T. & Subervi, F. (2008, August). *Assessing the diversity of Latino-oriented media in Central Texas.* Paper presented to the Minorities and Communication Division, Association of Education in Journalism and Mass Communication (AEJMC) National Convention, Chicago, IL.

Padilla, F. (Ed.). (1994). *Sociology.* Volume 3 of *Handbook of Hispanic Cultures in the United States,* general editors N. Kanellos and C. Esteva-Fabregat. Houston, TX: Arte Público.

Pease, T., Smith, E. & Subervi-Vélez, F. A. (2001). *The news and race models of excellence project. Overview: Connecting newsroom attitudes and news content.* St Petersburg, FL: Poynter Institute.

Subervi, F. (2004). *NAHJ Survey of news professionals at Spanish language media in the U.S.* [Encuesta de la NAHJ en torno a los profesionales de noticias en los medios en Español en los Estados Unidos]. Washington, DC: National Association of Hispanic Journalists.

Subervi, F., Torres, J. & Montalvo, D. (2004). *Network brownout 2004: The portrayal of Latinos in network television news, 2003.* Washington, DC: National Association of Hispanic Journalists.

Subervi, F., Torres, J. & Montalvo, D. (2005). *Network brownout 2005: The portrayal of Latinos in network television news, 2004, with a retrospect to 1995.* Washington, DC: National Association of Hispanic Journalists.

Subervi-Vélez, F. A. (1999). Spanish-language television coverage of health news. *Howard Journal of Communications, 10*(3), 207–228.

Subervi-Vélez, F. A., Vargas, L. & Brady, L. A. (1998). *What's the diagnosis? Latinos, media and health. A study of health coverage in Latino newspapers, television and radio news, 1997–1998* [Title of Spanish version released simultaneously: ¿Cuál es el diagnóstico? Los latinos, los medios de comunicación y la salud: Estudio sobre la cobertura de la salud en noticias difundidas en periódicos, televisión y radio latinos, 1997–1998]. Menlo Park, CA: Kaiser Family Foundation.

19
Advertising in Spanish Language Media

Cristina Etayo
University of Navarra, Spain

and Ángela Preciado Hoyos
Universidad Pontificia Bolivariana, Colombia

Introduction

The advertising industry constitutes a sector which has gradually been acquiring a larger importance in many national economies. According to a report produced by the International Advertising Association (IAA), in 2007 the world's advertising investments totaled $455,119 million. This represented a growth of 5.19 percent in relation to the previous period. Within a global context, Spanish-speaking countries have been part of this phenomenon. For example, despite the fact that the Latin American advertising sector is still in a developmental stage, in 2007 over $22 million were allotted to advertising. While the advertising sector is gaining importance within the Spanish-speaking economies, there are no works describing their global situation in the different countries. Therefore, the purpose of this chapter is filling this gap, and describing the main features of this industry, which has a vital importance for the media.

For this purpose, we first analyze the role played by advertising from a macroeconomic point of view, by examining the evolution of advertising expenditures in the different countries, as well as its relation to the economic cycle. Next, we analyze the specific situation of the main advertising supports, the preferences of some media over others in some countries, and the factors that may explain this larger commitment. Then we will describe the main agents that participate in the advertising processes in the region, namely advertising agencies, media agencies, advertisers and service providers. Finally, we will present the main conclusions of this chapter.

The Advertising Sector in the Economy

The advertising sector has become an important industry within national economies, primarily due to three reasons: its significant contribution to the gross domestic product (GDP), the economic impact it generates by adding value to the goods and services advertised, and the influence it exerts on the behavior of the media and consumers. In order to analyze the relevance of advertising investments in Spanish-speaking countries, we first consider the percentage of GDP allotted to advertising in conventional media. Table 19.1 reflects the values of this ratio from 1995 to 2004 for the main Spanish-speaking countries. Data referring to Japan, the United Kingdom and the United States are also included, so as to facilitate an inter-country comparison.

Table 19.1 Percentage of GDP Allotted to Advertising per Country, 1995–2004

	1995	1996	1997	1998	1999	2000	2001	2002	2003	2004	Mean	SD
Argentina	1.03	1.03	1.08	1.09	1.25	1.20	1.86	1.37	1.72	1.85	1.35	0.33
Chile	0.95	1.07	0.95	0.84	0.79	0.77	0.70	0.71	0.68	0.64	0.81	0.14
Colombia	2.10	2.25	2.35	2.99	1.78	1.86	2.17	2.12	1.95	1.83	2.14	0.35
Costa Rica	1.24	1.19	1.19	1.20	1.12	1.35	1.38	1.53	1.43	1.28	1.29	0.12
Honduras	1.15	1.51	1.90	1.95	2.38	3.00	2.64	2.20	2.21	2.43	2.14	0.53
Mexico	0.64	0.73	0.88	0.97	1.55	1.79	1.84	1.74	1.88	1.94	1.39	0.52
Nicaragua		1.15	1.04	1.26	1.39	1.46	1.49	1.43	1.51	1.57	1.23	0.17
Paraguay						1.37	1.49	1.16	1.29	1.27	1.32	0.12
Peru		1.91	1.83	1.74	1.74	1.51	1.63	1.47	1.44	1.13	1.44	0.24
Spain	0.78	0.76	0.76	0.81	0.85	0.87	0.79	0.73	0.70	0.72	0.78	0.05
Uruguay						3.39	3.01	3.10	3.48	3.73	3.34	0.29
Venezuela	1.03	1.18	1.01	1.35	1.32	1.27	1.28	1.34	1.11	1.63	1.25	0.18
Japan	0.73	0.77	0.78	0.75	0.75	0.80	0.80	0.75	0.75	0.78	0.77	0.02
UK	1.14	1.16	1.20	1.24	1.25	1.31	1.19	1.14	1.12	1.15	1.19	0.06
USA	1.24	1.27	1.29	1.33	1.35	1.47	1.29	1.27	1.25	1.24	1.30	0.06

Source: Compiled by the authors from World Advertising Trends and World Bank

As seen in Table 19.1, there are significant differences within these countries in regard to the importance assigned to advertising in conventional media. The data show that the Spanish-speaking countries which allotted the largest percentage of their GDP to investments in advertising during the period 1995–2004 were Uruguay (3.73 percent), Colombia (2.14 percent) and Honduras (2.14 percent). Uruguay holds the highest values. Even when the series began in the year 2000, it can be seen that it was the country with the highest percentage of its GDP allotted to advertising. Colombia underwent a significant decline in advertising spending during this period. Honduras followed the opposite path. Starting from low values at the beginning of the period, it accomplished a quite high percentage at the end.

On the other extreme are Chile and Spain, with percentages lower than 1 percent. It must be taken into account, however, that the rates shown here make reference to investments only in conventional media, because they have been the media traditionally used by firms for the diffusion of their advertising messages. They are newspapers, magazines, television, radio, outdoors, cinema and Internet. Non-conventional media include direct marketing, phone marketing, point of purchase, gifts, trade fairs, exhibitions and sponsorship.

The great dispersion of these media and the recent development of some of them make it difficult to acquire aggregated data on advertising investment. The rest of the conventional media are not included because of their low participation on the whole as well as for the lack of homogeneous data for the countries analyzed. However, for the Spanish case, where these non-conventional media have experienced a fast development, if the total advertising investment were analyzed, the results might show some differences. In recent years there has been a transfer of conventional to non-conventional media advertising. As a result, the importance of the former has experienced a sharp decline. Nevertheless, despite the exclusion of non-conventional media in this study for lack of data availability, it can be seen how the advertising sector is considered differently across the Latin American countries.

If we make a comparison with other countries, with the exception of Japan, where the weight of conventional advertising investment is sensibly lower, the United Kingdom and United States data do not substantially differ from those of Spanish-speaking countries. However, it must be taken into account that, as in the case of Spain, non-conventional media had already unfolded in these countries. Consequently, the rates only show the advertising investment in conventional media.

It is interesting to analyze the standard deviation of advertising intensity throughout the period considered (investment in conventional media over GDP), since it supplies us with information about the degree of consolidation of the companies' advertising budgets in the different countries. Non-Spanish-speaking countries have standard deviations of between 0.02 and 0.06, which indicates that the advertising investment levels in relation to the GDP are stable over time. The same happens in the case of Spain (coefficient of 0.05). Investments in advertising in conventional media have reached certain levels which, with the exception of slight variations, have remained constant. However, if we observe the values for the rest of Spanish-speaking countries we find a clearly different situation, which reaches extreme levels in the cases of Honduras, Mexico, Colombia and Argentina. In other countries, such as Paraguay and Costa Rica, the deviation is small.

In order to analyze how the importance of advertising within the GDP has evolved over time, we will analyze the correlation between the average of advertising intensity (measured as advertising investment in conventional media over GDP) and time within the different Spanish-speaking countries (see Table 19.2).

As seen in Table 19.2, there are countries where the advertising intensity has clearly increased over time. Mexico, Nicaragua and Argentina show high correlations. This means that the percentage of GDP allotted to advertising has been constantly growing in these countries during these years. The intensity has also grown in Honduras, Costa Rica, Venezuela and Uruguay, though less regularly. In countries such as Peru and Chile the trend is exactly the opposite. There has been a significant reduction in advertising investment in conventional media. A likely explanation is that the advertising sector in these countries is in its first development stage and has not yet started growing. It is also possible that the sector has reached its zenith, and will experience limited future growth. In this case, there could be other factors different to time that have an impact on advertising intensity and are related to the economic situation or population growth. A similar negative correlation can also be seen in Paraguay, Colombia and Spain, even when the decline is not so sharp.

The macroeconomic effects of advertising have been the object of strong controversies, miscellaneous studies and reference searches. When making decisions on economic policy, it is useful to determine whether these effects can be quantified as well as the magnitude of their influence (Jacobson & Nicosia 1981). For instance, Galbraith (1967) proposed the use of advertising as a tool to smooth down the economic fluctuations.

Some studies (Dhalla, 1980; Howard, 1980) analyze the role of advertising as an anti-recession resource. Empirical evidence has not yet provided foundations to determine the relationship between advertising and GDP. It is uncertain if advertising is a cause or effect of a country's GDP. Some studies have used different techniques in order to deduce these associations, such as causality analysis (Ashley, Granger & Schmalensee, 1980; Sturgess & Wilson, 1984) or co-integration analysis, that takes into the account the effects of time on the variables analyzed isolating the impact of spurious correlation (Baghestani, 1991).

Table 19.2 Correlation between Advertising Intensity and Time, 2008

Argentina	0.86
Chile	−0.94
Colombia	−0.42
Costa Rica	0.64
Honduras	0.70
Mexico	0.94
Nicaragua	0.90
Paraguay	−0.53
Peru	−0.94
Spain	−0.41
Uruguay	0.62
Venezuela	0.63

Source: Compiled by the authors from World Advertising Trends and World Bank

There is a lack of studies that analyze the influence of economic cycles on advertising expenditures. The only exception is Picard (2001), which examines the effects of economic recessions on advertising expense in nine countries. In order to determine whether there is a relationship between the growth of the advertising investment and the GDP, Table 19.3 shows the correlation coefficients between both advertising investment and GDP.

Table 19.3 shows a positive correlation coefficient for most of the countries. As GDP grows, advertising also grows, and when GDP declines, advertising declines. This illustrates the cyclical character of advertising. Uruguay, Honduras and Venezuela are the countries where advertising is most in tune with the economic situation, with correlation coefficients of over 0.8. Nicaragua, Mexico, Colombia, Chile and Paraguay occupy an intermediate position, with correlation coefficients

Table 19.3 Correlation between Growth in Advertising Investment and GDP, 2008

Argentina	0.14
Chile	0.42
Colombia	0.59
Costa Rica	−0.12
Honduras	0.85
Mexico	0.67
Nicaragua	0.78
Paraguay	0.40
Peru	−0.10
Spain	−0.07
Uruguay	0.97
Venezuela	0.83

Source: Compiled by the authors from World Advertising Trends and World Bank

between 0.4 and 0.8. However, despite this general pattern, there are countries such as Argentina, Spain, Peru and Costa Rica, where advertising bears only a small relationship to the economic cycle. In Spain, Peru and Costa Rica the coefficient is negative, even though there is no relationship. Spain can be explained by the fact that advertising in conventional media underwent a development period in the 1980s, and then stabilized. In this country, companies are becoming increasingly aware of the need of planning their advertising investments in the long term. In other words, they realize they need to consider advertising disbursements as actual investments and not as spending, which is the current trend. During economic crises, advertising is one of the first expenditure items that companies cut. With the growing development of communications, this practice goes against certain objectives, such as branding and permanence in the consumers' minds. Perspectives on advertising have changed. This has made its percentage in relation to the GDP in advanced economies to be lower than in the past.

Figure 19.1 shows a summary of the overall situation, as well as of the structure and features of the advertising sector in each country. The figure shows data from the Spanish-speaking countries, divided into four groups. The first group in the top-right quadrant includes Uruguay, Honduras, Venezuela, Nicaragua and Mexico. These countries feature an advertising sector which has grown during the period of analysis, and which bears a close relationship with the behavior of the GDP. That is, it grows when the economic situation is sound, and tends to diminish when it stagnates. These countries, therefore, have a growing, though still not fully developed advertising sector. The other group includes Argentina and Costa Rica. While these two countries are not in the same quadrant, their situation is very similar because the correlation between advertising intensity and time is high, and they do not depend so heavily on the GDP: so, in these two countries, the advertising sector is less influenced by the economic situation.

The countries in the second quadrant are Colombia, Paraguay and Chile. Their main feature is a negative correlation between advertising intensity and time. In these countries advertising has not grown over the time examined. The evolution of the advertising sector is different for one of two reasons: either because they have completed their development or entered a consolidation stage; or because the sector has not yet reached full development.

The countries in the third quadrant are Spain and Peru. As Figure 19.1 shows, there is no correlation with the GDP, and the correlation over time is negative. This fact is especially significant in the case of Peru, which has experienced a large reduction in investment rates. As for

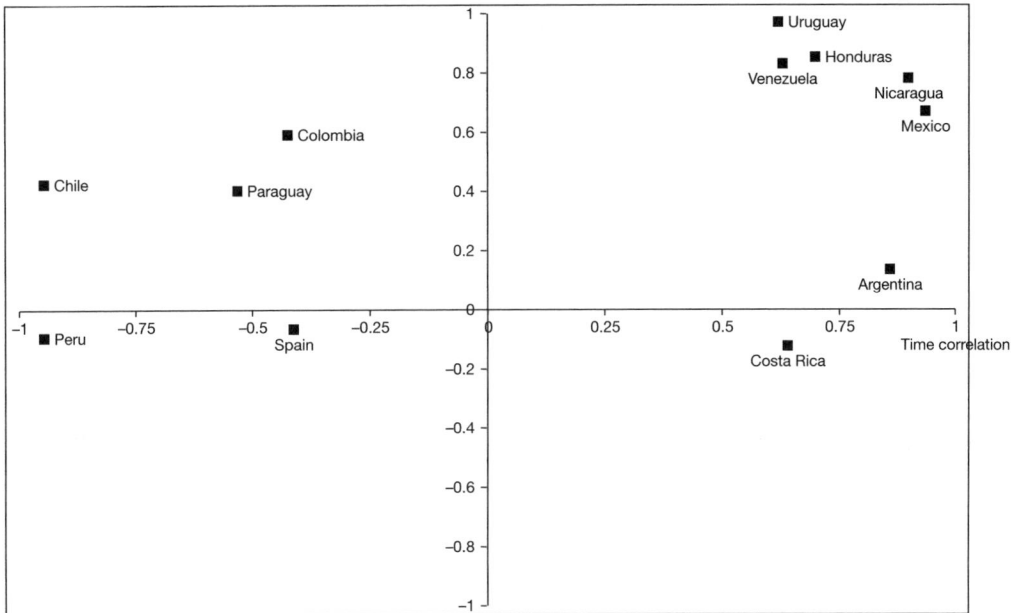

Figure 19.1 Advertising Intensity in Relation to Time and GDP in Each Country

Source: Compiled by the authors from World Advertising Trends and World Bank

Spain, the reduction in conventional media investments is lower, and has been due to a budgetary shift to non-conventional media.

Advertising Media

Having analyzed the advertising sector as a whole, we now consider advertising investments in the different media in each of the countries. Table 19.4 (p. 254) shows the investments in each one of the conventional media in relation to the total investment in each country. The purpose is to see whether there are significant differences regarding the media preferred by advertising clients across the different countries.

The differences between the Spanish-speaking countries and the three non-Spanish-speaking countries considered are relevant. If we compare the average commitment to the different supports of both groups of countries, we see the investment in newspapers and magazines is much higher in the case of the non-Spanish-speaking countries. Nevertheless, in audiovisual media (radio and television) the situation is the opposite. Television advertising is especially interesting. In the Latin American countries television receives almost two-thirds of the total advertising budget. In all the Latin American countries, investments in television advertising largely exceed those of Spain, Japan, the United Kingdom and the United States. The case of magazines is also surprising. In all of the Spanish-speaking countries advertising investments in magazines are much lower than in Spain.

Another interesting fact regarding the Latin American countries is that four media (newspapers, magazines, television and radio) capture almost 100 percent of the budget in conventional media, whereas in non-Spanish-speaking countries this percentage is 90 percent, due to the weight of other significant conventional media (cinema, out-of-home and Internet advertising).

Table 19.4 Participation of Each Media in the Total Investment, 2008

Country	Newspapers	Magazines	Television	Radio
Argentina	32.17	7.28	49.03	6.88
Chile	32.79	4.27	45.98	9.89
Colombia	15.28	4.33	56.51	23.87
Costa Rica	30.26	5.05	47.61	15.44
Honduras	37.04	0.68	58.10	4.47
Mexico	9.45	4.12	65.89	20.53
Nicaragua	24.92	0.27	60.66	14.31
Paraguay	30.86	2.92	64.28	9.69
Peru	12.35	2.42	81.31	3.92
Spain	32.07	11.82	40.19	9.13
Uruguay	21.03	0.89	78.08	
Venezuela	20.13	1.78	72.47	2.87
Average Spanish-speaking countries	24.86	3.82	60.01	11.00
Japan	27.68	9.78	43.98	4.74
UK	40.05	16.64	31.43	3.94
USA	34.25	11.38	37.59	12.14
Average non-Spanish-speaking countries	33.99	12.60	37.67	6.94

Source: Compiled by the authors from World Advertising Trends

In addition to these substantive differences between both groups of countries, there are also many differences referred to media commitment among the different Latin American countries. In regard to newspapers, Argentina, Chile and Honduras have percentages over 30 percent, similar to Spain, Japan and the United States. In the United Kingdom the percentage is higher (around 40 percent). The rest of the countries feature much lower levels. Regarding magazines, even when the levels are low, there are differences. Argentina is the Spanish-speaking country with the largest advertising investment in magazines, at 7.28 percent.

In regards to television, Peru, Uruguay and Venezuela display high investment levels, as do Mexico, Nicaragua and Paraguay. The Latin American countries with the lowest investments in television are Chile, Argentina and Costa Rica. Likewise, radio advertising also shows differences among countries. Mexico and Colombia feature the highest investment in radio advertising, whereas the investment is almost nil in Honduras and Peru.

Newspapers

Newspapers and the press in general have been the object of many research works aimed at foreseeing future behavior and evolution. Will the printed press have a future after the Internet? Can magazines compete against their own information on the Internet? These issues have in no way been settled. It is a fact that the press has declined in circulation, but, have advertising investments in newspapers followed the same path? Table 19.5 shows data on this evolution.

The data in Table 19.5 on newspaper advertising are not very encouraging. Advertising budgets that used to be assigned to newspapers have been reassigned to other media. In view of the reduction in newspaper circulation, advertisers are rethinking their investment in newspapers. This is a common trend in all the countries with a more or less sharp decline in newspaper circulation, even when the results have in all cases depended on the initial situation.

Table 19.6 shows the correlation coefficients between the participation of newspaper investment in total investment and time. In almost all Spanish-speaking countries there is a negative relationship over time. However, two countries display a different pattern. Peru and

Table 19.5 Evolution of Advertising Commitment to Newspapers, 1995–2004

	1995	1996	1997	1998	1999	2000	2001	2002	2003	2004
Argentina	34.60	35.01	36.27	38.05	38.92	33.66	24.86	27.53	27.01	25.81
Chile	35.28	33.60	35.11	34.96	35.98	34.49	30.59	30.01	28.27	29.56
Colombia	16.61	15.89	14.77	11.74	17.74	15.61	14.97	14.37	15.32	15.83
Costa Rica	29.78	30.63	30.44	35.10	35.61	32.38	29.84	25.90	26.28	26.60
Honduras	45.14	48.96	38.26	37.93	34.50	27.68	36.26	34.96	36.68	29.99
Mexico	19.03	14.91	13.46	11.90	7.14	6.63	5.96	5.94	5.05	4.52
Nicaragua		23.84	26.05	24.90	25.04	23.73	21.65	24.73	25.16	29.18
Paraguay						38.11	33.26	33.17	25.06	24.70
Peru		10.27	9.51	10.99	12.21	11.88	12.28	13.35	13.94	16.70
Spain	34.20	34.12	33.80	32.59	32.90	33.10	31.79	30.82	29.31	28.11
Uruguay						25.62	27.70	22.07	14.98	14.81
Venezuela	13.14	14.24	25.83	26.14	22.80	22.48	25.61	19.43	16.72	14.90
Average Spanish-speaking countries	28.47	26.15	26.35	26.43	26.28	25.45	24.56	23.52	21.98	21.73
Japan	29.59	29.32	28.88	28.05	28.02	28.12	27.58	26.35	25.86	25.06
UK	41.42	40.40	39.93	39.62	39.66	40.20	41.26	40.38	39.40	38.29
USA	37.95	36.98	37.23	36.58	35.64	32.57	32.33	31.52	31.05	30.67
Average non-Spanish-speaking countries	36.32	35.57	35.35	34.75	34.44	33.63	33.72	32.75	32.10	31.34

Source: Compiled by the authors from World Advertising Trends

Table 19.6 Correlation between Newspaper Advertising and Time, 2008

Argentina	−0.771
Chile	−0.828
Colombia	−0.064
Costa Rica	−0.541
Honduras	−0.728
Mexico	−0.938
Nicaragua	0.338
Paraguay	−0.952
Peru	0.930
Spain	−0.935
Uruguay	−0.911
Venezuela	−0.002
Japan	−0.967
UK	−0.553
USA	−0.966

Source: Compiled by the authors from on World Advertising Trends

Nicaragua are the only countries where advertising investments in newspapers have grown over time. In Venezuela, Colombia and Costa Rica, the situation has been more stable and less volatile over time.

Magazines

Table 19.7 details the percentage of advertising in magazines in each country. Advertising in magazines in Spanish-speaking countries is remarkably scarce. Only a tiny part of the total investment is assigned to magazines. In Spain and in several non-Spanish-speaking countries, advertising in magazines is less than 10 percent of the total investment, whereas in Latin American

Table 19.7 Evolution of Advertising Commitment to Magazines, 1995–2004

	1995	1996	1997	1998	1999	2000	2001	2002	2003	2004
Argentina	7.70	7.99	8.32	8.95	8.67	7.66	6.59	5.00	5.50	6.38
Chile	3.54	5.54	4.47	4.49	3.59	5.04	4.51	4.15	3.84	3.48
Colombia	4.34	3.83	3.86	3.67	5.75	4.99	3.93	3.87	4.35	4.75
Costa Rica	5.79	5.44	4.61	4.48	3.86	3.72	3.97	5.63	6.26	6.75
Honduras					0.11	0.56	0.84	0.59	1.13	0.85
Mexico	6.25	6.74	6.55	6.51	2.74	2.46	2.93	2.39	2.05	2.59
Nicaragua				0.42	0.16	0.27	0.24			0.26
Paraguay						3.49	2.91	3.07	2.57	2.54
Peru		1.92	2.92	2.90	2.61	2.75	2.79	1.91	1.85	2.15
Spain	13.16	12.90	12.84	11.98	11.38	11.31	11.56	11.10	11.00	11.02
Uruguay						1.44	0.16	0.80	0.83	1.19
Venezuela	1.46	1.48	2.37	1.77	1.66	1.78	2.19	2.07	1.61	1.42
Average Spanish-speaking countries	6.03	5.73	5.74	5.02	4.05	3.79	3.55	3.69	3.73	3.62
Japan	9.44	9.61	9.99	10.10	10.12	9.81	9.56	9.94	9.89	9.37
UK	17.44	18.10	18.12	18.03	17.04	16.19	16.69	15.73	14.84	14.25
USA	12.41	12.06	12.15	11.89	11.71	11.21	11.13	10.48	10.46	10.29
Average non-Spanish-speaking countries	13.10	13.26	13.42	13.34	12.96	12.40	12.46	12.05	11.73	11.30

Source: Compiled by the authors from World Advertising Trends

countries it is less than 5 percent, with the exception of Argentina (7.28 percent). All of the countries kept investments low during the period reviewed, with slight increases and decreases.

Table 19.8 shows the correlations between magazine advertising and time. Most of the countries (Paraguay, Mexico, Argentina, Peru, Chile) show negative relationships. Costa Rica and Colombia show slightly positive coefficients indicating little growth over time. The coefficients of Uruguay, Venezuela, Nicaragua and Chile indicate that these countries have maintained low investment levels in magazines. The only country where advertising in magazines have grown is Honduras, but analysis of the data indicates that it started from a level next to zero, and so a certain level of growth seems logical. This same trend can be observed both in Spain and in non-Spanish-speaking countries (with the exception of Japan, which has maintained constant levels).

Table 19.8 Correlation between Magazine Advertising and Time, 2008

Argentina	−0.737	Peru	−0.405
Chile	−0.338	Spain	−0.928
Colombia	0.207	Uruguay	0.054
Costa Rica	0.306	Venezuela	0.024
Honduras	0.792	Japan	−0.057
Mexico	−0.863	UK	−0.912
Nicaragua	−0.292	USA	−0.979
Paraguay	−0.905		

Source: Compiled by the authors from World Advertising Trends

Television

Television advertising is just the opposite of the situation with magazines. Latin American countries allocate most of their advertising budgets to television. Television in Latin America is the most typical advertising media, ranging from 45 percent in Chile to 81 percent in Peru. The countries with the highest investment levels are Peru, Uruguay and Venezuela. These data raise a question: is television becoming the main advertising medium in Latin America, to the detriment of print media, or was it already so and now there is an evolution into a more balanced distribution of investment in conventional media? The data suggest acceptance of the first proposition.

Table 19.9 shows that during the period considered, the advertising budget has in no way been more evenly distributed. Instead, in many countries the percentage assigned to television has undergone a significant growth.

Table 19.9 Evolution of Television Advertising Commitment, 1995–2004

	1995	1996	1997	1998	1999	2000	2001	2002	2003	2004
Argentina	42.79	40.73	40.83	38.60	39.32	47.68	56.52	58.51	62.15	63.12
Chile	46.34	42.94	42.60	42.92	43.73	42.79	47.60	49.59	50.80	50.53
Colombia	62.55	63.32	62.49	66.27	46.53	49.32	55.88	54.28	54.03	50.43
Costa Rica	49.71	48.80	50.41	46.08	45.65	47.86	46.83	49.01	46.82	44.95
Honduras	49.31	45.91	57.35	58.42	61.35	69.86	59.19	60.96	57.76	60.86
Mexico	59.03	56.39	62.69	58.77	60.32	62.56	77.46	77.75	71.88	72.11
Nicaragua		62.85	60.78	60.04	57.72	62.00	64.72	60.05	60.89	56.88
Paraguay						58.40	54.14	63.76	72.37	72.75
Peru		84.02	83.48	82.61	80.69	81.44	81.45	81.02	80.89	76.19
Spain	37.53	37.78	38.28	40.74	41.51	41.60	39.24	40.15	41.63	43.45
Uruguay						72.95	72.14	77.13	84.19	83.99
Venezuela	82.48	81.31	67.30	66.47	69.94	68.81	62.46	71.09	75.05	79.79
Average Spanish-speaking countries	53.72	56.41	56.62	56.09	54.68	58.77	59.80	61.94	63.21	62.92
Japan	41.92	42.72	43.20	43.70	43.73	44.15	44.66	44.87	45.19	45.66
UK	32.53	32.50	32.35	32.21	32.55	31.67	29.71	30.99	30.16	29.65
USA	37.19	38.58	37.25	37.35	36.70	36.56	36.54	38.26	38.53	38.91
Average non-Spanish-speaking countries	37.21	37.93	37.60	37.75	37.66	37.46	36.97	38.04	37.96	38.07

Source: Compiled by the authors from World Advertising Trends

Table 19.10 shows the correlation coefficients over time. In most of the Latin American countries television advertising is high and has been growing over time. The only exceptions are Colombia and Peru.

Table 19.10 Correlation between Advertising Commitment to Magazines and Time, 2008

Argentina	0.889	Peru	−0.841
Chile	0.756	Spain	0.802
Colombia	−0.659	Uruguay	0.930
Costa Rica	−0.594	Venezuela	−0.166
Honduras	0.599	Japan	0.988
Mexico	0.816	UK	−0.876
Nicaragua	−0.312	USA	0.357
Paraguay	0.895		

Source: Compiled by the authors from World Advertising Trends

Radio

Table 19.11 displays data regarding radio advertising. In Latin America there is a preference for advertising in audiovisual media; radio follows the same path as television. In Latin American countries radio advertising investments are higher than in non-Spanish-speaking countries, even

Table 19.11 Evolution of Commitment to Radio Advertising, 1995–2004

	1995	1996	1997	1998	1999	2000	2001	2002	2003	2004
Argentina	7.70	8.06	6.96	6.59	5.78	7.39	9.67	6.64	5.33	4.69
Chile	7.92	11.32	11.20	11.04	9.75	10.53	10.16	9.50	9.21	8.29
Colombia	16.51	16.97	18.88	18.31	29.98	30.08	25.22	27.47	26.30	29.00
Costa Rica	14.72	15.14	14.53	14.34	14.88	13.27	16.02	16.30	17.24	17.98
Honduras	5.56	5.13	4.39	3.72	3.98	1.90	3.67	3.53	4.47	8.33
Mexico	15.69	21.96	17.31	22.81	29.79	28.36	13.65	13.92	21.03	20.78
Nicaragua		13.31	13.47	14.85	16.91	14.13	13.38	15.23	13.95	13.58
Paraguay							9.69			
Peru		3.76	4.10	3.49	4.49	3.93	3.48	3.72	3.36	4.95
Spain	9.77	9.84	9.70	9.36	8.71	7.37	9.13	9.13	9.30	8.96
Uruguay										
Venezuela	1.46	1.48	1.42	3.55	2.29	3.37	5.88	3.94	3.08	2.22
Average Spanish-speaking countries	9.92	10.70	10.20	10.81	12.66	12.03	10.90	10.94	11.33	11.88
Japan	5.19	5.07	5.04	5.05	4.89	4.59	4.52	4.45	4.37	4.19
UK	3.31	3.50	3.64	3.93	4.11	4.30	4.10	4.13	4.26	4.09
USA	11.34	11.30	11.52	11.89	12.57	12.24	12.50	12.94	12.67	12.42
Average non-Spanish-speaking countries	6.61	6.62	6.73	6.96	7.19	7.04	7.04	7.17	7.10	6.90

Source: Compiled by the authors from Advertising Trends

though in the United States a large percentage of the GDP is assigned to radio advertising, similar to Spain. However, is the media finding a common behavior pattern is more difficult. It would be necessary to analyze the key variables that exert influence on radio investments in each country.

Colombia and Mexico assign a very high percentage of their advertising investments (between one-fourth and one-fifth) to radio. In contrast, countries such as Venezuela, Peru and Honduras spend a lot on television and very little on radio advertising.

Table 19.12 illustrates how radio advertising investments have evolved over time. The correlation coefficients show that Colombia, Costa Rica and Venezuela have experienced the most growth in radio advertising. Argentina, Spain and Chile have seen a decrease. The other Latin American countries experienced no significant increases or decreases.

Table 19.12 Correlation between Radio Advertising and Time, 2008

Argentina	−0.470	Peru	0.177
Chile	−0.337	Spain	−0.410
Colombia	0.794	Venezuela	0.506
Costa Rica	0.722	Japan	−0.978
Honduras	0.151	UK	0.841
Mexico	−0.022	USA	0.870
Nicaragua	−0.010		

Source: Compiled by the authors from World Advertising Trends

Advertising Institutions in Spanish Language Countries

Here we examine the primary advertising institutions found in Spanish-speaking countries. These include advertising agencies, media agencies, the advertisers and services for the advertising sector.

Advertising Agencies

Advertising increases brand value and helps create product positioning in the minds of the public. Advertising agencies are organizations which generate messages and campaigns with creative ideas for advertisers. In developing strategic concepts and ideas, agencies offer their customers specialized services, account management, analysis and planning of advertising media, and in some cases, research and data on media audiences.

In the Latin American market miscellaneous agencies coexist (especially those at the local level) with large multinational companies belonging to media groups. Some of them have been in the region for more than three decades, but the acquisition of local agencies by global groups generalized by the end of the 1990s. Most large agencies operate from a central office or hub where they manage the operations for the region through *clusters*. This structure follows a trend towards market integration. One of them is the "Andino" cluster, which includes Colombia, Venezuela, Ecuador, Peru and Bolivia. In isolation, these countries lack an advertising investment as strong or representative as, for example, Mexico. Working together, they consolidated to form a larger potential market, as well as reduce costs for personnel and offices. There is a second organization model which includes a head office for the region, and ancillary offices with a certain level of autonomy in each country.

Multinational agencies acquire the largest percentage of advertising dollars. They are the largest companies in terms of personnel and they manage the most renowned brands in each country. Their entrance into the Latin America market has made it possible to enlarge the number of advertising services, among them market research, sales promotion and the development of public relations programs, since they have proved that they can deal with any marketing and communications requirements in general.

Spanish agencies render basically the same services as Latin American entities. They feature consolidated business integration models specialized in research, marketing plans, interactive advertising, point of sales advertising and, in general, non-conventional media. Most of the large Latin American countries, especially Brazil, Mexico and Argentina, follow the full service agency model.

Table 19.13 (p. 260) includes some of the agencies that participate in the advertising market in Spanish-speaking countries. The presence of multinational commercial communication groups is strong in the region. Local entities play similar, but smaller roles.

The election of advertising agencies by advertisers in the Spanish-speaking market is made using different criteria. These include the types of operations handled, the ability to deal with the requirements of each campaign, the relationship among quality, effectiveness and cost, the image of each agency, creative capacity and international guidelines. All of these elements are used to suggest specific agencies to multinational companies.

The creativity factor has been the object of diverse analysis, as a result of the concern caused by the very few awards won by Latin American advertising agencies in contests and events that reward advertising creativity within a global context. In 2007 the region obtained just four awards in Clio, One, and Design and Art Direction (D&AD) festivals. The limitation on results might be explained for the following reasons: first, the more advertising a country produces, the greater the possibilities of making a good selection of commercials to participate in the festivals; second, some international festivals accept only commercials in English; and third, Latin American countries still do not perceive that ideas generate economic development.

Table 19.13 Advertising Agencies with Presence in Spanish-Speaking Countries, 2008

Argentina	BBDO, Oyster Group, McCann Erickson, One 7 Group, JWT, DDB, Vegaolmosponce, Leo Burnett, Del Campo Nazca Saatchi & Saatchi, Euro RSCG, Grupo PMG S.A., Ogilvy & Mather, Gallo Mendoza & Asociados, Publicis Graffiti, La Negra, Young & Rubicam, Buró creativo, Ferrari Chiappa.
Bolivia	Nexus Publicidad, DDB, Publicis, JWT.
Chile	Cuatro monos, Armstrong y Asociados, BBDO, DDB, Prolam Young & Rubicam, Grey Chile S.A., JWT Chilena, Leo Burnett, Publicis, Saatchi & Saatchi, Euro RSCG, Ogilvy, Publicis.
Colombia	Sancho BBDO, Toro Fisher, DDB Colombia, Ogilvy & Mather, Lowe SSP3, Leo Burnett, Young & Rubicam, McCann Erickson, JWT, Rep Grey, Publicis, Jua Publicidad, Pérez y Villa, Harold Zea & Asociados, Euro RSCG.
Costa Rica	Garnier BBDO, DDB, Saatchi & Saatchi, Euro RSCG, Ogilvy, JWT, Young & Rubicam.
Dominican Republic	Pages BBDO, Saatchi & Saatchi, Euro RSCG, Publicis, Young & Rubicam.
Ecuador	Garwich Ecuador, DDB, Saatchi & Saatchi, Euro RSCG, Ogilvy, Publicis, JWT, Young & Rubicam.
El Salvador	Apex BBDO, DDB, Euro RSCG, Molina Bianchy Ogilvy, JWT, Young & Rubicam, McCann Erickson, J. M. Creativos & Asociados, Angle Group, Publinter, Crea, Lowe & Partners.
Guatemala	BBDO Guatemala, DDB, Nazca Saatchi & Saatchi, Euro RSCG, Leo Burnett, Ogilvy, Publicis, TBWA, The Ad Company, Publicentro, Lowe and Partners, Publicis, JWT, Young & Rubicam.
Honduras	BBDO Honduras, DDB, Saatchi & Saatchi, Euro RSCG, Ogilvy, JWT.
Mexico	BBDO México, DDB, Saatchi & Saatchi, Euro RSCG, Ogilvy, Publicis, JWT, Young & Rubicam.
Nicaragua	BBDO Nicaragua, DDB, Euro RSCG, Ogilvy, JWT.
Panama	BBDO Panamá, DDB, Euro RSCG, Ogilvy, JWT, Young & Rubicam.
Paraguay	Ogilvy, Publicis, JWT, Biederman, Sistema siete, Mass, Estudio Uno.
Peru	Garwich Perú, DDB, Saatchi & Saatchi, Euro RSCG, Ogilvy, JWT, Young & Rubicam.
Puerto Rico	BBDO Puerto Rico, Saatchi & Saatchi, Euro RSCG, JWT, Young & Rubicam.
Spain	McCann Erikson, Young & Rubiam, DDB, FCB Tapsa, Bassat & Ogilvy, Tiempo BBDO, Euro RSCG, Grey & Trace, Delvico Red Cell, Contrapunto, Publicis, JWT, Lowe, SCPF, Shackleton, TBWA, Vitruvio Leo Burnett.
Uruguay	DDB, Euro RSCG, Ogilvy, Publicis, JWT, Young & Rubicam.
Venezuela	BBDO Venezuela, DDB, Saatchi & Saatchi, Euro RSCG, Leo Burnett, Ogilvy, Young & Rubicam.

Source: Compiled by the authors from websites of advertising agencies and associations of advertising agencies in Latin America

Media Agencies

Media agencies did not have an easy entrance into the Latin American market. Despite having consolidated as specialized businesses in the advertising sector since the end of the 1990s, they have not yet won the advertisers' hearts. In many cases, their profits have diminished since all types of rates are offered in the market. This makes it necessary to choose between being more competitive or more profitable. In many cases, advertisers ignore the service they render, and consider them to be more a cost than an investment. For them, media agencies are but another intermediary in the market, and in this sense, an agent that adds to the cost of the advertising investment. Since price is a key business factor, customers need to be convinced of the service offered, so that advertisers stop seeing media agencies as a cost.

Some of the services offered include research, surveys on audiences and preferences regarding media content, and the effectiveness of advertising tools. Based on a thorough knowledge of the media market, theme specialization and recognized experience in the sector, they organize themselves in areas oriented at the local market, the analysis of media by audience segments and commercial planning. In general, they are structured in areas of sales, technological support and information systems. Table 19.14 shows a list of media agencies with operations in Iberian America. These compete against other local media agencies, among them commercial agencies

Table 19.14 Media Agencies in Spanish-Speaking Countries, 2008

Argentina	Mindshare, OMD, Universal McCann, Brand Connection, Carat, Gustavo Quiroga, Ignis Argentina, Initiative, Starcom, Havas Arena, Mediaedge:cia, Zenith Optimedia.
Bolivia	OMD.
Chile	Mindshare, OMD, Mediawise, Starcom, Universal McCann, Havas Arena, Initiative, Mediaedge:cia, Zenith Optimedia.
Colombia	OMD, Universal McCann, Starcom, Mindshare, Mediaedge:cia, Initiative Group, MPG, Arena Communications, Beat, Mediawise, Massive, Jua Publicitaria, United, Havas Arena, Carat, Initiative, Zenith Optimedia.
Costa Rica	OMD, Mediawise, Starcom, Universal McCann, Mediaedge:cia.
Dominican Republic	OMD, Initiative, Mediaedge:cia.
Ecuador	Mindshare, OMD, Universal McCann, Initiative, Mediaedge:cia, Zenith Optimedia.
El Salvador	OMD, Mediawise, Starcom, Initiative, Mediaedge:cia.
Guatemala	Starcom, Mediaedge:cia.
Honduras	OMD, Starcom.
Mexico	Mindshare, OMD, Mediawise, Starcom, Universal McCann, Havas Arena, Carat, Initiative, Mediaedge:cia, Zenith Optimedia Media Planning, Universal Media Mediacom y Zenith Media.
Nicaragua	OMD, Starcom.
Panama	OMD, Universal McCann, Mediaedge:cia, Zenith Optimedia.
Paraguay	OMD.
Peru	Mindshare, OMD, Starcom, Universal McCann, Carat, Initiative, Mediaedge:cia, Zenith Optimedia.
Puerto Rico	OMD, Universal McCann, Initiative.
Spain	Havas Arena, Zenith Optimedia, Carat España, Initiative, Mediaedge:cia, MPG Direct, OMD. España, Starcom Worldwide, Veritas, Magna Global.
Uruguay	Mindshare, OMD, Starcom, Carat, Initiative, Zenith Optimedia.
Venezuela	Mindshare, OMD, Starcom, Universal McCann, Initiative, Zenith Optimedia.

Source: Compiled by the authors from websites of advertising agencies and associations of advertising agencies in Latin America

created by the media themselves, as a way of defending their interests in the advertising market, and participating in the profits generated by commissions for the presence of advertising spots. In some countries, media owners have been the main opponents to the proliferation of media agencies.

Advertisers

The leading advertisers in Latin America are the companies which offer personal hygiene items, food and drink, as well as telecommunications and financial services. In Argentina the top advertisers are Danone and Unilever, as well as by national supermarket brands, including Coto, Jumbo, Disco, Vea, Carrefour and Norte. Other key advertisers include Johnson & Johnson, Quilmes, Coca-Cola and Pepsi. Other advertisers come from the financial, insurance, trade, tourism, services and tobacco sectors (Ibope, 2008).

The Colombian market features significant national companies, as well as multinational companies. Among the leaders are Comcel, Bancolombia, Unilever Andina, Postobón, Procter & Gamble, Bavaria, Colgate-Palmolive, Colombia Móvil, Telefónica Movistar, Coca Cola, Almacenes Éxito, Alpina and Sofasa. In Chile the leading advertisers are Unilever, Falabella (the most popular department stores in the country), Procter & Gamble, Almacenes París and Nestlé. In Mexico, the top advertisers are led by Pepsi, Liverpool, Colgate-Palmolive, Genomma Labs, Grupo Bimbo, General Motors, Procter & Gamble, Banorte and Grupo Carsa's companies, and Telmex.

Personal care products, drinks and foods, and telecommunications services are the main advertisers in Venezuela. In this country, the largest advertisers are Procter & Gamble, Unilever, Nestlé, Cantv, Movilnet, Movistar, Coca-Cola and Pepsi. In Spain the leading advertisers include Telefónica, Procter & Gamble, L'Oréal, El Corte Inglés, Volkswagen-Audi, Vodafone, Renault, ING Direct, France-Telecom España and Danone.

In each of these countries, advertisers organize themselves in associations aimed at carrying out studies and research activities about the media with the purpose of facilitating the decision-making process in regard to optimizing advertising investments. Advertisers also want to represent the interests of the sector, as well as the promotion, development and sponsorship of events tending to increase and strengthen the prestige of the advertising industry.

Services for the Advertising Sector

In addition to the advertising agencies, the media agencies and the advertisers, there are some organizations associated with the advertising market. These include those in charge of researching and collecting data related to advertising, the regulatory bodies, and the associations of advertising agencies, which, in general, are in charge of generating self-regulatory mechanisms.

Audience research and measurement

The Instituto Brasileño de Opinión Pública y Estadística (Ibope: Brazilian Institute of Public Opinion and Statistics) has an important presence in Latin America. A multinational company specialized in media, market and opinion media, it acts through media committees and purchasers distributed in the countries where it performs operations, among them Argentina, Bolivia, Brazil, Chile, Colombia, Costa Rica, Ecuador, Guatemala, Mexico, Panama, Paraguay, Peru, Uruguay and Venezuela (Ibope, 2008).

Ibope's services are financed by the media, the media agencies and advertising agencies. The information obtained by the studies has a restricted circulation, and is shared only with those who pay for it. Television audience measurement is made through mechanisms such as the People Meter, which is installed on a certain number of receivers located in different cities of each country. The People Meter records, minute by minute, the viewers' habits, among them the time television sets remain on or off, and the most watched programs. The data are sent to Ibope's regional reception centers, where the information is analyzed and issues a report about the previous day's television audience. This technology is also used by companies such as Nielsen and AGB.

Ibope's study is, in many cases, the only support for the countries to obtain official statistics about the daily preferences regarding television. This can be a difficult task. In May 2008 Colombia was left without official data, since the private channels who broadcast openly withdrew from the group of companies that hires Ibope's services. The conflict arose when this organization introduced television for subscribers in the sample used for audience measurement. This television mode is significant in countries such as Argentina and Colombia, with a penetration of 75 and 65 percent, respectively (Lamac, 2008). This automatically reduces the rating of free television and affects its appeal for advertisers.

Ibope conducts the Target Group Index (TGI) with different companies in each country. It has also introduced the WebLatam service, which consists of a detailed study about the use of Internet in Argentina, Brazil, Chile, Colombia and Mexico, countries which represent 91 percent of the GDP and 87 percent of the total population of Latin America. The measurement services, supported by the people meter technology, are also rendered by AGB in the Dominican Republic, Mexico and Venezuela (Ibope, 2008).

The Estudio General de Medios (EGM: General Media Study) is another important reference instrument for audience measurement. The difference in the activities performed by Ibope lies in the methodology it uses and the time periods it covers. In Colombia the EGM is performed by the Asociación Colombiana de Investigación de Medios (ACIM: Colombian Association of Media Research), a non-profit organization whose purpose is carrying out audience research, measurement and control activities, and studying the behavior of the different media. Its services are hired by media agencies and centrals, advertisers and media.

The Interactive Advertising Bureau (IAB) is another organization offering specialized services. This association, founded by the United States in 1996, is currently present in thirty countries, among them Mexico, Puerto Rico, Colombia, Peru, Argentina, Chile and Spain. It performs specific studies and analysis for interactive media. Agencies, media agencies and publishers of Internet sites take part in this organization. Members receive information about trends in the use of these media and access to publications and reports.

In Mexico there is a wide range of market research, public opinion surveys and audience data. These entities are grouped by the Agencias de Investigación de Mercados y Opinión Pública (AMAI: Agencies of Market and Public Opinion Research). Ibope, Nielsen and Arbitron, among others, belong to the group.

In Spain, the OJD is a private association of media, agencies and advertisers. It obtains and facilitates information referred to the distribution and dissemination of periodicals. It operates on the basis of information delivered by the companies themselves, which supply OJD with data on the number of issues, subscriptions, total sales and distribution in a given period. Once the data are verified, OJD authorizes its dissemination. INFOADEX, an organization which offers qualitative and quantitative research services regarding media, agency, publishing group, and advertiser rankings, analyzes the investment in advertising and the media content.

The Asociación para la Investigacion de Medios de Comunicacion (AIMC: Association for the Investigation of Communication Media) produces a General Media Study (EGM). This institution was founded by advertisers, advertising agencies and media centrals. Its purpose is to perform audience and other studies related to the media structure and their supports, so as to make comparisons, analyze trends and collect significant data for media planning. Spanish media finance 75 percent of the AIMC's work; the remaining 25 percent comes from subscriptions of members of the association. Some Spanish-speaking countries lack independent organizations able to verify the circulation of printed media or audience ratings.

Associations of advertising agencies
In all of Latin America and Spain there are associations or federations of advertising agencies. One of the main roles they play consists of developing ethical and self-regulation codes for the sector. They also produce and disseminate reports, issue publications such as *El libro de oro de la publicidad* (The golden book of advertising) and negotiate programs before public or private bodies, to the benefit of the advertising industry in each country.

There are also federations which group together the different agents of commercial communications. In Mexico the Asociación de Agencias de Medios (AAM: Association of Media Agencies), the Asociación Mexicana de Agencias de Publicidad (AMAP: Mexican Association of Advertising Agencies), the Asociación Mexicana de Agencias de Promociones (AMAPRO: Mexican Association of Promotion Agencies), the Interactive Advertising Bureau, Mexico Chapter, the Asociación Mexicana de Internet (Mexican Internet Association) and the Asociación Mexicana de Mercadotecnia (Mexican Association of Technical Market) are part of the Confederación de la Industria de la Comunicación Mercadotécnica (CICOM: Confederation of the Industry of Technical Market Communications).

There are also associations per type of media. An example is Andiarios in Colombia, an institution consisting of the main daily print media in the country, and organizations such as Lamac, which is in charge of the sale of advertising spots for international television channels. Its headquarters are in Mexico and Colombia, and some television subscription channels are members, among them Fox for Latin America, Discovery channels (Home and Health, Kids, Travel and Living), ESPN, National Geographic, CNN (in Spanish and International) Warner Channel, Cartoon Network, TNT, Sony Entertainment and MGM.

Conclusions

This chapter has presented an overview of the advertising sector in the Spanish-speaking countries. The topic was approached both from a macroeconomic and a micro-organizational point of view, by analyzing the main entities related to the advertising sector.

The study shows, in general terms, that the advertising sector has not yet consolidated within the national economies in the Spanish-speaking countries. It is at the beginning of its development stage and, as a consequence, is heavily dependent upon economic circumstances.There are other common patterns, such as the decline of newspaper advertising. In the Latin American economies there is a clear preference for television as an advertising media, and so advertisers rely heavily on this medium. In general, audiovisual media are preferred to print media, due to cultural circumstances and to the idiosyncrasy of these countries.

The differences existing between Spanish-speaking and non-Spanish-speaking countries at the macroeconomic level found in the chapter countries are also worth mentioning. For example, investment in advertising is much lower in Spanish-speaking countries. Moreover, it was found that in each country the advertising industry has its own characteristics.

As a limitation of our analysis it must be said that a deeper knowledge of the situation of the advertising industry in Spanish-speaking countries requires a greater availability of homogeneous data in order to make more precise comparisons. In this sense we must mention the lack of data on investment in non-conventional media. Although in the majority of these countries their importance probably is still moving at low levels, it is expected that in the future these media reach the degree of advertising spending they have achieved in more developed countries.

Another aspect where more data and research are needed has to do with people's attitudes towards advertising. Whereas in this chapter we have offered an overview of advertising from the macro, sector and firm level, in the future special efforts should be devoted to analyze how individuals in Spanish-speaking countries think, believe and act in relation to advertising. Among these aspects that have been studied for other countries, we could mention preference towards advertising, valuation of its informational content, entertainment role, advertising avoidance behaviour, etc. Studies should focus on the interrelationships between these variables and on the existence of differences in them among countries. The results of this line of research would be especially useful for advertising companies. As we have reported in this chapter, many advertising agencies launch the same campaigns in many Spanish-speaking countries for cost-savings reasons, supposing that attitudes towards advertising and, therefore, the effects of their actions, are the same. A rigorous analysis of this question would confirm the validity of this practice or would stress the need of a particular approach involving country segmentation.

References

Ashley, R., Granger, C. W. J. & Schmalensee, R. (1980). Advertising and aggregate consumption: An analysis of causality. *Econometrica, 48*(5), 1167–1980.

Baghestani, H. (1991). Cointegration analysis of the advertising–sales relationship. *Journal of industrial economics, 39*(6), 671–681.

Dhalla, N. K. (1980). Advertising as an anti recession tool. *Harvard Business Review, 58*(1), 158–165.

Galbraith, J. K. (1967). *The new industrial state.* Boston, MA: Houghton Mifflin.

Grupo Consultores. (2004). *Estudio de agencias. Research report.* Madrid: Grupo Consultores.

Howard, N. (1980). Advertising versus recession. *Duns Review, 115*(4), 126–129.

Ibope. (2008). Retrieved August 10, 2008, from www.ibope.com.

Jacobson, R. & Nicosia, F. M. (1981). Advertising and public-policy: The macroeconomic effects of advertising. *Journal of Marketing Research, 18*(1), 29–38.

Lamac. (2008). Retrieved August 16, 2008, from www.lamac.org.

Picard, R. G. (2001). Effects of recessions on advertising expenditures: An exploratory study of economic downturns in nine developed nations. *Journal of media economics, 14*(1), 1–21.

Sturgess, B. T. & Wilson, N. (1984). Advertising expenditure and aggregate consumption in Britain and West Germany: An analysis of causality. *Managerial and decision economics, 5*(4), 219–227.

World Advertising Trends, several years, WARC.

World Bank from www.worldbank.org/data.

20
Hispanic Advertising, Marketing and New Media

Lauren Boyle
Grupo Exito, Dallas, TX, USA

Introduction

Since the late 1990s, the Hispanic population in the United States has grown exponentially. Hispanics are now the largest minority group in the United States.[1] Population estimates from the US Census Bureau state that there are more than 45 million US Hispanics representing approximately 15 percent of the total US population; thus one out of seven persons living in the United States is Hispanic. In addition to their sheer number, Hispanics have a spending power of almost $750 billion annually (Advertising Age, 2007; HispanicAd, 2008).

This rapidly growing segment of the consumer population has been captivating corporate America's attention. As a result, there is a high demand for Spanish language media outlets to reach US Hispanics. Spanish language media are now an integral part of the general market media mix as advertisers look toward this lucrative market.

Despite the decline of overall ad spending in 2007 and 2008 due to economic concerns, Hispanics are still spending money on big-ticket items such as new vehicles, flat-screen high-definition televisions HDTVs), digital cameras, iPods, laptops and gaming units (Sullivan, 2008). Hispanic advertising spending is still on the rise as a result. In November 2007, Nielsen posted on HispanicAd.com a study demonstrating total advertising spending for the first half of 2007 was up 2.3 percent over the same period in 2006. The principal drivers were Internet, Spanish language television and national magazine spending (HispanicAd, 2007e). Even though overall US advertising spending was flat in 2007, Spanish language television was up 7.7 percent demonstrating the Hispanic market is still strong and on the upswing (PR Newswire, 2008).

The 500 largest print and television advertisers' Hispanic expenditures surpassed $5 billion in 2006—an increase of 42 percent since 2003 (Advertising Age, 2007). There is no doubt that as this population increases, so does the list of key brands that want a piece of the pie and more media outlets to fulfill their marketing needs.

Research by both Advertising Age and Nielsen reveals the largest advertiser categories targeting the Hispanic market are automotive, retail and wireless telephone services (Advertising Age, 2008; Nielsen, 2007).

Hispanics consume all facets of media in their daily lives and the growing Hispanic population makes it a more complex media mix as options continue to grow as do the number of Hispanic

Internet users. The majority of growth in Hispanic media is in online offerings, events and promotions (Faura, 2006; HispanicAd, 2007d).

This chapter highlights Spanish language advertising, Hispanic Internet growth, user trends, and new media utilized to reach this ever-growing market segment.

Hispanic Advertising

The basic principles that apply in communicating with average market consumers generally work just as well when dealing within a specific Hispanic market. The cultural approach that needs to be taken, however, is notably different.

Demographic characteristics provide only a foundational knowledge of the US Hispanic market. In order to succeed in reaching this population, one must go deeper than surface demographics, taking into consideration factors such as language, country of origin, culture, level of assimilation, traditions and socioeconomic characteristics. All of these combined factors must be understood in order to target effectively in this very complex market. Below is a sample of what a basic Brand Brief and Advertising Brief would generally look like (Kreativa Solutions, 2008):

Brand Brief

Brand: defined as "The name of the brand being marketed"
Brand History: defined as "How the brand got started and where it is today"
Brand Values: defined as "The basic pillars of the brand essence"
Brand Positioning: defined as "The single position the product owns in the mind of the Hispanic consumer"
Marketing Objectives: defined as "What the client wants the brand to achieve in the Hispanic marketplace"
Marketing Strategy: defined as "The clever plan to achieve the Marketing Objective that appeals to the Hispanic consumer"
Source of Business: defined as "Where the sales will come from."

Advertising Brief

Targeted Consumer: defined as "Whom we must convince" (such as language preference, age group, level of assimilation and lifestyle)
Consumer Benefit: defined as "What we can promise the Hispanic consumer that they need and want"
Consumer Insight: defined as "What single understanding we have about the Hispanic consumer's behavior and needs that will make them receptive to the promise"
Reason to Believe: defined as "The single most compelling reason for the Hispanic consumer to believe the promise"
Media Outlets: defined as "What media outlets are available to reach this particular consumer."

All of the points above must be acknowledged in order to effectively make an evaluation as to how to reach this unique consumer base.

As Hispanic advertising and media continue to outperform their general market counterparts, alongside the rising costs of traditional media advertising, marketers and advertisers are looking to more alternatives to reach the Hispanic consumer. According to the Advertising Age (2007) *Hispanic fact pack*, Hispanics are heavy consumers of radio, television and online properties.

In addition to evolving online opportunities, integrated media and promotional initiatives are increasing to target this market. Companies and advertisers are looking for innovative ways to reach this consumer in a more personal and engaging way.

Industry professionals dealing with the Hispanic market agree that all marketing, media and promotional efforts must be culturally relevant and the general message must connect with the consumer. Complete integration of the strategic platform is crucial to implementing successful advertising campaigns within the Hispanic Market (Advertising Age, 2007; HispanicAd, 2007d).

The Association of Hispanic Advertising Agencies (AHAA) is the leading national organization of companies that specialize in Hispanic marketing and advertising. The spring 2007 AHAA conference focused on three key themes: acculturation, technology and accountability. The underlying message of the conference was that advertising to US Hispanics has grown beyond placing commercials in traditional Spanish language media.

Advertising agencies were encouraged to explore new platforms, with heavy emphasis on adapting media plans to include new digital technologies (Internet, text messaging, out-of-home, etc.). Hispanic agencies at the conference were also encouraged to begin producing commercials in English, which could reward them with expanded projects from advertisers. In addition, account planning for Spanish is now working alongside its English counterpart with a goal of 360° marketing.

A great deal of discussion at the conference was directed towards the aspect of "inter-acculturation"—immigrant culture becoming more like host culture, as the host culture adapts to assimilate the immigrant culture. "American culture has a huge influence on Latins and how they act," said Cynthia McFarlane, Conill's managing director at the AHAA (2007) conference. "Conversely, Latins are having a huge influence on mainstream culture as well."

A case study presented by Conill New York shared the ideation and strategy implemented in the 2006 Toyota "Yaris" launch. Conill helped take the car from unknown to a 30 percent share of the entry-level subcompact automotive segment in the Hispanic market by targeting young Hispanics who view themselves as trendsetters leading the way in a new, multicultural world.

The Yaris launch partnered Telemundo, Univision, Mun2, SíTV and Batanga as the integrated campaign utilized online, TV and print, focused on English-language outlets that reflected Latino lifestyles such as SíTV and *Urban Latino* magazine. MundoYaris.com, the website Conill created where visitors could mix music and create personal ring tones, also included a Yaris Design Lab for making films, music and art, and a sweepstakes to win an in-home performance by the African-Latin band, Ozomatli (AHAA, 2007).

The 2008 AHAA conference, ClickAltDelete continued that theme focusing on technology and new media in the Hispanic market. Advertisers, agencies and traditional media were again encouraged to incorporate new media into their overall marketing campaigns and media awards were given out in categories such as Best Plan Using the Internet, won by the Chicago agency Tapestry for their work with Miller Light (AHAA, 2008).

Advertising agencies are encouraging the media to build greater partnerships through designing multimedia platforms and forming partnerships with other media properties. For many major household brands, Hispanics are a big business opportunity (Faura, 2006). Hispanics aged 18–34 are the largest piece of that pie representing approximately 12 million consumers, willing to try new products, and embrace new trends and technology (Advertising Age, 2007; Cancela, 2007). In 2008, Univision established an $80 million cross-platform agreement with Miami-based Zubi Advertising—a record-breaking deal between a Hispanic media agency and Hispanic television network (Consoli, 2008).

Hispanic Business in September 2007 released a new study conducted by AHAA and Simmons Market Research, which identifies this young, Hispanic profile, revealing that 68 percent of Hispanics aged 18–34 are Spanish-dominant or bilingual, speaking primarily Spanish at home (Hispanic Business, 2007). Additional findings in this study regarding 18–34-year-old Hispanics:

- They consume Spanish and English broadcast media in equal portions, with Spanish language television and radio outpacing English language television and radio.
- Young Hispanics are more likely to be impulsive shoppers and shop at more stores than their non-Hispanic counterparts.
- They are heavy readers of lifestyle, entertainment, automotive and sports magazines.
- They are more persuaded and loyal to brands which advertise in Spanish.
- They like to try new things as most have not developed brand loyalties.
- They are impulsive purchasers.
- They are trendy, frequently purchasing clothing, health and beauty products, food and beverages, electronics, entertainment and home furnishings.

Companies such as Coca-Cola, Pepsi, Nissan, Wal-Mart, McDonald's, Anheuser-Busch, Pennzoil and Frito Lay are all targeting this Hispanic youth segment and are receiving significant return on their investments (Hispanic Business, 2007).

Hispanic media in the United States is a hot topic among advertisers and general market media alike. In 2008, Radio Disney formed an alliance with Azteca America in Orlando for Hispanic outreach in that market (ExtraNews, 2008).

Spanish Language Internet and New Media

There is no question that Internet usage has changed the world as we know it, and now, any time anyone needs information, they look first to the Internet for a solution. Whether on cellular phones or another mobile device, the Internet is now at the user's fingertips.

There is no exception to the Internet proliferation within the US Hispanic population. Nielsen noted the US Hispanic online market is the fastest growing segment online. As the group's population increases, so too will the need for more target specific Internet services. It is imperative that strategies and tactics in US Hispanic media today should include website development and online marketing. For companies looking to reach more affluent US Hispanics, the online arena offers a cost-effective opportunity when compared to traditional radio and television advertising (Hispanic Business, 2007; Nielsen, 2007).

Some companies and advertisers have underestimated Hispanics' Internet usage, thus not offering Spanish language versions of their websites: this is a gross mistake (Earth Times, 2008). According to Advertising Age (2007), they have overlooked that approximately 65 percent of US Hispanics own a computer—a very high number for a group who, until recently, have been underserved online. With the growth in Hispanic Internet usage, online video advertising is growing at a rapid pace with increased brand awareness (Advertising Age, 2007). Clients are now utilizing Internet banners, blogs, social networking sites, text messaging and email marketing in tandem with their television, radio and print campaigns.

In fact, a report in the Advertising Age (2008) *Hispanic Fact Pack* detailed just how strong usage of new media by US Hispanics is. According to the report, 19.62 percent of Hispanics download music versus their general market counterparts at 17.08 percent; 11.3 percent listen to online radio versus 10.18 percent of non-Latinos; 7.3 percent visit chat rooms versus 4.14 percent; and 2.3

percent of Latinos blog versus 3.72 percent. These are strong indicators that Latinos are as tech savvy as non-Latinos (Advertising Age, 2008).

Spanish versus English Online Content

There have been many debates among industry professionals as to the importance of Spanish language offerings online. Some have argued that those US Hispanics who have access to a computer speak English, so why the need for in-language content?

The Search Engine Strategies Latino Conference and Expo in Miami in June, 2007, discussed Spanish versus English online content. Portada.com released some interesting research that Google shared with the expo on Internet content and the Hispanic market (Portada, 2007f):

- Spanish content must be unique and relevant.
- Spanish performs at a higher level than English.
- Spanish appears more authoritative.
- US Hispanics skew younger with smaller households and 49 percent speak Spanish fluently.
- Hispanics are more usage intensive with 25 percent more pages viewed daily and spend 20 percent more time online than the general market.
- Around 61 percent of US Hispanics own cell phones.

Spanish Language Online Content Growth

Many popular sites such as MySpace, YouTube, iTunes and Wikipedia offer Spanish language options to reach Hispanics, while Spanish language specific sites like Que Pasa, Telemundo, Batanga, PlanetaTV.com and VoyTV.com are holding their place among the top ten most visited sites by Hispanics (Advertising Age, 2008).

Based on population growth and buying power, US Hispanic specific content is still lacking, but advertisers and media groups are continually looking for new ways to reach this consumer and quickly, leaving a lot of room for growth for new online properties (Pew Internet, 2007). Market researchers have created four prime categories of Hispanic Internet usage: information, entertainment, financial transactions and communications.

ComScore Media Metrix, an industry leader in Internet measurement and ranking, ranked the top ten most visited web properties among Hispanic users; the top five were Yahoo! Sites, MSN Microsoft, Google, Time Warner and eBay (Advertising Age, 2007).

The year 2007 presented many new Hispanic-targeted website offerings, with a variety of content and services emerging to take advantage of this lucrative market; from new online initiatives from health-related social networking sites, banks and financial web portals, to larger more mainstream sites such as Best Buy, Dell, MySpace and BabyCenter. The launch in 2007 of ClickOcio.com, meaning "ClickLeisure" in English, provides US Hispanics with the first 100 percent Spanish language consumer website selling flights and Broadway theater tickets (Portada, 2007d).

BabyCenter, the largest global online resource for expectant and new parents, also launched BabyCenter en Español in 2007. In an interview on Hispanic PR Wire, Isidra Mencos, editor and chief of Baby Center en Español, said, "BabyCenter en Español was conceived to deliver relevant content in Spanish, geared specifically for Hispanic Moms who are online" (Hispanic PR Wire, 2007).

CosmeticSEO.com is another targeted site that launched in mid-2008 offering a site where plastic surgeons can market their services to Latinas (Emedia Wire, 2008). In July 2008,

MasterCard launched an integrated campaign by relaunching its MasterCardenespanol.com website, along with a television ad entitled "Luchador" (a Lucha Libre themed spot) and incorporation of its famous "Priceless" campaign (Webwire, 2008).

Internet TV is an important revenue driver in US Hispanic media. For Terra, one of the largest Spanish language online portal companies, Internet TV generated 17 percent of its online advertising revenues in 2006. Terra has more than 8 million unique visitors per month and offers a variety of services and resources (Portada, 2007c).

However, the influx of digital media has meant a detracting from radio, television and traditional print sources; the ability to be seen and heard is now a greater challenge. Spanish language television and radio stations are utilizing their websites to promote their events, programming, clients and contests.

Telemundo is trying to capitalize on the popularity of its *telenovelas* by repurposing its content on its website and creating discussion forums around the programming where viewers can exchange feedback, commentary, download clips and view excerpts from the shows. Additionally, Telemundo is introducing interactive ways for engaging viewers with its programming online. It invites people to send in videos interpreting some aspect of the popular hit *telenovela*, *Zorro*, through song, dance or other interpretive form and posting it on the website (Portada, 2007g; Shields, 2007).

In 2007, Univision launched a video portal on Univision.com, where users can access clips from TV shows, celebrity interviews, music videos and news clips. Univision is launching a social networking service in addition to a wireless video subscription service through its new mobile initiative, Univision Movil.

Univision has also created a web-only novela, co-produced with Unilever's Caress body-care brand following extensive Unilever research to tap into a growing young Hispanic female audience and consumer group (Portada, 2007h; Univision, 2007).

Hispanic Youth Online

Portada.com, a leading Spanish language Internet research and blog site, noted that Hispanic teens have an affinity toward cutting-edge technological features with the fastest emerging platform to reach them, mobile marketing. MTV network's Slivered Screen Research demonstrated that 63 percent of Hispanics in the United States own a media-capable cell phone (compared to the non-Hispanic percentage at 46 percent) and are 23 percent more likely to use them to watch video content and programming than the general population. Responding to such compelling data, MTV Tr3s launched a multi-carrier, bilingual mobile channel for Hispanic youth in March, 2007, with ringtones and video content from hot Latin artists (Hispanic Business, 2007).

Social Networking and Blogging

Social networking has become a wildly popular phenomenon, with Forrester Research indicating that social online networking among Hispanics tripled between 2005 and 2006. The report demonstrates that half of online Hispanics are involved in at least one out of five social Internet activities, including blogging, personal web pages and involvement on discussion boards. According to the study, MySpace ranks first with 31 percent of Hispanics visiting at least monthly (Advertising Age, 2007). A study in 2008 by Synovate supplemented this discussion as this study took it to a different level with gender. According to this study, males are twice as likely as females to engage in social networking (Earth Times, 2008).

Another interesting growth mechanism on the Internet is blogging. Scarborough Research reported that Austin, TX, Portland, OR, San Francisco, CA, and Seattle, WA, are the top markets for people to read or participate in blogging activities. According to Scarborough's findings, these cities are the leaders because they are youth driven and tech savvy. Interestingly, half of these markets are heavy Hispanic growth markets, so it is no surprise that new research is currently being conducted on Hispanics and blogging habits (HispanicAd, 2007a).

Hispanic Who Are Not Online

A study conducted by the Pew Hispanic Center indicates that a lack of access is the most prevalent reason for Hispanics not utilizing the Internet with 53 percent of the respondents claiming they do not have Internet access available. Interestingly, only 6 percent percent of the respondents claimed cost as a barrier. The study also indicated that about one-fifth claimed that they are simply not interested in accessing the Internet, leading industry professionals to believe that there is a great lack of relevant and compelling content to engage them (Pew Internet, 2007).

Utilizing New Media Opportunities

Complete integration of the strategic platform is crucial to implementing successful advertising campaigns within the Hispanic market. The key industry buzzword in 2007 was "integration" and in 2008, it was "technology" or "new media" (AHAA, 2008). Trade resources and the Internet are the best tools for discovering ways to market using new media. Industry trade publications and trade conferences are also used in looking for ways to expand technologies and marketing possibilities.

Convincing the client who is skeptical of new media is a challenge, and the best defense is research and empirical proof of effectiveness. For clients that have grown accustomed to traditional advertising over the years, research, success stories and innovative ideas are keys to persuading clients of the benefits of the new media. When clients see the numbers produced by Internet users, they are usually sold.

In reality, it is difficult to imagine a circumstance where new media would not be a viable or even key component of an advertising campaign. Ignoring new media is comparable to thinking that not everyone benefits from television advertising. Unless the core target demo is primarily over the age of 70, new media can always be a relevant tool. Another advantage is that new media campaigns can be tracked instantaneously with many tools available to track the number of hits and click-through rates to assess effectiveness.

Mobile Marketing

As the mobile phone is rapidly becoming the most effective tool in advertising due to its cost-effectiveness, companies are now learning this new technology and what it has to offer. There are a handful of companies that offer the technology necessary to deliver content and messaging via the mobile handset—regardless of carrier. This is very different than what Univision and Telemundo are offering with their mobile technology, because what they offer is setting a call to action (such as Text Casa to 12345) on their television station or website in order to do what they call an "opt in."

This method of having a consumer opt in (whereby they grant permission to contact them by virtue of their input) is one of the most valuable aspects of the entire mobile marketing concept.

They are allowing a company the ability to establish one-on-one relationships with them, or allowing a company to provide them information on demand, when they are most likely or most receptive to accept an offer or receive information.

The process of opt-in is what is necessary to drive the most into the mind of the customer, be it an agency or a brand, because it is what makes advertising finally a two-way process of communication, while at the same time providing measurable results rarely seen from most advertising campaigns. Independent mobile platform delivery companies are more flexible and can work with all types of traditional advertising, allowing advertisers to attach a call to action on whichever media they see fit. Below are five reasons why mobile marketing works:

- because text messaging is the fastest growing communications channel due to its portable mobility
- because it is opt-in or permission-based without the danger of spam
- because it has a viral element, when messages and content are forwarded to another handset
- because it is interactive and engaging to the consumer
- because it allows you to create a database and is measurable.

The United States is the global leader in mobile Internet adoption with 40 million US mobile users; 26 percent of them view ads via their handset (Nielsen Mobile, 2008). Nielsen data indicate that Hispanics over-index on mobile phone usage in terms of downloading applications, accessing news and information, and watching video.

From January to August 2007, mobile video usage increased 36 percent, representing 6.8 million viewers in the United States (M:Metrics, 2007). A study on the Internet and American Life by the Pew Foundation found that Hispanics outpace both Anglos and African Americans in the use of cell phone applications (Pew Internet, 2008).

The Response to New Media Approaches

Many clients openly embrace new media, while others assume that Hispanics do not use computers, but the new media marketing results are quantitatively excellent. According to Portada.com, Hispanic teens have an affinity for cutting-edge technological features and the fastest-emerging platform to reach them is via mobile marketing.

In order to succeed with online marketing efforts, though, developing an integrated Hispanic online marketing program that delivers the customer value and achieves business objectives is imperative. The goals of the traditional marketing campaign should not be abandoned simply because of changes in technology and advertising media.

Face-to-Face Promotions

With the rising costs of traditional advertising and "clutter" within the marketplace, marketers and advertisers look for a fresh and often lower cost alternative to reach the Hispanic consumer in addition to new media. Event marketing and promotions can be an inexpensive way to market a product or service to the Hispanic market: it really takes a lot of planning to create a cost-effective way of reaching a consumer with direct person-to-person contact.

What may be saved in production and media expenditures is lost in site fees, staffing and management of the project. Site fees for an event in 2008 can range anywhere from $1,000 for a 10ft × 10ft booth space in a small event in Boise, ID, to upwards of $100,000 for major events and title sponsorships in Los Angeles. Title sponsorships generally come with large pavilion space, signage and media support. Grass-roots promotions and events are very labor intensive and staffing costs can quickly escalate; however, an efficiently planned, timed and executed event can be quite cost-effective. There are a few companies in Hispanic media that offer this niche service, but there is scope for many more.

Promotional efforts can pay off well in the long run—better than traditional media when correctly executed. A media impression only lasts so long and then it is forgotten, but a personal connection with a brand, through grass-roots promotional efforts, can last forever. Industry leaders forecast a large growth in promotional efforts pertaining to the Hispanic market over the next several years.

The most important part of a promotional campaign is the promotional strategy in targeting the Hispanic consumer. An analysis of a product's performance takes into account both surface indications and underlying problems facing the brand. Below are essential considerations in planning a good promotional strategy:

1. *Customer Attitudes and Buying Behavior*: determine who your customers are demo-graphically and psychographically, personal characteristics, age group, level of assimilation, income, etc.
2. *Brand Strategy*: consider the product's level of dominance in its category. How will a sales promotion factor into the performance? What are the strengths and time period before returns are realized?
3. *Competitive Strategy*: evaluate past performance of the brand and its competitors as well as determine what activities, levels of spending and time periods produced the best results.
4. *Trade Environment*: what are the distributors' attitudes toward the brand and its competitors? If the trade environment is lacking, so will the promotional efforts.

Many brands and advertisers use sales promotions in order to move the sales needle. The typical sales promotion has an offer of some type, such as a buy one get one free, or gift with purchase. The three basic elements of a sales promotion are:

1. The offer.
2. The media to communicate the offer.
3. The creative "hook"; the message or theme that moves the consumer toward the desired response—the purchase.

Markers must consider the compatibility with the brand's objectives and budget parameters. Basic promotional tactics that are used are as follows:

1. *Coupons*: these short-term price incentives persuade consumers to purchase a particular product or service. Not only do they save the consumer money, but also they are effective ways of introducing new products to the public. Coupons stimulate trial and conversion, retain current consumers and serve as a sales tactic.
2. *Sweepstakes*: sweepstakes are promotions wherein winners are determined by a random drawing in a chance event where the participants exercise no control. Sweeps generate awareness and involvement with a brand. The most cost-effective sweepstakes prize is travel, which has a substantially higher perceived value than its cost.

3. *Sampling*: sampling allows the consumer to decide whether or not a product satisfies a need. If the results are favorable, there are often product inventories available for purchase. In-store sampling is key for fast-moving consumer goods (FMCG) brands as the product is at the point of trial.

From events to sales, promotions are key in driving a consumer to purchase.

Conclusion

In summary, the Hispanic market has become increasingly global in scope and consumers are drawing information from more media outlets than ever. We have seen the influx of digital media and general market initiatives detracting from Spanish language radio, television and print. Combined with English language agency roles, the ability to be seen and heard is a greater challenge. Corporations looking to reach these consumers need to have messages that are not only in English, but also in Spanish and are culturally relevant in order to penetrate this complex audience. Many brands are using their Hispanic campaigns to cast a wider net in the general market, creating a multicultural message that is effective and cross-cultural.

While many are jumping on to the Hispanic bandwagon, there is still tremendous growth opportunity for promotions and new media such as online, mobile and integrated advertising. Companies are utilizing Internet and mobile advertising almost as often as they use radio, and usually in tandem with radio, television, print, email marketing, and blogging.

The marketplace has diversified as television and radio options continue to grow and marketers are seeking new and innovative avenues to reach US Hispanics. As lives become more hectic and people spend less time in front of the television and more time online using Internet and mobile devices, marketers will continue to move toward a digital, mobile and integrated advertising approach.

Note

1   In this chapter the term Hispanics is used to represent the Spanish-speaking audience in the United States, but the information also applies to Latinos as well.

References

Advertising Age. (2007). *Hispanic fact pack: Use of technology*. Retrieved July 23, 2007, from www.adage.com/images/random/hispfactpack07.pdf.

Advertising Age. (2008). *Hispanic fact pack: Digital media usage*. Retrieved July 25, 2008, from www.adage.com/images/random/hispfactpack08.pdf.

Association of Hispanic Advertising Agencies (AHAA). (2007, April 25–27). The Mutant Latino Conspiracy Conference; Chicago, IL.

Association of Hispanic Advertising Agencies. (2008, April 16–18). ClickAltDelete Conference. San Antonio, TX.

Cancela, J. (2007). *The power of business en Español*. New York: HarperCollins.

Consoli, J. (2008, June 24). *Univision cuts huge cross-platform deal*. Retrieved June 25, 2008, from www.hollywoodreporter.com/hr/content_display/news/e3i39a618183fe30fd5aa736f4.

Earth Times. (2008, June 2). *Synovate study compares online behavior of connected Hispanics, African Americans and general market consumers*. Retrieved June 3, 2008, from www.earthtimes.org/articles/show/synovate-study-compares-online-behavior,415749.

Emedia Wire. (2008, June 3). *Plastic surgery marketing services for physicians unveiled by Cosmeticseo.com*. Retrieved June 3, 2008, from www.emediawire.com/releases/plastic-surgery-marketing/marketing-kit/prweb988754.

ExtraNews. (2008, June 24). *Azteca America central Florida and Radio Disney form a partnership in Orlando*. Retrieved June 25, 2008, from www.extranews.net/news_pr.php?nid=11808.

Faura, J. (2006). *Hispanic marketing grows up*. New York: Paramount Market.

HispanicAd. (2007a, October 31). *Austin, Portland, San Francisco and Seattle are the top blogging markets.* Retrieved November 1, 2007, from www.hispanicad.com/cgi-bin/news/newsarticle.cgi?article_id=23018.

HispanicAd. (2007b, November 15). *Best Buy offers new bilingual online and in-store presentation.* Retrieved November 19, 2007, from www.hispanicad.com/cgi-bin/news/newsarticle.cgi?article_id=23110&search_string=advertising&criteria=Any.

HispanicAd. (2007c, October 18). *Coors Brewing Company unveils advertising campaign celebrating Hispanic community leaders.* Retrieved November 19, 2007, from www.hispanicad.com/cgi-bin/news/newsarticle.cgi?article_id=22919&search_string=advertising&criteria=Any.

HispanicAd. (2007d, November 15). *My (early) predictions for 2008.* Retrieved November 19, 2007, from www.hispanicad.com/cgibin/news/newsarticle.cgi?article_id=23096&search_string=advertising&criteria=Any.

HispanicAd. (2007e, September 11). *U.S. Advertising expenditures decreased 0.3 percent in first half of 2007.* Retrieved November 19, 2007, from www.hispanicad.com/cgi-bin/news/newsarticle.cgi?article_id=22684&search_string=advertising&criteria=Any.

HispanicAd. (2007f, November 19). *Word-of-mouth marketing spending to break $1B in 2007.* Retrieved November 19, 2007, from www.hispanicad.com/cgi-bin/news/newsarticle.cgi?article_id=23129&search_string=advertising&criteria=Any.

Hispanic.Ad. (2008, May 1). *U.S. Hispanic population surpasses 45 million . . . Ajua!* Retrieved May 1, 2008, from www.hispanicad.com/cgi-bin/news/newsarticle.cgi?article_id=24257.

Hispanic Business. (2007, September 12). *New insight on advertising's holy grail: Young Hispanics.* Retrieved November 26, 2007, from www.hispanicbusiness.com/news/newsbyid.asp?id=12515.

Hispanic PR Wire. (2007, September 27). *BabyCenter gives birth to a new Spanish language website.* BabyCenter(R) en Español. Retrieved October 20, 2007, from www.hispanicprwire.com/news.php?l=in&id=9611&cha=8.

Kreativa Solutions. (2008, September 15). *Brand and advertising briefs.* Dallas, TX: Kreativa Solutions Llc.

M:Metrics. (2007, August). *US mobile video usage.* Retrieved September 21, 2008, from www.marketingcharts.com/television/us-mobile-video-audience-usage-expanding-rapidly-2186/m-metrics-mobile-video-usage-us-august-2007jpg/.

Nielsen. (2007, November 6). *Spanish language ad spending remains strong, Nielsen reports.* Retrieved November 6, 2007, from www.nielsen.com/media/2007/pr_071106.html.

Nielsen Mobile. (2008, July). *Critical mass: The wordwide state of the mobile web.* Retrieved September 20, 2008, from www.nielsenmobile.com/documents/CriticalMass.pdf.

Pew Internet. (2007, March 14). *Latinos online.* Retrieved November 1, 2007, from www.pewinternet.org/pdfs/Latinos_Online_March_14_2007.pdf.

Pew Internet. (2008, March). *Mobile access to data and information.* Retrieved September 25, 2008, from www.pewinternet.org/PPF/r/244/report_display.asp.

Portada. (2007a, June 18). *Access, language still barriers to Hispanic Internet usage.* Retrieved October 16, 2007, from www.portadaonline.com/productdetails.aspx?productID=2366.

Portada. (2007b, April 11). *Content preferences of Hispanic teens.* Retrieved October 17, 2007, from www.portada-online.com/productdetails.aspx?productID=2258.

Portada. (2007c, May 21). *Hispanic Internet TV to grow substantially in '07.* Retrieved October 16, 2007, from www.portada-online.com/productdetails.aspx?productID=2309.

Portada. (2007d, October 9). *New web launches.* Retrieved October 17, 2007, from www.portada-online.com/productdetails.aspx?productID=2479.

Portada. (2007e, September 4). *Social networking among Hispanics tripled between 2005 and 2006.* Retrieved October 17, 2007, from www.portada-online.com/productdetails.aspx?productID=2446.

Portada. (2007f, June 25). *Spanish vs. English content, searching in Spanish, mobile search.* (Conference Review: SES Latino). Retrieved October 16, 2007, from www.portada-online.com/productdetails.aspx?productID=2372.

Portada. (2007g, March 14) *Telemundo repurposes broadcast content online.* Retrieved October 16, 2007, from www.portada-online.com/productdetails.aspx?productID=2219.

Portada. (2007h, June 18). *Univision launches video portal.* Retrieved October 16, 2007, from www.portada-online.com/productdetails.aspx?productID=2367.

PR Newswire. (2008, June 16). *U.S. advertising spending is flat in first quarter 2008, Nielsen Reports.* Retrieved June 16, 2008, from www.prnewswire.com/cgi-bin/stories.pl?ACCT=104&story=/www/story/06-16-2008.

Shields, M. (2007, November 5). *Telemundo to offer full shows on Yahoo!* Retrieved November 5, 2007, from www.mediaweek.com/mw/news/interactive/article_display.jsp?vnu_content_id=1003668189.

Sullivan, L. (2008, June 9). *Despite downturn, Hispanics still buying big ticket items.* Retrieved June 9, 2008, from http://publications.mediapost.com/index.cfm?fuseaction=Articles.showArticleHomePage.

Univision. (2007). *Wins big at Promax/BDA Latin America.* Retrieved October 15, 2007, from www.univision.net/corp/en/pr/Los_Angeles_08012007-3.html.

Webwire. (2008, July 8). *MasterCard launches new U.S. Hispanic marketing campaign.* Retrieved July 8, 2008 from www.webwire.com/ViewPressRel.asp?aId=69508.

21

The Potential of Book Publishing in Iberian American and African Countries
The Portuguese Perspective

Paulo Faustino
Portuguese Catholic University, Lisbon, Portugal

Introduction

This chapter explores the relationship of the Portugese language to Spanish language media, with a focus on book publishing. Portugal and Spain make up what we know as the Iberian Peninsula. Both countries throughout their histories spread their culture and influence to other regions of the world: Spain to Latin America, and Portugal to Brazil and the African region. Except for Brazil, all countries in Latin America speak Spanish. Some African countries that speak Portuguese are not part of this discussion, namely Mozambique, Angola, Guinea-Bissau, Cape Verde, São Tomé, Príncipe and East Timor. This way, in order to define the concept of a regional market with linguistic affinity with Portugal and Spain, one should consider the Iberian American and African Region (IAAR—a term conceived by the author) market. This chapter identifies issues observed in the media and cultural industries—mainly book publishing—in Portugal and Spain, and analyzes commercial relations between Iberian book publishers, as well as larger extensions to Hispanic and Lusophone (countries and regions that use Portuguese) communities.

The Research

Five initial questions were defined for the research:

1. In what way do capital-sharing relationships exist between companies operating in the Portuguese and Spanish markets?
2. What are the main market issues and corporate management practices observed in the media content industry in the Iberian Peninsula?
3. In what way does geographical and cultural proximity influence the publishing strategies of the Iberian American market?
4. What is the importance of the Spanish and Portuguese languages as a content market in the Iberian Peninsula?
5. How are Iberian companies facing the globalization phenomenon and sustaining growth strategies?

Subsequently, in order to answer these research questions, it is assumed that one is facing an activity sector whose strategic mission—economically and culturally—is the production and sale of products and services susceptible of creating and/or molding opinions, tastes, intuitions, values and behavioral patterns. The media and creative industries (see Florida, 2002) comprise a large group of segments, companies and agents, where there is a unique crossing. Some are committed to economical results and others are more focused on the ability for intellectual creation. Therefore, by studying this industry one acknowledges two different domains: culture and industry; being that culture can be perceived as inherent to what the human being produces as a symbol of his existence. This activity is an integral part of a production, distribution and marketing system that delivers these cultural products to the consumer (Lampel, Shamsie & Lant, 2006). One of the more common ways to analyze this industry is through the distinction between printed products (newspapers, magazines and books) and electronic products (television, movies, radio, music, games, Internet and mobile-phone equipment). One can even consider another approach, based on separating entertainment and leisure products and services (movies, music, games) from those concerning information and knowledge (such as newspapers, books, magazines and documentaries). However, all these classifications are threatened by technology and financial means and supports.

Although this study's range is more focused on the classic media industry section (radio, television, press and printed books) that produces knowledge and entertainment through the written word, there are several common elements that integrate the media's activity. According to Aris and Bughin (2005), the great majority of media businesses and entertainment, including books, face very similar challenges, namely:

> i) Manage products and services whose majority has a short lifetime, mainly most *best-sellers*; ii) Surpass the volatility inherent to the products' life cycles, which are becoming shorter; iii) Answer the complexity of a market set on three pillars: end consumers, authors and advertisers; iv) Deal with multiple local markets, instead of an actual international market; v) Reach balance between the economical objectives and commitments and the cultural and social ones.
>
> (Aris & Bughin, 2005, p. 3)

This chapter presents some essential characteristics of the content market, especially in regards to book publishing in Portugal and Spain, and their corporate perspective. Besides the general profile of the sector, some main market issues and tendencies of business development can also be identified. In order to better understand the relation between media/content companies and book publishers operating in Portugal and Spain, and to observe strategies for a common Iberian market, this work begins with a review of the situation regarding the interest showed by Spanish companies for the Portuguese market and by Portuguese companies for the Spanish market. The investigation is structured in three parts. First, it uses an economical and cultural approach associated with the concept of *Iberismo* (the Portuguese and Spanish term used) to describe issues concerning the Iberian content market and some globalization situations and possibilities are identified for countries with linguistic affinity. Second, it presents the book industry in an international and Iberian context. Some management practices, tendencies and issues are also identified in the market, including current and potential relations with other Lusophone and Hispanic markets. Third, it discusses the main ideas and conclusions concerning the state of the Iberian content industry art and development opportunities, including ideas for future research regarding the Iberian content market.

In regards to methodology, this chapter is based fundamentally on documented research; namely books, company reports, sector reports, scientific magazines and published articles in the press, with a greater emphasis on the Portuguese and Spanish reality. As the author is both a businessman (publisher) and adviser in the media area, this position as an active observer allows for the gathering of information reflected by the research approach. Interviews were also carried out with specialists in the communications industry area, namely university professors, executives, business executives and directors with connections to Portugal and Spain. Due to space limitations, it was not possible to include empirical results in this chapter. The questions were focused in four areas: existence or emergence of an Iberian market of cultural and media content; management practices, strategies and issues concerning the content market of Iberian companies; corporate connections and relations between book publishers and media companies operating in the Iberian market; and strategies and possibilities of internationalization of Iberian content companies near markets with larger cultural affinities.

Twelve interviews were completed involving six Spanish and six Portuguese subjects. Interviewer profiles were divided in two categories: communication company professionals and communication science professors. In terms of specific occupations, the interviewees performed the following functions: four university lecturers, three journalists, three managers and two directors. All subjects have extensive knowledge of the industry, both from corporate and academic perspectives. Interviews were performed between July and August 2008, with an average time of 30 minutes. Four interviews were face-to-face, two completed by telephone and two by email.

Four main questions were asked:

- To what extent do shareholdings exist between media companies and publishers operating within the Portuguese and Spanish markets?
- What are the main market dynamics in the media content market and corporate management practices observed in the Iberian Peninsula?
- How does geographic and cultural proximity influence publishing and corporate strategies within the Iberian content market?
- How are Iberian companies facing globalization and developing strategies aimed at Latin American and African countries?

In general terms, the main conclusions drawn from the interviews points to increased acknowledgement of the Iberian American and Iberian African markets, and the need to promote economic and social cooperation, aimed at increasing the potential of these countries and regions.

This chapter was generally structured with the objective of identifying and understanding issues observed in the Iberian content market, especially in the book sector. On the other hand, the research provides a perspective on development issues of the industry in regards to internationalization opportunities with emerging markets (such as Lusophone and Hispanic communities) essentially in Latin America and Africa. This way, some thoughts were also considered—either as a result of research or investigation—concerning opportunities and threats towards internationalization processes of countries with larger cultural affinities with Portugal and Spain.

Culture and Dynamics in Latin American and Portuguese-Speaking Areas

The Development of an Iberian Culture: Between Economy and Culture

As in all nations, the origins of Portugal are to be found in foundation myths and traditions related to the people who have dwelt in this territory. Its evolution results from the cultural confrontation between dwellers from different historical eras, some peaceful, some violent. As affirmed by Carneiro (2004), the fact that the desires embodied by different cultures, still in violent conflict in other areas of the world, are centred in the Iberian Peninsula and its transcontinental areas of influence is very significant: these are cultures emerging from Jewish monotheistic branches, as well as Christian and Islamic cultures. We believe that one sole original action of Iberian people led to the almost dialectic resolution of the differences between these cultures, so close yet so far apart. As suggested by Faustino (2006), culture is usually mediated by the masses, which means that people share experiences, religious ideas, values and personal feelings, intellectual concepts, attributes shared via texts and symbolic artifacts and mass media contents consumption.

Culture needs to be examined as a primary factor. Media and telecommunications play a key role in organizing different cultures. The mass media may or may not contribute towards social integration. The role of politics in supporting the mass media with a view to achieving social integration may be active or passive. Politics may or may not succeed in achieving this objective. But, more importantly, different ways of using the mass media as a social-integration driver exist; forces such as globalization has made this integration difficult.

The issue of media impact on cultural identity is doubtless related to discussion on cultural identities. The Iberian cultural identity, within the context of political and economic cooperation, is fundamental to understanding the dynamics for the communications market in the Iberian zone of Latin America and the Iberian Peninsula. Schlesinger (1994) suggests that, before making any attempt at assessing media effects on cultural identity, it is crucial to conceptually define this same identity. According to Rocca (2006), main daily newspapers, such as *El País*, make an effort to spread the idea of a Spanish identity within the existing Iberian Peninsula constitution and identity, including its Latin American "brothers." The weight of the media in forming this Iberian identity and narrowing ties with Latin America has been constant for many years. The joint entry of Spain and Portugal into the European Economic Union in 1985 strengthened cooperation in order to create an "Iberian zone" within the European market. The historical and cultural connection between both countries united economic and political interests.

Spain followed two strategic lines within the new Europe. First, to strengthen the so-called "Mediterranean Axis," together with France, Italy and Greece, and second, to create a bloc with Portugal, aimed at defending common issues as well as counterbalancing Eastern countries of Slavic origin and German influence. Iberian identity, as a genuine identity within the European Union, attempts to promote Iberian Peninsula values and culture within the future European identity. The media have also participated in this integrating process between Spain and Portugal. For example, Prisa, in its 2005 annual report, presented itself as the leading communications group in Iberian America (Spain, Portugal and Latin America). The acquisitions and attempts made by Prisa in Portugal, as well as the efforts of the company to expand its book publishing to Santillana, a very relevant operation in all Latin American countries (Grupo Prisa, 2005).

Therefore Iberianism, as advocated by Enrique Calpe (2008), Spanish Ambassador in Portugal, should be understood as the interaction between two neighboring countries found on the edge of the European Union (EU), with similar geographic and political characteristics, needing to position themselves as two states integrated in Europe. In this context, the future of both countries may be projected on an international level, through common actions, integrated by other states, including Iberian America. It is fundamental for both countries to position themselves as a large economic bloc within the EU. The economic level assumes special importance such as the partnership between Portugal Telecom and Telefónica, as well as mobile company Vivo, in Brazil and Morocco.

Some activity may already be observed from an Iberian and Latin American perspective, within the particular case of the content industry (media and books). From a market perspective, the internationalization trend is more focused on markets/countries with greater cultural affinity; Spain preferably promotes relations with Spanish-speaking countries (Mexico, Chile, Argentina, Venezuela, Colombia, etc.), whereas Portugal has focused its attention on economic relations within Portuguese-speaking communities (Brazil, Angola, Mozambique, Cape Verde, Guinea-Bissau, São Tomé and Príncipe).

Resulting from the need to widen economic, social and cultural cooperation, the concept of an Iberian area has also been associated to Latin American countries. In this context and as proposed by Nosty (2007, p. 13),

> in communication, the Iberian-American area is associated to a heterogeneous political and economic geography, which is why caution must be taken in separating cultural and communication dimensions, from which certain common values stem, in a broader context, without denying the interaction of these separate variables on the whole context.

The Latin American area includes many complex realities, where more developed social and economic structures coexist with structurally fragile cultures. According to Hallin and Mancini (2007) it is not surprising in terms of cultural expansion as a sign of development, that media systems in Latin America resemble the polarized pluralist model more closely than other redesigned models. The Iberian American press evolved according to Iberian models. In order to consolidate the concept of Iberian American area, the Iberian American Cultural Charter was also approved in 2006 in Montevideo, Uruguay. This initiative reflects the commitment of the different countries towards cooperation, in order to develop a cultural system with an individual identity, characterized by a series of recognizable and differentiating values and cultural expressions. Table 21.1 (p. 282) shows the main guidelines for this initiative. Various examples also exist for the concrete case of media and entertainment, such as cultural initiatives associated to communication, symbolizing cooperation with a view to strengthening political, economic and social interchange between Iberian American countries.

Cultural Iberian American television consists of various channels whose main objective is to promote cultural and artistic values within the Iberian American area. In order to understand the potential of the cultural area and media system, a Delhi study was carried out in 2006, with the objective of analyzing the extent to which Iberian American media may contribute to a regional process of media and cultural convergence. According to Ventura (2007), it was concluded that the future regarding culture and media area depends largely on the capacities of the various countries to overcome the digital gap that exists, in relation to other economic areas, both on the level of existing broadband infrastructure and access and volume of its own content circulating on the Internet. Several studies were undertaken within the scope of the research, identifying opportunities and threats to cultural and media cooperation within the Iberian American area. Table 21.2 (p. 282) presents the primary conclusions.

Table 21.1 Objectives of the Iberian American Cultural Charter, 2006

1. To affirm the central value of culture as necessary basis for human development, in order to overcome poverty and inequality.
2. To promote and protect the cultural diversity originating the Iberian American culture, on which this culture is based, as well as the numerous identities, languages and traditions integrating it.
3. To consolidate Iberian American culture as having an individual and differentiating scope, based on solidarity, mutual respect, sovereignty and plural access to knowledge, culture and cultural exchange.
4. To promote exchange of cultural goods and services within the Iberian American culture, as well as promote solidarity ties and cooperation with other world cultures.
5. To promote protection and diffusion of the Iberian American natural and cultural heritage, both tangible and intangible, through cooperation between countries.

Source: Adapted by the author from Declaração de Montevidéu (2006)

Table 21.2 Opportunities and Threats within the Iberian American Area

Opportunities	Threats
1. Language, historical and geographic proximity	1. Corporate-structure and financial-capacity weaknesses
2. New communication technologies based on cooperation	2. Access levels to culture and new technologies
3. Emergence of new cultures not linked to physical areas	3. Need for broadband infrastructures
4. Digital television and multi-channel offer	4. Economic dimension of the area
5. Ability of the Internet to converge with other media	5. The universal character of the English language
6. Cultural expansion linked to migration phenomena	6. Corporate capacity of external corporate groups
7. Local culture diversity and wealth	

Source: Adapted by the author from Nosty (2007), p. 160

Within the scope of cooperation initiatives between the Iberian countries, the Comunidade dos Paises de Lingua Portuguesa (CPLP: Community of Portuguese Language Countries) should be emphasized. This community includes a population of over 230 million people, and a total area of over 10 million square kilometers (larger than Canada). The cumulative GDP for all countries exceeds US$1.700 trillion. The CPLP is a multilateral forum for strengthening mutual friendship and cooperation between members; it is a juridical entity and is financially autonomous. The general objectives of this organization include political and diplomatic coordination between member states; cooperation at all levels of society; and projects aimed at promoting the Portuguese language. The CPLP differentiates itself not only through use of the same language in different countries, but also through differences in evolution of the Portuguese language (spoken and written) in different cultures and societies. The following section describes the media market dynamics observed in the Iberian American and Portuguese-speaking areas, which are associated in terms of market logics, to the existing cultural and social affinities with Portugal and Spain.

Content Industry Dynamics and Trends within the Iberian Area

While the concept of Iberianism tends to establish itself as an economic bloc, a brief analysis of corporate dynamics within the Iberian contents market leads to the conclusion that the presence of Spanish media companies in the Portuguese market is increasing, whereas the presence of Portuguese companies in the Spanish market is of little relevance. From a market perspective, reality indicates a unidirectional economic flow, that is from Spain to Portugal. According to the Spanish newspaper *El País* (quoting data from the Spanish–Portuguese Trade Chamber), trade between Spain and Portugal reached €24,000 million in 2006, with approximately 1,050 Spanish companies with operations in Portugal, compared to 400 Portuguese companies operating in Spain, which is Portugal's main customer and supplier. Spanish domination is evident in the banking sector, through Banco Bilbao Viscaya e Argentaria (BBVA) and Banco Santander Central Hispanico (BSCH). In 2006, 1.1 million Spanish citizens spent holidays in Portugal. In 2003, Portugal imported €13.22 million in goods from Spain, whereas Portuguese exports to Spain represented €5.92 million.

However, according to Calpe (2008), it should be noted that despite the fact that the Spanish presence in Portugal is more significant than the Portuguese presence in Spain, more detailed analysis reveals that Portugal is comparatively advantageous. Approximately 1,050 Portuguese companies have Spanish capital, compared to 400 Spanish companies with Portuguese capital. Regarding the media sector, the acquisition of Media Capital Group (MCG) by the Spanish group Prisa in 2005 symbolizes the increasing presence of Spanish media companies in the Portuguese market. Faustino (2007) states that the experience acquired by Prisa in the press, radio and television segments helped MCG continue its growth, as well as exploit synergies and develop joint ventures. Media Capital has a strong shareholder base, which joins the main media group in Spain and one of the biggest in Latin America. The arrival of the Prisa group in the Portuguese market indicates increasing interest in the Portuguese market by Spanish companies.

Several international groups operate in Portugal, some with important branches in Spain: Prisa, Edipresse, RCS Mediagroup (through Recoletos), RBA, Gruner + Jahr (through Motorpress) and Lagardère (through Hachette Filipacchi Médias) are the most representative examples, complemented by the branches of other companies, such as Endemol and Fremantle Media, and channels such as TV Record, MTV, Panda and the History Channel. The Portuguese media market is increasingly perceived as a sub-region where the most diversified companies and products coexist in an increasingly global business universe. The interest shown by international groups in Portuguese media assets is a phenomenon that may be explained by the Portuguese market's growth potential and entryway to a universe of 500 million Portuguese-speaking people, as well as the Spanish-speaking market. Therefore the Iberian market represents a natural extension of media and entertainment group portfolios.

One of the few examples of investment in the Spanish market by a Portuguese media company is Impala, through Euroimpala Editores, which launched two magazine titles: *Secretos de Cocina* and *Lineas y Puntos*. This company was already publishing books in Spain. Zon Multimedia, which has business in the area of film exhibition and distribution in the Spanish market, through Lusomundo Spain, is another. The entry into the Portuguese market of the Prisa Group, RCS and Gruner + Jahr provide evidence that the national media market will be increasingly exposed to new international players, often within the scope of a business management logics, through direct and indirect acquisitions in Portugal.

These examples illustrate the increasing interest of Spanish companies in the Portuguese market. However, the Spanish company dynamics are not counterbalanced by a similar trend with Portuguese companies. In fact, despite the existence of some cases of Portuguese media companies with a presence in the Spanish market, the magnitude of investment is very dissimilar. Table 21.3 (p. 284) summarizes the investments of Spanish companies in Portugal.

Obviously, the interest in the Portuguese market should be viewed from a broader market perspective. There are two large regions associated with Iberianism (Portuguese-speaking and Spanish-speaking countries), which are natural markets for Portugal and Spain. In a broader context, it may be affirmed that two large regions exist (Latin America and Africa) whose cultural heritage is associated with Portugal and Spain and that, despite differences in language, some

Table 21.3 Revenues of Spanish Companies in Portugal, 2007–2008 (€000)

Media and advertising subsectors	Communication companies	Revenue 2007	Revenue 2008	Number of employees
Media	Media Capital	222,235,630	213,297,000	1200
Media	Media Luso	16,274,580	101,670,065	35
Advertising	Media Planning	n.a.	152,251,803	

Source: Bastos, Marques and Fonseca (2007)

Table 21.4 Global Media and Entertainment Markets by Region, 2007–2012 ($US millions)

Region	2007	2008	2009	2010	2011	2012	2008/2012
United States	600,746	622,534	646,925	683,501	714,931	758,877	
% change*	4.2	3.6	3.9	5.7	4.6	6.1	4.8
EMEA**	569,691	609,784	649,244	699,296	740,869	791,780	
% change	6.8	7.0	6.5	7.7	5.9	6.9	6.8
Asia Pacific	333,114	370,102	398,202	433,552	469,270	508,266	
% change	9.4	11.1	7.6	8.9	8.2	8.3	8.8
Latin America	51,278	57,280	63,199	70,416	76,971	84,744	
% change	11.5	11.7	10.3	11.4	9.3	10.1	10.6
Canada	40,719	42,821	45,325	49,274	51,095	54,089	
% change	5.2	5.2	5.8	8.7	3.7	5.9	5.8
Total	1,595,548	1,702,521	1,802,895	1,936,039	2,053,136	2,197,756	
% change	6.4	6.7	5.9	7.4	6.0	7.0	6.6

Source: PricewaterhouseCoopers (2008)
Notes: * Percentage changes are from the previous year
** EMEA = Europe, Middle East, Africa

cultural similarities exist. As seen in Table 21.4, a comparative analysis of the media and entertainment industry in the various continents reveals that projections through 2010 show Latin America (including Brazil, whose GDP growth rate is approximately 4 percent) as one of the regions with better growth perspectives, surpassed only by the Asia and Pacific region. It is foreseeable that media companies based in Portugal and Spain will tend to increasingly base their internationalization strategies on Latin American and African countries.

Due to the difficulties faced by media companies operating in Portugal and Spain in entering the European market, approaching the Latin American and African markets provides more opportunities. Language is another entry barrier associated with the European market.

In the Portuguese book industy, there is an increased presence of Spanish publishers in the market. It should also be noted that content and capital circulation within the Iberian American and Portuguese-speaking areas are not solely based on the Iberian Peninsula. Investments are also being made by companies from Brazil, Venezuela, Colombia, Angola, Mexico and other Latin American countries, both in Portugal and in Spain. One can expect content and capital circulations to become bidirectional, as both the Spanish and Portuguese media markets move towards consolidation. These are discussed in more detail in the following section.

Book Publishing Market

Book Publishing Economics and Market Dynamics

Books share characteristics with other cultural products: irregular demand, short (profitable) lifespan, unlimited variety and vertical differentiation. From an economic perspective, books are private products, since their consumption entails exclusiveness. The book sector is based on a traditional production, distribution and sales chain, with a large number of companies and considerable competition at all stages of the value chain. Market structure fluctuations are also frequently observed (both regarding market shares and corporate strategies), as well as market entry and exit movements.

According to Canoy, van der Ploeg and van Ours (2005), in the book industry market structure value depends on experience and may be determined only after reading. Fixed production costs are high, while marginal costs (associated to producing extra units) are relatively low. Commercial success is very difficult to forecast; some books may become best-sellers, while others flop. Price flexibility is rather low compared to other goods; the quantity of books sold is not significantly affected by price variations. Consumption may be considered a cultural investment, instead of consumer behavior.

Despite being private goods, books also display some of the characteristics of public assets, namely associated with their cultural value. Among these values are such things as national identity, justice and peace, social cohesiveness, national prestige, creativity, critical thought and enterprise, among others. These values are not fully reflected in book prices, which are clearly inferior to their sum (Canoy et al., 2005). From an industrial economics perspective, the book sector displays monopolistic competition characteristics in that each book is a new product or commodity. The publisher holds exclusive rights (legally protected) to a book, which will be directly competing with other books of the same genre. Book prices are set by publishers, which position themselves as price-makers. A large number of sellers exist, each ignoring the price decisions by its competitors.

In the book business, a trade-off exists between efficiency, resulting from producing more books of the same type and searching for scale and range economies, extending production to new areas and titles. Despite the fact that books are referred to as an example of a monopolistic competition model, the sector displays unique characteristics. In a traditional monopolistic model, the strategic decision made by each producer is to decide on the quantity to produce where fixed costs are irrelevant. However, in book publishing, a totally different scenario is observed. The strategic decision with which publishers are faced consists of whether or not to publish a particular book, based on risk analysis, which includes the terms of the agreement established with the corresponding author and fixed costs.

Some books will be more successful than others. According to Earp and Kornis (2005), it is estimated that only 10 percent of published books are profitable, 20 percent are able to cover production costs and the remaining 70 percent represent financial losses. The larger a publisher's portfolio, the greater the probability profits will cover the losses. However, uncertain demand leads to difficulties in forecasting sales. In addition to minimizing commercial risks, publishers engage in portfolio diversification, attempting to exploit range economies which consists of reducing average production costs within a given unit (or company) by producing a range of products.

Book Publishing Managerial and Corporate Strategies

During most of the twentieth century, the book publishing business was understood as a break-even business, whose objective was essentially to cover costs in order to avoid losses. However, publishers increasingly use economic and financial criteria in deciding which books to publish, or what Schiffrin (2000) refers to as "market censorship." The ultimate goal of the book business is the same as any other business—to generate profits. Similar to other consumer goods, book sales are seasonal and purchase patterns exist. For example, sales are highest for most retailers preceding the Christmas season.

Each publisher defines its target audience, its niche, in a unique way. Publishers adopt somewhat complex business models, due to the difficult balance between production costs and sales revenues. Books have characteristics different from other consumer goods: they are not recognizable by a brand, but by their title or author. The weight of publisher brands in consumer choice is reduced (when compared to other economic activities), with the exception of some particular segments, such as children's books and travel guides. Despite the differences and specific characteristics of each market, business models and management practices reveal some common trends, including the Iberian book market, which will be discussed later.

International Book Business Trends

According to Vogel (2004), the editing and publishing sector represents approximately one-quarter of total entertainment industry revenues. The market consists of two main sub-sectors: educational/professional and general interest, each characterized by specific demand and an economic and financial profile. Analysis of the various segments (see Tables 21.5 and 21.6) reveals that average sales of general interest books have grown at a slightly higher rate relatively to educational and professional books, which appears to suggest increased competition by other media, namely the Internet. PricewaterhouseCoopers estimates that book revenues in the United States, EMEA (Europe, Middle East, Africa), Asia Pacific, Latin America and Canada will grow at a 2.8 percent compound annual rate through 2012. Asia Pacific will be the fastest-growing region, expanding at a 3.9 percent annual rate, to $29.7 billion in 2012. EMEA will increase at a 2.5 percent compound annual rate, reaching $56.2 billion in 2012. The United States will rise to $37 billion in 2012, growing at a 2.5 percent average annual rate. Spending in Latin America will rise at a 2.4 percent annual rate, totaling $5 billion in 2012, while Canada will expand to $1.9 billion in 2012, growing at a 3.3 percent compound annual rate (PricewaterhouseCoopers, 2008).

In general terms, the book industy is a mature sector. Despite a slowdown in previous decades, world book market sales remain at good levels, with no dramatic falls, despite competition by other media. Table 21.5 displays some market trends, by continent.

Book Business Trends within the Iberian Market

The Spanish and Portuguese markets exhibit common trends in that both are mature markets experiencing constant change, and concentration among publishers continues. Portuguese and Spanish publishers are intensifying their globalization strategies, and management practices are progressively orientated towards the market. Finally, there is increased importance on large supermarkets or "hypermarkets" as privileged locations for the sale of books aimed at mass audiences. However, some differences are also observed in that the Spanish market is four times larger than the Portuguese market, and Spanish publisher globalization strategies are more oriented towards Spanish-speaking countries, whereas Portuguese publishers preferentially bet on

Table 21.5 Book Publishing Market Trends, 2003–2012 (US$ millions)

Region	2003	2004	2005	2006	2007	2008	2009	2010	2011	2012	2008–12 CAGR
United States	28,877	28,871	31,085	30,579	32,740	32,114	33,062	34,232	35,584	36,996	
% change	*6.4*	*0.0*	*7.7*	*-1.6*	*7.1*	*-1.9*	*3.0*	*3.5*	*3.9*	*4.0*	*2.5*
EMEA	44,152	44,868	46,781	47,034	49,570	49,874	51,210	52,771	54,405	56,183	
% change	*1.6*	*1.6*	*4.3*	*0.5*	*5.4*	*0.6*	*2.7*	*3.0*	*3.1*	*3.3*	*2.5*
Asian Pacific	19,761	20,512	21,294	22,570	24,503	25,775	26,907	27,906	28,879	29,667	
% change	*1.7*	*3.8*	*3.8*	*6.0*	*8.6*	*5.2*	*4.4*	*3.7*	*3.5*	*2.7*	*3.9*
Latin America	4,066	4,129	4,229	4,341	4,471	4,591	4,706	4,819	4,930	5,041	
% change	*0.4*	*1.5*	*2.4*	*2.6*	*3.0*	*2.7*	*2.5*	*2.4*	*2.3*	*2.3*	*2.4*
Canada	1,445	1,457	1,516	1,537	1,615	1,641	1,704	1,769	1,835	1,904	
% change	*-0.2*	*0.8*	*4.0*	*1.4*	*5.1*	*1.6*	*3.8*	*3.8*	*3.7*	*3.8*	*3.3*
Total	98,301	99,837	104,905	106,061	112,899	113,995	117,589	121,497	125,633	129,791	
% change	*2.9*	*1.6*	*5.1*	*1.1*	*6.4*	*1.0*	*3.2*	*3.3*	*3.4*	*3.3*	*2.8*

Source: PriceWaterhouseCoopers (2008)

Table 21.6 Book Industry Trends in the Iberian Region, 2003–2012 (US$ millions)

Iberian Region	2003	2004	2005	2006	2007	2008	2009	2010	2011	2012	2008–12 CAGR
Book publishing market*											
Consumer and educational book market											
Portugal	256	256	261	263	270	268	271	274	277	279	0.7
Spain	4,658	4,801	4,892	4,999	5,174	5,246	5,370	5,495	5,624	5,754	2.1
Professional book market											
Portugal	25	25	25	25	25	25	26	26	26	26	0.8
Spain	656	643	644	647	650	651	653	655	658	661	0.3

Source: PriceWaterhouseCoopers (2008)
Note: * At average 2007 exchange rates

Table 21.7 Consumer and Educational Book Publishing Market, 2003–2012* ($US millions)

Latin America	2003	2004	2005	2006	2007	2008	2009	2010	2011	2012	2008–12 CAGR
Argentina	175	181	188	194	202	209	218	224	231	237	3.2
Brazil	2,752	2,798	2,869	2,943	3,031	3,108	3,182	3,254	3,326	3,398	2.3
Chile	145	150	154	159	164	170	175	179	184	188	2.8
Colombia	165	168	173	179	186	194	202	210	217	224	3.8
Mexico	811	814	827	846	868	889	908	929	949	970	2.2
Venezuela	18	18	18	20	20	21	21	23	23	24	3.7
Total	4,066	4,129	4,229	4,341	4,471	4,591	4,706	4,819	4,930	5,041	2.4

Source: PriceWaterhouseCoopers (2008)
Note: * At average 2007 exchange rates

Portuguese-speaking countries. Sales points in Portugal are concentrated in a few bookshop chains, whereas in Spain bookshops are more scattered by region. The main book publishers in Spain are part of media groups, whereas publishing groups are autonomous in Portugal. Finally, pocket-book editions do not generate significant sales in Portugal, whereas this segment is increasing in Spain. Table 21.6 shows some market trends in the two Iberian countries.

An analysis of natural markets reveals greater potential for the Hispanic market, yet the Portuguese-speaking market should not be ignored, especially in Brazil, the largest South American market, with over 186 million people. Table 21.7 details the consumer and educational book publishing market in Latin America, a market expected to continue to grow, due to several factors. These include better economic conditions and increased government funding for educational books. However, low readership levels and piracy will restrict the market.

In summary, the publishing sector has become significantly concentrated in order to respond to a global market and as a strategy to face increasingly concentrated distribution, with greater discount and deadline demands. In the case of Spain, main publishing groups operating in this market are generally market leaders also in Latin America. Publishers from Spanish-speaking countries find a market unified by the Spanish language. In the case of Portugal, the book market presents more modest performances, not only regarding the domestic market, but also regarding internationalization strategies to Portuguese-speaking communities. In the nineteenth century, Portuguese poet Fernando Pessoa was already alerting publishers to the need for international-ization and attracting the moderately cultured audiences, both in Portugal and Brazil (in Fernandes, 2007). The fact that Portugal has only 10 million inhabitants (approximately four times less than Spain) partly explains the smaller dimension of Portuguese publishers and their smaller international competitiveness. However, between 2006 and 2008, the Portugese publish-ing market has become more professional, focusing on the creation of publishing groups with increased capacity to develop more aggressive corporate strategies, both in the domestic market and across the Portuguese-speaking countries.

Discussion and Conclusions

The main objective of this research was to analyze issues and dynamics observed in the Iberian media and cultural content market, with an emphasis on the book publishing sector, and to identify tendencies regarding the economy and management of media and press companies, especially globalization strategies in the Lusophone and Hispanic communities. For this purpose, several investigation techniques were employed, utilizing reports, surveys and interviews. Several conclusions are drawn from this research:

- The concept of an Iberian content market is yet to be fully established, especially for Portugese companies.
- Investment levels in the Iberian content market indicate a one-way flow from Spain to Portugal.
- The Iberian content market adopted management practices designed to surpass competition.
- The markets associated with Lusophone (Portuguese language) and Hispanic (Spanish language) communities are considered a strategic international priority.
- Future capital exchanges were predicted between Iberian companies and African companies (of Portuguese language) and Latin America.
- There are civic and political movements towards reinforcing cultural and economical cooperation to strengthen the Iberian American market.
- There are many differences between the spoken Portuguese in Portugal, Brazil and Africa that cause repercussions in media products.
- There are also differences between the spoken Spanish from Spain and that in Latin America, but these are much less evident than in the case of Portugal.

In the case of the Iberian book market, other distinctions were noted. In Portugal the majority of book publishers are not related to media companies, while in Spain the opposite is the case. For example, the publisher Santillana is integrated in the Prisa group and the Barcelona-based publisher Planeta also holds several products and media companies. The book industry in Portugal and Spain is not very different from that observed in other Western countries, even though there are differences in terms of market dimensions. Some other trends were noted in the Iberian book market, which are, in many aspects, also extendable to other media content businesses. Three areas are noted below.

First, books are no longer simply a cultural manifestation. Books are above all a business product, in part due to a series of successive transformations and reforms of the corporate and market structure at a level of demand, as well as production, distribution, commercialization, marketing, new technologies, promotion, competition and so on.

Second, the book market has a well-defined and transparent value chain. In terms of industrial structure the sector corresponds to a monopolistic competition model, considering each book as a new product, whose price is unilaterally settled. The strategic decision is not what price is chosen, but the decision to publish a given book.

Third, the relationship between publishers and retailers is above all underlined by the difficulty associated with commercial uncertainty. The return mechanism is the last indicator of this difficulty. There is also in retail a trade-off between efficiency (fewer stores with a large dimension) and diversity (i.e. geographical diffusion). A strong focus on retail is also critical.

Regarding the research questions posed in the introduction, we can now answer these in a more systematic manner to conclude the chapter.

1. In what way do capital-sharing relationships exist between companies operating in the Portuguese and Spanish markets?
The concept of an Iberian media market is not yet established and essentially reflects a hegemony in the investment from Spanish media and communication companies in the Portuguese market

as compared to Portuguese investment in Spain. The larger dimension of the Spanish media market enables more scale economies, a bigger investment capacity and development of synergies, in terms of corporate practices and content production. Concerning the book business, the tendency also points to larger investment dynamics from publishers with Spanish capital in the Portuguese market. In fact, just the participation of Prisa group of Media Capital (until 2005 dominated by Portuguese capital) is sufficient to demonstrate the difference between exposure of Portuguese and Spanish companies in the Iberian content market. Therefore, from an economical point of view the Iberian market is characterized by a "force game" clearly superior to Spain, and from a social or cultural point of view conditions are favorable for these two countries to be perceived as a sub-region of Europe. Although *Iberismo* is far from being incorporated by the population, there are political initiatives to reinforce this concept, including the EU. With an EU dominated by Anglo-Saxon and French-German regions, the importance of the Iberian language and culture tends to be revaluated on a political, economical, social and cultural point of view.

2. What are the main market issues and corporate management practices observed in the media content industry in the Iberian Peninsula?

The reality of the Iberian market has very distinct aspects, yet this also presents some dynamics common in media and cultural content businesses. For example, in the book sector, the following tendencies stand out: concentration of large groups; increase of the rhythm of book revenues returns; implementation of pocket-book editions; obsession for best-sellers in order to increase income; the need for booksellers to include titles with high rotation; technological revolution as a business driver; an active market of rights and globalization; growing interest for specialized niches; distribution of increasingly complex products; introduction of multimedia products; and an overabundance of new titles and fewer average releases.

In the case of media content, the keywords that are best associated with new market dynamics are concentration, consolidation and globalization. Companies are more and more pressured by the growth limitations of their domestic markets and the corporate initiatives point towards the adoption of management practices that support the promotion of synergies and profitability of companies and media products. In the Iberian Peninsula book publishing is characterized more and more by the internalization of economic products (instead of the cultural industry perspective) that must acquire profits, like other economical sectors. This concept arrived late in Portugal, especially if one compares the situation in Spain. This perspective, with a larger focus on the market and profitability, is associated with a growing professionalism at the top levels of management. It is inside the boardrooms of corporate management that media and book marketing have been gaining a new focus in regard to operational and strategic management of this industry.

3. In what way does geographical and cultural proximity influence the publishing strategies of the Iberian American market?

In order to understand the cultural processes in Latin America, one must observe concepts such as globalization, internationalization and transnationalization and how these are incorporated in this social universe. In the twentieth century, Latin American countries experienced social and economic transformations at all levels. The globalization process has allowed the formation of industrial conglomerates and financial corporations, including the media industry. In the cultural and media content field, the market's reorganization results not only from an economical, political and technological process, but also from a global articulation of the commercial, publishing and academic objectives. In this new scene there is a tendency of media and culture institutions to participate in the industrialization of created outputs. With linguistic issues, the publishing industry permits cultural exchanges, while cinema and television, music and information technology function in a market with easier worldwide amplitude.

4. What is the importance of the Spanish and Portuguese languages as a content market in the Iberian Peninsula?

The Lusophone and Hispanic markets are fundamental to support the development strategies of the media content industry operating in the Iberian market, which is under a maturing cycle. At the publisher company level, one can state that in the Portuguese case some weaknesses exist in terms of corporate structure, market dimension and management efficiency, which has created difficulties in moving towards more globalization opportunities. The book industry seems to be changing towards a greater corporate dynamic, evidenced by concentration of publishers, more aggressive management and marketing practices, internationalization strategies and sale of the author's copyrights. On the other hand, Spanish publishers are on a more advanced stage regarding internationalization strategies for Latin America. Brazil is already the largest market in terms of book volumes for Santillana, surpassing Spain where the publisher originated. The Iberian American and African market's dimensions, social and economic development, cultural affinities with Portugal and Spain, and the relative stagnation of the Iberian market of media and publishing constitute the main motivational drivers for focusing internationalization strategies in these markets.

5. How are Iberian companies facing the globalization phenomenon and sustaining growth strategies?

As discussed in this chapter, the Iberian content industry is engaged in internationalization strategies. Like other countries, Portuguese and Spanish companies center growth strategies in the domestic market, and on a second stage at an international level. Some entities operating in the Iberian market integrate national groups of considerable dimension, although the situation favors Spain over Portugal. A national and international focus is also important for the book industry, to meet growing competition and improvement of financial performance and investment capacity. The search for growth patterns, mechanisms and models based on the market's expansion, namely globalization, is an absolute need in order to compensate the relative apathy of domestic markets, which are generally in a stage of maturity. However, this foreign entry process in the media sector will not have the celerity sometimes desired by international investors. In the case of book publishing, this explains the bigger presence of multinationals in the Iberian American and African market, including publishers originating from Portugal and Spain.

Consequently, the Lusophone and Hispanic markets seem to constitute a natural extension whose main driver are cultural affinities and represent a big opportunity to provide greater strength to the Iberian content industry. This does not mean that there is an absence of investment opportunities in the domestic markets in Portugal and Spain. However, it is important to point out some substantial differences observed between the development level of the Latin American and African markets of Iberian language. While the first region (Latin America) clearly reveals itself as an emerging market, the second (Portuguese Africa) is a market with development potential tied to political reforms and challenges with low education levels in Africa. In this respect, the corporate dynamics of Iberian book publishers constitute a good example of the potential that the Iberian American and African markets represent. Book publishing, which is characterized by the production of products whose main value is cultural property, is still a target of purchase and sale in the international market, particularly the author's copyrights. However, in the case of the Iberian American and African markets, it seems that there is no correlation between the exposure of the financial capital and the intellectual capital applied to book production, meaning there is not a direct relationship between the concentration of capital and the concentration of authors.

Directions for Future Research

More investigation and analysis is needed on the Iberian American market, and the role that Portugal will play in Spanish language media. In assessing directions for future research, these topics deserve attention by scholars:

- Extend empirical research in Latin American countries and African Portuguese-speaking countries.
- Explore in a more systematic way the relationship of the cultural and creative industries in the Iberian American regions.
- Develop cultural initiatives between these regions that relate to media content projects.
- Identify and analyze data to assess markets trends in the Iberian American and African regions.

In conclusion, the cultural and commercial cooperation between Portugal and Spain (Old World) and Latin American and Africa (New World) is growing because of economic potential, especially in regard to media products. In these countries opportunities exist because of the size of the market, a similar language and cultural links. However, this is not enough to develop a competitive advantage. It is essential to promote economic, social and cultural cooperation among governments, non-profit organizations and private-sector companies. The opportunities will come for the media and creative industries to establish a long tail (Anderson, 2006) to explore in the Iberian American and African regions.

References

Anderson, C. (2007). *The long tail. The revised and updated edition: Why the future of business is selling less of more.* New York: Hyperion.
Aris, A. & Bughin, J. (2005). *Managing media companies: Harness in creative value.* Chichester, UK: John Wiley & Sons.
Bastos, I., Marques, S. & Fonseca, C. (2007). Dinamismo Ibérico no sector da comunicação. In *Actualidad e Economia Ibérica* (pp. 38–43). September, 118. Lisbon: Câmara de Comércio Luso-Espanhola.
Calpe, E. (2008). Cooperação Ibérica. *Diplomática magazine,* June–July, 19–21.
Canoy, M., van der Ploeg, F. & van Ours, J. (2005). *The economics of books.* Centre for Economic Policy Research (CEPR) discussion paper no. 4892, London. Retrieved March 8, 2009, from http://ideas.repec.org/p/dgr/kubcen/200513.html, from.www.cepr.org.
Carneiro, A. (2004, April). *Pensar Iberoamérica.* Retrieved March 8, 2009, from www.oei.es/pensariberoamerica/ric05a03b.htm#1a.
Declaração de Montevidéu (Carta Cultural). (2006, July 13–14). *IX Conferência Ibero-Americana de Cultura,* Uruguay. Retrieved March 8, 2009, from www.oeibrpt.org/ixcic.htm.
Earp, F. S. & Kornis, G. (2005). *A economia da cadeia produtiva do livro.* Rio de Janeiro: Banco Nacional de Desenvolvimento Econômico e Social.
Faustino, P. (2006). *O alargamento da União Europeia e impactos nos media e identiadades locais.* Lisbon: Media XXI/Formalpress.
Faustino, P. (2007). Becoming a broadcasting leader in 10 years: A case study of Portugal's TVI/Media Capital Group. *International journal on media management, 4,* 151–164.
Fernandes, F. (2007). *A gestao segundo Fernando Pessoa.* Lisbon: Oficina do Livro.
Florida, R. (2002). *The rise of the creative class and how it's transforming work, leisure, community and everyday life.* London: Basic Books.
Grupo Prisa. (2005). *Informe Anual 2005 del Grupo Prisa.* Retrieved March 8, 2009, from www.prisa.com/upload/ficheros/cuentas-anuales/memoria2005/memoria_2005.html.

Hallin, D. & Mancini, P. (2007). Un studio comparado de los medios en América Latina. In D. Nosty (Ed.), *Anuário: Tendências 2007 dos médios de comunicación—el escenario iberoamericano* (pp. 89–91). Spain: Fundación Telefónica.

Lampel, J., Shamsie, J. E. and Lant, T. (2006). *The business of culture: Strategic perspectives on entertainement and media.* Mahwah, NJ: Lawrence Erlbaum Associates.

Nosty, D. (Ed.) (2007). *Anuário: Tendências 2007 dos médios de comunicación—el escenario iberoamericano.* Spain: Fundación Telefónica.

PricewaterhouseCoopers (PWC). (2006) *Global entertainment and media outlook: 2006–2010.* New York: PWC.

PricewaterhouseCoopers (PWC). (2008) *Global entertainment and media outlook: 2008–2012.* New York: PWC.

Rocca, J. (2006). A perspectiva Espanhola e Ibérica no contexto Europeu. In P. Faustino (Ed.), *Alargamento da Uniäo Europeia e impactos nos media e identiadades locais* (pp. 123–142). Lisbon: Media XXI/Formalpress.

Schiffrin, A. (2000). *The business of books.* London: Verso.

Schlesinger, P. (1994). Europe's contradictory communicative space. *Daedalus, 123*(2), 25–52.

Ventura, R. (2007). Espacio cultutao y sistema de medios. In N. Diaz (Ed.), *Anuário: Tendências 2007 dos médios de comunicación—el escenario iberoamericano* (pp. 151–163). Spain: Fundación Telefónica.

Vogel, H. (2004). *Entertainment industry economics: A guide for financial analysis* (6th ed.). London: Cambridge University Press.

22

Assessing the State of
Spanish Language Media
A Summary and Future Directions

Alan B. Albarran
University of North Texas, USA

The Handbook of Spanish Language Media is a research volume designed to address two primary goals: to provide a baseline of information and research on the media industries in the many Spanish-speaking countries, and to provide directions for future research within individual country chapters, and those chapters offering exploration in to specific topics. As the editor of this project, it is my hope that working with the approximately forty contributors to this volume we have accomplished these goals.

This final chapter offers an overall summary and synthesis of this research effort by looking at the subject of Spanish language media from a macro perspective. To this end this chapter considers three broad research questions to assess the state of the Spanish language media market:

1. What are the strengths of the global Spanish language media market?
2. What are the limitations of the global Spanish language media market?
3. What research is needed to better understand the global Spanish language media market?

Strengths of the Global Spanish Language Media Market

A review of the various country-by-country chapters reveals a global market that is unified by a common language (recognizing that many regional influences, dialects and customs exist from nation to nation), quite large and continuing to grow. As of late 2008, the global Spanish language market represents approximately 452 million people (see Worldwide Spanish, 2008), with growth rates varying from country to country. The five largest countries in terms of population—Mexico, Colombia, the United States, Argentina and Spain—reflect the broad geographical segments of this market in North America, South America and Europe, home of "mother" Spain which brought the language to the western hemisphere centuries ago.

An important statistical indicator of population growth is a nation's birth rate. Birth rates are usually considered as the number of births per thousand people at mid-point of each year; this is also known as the "crude" birth rate, but it does reflect anticipated growth of a population.

Table 22.1 Highest and Lowest Birth Rates among Spanish Language Nations, 2007

Highest birth rates	Lowest birth rates
Guatemala (29.09)	Spain (9.98)
Paraguay (28.77)	Cuba (11.44)
Honduras (27.59)	Puerto Rico (12.79)
El Salvador (26.13)	Uruguay (14.41)

Source: Nation Master (2008)

Table 22.1 lists those countries with the four highest and four lowest birth rates based on 2007 data.

Countries not included in this abbreviated table have birth rates that are also strong and clustered close together, ranging from the Dominican Republic (22.91) to Peru (20.09). While the United States has a national birth rate of 14.16, it is impossible to exactly pinpoint the Latino/Hispanic birth rate because of the presence of undocumented aliens in the country. But there is general consensus that the birth rate among Latinos and Hispanics in the United States is much higher in comparison to Anglos or African Americans.

Clearly, the size of this market and future growth potential has the attention of advertisers, as evidenced by the examinations in this volume by Boyle (Chapter 20) in the United States, and by Etayo and Preciado (Chapter 19) throughout Spain and Latin America. Total global advertising across all media is estimated at approximately $668 billion in 2008 according to Coen (2008). As best as can be discerned, the total amount of advertising in Spain, Latin America and Spanish language media in the United States probably totals about $6 billion for 2008. Clearly, with such a growing market there is plenty of upside potential for the Spanish-speaking market; no doubt these countries will continue to attract advertising dollars across all types of media and distribution platforms.

As of late 2008, the world was reeling from an economic crisis, which impacts just about every nation's gross domestic product and future growth projections. However, there has been strong growth across the Latin American region and in Spain in the twenty-first century. As a region, Latin America's GDP grew by 5.5 percent in 2007, an estimated 4.5 percent in 2008, and 3.25 percent in 2009 (London South East, 2008). Spain's GDP for 2007 was a healthy 3.8 percent, but the economic crisis lowered projections for 2008 to 1.6 percent and 2009 to 1.0 percent (The Economist, 2008). It is safe to say the global Spanish language market will continue to attract global trade and commerce, not only through existing trade agreements, but with new opportunities as well.

Limitations of the Global Spanish Language Media Market

A review of the chapters in this handbook provides considerable insight to the limitations impacting the global Spanish language market. There are differences however, when considering the United States, Spain and Latin America, so each area will be addressed separately.

The United States represents one of the fastest growing Spanish language markets in the world, yet many advertisers are still hesitant to invest in the market due to two negative perception: that this segment lacks financial resources, and that many members are undocumented. Both of these perceptions are fallacies. The Hispanic/Latino population in the United States has a higher per-capita household income than African Americans. The United States certainly has a large population of undocumented Hispanics and Latinos, but no one knows exactly what the number is, although most demographers suggest it is somewhere around 10–15 million people. Regardless, there are over 45 million *legal* Spanish-speaking people in the United States. Even the undocumented residents eat food, buy gasoline and other products, and are active consumers. This means the United States is actually the second-largest Spanish language market in the world behind Mexico.

The growth of the Spanish-speaking population in the United States has also led to controversies over a number of public policy issues, ranging from immigration reform to health care to bilingual education to state-mandated efforts to make English a required language. Spanish language media in the United States has been at the forefront in presenting these issues, and informing their audiences. In the United States, one out of every four people will be of Hispanic/Latino descent by 2050 (Advertising Age, 2007), so these cultural issues will continue to exacerbate and be played out in the media.

Spain faces a different set of challenges. The end of the Franco regime, as documented in Chapter 2 on Spain by Arrese, Artero and Herrero, marked the beginning of a complete transformation of the media system in the country to one participating in market forces. As such, the media in Spain has in reality been operating independently for only a little over thirty years, and is continuing to develop. The Spanish language market in Spain is limited to just the Kingdom of Spain. Spain is not only part of the European Union, but also part of the global Spanish market, although its separation from both North and South America prevents closer interaction. However, many Spanish-based companies such as Telefónica and the Prisa Group are active in Latin America and moving in to other sectors of the economy in the United States.

Still, Spain represents a country with an aging population base, low birth rate, high unemployment, growing inflation and challenges with immigration from many African and Eastern European countries. For media companies to grow in Spain, the nation's best option is to continue to pursue expanding market share through globalization, most notably in Latin America, and as Faustino reports in Chapter 21, some opportunities in the Portuguese-speaking market.

Latin America has its own unique set of limitations. Many of the countries detailed in this handbook have a history of political unrest, government corruption, instability within their economic system, cultural challenges among indigenous populations and infrastructure issues. Other countries continue to deal with the farming of illegal drugs and drug trafficking.

While many countries are making progress in developing democratic values and improving their business activities, efforts to nationalize different areas of business and industry (including the media) in Venezuela, Bolivia and Ecuador, troubled countries in the region as well as trade and commerce partners outside of Latin America. The use of military force remains a threat for many countries in the region.

All of these concerns clearly impact potential business investment within the different countries that make up Latin America. The World Bank produces an annual survey of 184 nations indexed for the best places to do business (World Bank, 2009). Note that this report concerns all business activity, and focuses on government reforms that enable greater business activity. Table 22.2 lists the countries covered in this summary report, along with Brazil.

As Table 22.2 illustrates, there is a wide variance among the countries examined in this text. As far as Latin America is concerned, the economies of Chile, Colombia, Mexico and Peru are the highest in the region, while Honduras, Ecuador, Bolivia and Venezuela rank near the bottom of the index. Not surprisingly, the latter three countries have had the greatest political instability and forced nationalization of several industries.

Another tool to gain insight in to the business climate in various economies is to look at entrepreneurial activity. The Global Entrepreneurship Monitor (GEM) is a non-profit consortium

Table 22.2 Best Places to Do Business (country followed by 2009 ranking)

United States (3)	El Salvador (72)	Paraguay (115)
Puerto Rico (35)	Panama (81)	Costa Rica (117)
Chile (40)	Dominican Republic (97)	Brazil (126)
Spain (49)	Nicaragua (107)	Honduras (133)
Colombia (53)	Uruguay (109)	Ecuador (136)
Mexico (56)	Guatemala (112)	Bolivia (150)
Peru (62)	Argentina (113)	Venezuela (174)

Source: Adapted by the author from World Bank (2009)
Note: Cuba is not ranked by the World Bank

of entrepreneurial activity that has been conducted annually since 1997. For the most recent report in 2007, the GEM used a subset of Latin American and Caribbean nations for data analysis: Argentina, Brazil, Chile, Colombia, Dominican Republic, Peru, Uruguay and Venezuela (Bosma, Jones, Autio & Levie, 2008). While the GEM report is quite detailed, the 2007 data indicate that several Latin American counties rank highly in terms of early stage entrepreneurial activity. Peru ranked second among all countries examined, followed by Colombia and Venezuela. In terms of the percentage of the population that is involved in different stages of business ownership and management, all of the eight countries except Uruguay ranked in the top ten. However, Uruguay was ranked in twelfth place (see Bosma et al., 2008).

Another area of concern for the Latin American countries that emerges from this work is the continuing threat and safety of journalists working in the region. Slocum details this problem in the countries of Mexico, Colombia and Spain in Chapter 16, and several authors allude to the safety of reporters in many countries represented in this handbook. Latin America has been a dangerous place to be a journalist. The Committee to Protect Journalists (CPJ) has tracked data on journalists killed since 1992. Since then, CPJ has identified forty journalists who died in Colombia and another fourteen in Mexico (Committee to Protect Journalists, 2008), as well as many other countries. The World Association of Newspapers (WAN) also tracks the number of journalists killed each year; in 2008 alone the WAN identified three journalists killed in Mexico, and one each in the countries of Bolivia, Brazil, the Dominican Republic, El Salvador, Guatemala, Honduras and Venezuela (World Association of Newspapers, 2008).

Finally, several nations in the handbook indicate challenges of growing their technological infrastructure and working to avoid a digital divide that affects their respective populations in terms of socioeconomic class. While this situation is a global challenge, there is wide disparity among many Latin American nations as found in these chapters in terms of access to computers and to the Internet. It is a problem that can only be addressed only through cooperative agreements between governments, industry and education.

Future Research on the Global Spanish Language Media Market

There are many possible directions for future research on the global Spanish language market. In most of the chapters in the handbook, the authors have detailed specific research directions for individual countries and specialized topics. In the final section of this chapter, I suggest some potential areas for research involving the entire Spanish language regions, with the hope of promoting more macro-driven and cross-cultural studies. In no particular order, there are five directions that would help fill in some of the existing gaps identified within the handbook.

Studying Trends and Patterns in Spanish Language Media

The size and potential of the global Spanish-speaking market demands more study on media usage (ratings for audiovisual and circulation for print), advertising investment, consumer habits and preferences, technology diffusion, and a host of other possible topics for study. I hope that this volume will help to offer initial research on the global Spanish language market, but much more work needs to be done. Not only would this provide insight in to changing patterns and trends, but also it would elevate our understanding of this important market.

Case Studies of Successful Media Companies and Enterprises

Most of the knowledge of successful media companies and their best practices are limited to a handful of well-known enterprises: Univision and Telemundo in the United States; Telefónica and Prisa in Spain; Grupo Televisa and Grupo Azteca in Mexico; Carrolco in Colombia; and Venevision in Venezuela. We also know that major advertisers such as Procter & Gamble, Unilever, Coca-Cola, Nestlé, Colgate-Palmolive and other well-known brands are among the leading advertisers in global Spanish language media. Yet our knowledge is limited to the major countries, and most of the information is descriptive as opposed to analytical. We need case studies of new and growing indigenous media companies seeking to enter different aspects of the market, and analysis of companies that are both successful and those that fall short of their goals. This will help improve our understanding of the market, and the unique business practices associated with Spanish language media.

Improving Data Sources on Spanish Language Media

This is a problem primarily confined to Latin America, and one that needs to be addressed in order to improve broader research efforts. There are numerous opportunities here that exist for both businesses engaged in research and university or educational partners. Media companies can help create specialized organizations to track key data like advertising, ownership and industry revenues. Governments in these countries can also get involved by funding bureaus and agencies that can gather and organize data on an annual basis. Universities can create research consortiums or centers and institutes that devote their efforts to improving data sources. It is very challenging to conduct research without access to data, and this is a huge challenge in moving the research agenda in Latin America forward.

Transitioning to a Digital Environment

Many Spanish-speaking countries are in the process of transitioning to a digital environment, and in a number of countries, the pace of technological change is moving at a fast rate of diffusion. At the same time, the mobile phone is rapidly emerging as the most affordable technology to access the Internet, and could prove to be a great enabler for many people in the lower economic strata. The implications of moving to a digital environment, and its impact on traditional media, raise a number of research issues that will deserve more investigation.

The Impact of Economic, Political, Social and Globalization Forces

The Spanish language market will continue to be affected by shifting economic, political, social and globalization forces. This confluence of external forces will impact the media industries operating in the Spanish-speaking nations, their advertisers, and most importantly, their audiences. Research will be needed to analyze and assess these macro forces on the media and their constituencies, taken from an objective and unbiased view.

Final Thoughts

As with any research effort, the final product leaves us with more questions that need to be answered rather than a set of tidy explanations. Such is the case with *The Handbook of Spanish Language Media*. The countries and issues explored in this edited volume help to answer a number of questions about the global Spanish language market and provide a baseline on which to build, but it also leaves us wanting more. That is the challenge for you, the reader, and other students, professors and industry practitioners wanting to know more. Our work is far from over, and we need more research and collaboration to have a better understanding of the important role played by Spanish language media throughout the world.

References

Advertising Age. (2007). *Hispanic fact pact.* Retrieved March 7, 2009, from www.adage.com/images/random/hisp factpack07.pdf.

Bosma, N., Jones, K., Autio, E. & Levie, J. (2008). *Global entrepreneurship monitor. 2007 Executive report.* Retrieved October 25, 2008, from www.gemconsortium.org/about.aspx?page=pub_gem_global_reports.

Coen, R. J. (2008, July). *Insider's report.* Retrieved October 30, 2008, from www.magnainsights.com/docs/Coen_Insider's_Report_June_2008.pdf.

Committee to Protect Journalists (CPJ). (2008). *Journalists killed: Statistics and background.* Retrieved March 8, 2009, from www.cpj.org/deadly/index.html.

Doing Business. (2009). *Doing business 2009.* Retrieved October 28, 2008 from www.doingbusiness.org/Features/Feature-2008-22.aspx.

The Economist. (2008, September 30). *Spain forecast.* Retrieved October 31, 2008, from www.economist.com/COUNTRIES/Spain/profile.cfm?folder=Profile-Forecast.

London South East. (2008). Latin American GDP growth to slow, October 8. Retrieved October 26, 2008, from www.lse.co.uk/MacroEconomicNews.asp?ArticleCode=75a2wr6jjhcvz5j&ArticleHeadline=latin_american_gdp_growth_to_slow_imf_says.

NationMaster. (2008). *People statistics: Birth rate.* Retrieved October 31, 2008, from www.nationmaster.com/graph/peo_bir_rat-people-birth-rate.

World Association of Newspapers (WAN). (2008). *Press freedom.* Retrieved March 8, 2009, from www.wan-press.org/rubrique.php3?id_rubrique=922.

World Bank. (2009). World Bank website: www.world.bank.org/data.

Worldwide Spanish. (2008). *Worldwide Spanish speaking population statistics.* Retrieved October 26, 2008, from www.spanishseo.org/resources/worldwide-spanish-speaking-population/.

Contributors

Alan B. Albarran is Professor of Radio, Television and Film and Director of the Center for Spanish Language Media at the University of North Texas. His research interests revolve around the management and economics of the media industries and Spanish language media. He has authored or edited eight previous books in the areas of media management and economics, and served as the editor of two journals.

Ángel Arrese is Associate Professor of Marketing and Economic and Business Journalism at the School of Communication, University of Navarra, Spain. His main research interests are media marketing issues and the economic and financial news industry. He is the author of *La identidad de The Economist* (1994), *Economic and Financial Press* (2001) and *Prensa económica* (2002). He co-edited *Time and Media Markets* (2003) with Alan Albarran. He is the former editor of *Comunicación y Sociedad*, the leading academic communication journal in Spanish.

Juan Pablo Artero is Assistant Professor of Media Management and Structure of Media Industries at the School of Communication, University of Navarra, Spain. He holds a PhD in Public Communication from University of Navarra and an MSc in Management from Cass Business School (City University, London, UK). He is the author of *Modelos estratégicos de Telecinco (1990–2005)* (2007) and *El mercado de la televisión en España: oligopolio* (2008). He was a visiting fellow at the Institute for Media and Entertainment and Fordham University, New York.

Luz Carmen Barrera Avellaneda is a lecturer in the Faculty of Communication at Universidad de La Sabana, Colombia.

Ligia García Béjar is Academic Secretary and Graduate Studies Coordinator at Universidad Panamericana, in Guadalajara, Mexico. She is an MA candidate in Radio Television and Film at the University of North Texas, and holds a Certificate in Hispanic Marketing Communication from Florida State University.

Cristóbal Benavides is Professor of Media Management at the School of Communication of the Universidad de los Andes, Santiago, Chile. He is a journalist and has a Master's degree in Media Management from University of Navarra, Spain. His research interests include leadership and innovation in media companies.

Lauren Boyle is President of Grupo Exito, a Hispanic marketing and advertising firm in Dallas. With more than fifteen years' experience in US Hispanic media, she has held directorship positions at global advertising firms and has won several international awards for her work. She has directed numerous blue chip advertising accounts. She holds a Master's degree in Broadcast Media from the University of Arkansas, and has taught as an adjunct professor at the University of North Texas.

Lucila Carbajal teaches courses in Broadcast Journalism in the Communication School at the University of Montevideo, Uruguay.

Liliana Gutiérrez Coba is a lecturer in the Faculty of Communication and director of the Journalism Research Group at Universidad de La Sabana in Colombia.

Amy Jo Coffey is an assistant professor in the College of Journalism and Communications at the University of Florida where she teaches audience analysis, telecommunications management, and telecommunications programming. Her research interests include audience economics and language, with an emphasis on foreign language programming within the United States, as well as market segmentation and other strategic competition issues. She received her PhD from the University of Georgia, and holds an MA in journalism from the Ohio State University.

María Ignacia Errázuriz is Dean of the School of Communication at Universidad de los Andes in Chile. She is a journalist and holds a Master's degree in Journalism from the Pontificia Universidad Católica de Chile (Santiago). Her research interests include television production and quality in television and multimedia.

Cristina Etayo is a lecturer in the School of Communication, University of Navarra, Spain in the Department of Media Management where she teaches courses in media management and sales promotion. Her PhD was completed in the field of economics.

Paulo Faustino teaches media management, economics and marketing in the Portuguese Catholic University and Polytechnic Leiria Institute, Portugal. He is president of Formalpress (a publishing and consulting company). He is director of Media XXI Magazine and is an editorial board member of the *International Journal on Media Management* and board member of the European Media Management Association.

Germán Arango Forero is Chair of the Audiovisual and Multimedia Communication program at Universidad de La Sabana in Colombia. He is also a researcher at the Media Observer and a television journalist.

Guillermo Gibens is Associate Professor of Communications at William Penn University in Iowa. He gained a BA from Catholic University Andrés Bello of Caracas, Venezuela, and an MA in Communication Studies from the University of Kansas. After working for several years as a journalist, he went back to college and earned a PhD in Communication Studies at Bowling Green State University, Ohio. He also teaches communication at the Institute of International Studies at Ramkhamhaeng University in Bangkok, Thailand.

Alfonso Forero Gutiérrez is a lecturer in the Faculty of Communication at Universidad de La Sabana, Colombia.

Mónica Herrero is Associate Professor of Media Economics at the School of Communication, University of Navarra, Spain. She holds a Master's degree in Media Management from the University of Stirling, Scotland. Her research focuses on television economics, especially the main implications of direct viewer payments for the economics of the television industry. She is the author of *Programming and Direct Viewer Payment for Television* (2003) and *El Mercado de la televisión de pago en España* (2007).

Ángela Preciado Hoyos earned her PhD in Communication from the University of Navarra, Spain. She is a lecturer at the Social Communication School, Universidad Pontificia Bolivariana, Colombia, and teaches courses in communication management and corporate communication.

Eileen Hudson is Dean of the School of Communication School at the University of Montevideo, Uruguay.

David Kimber is Professor of Marketing at the School of Business and Economics of the Universidad de los Andes, Santiago. He has a degree in Economics and Business Administration and holds an MBA from the Pontificia Universidad Católica de Chile (Santiago). His research interests include marketing research, advertising research and quality in television.

Allen Panchana Macay is a professional journalist, the regional director of Ecuavisa (a TV Station) and Professor of the Communication Faculty of La Universidad Católica de Guayaquil in Ecuador.

Rodolfo Prada Penagos is a lecturer at the Faculty of Communication at Universidad de La Sabana, Colombia.

Juliet Pinto is an assistant professor in the Department of Journalism and Broadcasting at Florida International University. Her research interests include media and democratization processes in Latin America, Hispanics and media use, and environmental journalism. She received her PhD from the University of Miami, Florida.

Rosa Zeta de Pozo is Professor of Public Communication, Information Deontology and Communication markets in the School of Communication at the Universidad de Piura, Peru, where she is also the Director of Research and editor of the Communication magazine, Peruvian. She holds a PhD in Public Communication, an MA in Liberal Arts from Universidad de Navarra, Spain.

María Elena Gutiérrez Rentería is Dean of the School of Communication at Universidad Panamericana, Guadalajara, Mexico. She earned her PhD in Public Communication from the Universidad de Navarra, Spain. She is a member of the National System of Researchers in Mexico.

Adriana Guzmán de Reyes is Dean of the Faculty of Communication at Universidad de La Sabana, Colombia.

Fernando Salas is in charge of courses related to Sociology and Political Science at the University of Montevideo, Uruguay.

Catherine Salzman holds an MS in Radio, Television and Film from the University of North Texas. She resides in Dallas, Texas, where she works for a private research organization.

Ryan Salzman is a PhD student in Political Science at the University of North Texas. His research interests revolve around Latin American comparative politics, political culture, media, corruption, and democracy studies. He received his BA degree in Political Science from Texas Christian University.

Isabel Santa María is Professor of Print Journalism at the School of Communication of the Universidad de los Andes, Chile. She is a journalist and worked as a publisher of the National Newspaper Association magazine. Her research interests include newspaper journalism and television quality.

Luciana Silvestri is a researcher at the IAE Business School's Media and Entertainment Research Center for Latin America. She was a consultant at Accenture for the telecommunications and media and entertainment industries and later a consultant at Aventeon, a Munich, Germany, Seattle, USA, and Bangalore, India based start-up for mobile technologies.

Phyllis Slocum is a lecturer in the Department of Radio, Television and Film and the Station Manager of North Texas Television at the University of North Texas.

Gonzalo Soruco is Associate Professor in the School of Communication at the University of Miami. His research focuses on Latin American mass media, freedom of expression, and advertising. He has worked on Hispanic mass media and Hispanics' media uses, particularly among the populations of South Florida.

Federico Subervi is Professor and Director of the Center for the Study of Latino Media and Markets at the School of Journalism and Mass Communication, Texas State University-San Marcos. For more than 25 years, he has been teaching and conducting research on a variety of issues related to the media and ethnic groups, particularly Latinos in the United States. His research interests also extend to Latin America, where he has conducted studies about Blacks in the media of Brazil, and about the media system of Puerto Rico, his country of origin.

Rodrigo Jordán Tobar is a senior consultant for BO Communications of Quito and Quantum Inform. He is also a journalist and Principal Professor of the Communication Faculty of La Universidad de los Hemisferios in Ecuador.

Florencia Traibel teaches Broadcast Journalism in the School of Communication at the University of Montevideo, Uruguay.

Jairo Valderrama Valderrama is a lecturer in the Faculty of Communication at Universidad de La Sabana, Colombia.

Roberto S. Vassolo is Associate Professor of Strategy at IAE Business School in Buenos Aires, Argentina, and the Director of its Media and Entertainment Research Center for Latin America. He received his PhD from Purdue University, Indiana.

Aldo van Weezel is a doctoral candidate at the Media Management and Transformation Centre at Jönköping International Business School (Jönköping, Sweden). He holds a MSc in Engineering and a Master's degree in Media Management. His research interests are strategy and entrepreneurship in media companies.

Kenton T. Wilkinson is Regents Professor in Hispanic and International Communication in the College of Mass Communications at Texas Tech University. His international communication interests include mass media and free trade, and cultural-linguistic media markets. He also specializes in US Spanish language media and its Latin American connections, especially in Mexico.

Index

Abadía Méndez, Miguel, 70
ABC, 83, 154, 184, 228
access to media, 59–61, 70, 98–9, 156–7, 166, 219
 see also device ownership; internet access
ACIM, 66, 69, 263
ACIR group, 39
Acosta-Alzuru, C., 85
ACPV (Acció Cultural del País Valencia), 223
AD (Democratic Action), 79–80, 85
ADN, 24, 71, 148
advertisers, 84, 261–2, 268–9, 271, 295, 298
advertising, 37, 116, *126*, 129, 176–7, 185, 187,
 210–13, 259–60, 263–5; Argentina, 251–2, 254,
 256, 258–9, 261–3; Bolivia, 93, 98; Central
 America, 53, 56–7; Chile, 144–6, *145–6*;
 Colombia, 71, 228; and the economy, 249–53,
 250–3, 251; Hispanic, 12, 214, 267–9, 272;
 institutions, 258–64, *260–1*; intensity, 251–2,
 253; magazines, *254*, 255–6, *256*; newspapers,
 253–5, *254–5*; political, 225, 227; radio, *254*,
 257–8, *258*; Spain, 24, 26–7, 31, 250–4, 258,
 262–3; television, 209–13, 253–4, *254*, 256–7,
 257; United States, 6–8, 13, 209–15, *210–13*,
 231, 240, 242, 249–50, 253–4, 258, 263, 266,
 273
Advertising Age, 8–9, 12–14, 266, 268–71, 296
AEDEP, 106, 118–19
Africa, 279, 281, 284, 286, 291–2
African Americans, 207–8
age differences, 121, 135, 162–5, *165*, 167, *167*
Agosta, D. E., 61
agrarian economies, 48–9, 52, 55, 63, 68, 78, 89,
 103, 152, 183, 193
AHAA, 12, 214, 268–9, 272
Ahora, 193
AIMC, 31, 263
Ajá, 127–9, 136
Alarcón Costa, Cesar, 112
Albarran, A. B., 56–7
Alemán Valdes, Miguel, 57, 224
Alexander, Alfredo, 94
Aljovín, Cayetana, 134

Alvarado-Roca Group, 111–13, 115
AMAI, 36, 263
AMARC, 185
Amazonian Network, 118
AM Center, 83
América Movil, 43, 110, 186
América Televisión, 132–3
ANDA (National Association of Advertisers,
 Venezuela), 82
Angola, 281, 284
Anselmo, Rene, 9
Antena 3 group, 21–2, 26
Anzola, Edgar, 83
Apoyo, 128, 133, 135
Aramayo, Felix Avelino, 90, 93
Arbitron, 8, 197, 263
Arce, Armando, 94
Argentina, 151–5, 168–70, 294; advertising, 251–2,
 254, 256, 258–9, 261–3; social fragmentation,
 152, 155–68, *156*, *158–62*, *164–5*, *167*; television,
 154, 238, 242
Arias, Oscar, 55
Aris, A., 278
de Armas Bloc, 82
armed militias, 63–4, 95
Arráiz Lucca, R., 78–81
Arrese, A., 27, 296
Arroyave, J., 228–9
Artero, J. P., 27, 296
ARVM, 36–7, 39
aspirations, 52, 89, 151, 157–8, 160, 162–3, 165, 169
assimilation, 4, 62, 267–8
audiences, *29*, 58–61, 66, 131–3, *160–2*, *164–5*, *167*
 see also People Meters; press circulation; user
 profiles; ratings, 9–11, *27*, 30, 69, 140, 213–14;
 research, 15, 66, 114, 243, 262–3; segmentation,
 6, *37*, 39, 45, 74
audiovisual media legislation: Chile, 140, 148–9;
 Colombia, 68; Ecuador, 115, 118; Mexico, 34,
 37, 225; Peru, 130–1; Spain, 28, 223; Uruguay,
 174, 180; Venezuela, 86
Auna, 28

authoritarian regimes, 17–18, 79–82, 85, 89, 95–6, 100, 104, 174–7, 183, 189, 192–3, 199, 220–1
autonomies, 19–20, 30
Aymara, 91
Ayoreo, 185
AYRE (Broadcasting Central de Caracas), 82–3
Azcárraga, Emilio, 239–40
Azcárraga family, 38, 224
Azcárraga Vidaurreta, Emilio, 9
Aznar, José María, 23
Azteca América, 11, 13, 213–14, 231–2, 242, 269, 298

BabyCenter en Español, 270
Bachman, K., 11, 14
Baptista, Mariano, 92
Barrera Tyszka, A., 85
Barrios, M., 228–9
Basques, 18, 24, 30, 221–2
Batanga, 268, 270
Batlle Berres, Luis, 171
Batlle y Ordóñez, José, 173, 176
BBC, 116, 141, 219, 223, 226–7
Bednarski, P. J., 242
Beltrán Ramiro, L. R., 91, 93, 95
Bendixen and Associates, 5, 9
Benitez, J. L., 58
Betancourt, Rómulo, 79, 82
bilingualism, 3, 12, 14–15, 213, 215, 241, 243, 269–70
Billiken, 153
birth rates, 172, 208, 294–5, 295
Bisbal, M., 81–6
blogging, 136, 271–2
El Bocón, 127–8, 136
Bohemia, 190
Bolivia, 88–9, 100–2, 259, 262, 296–7; 21st-century challenges, 99–100; political factors, 96–9; press, 89–96, 98; television, 99, 99
book publishing, 148, 178, 277–9, 292–3; content industry dynamics, 282–4, 284; Iberian culture development, 279–82, 282; market, 285–92, 287–8
Booth, J. A., 47–9, 52, 59
BOP consumers, 155–7, 168–9
Boyacá 7 días, 64, 72
Boyle, L., 215, 295
Brazil, 242, 259, 262, 281, 284, 288, 291, 296–7
Breiner, James, 98
broadband, 13, 31–2, 75, 99, 121, 144, 154–5, 215, 281
broadcasting legislation see audiovisual media legislation
Broadcast Media Partners, 10, 241
Bucaram, Abdalá, 104
Buen Hogar, 109, 143
Bughin, J., 278
Buscando Estrellas, 238
business environments, 230, 232, 296–7, 297
Búsqueda, 176–7

Caballero Spanish Media, 8
cable television, 12, 22, 28, 58, 132–3, 179–80, 185, 209, 215; Cable TV, 128; Cablevisión, 37, 84, 154; Sogecable, 27; Supercable, 65, 84; TV Cable, 65, 115; TV Cable Group, 110
La Caceta de Chuquisaca, 93
Caetano, J., 173
Café 7 días, 64, 72
CAFTA, 57
Caldera, Rafael, 79–80, 82
Calderon, Felipe, 225
The Call of Oboe (Paraguay-Brazil), 186
La Calle, 94
Calpe, E., 280, 283
Cambio, 71
Canelas, Demetrio, 94
Cano, Guillermo, 65
Canoy, M., 285
La Capital, 153
capital-sharing relationships, 289–90
Capriles Network, 82
Caracol, 64–5, 68–70, 228
Caras, 73, 109, 120, 142–3, 146
Caras y Caretas, 153
Carat, 219
Cardenas, Victor Hugo, 97
Caretas, 135
Caribbean, 189–99, 297
Caribbean Business, 196
Carneiro, A., 280
Carocol, 65
Carrasco, José, 93
Carso Group, 35, 43, 261
Cartagena, C., 66, 208, 210
Casa Editorial El Tiempo (CEET), 64, 71–2
Castillo, Ruben, 174
Castro, Fidel, 97–8, 189–90
Castro, Julián, 79, 81
Castro, Raul, 193
Catalá, J. A., 82, 86
Catalans, 18, 24, 30, 221–2
Catalunya Radio, 30
Catholic Church, 20–2, 94, 117, 147, 190
CBS, 84, 141, 154
El Censor, 93
censorship, 19, 48, 54, 82, 86, 92, 95–6, 174, 190
census data, 103–4, 113, 125, 203, 208–10, 213, 223, 238, 266
Center for Spanish Language Media, US, 247
Central America, 61–2; advertising, 53, 56–7; audiences, 58–61; demographics, 50–1, 50–1; economic development, 49–50; globalization, 57–8; history, 47–9, 51–2; media oligarchies, 52–3; press freedom, 53–6
Cepero, I., 190
Cero Corá, 186
Céspedes, Augusto, 94
Cevallos, D., 225–6
Chabran, R., 220–1
Chaco War, 94–5

Chamorro family, 52
Chan-Olmsted, S. M., 56–7
Chávez, Hugo, 78, 80–2, 84–6, 97, 104
Chile, 139, 149–50, 250–2, 254, 256, 258, 261–3, 296; advertising, 144–6, *145–6*; internet, 144, *145*; ownership, 146–8; press, 141–3, *142*, 148; radio, 143, *143*, 146–9; television, 140–1, 144, 146–9
CIA, 48–9, 51, 59, 78, 152, 184, 189, 193–6
Cine en Español, 238
cinema, 186–7, 238, 241–2
Cisneros, Diego, 83
Cisneros group, 69, 84–5
Cisneros, Gustavo, 85
Cisneros, Henry, 10
civil conflict, 48, 63–4, 75, 79–80, 88, 92, 94–100, 104–5, 220, 227, 229, 296
Claridad, 196
Clarín Group, 152, 154
Claro Group, 140, 147, 155, 186
Claro, Ricardo, 147
class differences, 38, 142, 151, 155, 162
Clave, 193
Clear Channel Group, 8, 39
ClickOcio.com, 270
CMET, 144
CMT, 31
CNN en Español, 208, 231, 264
CNP journalists' guild, Venezuela, 86
CNR National Radio Coordinator, Peru, 132
CNTV, 65, 69, 140–1, 149, 227
COB workers' center, Bolivia, 95
Coca-Cola, 84, 261–2, 269, 298
CODESI, 134
Coen, R. J., 295
Coffey, A. J., 207, 214–15
Cold War, 96
Colgate-Palmolive, 261, 298
Colmenares, Fabiola, 85
Colmundo, 65
Colombia, 48–9, 74–6, 110, 233, 251–2, 254–5, 257–9, 262–4, 284, 294, 296–8; consumer trends, 66, *67*; history, 63–4, 227; internet, 73–4; ownership, 64–6; press, 64, 71–3; radio, 64–5, 70–1; television, 64–70, 75, 219, 226–30, 233
Colombia Móvil, 261
El Colombiano, 71–2
colonial rule, 47–9, 78, 89, 93, 110, 193, 224, 227
Columbia Pictures, 241–2
Comcel, 261
El Comercio, 119, 126–30, 136
El Comercio Group, 111–13, 116, 120–1, 129–30
commercial radio, 8, 22, 70, 83, 95, 116–17, 173
commercial television, 19, 21, 36–7, 83–4
Communication Act (US), 9
communication firms Mexico, *44*
Communism, 64, 79–80, 85, 122, 177, 189–90
community radio, 61, 70–1, 84, 95, 118, 132, 175, 185

community television, 84, 115
competition, 10, 24, 26–7, 38, 43, 45, 51, 110, 122, 214–15, 231–2, 237
complementary research, 246–7
ComScore Media Metrix, 270
CONARTEL, 115, 117
CONATEL, 83, 185–6
El Condor de Bolivia, 93
conferences and festivals, 187, 259, 268, 270
Constantakil-Valdéz, P., 241–2, 245
El Constitucional, 81
consumers, BOP, 155–7, 168–9
consumer trends, 20, 37–8, 58, 66, 72–3, 113–14, 156, 179, 181; books, 286–8, *287*; Colombia, 66, *67*; Ecuador, 113–14, 119; Hispanic, 266–7; Paraguay, *184*; Peru, *126*, 128–9, 131–2
convergence, 10–14, 37, 45, 72–3, 135–6, 152, 155, 181, 188, 221, 281
Convergencia, 152, 154–5
COPACO SA, 186
COPE Group, 21–2, 30
COPEI (Social Christian Party), 79–80, 85
Copesa Group, 143, 148
CORAPE, 117–18
Cordovez Borja, Carlos, 116
corporate strategies/practices, 286, 290
Corporativo Mina, 42
Correa Delgado, Rafael, 103–6, 108, 115, 121
Correo, 127–9, 136
El Correo del Orinoco, 81
Correo group, 20, 22–3
corruption, 50, 55–6, 80, 86, 183, 224, 226–7
Cosas, 120, 143, 146
CosmeticSEO.com, 270
Cosmopolitan, 43, 143
Costa Rica, 48, 50–5, 58–61, 251–2, 254–6, 258, 262
Costumbrismo, 220
coups d'état, 79, 85, 95, 154, 173
CPI, 129, 131, 133
CPJ, 225–6, 297
CPLP, 282
CPN, 128, 131
credibility issues, 98, 105, 116, 121, 178, 229
Cromos, 65, 73
Crónica (Ferretjans), 176, 184
El Cronista Comercial, 153
La Cuarta, 142, 148
Cuatro, 27
Cuba, 97, 189–90, 199; internet, 192–3; press, 190–1, *191*; radio, 191–2, *192*; television, 192, *192*
Cubavisión, 192
cultural identity, 3, 30, 207, 209, 221, 241–2, 278, 280–1, 284–5, 290–1

daily papers, 5, 22, 24, 41, 128, *128*, 129–30, 176–8; Mexico, *41–2*; Peru, 129–30
D'Andrea, G., 156–7
DANE, 73–4
Danone, 261–2

debt issues, 49, 91
decentralization, 19, 129, 136
defamation laws, 54, 94, 99–100, 223, 225
Delta Publicity, 112
democracy/democratization: Bolivia, 93, 96–7;
    Caribbean, 193, 199; Central America, 50, 53–4,
    62; Chile, 139; Ecuador, 104, 106–10, 118, 122;
    Mexico, 36, 41, 45; Paraguay, 187–8; Spain,
    17–19, 21; Uruguay, 172, 174; Venezuela, 78–80
Democratic Corporatist model, 219–20, 222
demographic factors: Argentina, 161; Central
    America, 50–1, *50–1*; Colombia, 63; Mexico, 36;
    Peru, 125; United States, 4, 6, 12, 14, 204,
    208–9, 214–15; Uruguay, 172–3, 175;
    Venezuela, 77, 86
Dennis, E. E., 81, 84
deregulation, 35, 152
desacato laws, 100
device ownership, 58–61, *59*, 83–4, *126*, 135, 143,
    185, 187, 219
El Día, 176
Dial, 148
Diario, 93, 176
Diario 16, 20
Diario Clarín, 153
Diario de Lima, 126
Diario Financiero, 142, 147
Diario Hoy, 112–13, 121
Diario La Prensa, 5
Diario Super, 120
Díaz Ordaz, Gustavo, 34
Díaz, Rámon, 177
Díaz Rangel, E., 81–2, 86
dictatorships *see* authoritarian regimes
Digital +, 28
digital media, 12, 22–4, 45, 112–13, 281; Chile, 149;
    Colombia, 66; United States, 12–14
digital television, 27–8, 134, 149, 181, 215, 221
Dinediciones, 108, 112
Diners World, 108, 112, 120
Direct TV, 84, 140, 154, 180, 232
Discodromo, 174
Discovery Channels, 12, 208, 264
Disney, 228
Dolan, K. A., 240
Dominican Republic, 196, 199, 262, 295, 297;
    internet, 195, *195*; press, 193–4, *194*; radio, 194,
    194; television, 194–5, *195*
Dominican Times, 193
drug trafficking, 64, 96–7, 183, 225–7, 229–30
dual product market, 56, 210

Earp, F. S., 285
economic crises, 179, 220, 232, 251–2, 295;
    Argentina, 151–3; Bolivia, 91, 96; Chile, 144;
    Ecuador, 104–5, 116, 121; Spain, 23; Uruguay,
    173, 179
economic factors, 56, 126, 139, 151, 199, 224, 232
    see also economic crises; macroeconomics;
    advertising, 249–53, *250–3*, 251; agriculture,

48–9, 52, 55, 63, 68, 78, 89, 103, 152, 183, 193;
    book publishing, 285; Central America, 49–50;
    instability, 89, 296; mining, 78, 89–95, 100;
    Uruguay, 171–2; US TV news, 230–1
The Economist, 139, 151–2, 169, 228, 295
Ecuador, 103–6, 122–4, 259, 262, 296; consumer
    trends, 113–14, 119; democratization, 104,
    106–10, 118, 122; internet, 120–1, *120–1*; media
    groups, *111*, 111–13; press, 109, 118–20, *119*;
    Quito-Guayaquil Axis, 110–11; radio, 105,
    108–9, 116–18, *117*; television, 105, 108–9,
    114–15, 114–16
Ecuadorinmediato, 113
Ecuador TV, 114
Ecuavisa, 112–14
Ediciones PLM, 42
Edipresse group, 26, 283
Editora Cinco, 42
Editora Peru, 128
Editora Sindesa, 127–8
editorial stances, 39, 81, 85, 93–4, 106, 108, 177,
    223
Editorial Televisa, 42, 109, 142
Editorial Vid group, 42
education, 20, 51, 68, 125, 227
Edwards family, 147–8
EFE news agency, 223
Egas, Fidel, 108, 112
Egas Group, 113
EGM, 25, 31, 66, 71–2, 74, 263
Elite, 82
Eljuri family, 112
Ellingwood, K., 225–6
ELN (National Freedom Army), 64, 227
El Salvador, 48, 50–5, 57–9, 61, 297
emerging markets, 156, *156*, 157, 279
La Encuesta, 135
Endemol, 23, 283
entertainment, 51, 114, 156, 158, 160–3, *162*, 166,
    180, 238, 243, 246, 278
Entravision Communication, 8
EPENSA, 127–9
Equity Media Holdings Corp., 232
Escala, 43
Escalier, José Maria, 93
El Espectador, 65, 72, 174, 176
ESPN, 12, 264
ESPN Deportes, 6, 12
Estrategia, 142
ETA (Euskadi ta Askatasuna), 222–3
Etayo, C., 295
ethnic issues, 88–92, 97–8, 100, 204
European Union, 18, 21–2, 172, 280–1, 296
Expansión group, 42
Expreso, 112, 128, 136, 196
Extra, 112, 119, 128

face-to-face promotions, 273–5
family ownership, 52–3, 65, 71–2, 147–8, 179,
    224–5, 228

FARC (Colombian Revolutionary Armed Forces), 64, 227
Fasano, Federico, 177, 180
Faura, J., 267–8
Faustino, P., 280, 283, 296
FCC, 9, 209, 230, 239
Federal War, Venezuela, 78–9
Federation of Jounalist Trade Unions, 221
Ferreira, L., 95, 224
Ferretjans, Álvarez, 176–7
festivals and conferences, 187, 259, 268, 270
Fidel Egas Group, 111–12
Filanbanco, 105–6
Filgueira, Carlos and Fernando, 171
First Chicago, 9–10
Fisher, C., 240
Flores Perez, Francisco, 57
FMLN (Farabundo Marti National Liberation Front), 49
focus group interviews, 158–61, *159–61*
Fontaina, Raul, 179
foreign capital/investment: Bolivia, 95–6, 98; Central America, 50, 53, 57–8; Colombia, 64, 72, 75; Ecuador, 109–10, 121; Mexico, 35; Spain, 18, 21–2, 26
foreign ownership policies, 8–9, 21, 107, 130–1, 140, 148–9, 152, 239–40
Forrester Research, 13, 271
Fouce v. SICC (1976), 9
Fox Latin America, 12, 264
Fox Sports en Español, 12, 208, 231
Fox, Vincente, 226
fragmentation factors, 157, 162, 168, 242 *see also* horizontal fragmentation; social fragmentation; vertical fragmentation
Franco, Francisco, 17–19, 220–1, 296
Frecuencia Latina, 132–3
Freedman, J., 91
Freedom House, 50, 53–4, 88, 94, 98
freedom of information/expression, 232–3 *see also* press freedom; Bolivia, 93–4, 99; Caribbean, 190, 199; Central America, 53, *55*; Chile, 148–9; Colombia, 75, 227, 230; Ecuador, 106–7, 118–19; Peru, 127; Spain, 19–21; Uruguay, 174, 176; Venezuela, 80
Freedom of the Press Index, 53–4
free newspapers, 24, 40, 119–20, 142
free-to-air television, 23, 26–8, 132
Frente Nacional, 63
frequency concentration: Ecuador, 117–18
FTA, 141
Fucsia, 108, 112
Fundación Cinematica, 186
Fundación Telefónica, 38, 183–5, 187
future research: advertising, 264; book publishing, 292; Colombia, 75; Ecuador, 122; globalization, 297–9; LaMP, 247–8; Peru, 137; United States television, 215; Venezuela, 86

La Gaceta di Puerto Rico, 196

gaceta press, 93
Galavisión, 11–12, 230, 237
Galbraith, J. K., 251
Galeano, Eduardo, 66
Galicians, 18, 30, 221
Galvis group, 65–6
Gamarra, H., 186–7
Gama TV, 105, 114
García-Avilés, J.A., 73
Garnica, A., 38
The Gate of Dreams (Paraguay), 186–7
La Gazeta de Caracas, 81
GEM (Global Entrepreneurship Monitor), 296–7
Gems, 12, 84
gender differences, 38, 143, 151, 162–3
General Electric, 69, 225, 237
Gestión, 129–30, 135
Gestión Group, 127–30, 135
Giampietro Scheck family, 179
Gill, J., 222, 228
Ginsberg, L., 227–9
globalization, 10, 13, 18, 35, 43, 57–8, 62, 66, 89, 181, 283, 291, 294–9; future research, 297–9
Globo Brazil, 180
Globovisión, 85
GLR Networks, 146, 148
Godó group, 24
Gómez family, 72
Gómez, Juan Vicente, 79, 81–2
González, Ángelo González, 53, 57–8, 61, 69, 109, 140
Gonzalez, Felipe, 22
government pressure, 71, 126, 154, 176, 185, 220; Bolivia, 92–3, 95–6, 99–100; Central America, 54, 57; Cuba, 190, 192–3; Ecuador, 105–6, 118; Mexico, 34–5, 40, 224; Venezuela, 81–2, 85–6
El Gráfico, 40, 153
Gráficos Nacionales SA Group, 112–13
Granda Centeno, Antonio, 108
Granda Garcés, Eduardo, 108
Granma, 190
Guadalupe-Hidalgo Treaty, 5
Guaraní, 91, 183–5
Guatemala, 50–5, 57–61, 262, 297
guerrilla groups, 63, 75, 79–80, 173, 226–7
Guisti, Roberto, 85
Gutiérrez, F. F., 7–8, 240
Gutiérrez, Lucio, 104
Gutiérrez, M., 34–5, 223, 225
Guzmán Blanco, Antonio, 78–9

Hachette, 20, 26
Hallin, D., 219–20, 223, 226, 230, 232, 281
Hallmark Cards, 9–10, 240
Hanson, S., 222, 227
The Havana Post, 190
HBC, 215
Herrán, M., 71
Herrero, M., 27–8, 296

HispanicAd, 266–8, 272
Hispanic Advertising Agencies Association, 12, 214, 268–9, 272
Hispanic Broadcasting, 8
Hispanic Business, 6, 8, 269, 271
Hispanic communities, US, 3–4, 14, 203–4, 208–9, 238–9, 266, 295–6
Hispanic consumer trends, 266–7
Hispanic markets, 288, 291
Hispanic PR Wire, 228, 232, 270
Hispanic subgroups, 242–3
Hispanic votes, US, 3–4
Hochschild, Mauricio, 90, 94
Hogar, 112, 153
Hola group, 25–6
holamun2.com: El Show, 13
Honduras, 50, 52–5, 58, 60, 251–2, 254, 256, 258, 296–7
La Hora, 110–11, 119, 121, 142, 148
La Hora-Editorial Minotauro Group, 112
horizontal fragmentation, 135, 151, 156–60, *159*, 162–5, 207
Hoy, 71–2, 94, 108
Hoy Group, 112–13, 120
Hoyos, Rodolfo, 7

Iberian culture development, 280–2, 291–2; book publishing, 279–82, *282*; markets, 279, 288–9, 292
Ibope, 39, 69, 113–14, 119, 261–3
ICRT, 191–2
ideological polarization, 29, 52, 63, 81–2, 85–6, 88, 93–5, 97–8, 104, 227
illegal production/consumption, 58, 86, 154, 175, 185, 187–8, 190, 192
Imagenio IPTV service, 28
Imevisión, 11
IMF, 103, 151–2
immigrants, 4–5, 208, 238
Impala, 283
imported programming, 57–8, 141, 181, 198, 228, 238–40, 243
ImpreMedia, 5
Impulsa TDT, 28
independence struggles, 4, 48–9, 78, 81
Index scores: Central America, *51*
indigenous peoples, 47–8, 88–93, 95–8, 100, 104, 118; activism, 96–9
La Industria, 128, 136
INEC, 103–4, 113
INEI, 125–6, 134–5
inequalities, 35, 48, 55, 74, 88–93, 97, 100, 151, 155
Infoadex, 31, 263
Informative Network, 118
institutionalization, 7–8
interactivity, 13, 40, 154, 175
Inter American Press Association, 105, 226
International Advertising Association, 249
internationalization, 223, 232, 279, 281, 284, 288
international markets, 10, 26, 38, 41, 57, 69, 239–40

internet, 23, 37, 58–9, 64, 75, 105, 112–13, 146, 174, 190, 254, 269–72 *see also* online media; access, 52, 73–4, 86, 99, 120, *120*, 134, 144, 192–3, 272, 281; Argentina, 154; blogging, 136, 271–2; Chile, 144, *145*; Colombia, 73–4; Cuba, 192–3; cyber cafés, 52, 120; Dominican Republic, 195, *195*; Ecuador, 120–1, *120–1*; Paraguay, 187; Peru, *133–4*, 134–6; Puerto Rico, 198; Spain, 31–2, *32*; web traffic, 31–2, *32*, 121, *121*
Interviú, 20
IPTV, 28, 140
Isaías group, 105–6, 110–11, 113, 115
Isidra Mencos, 270
isolation, 91, 95, 183
IVM, 40–1
Izarra, A., 85

Janus, N., 48, 51–2, 57–8
Japan, 249–50, 253–4
Jara, E., 38
Jimenez family, 53
Jiménez, Marcos Pérez, 79, 82
John Blair & Co., 241
journalism, 39, 174–5, 178, 190, 219, 221–2, 245–6; risk factors, 54, 57, 81–2, 86, 93–4, 96, 98–9, 222–6, 228–30, 297
Juventud Tebelde, 190

Kanellos, N., 4–5
Katz Hispanic Radio, 8
KCOR, 7, 238
Kichwa Network, 118
KMEX-TV, Los Angeles, 10, 241
Kornis, G., 285
Kumar, K., 62
KVEA, 10

Lamac, 262, 264
LaMP, 245–8
language metrics, 214
language use variations, 3, 7, 12, 242–3
Latin America, 279–80, 284, 286, 288, 290–2, 297 *see also individual countries and regions*
Latino Print Network, 5
LATV, 213, 215
left-wing politics, 18, 63, 152, 172 *see also* Communism; Socialism
legal structures: Peru, 130–1, 134
legislation *see also* audiovisual media legislation; defamation laws: audiovisual media SUBS, 37, 68, 86, 115, 118, 130–1, 140, 148–9, 174, 180, 223, 225; internet, 134; press, 54, 94, 99–100, 106–7, 127, 178, 223, 225, 227; telecommunications, 35, 43, 73
Leoni, Raúl, 79
El Liberal, 65, 81
liberalization, 19, 43, 80
Liberal model, 219, 230
Liberman Broadcasting, 8
Liberty Global, 147, 152

Liberty Media, 11, 140
Libro Policiaco, 42
Libro Semanal, 42
Libro Vaquero, 42
licensing, 21, 27, 54, 69–70, 130, 140, 149, 180, 220,
    224, 228, 230, 239–40
lifecycle stage differences, 151, 162–5, *165*, 167,
    167
Lineas y Puntos, 283
Lippmann, Walter, 92
Listin Diario, 193
literacy, 51, 78, 125, 184, 220
Llano 7 dias, 64, 72
Lloreda family, 72
local media: press, 40, 43, 65, 109, 111–13, 120,
    126, 129; radio, 29, 40, 116, 131–2, 175, 191;
    television, 26, 68–9, 84, 114–15, 141, 154, 192,
    208–9, 218, 238
local news, 93, 175, 231–2
Los 40 Principales Ecuador, 109
Lotus Hispanic Reps, 8
Lugo, Fernando, 183, 185
Lusophone communities, 277, 288, 291

macroeconomics, 35–6, *36*–7, 43, 249, 251
The Magazine, 111
Magazine Cosas, 109
magazines, 42–3, 72–3, 120, 129, *142*, 142–3, 146,
    153, 253–4, *256 see also* online media; print
    genres; advertising, *254*, 255–6, *256*; Caribbean,
    190–1, *191*, 193–4, 196; Spain, 20, 25–6, *26*;
    United States, *6*, 6–7
Mahaud Witt, Jamil, 104–5
Mallorquin, Gonzalo, 105
Management, 108, 112
managerial mass media, 21–4
managerial strategies/practices, 286, 290
La Mañana, 81, 176
Mancini, P., 219–20, 223, 226, 230, 232, 281
Mantilla family, 111–12
Manzanera, Miguel, 100
Marca, 20, 22
Marcano, C., 85
María Escobar (Paraguay), 187
Marich, R., 242
market maturation, US, 214–15
Marsh, M., 90–1
Marti, Jose Martí, José, 190
Martinez Ruiz-Velasco, L., 13–14
Marxism-Leninism, 64, 122, 177
MAS (Movimiento al Socialismo), 98–100
MasterCardespanol.com, 271
Mata family, 81
Maxwell, R., 21, 220
McFarlane, Cynthia, 268
MCG (Media Capital Group), 283
McQuail, D., 215
media agencies, 260–1, *261*
media groups, 19, 24, 65, 107, *111*, 111–13, 127,
    146, 175, 183–4, 228, 259

media models, 219, 225; Hallin and Mancini, 223,
    226, 230, 232, 281
Media Observatory, 122
media oligarchies, 52–3
Mediapro, 27
Mediaset Group, 21, 23, 26
Mediterranean Axis, 280
Mega, 141, 147, 242
melodramas, 38, 83, 141, 242–3, 271
Méndez, M., 40, 42
El Mensagero Lusianés, 4
MERCOSUR, 172, 183, 185–7
El Mercurio, 141, 146–7
El Mercurio Group, 147–8
Mercurio Peruano, 126
mergers and acquisitions, 8–9, 11, 26, 28, 64–6,
    140, 147–9, 240–2, 283
Mesa, Carlos, 97
Metro, 24, 142
Metrohoy, 112, 119–20
Metropolis Intercom, 140, 147
Metroquil, 112, 120
Mexican-Americans, 5, 238
Mexican Federal Elections Board, 225
Mexico, 34–8, 43–6, *44*, 58, 61, 224, 284, 294,
    296–8; advertising, 251–2, 254, 256, 258–9,
    261–4; macroeconomics, 35–6, *36*–7;
    newspapers, *41*–2; press, 40–3, *41*–2; radio,
    39–40; television, 38–9, *39*, 219, 223–6, 233; and
    United States, 5, 35, 39, 41, 238, 240, 242
Migration Network, 118
mining industry, 78, 89–91, 93–5, 100
Miró Quesada family, 127
El Misisipí, 4
MNR (Revolutionary Nationalist Movement), 94–6
mobile communications, 13–14, 23, 112, 135, 155,
    181, 186, 272–3
modernization, 17–18, 79, 91
monopolies, 18, 21, 27, 35, 38, 43, 57, 65, 107, 109,
    224–5, 285
Montenegro, Carlos, 94
de Moragas, Gramunt, 95
Morales, Evo, 88–9, 96–100, 104
El Mosquito, 153
Movistar, 110, 155, 262
MTV, 12, 213, 231, 242, 283
Multicanal, 154, 180
multimedia groups, 21, 45, 112–13, 122, 149, 175,
    240, 243
Multivisión, 192
Mun2, 12, 213, 215, 237, 242, 268
El Mundo, 22, 24, 82
music industry, 8, 30, 40, 116, 175, 187, 197, 237
Muy Interesante, 43
MVS Radio, 39, 43
MySpace, 270–1

La Nación: Argentina, 153; Chile, 148; Paraguay,
    184
El Nacional: Cuba, 193; Venezuela, 82, 84

Napoleón Franco survey, 69
Nardone, Benito, 173
National Association of Broadcasters, 215
National Association of Hispanic Journalists, 231, 245–6
National Constitutions: Bolivia, 96, 99–100; Chile, 148–9; Cuba, 189–90; Ecuador, 104–8, 121; Mexico, 224–5; Peru, 127; Spain, 221; United States, 230; Uruguay, 174
National Geographic, 109, 143, 264
nationalism, 18, 20
nationalization, 95, 220
national radio/television: Venezuela, 83
national security, 118, 127
natural resources, 90–2
NBC, 11, 13–14, 83, 154, 213, 215, 225, 231, 237, 242
Nearing, S., 91
Negocio, 24
neoliberalism, 35, 49–50, 96–9
Nerone, C., 96
Nestlé, 261–2, 298
Net TV, 27
Network Communicators for Teens, 118
newspapers *see also* daily papers; free newspapers; print genres; regional press; tabloids: advertising, 253–5, *254–5*; Argentina, 153; Bolivia, *98*; Caribbean, 190, *191*, 193, *194*, 196; Central America, 51, 58; Chile, 141–2, *142*, 144, 146; Colombia, 65–6, 71–2, 74; Ecuador, 110–11; Mexico, 40–2, *41–2*; Peru, 126–7, *128*; Spain, 20, 22, 24, *25*, 220; United States, 4–6, *6*; Uruguay, 176–7; Venezuela, 85
NHTI, 207, 213–14
Nicaragua, 48–53, 55–8, 60, 251–2, 254–6
Nicolás, Emilio, 238
Nielsen Media Research, 32, 156, 207, 214, 263, 266, 269, 273 *see also* People Meters; People Meters, 69, 114, 213, 262
non-conventional media advertising, 250–1
Noriega, Manuel, 54
Nosty, D., 281
El Nuevo Día, 196

OAX, 131
objectivity MORE, 178
El Observador, 177–8
Observatorio de Medios, 69, 71, 75
Ocampo, E., 93–4
Ocampo, M. C., 66
O'Farrill family, 224
OJD (Audit Bureau of Circulation), 32, 263
Ojo, 127–9, 136
oligopolies, 27, 43, 52–3, 56, 107, 179–80
Olivares, Francisco, 85–6
Onda Cero group, 22–3, 29–30
Ondas del Lago Televisión, 83
online media, 31–2, 41, 70, 75, 130, 135–6, *136*, 137, 148, 174, 190, 215, 237, 271
Ono, 28, 31

open access television, 36, 38
Open Mobile Video Coalition, 14
La Opinión, 5
opt-in advertising, 272–3
Organización Radiorama, 39
organized crime, 225–6
Ortega, Daniel, 55–6
Otero family, 82, 85
Over the View TV, 179
ownership of media, 7, 10–11, 29, 57, 64–6, 105, 107–11, 117, 127, 146–8, 226, 230 *see also* family ownership; foreign ownership policies
ownership policies, 21, 107, 130–1, 140, 148–9, 152, 239–40

Páez, José Antonio, 78, 81
El País, 20–1, 24, 32, 41, 71–2, 176–8, 280
Panama, 48–50, 52–4, 56, 60–1, 262
PAN (National Action Party), 34, 224
Papel Periódico de la Habana, 190
Pappas Broadcasting, 11
Paradizábal, Sebastián, 173
Paraguay, 91, 183–8, 251–2, 254, 256, 262
Paraguay Ahora, 184
Paraguayan Visual Archives, 186
paramilitary organizations, 64, 75, 226–7, 229–30
Park, Robert, 92
party influence, 71, 126, 154, 176, 185, 220; Bolivia, 92–3, 95–6, 99–100; Central America, 54, 57; Ecuador, 105–6, 118; Mexico, 34–5, 40, 224; Venezuela, 81–2, 85–6
party press, 93, 220, 223–4
Patiño, Ricardo, 106
Patiño, Simon, 90, 93
Patria, 94, 190
Paula, 143, 146, 148
pay television, 11, 13, 21, 27–8, *29*, 37–8, 43, 69, 75, 141, 154, 179–80
Paz Estenssoro, Victor, 95–6
Pazos Kanqui, Vicente, 93
PBT, 153
PCC (Cuban Communist Party), 189–90
PCV (Venezuelan Communist Party), 79
Pecado Cozza family, 53
Peirano, Ricardo, 177
penetration: Argentina, 154–5; Caribbean, 194–5, 198; Central America, 51; Chile, 144; Colombia, 71, 73, 75; Mexico, 38, 43; Paraguay, 184–5, 187; Spain, 24, 28, 31; Uruguay, 174, 179
People Meters, 11–12, 69, 114, 213, 262
Pepsi, 261–2, 269
Perenchio, A. Jerrold, 10, 240–2
Pérez Alfonzo, Juan Pablo, 79, 82
Pérez, Carlos Andrés, 80, 82
Pérez family, 111
Pérez-Linan, A., 219
Periódicos Asociados, 72
Personal, 155, 186
Peru, 125–6, *126*, 136–8, 251–2, 254–9, 262–3, 295–7; internet, *133–4*, 134–6; press, 126–30,

128, *134*, 135–6; radio, 131–2, *132*, 136;
    television, 130, 132–4, *133*, 136
Perú, 127, 129, 136
El Peruano, 126–8, 135
Peruvian Radio Corporation, 131–2
Peruvian Scientific Net, 134
Pessoa, Fernando, 288
Pew Hispanic Center, 208, 231, 272
Pew Internet, 270, 272–3
Phelps/Granier Group, 83–5
Picard, R. G., 56, 252
Piñera, Sebastián, 140
Planeta group, 26, 29–30, 64, 69, 71–2, 289
Planimedios, 112
Plus, 131–2
Polarized Pluralism, 219–20, 222–3, 226, 281
political advertising, 225, 227
political background: Bolivia, 96–9; Uruguay,
    173
political bias, 19, 29, 39, 51, 81, 92, 106, 148,
    176–7, 185, 224
political debate, 19, 75
political instability, 56, 89, 104
political journalism, 22, 126, 153, 177–8
political pluralism, 45
political upheaval, 22, 151, 296
Polity IV, 50–1
Popular, 120, 128–9
Popular group, 29–30
Popular Mechanics, 109, 143
population size, 36, 125, 172–3, 204, 208–13,
    294–5 *see also* birth rates; demographic factors
Portada.com, 270–1, 273
Portafolio, 64, 72
Portugal, 277–84, 288–91
Portuguese language, 277–93, 296
poverty, 48, 52, 55, 88–9, 91 *see also* inequalities
Prahalad, C. K., 155
Preciado, A., 295
La Prensa, 48, 52, 81, 94, 126, 153
La Prensa del Movimiento, 19–20
Prensa Ibérica group, 24
Prensa Latina, 190
press *see also* magazines; newspapers; press
    freedom; print genres: Argentina, 153; Bolivia,
    89–96; Chile, 141–3, *142*, 148; Colombia, 64,
    71–3; Cuba, 190–1, *191*; Dominican Republic,
    193–4, *194*; Ecuador, 109, 118–20, *119*; Mexico,
    40–3, *41–2*; Paraguay, 184; Peru, 126–30, *128*,
    134, 135–6; Puerto Rico, 196, *197*; Spain, 20, 22,
    24–6, *25–6*, 220–1, 223; United States, 4–7, *6*,
    6–7, 230, 232; Uruguay, 176–9; Venezuela,
    81–2, 86
press circulation, 25, 32, 40–1, 128–9, 141, 153,
    184, 263
press freedom, 233 *see also* freedom of
    information/expression; Bolivia, 88–9, 93–4, 96,
    99–100; Central America, 53–6; Chile, 149;
    Colombia, 227; Colombia, 75; Mexico, 224–5;
    Spain, 220–1, 223; Venezuela, 80, 85

press law, 54, 94, 99–100, 106–7, 127, 178, 223, 225,
    227
PRI, 34, 224
price concessions and tariffs, 115–16
PricewaterhouseCoopers (PwC), 286
print genres, 6, 42, 128, 143, 153
Prisa group, 21–4, 27, 30–2, 64, 69, 98, 148, 280,
    283, 289–90, 296, 298
privacy laws, 54, 127
privatization, 18–20, 22–3, 35, 68, 96, 105
Procter & Gamble, 261–2, 298
professionalization, 45, 94, 178–9, 181, 221–2
programming genres, 38, 69, 71, 114, 131, 141, 175
promotional practices, 24, 274–5
Pronto, 25
propaganda, 19, 174, 185–6
Público, 24
public opinion, 22–3, 39, 41–3, 73, 94, 119, 154
public radio, 70–1, 83, 117, 185
public television, 21, 23, 26, 38, 68, 84, 105, 115,
    132, 180
Publimetro, 142
Publipromueve, 112
El Pueblo, 128
Puerto Montt Channel 7, 147
Puerto Rico, 196–7, *197*, 197–8, *198*, 198–9, 237,
    241, 263

quality, 114, 141, 175, 181, 192, 243
Qué!, 24
Quechua, 91
Qué Pasa, 143, 146, 148, 270
Quesada, Vicente Fox, 34
Quintos de Jesus, Melinda, 219
Quito-Guayaquil Axis, 110–11

El Radical, 93
radio: advertising, *254*, 257–8, *258*; Argentina,
    153–4; Bolivia, 95, 98; Central America, 51, 58,
    61; Chile, 143, *143*, 146–9; Colombia, 64–5,
    70–1; Cuba, 191–2, *192*; Dominican Republic,
    194, *194*; Ecuador, 105, 108–9, 116–18, *117*;
    Mexico, 39–40; Paraguay, 184–5; Peru, 131–2,
    132, 136; Puerto Rico, 196–7, *197*; Spain, 20–1,
    23, 29–31, *30–1*; United States, 7–9; Uruguay,
    173–6; Venezuela, 82–3
Radio and TV Martí, 192
Radio Caracas, 83–4
Radio Casa de la Cultura, 105
Radio Centro group, 37, 39
Radio Chilena, 147
Radio City (regional), 111, 113
Radio Comas, 132
Radio Disney, 109, 269
Radio Enciclopedia, 191
Radio Exa Ecuadoris, 109
Radio Fórmula group, 39
Radio Havana, 191
Radio Illimani, 95
Radiolandia, 153

Radio Mix (Radio A), 131
Radio Moda, 131
Radio Musical Nacional, 191
Radio Nacional: Ecuador, 105; Paraguay, 185; Peru, 128
radio news, 7, 22, 116–17, 220
Radio Panamericana, 131
Radio Progreso, 191
Radio Quito, 111, 116
Radio Rebelde, 191
Radio Reloj, 191, 197
Radio San Borja, 132
Radio Sarandí, 174, 176
Radio Taíno, 191
Radio Top FM (Radio Inca), 131
Radio Valencia Televisión, 83–4
Radio Vigía de la Policía Nacional, 105
Radio Ya, 51
Ramos, Angel, 241
Ramos, Jorge, 242
La Razón, 93, 98, 136, 153
RBA group, 26, 283
RCN Group, 65, 68–70, 228
RCTV, 85
Reagan, Ronald, 96
Rebeca, 13
Recoletos Group, 20, 22–3, 147
Red Privada de Comunicación, 184
Red Uruguaya de Televisión, 179
Reforma group, 41
Reggaetón, 8
regime change, 36, 53–4, 78–9, 104, 152
regional divisions, 90–1, 110–11
regional press, 4, 24, 40, 43, 72, 110–11, 153
regional radio, 116, 175
regional television, 83–4, 92, 115, 132, 147
regulation, 27, 53, 70, 185
Relad, 112–13
Reliance Group, 241–2
religious organizations, 118, 197
Reporters Without Borders, 53–4, 88, 222–3, 225–6, 229
La República, 92, 128–9, 135–6, 177–8, 180
Research Internacional, 177–8
Retevisión, 23
Revista Dominicana, 193
right-wing politics, 18, 22–3
Rilla, José, 173
Del Rio, José Pérez (Pepe), 238
risk factors for journalists/media workers, 54, 57, 81–2, 86, 93–4, 96, 98–9, 222–6, 228–30, 297
Rivas family, 112
Rizzoli-Corriere della Sera group, 22
RNE (Radio Nacional de España), 29–30
Rocca, J., 280
de la Roche, Bernardo Tobon, 70
Rockwell, R., 48, 51–2, 57–8
Romay Salvo Group, 179
Romero, S., 227, 229–30

La Rosca, 90, 92, 94–5
RPP Group, 131–2, 136
RTS (Red Telesistema), 109, 112–13, 117
RTU Group, 112
RTVE Group, 26, 29
Rubio, Carlos García, 179–80
Rueda, Nancy, 110

Sabado Gigante, 10
Sabés, F., 196
Sacassa family, 52
Saeta TV, 179–80
Saieh family, 148
Salamanca, Daniel, 92
Salinas Pliego family, 11
Salinas Pliego, Ricardo, 38
Sandanistas, 49, 51, 57
Sanguinetti, Julio María, 180
San Juan Star, 196
Santillana, 289, 291
Santo Domingo Group, 65, 72, 228
Santo Domingo, Julio Mario, 64, 228
Santos family, 72
Santos, Máximo, 176
Sanz, Raúl, 85
Saporiti, 153
Saralegui, Cristina, 10
satellite systems, 12, 22, 28, 84, 180, 185, 215
SBS, 197
Scarborough Research, 272
Schement, J. R., 7–8, 240
Schlesinger, P., 280
Scolari, C., 222
Secretos de Cocina, 283
segmentation strategies, 42, 207, 209, 214–15
La Segunda, 142, 147
Selecciones, 6, 43
self-censorship, 57, 82, 86, 226, 229
Semana, 72–3, 112
Semana Group, 73
sensationalism, 40, 42, 82, 111, 177
SER Group, 21–2, 30
Servicios Editoriales Sayrols, 42
La Sexta, 27
El Show de Cristina, 10
El Show Hispano, 238
SICC, 9–10, 239–40
Siles, Hernan, 96
Silverman, Henry, 241
Simmons Market Research Bureau, 3, 269
SIN, 9–10, 203, 230, 239–40
Sitges agreement (1957), 63
SíTV, 12, 112, 213, 215, 268
Sky Latin American, 180
Slim Helú, Carlos, 43, 110
Slocum, P., 231, 297
soap operas, 38, 83, 141, 242–3, 271
social cleavages, 35, 38, 48, 55, 88–93, 97–8, 100, 155
social embeddedness, 151, 157, 162, 168

social fragmentation, 27, 69, *152*, 155–68, *156*, *158–62*, *164–5*, *167*
Socialism, 21–3, 27, 96–8, 104, 189–90, 199 *see also* 21st-Century Socialism
social networking, 156, 215, 269–71
social roles of media, 36, 71, 175, 184, 229, 231
socioeconomic levels, *36*, 129, 133, 151, 155–8, *156*, *158*, 166–8, *167*, 177, 242
SODRE, 174
Soho, 73, 108, 112
Sony, 11, 264
Spain, 17–24, 220–1, 223, 294, 296–8; advertising, 24, 26–7, 31, 250–4, 258, 262–3; Iberian culture development, 277–9, 281–4, 289–91; internet, 31–2, *32*; press, 20, 22, 24–6, *25–6*, 220–1, 223; radio, 29–31, *30–1*; television, 20–1, 26–9, *27*, *29*, 238, 242; TV news, 219–23, 233
Spanish Broadcasting System, 8
specialized content, 22, 24, 27, 30, 42–3, 45, 74, 128, 142–3, 215
Spencer, D., 224
sport, 114, 132, 242
standardization, 7–8, 242–3
Stanford Institute, 74
state control *see also* government pressure: Argentina, 154; Chile, 148; Colombia, 66–8, 70, 227; Cuba, 190–3; Ecuador, 105–6; Mexico, 38; Spain, 19, 21–3, 26, 220–1; Venezuela, 84–6
Steckel, Adrian, 232
Steinberg, Saúl, 241
Stepp, Carl Sessions, 178
Straubhaar, J., 224
Suberví, Federico, 245–7
Suberví-Vélez, F. A., 238–42, 246
subscriptions MORE, 136
subsidies, 28, 56, 240
SUBTEL, 140, 144
Super, 65, 111
SUPERTEL, 111, 113, 115, 120, 122
supply and demand, 203, 213, 215
Synovate, 271

tabloids, 71–2, 128–9, 142
Táchira state generals, 78–9
Tadeo Monagas, José, 78
talk radio, 39–40, 185, 196
Target Group Index, 262
TC Television, 105, 114
technology factors, 297; Argentina, 152, 157, 161–4, 167, *167*; Bolivia, 95; Caribbean, 198; Chile, 140, 149; Colombia, 66; Ecuador, 117, 120; Paraguay, 184, 188; Peru, 126, 131, 134; Spain, 27–8, 221–2; United States, 9; Uruguay, 174–5, 180–1
Tele 5, 21, 23
Teleamazonas, 108, 112, 114
TeleBoconó, 84
Telecinco, 26–7
Telecom, 152, 154–5, 281
telecommunications, 22–3, 35, 37, 65, 84, 110, 120

Teledoce, 179–80
Telefónica Group, 261–2, 281, 296, 298; Argentina, 152, 154–5; Chile, 140, 144; Colombia, 65; Ecuador, 110, 120; Peru, 128, 132; Spain, 22–3, 28, 31
Telefutura, 185, 213, 230, 237
El Telégrafo, 93, 105
Telemundo, 10–14, 65, 69, 198, 213–15, 225, 231, 237, 241–4, 268, 270–2, 298
telenovelas, 38, 83, 141, 242–3, 271
Tele Rebelde, 192
Telesistema Mexicana, 9, 224, 239
Televisa Group, 298; Central America, 53, 57; Chile, 142, 147; Colombia, 65, 69; Mexico, 37–8, 42–3, 219, 224–6; United States, 9–11, 239–41; Uruguay, 180; Venezuela, 83
television: Argentina, 154, 238, 242; Bolivia, 99, *99*; Central America, 51–2; Chile, 140–1, 144, 146–9; Colombia, 64–70, 75, 219, 226–30, 233; Cuba, 192, *192*; Dominican Republic, 194–5, *195*; Ecuador, 105, 108–9, *114–15*, 114–16; Mexico, 38–9, *39*, 219, 223–6, 233; Paraguay, 185; Peru, 130, 132–4, *133*, 136; Puerto Rico, 197–8, *198*; Spain, 20–1, 26–9, *27*, *29*, 238, 242; United States, 9–12, 203–17, *204–7*, *210–13*, 237–44; Uruguay, 179–81; Venezuela, 83–5
television advertising, 209–13, 253–4, *254*, 256–7, *257*
Televisión Nacional del Perú, 132
television network growth, 204–8, *205–7*
Television Serrana, 192
television station growth, 208–9
Televisora Nacional, Colombia, 68
Telmex, 35, 37, 43, 65, 110, 115, 140, 152, 155
La Tercera, 141, 143, 148
Terra, 144, 271
Terrazas, Julio, 100
territorial disputes, 4, 91–2, 94–5
terrorism, 54, 222–3
El Tiempo, 64, 71–3, 129, 136
title sponsorships, 274
TNS Media Intelligence, 203–4, 209
TNT, 12, 264
Todelar, 65, 70
Tolima 7 dias, 64, 72
topographies, 63, 90, 103, 125, 171
de La Torre, H. S., 116, 118
Torrijos, Martín, 54
Toyota 'Yaris' launch, 268
transparency, 34, 40, 55, 180, 227
Trinidad, La Voz de la Gente, 185
triple play services, 37, 43, 45, 110
Trome, 127–9
Trujillo, Rafael Leónidas, 193
Tú, 43, 109
Tunstall, J., 242–3
TV3, 222–3
TV America, 127–8
TV Azteca, 11, 37–8, 43, 213, 219, 224–6, 232
TVC, 180, 228

TVE, 19
TV Grama, 143, 146
TVN, 140–1, 146, 148
TV news: Colombia, 226–30; impact, 218–20;
    Mexico, 219, 223–6, 233; Spain, 219–23, 233;
    United States, 223–4, 229–33
TV Notas, 42
TV Quality Index, 141
TV y Novelas, 6, 42, 72, 109, 143
20 Minutos, 24
21st-Century Socialism, 80, 85, 104

UCTV, 140–1, 146–7
UCV, 132, 140, 147
Ulanovsky, C., 153–4
Última Hora, 94, 184
Últimas Noticias, 82, 111, 120, 142, 147, 177
Umstead, R. T., 207
UN, 50, 52, 58–9
Unedisa, 20, 22
Unidad Editorial group, 24
Unilever, 261–2, 271, 298
Union of Distributors, Mexico, 41
Unión Radio, 64, 83, 148
United Kingdom, 249–50, 253–4
United States, 3–4, 12–16, 64, 230, 286, 294–6, 298;
    advertising, 6–8, 13, 209–15, *210–13*, 231, 240,
    242, 249–50, 253–4, 258, 263, 266, 273; and
    Bolivia, 91, 94, 96–7; and Caribbean, 190,
    192–3, 196–9; and Central America, 48–9, 58;
    magazines, 6–7; market maturation, 214–15;
    and Mexico, 5, 35, 39, 41, 238, 240, 242;
    network growth, 204–8, 213–14; newspapers,
    4–6, *6*; population growth, 204, 208–13; press,
    4–7, *6*, 6–7, 230, 232; radio, 7–9; television,
    9–12, 203–17, *204–7, 210–13*, 237–44; TV news,
    223–4, 229–33
El Universal, 40, 65, 81–2, 85, 92
universities, 140, 147, 245–8
University of Texas, 246
El Universo, 119–21
El Universo Group, 111, 113, 115, 119–21
Univisa, 111–12, 115
Univision Group, 8, 10–11, 13–14, 203, 213–15,
    298; advertising, 268, 271–2; Caribbean, 197–8;
    Colombia, 65; history, 239–41; and Telemundo,
    237–9, 241–4; TV news, 224, 230, 232;
    Venezuela, 84
Uribe Vélez, Álvaro, 64
Uruguay, 171–2, 181–2, 250–2, 254, 256–7, 262,
    281, 297; population trends, 172–3; press,
    176–9; radio, 173–6; television, 179–81
user profiles, 31, 38, *59*, 119, 129, 134–5, 140, 161,
    161
UTECA, 26, 221

Vacaflor, Humberto, 98

Vanden Heuvel, J., 81, 84
Vanguardia, 112, 120
Vanguardia Liberal, 65, 71–2
Vanidades, 6, 109, 142
Velasteguí family, 117
Venevisión, 10, 83–5, 240–1, 298
El Venezolano, 81
Venezuela, 77–80, 84–7, 97, 240, 242, 251–2,
    254–9, 262, 284, 296–8; press, 81–2, 86; radio,
    82–3; television, 83–5
Ventura, R., 281
Veo Televisión, 27
vertical fragmentation, 48, 88, 90, 151, 155–7, *156*,
    161–2, 166–8
Villafane, Veronic, 231
Villarruel, M., 109
Vinasco, William, 65
violence, culture of, 49, 54–5, 57, 63–4, 86, 98, 222,
    225–7, 229–30
Visión 20, 132
Vistazo, 112, 120
Vivanco family, 112
Vocento Group, 20, 24
Vogel, H., 156, 286
Vorhauer, Eduardo, 40
Voz de los Andes, 116
VTR, 140, 144, 147
VTV, 84, 180

Wade, C. J., 47–9, 52, 59
Waisbord, S., 89, 98
Walker, T. W., 47–9, 52, 59
War of the Worlds (Wells), 116
Washington Consensus, 96
web traffic, 31–2, *32*, 121, *121*
WNJU, 241–2
World Association of Newspapers, 297
World Bank, 55–6, 97, 296
World Factbook (CIA), 50, 59
World Press Freedom Index, 53–4
World Statistics Pocketbook (UN), 58
World War I, 90
World War II, 116
La WV Radio, 65

Yahoo!, 242, 270
Yashar, D., 95, 97
Yezers'ka, Lyudmyla, 136
Yunda, Jorge, 117
YVKE Mundial, 82, 84

Zapatero, José Luis Rodríguez, 29, 222–3
Zaracay Group, 117
Zeta group, 20, 22, 24, 26, 82
Zeta, R., 129, 134–5
Zon Multimedia, 283
Zorro, 271